# Telltale Hearts

# Telltale Hearts

■

## *The Origins and Impact of the Vietnam Antiwar Movement*

Adam Garfinkle

**St. Martin's Press**
**New York**

ISBN 0-312-12520-8

**Library of Congress Cataloging-in-Publication Data**
Garfinkle, Adam M., 1951-
    Telltale hearts : the origins and impact of the Vietnam antiwar
movement / Adam Garfinkle.
        p.  cm.
    Includes bibliographical references and index.
    ISBN 0-312-12520-8
    1. Vietnamese Conflict, 1961-1975—Protest movements—United
States. 2. United States—Politics and government—20th century.
Radicalism—United States—History—20th century. I Title.
DS559.62.U6G37  1995
959.704'3373—dc20                    94-39655
                                     CIP

Book Design by Acme Art, Inc

First Edition:  July 1995
10  9  8  7  6  5  4  3  2  1

# Contents

Foreword by Stephen E. Ambrose . . . . . . . . . . . . . . . . . . vii

Preface . . . . . . . . . . . . . . . . . . . . . . . . . . . . . . ix

Introduction . . . . . . . . . . . . . . . . . . . . . . . . . . . 1

1. Ironies of Protest . . . . . . . . . . . . . . . . . . . . . . 7

2. American Traditions of Dissent and the Vietnam Generation . . . . . 33

3. Evolution of the Movement: Liberals and the Left . . . . . . . . . 57

4. Groundswell . . . . . . . . . . . . . . . . . . . . . . . . . . 85

5. Sources of Sixties Radicalism . . . . . . . . . . . . . . . . . 117

6. Best of Times, Worst of Times . . . . . . . . . . . . . . . . . 149

7. Denouement: Tin Soldiers and Nixon Coming . . . . . . . . . . . 181

8. Vietnam as Metaphor, 1975–92 . . . . . . . . . . . . . . . . . 209

9. Back in the Street: Vietnam and the Kuwait War . . . . . . . . . 237

10. Truths and Consequences . . . . . . . . . . . . . . . . . . . . 265

Epilogue: McNamara's Lament . . . . . . . . . . . . . . . . . 299

Notes . . . . . . . . . . . . . . . . . . . . . . . . . . . . . . 303

Bibliography of Cited Works . . . . . . . . . . . . . . . . . . . 341

Subject Index . . . . . . . . . . . . . . . . . . . . . . . . . . 361

Name Index . . . . . . . . . . . . . . . . . . . . . . . . . . . 367

*This book is dedicated to my children,
Gabriel, Hannah, and Nate, in the hope
that their souls will never be so empty
that they mistake politics for life.*

# Foreword

## by Stephen E. Ambrose

The Vietnam War is a painful subject, not just because we lost it but because of the way we fought it and because of the effect it had back home. The length of the war, the methods used to fight it (ranging from B-52's to Lieutenant Calley at My Lai) and the questionable cause (a corrupt, undemocratic government in Saigon) combined with other factors to create an antiwar movement that, between 1965 and 1973, played a critical role in dividing and changing the nation in drastic and fundamental ways.

Every American war (except World War II) has spawned a significant antiwar movement, but none was so widely based, so greatly influential on American life, or so ineffective in shortening the war. The movement began when the counterculture began—it is difficult to say which came first—and the two fed on each other to the point that neither one is imaginable without the other.

Given the widespread unpopularity of the war, its duration, media coverage, and other factors, however, what stands out about the antiwar movement is how little influence it had on events. It could have been a well-organized mass political opposition drawing its strength from its numbers and the variety of different politics and groups it represented, concentrating single-mindedly on ending the war. Instead it was a movement of competing visions, of groups with their own agendas, from the old line Communist ranks to the hippies of the Age of Aquarius, from Quakers to idealistic socialists. For that reason, and others, it could never agree on a goal. Stop the bombing of the North? Or all bombing? Pull back all but service troops? Pull out everybody? Elect Democrats? Overthrow the society? Have a revolution?

The antiwar movement had a chance to create a genuine party of the left in America, but instead it took its opportunity to print a license to riot, to scandalize, to do drugs and group sex, to talk and dress dirty, to call for revolution and burn flags, to condemn parents and indeed anyone over 30 years of age, in an excess of free will and childish misjudgment seldom matched and never exceeded. To the participants, it provided intensity of feeling and was great fun. To the potential antiwar members of the middle class, it was a turn-off.

I was in the antiwar movement. I attended teach-ins and rallies. I opposed the war for many reasons, including the way it was being fought and some serious questions about the wisdom and justification of the cause.

I also objected strongly to the military policy. In the late 1960s and early 1970s I was studying World War II from Eisenhower's point of view. It seemed to me that we were never going to win without invading North Vietnam and taking Hanoi, as Ike had invaded Germany in 1945. You can't win wars fighting on the strategic defensive.

It was obvious that we were not going to invade North Vietnam, not after the experience of approaching China's border with Korea in the fall of 1950, when Mao put a million men into the campaign. Nobody wanted any part of that again. So if we weren't going to fight to win, we shouldn't fight at all, was my feeling, based on what I was learning from Eisenhower in my research.

What I found in the antiwar movement, however, was not an understanding that the Army had been given an impossible job to do by the civilian leadership, but rather a hatred for the Army and its personnel. This was a terrible thing. It was also ironic because the U.S. Army was the most thoroughly integrated organization in the world, the organization that offered the most opportunity for advancement, based on merit, to working-class youngsters, conspicuously free of major scandal and religiously committed to the principle of civilian control. How it could have been despised by the New Left I have never understood.

Recently I attended a symposium held on the 25th anniversary of My Lai. The left wing of the antiwar movement was well represented, with some older Communists of various factions, some younger socialists, one Weatherman, a couple of SDS alumni—the usual suspects. They have somehow convinced themselves that they stopped the war; they remain certain of their moral superiority; they continue to hate the Army. They condemn the United States, which has so bitterly disappointed them by not living up to their image of what it should be.

The permanent influence of the antiwar movement was not to shorten the war but to pave the way for and extend the boundaries of the counterculture. How that happened, and why the movement was never able to become a serious political force, is the subject of this brilliant book.

If you were there, you will find yourself here. Adam Garfinkle covers us all, using our own words to describe ourselves, from professors to students, old Left to New Left, SDS to Weathermen. The emotion and heartache, the posturing, the tripping on rock music and drugs, the intense debates in the early hours at teach-ins are all here, along with much more. You may more than once find yourself exclaiming, "Ouch! That hurts. That was me."

Garfinkle's analysis of the actions of the antiwar movement is thought-provoking, instructive, opinionated and lively, adding to the pleasure and the pain of reading this book. On his central point, that the antiwar movement had little impact on how the presidents carried out the war, he is thoroughly convincing. And he is quite fascinating in his speculation on how the war might have been fought differently and won.

Altogether a damn fine piece of work.

Stephen E. Ambrose
New Orleans
December 1994

# Preface

Nearly every adult English-speaker has read or knows the gist of Edgar Alan Poe's 1843 short-story masterpiece "The Tell-Tale Heart." A murderer hides a corpse under his living room floor, but when the police come to ask questions, the murderer, inexplicably, begins to hear the victim's heart beating ever more loudly beneath his feet. The guilty man soon cracks and confesses all, even though no one hears the "tell-tale heart" except the murderer.

I have titled this book *Telltale Hearts* not to invoke magic and mystery, to imply murder, or to preach about the power of a guilty conscience, even though many deaths and inner doubts do inhabit this story. I chose the phrase only to suggest that some things from the past that are literally dead and buried are not as inert in our lives as we sometimes think.

It took several years to reduce my thinking about the Vietnam antiwar movement to two words. In the mid-1980s I was asked to address the subject for a conference whose theme was retrospection on the war ten years after the fall of Saigon. I was slow to accept, pleading that I had never really studied the movement, that all I knew about it flowed from my own college experiences in the late 1960s and early 1970s. I was told that my approach to the nuclear-freeze movement in a 1984 book was a good model for my new assignment, since what I was to do for the conference, as I had done for the book, was examine the influence of domestic political culture on an episode in the foreign or security policy of the United States. I was intrigued. (I also needed the money.) I accepted.

I then did nothing for a long time, and wondered why. The answer soon became obvious: Vietnam and everything about it just bothered me. From this modest reflection, and with the conference deadline close at hand, I began work and suddenly found myself engrossed in a subject I had assiduously avoided for years. As I worked, a new discomfort arose. Most people are uncomfortable when they recognize that important beliefs they hold are inconsistent. In this case, my inclination to *realpolitik* foreign policy analysis did not square with the conventional "hawkish" understanding of the antiwar movement and the Vietnam War. I knew I wasn't alone: Only a minority of "hawks" then under 40 years of age were of the same feather as those several years older. I figured that the reason had to have something to do with Vietnam.

The conference essay grew to book length over the next two years but before I could complete it I was diverted by other obligations as my professional attentions focused mainly on that part of the world lying roughly between

Khartoum and Kabul. Then the Cold War suddenly ended and the Kuwait War came and went, both changing the outer context of the study in interesting ways. This turned into an opportunity, for, like every ending, it changed the sense of what went before. Many reminders of my negligence pushed me forward, including President George Bush's March 1991 proclamation that the Kuwait War had put an end to the Vietnam syndrome. Other goads arose; the flap during the 1992 presidential primary season over Governor Bill Clinton's avoidance of military service in Vietnam and the diverse range of comment about it was a stellar example. In reference to that flap, a friend remarked in passing: "Won't that damned war *ever* end?" That's when I resolved to finish, and now, finally, I have.

Some thanks are now in order. Many colleagues read parts of early versions of the text and discussed its contents with me, for which I thank them even if some can no longer remember having helped: Patrick Clawson, Peter Collier, Mark Falcoff, Paul Hollander, Guenter Lewy, Douglas Pike, Judith Shapiro, and Marc Trachtenberg. Walter A. McDougall and John E. Mueller offered especially helpful critiques on more advanced drafts.

My thanks are also due to Bill Bodie, then of the Smith Richardson Foundation, who took an interest in my work and got his employer to support it. I don't want to give the wrong impression about foundation support, however. It was modest, occurred early in the process, and it might also be that some of the folks still at the foundation will want their money back when they see what I've written. (Fortunately, that's impractical.)

Given the modest foundation support I enjoyed, thanks are due to two institutions whose generosity, or inattention, allowed me to work on this book over the years. One is the Dayan Center for Middle Eastern and African Affairs at Tel Aviv University, where I spent 1992-93; my thanks go out to its head, Asher Susser. The other is the Foreign Policy Research Institute, where I worked before and since Tel Aviv, and whose current president, Harvey Sicherman, I count as a friend of more than 22 years' standing.

During the time when I was not working actively on the book, I was fortunate enough to be able to teach two courses on the subject at the University of Pennsylvania, an opportunity for which I thank my students and the university's political science department. Speaking of students, I also owe thanks to a baker's dozen of my interns at the Foreign Policy Research Institute; they helped me over the years chase down books and essays from libraries near and far, complete notes, and, most important, ask usually innocent and thus penetrating questions about the subject matter.

Thanks are due also to Simon Winder, until recently St. Martin's editor for reference and scholarly books. Simon was among those who pestered me about the book over a long period, and told me when I finally sent him the manuscript that he'd been waiting more than three years for it. Simon is also responsible for having assigned copyediting duties to Ms. Deborah Manette, a skillful copyeditor whose sharp eye and sharper pen led to manifold improvements in clarity. I thank her for each and every one, and also thank Roger Donway, managing editor of *Orbis,* for his many helpful comments. Michael Flamini, Simon's capable successor, and Nancy Hirsch, Michael's omni-talented deputy, saw the book through to completion.

As may be imagined from the foregoing, this book, though within the scholarly canon in style and substance, has a personal dimension. That being so, I hope the reader will indulge me in a last personal reflection.

I am a fringe member of the Vietnam generation, having finished high school at age 18 in 1969. Thus, during the Tet offensive and the mayhem in Chicago, I was on the threshold of college, but not in it. I was, however, political at a young age; the day after the 1968 election I wore a black armband to school, where our Republican librarian excoriated me for so doing. As a high school junior I tried to institute mandatory student evaluation of teachers; some young faculty members encouraged me but an older group thought me mad. I joined a group that tried unsuccessfully to convince the class to do something socially useful with the money intended for a lavish prom. I grew a beard and ignored several teachers' suggestions that I shave it off. I refused to cut my hair, too.

All of this took place in Arlington, Virginia, the bedroom of the federal government, a place where local news and national news seemed to be more or less the same news. This enabled me and some friends—some of whose fathers were administration appointees and high-ranking military officers—to attend national antiwar demonstrations just by biking along the Potomac, over Memorial Bridge, and on to the Ellipse. Getting to the Pentagon in October 1967 was even easier. During the second semester of my freshman year at the University of Pennsylvania, the invasion of Cambodia, the Kent State killings, and the largest spontaneous college strike in American history took place. So youth that I was, I didn't miss it all.

Several observers have suggested that it would probably take someone a bit younger than the archetypal protester who did not really care that much about the antiwar movement from a personal perspective to give a proper account of it. I hope I'm that person.

In any event, by 1969 it was clear to me—being still a teenager, perhaps *too* clear—that the Vietnam War was a fiasco. But it didn't make me a radical. My view, then and now, is that the war was a mistake born of noble intentions, not a crime born of sinister ones. I went to antiwar rallies but usually disagreed with the speeches. This may have been because my father, born in January 1905, was a Teamster who had taught me about Communists and "other lying scum" in the trenches of the labor movement. He also warned me about Richard Nixon, a man who, said my father, was not to be trusted. Teenagers typically demonstrate enormous willpower when it comes to resisting parental advice and views; I have a teenage son and no one can persuade me otherwise. But, somehow, what my father told me sunk in; I think I was about as well prepared for college in 1969 as an 18-year-old naif could have been.

Nonetheless, what follows is not primarily personal reflection. Nor is it meant as a history, encyclopedic or otherwise, although much chronicling is found within. Rather it is meant as an interpretation of a broad swath of interconnected material. The extracts and specific descriptions I bring are meant to exemplify, not exhaust, the subjects they illustrate; other, much longer, books on narrower aspects or more constricted time periods contain much more detail. While I have made ample use of these books, it has never been my aim to compete with them. My attention has thus been selective but wide ranging.

I have tried to keep the narrative as direct as possible, resorting to discursive and plentiful notes to satisfy scholars but spare others the tedium of bibliographical name-dropping and academic jousting. The notes will, I hope, allow serious readers a better opportunity to evaluate my judgments and enable future writers to see the sources of errors and insights. Such errors could include errors of omission; it is impossible by now to read everything on the subject, and my bibliography, although large, surely doesn't include even half of the existing literature.

Two words about tone, if I may. First, arguments about causality in a social analysis like this one are best thought of as interpretations, not proofs. (But no, they are not *just* "texts.") In Chapter 5, where I try to examine the social-psychological roots of 1960s radicalism, I venture into terrain nearly unresearchable by conventional means, and there "interpretation" is a generous word; "speculation" might be more honest. There are simply too many variables and too little hard data to claim certainty over topics like these, however strong one's intuition may be. This leads me to make the kinds of conditionalized statements that drive editors mad and lead to their picking up large black markers. So I apologize in advance for any statements that seem confident well beyond evidence; they do not mean that I have mistaken the basic nature of the subject.

Second, the origin and impact of the Vietnam antiwar movement do not compose an inherently dry subject. It is not analogous to, say, "glassblowing in colonial times" and there is no sense pretending otherwise. There are already several long narratives about the antiwar movement in print, and every one of them is written from a position generally sympathetic to the antiwar movement. As becomes clearer later, I believe that wishful thinking and the dynamics of ego protection have played a role in misleading these authors as to the essence of what the antiwar movement did and did not achieve. Most of these authors openly tell readers what their sympathies are and, having done so, often pour no little scorn on two or more American presidents, their aides, their administrations, their supporters, and sometimes their basic integrity. I have a point of view, too, and, like authors of another persuasion, I have not been shy about expressing it.

Still, I have tried to restrain myself from gratuitous aspersion, and it is no part of my intention to scorn or irritate anyone just for the sake of it. But I have also tried to preserve the full flavor of my interpretations, and I would be less than honest if I denied an ambition to put some readers through a trying experience in order to stimulate a rethinking of old, comfortable assumptions. I hope I have struck a reasonable balance in this.

Last, I confess to having found little joy in this project. The discomfort I sensed at the start never left me. I wish there had been no occasion to write this book because I wish there had been no war in Southeast Asia, especially one involving the United States. But wishes can't change history. We inhabitants of this bloody twentieth century have paid a heavy price for the privilege of looking reality straight in the eye. We should try to get our money's worth.

Adam Garfinkle
Philadelphia
January 30, 1995

# Introduction

*He who confronts the paradoxical exposes himself to reality.*
—Friedrich Dürrenmatt

This book argues three propositions about the Vietnam antiwar movement: One concerns its impact on American decision making during the war, a second is about the sources of the era's youthful radicalism, and a third focuses on the movement's longer-term impact on American political culture. The three are linked historically by the obvious fact that they all concern the Vietnam War and its times. They are linked, too, in that the state of the American commonwealth, the condition of the hearts and minds of its citizens, and relationships between public opinion and policy making remain, one hopes, issues of contemporary interest. Last, all three are liable to strike many readers as counterintuitive and give rise to some skepticism. It is my hope that, upon reflection, skepticism will give way to an appreciation of paradox, so often the subtle garb of truth in political life.

The first thesis is this: Contrary to the great weight of common knowledge, the Vietnam antiwar movement at its radical height was counterproductive in limiting U.S. military operations in Southeast Asia. It was not decisively counterproductive; other factors strongly drove American public opinion against the war: mounting casualties, mounting costs, the failure to win, the credibility gap, shifts in administration policy, and more besides. But the antiwar movement, at least between 1966 and 1969, was not among these factors. It did not help stop the war but rather helped prolong it.[1]

My fuller argument on this point holds that the antiwar movement moved through three phases along with the war itself. In the first phase, before 1966, opposition to expanding the U.S. role in Vietnam was predominantly liberal in inspiration, was well represented inside both the Kennedy and Johnson administrations, and was strongly held by many of those in the press and elsewhere to whom principals of those administrations listened. In this very broad constellation it was effective too in limiting U.S. military activity: The escalation of the war in 1965 might have taken place in 1962, 1963, or 1964. The rationale for escalation in those years was not different in kind, only in degree, from the one that propelled American action in 1965.

In the second phase, between 1966 and 1968-69, the antiwar movement's center of gravity grew increasingly radical and counterproductive to its goal of stopping U.S. military activity in Southeast Asia. At the very time when the war's unpopularity was growing in the country at large, the image of irresponsibility and willful antipatriotism conveyed by the antiwar movement had the general effect of muting the expression of disaffection. Lyndon Johnson made his famous March 31, 1968, speech on national television reversing American policy and admitting personal political weakness not because the movement had taken to the streets, but despite the fact that it had.

The antiwar movement's impact in this phase was doubly hurtful because U.S. military activity in Southeast Asia was itself unwittingly counterproductive to American war aims at this stage of the war. The antiwar movement's inadvertent role in bolstering the Johnson administration's own stasis thus not only helped prolong the war but also contributed to losing it.

In the third phase of the war and the antiwar movement, from 1969 to the fall of Saigon in 1975, the redomesticated, more liberally centered movement was again moderately effective in limiting U.S. military activity in Southeast Asia, mainly through actions taken by Congress designed to hem in the Nixon administration militarily and politically. But electoral dynamics were mainly responsible for the movement's renewed effectiveness in its return to mainstream American politics. Democrats were now in the opposition, and their reluctance to criticize the war  · evaporated when Vietnam became Nixon's and the Republicans' war instead of their own. The great tumult within the party in 1968, of course, had primed the Democrats well for this new role.

But this phase of the antiwar movement was injurious too, because, after the Tet offensive, the war entered a postinsurgency phase for which U.S. military power, operating under a reconceived strategy, was much better suited. Had the political situation in the United States allowed it, the U.S. military, acting as a deterrent to conventional aggression, probably could have achieved the main task at hand: building a shield to protect the construction of a self-sustaining non-Communist government in Saigon. This could have been done in more or less the same way that such a government was constructed in Seoul under the wing of U.S. military protection after the Korean armistice in 1953.

The failure to proceed along such lines during the Nixon administration does not rest mainly—as most believe—on the antiwar movement's influence over the Congress, which is beyond doubt.[2] The Congress was unhelpful, but ultimately it was the Nixon administration itself that elected not to take the time or spend the political capital necessary to save South Vietnam. Strong congressional opposition to helping Saigon was less important than the administration's broader global foreign policy vision, which required putting the war behind and moving on. There was Watergate too and the ever-present impact of electoral politics: Richard Nixon's determination to win the 1972 election and subsequently choose his own successor for 1976. Just as fear of the electorate had restrained Democrats in the White House before 1964, the same fear restrained Republicans after 1969.

These utterly normal contours of American politics—together, of course, with the battlefield situation—better explain American decisions about escalation and de-escalation in Vietnam than anything the antiwar movement did in the streets either before or after Richard Nixon became president. Those observers, such as historian Tom Wells, who still believe that the antiwar movement "played a major role in constraining, de-escalating and ending the war," are wrong.[3]

The book's other two theses may also seem counterintuitive to some. The first is that while the war in Vietnam was the main catalyst for 1960s radicalism, especially among selected groups of youth, it was not the cause. The real causes lay in the generic difficulties of coping with the revolutionary social life of post–World War II America—even in the supposedly somnambulistic 1950s—and the result was to produce what, for want of a better term, was a religious movement among youth. Human beings are meaning-making animals. Postwar youth, affluent and idealistic beyond prior generations, sought a new godhead in the face of the subtle but pervasive banishment of the sacred from everyday life in the on-rushing technetronic age. That chiliastic search turned to politics, where the impulse to the sacred has often come to reside in modern times, even if it has often done so incognito. In some respects, the antiwar movement was a modern children's crusade, with similarly depressing consequences.

The final thesis is that the main impact of the antiwar movement was not felt in Southeast Asia but in the United States. The impact has also transcended politics as conventionally construed, for the antiwar movement cannot be analyzed apart from larger trends in American culture. Relatedly, the impact of the movement cannot be discussed entirely in the past tense. As time passes and one set of experiences is overlaid by others, sifting the effects of moments frozen in time 25 years ago is a delicate task. Perceptions and accounts that have come down to us today about both the war and the antiwar movement are necessarily influenced by ideas, events, and edited memories from well after the fall of Saigon. When we speak today about the impact of the Vietnam War and the antiwar movement, we have to mean not only what happened between 1964 and 1975 but also what has been said and written about it since and even subsequent actions taken on the basis of those sayings and writings. Grasping this mixed class of phenomena is quite difficult.

Hence, since both the origin and impact of the Vietnam antiwar movement have been broad, approaches to understanding it need be broad as well. This book takes a roughly chronological approach following Chapter 1, "Ironies of Protest," which tries to explain more fully why common knowledge about the antiwar movement's impact on the war is so much at variance with the available data. The

chapter also details my argument about the war itself, and thereby undergirds the
subsequent analysis of the antiwar movement.

Chapter 2, "American Traditions of Dissent and the Vietnam Generation,"
outlines the origins of American anti-establishment movements and briefly describes
their variations through time. It then looks at the most proximate social origins of the
antiwar movement—nuclear pacifism and the civil rights struggle. In doing so, the
chapter defines the dominant value structure of the Vietnam generation.

Chapter 3, "Evolution of the Movement: Liberals and the Left," begins with
a typology of opposition to U.S. policy in Southeast Asia: old Leftist, New Leftist,
liberal, and pacifist.[4] It distinguishes their agendas and understanding of the war,
and shows how the center of gravity of antiwar activism shifted by mid-1965 away
from liberal organizations and toward radical ones. Thereafter, the chapter details
the relations between the Johnson administration and the antiwar movement; it
also analyzes continuing conflict within the movement between radicals who saw
the war as an outgrowth of evil American corporate capitalism and liberals who
saw it as an aberration.

Let me stress that the tale of the New Politics—the cumulative effect of the
antiwar movement once it became ensconced mainly in the Democratic Party after
1968—has been well told by other authors; no purpose is served by repeating that
analysis here. This book concentrates more on the impact of the radical or left-wing
part of the movement mainly because I think that radicals were more important
than generally acknowledged in explaining the general direction the movement
took over the period as a whole. Still, that doesn't mean that the more liberally
oriented parts of the movement were unimportant. In Chapter 10, I accuse the
press of having had a morbid fascination with the radical part of the movement and
of exaggerating its impact; I open myself to a similar accusation unless I repeat
clearly and unequivocally here at the outset that, yes, at those points when it was
dominated by liberals, the movement was at least marginally effective.

Chapter 4, "Groundswell," continues the themes of the previous chapter as
the antiwar movement passed more decisively to radical elements in 1966 and
1967. Many formerly liberal activists were converted in this phase, and many new
radicals emerged from the campuses. Yet sectarianism in the Left limited its
effectiveness. A paradox emerged: The more that radicalism triumphed within the
inner core of the antiwar movement, the less organizationally coherent the growing
movement became. This phenomenon was obscured at the time by the swelling
ranks of the antiwar movement at the political margins, which suggested to those
who supported the war that the movement had greater organizational strength than
it really possessed.

Despite the movement's organizational incoherence, antiwar sentiment in
the population at large did broaden as the war dragged on. Antiwar factions
competed to mobilize this sentiment on behalf of their own political agendas. They

also competed to ally with an evolving black nationalism, which had a disproportionate influence on the radical antiwar movement as a whole. The chapter also
traces the flows of influence within the movement among literati, activists, faculty,
and students.

Chapter 5, "Sources of 1960s Radicalism," departs from the chronological and
considers the deeper origins of radicalism in the 1960s, especially the versions most
popular among the young. It argues that generational conflict and social changes that
few understood at the time were crucial in the broader social and intellectual roots of
radicalism. It suggests a reason that the impact of 1960s radicalism continues today,
not in politics narrowly construed but in the broader domain of political culture. The
real roots of New Left radicalism also help explain why its political aspect was
unsustainable, as described in Chapter 6.

Chapter 6, "Best of Times, Worst of Times," begins with a discussion of the
October 1967 March on the Pentagon, then concentrates on the impact of the Tet
offensive and the breakup of the radical core of the antiwar movement in 1968-69.
Tet provided a synapse between President Johnson's most trusted advisors—the
Wise Men—and the antiwar movement, with dramatically expressed opposition to
the war reinforcing inner doubts among the Wise Men. Doubts were not limited to
the White House, however. As sectarianism ravaged the inner core of the movement, the schism between New Left and old Left widened, with militant pacifists
stranded in the middle. Within the New Left, divisions worsened among Students
for a Democratic Society, Yippies, Maoists, and several anarchist groups. Even
within the old Left, new schisms erupted between conventional and independent
Communists on the one hand and the Troskyites of the Socialist Workers Party,
who saw themselves as a vanguard within the vanguard, on the other. These
ideological and tactical differences, based more on the desire to promote parochial
interests than to stop the war, limited the radical movement's success at the time
and eventually tore it to shreds.

Chapter 7, "Denouement: Tin Soldiers and Nixon Coming," picks up the
chronological narrative after the self-immolation of the New Left and the radical
center of the antiwar movement. It briefly charts the re-ascendance of liberal
antiwar activism, first epitomized by the presidential candidacies of Democratic
Senators Eugene McCarthy and Robert F. Kennedy in the 1968 election. It discusses
the capture of the movement's core by sectarian Communists and, strange as the
term sounds, "militant pacifists." It relates why the Vietnam Moratorium, which
issued from the liberal side, or right wing, of the movement in 1969 was more
successful at mobilizing growing antiwar sentiment than the Spring Mobilization,
the radical project of the year. It also looks at the balkanization of radicalism and
the emergence of the "identity politics" that have transformed the psychology of
American politics and given rise to today's "multicultural" movement. Last, it
examines the reasons for the "curious calm" near the war's end.[5]

Chapter 8, "Vietnam as Metaphor, 1975-92," charts the passage of Vietnam from practical policy problem to cultural metaphor, showing how the Vietnam War and the antiwar movement have been ingested and interpreted within American political culture. The uses to which Vietnam was put may shed little light on the war, but they profoundly influenced the political debate of the first post-Vietnam decade in U.S. foreign policy and more besides. In particular, the academy and the adversary culture have never been the same.[6]

Chapter 9, "Back in the Street: Vietnam and the Kuwait War," looks at a special case of the uses of Vietnam.[7] The Kuwait crisis marked the first time since the end of the Vietnam War that U.S. forces could have been tied down in an unpopular, protracted, and bloody conflict overseas. As a result, buds emerged of both an antiwar movement and an anti-antiwar movement. The brevity of the war and the clear-cut military victory short-circuited full development, but both parallels and differences between the Vietnam and Kuwait wars were striking. Most interesting were attempts to answer still-open questions about Vietnam on the basis of what did or did not happen in the Persian Gulf—a curious business, indeed.

Chapter 10, "Truths and Consequences," asks and tries to answer basic questions: How much did the movement affect the war's ultimate impact on Southeast Asia? How much did it and the counterculture affect American political culture itself? To answer these questions, I briefly track the impact of the movement on the Democratic Party, congressional assertiveness, pollsterism, the role of the press, the academy, and the adversary culture. I conclude with a reflection on the politics of memory and a note on the erstwhile former secretary of defense, Robert McNamara.

# Ironies of Protest

*Everyone complains of his memory,*
*no one of his judgment.*
—François, duc de la Rochefoucauld

I t is all too easy to confuse correlation with cause, especially if one has been personally involved in the events under analysis. But just as high mortality rates in Florida do not prove that it is a dangerous place to live, the fact that there was a great crescendo of radical antiwar protest between 1965 and 1970 does not prove that it was the reason American public opinion generally turned against the Vietnam War or that the U.S. government dramatically changed policies toward that war. People believe things about past politics for lots of different reasons, only some of which have much to do with what actually occurred. The dueling mythologies of the Vietnam War, whether about the antiwar movement or the war itself, remain a case in point.

## DUELING MYTHOLOGIES

Contending versions of the Vietnam War and the antiwar movement began to develop even before the war ended. The hawks' version, then and now, holds that the war was winnable, but that the press, micromanaging civilian game-theorists in the Pentagon, and antiwar hippies lost it. Had military professionals been given free rein, the argument usually goes, the battle would have been won before the antiwar movement arose to complicate the politics of the war.[1]

The doves' version, contrarily, remains that the war was unwise and unwinnable no matter what strategy was employed or how much firepower was used. The United States was on the wrong side, fighting a righteous peasant uprising against a tyranny. The antiwar movement thus saved the country from further immorality and failure, saving American and Asian lives in the process.[2]

Both of these versions of the war and the antiwar movement as they have come down to us are better termed myths than versions of history because they function less as explanations of reality than as new justifications of old positions and the emotional investments that attended them. As a consequence, these paradigms of interpretation have often become more rigid as they have aged. Both myths miss the war's essential reality.

The hawks are right to say that the Vietnam War was winnable within a reasonable definition of victory. But the military strategy adopted by the United States in late 1964 and doggedly pursued into 1968 was, on balance, counter-productive to America's own war aims. More brainpower, not more firepower, is what was needed. Neither the press nor micromanaging civilians lost the war; U.S. civilian and military leaderships did—especially the latter.

As for the antiwar movement, the hawks' myth about it is wrong at almost every turn. Many hawks believed that the movement was subversive and, though seemingly led by students, was both guided and manipulated by Communists through a variety of popular front tactics. But the antiwar movement was neither homogeneous nor static, and it was never Communist in any meaningful sense. True, students did not lead the movement—rather they were its mass and its target simultaneously—and adversary culture professionals *did* lead it for several years insofar as it was led at all. But only a minority of those adversary culturalists were Communists and these were divided among Trotskyites, Stalinists, Maoists, and varieties of "independent" radicals. Moreover, militant pacifists and, at times, angry liberals were equally important. Even the New Left, while it eventually developed an authoritarian Marxist spirit, contained a deep streak of nativist North American anarchism. This amalgam of influences helps explain the self-destruction of the movement's radical core and its balkanization after 1969, something that could never have happened to a mere Soviet front. Such an internally contentious and ultimately self-destructive movement did not "lose" the Vietnam War.

Former supporters of the war usually contend that the war and the draft were the underlying reasons for student radicalism and countercultural abuses, not any principled or well-thought-out critique. The movement was self-indulgent, they aver, and just plain ill-mannered. In many cases, the war and the draft did supply the occasion for political protest and cultural nonconformity, but they were not the cause, and principles *were* involved as well. Student protestors were not all psychological aberrants who hated their parents. The social disconnections, alien-ation, and anxiety of the baby-boom generation were real. The moral underpinning of American public life in the 1950s and early 1960s seemed to clash head-on with both the newly exploding recognition of racial prejudice and the passionlessness of the technocratic style. Despite the appearance of calm and stability, it was an experimental age, and, like all such ages, it produced special forms of anxiety.

As for the doves' myth, no, the antiwar movement did not save lives but instead probably cost them. This was done not by substantially aiding the enemy but by unwittingly abetting the paralysis of the Johnson administration. The fact that U.S. policies were blemished does not make the antiwar movement pure; and the fact that the antiwar movement also was blemished does not absolve the failures of two and perhaps three administrations (if one counts Kennedy's) through different stages of intervention and withdrawal. Indeed, two wrongs usually do not make a right; usually they make a mess.

In retrospect, it is clear that both the Johnson and Nixon administrations *and* the antiwar movement made long-lasting and generative errors about what was going on in Southeast Asia and about each other. Indeed, the government's and the antiwar movement's mutual misperceptions contributed to an interlocking spiral of error.

The Johnson administration underestimated the intellectual frailty of its own military establishment whose errors were unwittingly helping the Vietcong and Hanoi. Movement radicals, on the other hand, misconstrued the effects of their own actions, which unwittingly helped the Johnson administration. Later, at the crucial moment of the Tet offensive (January 1968), the movement underestimated the Johnson administration's irresolution and confusion while, at the same time, the administration and its Wise Men may have misjudged the movement's impact on public opinion, according it more impact than it really had and thus giving it more influence than it deserved.[3]

Had more than 58,000 Americans not gotten killed as a result, this sequence of mutual misperception would almost be amusing, a sort of negative version of O. Henry's "The Gift of the Magi," in which the wife sells her hair to buy the husband a watch chain, and the husband sells his watch to buy the wife combs and brushes. These are the ironies of war and protest, and only when those Americans who lived through those times recognize these ironies for what they are will we ever forgive ourselves for what we have said and done to each other these many long years.

## A CONCORD OF OPPOSITES

Especially ironic is the fact that, of all the lessons drawn by hawks and doves, the only one held more or less in common is flat wrong. That is the widespread assumption that the antiwar movement was successful, even decisively instrumental, in limiting and ultimately stopping U.S. military activity in Southeast Asia. Testimony to this view is ubiquitous.

Tom Hayden, former SDS president and perhaps the archetypal 1960s antiwar radical, boasted in 1977: "We ended a war, toppled two Presidents, and desegregated the South."[4] Similarly another former radical protestor, Irwin Unger, claimed in 1974 that the antiwar movement "forced the United States out of Vietnam."[5] Joshua Muravchik, a former radical turned neoconservative political analyst, wrote in 1989 that the New Left achieved "the withdrawal of the United States from Indochina."[6] Yippie cofounder Jerry Rubin put it this way in 1990: "Our nationwide campaign to build public opposition to the Vietnam War succeeded, and the war ended."[7] *New York Times* editorialists credited "youth" generally with this success as recently as 1994: ". . .the Sixties saw an exercise in mass sanity in which a nation's previously voiceless citizens—its young—overturned a war policy that was, in fact, deranged."[8]

Writing after the Paris Accords but before the fall of Saigon, writer and former protestor Thomas Powers asked more specifically: "What kinds of opposition worked? The answer seems to be that every kind worked, but in general those worked best that cost the most in a personal sense, and they worked best the first time or two, before the national consciousness learned to accept and then to ignore them. . . . The opposition often seemed pitifully weak compared to the power of the presidency, but in the end it prevailed."[9]

Similarly, David Horowitz wrote that the radical Left of the 1960s "began as a fringe movement" but in the end

> our ranks continued to swell until finally we reached what can only be called the conscience of the nation. . . . Because the American people became so troubled, the American government lost its will to continue the war, and withdrew. . . . We changed national policy in the most dramatic way on the most important issue: the issue of war and peace. . . . [I]n all the history of war, there was no other case of a power so great retreating from the field of battle because of the moral protest of its people.[10]

In other words, eventually the mass opinion of the country came to correspond with that of the radical antiwar movement, and in the end the latter became more or less representative of the former.

Claims have been made about the deeper impact of the antiwar movement on the postwar era, too. Journalist Charles Kaiser asked, "What did we accomplish?" His answer: "There have been no more Vietnams since 1968. That is our generation's finest achievement. The 58,021 Americans who perished in Southeast Asia did not die in vain: their sacrifice saved the lives of hundreds of thousands who came after them, who thus far have been spared the folly of similar adventures."[11]

Just as striking, this view of the success of the antiwar movement is held in retrospect by many committed observers who explicitly acknowledge that the antiwar movement "turned off" lots of people, which is to say that it produced what professional analysts of opinion refer to as a negative follower effect.[12] One of the most interesting comments in this regard is that of George McGovern, former U.S. Senator and the antiwar Democratic standard bearer in the 1972 election.

"In dividing the Democratic party between 'hawks' and 'doves,'" wrote McGovern of the radical side of the antiwar movement,

> it probably contributed decisively to the election of Richard Nixon in 1968
> and his reelection in 1972. In 1968 Democratic doves tended to sit on their

hands after the defeat of Senator McCarthy and the assassination of Senator Robert Kennedy.[13]

Then, directly after admitting that the antiwar movement helped elect Richard Nixon to the White House twice, McGovern was still able to write:

> My biased conviction is that the antiwar movement finally saved America from a moral, political and economic disaster. It is said by supporters of the Vietnam War that the war was not lost in Vietnam but in the antiwar movement in America. *I hope that is a correct analysis.* It would be the highest tribute both to the antiwar movement and to American democracy if it could be firmly established that organized public opinion and political actions were responsible for correcting the enormous blunders of the leaders who took us unto the jungles of Vietnam.[14]

McGovern is not the only one to make reference to the negative follower effect of the antiwar movement in one breath and discount its impact in the next. David Farber, another former radical leader, wrote in 1992 of the violent actions the movement undertook: "Though few in number, such zealots gave antiwar protests a negative image and provided ammunition to administration supporters struggling to discredit the movement as anti-American."[15] Todd Gitlin, a former SDS leader and now a sociologist at the University of California, admitted that, to the shock of the protestors present, most Americans sided with the police in the Chicago mayhem of 1968. He understands in retrospect how wrong antiwar radicals had been to imagine the Chicago riots as some sort of victory:

> To our innocent eyes, it defied common sense that people could watch even the sliver of the onslaught that got onto television and side with the cops— which in fact was precisely what the polls showed. As unpopular as the war had become, the antiwar movement was detested still more—the most hated political group in America, *disliked even by most of the people who supported immediate withdrawal from Vietnam*. . . . [W]hoever swung the clubs, we were to blame.[16]

But does Gitlin thus conclude that the long phase of the antiwar movement in which radicals were ascendent was counterproductive to stopping the war? No. Sam Brown, another prominent antiwar leader who resisted full radicalization toward the end of the 1960s, admitted in 1975 that the movement had failed to have a major influence.[17] But did he consider that it might have been counterproductive overall? No.

Sympathetic academics have made similar constructions. Melvin Small and William D. Hoover, noting the diversity of the antiwar movement coalition, observed:

> The practical, no-enemies-to-the-Left approach, which guaranteed huge turn-
> outs at periodic rallies and marches, nevertheless contributed to bitter fac-
> tional disputes and drew the media's attention to the most extreme and bizarre
> protestors.

Absolutely correct. But then they continue:

> Yet one wonders what other approach could have produced *the relatively
> successful record* of the Vietnam antiwar movement.[18]

Relatively *successful* record? One wonders, indeed.

In an earlier book, Small engaged in an even more exasperating exercise.[19]
He identifies himself as a former protestor, "a foot soldier and petition signer for
antiwar causes" who later wondered as a professional historian whether the protests
had an impact. To find out, he interviewed a great many people and searched a
good many archives. What did he learn?

Small reported, plainly and persuasively, that Johnson administration principals Clark Clifford, McGeorge Bundy, Walt Rostow, Dean Rusk, and several others
all told him that the protests had little or no impact on their decisions. The same basic
message came from the archives. Small acknowledged, too, that in any event it is hard
to calculate the impact of opinion on presidential (or any key executive branch)
decisions. He also noted the negative follower effect of the radical antiwar movement
and mentioned scholarly arguments that the movement may well have prolonged the
war as a result, even citing much of the same literature cited here.[20]

Yet despite all this, Small concluded the reverse, that the movement did
contribute to the pressures that produced U.S. withdrawal. How? Because "most
analysts give it high marks for its effectiveness."[21] But the "analysts" Small cites to
support a view he would like to believe cannot stand against the opposing
scholarship he himself cites. To describe "most analysts" he mentions specifically
only: Irving Louis Horowitz and Peter Berger, two scholars, neither of whom had
systematically studied the issue or even claimed to have done so;[22] James O'Brien
and Jonathan Schell, two left-wing journalists not known for their scholarship or
their objectivity; and U. S. Grant Sharp, William Westmoreland, and Richard
Nixon, two high-ranking military officers and a former president, all with a vested
interest in blaming something or someone else for their own mistakes.[23] Beyond
that, Small's argument amounts to more or less logical but ultimately strained
conjecture. Sentences like this are typical: "Nevertheless, sitting in the White House
on a Sunday morning, leafing through the *New York Times,* Nixon aides had to be
disheartened by the numbers of important educational and cultural leaders who
continued to add their names to those [antiwar] petitions."[24]

Neither radicals of old nor their sympathizers today can bring themselves
to move from specific observations of the negative follower effect to a general

conclusion that the overall impact of radical antiwar protest was negative. But the truth is that, while it wasn't easy, the radical antiwar movement made even the Johnson and Nixon administrations look good.

How is it possible for the same individual to acknowledge the antiwar movement's strong negative follower effect and still insist that the movement limited or halted U.S. military activity in Vietnam? It is possible only when the needs of ego protection triumph over common sense. Common sense suggests that it is one thing to tell average Americans that their government has made a mistake, quite another to tell them, as antiwar movement radicals did, that their lives are empty, their values criminal, and everything they cherish as worth loving and protecting is the scourge of mankind. The former is a believable proposition of patriotic dissent in an era in which the country as a whole was struggling to shake off the legacy of racism and segregation. But the idea that the government did not err, but was committing crimes abetted by a diseased society of which the average American was both product and subsequent cause is something else again. Shout such a message, bedecked with sufficiently loud and vulgar obscenities, into the ear of middle America for long enough and no group of dissenters should expect to win any popularity contests. And they didn't; that is no mystery. The mystery is that so many people who ought to recognize such a simple fact don't—or won't.

## PUBLIC OPINION AND THE ANTIWAR MOVEMENT

Common sense is joined with much data, which suggest strongly if not conclusively that the war would have been even more unpopular than it was, sooner that it was, among a broader and more politically salient segment of the American people had radical-led protests *not* occurred.[25] Claims to the contrary, such as those made by Hayden, Powers, Horowitz, Rubin, Unger, Small, Kaiser, and others sound right partly because we are so used to hearing such things. But it was not true, as Powers claimed, that the more radical or personally sacrificial the act, the more it worked to stop the war; the reverse was more likely the case. It is not true that the national consciousness ever accepted such acts, and it certainly did not learn to ignore them. Indeed, the backlash against the antiwar movement created by radicalism's excesses was immense, so much so that one wonders how such statements could ever have been written with a straight pen, whether in 1968, 1986, or thereafter.

The public opinion data we have indicate that the antics of the radical antiwar movement deterred more Americans from opposing the war sooner because they were afraid of the company they would have to keep by so doing.[26] Radical protestors formed a strong negative reference group, producing a rally-around-the-president phenomenon not entirely unlike the boost in support presidents receive when force is used to protect the nation's honor or interests from perceived assault.

Importantly, the negative reference group affect worked on Democrats as well as Republicans; the working-class members of the former were otherwise more likely to oppose a distant war in which their sons were far more likely to get killed than the sons of the wealthy. As labor movement analyst Kenneth Heineman concluded: "By alienating working- and lower-middle-class white Democrats, campus activists discredited the causes of peace and civil rights within that important political constituency."[27]

In short, the radicalization of the antiwar movement in the 1965-69 period seems to have strengthened the prevailing "middle" view that the United States should neither leave Vietnam nor escalate the war sharply, but should keep U.S. troops there and simultaneously try to end the war by negotiation.[28] Public opinion therefore, does not seem to have materially limited the U.S. government beyond the self-imposed limits set earlier on, at least not during the Johnson administration.[29] Insofar as it had impact at all, the tenor of public opinion is most likely to have reinforced administration stasis during this period.

Illustrating this argument requires data attesting to the strength of this ambivalent "middle" position within U.S. public opinion and to the role of the antiwar movement in helping to shape it. There is reasonably good statistical evidence on the first score, less on the second.[30]

Clearly, rising antiwar sentiment in general was not the same as antiwar activism, and there is no evidence that the former was generated by the latter. Contrary to received opinion about the existence of a lockstep relationship between the war's dragging on, the rise of radical protest, and Lyndon Johnson's unpopularity, the data suggest more subtle relationships. John Mueller, a University of Rochester political scientist, has shown that: opposition to the war tended to slow after the initial phase of Americanization in 1965 despite continuing casualties; President Johnson's unpopularity was not a direct consequence of the war; public opinion was not especially sensitive to major events; and antiwar sentiment was not more widely spread, even among young people, during the Vietnam War than it was during the Korean War—it was only more vocal.[31]

Moreover, Mueller shows that no single, simple hypothesis explains support and opposition for the war. It cannot be demonstrated that support declined because the war dragged on and casualties mounted, although some diminution of support probably had that source and there is a strong correlation between the two.[32] Nor can a sunken-cost source of support for the war be ignored, which leads in the opposite direction. Of those academic specialists who have looked closely at the data, absolutely no one has argued that antiwar protest was an important factor in the shaping of public opinion.

So what did shape it? Four things, mainly, in various combinations: party loyalties and partisanship, patriotism expressed largely in terms of support for the president, sensitivity to the war's costs as against potential benefits, and shifts in

administration policies. Overall, though support for the war fell fairly sharply after
the Americanization of the effort in 1965, for a time thereafter it still remained
relatively high. But by the second half of 1967 this level of support gave way and never
recovered. Until March 1968, however, the continuing decline was quite gradual and
the sharpness of opposition quite muted. At the same time, the president's rating
over Vietnam in a January 1966 Gallup poll was 56 percent approval, 26 percent
disapproval, and 18 percent no opinion. But by August 1967, only 39 percent
approved, 47 percent disapproved, and 14 percent had no opinion.[33]

If we look within this general opinion trend, some interesting relationships
emerge. For one thing, not all lack of support for the war policy was dovish; reading
the data that way is a serious error. This is shown by the fact that support for escalatory
policy options as a way out of the stalemate remained fairly high. On January 9, 1966,
for example, a Gallup poll asked: "If you could sit down and talk to President Johnson
and ask him any question you wanted about Vietnam, what would you ask him?" The
results favored the hawks and the ignorant as answers fell largely into two categories:
"Why don't we step up our effort in Vietnam?" and "Why are we fighting in Vietnam?"
A September 1966 poll reinforced this finding. Asked "What should the U.S. do in
Vietnam?" fully 55 percent answered "increase the strength of attack." Equal numbers
(18 percent) answered that we should "maintain current policy" and that we should
"begin to withdraw." Seventeen percent had no opinion.

In short, not surprisingly, American opinion was ambivalent, as it is on many
issues. On the one hand, the American people wanted, it seems, either to win or
to leave. On the other, they were not about to turn against their president or their
country if either withdrawal or victory could not be quickly accomplished. The
people, then, were in more or less the same quandary as the administration and its
generals, who were faced with excruciating choices and painful, even debilitating,
moral dilemmas.[34]

A Gallup poll done in April 1966 summed up the matter fairly well.[35] When
asked "What are your overall feelings about the Vietnam situation?" the data broke
down like this:

| | |
|---|---|
| necessary evil | 43 |
| U.S. should get out | 15 |
| be more aggressive | 12 |
| general fear of war | 11 |
| wish for a quick ending | 10 |
| too many lives being lost | 6 |
| other reasons | 6 |
| don't know | 6 |

Thus, despite the desire for closure, most people expected the war to go on for
some years. Despite this grim expectation, however, the number of those who

favored unilateral withdrawal before Tet remained modest: between 15 and 24 percent.

The same ambivalence expressed in this data appears in a June 5, 1966, Gallup poll. It asked the most famous of all polling questions: "Did the United States make a mistake by entering Vietnam?" Fully 49 percent said no, 36 percent said yes. Of these 36 percent, however, considerably fewer than half favored unilateral withdrawal. In September Gallup asked if sending troops to Vietnam had been an error. The results were almost identical: 49 percent said no, 35 percent said yes, 16 percent had no opinion. On February 26, 1967, Gallup asked if the bombing of North Vietnam should be halted—one of the central demands of the antiwar movement at the time. Fully 67 percent said no, only 24 percent said yes. Again, these views were not entirely dissimilar from those of individuals who were then busy writing the internal memos that eventually ended up in *The Pentagon Papers*. Policymakers and the attentive public alike seemed cognizant of both antecedent error and future danger, but they were convinced that with considerable costs already sunk, the only way to go was forward. This ambivalence was neither irrational nor surprising; given the choices available as the war wore on, it was quite natural.

Perhaps most striking of all, and more to the point of our purpose here, opinion data after 1966 show relatively sharp discontinuity in the direction of not supporting the war effort only *after* the shock of the 1968 Tet offensive had sunk in, and especially after President Johnson's March 31, 1968, speech.[36] It then shows another relatively sharp drop after the Nixon administration placed itself squarely on the rhetorical path of winding down the war. This is suggested in the data for the following question: "Which of the following do you think we should do in Vietnam?" The alternatives given were:

1.   pull out of Vietnam entirely
2.   keep our soldiers in Vietnam but try to end the fighting
3.   take a stronger stand, even if it means invading North Vietnam
4.   other; depends
5.   don't know; not ascertained

The answers given to this question in 1964, 1966, 1968, and 1970 show that an outright majority of Americans always opposed unilateral withdrawal (options 2 and 3), but that after President Johnson himself changed course that majority shrunk significantly.[37] Similarly, those in favor of unilateral withdrawal only rose sharply after Johnson's abrogation of the initial U.S. mission in Vietnam. The same was true in the Congress; as then-Secretary of State Dean Rusk pointed out in his memoir, before March 1968 the administration's main trouble from the Congress came from those who wanted to escalate the war further, not those who wanted to end American participation by withdrawal.[38] Public opinion remained opposed to unilateral withdrawal even in 1970 despite the fact that the percentage of those who favored such action nearly doubled in two years.[39] So much, then, for the claims that the antiwar movement reached the conscience of the American people while it was at its radical height.

But what about the data on the antiwar movement and its influence on public opinion? Although these data are not very reliable or abundant, what there is reveals that the radical phase of the antiwar movement was deeply offensive to the majority of attentive Americans, Democratic as well as Republican. It cannot be argued on this basis, however, that dislike of the antiwar movement had a direct causal impact on opinion—in other words, that the negative follower effect was large or always simple in its workings. It seems instead that most people interpreted antiwar radicalism within the framework of their own views, which were formed on the basis of other, more central judgments. In other words, radical antiwar protests stimulated people to run their perceptions of the antiwar movement through a filter composed of their fundamental views of the war.

When hawks did this, they were prone to conclude that escalation was the best option in Vietnam partly because the antiwar movement and the counter-culture were undermining American resolve, cheering Hanoi, and exposing youth to the clever blandishments of Communists. Those already dovish by inclination, but not out on the street protesting for a change in policy, could bolster their preference for withdrawal on the basis that massive dissent was tearing the nation apart from within. Most important, party partisans and "followers" interpreted antiwar agitation within the frame of their loyalties, and since the antiwar movement was vociferously against both Presidents Johnson and Nixon and against both main-stream parties, these interpretations must have been generally negative.

As prior analysis has shown, the phenomena of partisans and followers were more significant in shaping overall opinion than that of the hawks vs. doves dichotomy. So it was in the great middle of American opinion, among the ambivalent many who supported the Johnson administration's basic view of what to do but were at the same time dissatisfied with how the administration was doing it, that the radical antiwar movement probably had the greatest impact. Overall, as we have seen, the longer the war went on, the more opinion in the middle moved from ambivalently hawkish to ambivalently dovish. But, if anything, antiwar radicalism served as a brake to such movement. Here we take up the aforementioned phenomenon of the negative reference group.

Mueller shows that superficial support for the war was relatively easily eroded and that is why the drop in support for the war was so sharp in 1965. Better-educated or more hardened supporters resisted moving into opposition thanks to a well-known psychological sunken-costs phenomenon.[40] Since convert-ing such individuals is more difficult, and since such supporters came to make up a higher percentage of the war's supporters by 1966-67, it follows that any factor tending to push such individuals toward support for the war policy would be significant. The radical antiwar movement was precisely such a factor. As Mueller put it:

> For a war . . . public opinion is going to be influenced by who is for it and who is against it. Now it happens that the opposition to the war in Vietnam came to be associated with rioting, disruption, and bomb throwing, and war protestors, as a group, enjoyed negative popularity ratings to an almost unparalleled degree. . . . That negative reference groups can harm a cause's impact, a sort of negative follower effect, is quite clear.[41]

Put less in the language of opinion analysis, George Herring, a political scientist, made more or less the same point:

> Public opinion polls make abundantly clear . . . that a majority of Americans found the anti-war movement, particularly its radical and "hippie" elements, more obnoxious than the war itself. In a perverse sort of way, the protest may even have strengthened support for a war that was not itself popular.[42]

Exactly so.

In short, to be associated with a general revolt against authority, with irreverence and illegality, was too much for middle America, regardless of its own doubts about Vietnam. By the 1968 election, the counterproductivity of the radical antiwar movement was already clear. Undoubtedly the backlash against the hippies and flag burners contributed to Richard Nixon's narrow victory, not to speak of what it did for the national political career of Alabama governor George Wallace.[43] In a mid-1970 Gallup poll, Students for a Democratic Society (SDS) was named as a "highly unfavorable" group by 42 percent, higher even than the John Birch Society. The Black Panther "highly unfavorable" rating was 75 percent, about the same as that of the Ku Klux Klan.[44] A University of Michigan study in 1968 asked respondents to place personalities and groups on a 100-point scale. Antiwar protestors received a zero from a third of all respondents; only 16 percent put them anywhere in the upper half.[45]

As suggested in passing earlier, however, the most significant aspect of the counterproductive influence of the radical antiwar movement may have been within the Democratic Party, the party of labor and the working class, and it probably occurred *before* the 1968 election. There was more latent dovish sentiment among Democrats than Republicans; what happened after the election shows that beyond doubt. But Democratic partisans were reluctant to betray their party leadership and their president even though the impulse to do so grew as time passed. It probably would have grown faster and stronger had it not been for the radicalization of the antiwar movement. If so, then what happened inside the party in 1968 might have happened earlier, perhaps a full year earlier. Had that been the case, Lyndon Johnson's decision to reverse course in March 1968 might have come before the majority of American combat casualties were suffered, and it might have come without his having to leave the presidency. Had that occurred, Richard Nixon might not have won the Republican nomination with a "secret plan" to end a war that would have been growing politically less salient. Even had Nixon won the nomination, it would have been far more difficult to win the White House in November 1968 running against the incumbent.

In sum, by slowing the flow of dissent against the war into normal political channels, the antiwar movement abetted the paralysis of the Johnson administration in Vietnam. By giving the administration more time to fail, as it were, it contributed at least something to the conditions under which American soldiers were being killed by the thousands each and every year.

At the time, of course, Johnson administration officials did not know that they would fail in the war. While the antiwar movement was hardly their main worry, they did have its effect pegged about right. National Security Advisor McGeorge Bundy wrote to President Johnson in November 1967, just after the famous March on the Pentagon: "One of the few things that helps us right now is the public distaste for the violent doves . . ."[46] Bundy may have been mistaken about many things concerning the war, but about the antiwar movement he was right on target.

Antiwar protests may have been counterproductive to limiting U.S. military activities in Southeast Asia in yet another way. Some observers believed at the time that antiwar protest in the United States encouraged Hanoi to press on: Richard Nixon made this point repeatedly throughout 1966 and 1967, as did Secretary Rusk.[47] Even liberal *New York Times* columnist James Reston argued that "lawless" demonstrations "are not promoting peace but postponing it. They are not persuading the President or the Congress to end the war but deceiving Ho Chi Minh and General Vo Nguyen Giap into prolonging it."[48] It follows that had antiwar protests not occurred, the war could have been stopped by negotiation or won outright in a much shorter time. The only problem with this view is that there is no evidence for it. The North Vietnamese doubtlessly looked with favor on the protests, and after 1965 they encouraged political pilgrimages to Hanoi, but they have since revealed that they expected U.S. military failure to produce broad antiwar sentiment in the United States, not the other way around.

If the antiwar movement did not drive public opinion against the war, or hearten Hanoi, it nevertheless may be true that the movement indirectly helped stop the war in a third manner: by influencing the judgment of President Johnson and his closest advisors, the Wise Men, during the crucial weeks after the Tet offensive. As reviewed in detail in Chapter 6, President Johnson and his senior Democratic colleagues may have misread both public opinion and the power of the antiwar movement at a key moment in the aftermath of Tet, mistaking the relationship between street protest and the ever-plummeting popularity of the war and the administration. A blip in opinion polls, encouraged by popular television news anchorman Walter Cronkite's first public expression of deep pessimism about the war, appeared to the administration to be a more profound shift probably because their own views had undergone one as well. This shift among the Wise Men led not to an adjustment of U.S. objectives in Vietnam, as it might have, but to the essential abandonment of those objectives.

Whether the antiwar movement was a major cause of this, one of several catalysts, or not important at all, is difficult to know. Most likely, the Wise Men changed their own minds and used the polls and the antiwar movement to bolster their own beliefs and help make their arguments to their peers. Even if the antiwar movement had an impact on the Wise Men, its effect on the war was not at all what either its main detractors or its main devotees attribute to it. If anything, the movement served as a once- or twice-removed psychological factor in the irresoluteness of a small group of important people already tormented by their own doubts.

So neither by driving opinion against the war, nor by bolstering Hanoi's morale, nor by stunning the Wise Men into a change of heart did the antiwar movement lead to President Johnson's decision of March 31, 1968, to abandon fixed U.S. policy goals in Southeast Asia. What it was able to achieve later on during the long period of winding down and negotiating, after the self-destruction of the radical part of the movement, is another matter.

## A CONVENIENT AMNESIA

Looking at the juxtaposition of common knowledge about the antiwar movement on the one hand and the best data we have about it on the other, the obvious question is: How is this wide divergence possible? How could such a relatively straightforward dynamic as that of the negative follower group have been overlooked for so long, and romantic myths of one kind or another instead have taken pride of place? Why has no one in the academy tried to marry an interpretation of the antiwar movement as a whole to the available public opinion data, either in raw or processed form.[49] Why has the movement as a whole escaped all but the most reserved and genteel critical attention?

Of course, there have been critiques but they have not sought synoptic interpretation, nor have they all been astute, even in their limited scope. Melvin Lasky, a British intellectual, believes that there has been no serious critique of the ideas of the New Left because it never produced any serious ideas in the first place. The 1960s generation left no "meaningful record of self-understanding" because, he wrote, "They had no real idea of what they were doing, and no thoughtful comprehension of why they have changed, or how society has become different, or both. . . . [W]here there are no ideas there can be no continuing discussion."[50]

Not that there were so many intellectual luminaries in 1960s social move-ments, but a paucity of ideas does not explain the absence of a critique. Lasky confused the unconventional expression of thought with its absence, and heady times are always unkind to normal rules of evidence and logic. As Joseph Conrad put it in 1912: "The revolutionary spirit is mighty convenient in this, that it frees one from all scruples as regards ideas."[51]

No, the absence of a critique has more to do with questions of self-definition and self-esteem among those most likely to write about the antiwar movement—the Vietnam generation itself. Put simply, the 1960s are for many a paradise believed not quite lost, not yet anyway. It is hard to be candid with others or honest with oneself when protected memories of youthful enthusiasms are at stake. This is why there are so many people in high positions in the academic world, in elite journalism, and in government who have broken intellectually with the halcyon days of the 1960s but who cannot break away from them emotionally. There are political activists of nearly every description who may be counted as refugees or graduates from the antiwar movement and the counterculture, and today they include both the president and vice president of the United States. Any subject may be a target of their wit and intellect except the antiwar movement, which, enveloped in benign myth, seems perfectly immune.

Since political idealism and student protest are central elements within the self-images of the 1960s generation, to critically examine the antiwar movement is to scrutinize one's myth of personal development, the very anchors of one's public self-image. Most people do not want to do such things, at least not in public. Todd Gitlin's attitude is characteristic: "Say what we will about the Sixties's failures, limits, disasters, America's political and cultural space would probably not have opened up as much as it did without the movement's divine delirium." Gitlin assumes that this opening up was inherently good. The changes wrought by the 1960s, he says, "averted some of the worst abuses of power, and made life more decent for millions. The movement in its best moments and broadest definition made philosophical breakthroughs which are still working themselves out: the idea of a politics in which difference (race, gender, nation, sexuality) does not imply deference; the idea of a single globe and the limits that have to be set on human power."[52]

So whether in a reflective or an unexamined, assumed form, heady days of involvement in the movement are remembered, sometimes bashfully, usually wistfully, while the central questions of responsibility and judgment are parried with the circumlocutious language of inevitability to the effect that the war was unwinnable in any event, and that, despite youthful excesses, the movement did far more good than harm.[53] Especially for those still on the Left, ideological exuberance is interpreted retrospectively as having had no real price, neither to the person nor to the nation.[54] As the late Abbie Hoffman put it: "We were bold, we were reckless, we were impatient, we were excessive . . . but goddamn it, we were right."[55]

Even some of those with real doubts about the consequences of what they did cannot shake the emotional leaves loose from their branches. David Lehman, who participated in the 1968 upheavals at Columbia University, provides a good example. "Some experts maintain," he wrote:

> that the protests did little to alter the conduct or course of the war in Vietnam but had a devastating effect on our own political and social institutions. There are people I respect who hold it as an article of faith that many of the ills of our education system—and indeed of our culture at large—may be traced to the 1960s. . . . Still, I can't quite bring myself to disown what I did back then—or to condemn, from the historical remove of a quarter of a century, the excess of zeal that inspired us all. You must remember that I was young.[56]

Thus, no serious critical study of the antiwar movement by a member of the Vietnam generation exists because the movement cannot be thought of in the historical past tense as easily as can the more strictly military and high political aspects of the war. Memories can be and often are embarrassing—hence the selective editing process that comes with age, and hence the wisdom of la Rochefoucauld's aphorism, that everyone complains of his memory, no one of his judgment.

Avoidance of the subject may also have something to do with wanting to ignore both the flirtations with violence and the near incoherent ideological extremism that was a hallmark of the times. This is done most easily by denying the existence or significance of violence or the radicalism itself. Former antiwar radical Norman Birnbaum did the former. Still enthusiastic about the 1960s in 1989, if not still today, he called for a new New Left even as he has minimized the excesses of the old New Left. "Some groups in the New Left," he wrote in *Salmagundi,* "bitterly disappointed that the movements brought no total transformation of society, turned to terror."[57] But Birnbaum blamed much of the terror on FBI agents provocateurs.

Gitlin does the latter; his earlier-cited remark supplies a good example of this latter sort of avoidance. Where he is specific—say, on the matter of civil rights—he accepts change as a radical achievement even though it was more a part of a liberal agenda. One could argue that radicals, by holding liberals' hands to the fire when their moral impulses were found suddenly to conflict with their class interests, forced the issues toward successful resolution. But Gitlin argues nothing of the sort. Where he is vague, with talk about one world and limits to human power, he is either revisiting the utopianism of the 1960s or accepting quintessential elements not of a radical or Leftist character but of an old-fashioned American moralist one. Of the essence of the New Left's paradigm—the Satan of American corporate capitalism—Gitlin says little of a critical nature in more than 400 pages. This is a revealing position for a former radical who wrote in 1966 in "The Radical Potential of the Poor" that "the phrase 'imperialist monopoly capitalism' is rich with meaning."[58]

When it comes to Vietnam, denying the significance of the adversary culture's ideological radicalism often reverts from present tense to what might be called the past personal. Here the reluctance to reopen carefully packaged personal mythologies merges with the assumed insignificance of the adversary culture. No one likes to be used and no one likes to be told that they have been used, especially if there is any private suspicion that it might be true. The antiwar movement was a shifting coalition of ideologies, organizations, personalities, and tactics. Even the radical core of the movement, the professionals of the adversary culture who made the essential decisions that shaped the protest agenda, was neither stable nor harmonious. Self-conceived vanguard groups, Marxist and radical pacifist, were deeply involved in the movement and there were even self-styled bolshevik factions within those vanguards. For such groups and such people, the war and the antiwar movement were less the central problem and the central solution for it, respectively, than a combined means to radical sectarian ends. How much influence such groups really had, and whether parochial and sectarian ends were significantly advanced through the antiwar movement, is a subject over which honest disagreement is possible. But not to discuss the question is an evasion, and most of the academic literature does not discuss it. There is no reckoning.

For those still on the Left, and that includes much if not most of the middle-aged academics who write of such matters, the absence of second thoughts about the 1960s is truly telltale. As Peter Collier and David Horowitz, former radicals turned penitent conservatives, put it:

> [R]eckonings are conservative. They counsel against the heedless rush to try to redeem the ambiguous and mottled realities of the human condition. They prove that life is made better only incrementally and with great difficulty, but it is made worse—much worse—very easily. Reckonings examine the toxic waste revolutionary enthusiasms leave in their wake. Reckonings open the mass graves to examine the shards of bone that are all that is left of the New Men and Women created by utopias past.[59]

Even after the end of the Cold War, even after confirmation by former Communists of atrocities generally underestimated in the West, many left-wing academics born of the Vietnam generation are busy declaiming how the Soviet collapse indicts Western policy for overestimating Soviet strengths, denying that containment had anything to do with the outcome of the Cold War, and searching for ways to make the world safe for socialism now that communism is dead.

Getting beyond the lingering symbolic wounds of Vietnam will take time. Probably generations must pass, as with the Civil War, which did not settle comfortably into the national memory until all those who fought in it were dead. Some radical protesters from that era will never admit they were wrong about America in the 1960s. Few liberals will admit that their radical experiments may have permanently disfigured the liberal project and even the meaning of the word, or that they may have been duped by the sectarian Left. It is equally doubtful that many war supporters, including many Vietnam veterans, will ever accept that most of the suffering and death was made vain not by hippies or an adversarial press, but by hubris in Robert S. McNamara's Pentagon and the failures of William Westmoreland and his General Staff. Unfortunately perhaps, there is no statute of limitations on these kinds of arguments.

## WHY IT MATTERS

But so what? What difference does it make if the Vietnam generation avoids serious reflection and that most Americans believe the mythical common knowledge that the antiwar movement limited and finally stopped U.S. participation in the Vietnam War? If it is true that people learn nothing from history, then it probably makes no difference at all. But that isn't true. Both the study of the past and the creation of impressions about it facilitate a process of reasoning by analogy, a dangerous but popular kind of thinking that policymakers and ordinary citizens alike find irresistible.

It matters in even more obvious ways. Because of mislearned lessons of the antiwar movement, a small but not insignificant number of individuals believed that large street demonstrations against U.S. policy after the Iraqi invasion of Kuwait in 1990 could have defeated the Bush administration's policies and plans. But if Vietnam was any guide, the reverse would more likely have been the case; thankfully, the Kuwait War was so short that we will never know.

Some believe that the example of the antiwar movement can be moved across oceans. Referring to Israeli domestic politics, David J. Forman, a transplanted American, wrote:

> Public opinion is often shaped by the force of a creative protest movement.
> This was the case in the late 1960s in America, when the anti-Vietnam War
> movement effected major policy changes on the part of the U.S. government.[60]

As noted, this conclusion is simply wrong.

More important, to misunderstand the antiwar movement is to misunderstand American political culture over the last quarter century, and here we come again to the adversary culture. Most U.S. foreign policy analysts have an enduring blind spot for domestic political variables, and few scholars have taken fringe political groups very seriously. Work on them has usually fallen either to their acolytes or to researchers inclined toward the offbeat. But the significance of such groups lies not in how many street demonstrations they mount or in the likelihood they will seize power, but because of what marginal intellectual streams always represent and how they interact with the mainstream.

Because such groups develop political understandings outside the political mainstream, they form the boundaries of that stream, offering alternative explanations of reality when mainstream ones fail to satisfy, as they invariably do from time to time. In America's past, fringe forces in politics have intersected continuously, albeit with different intensities, with mainstream views, and in the main American society is not the worse for it—the abolitionist, suffragette, and labor movements were all, in their origins, far outside the political mainstream, and few Americans today wish to return to a social status quo with slavery, an all-male franchise, and no rights for workers to organize and strike. Before analysts label radical agitators as "flakes" and dismiss their significance, they should take a closer look at American social history.

Today, it is true, the relative invisibility of the adversary culture, which has come with the end of the Cold War and its brief and unsuccessful attempt to use the Kuwait War to mobilize support, has convinced most observers that if it was dead in the latter part of the 1980s, it is dead and buried now.[61] But in fact the adversary culture remains significant, still intertwining with mainstream views and still affecting them as it has always done.[62] Indeed, thanks to the experience of the antiwar movement, the adversary culture has established greater and long-lasting bonds to the mainstream of American life despite an decline in overt extraparliamentary protest in the 1980s and early 1990s. Many previously liberal organizations, such as the National Committee for A Sane Nuclear Policy (SANE), Clergy and Laity Concerned, and Women's International League for Peace and Freedom among many, have not been liberal for years—at least not as that term was understood in the early to mid-1960s. More important, those New Leftists who never abandoned political radicalism, and who teach in elite American universities, are now part of a new "old" Left.[63] In time the metamorphosis of the antiwar movement also created eco-anarchism, the new paradigm of American radicalism, which may turn out to be the movement's single most important legacy. These are not matters of the past tense but of the present and the future, and the only way to understand them fully is to look back to the antiwar movement.

Other legacies of the antiwar movement are with us, too, including the counterculture. The counterculture both reflected and deepened an already significant generational discontinuity in American society and politics, the result of which is a society probably less at peace with itself and hence simultaneously less satisfied and less governable overall. Some contend that the absorption of countercultural energies into the mainstream of American society created new social space and, ultimately, an expansion of individual creativity and liberty. Others howl with horror at the thought that what the United States retains from this period could possibly be beneficial. But even things that hurt sometimes do us a lot of good.

In that regard, study of the antiwar movement has much to teach us about the role of dissent in an open society. For all the trouble and love lost as a result of the antiwar movement, it was in retrospect a small price to pay for protecting American liberty. Wars generally do nasty things to tolerance and public liberality, which is why dissent and protest have a vital role to play in any open society. Most people who opposed the war sensed correctly that something was amiss, even if most were wrong about what it was. From this we ought to learn that in future foreign policy disputes, especially those involving blood and honor, we cannot expect to be prophetic or even wise. But if we can learn to be humble about our convictions and civil in how we express them, then reflections on Vietnam and the antiwar movement will do us all some good. That is why getting the origins and impact of the antiwar movement straight matters.

All that is left to do before proceeding to chronicle, then, is to fulfill the promise made earlier to lay out in more detail the nature of the Vietnam War itself. This follows directly.

## THE REAL WAR

The Vietnam antiwar movement was, obviously, a reaction to the Vietnam War itself; in essence, the movement's judgments were judgments about others' judgments—those of the administration in Washington and its supporters. It is impossible to assess the former without reference to the latter.

On the simplest level, for example, if one thinks the war was right and honorable, then a social movement that opposed it is liable to be cast in unflattering terms, and vice versa. But if one takes a more subtle approach to the war—if one looks at the real war rather than the war of contending mythologies—then one's approach to the antiwar movement needs to be more subtle too.

Subtlety must contend with uncertainty too. The key question—Was the war winnable, and if so, how?—is open-ended because perfect proofs of historical causality are impossible. Uncertainties pile up on one another and, ultimately, arguments boil down to interpretations. We will never know for sure that the war was winnable, or that it wasn't. The fact that one U.S. strategy lost the war does not mean that another available strategy might not have won it. This is crucial, for if it could be proven that the war was not winnable, then the movement may have saved American lives at least in its first and third phases. If the war was not winnable, then what befell millions of Southeast Asians under Communist rule after 1975 was unpreventable. But if the war was winnable, then a hypothetically effective antiwar movement was the agent of unnecessary catastrophe in Vietnam, and worse, mocked the purpose for which more than 58,000 American soldiers died. This is a lot not to know.

Still, since no analysis of the antiwar movement can logically proceed devoid of a view about the war itself, it's best to be open and direct about the premises from which one begins.

The vast majority of the members of the antiwar movement and, later, many members of a contrite and chastened establishment, came to believe that the Vietnam War was unwinnable. What various people meant by that differed in important ways, however. Some meant it could not be won because Vietnamese morale was higher than American morale and that Hanoi would thus be willing to pay any price to outlast Washington. Others meant it could not be won in the sense that gains would, in the end, not outweigh the costs in money, lives, morale, and the American reputation for pursuing a moral foreign policy.

Neither version of this point of view is compelling. Most likely the war could have been won, and won at reasonable cost, had a wiser, politically oriented approach been taken at the outset.[64] But the American approach to the war made it increasingly difficult to win as time passed. Search-and-destroy tactics hurt innocents and created millions of internal refugees, driving Vietnamese peasants by the tens of thousands into the arms of the Vietcong (National Liberation Front/NLF). The higher enemy body counts went, the larger the growth in Vietcong recruits. The "better" the U.S. military did as defined by General William Westmoreland, the worse the American situation became.

This confused the U.S. general staff to the point that they simply did not realize or believe it. The sorts of tactics they were using worked for the British in Malaya a few years earlier, and they worked against the Huks in the Philippines and, arguably, the Communists in Greece. The Vietnamese willingness to accept very high casualties was unexpected, and the weak nationalist credentials of the Saigon government were unappreciated. The general staff cannot be blamed for beginning as it did; it can be blamed for not adjusting far more quickly when the strategy was found wanting.

There were dissenting voices about U.S. military strategy from the start, but too few. General James M. Gavin, for example, warned against the attrition strategy at the time, but he was heckled and dressed down.[65] As a consequence of U.S. actions, by 1968 if not earlier the war had *become* very hard to win, unless the United States was prepared to spend another decade and countless lives in the process of reversing the impact of the mistakes it had made.

In short, there was nothing deterministically unwinnable about the Vietnam War before the United States fully engaged in it. Surely, there was nothing inevitable about the extraordinary obtuseness of U.S. military tactics in Vietnam. In all, the way the United States approached the war contradicted its basic aims: the creation of a secure, independent, non-Communist government in South Vietnam.

As to motives—another highly contentious point—I believe that the main impulse that drove America to Vietnam in the early 1960s was a moral one that was unexceptional in intended virtue; but moral impulses are poor guides for making judgments about where and when the U.S. government should commit itself to military campaigns of strategically dubious value. Nor is moral impulse enough to offset the damage done by inept and counterproductive military planning. The impulse that sent the antiwar movement into action against the U.S. government was also unexceptional in intended virtue but, again, moral impulses alone cannot influence public policy in a benign direction. Nor can a moral impulse predict its own history as intentions mingle with the conundrum of reality.

Clearly, it was on the basis of moral impulses that both the government and its opposition arrayed its core judgments about the war. In this sense, Vietnam was like every American war—moral from top to bottom, start to finish, inside government and out, in support or in opposition. The moral content of such judgments tends to make them rigid. Thus, if the administration defined the moral task to be defeating Communist aggression, then it was not free to consider that the war might be unwinnable. If the antiwar movement defined its moral task as stopping the war and purifying American society of racism and other evils, it was not free to suppose that its actions might have counterproductive results.

Neither high-minded intentions, nor the fact that the war was probably winnable, necessarily justifies the U.S. commitment in the first place, of course. It is easy to say after the fact that the commitment was not worth making because we now know its cost. Even if the war had been won, a similar verdict could be reached, again based on costs now known. But in 1964 or 1965, the costs that were eventually incurred were unimaginable to official Washington; hubris played its blinding role well. It is hard to disagree with former Secretary of State Henry A. Kissinger; when asked directly whether the war was a mistake he answered: "The depth of our involvement was a mistake, and surely a mistake if we were not prepared to win. Was it justified? I think the fundamental analysis was wrong, that [the Communist challenge in Vietnam] was the cutting edge of the world revolution."[66]

There is another irony in waiting here, not about protest but about war. The American phase of the Vietnam War, 1963-73, was really two wars. The first, from the assassination of South Vietnamese President Ngo Dinh Diem in early November 1963 to the reversal of U.S. policy in late March 1968, was fought primarily against the Vietcong. The second, between about 1969 and 1975, was fought mainly against North Vietnamese regulars. The difference was not trivial.

The first war was an extremely difficult one for the U.S. military. It did not understand enemy tactics, did not know the terrain, fought with unreliable allies, and used equipment mostly inappropriate for the task at hand. But despite counterproductive tactics, a victory of sorts may have been within reach after the decisive battle of Tet—a triumph of U.S. firepower over U.S. tactical obtuseness, so to speak. All military analysts (including General Giap) have since agreed that Tet virtually destroyed the National Liberation Front (NLF) within South Vietnam. Admittedly, the victory, even had it been recognized as such in Washington, might have been only temporary had the same counterproductive strategy been resumed thereafter. But the breathing space it could have provided to the South Vietnamese government, while the Vietcong was licking its wounds in Cambodia, might have been crucially important. A good deal more political progress was being made in South Vietnam than was generally appreciated at the time.[67]

But though nearly won on the battlefield, Tet was a political disaster in Washington, not primarily because of the press coverage given to it, as some have claimed, and certainly not because of the antiwar movement, but because the Tet offensive made nonsense of then-recent U.S. military claims that the NLF was done for, and that it had been defeated by a stringently limited U.S. effort. Consider the sequence of events.

General Westmoreland had claimed at the end of 1967 that the Vietcong was virtually dead, and on this he was proven wrong when it rose from the grave in Tet. It rose, however, only to be definitively dispatched by the U.S. Army between January 31 and early March 1968. Westmoreland took credit for this achievement but by then no reasonably intelligent observer believed much of anything the Johnson administration and its generals said about Vietnam. It amounted to crying wolf in reverse.

Tet convinced many circumspect and patient supporters of the war effort that if victory meant prevailing within limits established by the United States, then victory was farther away than ever. Thus a victory on the battlefield translated into a political defeat on account of a self-imposed definition of "reasonable limits." These limits were imposed not by the antiwar movement taking to the streets after 1965 but by the Pentagon and the White House between 1961 and 1964. Given the context, Tet was understood as a "loss" and, with it, the energy to stay the course dissipated irredeemably. Nothing any successor to Lyndon Johnson might have done could have reversed the impact of what the president said to the nation and the world on the evening of March 31, 1968. President Johnson did not just change tactics in order to reduce American casualties, as some have claimed. By combining a public willingness to negotiate with Hanoi with a halt in the bombing and a seeming admission of his own political weakness, he signalled the American people that the aim of U.S. policy was no longer to win the war, but only to exit it with minimal damage.

Then came the second war, the mainly conventional war fought between the United States and North Vietnam. This is the war the United States lost not because it could not fight, but because it chose not to fight. In the end, in March 1975, South Vietnam fell to a conventional North Vietnamese attack in open violation of the Paris Accords of January 1973. The United States could easily have blunted this attack had its military forces remained engaged, and it almost certainly would not have even occurred had U.S. forces remained engaged.

So what's the irony? This: that the United States nearly won a first hard war but thought it lost and therefore was not around to fight or deter a relatively easy second one.

The question of whether the war was winnable is therefore far more complicated than it seems. Some have argued that Vietcong willingness to take casualties was paramount, and that to assert the ability to win the war one has to deal with this matter. Not necessarily. If the United States had concentrated on holding territory and expanding it rather than in engaging and killing the enemy, the political dynamic of the war might have been changed without direct reference to relative body counts. The aim should have been to get most Vietnamese on the side of the Saigon government, not to alienate and then kill them.

Whether the war was winnable is important, for, as suggested earlier, simplistic myths about the impossibility of winning the war are crucial in the retroactive justification for virtually everything that was done at the time by the antiwar movement. In truth, even though U.S. policies through 1968 were flawed to the point of being counterproductive, antiwar radicals were not thereby made "right" by any intrinsic hopelessness of the effort.

A related issue concerns basic aims. The United States wanted two things in Vietnam: to stop Communism and, relatedly, to produce a self-sustaining, democratic South Vietnam. The former could have been accomplished without the latter simply by accepting South Vietnam as a "friendly tyranny"—a proxy state of authoritarian constitution—like a number of others the United States indulged as lesser evils during the Cold War.[68] Toward the end of the American engagement in Vietnam, the Nixon administration would have happily settled for a self-sufficient South Vietnam regardless of its form of government. Even this prospect rested, however, on how one saw the government in Saigon from the beginning and how one judged its evolution during the war.

The antiwar movement believed that the Saigon government from the start was a venal, backward, corrupt, and tyrannical regime, which would have fallen anyway in due course, and so was not worth defending. The American people as a whole were similarly minded almost from the beginning, if polls are to be believed.[69] Even the Johnson administration had its doubts, as *The Pentagon Papers* make clear.[70]

But despite its many weaknesses, the Saigon government was in fact a fairly successful modernizing regime under siege from a Communist insurgency.[71] Americanizing the war, however, undermined and corrupted that Saigon government, destroying whatever nationalist credentials it was entitled to claim. American enclaves, the enormous number of U.S. personnel, and the superabundance of war and war-related matériel provided a temptation to graft that the South Vietnamese found beyond their capacity to resist. Before the Americanization of the war, the South Vietnamese regime's main problem was not tyranny but impotence. But when the antiwar movement looked at Saigon after 1965-66, it saw not what was integral to South Vietnamese political culture but what the American war effort had created. This irony is almost wholly absent from the received mythology of the war. People remember the "tiger cages" and the photo of a summary execution by pistol to the head on the streets of Saigon, not the growing union movement, economic growth and diversification, the development of a free press, the opening up of the educational and electoral system, and eventual progress in electoral politics.

It is impossible to say if South Vietnam would have become democratic as well as non-Communist behind the shield of U.S. military protection. South Korea is close to such a transformation, although it has taken 40 years and is not yet complete.[72] So if South Korea, why not South Vietnam? Even in the fullest sense, then—that of producing a Southeast Asian democracy—the Vietnam War also may have been winnable.

# American Traditions of Dissent and the Vietnam Generation

*Every age, every culture, every custom and tradition has
its own character, its own weakness and its own strength, its beauties
and ugliness; accepts certain sufferings as matters of course, puts up
patiently with certain evils. Human life is reduced to real suffering,
to hell, only when two ages, two cultures, two religions overlap. . . .
Now there are times when a whole generation is caught in this way
between two ages, two modes of life, with the consequence
that it loses all power to understand . . .*
—Herman Hesse, *Steppenwolf*

Both the sources of the Vietnam antiwar movement and the movement they spawned were so heterogeneous that even to call it a movement, with connotations of a unified endeavor, is to stretch the common meaning of the word. We might compare it to a large gaseous planet, such as Saturn, with a solid core surrounded by swirls of intermixed and orbiting layers of gases of various densities. But no matter how modest the core in volume compared to the shell, in the antiwar movement as well as with Saturn, it was most significant in terms of weight.

To carry the metaphor a step further, Saturn's core is made of heterogeneous material, and so was the core of the antiwar movement. Three basic intellectual frameworks comprised that core: religious pacifism and its twentieth-century variations; religiously toned but secularized "liberal" peace activism; and Marxist or otherwise sectarian radical Leftism. Each of these frameworks had its own organizations, leaders, heroes, style, and temperament. All agreed that the war should be stopped, but they did not often agree on how to stop it or even on why to stop it.

Taken together, these three groupings composed the adversary culture in the United States as it existed in the 1950s and 1960s, a culture whose inner divisions gave the antiwar movement its basic architecture and one that was itself deeply influenced by its protracted effort in opposing the U.S. role in the Vietnam War. At the same time, it would be wrong to exaggerate the separateness of these paradigms, particularly as the war's duration changed the very shape of the adversary culture itself. The New Left, and Students for a Democratic Society (SDS) in particular, traversed all these adversarial paradigms at different periods of its meteoric but ill-fated career, starting off inclined toward liberal and pacifist lines but ending up neither liberal nor pacifist.

## THE ADVERSARY CULTURE IN THE
## TWENTIETH CENTURY: A THUMBNAIL HISTORY

For the adversary culture, as for the political culture as a whole, the Vietnam era was one of accelerated experience, where even business as usual was unusual business. But the war in Vietnam was not the first time the various elements of the adversary culture worked together even as they struggled over who should lead a swelling of national dissent and in what direction. In this century the three main pulses of the adversary culture have merged, diverged, and re-merged many times in a process that has influenced both its intellectual and institutional dimensions. The main catalysts of this process include the Spanish-American War, World War I, the Great Depression, World War II, the dawn of the nuclear era, the struggle for civil rights, and, of course, the Vietnam War.[1]

The intellectual origins of the adversary culture can be traced to religious pacifism and nonconformist philosophical movements in American society as far back as the transcendentalists of the nineteenth century. For our purposes, the adversary culture's proximate institutional origins emerge from the development of the social gospel movement of the Progressive Era, punctuated by the Spanish-American War and the war in the Philippines, and the maturation of the "liberal peace reform" during and just after World War I. To this, a decade later was added the beginnings of secular radicalism, both anarchist and Marxist.

In different ways, all three streams of the adversarial subculture reflect the secularization of the religious impulse, as the twentieth century careers of Abraham Johannes Muste, Dorothy Day, Emma Goldman, and many others illustrate.[2] Twentieth-century examples of this process should not surprise students of either eighteenth-century French Jacobins or nineteenth-century European Marxists, for both sets of adversary culture precursors represented prior secularizations of the Christian ethic, the "this-worlding" of classical Christian millenarian eschatology. As the historian Paul Johnson put it in discussing modern times: "Most twentieth-century intellectuals have no religious faith; their politics, which dictate their ethical assumptions, form a substitute for it. The undertone is Calvinist; they think in terms of sin and damnation . . . rather than goodness and salvation."[3]

The modern impulse to secularize and politicize religious ideals is strengthened in America by the abstract character and moralist base of American nationalism. This nationalism was born as a principled dissent in a revolution seen then as well as now as having been based more on values than on interests. Moreover, by nature American nationalism is sufficiently detached from antique claims of tribe or race that the search for moral consensus, and the self-consciousness of politics as a moral enterprise, have been *constitutive* of social cohesion—instead of being a result of it, as is the case in most societies.[4] The United States thus needs a civil religion more than most societies because it lacks a standard national mythology. And yet the basic ideas of this civil religion—liberty, democratic constitutionalism, self-reliance—must be kept alive amid a population of great and growing ethnic and religious diversity if the United States is to endure with the basic constitutional structure it has carried since its inception.[5]

The standard civil religion, however, has never been enough for some Americans. Abstractions tend to beget other abstractions, schisms further schisms, idealism still headier idealism. American religious idealism and the political romanticisms it spawned persisted in various intellectual and institutional incarnations throughout the nineteenth century. The abolitionism of the 1850s and 1860s, the evolution of "conscientious objection" during the War Between the States, the expansion of Quaker peace activism in the 1870s and 1880s (as opposed to its more traditional quietism),[6] and the emergence of the social gospel movement of the northern Protestant churches around the turn of the century all contributed to the growth and diversification of an anti-establishment ethos within American political culture. This ethos was initially centered in Puritan New England and Quaker Philadelphia, and it spread as the country grew. It was also consistent with the "low church" Protestant traditions of colonial New England, in particular, which had formed in the sixteenth and seventeenth centuries. That both sides in these old American arguments—"low church" Protestants and "high church" Episcopalian/Anglicans—had English Protestant origins reflects, among other things, the irrepressible cultural dialectic in which adversarial groups and those they oppose often share more than either side cares to admit. This contributed much to the bitterness of their enmity, for each declared itself to be the rightful interpreter of abstract values held in common. This argument did not end with the coming of the railroads or even the space age. As we will see, this same dynamic played itself out in secularized form during the Vietnam War, when liberals opposed a liberal Democratic administration.

As to the first stream of the adversary culture, religious pacifism, its institutional seeds in America were few in the period before World War I. During and after that war, however, those seeds germinated and flourished. The American

Friends Service Committee (AFSC), founded in 1917, and especially the American branch of the British Fellowship of Reconciliation (FOR), founded in 1915, developed institutional bases in the early 1920s that remain today.

The four decades between the Civil War and World War I also gave rise to the second stream of the adversary culture—liberal peace activism, or what one observer termed the "cosmopolitan reform."[7] Descending from the religious institutions of preindustrial New England, a secularized "cosmopolitan movement" matured institutionally through the fight for the abolition of slavery and later took up the cause of women's suffrage. Peace also became a part of its program, to be approached less through the moral importunings and community good works of the church than through activist government working in tandem with the modern tools of science and law. It was during this era that the legalistic idealism that came to dominate American social science academia was born. Through prominent, aristocratic but "progressive" clergymen, activist women,[8] intellectuals, businessmen, and political figures such as Frederick Perry Stanton, James Gillespie Blaine, and William Jennings Bryan, the beginnings of what later became known as "liberal" peace activism emerged.

The coming of age of secular "peace activism" was itself a heterogeneous phenomenon, as the diversity of its origins and the number of its organizations illustrate. The Association for the Reform and Codification of the Law of Nations, the National Arbitration League, the refurbished American Peace Society, and even the Women's Christian Temperance Union were all involved. This diversity reflected the social specialization and institutional vivacity that is characteristic of modern democratic, urban-based civilization. It also stands as testimony to the American penchant for building what political sociologists call the mediating institutions of civil society.

The first watershed of the pre–World War I secular "peace" movement came in response to American imperialism aimed at the Caribbean and the Pacific. The critical event in this regard was the Spanish-American War. On June 15, 1898, the Anti-Imperialist League was formed in Boston. At its center was a group of older New England iconoclasts known as the Mugwumps, but the league came to embrace an improbable coalition of intellectuals, including Samuel Clemens (Mark Twain) as vice-president,[9] industrialists, labor leaders, clergymen, feminists, religious pacifists, white supremacists, Negro activists, educators, and lawyers. The Anti-Imperialist League was representative of the political coalition that William Jennings Bryan tried, but failed, to ride into the White House in 1896 and again in 1900.

Despite Bryan's defeats, the period between the Spanish-American War and the end of World War I, now known as the Progressive Era, witnessed the fuller emergence of the social gospel movement and the broad secular reform movement. In this period, 45 self-defined "peace" groups were founded, including the American Association for International Conciliation, the Carnegie Endowment for International Peace, the League to Enforce Peace, the World Peace Foundation, and the Women's International League for Peace and Freedom. "Liberal" peace advocacy became fashionable and (upper) middle class; it was also influenced by a variety of European radical ideas, including those of Russian philosopher and writer Leo Tolstoy.[10] It was in this period that small liberal "peace" constituencies organized around anti-imperialist and isolationist themes developed in the Republican and especially the Democratic parties. On balance, it was an optimistic movement that saw itself as thoroughly modern, quintessentially scientific, and morally noble— until World War I.

Finally, it was also during this period that the first self-consciously radical university student organization, the Intercollegiate Socialist Society, was founded by Upton Sinclair in 1905. The ISS was the forerunner of the radical American Student Union of the 1930s and, ultimately, of Students for a Democratic Society in the 1960s.

## THE ANTIWAR MOVEMENT AND ORGANIZED LABOR

In addition to the religious pacifist and liberal reform organizations of the nineteenth and early twentieth centuries, the "peace movement" added the labor movement to its aegis during and after World War I. The labor movement was pushed forward by the industrialization of the American heartland and by the arrival of hundreds of thousands of European immigrants who were not as isolated from the main currents of nineteenth-century socialist thought as the young American proletariat. Most, but not all, immigrants quickly lost whatever interest they might have had in radical politics. For a few, however, the political innocence of the American landscape, which was almost entirely free of secret police or a rapacious nobility, seemed a potential garden of revolutionary delights. World War I brought out both immigrant tendencies: new patriotism and revolutionism as well as peculiar mixtures of the two, such as the patriotic Yiddish-language song of Jewish anarchists that praised the Jewish "Sammies" fighting in the American Expeditionary Force against the evil autocracies of Europe.[11]

Most significant in this context, the war spurred on nascent radical socialist tendencies in the young labor movement. Although internationalist proletarian solidarity in Europe did not survive the first weeks of the Great War, the experience of simultaneously being in America and looking at Europe was a powerful goad to antiwar sentiment in the U.S. labor movement, as was, initially, the Russian Revolution. For a few years, from about 1918 to 1920, radical labor organizations nearly dominated the adversary culture, which was greatly aided by divisions in the U.S. Socialist Party and the mainstream labor movement over U.S. involvement in the Great War. While the Socialist Party hierarchy opposed intervention, Samuel

Gompers and the American Federation of Labor agreed to support it in return for sweeping governmental support for the union agenda.[12] As Socialist Party support was weaned away, Communists and anarchists of various descriptions filled the vacuum.

By the end of the war, the core of the American "peace" movement was increasingly socialist. Most of the "liberal" elements (liberal now being defined more or less in the familiar twentieth-century American way)[13] had put their faith in international law as the key to enforcing peace among nations and had followed President Woodrow Wilson into the crusade to end war. In retrospect, this was a striking development when set against the struggle between liberal and Leftist "peace" activists in the 1960s. The intense antiliberalism of non-Communist radicalism in both the 1920s and the 1960s drove it ever farther Left into the arms and influence of sectarian radicals with very different beliefs about peace and progress. In the end, this process of accelerating to the Left and of trying to hammer out common positions with differently minded radicals led not to the success of radical projects but to schism and virtual self-destruction a few years later.

Religious pacifists, radical socialists, and some social gospel clergymen—not quite pacifist and not quite Marxist, but enough of each to join them to the adversary culture—had vigorously opposed U.S. involvement in the Great War. In the 1920s, each group infused different proportions of the domestic reform aspirations of latter-day progressives and social gospelers with the internationalism of radical socialists and militant pacifists, and together they developed a new concept of "peace."[14] This synthesis quickly diluted the power of sectarian radicalism. On balance, after 1920-21 radical socialism was a minor movement in the United States before the Great Depression.

The unifying characteristic of peace activism in the 1920s and 1930s was the development of a synoptic and romantic vision of social change. For most Americans, peace was synonymous with isolation, but for adversary culture groups peace was seen as a social process with "justice" at home a precondition for a sound and active American peace policy in the world. Still, the vision differed at least slightly either in content or in temper among religious pacifists, liberal sympathizers of the social gospel clergy, and radical socialists. Ironically, in the earlier period, differences in social class were a large part of the reason for this, with the radical socialists coming largely from immigrant, and disproportionately Jewish, backgrounds, while the other streams of the adversary culture were largely upper-class patricians.

Differences in philosophy also coexisted with differences in the sense of tactics, with the latter differences sometimes overwhelming the former. The main tactical difference emerged between liberals and radicals, with liberals, by definition, seeking change from within by winning control of government and radicals seeking to achieve change by overturning government from without.[15] Anarchists, in turn, had an entirely different attitude: Revolutionaries should not control government from within or without but should withdraw allegiance from it and establish independent institutions from the bottom up.

Despite such differences, self-styled progressive visions moved toward each other over time, partly because of basic ideals and aspirations held in common and partly because the events of the interwar period drove them together. The adversary culture as a whole developed a self-excluding distinctiveness outside the dominant conservatism of the period. Again, what happened from the mid-1920s to the mid-1930s resembled in some ways the reshaping of the adversary culture in the 1950s—the prelude to the Vietnam antiwar movement.

## CHANGING TIMES AND THE NEW PACIFISM

By the mid-1920s, with the return to "normalcy" and American isolationism, varieties of pacifism came to dominate the adversary culture. Its ranks were swelled by penitent liberals ashamed of their high-minded but, they now believed, futile and disastrous enthusiasm for U.S. intervention in the Great War. But the balance among pacifists, liberal activists, and radical socialists shifted twice between the mid-1920s and the mid-1940s. The first shift came with the Great Depression and the reradicalization of the labor movement; the second came with the onset of World War II.

Desperate times tend to generate desperate thoughts; hence the Leninist ideological link between "capitalism" and "war" made important inroads in the United States during the Depression. Several hundred thousand people joined and quit the U.S. Communist Party in the 1930s, and most of those who left probably did so for personal, not ideological, reasons.[16] Many others, neither formally nor fully radicalized, were influenced by the Nye Commission Report, a 1936-37 Congressional investigation that implicated U.S. arms manufacturers in American involvement in World War I. This was a harbinger of later notions of a demonic military-industrial complex pushing, pulling, and prodding the nation into war on behalf of profit-seeking "war industrialists." The fact that Senator Nye was a populist Republican from North Dakota takes on new interest as 1990s post–Cold War isolationism again features a blend of Left and Right variations.

At the same time, the transformation of the American economy after World War I, and especially the hardships of the social dislocations always caused by such transformations, captured the imagination of religious and once-removed religious pacifist groups as well, driving many toward a more Marxian social analysis. Pacifists did not accept Marxism as such nor its doctrine of class warfare, but many were swayed by the view that a society based on capitalist economic organization was necessarily unequal and, therefore, necessarily engendered coercive (i.e., violent) relationships.

The tragedies of the Great Depression, in particular, encouraged new mixtures of pacifist and radical socialist thought. A. J. Muste's career best exemplified the development of the New Pacifism. Born in Holland in 1885, Muste was ordained in the Dutch Reform Church in 1913, but soon lost his first pulpit because of his radical political inclinations. Muste then helped found the American branch of the Fellowship of Reconciliation (FOR) in 1915 and led it during a tumultuous time in the pacifist movement after World War I and the Bolshevik Revolution. Traditional pacifism had been characterized by a continuity of means and ends, to wit: Violent means cannot be used to support nonviolent ends any more than one can grow a rose from a cactus seed. While traditional pacifists hewed to this means-ends unity, others, like Muste, believed that one had to wage class warfare to prevent international warfare. Muste renounced his pacifism and became general secretary of the Communist League of America in the 1930s, a member of the Fourth International (Trotskyite). Although he eventually left communism and rejoined the FOR in 1937, he did so with a radically changed idea of pacifism, at the center of which was a novel definition of violence.

Muste believed that the economic, social, and political order was built up and sustained by violence, which he defined very broadly as any influence that caused someone's intrinsic interests to be violated. He believed that since most of the world's "violence," thus defined, was caused by forces of the status quo, it was unfair to focus on the small amount perpetrated by revolutionaries. Muste also argued that it was wrong for pacifists to advocate nonviolence to nonpacifist revolutionaries as long as pacifists benefitted from the existing order. Moreover, since the violence of the status quo was a prior violence, violence directed against it was not as bad, and could even be justifiable, since its aim was justice rather than exploitation.[17]

The encounter with socialist antiwar activism in the interwar period split and changed American pacifism forever. Some pure originalists held out for years; a few still do. But Muste brought about an enticing blend of proletarian internationalism propelled by the spirit of class warfare with religious pacifism motivated by the Christian ideal of turning the other cheek. This blend allowed the satisfying sense of moral absolutism to mix comfortably with the political vocabulary of a new era. The result was to transpose the Christian concept of martyrdom from an individual and theological level to a "class" and political level. The sufferings of Christ became the sufferings of the lower classes; redemption meant not being led to heaven by faith but building heaven on earth through revolutionary political devotion. Where it ended for most was reflected in the programmatic statement of the War Resister's League (WRL), a nonreligious offshoot of the FOR formed in 1923. The WRL was dedicated to political, economic, and social revolution by nonviolent means, but it supported the right of others to employ violence toward the attainment of just ends.

During the Great Depression, radical pacifism spread from the Protestant traditions to the Catholic one. In 1933 Dorothy Day and Peter Maurin formed an organization called The Catholic Worker.[18] They began with Houses of Hospitality to feed the hungry and house the homeless, but soon began publishing *The Catholic Worker,* an anarcho-pacifist journal that joined tógether an idolization of St. Francis d'Assisi with the ideals of the Industrial Workers of the World (IWW)—the Wobblies. Anticipating the basic themes of the counterculture by 30 years, Day and Maurin believed in a doctrine called personalism, which held that the megastructures of modern society were inherently corrosive of spiritual life and human dignity. They opposed capitalism and nationalism with equal vigor.

Naturally enough, *The Catholic Worker* favored the ill-fated syndicalists in the Spanish Civil War. After they were destroyed at the hands of fascists and Communists alike, the editors developed a strong antipathy to both main currents of European political thought in the 1930s—right-wing socialism (fascism) and left-wing socialism (communism). This antipathy in turn reinforced their anarchist approach to revolutionary theory and their isolationist approach to foreign policy.

The development and diversification of the new pacifism notwithstanding, the center of gravity in the adversary culture during the Great Depression moved away from "old" and "new" pacifists alike and back once more toward radical Left socialism. It also was a period in which the liberal "peace reform" of turn-of-the-century origins was itself partly radicalized and the remainder largely eclipsed, discredited from within and from without by having supported U.S. involvement in World War I. The fate of the still-small U.S. Socialist Party in this period is illustrative. Part was radicalized and eventually left the party for orthodox Marxism and Trotskyism; the remaining "liberal" anti-Communists fell either into irrelevance or into the larger Democratic Party, where, with interesting consequences, it has more or less remained ever since.

The second shift in the mix of adversary culture tendencies occurred with the onset of World War II, which was seen almost universally as a just war. As a result, the American body politic in effect adopted the discontinuity of the ends-means continuum of the new pacifism, turning from isolationism in the recognition that violence was necessary to defeat fascism, racism, and militarism. But the new pacifists opposed the war, thus falling into disrepute as Adolf Hitler's monstrous demonstration of evil became ever clearer.

Radical socialist antiwar agitators lost ground on two other levels. First, as American society came to more mature terms with its labor problems, agitators' tactics were increasingly resented by what was emerging as the mainstream of the labor movement.[19] That mainstream, moreover, was patriotic in the most basic sense; it was not prepared to look a national emergency in the eye, blink, and call it something that it was not. In contrast, the Molotov–von Ribbentrop, Soviet-Nazi Non-Aggression Pact of 1939 badly hurt the radicalized shard of the labor movement that, by then, was dominated increasingly by the pro-Moscow U.S. Communist Party. Second, the war did for the economy what the New Deal could not; radicalized labor lost ground because the raison d'être of desperation receded before the swell of new employment and higher wages as well as the pulling together of American society in the face of a clear and present danger.

What pacifists and Marxists lost as a result of "the good war," liberals regained. The Democratic Party welcomed lapsed pacifists, Marxists, and socialists with open arms. They were never the majority of the party, but they became enough of a coherent force to lead to Henry Wallace's independent presidential bid in 1948.

The only kind of pacifism that had held its own during the war was the old sort centered on the traditional "peace" churches: the Quakers, the Mennonites, and the Church of the Brethren. Conscientious objection during World War II was not common, but those conscientious objectors as there were, with their families and supporting religious communities, grew stronger in self-enforced isolation. After the war, while liberals worked to extend the New Deal and radical Left socialists cowered before Cold War McCarthyite excesses, traditional pacifists and new pacifists alike influenced the ban-the-bomb movement out of proportion to their numbers.

## FROM BAN-THE-BOMB TO VIETNAM

In the late 1940s and 1950s, the birth of the nuclear age infused all three streams of the adversary culture with new strength. Americans were afraid of the bomb and confused as to why, after they had won the war, there was still no real peace. Americans took out their frustrations on the Soviet Union, though, it must be said, this was not entirely without justification. Most Americans reacted to coping with the bomb and the Cold War in three ways: anesthetization, resignation, and protest.

Anesthetization was a most popular reaction, particularly after Americans had managed to live with the bomb for a few years—even through the Berlin Crisis of 1948—without incinerating the planet. The consumer boom, the hypnotic effects of television, which fuzzed the border between reality and image for many people (and still does), and the rhapsodic calm of "Grandpa" Ike playing golf while Soviet Premier Nikita Khrushchev blustered and bragged—all of this was very comforting in its own way. But, as many observers have contended, it was, or at least it seemed, hellishly dull. It was perhaps no coincidence that the younger musicians of the mid-1950s took the acoustic rhythms of the blues and boogie woogie and turned them into the electric rumble of rock and roll.

Another word about music is in order before moving on. The music of the 1950s had a brash, rebellious side to it, and it was political at least in the sense that it defined an early generation gap. When Elvis Presley shook his hips and pouted out his music, teens swooned and their parents blanched. Once popular music acquired such an image, it was a fairly short step to the increasingly politicized lyrics of the 1960s, which spread antiwar and antiauthority messages far and wide. Meanwhile, the mass production and consumption of music for young people was as novel as the designation "youth" itself. Charles Kaiser exaggerated only a little when he wrote that the teenagers of the 1960s generation were reared to become frustrated idealists who wanted to live apart morally from their parents and embrace causes larger than themselves, and that "neither impulse could have been satisfied without our two most powerful inspirations: the war and the radio."[20]

Songs with war-related or otherwise political themes were a particularly potent mixture. Though prior generations managed to revolt against their parents without rock or radios, music was extraordinarily important to the average student, radical and not so radical, of the 1960s generation, just as music seems to be important to every generation of youth. For the 1960s generation, the ideology of the times was expressed and conveyed less in books and pamphlets than in lyrics. Granted, such ideological expression is short on intellectual precision, but it is long on emotion—that is what music is for, after all.

In the 1950s and 1960s resignation ran a close second to anesthetization as a response to the nuclear age. Building bomb shelters became moderately popular not because people rated their chances of surviving a nuclear war to be very high, but because some chance was better than no chance at all in what many saw as the inevitable nuclear fire to come. Even resignation had its uses; cartoonist Jules Feiffer once depicted a would-be romeo making use of "rocket rattle" to bed down his female target of the moment under the pretense that if she didn't "let down her hair" now, she may never have the chance. This maudlin attitude, although drawn in jest, was not so far removed from those of later antiwar movement conclaves and demonstrations that combined fear and indignation with personal indulgences, sexual and drug-related.

Among traditionally religious rural folk, resignation had a millenarian edge: nuclear war was the apocalypse and the Cold War was the epochal struggle between Gog and Magog. This fateful notion, which is still prevalent within some evangelical churches and which once seeped into an open-microphone faux pas of President Ronald Reagan, found expression in the popular country music of the period. Here too music was important as a means of expression; it was epitomized by the Louvin Brothers's modern country gospel song "The Great Atomic Power," which climbed the country record charts in 1953.[21]

Then there was protest. From the new pacifism, represented by the FOR, AFSC, and WRL, came new efforts and projects organized around the bomb. These groups were active from 1946 onward but had little impact amid the *realpolitik*-minded consensus of the early Cold War period.[22] A bit later, the liberal section of the adversary culture gradually reemerged from the strange interlude of McCarthyite hysteria, and that is when the ban-the-bomb movement gathered strength.

Initially, liberal antibomb activism attached itself to existing organizations devoted to the ideal of transforming the United Nations into a world government through world law, namely the United World Federalists and the Federation of Atomic Scientists. But these organizations proved too timid, and their agendas too narrow, for those who wished to protest the bomb as a means to spread a broader political agenda.[23] SANE, the Committee for a Sane Nuclear Policy, was born from the AFSC in 1957 as the Provisional Committee to Stop Nuclear Tests. Its founders included Lawrence Scott, Norman Cousins, Clarence Pickett, Norman Thomas, and Benjamin Spock, all of whom ended up playing a role in the antiwar movement. Most had been associated with the new pacifism in the interwar period, and many were now Democratic Left-Liberal veterans of the 1948 Henry Wallace campaign. Some, like Thomas, were still connected to what remained of the U.S. Socialist Party.

In the late 1950s and early 1960s, SANE's leadership was torn between the standard Left-Liberal agenda, particularly nuclear disarmament and civil rights, and the more ambitious redemptive temptations of the new pacifism. For the most part, SANE's rank-and-file membership of a few thousand was increasingly composed of typical American liberals in the great age of American liberalism. SANE was hurt in the early 1960s when the Marxist old Left managed to penetrate a number of local chapters, particularly in the New York area. SANE's *primus inter pares,* Norman Cousins, became so alarmed at this that in 1960 he actually asked the FBI to investigate the organization and to inform the leadership of efforts to subvert it from within.[24] After dramatic Congressional hearings led by Senator Thomas Dodd, SANE purged its chapters. Leaving the organization's leadership in protest over what they saw as an artificial and ignoble narrowing of SANE's political base were A. J. Muste, AFSC stalwarts Bob Gilmore and Stewart Meacham, and Linus Pauling, some of whom then founded a "federative" organization called Turn Toward Peace, where Marxists and radical pacifists could breathe more freely.[25]

The early 1960s also witnessed the first real, if modest, merger of the Democratic Party's post-1930s Left-Liberal wing with the adversary culture's antibomb activism of the 1950s. One result of this merging was expressed by President John F. Kennedy's willingness to support the creation of the Arms Control and Disarmament Agency (ACDA) and to wage a "peace race" instead of an "arms race"—an idea coined by SANE member and Columbia University industrial sociologist Seymour Melman.[26] Kennedy staffed ACDA through the most liberal wing of the Party, which was positively disposed toward SANE in its post-purge phase. Thus, for example, Marcus Raskin joined ACDA in 1962. Raskin was soon disillusioned with government and in 1963 helped found the Institute for Policy Studies (IPS).[27] At its inception, IPS was already to the Left of the liberal consensus; by 1966 it had become an ecumenically radical institutional base for dozens of prominent antiwar activists.

There was another side to the Kennedy administration's liberalism, however, that gradually put it in direct confrontation with the Wallacite left wing of the party in the nuclear age. As the administration reworked the national security bureaucracy inherited from the Eisenhower administration, it brought into government the "best and the brightest."[28] Kennedy's trust in applied social science to provide solutions to poverty and racism—as in Project Camelot[29]—applied to national security too. Kennedy staffed the Pentagon with Robert S. McNamara, who brought on the computers and the "whiz kids" to run them. Civilian intellectuals centered around the RAND Corporation dominated strategic thinking in those young days of the nuclear era, in time producing the game-theoretical concepts of mutual assured destruction and graduated response. The former, the first serious intellectual attempt to come to grips with the novelty of the nuclear age, remained the mainstay of U.S. strategic thought through the doctrinal refinements of Defense Secretary James Schlesinger in 1975 and arguably until the promulgation of a Presidential Decision (PD-59) in 1979 revised the basis of U.S. strategic targeting doctrine. The latter notion, graduated response, was tested coldly in "technowar" in Vietnam.[30]

There was a certain irony in all this, for while the Kennedy administration's early rhetoric and SANE's relative restraint were drawing the Left-Liberal section of the adversary culture closer to mainstream American politics, and while liberal intellectuals joined government in high positions in unprecedented numbers, the administration was presiding over the largest buildup of strategic ballistic forces in the history of the nuclear era. It was also half-wittingly deepening the U.S. commitment in Southeast Asia and, through the strategic theology of graduated response, ensuring that the commitment would lead to disaster.

## THE CIVIL RIGHTS STRUGGLE
## AND THE VIETNAM GENERATION

There has been an adversary culture in the United States since at least the 1820s, its general influence waxing or waning as a function not only of its inner dynamic, but also of the general state of insecurity and change in society at large. Were it not for the challenge and confusion that periodically besets normal societies, political phenomena such as a civil rights or an antiwar movement could not attract the energies or absorb the adversary culture influence that they do. It seems obvious, therefore, that the growth of adversary culture influence in the 1960s clearly stemmed from the monumental social changes taking place at the time.

The American generation of the 1950s and 1960s—in other words, those born between the early 1940s and the early 1950s—that was molded by the civil rights movement and traumatized by Vietnam lived in unusual times. Its members did not see the Great Depression, the labor violence, and old Left deceits of that era, or experience directly the sacrifices and enthusiasms of World War II. Even the Korean War was for most a forgotten war in a far-off place. It is more useful to reflect, however, not on what this generation did not experience but on what it did experience in the 1950s and early 1960s.

Between 1947 and 1970 its members witnessed a sustained economic expansion unprecedented in Western economic history.[31] They saw the exponential growth of suburbia and the birth of the consumer society, two phenomena that in turn helped break down the authority of both the extended and nuclear family and the religious bonds that typically went with them. The new suburban churches and synagogues, in turn, bowing to the pressures of the secular consumer society, relegated God to footnotes and preached instead on social issues, self-help, and aesthetics. This Vietnam generation was the first to grow up with television, beholding the noble heroics of Mighty Mouse and the military caricaturing of Sergeant Bilko.[32] They were the first generation of the rock and roll era—featuring the Twist, the first dance in recent times where touching your partner was unnecessary—and the first generation of not "a chicken in every pot" but a two-tone automotive marvel in every driveway. A bit later, they also became the first generation of the new math, where suddenly it was not as important to work to get the right answer as it was to "understand the concept"—and so obtain instant wisdom. They became the generation of the sexual revolution, aided by the technology of birth control—and so they knew instant, (almost) worry-free gratification.

But they were also the first generation to grow up with the bomb. The raw materials of the age—waxing wealth, powerful cars, fast music, electronic entertainment, wild anomic dancing to rock and roll, and the ever-present but suppressed possibility of instant atomic death—came crashing together to form a unique generational personality. On the whole, it was a time of great hope and novelty, with the nuclear danger playing a descant in a minor key to the optimistic melody of the age. Todd Gitlin said that "It's that down-under-the-desk experience that was our sign that 'Ozzie and Harriet' was a lie."[33] But *Ozzie and Harriet* wasn't a lie; it was a coping mechanism.

By and large the 1950s seemed complacent times, even for the young. Few had any intimate contact with beatniks or their ideas—the role of Maynard G. Krebs on *The Many Loves of Dobie Gillis* was about as close as most got. Even James Dean's rebel star was a mild undercurrent before his death. The Vietnam generation was, after all, raised on a still-unspoiled faith in science and optimistic moral clarity. Racism was wrong, freedom was right. Communism was wrong, liberty was right. We could travel in outer space. We defeated polio. We *could* change our society for the better; we *could* defeat the Communist challenge by aiding the world's underdogs with the Peace Corps and foreign aid. The United States had never lost a war, nobody blanched at pledging allegiance to the flag, and it was taken for granted that the president and those in authority did not lie to you. To the stable political anchors of the domestic order was added a deep national consensus on foreign policy and military strategy. On the surface at least, things were okay.

Below the surface, however, the vast array of social and economic changes inherent in consumerism, suburbia, and the worship of technology that gave rise to both[34] produced notable cultural criticism in the work of writers Allen Ginsberg, Jack Kerouac, William S. Burroughs, Ken Kesey, and the rest of the beatniks. The beatniks were clearly the model against which the older cohort of 1960s radicals—those out of high school by 1960—modeled themselves on.[35] Some of the beatniks remained personally engaged in the movement too. Ginsberg was at the Pentagon in October 1967 and led an om chant while Abbie Hoffman led the attempt to levitate the building. Kesey was at Berkeley during Free Speech Movement times, although his influence was not very constructive.

A pertinent example of the beatniks' indirect influence concerns Tom Hayden. It was after reading Kerouac's *On the Road* that Hayden set out from Ann Arbor in June 1960 to go cross country in an effort to imitate the life of actor James Dean, the first rebel antihero of the American screen. In California he was politicized by some old Left acquaintances, and, by the time he returned to Ann Arbor a year later, Hayden had become a community "activist."[36]

Also, as sociologist Kenneth Keniston pointed out at the time, the post-war generation was the first to wear the social definition "youth," a novel classification somewhere between adolescence and responsible adulthood, made possible by great affluence and made necessary by the prolonged educational preparation demanded by the new "technetronic" society.[37] Its quarters were the hallowed confines of the university, but as a stage in life it was sui generis, without clear boundaries of expectations or trespass bequeathed by precedent. Little wonder, then, that the American university has never been the same since the postwar generation worked out its possibilities and limits on campuses throughout the nation in the 1960s.

This Vietnam generation may also have been affected, in ways we do not yet fully understand, by the explosion of vivid and colorful fantasies in movies and television. Mainly designed for children, movies such as *Cinderella* and *Peter Pan* may have given many members of the Vietnam generation extraordinarily high expectations of a normal life. No doubt against their better conscious judgment, many retain such expectations today. This is not just speculation; survey data strongly suggest it. Opinion expert Daniel Yankelovich concluded in 1985 that baby-boomers want a return to "good old-fashioned romance and happy endings, feel their lives are duller than they ought to be," and demand a life with more "sparkle and excitement."[38] Indeed, it may not be entirely frivolous to ask whether the proliferation of near-hysterical midlife crises among members of the Vietnam generation—particularly among men—is related to the childhood inculcation of highly unrealistic expectations of personal power, freedom, goodness, excitement, stimulation, and achievement.

In sum, most members of this Vietnam generation grew up with a sense of moral engagement, unlimited personal prospects, and social hopefulness virtually unfettered by any sense of a past. Anything that had happened before World War II might as well have happened before the Flood as far as most young people were concerned. This attitude amounted to a sort of invincibility. Not only that, but with so many instant marvels around, from soup to photographs, and with the increasingly ubiquitous cacophony of television advertising enthroning the pleasure principle beyond Freud's wildest dreams, one got the feeling that an all-pervasive progress was inevitable. Total automation was around the corner; hard work, sacrifice, and deferred gratification were passé. The Protestant ethic was something one read about in books, or that dripped with complaint from the mouths of grandparents and war veterans of a bygone age.

That is why the civil rights movement, or more pointedly, the problem of the denial of civil rights to Negroes,[39] was so important when it struck the consciousness and television screens of young America, starting in 1954 and accelerating into the early 1960s. It burst the bubble of optimism, progress, fantasy cum future, and, indeed, the sanitized sense of near-perfection that American children grew up with after World War II. The civil rights struggle was by far the most important and most proximate catalyst for the Vietnam antiwar movement.[40] American racism against Native Americans and blacks has been the greatest stain on an otherwise laudable historical record of adaptability and tolerance in domestic affairs. But the liberal, idealistic generation that came to political consciousness during the civil rights struggle saw the stain of racism so vividly, thanks in large part to the new power of television, that for many it obscured the broader view. Moreover, the awareness that the United States was flawed cast a shadow on other gilded truths to which the previous few generations had become inured, including the orthodoxies of containment and the Cold War. If things were not all to the good at home, it occurred to some that perhaps they might be all to the bad not only at home but also in the American role abroad.[41] It struck many that, as cartoonist Walt Kelley put it famously in his comic strip *Pogo,* "We have met the enemy and he is us"—or at least he is our parents.

The collision between idealism as bequeathed to youth by a lucky and benighted age with the flaws of modernity—the suffocating embrace of conformity, hypermaterialism, insensitivity to injustice—led to a crisis of belief. "Students simply do not know what to believe," wrote Joseph Califano in 1969, after the problem had persisted long enough to become clear. "Everywhere they look in the society around them—the church, the university, the world of business and politics—they see hypocrisy. And a significant number of students see hypocrisy more clearly in their own families than anywhere else."[42]

What may aptly be called the crisis of meaning for an agonized affluent generation was the source not only of a deep disaffection from the status quo, but also of a very powerful energy to change it. As we shall see too, the large role of the civil rights struggle in the initial confrontation with hypocrisy led, in the ensuing antiwar movement, to a romantic and blinding loyalty on the part of many white radicals to black perspectives and personalities via the Black Panthers organization and other expressions of black politics later in the 1960s.

It cannot be argued that the special socialization of the Vietnam generation was responsible in any simple way for the antiwar movement. The movement waxed and waned due to several independent variables; a remote factor such as basic socialization obviously cannot be directly correlated with a social movement that arose more than a decade later. But the Vietnam generation seems to have been predisposed to protest, to see official malfeasance, and to generate and then be lured by the enticements of the counterculture. As Francis Bacon observed in 1625, speaking "Of Seditions and Troubles": "If there be fuel prepared, it is hard to tell whence the spark shall come that shall set it on fire."[43] Had not civil rights and then Vietnam lit the fire, no doubt something else would have.

The Vietnam generation is still special. Although it has lost its innocence and much of its optimism, most of its members have retained their deep socialization into the pleasure principle. Yuppies are no more than the core cadres of the Vietnam generation entering middle age; hence the growing market for premature nostalgia, exercise without perspiration, diets without sacrifice, eating without having to cook, and opulence—through overextended credit—without having to save.

## FROM SELMA TO SAIGON

The civil rights movement, too, was clearly a product of an age of affluence and optimism, including even relative affluence and optimism among Negroes. But it was a product that, however nobly motivated and however widely endorsed by Negroes from leadership echelons to the street, might not have gotten very far—at least at first—without the broad support and sponsorship of white liberals, disproportionately Jewish liberals at that. The two seminal events that preceded the Birmingham bus boycott of 1955—the desegregation of the armed forces in 1948 and *Brown v. the Board of Education* in May 1954, which voided the separate but equal principle of segregated public schooling—were mainly the work of white liberals. Once the boycott took place, the civil rights movement became a true mass movement into which countless brave souls, mainly black but still also white, poured their energies and hard work, and even gave their lives.

To most liberals, the civil rights struggle was a necessary diversion from the ban-the-bomb movement, an obligatory and guilt-stained cleansing of the political soul. The radical Left and the new pacifism were soon involved in the civil rights movement too, but for different reasons. For the sectarian Left, civil rights was an issue to ride toward a radical politicization of Negroes and organized labor. For pacifists it was, to their everlasting credit, an old issue over which they had agonized and organized for more than a century.

The liberals' sense of moral stain, coupled with the idealism engendered in a new generation inspired by the youngest president in the nation's history, established the foundations of the early antiwar movement. Indeed, its sudden strength in 1964-65 is best explained by the coincidence of the institutional maturing of an essentially middle-class, midgenerational peace movement on the one hand and an equally middle-class but somewhat younger-generational civil rights movement on the other. Within this generationally two-tiered movement, the liberal establishment furnished the necessary respectability, the crucial organizational connections, and the well-honed political skills, while the younger generation—mainly college students— supplied the foot soldiers and the moral fervor, which youth seems to produce so effortlessly. The ban-the-bomb institutional base was very important too, but it was small. Had it not been for the experience of the civil rights struggle, liberals and Left-Liberals would never have been able to mount so rapidly an effective campaign against increasing U.S. involvement in Vietnam.

The sectarian Left and the new pacifists railed against U.S. involvement in the Vietnam War from the very start as part of their general opposition to U.S. foreign policy. Based on their own preexisting organizations and networks dedicated to both infiltrating and promoting the ban-the-bomb cause, radical groups sponsored and organized the first "peace" demonstrations as early as 1962 over an issue that had nothing to do with the bomb: They marched in support of Fidel Castro's Cuba and against American economic and (supposed) military pressures on him. Fidel was their hero, Columbia University sociologist C. Wright Mills was their prophet, and his recent book *Listen Yankee* was their gospel.

Before 1965, public demonstrations against the war were small and rare, and nearly all of them were sponsored by the organizations of the radical Left or of the new pacifism. A few were the work of still essentially liberal organizations—notably the Women's International League for Peace and Freedom (WILPF)—whose sense of proper and allowable tactics had been deeply influenced by the civil rights movement. There was also the Women's Strike for Peace (WSP), founded in 1961 on a ban-the-bomb platform. WSP was made up seemingly of archetypal suburban liberals, but it came to sound alternately like a vaguely Marxist or a vaguely anarchist group, depending on the spokesperson or the issue of the moment.

At the time, most liberals and most liberal organizations were far more concerned with the progress of the civil rights movement and with the lobbying campaign for a ban on atmospheric nuclear testing than they were with Vietnam. SANE was a partial exception. In September 1963, less than a month after the signing of the Partial Test Ban Treaty, the national board of SANE called publicly for U.S. "disengagement" from Vietnam.[44] But it sponsored no public protests and its view later became relatively more moderate.

SANE's position and tactics regarding U.S. involvement in Vietnam in these early years were colored by run-ins with more radical groups. In April 1963, for example, the annual ban-the-bomb march was held in New York City. It went under the name of the Easter Peace Walk and was held in sympathy with the British Aldermaston marches of the Campaign for Nuclear Disarmament (CND). Aldermaston was a weapons development and testing center in Great Britain, and on that day thousands of protesters marched from Aldermaston to London to protest the existence of nuclear weapons. The New York rally was larger by far in 1963 than it had been in previous years—perhaps as many as 7,000 people gathered in United Nations Plaza. There were two reasons for this: the possibility that an atmospheric test ban might be negotiated and signed so soon after the terrifying episode of the Cuban Missile Crisis and the fact that Pope John XXIII had only three days earlier issued an encyclical called *Pacem in Terris*. The encyclical was heady stuff for the American Catholic church in those days; it stated that "if civil authorities legislate for, or allow, anything that is contrary to [the moral] order, and therefore contrary to the will of God, neither the laws made nor the authorizations granted can be binding on the consciences of the citizens, since *we must obey God rather than men.*"[45]

The April 1963 rally was primarily a liberal and church-based affair; SANE was the *primus inter pares* of the sponsoring groups. But others showed up too, with signs protesting American involvement in Vietnam. The SANE organizers, reasoning that the Kennedy administration liberals they were trying to influence on nuclear issues would not be inclined to listen to critics of their Vietnam policy, demanded that the signs be put away. David Dellinger of the War Resisters League and Fred Halstead of the Socialist Workers Party (Trotskyite) refused. Even worse from SANE's point of view was that both Dellinger and the ubiquitous A. J. Muste were on the program, and, having been urged on by British philosopher Bertrand Russell, both chose to speak about Vietnam from the rostrum. The SANE board of directors was outraged and told Dellinger that he would never again be allowed to speak at a SANE-sponsored rally.[46] The April 1963 tussle was a harbinger of much competition and bitterness to come within the antiwar movement.

As this incident suggests, public protest over Vietnam was not part of the agenda of liberal groups, and it did not become a part until 1965. In 1963 and 1964, the effort by what soon became known as the right wing of the antiwar movement tried to restrain U.S. involvement in Southeast Asia through well-connected private conversation, newspaper articles and advertisements, by the social and professional networks of the ruling liberal elites, and through the voices of Senators Ernest Gruening and Wayne Morse. This effort was far more successful than has been generally recognized, although of course it did not stop the U.S. involvement in Vietnam in its tracks.

Public demonstrations that later became such a staple of the antiwar movement were far less frequent and less significant at the time; in fact, they went virtually unnoticed by the administration and the press corps. In August 1963, for example, at a march commemorating the destruction of Hiroshima and Nagasaki, Student

Peace Union (SPU) demonstrators, mainly from the University of Pennsylvania, marched in front of the federal building in Philadelphia. At the same time in New York, the Catholic Worker movement marched in front of Vietnam's permanent observer mission to the United Nations. Two men kept a vigil for ten days; they were then joined by about 250 other activists. An ABC film crew put it on the national evening news—another first. But hardly anyone noticed these actions for, in the same month, a quarter of a million people participated in the March on Washington and listened to Dr. Martin Luther King, Jr., as he spoke about "a dream."

Small-scale radical actions continued nevertheless. In October 1963, student radicals from the SPU and Students for a Democratic Society organized protests against the visit of President Ngo Dinh Diem's sister-in-law, Madame Ngo Dinh Nhu.[47] In April 1964, 200 WILPF and WSP protestors demanded an immediate cease-fire and tried to "expose the myth that South Vietnam is being invaded." Later in the month, the *National Guardian,* a New York paper of the old Left, carried a pledge from 87 university students of their resistance to serving in the military because of U.S. involvement in Vietnam. The advertisement was organized by Phillip Luce, who at the time was under federal indictment for defying a travel ban to Cuba and who was deeply devoted to the Cuban revolution.[48] Many "liberal" publications refused to carry the advertisement, probably because all the signatories were self-proclaimed Leftists, many from the Progressive Labor Party, the Maoist offshoot of the U.S. Communist Party. Later, in May, Luce managed to get a similar advertisement published in the *New York Herald Tribune,* by no means a Leftist paper, in which 149 men of draft age pledged not to go to Vietnam if called on to do so.

On May 2 a youthful Maoist group calling itself M2M (May 2nd Movement) organized about 1,000 radical Marxists in five cities to proclaim their refusal to fight "for the suppression of the Vietnamese struggle for national independence."[49] These actions had been planned some weeks earlier at Yale University by an offshoot group of the Progressive Labor Party, with the help and inspiration of history professor Staughton Lynd. In New York about 400 students gathered at 110th Street and Amsterdam Avenue at the Church of St. John the Divine and proceeded to march on Times Square and the United Nations. Along with Progressive Labor members were Trotskyites young and old from the Young Socialist Alliance and the Socialist Workers Party, respectively.

New pacifists were also involved. On July 3, 1964, the day that President Johnson signed the Civil Rights Act on the White House lawn, David Dellinger organized a demonstration across the street in Lafayette Park. With him were A. J. Muste, radical Catholic priests Philip and Daniel Berrigan, Rabbi Abraham Feinberg, and folksinger Joan Baez, among others.[50] There they read the "Declaration of Conscience," which was, in effect, a declaration of war against the Vietnam War through civil disobedience. It was modeled on the French *Manifeste des 121* written in 1960 by French Leftist intellectuals who opposed the Algerian War. The declaration had been put together by Dellinger, Muste, and black civil rights leader Bayard Rustin in the offices of *Liberation* magazine, the broadside of the WRL begun in 1956 by Dellinger.[51]

On August 6, 1964, Hiroshima Day, just a few days after the Tonkin Gulf incidents, where North Vietnamese gunners fired at U.S. naval vessels sailing in international waters, and one day before the final passage of the Tonkin Gulf Resolution in the Congress, a few hundred people gathered in Washington Square in New York to hear Rustin and Norman Thomas denounce U.S. involvement in the war. A few days later, M2M picketed the World's Fair in New York, and 16 out of about 60 people were arrested when they refused a police order to disperse—another antiwar movement first.

Later that month, in a mild harbinger of the 1968 Democratic National Convention in Chicago, 200 radical pacifists, mostly from New York, protested outside the Democratic National Convention in Atlantic City against "the immoral nature of U.S. policies in Vietnam." Inside the convention hall, the Democrats were determined not to let Senator Barry Goldwater, the Republican presidential nominee, make hay in the election by pointing to Democratic "weakness" over Vietnam. Senator William Fulbright of Arkansas sponsored a toughly worded resolution supporting President Johnson's Vietnam policies, evidently believing that it might help both to deter the North Vietnamese and, as important, to put the president in a stronger position to resist Goldwater's arguments for escalation. The radical pacifists standing outside either could not or would not understand the logic or the politics of the overwhelming vote in favor of the resolution.

Small demonstrations continued and more groups became involved in the nascent antiwar movement. They attracted little media attention and their impact on policy was insignificant, but they did refine the cooperative efforts of key adversary culture core groups who riveted their attentions increasingly on Vietnam to the exclusion of other issues. In October 1964, for example, 12 people from WSP, the SPU, the WRL, the FOR, and the Catholic Worker began a vigil against the war in Times Square. In the developing history of coalition-building among pacifist and Leftist groups, this was a small but significant watershed because, a year later, they were still there holding vigil. In November the WRL called publicly for "immediate and total" withdrawal of the United States from Vietnam, which was what radical groups had had in mind from the start—this was simply the first time any group had stated it so plainly. In reaction, perhaps, SANE sponsored its first public demonstration against the war. Over Thanksgiving weekend, some SANE members who were gathered in Washington for their annual convention marched in front of the White House. But their message was distinctly different. They called for negotiations, not immediate withdrawal. And only a minority of the convention showed up at the protest.

Finally, in December, a novel coalition was formed of three radical groups. The first was the War Resisters League, and the second was one of its offshoots, the Committee for Non-Violent Action (CNVA), which had been founded in 1957 to conduct "direct action" civil disobedience against "nuclear war targets." Third was a group of Catholic Worker pacifists. Together the three groups opened a campaign to resist the draft and obstruct the flow of "war munitions" on the grounds that U.S. policy in Vietnam was "a crime." One event was a rally held in New York at Washington Square on December 19. It was organized by David McReynolds of the WRL, by Muste in his CNVA capacity, and joined as well by the FOR.

The interesting thing about this particular rally was that Norman Thomas and A. Philip Randolph, who were more in the Left-Liberal to liberal camp than in the radical one, spoke as well. Everyone on the podium wanted an end to U.S. involvement in the war; deep disagreements over how it should end and how that ending was to be achieved were deliberately muted. In retrospect, the December 19 rally was one of the last rallies until 1969-70 during which the radical and liberal parts of the antiwar movement could sit more or less convivially on the same podium. One of the main reasons for this difficulty in maintaining broad antiwar coalitions was SDS, which, in different ways, frightened Left-Liberals, pacifist radicals, and old Left members alike. Chapter 3 discusses SDS in more detail.

## THE OPPOSITION WITHIN

The Arabs have a proverb that makes general sense: "All things start small except calamity." But it does not apply to Vietnam, which started small and became a calamity anyway. Yet the calamity did not happen all that easily, for opposition to expanding the American role there existed all along. But the opposition that mattered most in the early years of American involvement did not come from the street; it came from within the government.

The fact is that the United States did not rush into the Vietnam War with its saber at the ready and its heart set on violence. A basically liberal nation, governed by a liberal administration stocked with liberal intellectuals and supported overwhelmingly by organized labor, rather danced and dodged into Vietnam tentatively, anxiously, and about as unconsciously as could possibly be managed.[52] Despite President Kennedy's rhetoric about going anywhere and paying any price for liberty, nobody was looking for new San Juan Hills to be charged in Southeast Asia, and nobody of elevated stature in the White House, the State Department, or the civilian offices of the secretary of defense hoped to find any.

But as President Kennedy soon found out with Republican jousting over Cuba, the anti-Communist orthodoxy of the day was such that any action that might be seen as soft on the Communists had to be planned with the utmost caution. Some claim that Kennedy understood the dangers of getting involved in Vietnam and planned to reduce the U.S. commitment and disengage American prestige after he had won the 1964 presidential election, but dared not do so beforehand lest he lose that election.[53] Although his assessment is exaggerated, journalist Gary Wills captured the tone of the times:

> Over and over again in recent history Presidents have claimed that they had to act tough in order to disarm those demanding that they act tough. The only way to become a peacemaker is first to disarm the war maker by making a little successful war. And if the little war becomes a big one, it must be pursued energetically or the "hawks" will capitalize on the failure. If you are for it, you wage it. And if you are against it, you wage it.[54]

To some degree, the liberal administration's lack of enthusiasm for military adventures abroad was the result of many years' work by the adversary culture. To be sure, the adversary culture never dominated the country, whether before or after World War II, but it did affect various social attitudes all the same. The views of an establishment liberal in 1965 had much in common with the views of an anti-establishment radical in 1920 or 1930 because the establishment itself had changed; one has only to think of labor-management relations, views about the utility of international organizations, and attitudes toward race relations to get the point. When it came to war and peace, the legitimacy of using force and stealth in foreign policy had been eroded in official thinking over time.

The epic struggle over the Vietnam War was, or at any rate became, a struggle about the future of the American establishment. Would "progressive" views make further inroads into what was taken for granted as the status quo, or not? Would the United States push on into new seas, or would it throw its anchor over and rest in calmer waters? The Vietnam War, at least as it looked in 1961 when John Kennedy entered the White House, never figured to be a major theme in the epochal struggle of the New Frontier, the evocative label Kennedy gave to his programs in echo of Roosevelt's New Deal and Truman's Fair Deal. At the time, it was thought a minor matter, all things considered; it just didn't stay that way.

Radical groups cannot properly be said to have fomented the Vietnam antiwar movement or had much influence on it in the earliest stages.[55] Their turn came later. Particularly before February 1965, when the war was Americanized, the movement had the tone of the civil rights movement; it was an argument within the family so to speak, within the elite and the social strata from which the elite came. It was a civil protest motivated by a desire to reform and to purify, not to revolt or purge.[56] For this reason, opposition to expanding U.S. involvement in the Vietnam War penetrated easily into the governmental bureaucracy and into universities, for these were the bastions of the broadening American ruling elite.

Although the drama of later events and images has obscured it, the fact is that the antiwar movement's nascent period (before 1966)—if construed in its broadest sense to mean all those actions and agents devoted to restricting the U.S. commitment in Vietnam—was probably the movement's most effective phase in limiting U.S. military involvement in Southeast Asia. This may seem an odd remark considering the expansion of the U.S. role later on, but on reflection it is not so odd.

The United States could have expanded its military role well before February 1965; some military advisors urged it in 1961, but President Kennedy and his aides rejected the advice. Moreover, it was in this phase, in the years between 1961 and 1963, that limits were conceived and imposed on U.S. policy in Vietnam. These limits had the taste and smell of bureaucratic compromise and interagency dealing from the start, and, indeed, the arguments for and against expanded involvement assumed a shape early on that did not change fundamentally throughout the course of the war, at least until March 1968. Thus, crucial limits, restraints, and debates about U.S. policy in Vietnam were working within the bureaucracy long before that part of the antiwar movement that took to the streets ever existed. More important, when a more vocal and organized antiwar movement did come into existence, it did not do so in a vacuum; rather, it played into the fabric of an already existing bureaucratic web of arguments, judgments, and decisions. Administration principals understood most of the basic antiwar arguments better than the protestors; they had already heard them all *within* the system.[57]

Thereafter, as long as the center of the antiwar movement spoke in a moderate, patriotic, and at least vaguely *realpolitik* fashion, it carried a resonance within the administration that mattered. When it stopped talking in such a fashion, its influence on policy became less direct and less significant, and it came to constitute a negative blueprint.

It can be argued that what restrained U.S. intervention before 1964-65 was the lack of a pressing rationale, for the war was escalated sharply by the other side only in 1963-64, probably in consequence of Hanoi's interpretation of the U.S. agreement to "neutralize" Laos in 1962.[58] Still, the lack of an immediate military challenge does not change the fact that there had been a heated debate within the U.S. bureaucracy since 1961. That debate was dominated by relative doves—although the word "doves" had not yet been coined for this purpose—some of whom had connections with and sympathy for the liberal "peace" movement as it then existed, and who, it must be remembered, overwhelmingly thought of themselves as liberals too.[59] The odd truth, then, is that the first phase of the antiwar movement was largely *inside* the Kennedy administration and was distributed outside among groups and individuals familiar with the president's own priorities and philosophies. Dozens of small but dramatic and sincere public protests by "peace" groups of various persuasions had far less impact on the internal policy debate than the early private dissent within the bureaucracy of State and Defense Department officials such as George Ball and Townsend Hoopes, and by the gadflyish public dissent of Senators Morse and Gruening.[60]

# Evolution of the Movement: Liberals and the Left

*There are ways of conquering that quickly
transform a victory into a defeat.*
—Raymond Aron

The turning point from America the confident of the 1950s and early 1960s to America the disheartened of the late 1960s and 1970s was November 22, 1963. To the Vietnam generation, known more commonly as the baby-boomers, President Kennedy was a symbol of freshness and hope, of America facing its problems and moving to solve them. Kennedy was a vehicle of social catharsis and a beacon of vitality in a way that President Dwight D. Eisenhower could never have been. America would now go anywhere, do anything, pay any price—very youthful attitudes these were indeed.

After a shaky start—the failure of the U.S.-supported exile invasion of Cuba at the Bay of Pigs being the main cause of the shakes—things began to go well, or so most believed. A tax cut had worked to get the economy growing, progress against Jim Crow was thought to be accelerating in the South, the United States had held fast in Berlin and forced the Soviets to "blink first" in Cuba, as Secretary Rusk so memorably put it. The United States was on the verge of taking the lead in the space race, that test of superpower technological virility, and the President brought us the Partial Test Ban Treaty of 1963. The nation discovered physical fitness, the first lady was stunning, the kids were cute, and the President even managed to inspire admiring, respectful comedy.[1] When he was murdered, it was as if the new spirit of the nation dissolved. Even those who were little children at the time remember almost without fail exactly where they were and what they were doing when they heard the news. The only other event of this century that attained comparable powers of national psychic unification was Pearl Harbor. With Kennedy's murder also came the end of American restraint in Vietnam.

## PRELUDE TO ESCALATION

Lyndon Baines Johnson epitomized the old politics. Compared to Kennedy, he seemed a slightly vulgar Senate wheeler-dealer without a scintilla of charisma or a hint of romance. The inevitable backlash from Kennedy's desegregation policies hit Johnson just as the 1964 campaign heated up, stalling Kennedy's large stack of social legislation. In truth, President Johnson did a superb job of shepherding that legislation through the Congress, but his legislative successes on behalf of the liberal domestic agenda in the first seven months of 1964 won him only a short honeymoon with liberal constituencies. Before Johnson could build on these successes to shape an independent image as president, Vietnam emerged unexpectedly as a major issue.

It was unexpected in part because Southeast Asia had been the scene of what most observers took for granted as a Kennedy administration achievement—the sober "neutralization" of Laos in 1962. Moreover, it had seemed clear to insiders that the deposing of South Vietnamese President Ngo Dinh Diem in a bloody coup on November 1, 1963, had removed a main stumbling block to success in the war effort. Moreover, the war was not yet fully Americanized by 1964; at year's end there were only 23,300 U.S. military personnel in Vietnam. The administration of the war, however, had been Americanized in the immediate post-Diem epoch; that, plus a North Vietnamese–driven escalation of the war, made the next step almost inevitable.

In late 1964 American corpses started coming home and television showed them to us. Most notable in the political escalation of Vietnam as an issue was the November 1, 1964, Vietcong attack on the U.S. air base at Bien Hoa, during which five American soldiers were killed and six B-57 bombers destroyed. In an army of draftees, discontent in the military will find its way home just as surely as discontent at home will find its way into the military. Though few draftees were in Vietnam at the time, the fighting there frightened them wherever they were stationed. It was suddenly apparent that their situation was not even remotely analogous to Elvis Presley's spending a couple of uniformed years in Germany making movies, or to Mighty Mouse coming to save the day. This was war, with real bullets and real blood, and the invincible generation was afraid of dying.

Despite rising fears, however, the war was a strangely muted issue in the 1964 presidential campaign. It played a role, of course, but it is striking in retrospect how impoverished the scope of debate on Vietnam was. The Republican contender, Senator Barry Goldwater, knew the real question: Would the United States fight South Vietnam's war for it if South Vietnam could not? Goldwater never put it as bluntly as that, but he did say, in effect, that the choice would be between failure and escalation to a land war. Johnson knew the right question too; the looming choice between failure or escalation in fact set the terms of the internal administration debate if not the public one. And Johnson knew his probable choice as well, which was to escalate if he had to in order to prevent an American defeat that would reverberate, it was believed, from Bangkok to Bonn.

But Johnson would not say as much in public; instead he promised virtually the reverse. In Manchester, New Hampshire, on September 28, 1964, Johnson said about the use of force:

> I want to be very cautious and careful and use it only as a last resort, when I start dropping bombs around that are likely to involve American boys in a war in Asia with 700 million Chinese. So just for the moment I have not thought we were ready for American boys to do the fighting for Asian boys. . . . We are not going North and dropping bombs at this stage of the game, and we are not going South and run out and leave it for the Communists to take over. Now we have lost 190 American lives, and to each one of those 190 families this is a major war. . . . I often wake up at night and think about how many I could lose if I made a misstep.[2]

By September 1964 Johnson probably knew that if things were not improved in Southeast Asia by the end of the year, he would face a decision to bomb and to escalate. Perhaps he believed that things would change and direct U.S. force would not have to be used. Perhaps he lied. Either way, his not having been fully candid with the American people is not surprising under the circumstances; no president can afford to tell the enemy what he is thinking and may or may not do, and that is what being perfectly frank with the American people would have amounted to. Senator Goldwater had much greater freedom in this regard and he used it. Ironically too, as Powers put it: "Truth in government would later become a major political issue, but in 1964 Goldwater's honesty gained him nothing but abuse."[3]

This was why neither party had a strong antiwar plank; neither thought peace more important than the national honor and the integrity of the containment doctrine worldwide. The situation was, in fact, very difficult. No one was enthusiastic about escalation—the Korean metaphor was strong. But no one was willing to stand back while Communists defeated an American ally either. This dilemma led to the ever seductive middle position and to a kind of policy satisficing, which is to say choosing the first available option that solves the immediate problem but that need not be, and rarely is, the best option: Prevent an embarrassing defeat, do not overextend the United States in search of absolute victory, and take the first formula available to achieve this balance. The problem was that such a formula was maddeningly elusive; merely staving off defeat became more and more costly between 1961 and 1964, and then a different question arose: Is there a point at which the cost of preventing defeat, and potentially having to do it repeatedly, becomes so high that expanding the war in order to win once and for all involves relatively little increased risk?

The ambivalence prevalent in the Kennedy and Johnson administrations before the decision to escalate was finally implemented was also widespread among the foreign policy elite.[4] A Council on Foreign Relations poll revealed in February 1965, but undertaken some weeks earlier, showed that of 600 members who took part, 80 percent favored the policy of supporting South Vietnam and 90 percent were convinced that the policy was failing. But fewer than half wanted to pull out, and slightly fewer than that wanted to escalate.[5] The Council on Foreign Relations was split right down the middle in other words, just like, one imagines, the voices inside Lyndon Johnson's head. Meanwhile, overt antiwar sentiment in 1964 seemed restricted to select university faculties, the automatonic but barely audible slogan-eering Marxists of the old Left, the fringes of the Left-Liberal establishment represented by SANE, and the then entirely marginal new pacifism.

The fact that Senator Goldwater's views on Vietnam seemed excessively bellicose during the 1964 election campaign—despite long-standing Republican reluctance to get involved in a land war in Asia[6]—allowed the Democrats to emerge as the party of moderation. This situation rendered unnecessary any forced intro-spection about Vietnam, the sort of thing normally imposed by the healthy tensions of political competition. If anything, the nature of the Republican challenge over Vietnam gave the Johnson administration carte blanche to do anything it thought necessary militarily. There is no evidence, however, that opposition to the right persuaded the administration to escalate tactics on the battlefield. Instead, the contours of the election may well have reinforced the administration's self-conceived calculus of pursuing a limited commitment, at a limited price in treasure and blood, for a limited goal.

It is, in any event, fair to describe the Johnson administration's sensitivity to limits as acute—again, this despite the go-anywhere, pay-any-price rhetoric inher-ited from the New Frontier. One set of limits was financial; the president did not wish to starve Great Society programs of funds.[7] But the limits were also cautionary in the plainest sense, and, moreover, most civilian officials in the Defense Depart-ment and the National Security Council staff did not trust or feel comfortable with the high-ranking uniformed brass for both social and intellectual reasons. They also worried about political instability in South Vietnam following Diem's assassination. An excellent example is McGeorge Bundy's private memo dated June 30, 1965, to President Johnson in reply to a Joint Chiefs of Staff memo just after the initial February 1965 Americanization of the ground war.

The Joint Chiefs were pushing for a major expansion of the U.S. effort above and beyond the February deployment. They had posed to themselves the question noted above about the relative merits of sharp versus incremental escalation, and had opted against incrementalism. Bundy disagreed, writing the president that the military's request proposed a major new commitment to land warfare "at a time when our troops are entirely untested in the kind of warfare projected, proposes greatly extended air action when the value of air action we have taken is sharply disputed, proposes naval quarantine by mining at a time when nearly everyone agrees that the real question is not in Hanoi, but in South Vietnam."[8] Bundy concluded by saying: "My first reaction is that this program is rash to the point of folly. . . . This is a slippery slope toward total U.S. responsibility and corresponding fecklessness on the Vietnamese side. . . . If we need 200,000 now for these quite limited actions, may we not need 400,000 later? Is this a rational course of action? Do we want to invest 200,000 men to cover an eventual retreat?"[9]

The acute sense of limits expressed in Bundy's note, and the growing doubt from 1965 through 1968 that U.S. objectives could be achieved within established limits, were things the American people did not know about. In public, Bundy and other officials were upbeat. If the administration had been more frank about its own internal doubts, it might have won more sympathy from those liberals inclined to protest the war; its case might have sounded more authentic. But to have voiced such doubts publicly would have cheered Hanoi, undermined American military efforts and morale, and turned the bureaucracy into a leaking sieve of contention. Those who would criticize the administration too severely on this point lack a grasp of how hard it is to address multiple audiences simultaneously, a challenging necessity of successful leadership.

## ENTER SDS

The Johnson administration had its internal problems, to be sure, but so did the antiwar movement, and the stunning indecisiveness of Students for a Democratic Society was one of the reasons. A very short history of SDS is in order because, after 1964, nothing that can be said about the antiwar movement makes much sense without it.

As noted in passing earlier, SDS derived from the Intercollegiate Socialist Society (ISS), founded in 1905. The ISS more or less went out of business during World War I as the generation of its founders—who included such literary luminaries as Walter Lippmann, Norman Thomas, Upton Sinclair, Jack London, Clarence Darrow, John Reed, and Edna St. Vincent Millay—grew into middle age. After the war, it was brought into a second life as the League for Industrial Democracy (LID), with a student wing, the Student League for Industrial Democracy (SLID). SLID was always a small group, as was its parent organization. Both were essentially isolationist in the interwar period; ideologically, they were latter-day embodiments of the progressive spirit, which by then could aptly be described as a forerunner of democratic socialism. Both were, therefore, strongly anti-Communist. After World War II, with the GI bill and the expansion of the American university system, SLID was reduced to an obscure campus organization.

SLID changed its name to SDS in 1960 and, in that same year, fielded its first full-time paid staff member, Al Haber, courtesy of a $10,000 grant from the United Automobile Workers. The UAW's main motive, ironically enough as things turned out, was to support a pro-labor but anti-Communist organization on campus. The UAW also strongly supported the civil rights struggle, seeing in the effective emancipation of the South a great boon to organized labor there. A second staff member was added the next year and was sent to Atlanta. His name was Tom Hayden.

Before long, SDS had devoted itself to the central liberal passion of the day: civil rights. Involvement in the civil rights movement, and competition on campus from the Student Peace Union and other organizations farther to the Left, raised larger questions for SDS. In 1961 Haber decided that SDS needed a manifesto or an organizing document of some kind, and he asked Hayden to draft it. Hayden brought a version of his manifesto to an SDS meeting at a UAW camp at Port Huron, Michigan, in June of 1962. The delegates, mainly from a University of Michigan group called Voice, argued over it, and the UAW sponsors and LID overseers, including Michael Harrington, became uneasy as they sensed general and rapid movement to the Left, and particularly movement in the direction of abandoning anti-Communist sensibilities. A lockout of sorts was attempted, in the end unsuccessfully. A month or two later, after Hayden, then SDS president, had polished the draft, it was mailed to the membership and became known as the Port Huron Statement.[10]

The Port Huron Statement was idealistic and explicitly anti-authoritarian. It became immediately popular and influential among the few hundred young people who read it. Apparently it was one of those statements that put the right ideas into the right words at the right time. It summarized what a number of people had been talking about, diffusely and inarticulately, for some time. While it said nothing particularly new, it served as a unifying device for many a novice intellectual. It stood for decolonization, education, and civil rights. It was against poverty, elitism, American "Russophobia," the Cold War, and the "military-industrial complex." Haber's and Hayden's teachers at the University of Michigan had drilled them in the writings of C. Wright Mills, a radical sociologist, and lesser lights of similar disposition; indeed, Hayden's thesis had been on Mills's writings on the "power elite." In retrospect, there is little doubt that Mills was the principal intellectual influence behind the Port Huron Statement.[11]

The early New Left—also Mills's term, by the way—had found a radical thesis, but it was by no means a radical organization as the term was commonly understood at the time. In the 1964 election, for example, SDS's slogan had been "Part of the Way with LBJ." (SDS had been appalled by Barry Goldwater's remark that "extremism in the defense of liberty was no vice," but, of course, SDS took exactly the same attitude in defense of desegregation.) SDS's reluctance to break entirely with mainstream electoral politics owed something to the lingering charm of Kennedy liberalism and to the striking success of civil rights legislation in the Congress. But it also stemmed from the fact that few SDSers had had much contact with the old Left and few were themselves "red diaper babies," that is, the children of old-line Communists from the 1920s and 1930s. And most of those few who were red diaper babies had been disabused of the old Left either by the 1956 revelations about Stalin's crimes or by their parents' cultist sense of party loyalty—an unexpected manifestation of the generation gap.[12]

Nevertheless, the seeds of the New Left's eventual turn to Marxism-Leninism were there from the start. One seed germinated from Hayden's argument with Michael Harrington, which led to the inclusion of the condemnation of the "military-industrial complex" in the Port Huron Statement, and the conclusion that American economic organization—capitalism—was primarily responsible for the arms race. Other seeds, as social historian Maurice Isserman has pointed out, grew from the fact that there was a good deal more continuity, ideologically and biographically, between old and New Left than has generally been recognized.[13] While the New Left's minority of red diaper babies were not like their parents, they nevertheless had learned from them the basic vocabulary of Marxism and its essential metaphors of class revenge and had duly supplied them to their less well-tutored colleagues. Though at first consciously and conscientiously divorced from their older sectarian bases, these vocabularies and images unerringly steered the New Left back toward the old. Thus the Tom Hayden of 1962 talked of military-industrial complexes, but the Tom Hayden of 1968 talked of the need for forming a mass orthodox Marxist-Leninist revolutionary party.

In 1963 and 1964 SDS became increasingly engaged and devoted to the civil rights movement, notably through its Economic Research and Action Project (ERAP), which was active less in the South than in northern ghettos. Al Haber was suspicious of ERAP, calling it the "cult of the ghetto," but his soon became the minority voice. The ERAP projects, however, did not go well; the mostly subur-ban-bred, white-skinned participants were surprised to find their welcome in the ghetto strained at best. The experience did not radicalize the ghetto; rather, it frustrated and further radicalized the ERAPers who blamed the "system" for their failures.[14] By the time the Vietnam War began to emerge as a major issue in 1964, SDS was in a deep funk with a sharp tilt to the Left. Movement chroniclers Nancy Zaroulis and Gerald Sullivan, exaggerating a bit and romanticizing a bit more, describe what happened next:

> . . . at the very end of the year, on December 29 in New York City, in humble surroundings, with no media fanfare, with no celebrities attending, a momen-tous event took place: the antiwar movement was born. Its midwife was the maverick journalist I. F. Stone. The body which brought it forth was not, as might have been supposed, one of the traditional peace groups but a relatively new organization, Students for a Democratic Society.[15]

SDS met at the Cloakmakers Hall in New York City, at a meeting filled with old Left voyeurs.[16] I. F. Stone did indeed speak to the group. So electrifying was

his address, and so poorly were SDS's pet projects in the ghettoes going, that the
SDS leadership decided to sign on with full force to the annual Easter antiwar rally
then being planned, as always, by radical pacifist groups. The antiwar movement
was never again quite the same.

To put it simply, SDS as a vanguard representative of the New Left, was the
vehicle through which the counterculture—initially an antithetical force to the New
Left or any Left—was brought into an antiwar movement group. If one person can be
credited with producing this synapse, it was Jerry Rubin, initially a no-nonsense
political Leftist who saw counterculture styles as a way to politicize youth and widen
the movement. The vehicle that in turn brought SDS into contact with the center of
organized protest, and with the existing radical organizations of the sectarian Left and
the new pacifism, was also a person: David Dellinger. Dellinger imported both SDS
and the counterculture into the core of adults who had from the beginning been
directing antiwar movement traffic. Both Left-Liberals such as Norman Cousins and
sectarian Leftists such as Fred Halstead and Sidney Peck fought Dellinger and "his
kids" nearly every step of the way between 1967 and 1969—fought and lost. By the
time more orthodox Leftist hands had gotten back rough control of the movement
after the explosions of 1968-69, the damage had already been done: The antiwar
movement had become counterproductive to its own espoused cause.

## ON CAMPUS, 1965

In 1965 the Vietnam War truly became an American war. The air bombardment
campaign known as "Rolling Thunder" began in earnest, and the American contingent grew from 23,000 "advisors" to over 184,000 soldiers by year's end. It was the
year that body counts, including American bodies, became nightly news. Suddenly,
or so it seemed, over 600 American soldiers were dead. It was the year, as Secretary
of Defense McNamara had promised in October 1963, that "the boys would be
home for Christmas." But except for those who had come home in boxes, they were
not. It was the year, despite Secretary McNamara's telling the Congress a few years
earlier that the U.S. government could afford the war at current levels "forever,"
that the Johnson administration began to consider borrowing money to finance the
defense budget supplemental for Vietnam. It was the year that the government of
South Vietnam, between Big Minhs and Little Minhs and still littler Minhs for almost
anyone cared in America, began to look like the sad circus of venality and ineptitude
that it then was.

It was also the year when dissent against the war policy within the Demo-
cratic Party began to be expressed privately. In mid-1965, for example, McGeorge
Bundy sat down with five Democratic Senators privately in opposition to the policy:
Eugene McCarthy (Minnesota), Gaylord Nelson (Wisconsin), Stephen Young
(Ohio), George McGovern (South Dakota), and Frank Church (Idaho). Bundy

failed to persuade them to change their views. In consequence, the administration did the next best thing, mounting efforts to keep criticism private and within the Democratic camp. After the 89th Congress convened in 1965, Vice President Hubert Humphrey gave new members a welcoming speech during which he told them pointedly: "If you feel an urge to stand up and make a speech attacking Vietnam policy, don't make it. After you've been here a few years, you can afford to be independent. But if you want to come back in 1967, don't do it now."[17] And 1965 was the year that the antiwar movement organized itself to take its protest into the streets in a big way.

Whether liberal or radical, old Left or New, radical pacifist or traditional pacifist, the antiwar movement was still decidedly a minority movement, even among the young (and it probably remained so throughout the war). The top pop song of 1965 was Sergeant Barry Sadler's "Ballad of the Green Berets." Although public demonstrations before April 1965 may have been aided or even planned by young people, most were the doings of the scions of the old sectarian Left and the new pacifism. Most of the protesting was organized by professional activists of various stripes, not by students or other young people. It was not until the spring of 1965, following the sudden emergence of the Free Speech Movement at Berkeley in the fall of 1964 and the equally sudden notoriety of its young leader, Mario Savio, that relatively large antiwar demonstrations took place and that college campuses became an important focus of antiwar activism.[18]

The Free Speech Movement was important, not only because that is where Jack Weinberg uttered the immortal phrase "Don't trust anyone over 30," but because it was the first to aim at the university, the base of what radicals were soon to think was a revolutionary cadre in the making. It was also important because Savio brilliantly extended the metaphors of the civil rights struggle to young people who were, in his view, equally repressed. He was the first to conceive of all of America as the battlefield of protest, even before the Americanization of the war in February 1965. It is not hard to see how, from his vastly expanded concept of victimization—analogous to the new pacifism's vastly expanded definition of violence—it was natural to include the Vietcong as victims of "the system" along with blacks in the South and students at Berkeley.

Two general points may be made about the demonstrations themselves. First, some were now organized nationally; before 1965 they had been so organized only in the loosest of ways. The national demonstrations, in turn, increased the number of locally generated protests, which at the time were focused increasingly on university campuses. The reason was, in large part, that the draft had become a searing issue despite the famous II-S student deferment, which exempted virtually all university students from military service. Also important was that many campus protest leaders—mainly of SDS persuasions—were either veterans of the civil rights movement or those whose imaginations and hearts had been captured by the movement at a tender age. This is very important: The experience of the civil rights movement had taught the Vietnam generation that nonviolent public protest was a responsible, heroic, and effective way of expressing dissent. Through the civil rights movement, public displays of anger had become an accepted and even widely popular currency of political advocacy modeled on the Boston Tea Party. Tactics were borrowed directly from the civil rights movement too. For example, Savio happened to be the head of Friends of SNCC (the Student Nonviolent Coordinating Committee) when he launched the Free Speech Movement (or when it launched him), and he had spent the previous summer in Mississippi learning about organizing people by actually doing it. Outside of the civil rights movement, which was focused in the South, antiwar protests represented the first time Americans up north had witnessed such vast displays of public anti-establishment demonstration since suffragettes had taken to the streets before 1919.

Moreover, many SDSers, especially those who had gone South for voter registration drives in 1963 and 1964, explicitly linked desegregation and the Vietnam War in a variety of ways. After Savio's most famous speech in Berkeley, Joan Baez sang "We Shall Overcome," the theme song of the civil rights movement. In what may be an edited memory, Thomas Powers wrote in 1973:

> In November, 1963, I went to Mississippi with a group of students from Yale who had volunteered to help the Student Non-Violent Coordinating Committee run a mock election. I was plunged immediately into another world, fearing the police cars which waited on side streets at night with their lights off; fearing the white, thin-faced farmers in pickup trucks who followed us along dusty country roads; fearing the approach of strangers. Once in that world, the senses of oppression, injustice and physical danger were overpowering. I remember thinking, at the end of eight days, that I knew how the world appeared to the Vietcong.[19]

Another outtake with the same general theme was reported by John Doar, who worked for the Justice Department's Civil Rights Division in the early 1960s. He reported a confrontation with SDSers in Jackson, Mississippi, during which he was asked: "How is it that the government can protect the Vietnamese from the Vietcong and the same government will not accept the moral responsibility of protecting the people in Mississippi?"[20]

The second important point about the early large demonstration is that, SDS notwithstanding, civil rights movement–trained students did not take over the leadership of the antiwar movement. The Free Speech Movement at Berkeley and kindred movements elsewhere were added to antiwar activism and clearly bolstered it, but they were autonomous organizationally and had more to do with the university cum microcosm of American life than with a war in Asia. The leaders of the antiwar movement in 1965 were still professional adversary culture activists, and they were generally the same ones as in 1962, as the founding and history of the National Coordination Committee to End the War in Vietnam (NCCEWV) clearly shows. Universities became the main focus of protest and demonstration simply because they were filled with idealistic young people pragmatically terrified of the military draft. They were also filled with the most radical members of the American intelligentsia—the faculty. As a result, by the end of 1965 students were no longer the professional activists' audience but their allies, and SDS was the crucial but unpredictable organizational link in that new alliance. Now the nation—largely through the national media's capricious coverage of the antiwar movement—became the audience.[21]

Antiwar demonstrations on campus depended on three intermingled layers of workers. At the top were the professional organizers from the pacifist groups and from SDS, many of whose leaders after 1964 were not students in any commonly understood sense, certainly not undergraduates. These were the people who maintained links with the national organizations and particularly with the NCCEWV in New York, and who made the major tactical and related financial decisions. In the center was a larger group of more or less dedicated local volunteer workers, including graduate students and young faculty members, who put up posters, took out advertisements, addressed envelopes, picketed draft boards, wrote letters to newspaper editors, joined and tried to mobilize assorted campus organizations against the war, arranged for antiwar speakers, and proselytized younger students. The largest group was made up of those who came to rallies, chanted slogans, and enjoyed the heroic prose, live music, and the chance to feel very moral. Those in the third echelon occasionally moved into the second, to be replaced by ever more third-echelon members as the movement grew at the margins. But those in the second echelon only very rarely moved into the first. Even in its limited life span, the antiwar movement had its own career patterns and hierarchy.

## THE ARCHITECTURE OF DISSENT

More important than what was happening on campus was what was going on in the adversary culture itself. By the end of the winter of 1964-65, the antiwar movement leadership had taken on the fluid triangularity that was to characterize it through the end of the war. Indeed, probably the best way to describe the evolution of the movement is to show how the flow of tactical alliances among its three main elements reflected the shifting center of gravity of the movement as a whole. These three elements were: (1) the liberals and Left-Liberals, centered around SANE, Americans for Democratic Action (ADA), and, later, Clergy and Laity Concerned about the War in Vietnam (renamed in September of 1972 Clergy and Laity Concerned);[22] (2) the radical Left, now coming to be centered around the

New Left with SDS at its core, but also including the Socialist Workers Party (SWP) and its campus affiliate, the Young Socialist Alliance (YSA); and (3) the new pacifists, centered around the WRL, the CNVA, the FOR, WILPF, WSP, and the AFSC. Each element had a different view of what was at stake in Vietnam and of the ultimate aims of the antiwar movement, which in turn influenced its tactics and intergroup relations.

For Left-Liberals, antiwar protest was a necessary but diverting target from their main interest, which was the antinuclear weapons movement. Left-Liberal activists in those days felt like lovers scorned, for most liberals had supported the reelection of Lyndon Johnson in 1964—Benjamin Spock had led Doctors for Johnson—and they now felt betrayed. They supported a negotiated settlement that would include the Vietcong, a group they presumed indigenous to South Vietnam. Most had no overarching social or political agenda; they did not go out of their way to draw links among various issues, and it is not clear if many even believed such links existed. It was political adversarialism à la carte. They did believe firmly, however, that nonviolent, polite protest would have the greatest positive impact. They were, in truth, afraid of the real radicals, and they were—especially in SANE's leadership—divided over whether to try to co-opt, ignore, or oppose opposition to the Left. For most of them, the enemy was Cold War zealotry and the misguided attempt to "contain China" through a "militarized" foreign policy.

For the radical Left, the war in Vietnam was a revolutionary struggle by the Vietnamese, with help from friendly socialist states, against worldwide imperialism led by the United States. For the old Left, the real enemy was the corporate capitalist conspiracy of Marxist lore. For the New Left, it was something at the same time larger and more diffuse. SDS president Paul Potter, when once asked why he had not named capitalism to be the enemy in a speech he had given, answered: "I refused to call it capitalism because capitalism was for me and my generation an inadequate description of the evils of America—a hollow dead word tied to the thirties."[23] The New Left found a new word that summed up the evil, and that word was "Amerika," the curious spelling referring not to Franz Kafka's enigmatic novella of that name but to German fascism in the vaguest of ways—sometimes a swastika was substituted for the letter "k."

For both old and New Left, however, the real aim of the antiwar movement was to uncover the supposedly sinister face of reactionary capitalism at home. The war was the vanguard issue in the main struggle, which was revolution at home, and in which violence would play its "objectively necessary" part.[24] SDSers believed firmly that the antiwar movement could never stop the Vietnam War; they wanted, they said, to change and revolutionize American society and politics in order to stop the "seventh war from now." They despised liberals and Left-Liberals alike. Long before 1965, the New Left's ideological and tactical thrust led it to break decisively with the organized ban-the-bomb activism of the 1950s. SANE was the negative role model for the early New Left; liberals were "the pink bourgeoisie." This animosity endured into the Vietnam protest movement and grew to almost pathological proportions.

It is important to understand the depth of this hatred. As suggested earlier, the Vietnam generation started off as extraordinarily idealistic and optimistic. The Vietnam generation was reared to believe and to cherish the ideals of liberal humanism. But racism and Vietnam provoked an escalation of demands that led, in effect, to a total rejection of the ideas that were the source of the original idealism. Social critic Paul Berman put it well. The New Left

> had two phases, which were in perfect discord, like two piano strings vibrating against each other. The first was an uprising on behalf of the ideals of liberal humanism—on behalf of the freedom of the individual against a soulless system. But the second phase was entirely the opposite, at least philosophically. It was a revolt *against* liberal humanism. It said, in effect: Liberal humanism is a deception. Western-style democracy, rationalism, objectivity, and the autonomy of the individual are slogans designed to convince the downtrodden that subordination is justice.[25]

"Extravaganzas of cynicism" were substituted for belief in Western-style democracy, rationalism, objectivity, and the autonomy of the individual, and such cynicism lay at the center of a conviction that "we and the world are permeated by a gigantic, hidden, impersonal structure, the way that human forms in *The Invasion of the Body Snatchers* are inhabited by extraterrestrial beings."[26] It was, in short, close to a conspiracy theory, a matter to which we return later. Like all purveyors of conspiracy theories, New Leftists were hard to reason with, as both old Leftists and new pacifists soon discovered.

Also like such purveyors, the New Left saw themselves as victims. And they hated liberals because liberals refused to see themselves as victims too; they only saw *others* as victims. Here, perhaps, was the key difference between liberals and New Leftists. SDSer Greg Calvert put it this way:

> The liberal reformist is always engaged in fighting "someone else's battles." He does not sense himself to be unfree. Radical or revolutionary consciousness perceives contradictions in a totally different fashion. The gap is not between oneself and the underprivileged but is the gap between "what one could be" and the existing conditions for self realization. It is the perception of oneself as unfree, as oppressed—and finally it is the discovery of oneself as *one of the oppressed* who must unite to transform the objective conditions of their existence in order to resolve the contradictions between potentiality and actuality.[27]

The Marxist analysis seemed plausible to most new pacifists, but they did not accept the Marxist solution, and they certainly took exception to Marxist tactics. The enemy was not capitalism but violence itself, of which capitalism was but one expression. The temper of the new pacifism was also decidedly different, indissolubly linked as it was to religion and other concerns of the spirit. Generally speaking, talk of systems left pacifists cold. Rather, the reform and purification of individual souls would lead to the reform of society. To accomplish this, one "spoke truth to power." Moreover, the New Left was thoroughly fond of the Vietcong and their totalitarian supporters and, unlike the old Left, actually said so to anyone who would listen. But new pacifists were not so easily persuaded of the moral superiority of the other side.[28] Yet their fervent anti-establishmentarianism and their eagerness to form coalitions with anyone opposed to U.S. policy often obscured this nuance to those outside the movement. More important, however, was the fact that they were led to the Left by a sense of shared alienation, by their belief that they were oppressed in some fundamental spiritual way. Also important in the connection between the new pacifism and the New Left was a mutual sensitivity to the potential moral perils of abundance in an industrial society and to the related fear of technology and technocracy.

Even among pacifists there were tactical differences. Certainly by 1968, if not long before, David Dellinger was not above virtually any tactic, even if it might lead to violent responses—in this sense, at least, he was much like Mahatma Gandhi, an adopted patron saint of the WRL. On the other hand, A. J. Muste, who by 1965 was 80 years old, though no less a pacifist or a radical than Dellinger, was more contemplative about such matters. At times he cancelled or stopped ongoing demonstrations when it appeared they might lead to violence. Not so Dellinger, who by October 1968 was plainly promoting "trashings" on the streets of Chicago. These differences over tactics within the pacifist wing of the antiwar movement emerged less on account of ideology than on account of temperament.

Within the movement as a whole, the divisions that evolved are similar to the Protestant theologian Reinhold Niebuhr's distinction between hard and soft utopians. The former stood ready for austere and immediate militant action to force utopia into existence while the latter trusted in time and tide.[29] In the antiwar movement, the New Left and the old Left alike were the hard utopians. Left-Liberals were, for the most part, soft utopians. Pacifists were not split into two visions of what was good and right, but rather into hard and soft advocates based on their sense of urgency and therefore their preferred way of attaining their goals. Basically, the left wing of the movement aimed to end the war by disrupting the system through civil disobedience, draft resistance, and planned violence. The right wing sought constantly to widen the base of popular protest, and that meant avoiding all of the things the Left set out to do. The left wing believed Vietnam to be an inevitable by-product of an imperialist/capitalist society. The right wing believed Vietnam to be an aberration. As Sam Brown put it, perhaps too charitably: "For almost half a decade, each method garnered support and lived in uneasy alliance with the other."[30] More than that, one must be careful about taxonomies and labels.

However helpful they may be in theory, in practice idiosyncratic differences and the unpredictable mix of personalities and circumstances led to a situation in which ideology alone could not explain the views and behavior of many activists as the movement evolved month by month.

Despite the increasing interest of the Left, old and New, and of the new pacifism in variously penetrating, controlling, or influencing the antiwar movement, as of 1965 no one had succeeded in controlling anything. The bulk of those involved and the main programmatic direction of the antiwar movement was still a middle-class protest urging reform, not revolution. Radical protest was louder, more publicly demonstrative and evocatively symbolic, but in terms of impact, a dozen small radical "actions" did not have as much influence on elite opinion, for example, as a single SANE advertisement signed by a prominent scholar such as Hans Morgenthau, a disparaging remark by the author of the containment doctrine himself, George Kennan, or a powerfully signed doubting memo within the bureaucracy. The radical analysis of the war as a malignant outgrowth of a vicious capitalist society was very much a minority view, and the militant, totalist idealism of the new pacifism was more marginal still.

But the future of adversary culture groups was nevertheless growing brighter. The Vietnam War was becoming a problem for most people for much simpler reasons: the draft, the death, the inability to win quickly, the unreliability of our ally in Saigon, and vague fears of war with China based on memories of Korea. The most influential intellectual criticisms at the time were still those that questioned the war in *realpolitik* terms; that is: Was the defense of Vietnam a vital interest, or was it an unwise strategic diversion? Wasn't this really a *civil* war with little to do with the major Communist powers, and wasn't the war therefore insufficiently important to warrant such a sizable U.S. military commitment? The Left-Liberal center of the antiwar movement still demanded the de-Americanization of the war and a negotiated settlement, not the complete or the unilateral withdrawal of U.S. personnel and interests in South Vietnam.

There is every reason to believe that the Johnson administration was listening to this critique, particularly as it knew that it hardly had all the answers about Vietnam. Outside critics could not know it, but little of what they said was not still being raised by administration principals in private conclave. Thus, for example, when 85 college professors, liberal to a man, went to Washington on April 8, 1965, to meet with officials of the Democratic National Committee, the committeemen listened. Senators Jacob Javits and Robert Kennedy of New York met with the group, too, and said that the president's speech the previous day at Johns Hopkins University, in which he offered negotiations with the North, was prompted in part by "responsible" criticism of the war.[31] This was not surprising: Lyndon Johnson, a liberal, was prepared to listen to other liberals. But the antiwar movement had another growing, illiberal side.

## APRIL RALLY/JUNE RALLY

Divisions in the antiwar movement were reflected vividly in the public demonstrations of 1965. Early in the year, as the peace movement anticipated an April protest extravaganza, tactical divisions were evident. In February there were "actions" at the White House, the Pentagon, and the U.S. Mission to the United Nations staged by WSP, WILPF, SDS, the CNVA, the Catholic Worker, the WRL, and the SPU. SANE, on the other hand, sponsored not "actions" and demonstrations, but purchased newspaper advertisements in the *New York Times*.

At about this point, the Johnson administration gave an unintended but important helping hand to the antiwar movement. On February 27 the second State Department White Paper on Vietnam was released. It was so careful in its assessments, we now know, that it vastly underestimated North Vietnamese infiltration activity, as had the earlier 1964 White Paper. This allowed opponents of the war, notably I. F. Stone, to "prove" that U.S. actions were disproportionate to what the other side was doing, and that therefore the United States was primarily to blame for escalating the conflict.[32] Also in February, the bombing of North Vietnam began in earnest and U.S. Marines landed noisily at Da Nang, weapons at the ready and flak jackets buttoned as they emerged from their landing craft to be welcomed by banners, photographers, and native girls. If this was meant to impress and terrify the North or the Vietcong, it was an absurd gesture; they would have found out soon enough about the Marines. Back home, photographs of the landing doubly energized the antiwar movement, first because it was seen as an escalation, second because it was portrayed more or less successfully by the administration as a popular act.

One of the first responses to the escalation of the American presence in 1965 was the development of the teach-in movement. The first teach-in took place in late March at the University of Michigan in Ann Arbor; Arthur Waskow of the Institute for Policy Studies was the first main speaker, and he took a rather liberal tone, suggesting that the war was an aberration. Carl Oglesby of SDS was there too, however, and he suggested the reverse.[33] Organized by the faculty, the teach-in surprisingly attracted thousands of students, and the notion spread to other campuses. No one knows who came up with the word "teach-in," but it was clearly modeled on the "sit-in" of the civil rights movement and was the harbinger of a great many more "(fill-in-the-blank)-ins" to come. (This language construction, of course, was quickly captured and mummified by Madison Avenue, first with the popular *Laugh-In* television show and later with countless other variations.)

The major event of the spring, however, was the long-awaited April protest rally. On April 17, roughly 25,000 protestors came to Washington under the sponsorship of SDS for a truly remarkable event. When planning began months earlier under the familiar auspices of the FOR, the WRL, WILPF, SANE, and the rest, SDS had not yet discovered the war in Vietnam as the vanguard issue of its agenda. But by April, after the emotional pitch delivered by I. F. Stone, SDS had essentially hijacked the march from its originators. It was SDS members who had put out the call and who had worked tirelessly to double, nay, quadruple the size of the previous year's rally. But bigger size brought bigger problems too.

As the time for the rally drew nigh, SDS openly called for nonexclusionary sponsorship, which meant, in effect, explicit Communist participation. This issue split the original organizers right down the middle. Most of the new pacifist groups went along with SDS; the established Left-Liberal peace groups would not. Arrayed against SDS, in particular, were Norman Thomas and H. Stuart Hughes of SANE, pacifist Robert Pickus and Bayard Rustin, and, initially, A. J. Muste. Thomas, Hughes, and Rustin were impelled by the same tactical considerations that had been the font of their anger at Dellinger nearly two years earlier, namely that Communist participation would be politically counterproductive. Rustin was ready to hit the streets, as he told a rally in June, but not with M2M Maoists, Progressive Labor (PL), and the Communist Party at his side. On April 16 Rustin demanded that the march reject all these groups. But not even Norman Thomas would accept Rustin's language, and instead he offered a compromise that included anti-Communist tones but that did not ban any individual from participation.

Muste, along with Thomas, refused to sign the first document, and with Thomas agreed to sign the second. His motives were slightly different from those of the others. Here was a man who had been a Marxist and who had left Marxism *before* the Nazi-Soviet Non-Aggression Pact. Here was a man who had once embarrassed his Soviet hosts by staging a one-man demonstration in Red Square against Soviet nuclear testing. When Muste signed his name to a document that said, in part: "We welcome the cooperation of all groups and individuals, who, like ourselves, believe in the need for an independent peace movement, not committed to any form of totalitarianism or drawing inspiration from the foreign policy of any government,"[34] he did so because he really believed it. While Muste later regretted having signed the document because it reduced what antiwar solidarity there was, that does not change what his signature indicated about his views at the time.[35]

Arrayed against Thomas, Hughes, and Muste were Dellinger, Staughton Lynd, WRL leader David McReynolds, and others. They argued that to exclude anybody, *especially* Communists, gave in to the paranoia that caused the Vietnam War in the first place. With their help, SDS got its way. SANE then removed its sponsorship of the rally.[36] No doubt there would have been an argument over this matter, SDS or no SDS. But unlike the 1963 rally, where Dellinger and company were in the minority, and where SANE could and did dictate the slogans and control the rostrum, by April 1965 the balance of power had shifted markedly, with the escalation of the war providing the fuel and SDS providing the spark.

The rally itself clearly reflected the radicals' victory. Even though a U.S. Senator, Ernst Gruening of Alaska, addressed the rally speaking in relatively measured tones, so did Stone, Lynd, Robert Moses of SNCC,[37] and SDS president Paul Potter. Their tones were not measured at all. Potter said, for example, in the famous passage about naming the enemy noted in passing earlier:

> The further we explore the reality of what this country is doing . . . in Vietnam, the more we are driven to the conclusion of Senator Morse that the United States may well be the greatest threat to peace in the world today. . . . We must name the system [that led to the war]. We must name it, describe it, analyze it, understand it and change it. For it is only when that system is changed . . . that there can be any hope for stopping the forces that create a war in South Vietnam.[38]

He never did name the system, which old Leftists assumed to be capitalism. But that is not what Potter meant; he did not yet have a name for what was not a conventional ideology but a system of culture itself—a point to which we return later.

At 25,000-plus in attendance, the April rally was unprecedented in size despite the fact that SANE and other Left-Liberal groups officially boycotted the affair. It received unprecedented press coverage as well. Associations with the civil rights movement were in evidence and were cultivated. Robert Moses made explicit reference to the connection between violence in the South and violence in Southeast Asia. Joan Baez, Judy Collins, and Peter, Paul, and Mary, folksinging social troubadours whose fame rose during the civil rights movement, sang old songs and new, including the poignant Bob Dylan composition "Blowin' in the Wind."[39] The Freedom Voices, a SNCC trio, sang the "Battle Hymn of the Republic" and closed with a rousing "We Shall Overcome."

Nevertheless, despite the widening split in the antiwar movement, its left wing's hatred of liberals had yet to fully harden. Evidence comes from an attempt by seven radical activists or sympathizers—David McReynolds, anarchist scholar Paul Goodman, editor and literary critic Dwight Macdonald, former Workers Party follower of Max Schachtman and UAW activist Harvey Swados, Kay Boyle, Nat Hentoff of the *Village Voice,* and former Vermont Congressman William H. Meyer— to persuade one of their political heros, Adlai Stevenson, in June 1965 to resign his post as U.S. Ambassador to the United Nations in protest of the war. Stevenson refused. This event and a few others like it, accelerated the radicals' movement away from any dealings with liberal opponents of the war.[40]

SANE and the Left-Liberals sponsored their own antiwar rally at Madison Square Garden in June. It drew around 18,000 people according to its sponsors, but only about 10,000 according to police estimates. In Washington in April, Senator Gruening and I. F. Stone had called for immediate and total U.S. withdrawal, but in New York, Dr. Spock and Professor Morgenthau called for a mutual cease-fire and negotiations. Other speakers included Martin Luther King, Jr.'s wife, Coretta Scott King, who was a WSP member, Bayard Rustin, and Senator Morse. Rustin made the essential point of the day, again invoking civil rights experience and metaphors, telling liberals that they would have to compete with radicals for space on the street: "We know that the Wagner Act, which gave labor the right to organize and bargain collectively, was empty until workers went into the streets. The civil rights movement has learned this lesson. This is a lesson that must be applied now to the peace movement as well. We must stop meeting indoors and go into the streets."[41]

## HARBINGERS

Between the April and June rallies, which were ideologically and organizationally competitive but effectually complementary in a broader political sense, three significant events took place in the antiwar movement and one in the Congress. All were first tastes of things to come.

First, on May 15 a national teach-in took place in Washington, sponsored by the Inter-University Committee for a Public Hearing on Vietnam. Spreading from Ann Arbor in March, teach-ins had occurred on dozens of campuses. In coordination with SANE and other like-minded groups, faculty members arranged for a radio hookup from Washington to over 120 campuses to create a nationwide teach-in. SANE persuaded the administration to agree to debate; McGeorge Bundy promised to come. Extensive media coverage was arranged. SANE had secured Vietnam experts Bernard Fall, Seymour Melman, and Hans Morgenthau to present the antiwar case in patriotic, *realpolitik* terms. Speaking on behalf of the administration were Columbia University political scientist Zbigniew Brzezinski, administration official Walt Rostow, and the scribe of Camelot, historian Arthur Schlesinger, Jr. Bundy never showed up. Unbeknownst to the crowd, he had been called away by the ongoing crisis in the Dominican Republic, which was, at the time, about two weeks old.[42] But he did not send a replacement, and the White House refused to say where he was or to apologize for his absence. Schlesinger did speak, and while he criticized the administration on many points, he concluded by saying: "Indeed, if we took the Marines now in the Dominican Republic and sent them to South Vietnam, we should be a good deal better off in both countries."[43]

Here again, the budding divisions in the antiwar movement were in evidence. While liberals appreciated Schlesinger's wit, Staughton Lynd contemptuously rejected his position at the final local teach-in of the spring semester on May 21-22, which took place in Berkeley. Lynd said that heeding Schlesinger's call to compromise and conciliation would be like making "a coalition with the Marines."[44] He used the same phrase in reference to Bayard Rustin, with whom he was furious over his attempt to "purge" the April 1965 rally. Rustin was equally furious at Lynd; their "public" correspondence in 1965-66 is perhaps the clearest expression of the differing points of view of the two wings of the antiwar movement and the best illustration of its internal passions.[45]

Coming on the heels of the Washington national teach-in and the April rally, as well as the Free Speech Movement, which had created a feeling of permanent mobilization on campus, Berkeley's Vietnam Day on May 21-22 took on a national dimension. Aside from Lynd and locals, speakers included Senator Gruening, Dr. Spock, Trotsky's biographer Isaac Deutscher, Norman Thomas, Paul Potter of SDS, Robert Moses, and many others. Among them was David Dellinger, who called for nonviolent civil disobedience. While a Leftist combination had not mixed well back East, after the April rally the movement was in general flux, and the edges of old antipathies seemed softer in California. In addition, new voices were heard, including those of black comedian Dick Gregory (who more or less stole the show) and novelist Norman Mailer.

But the good feeling did not last long. The mainstream liberals' response to the Berkeley Vietnam Day was similar to the radicals' response to Schlesinger and Morgenthau. Robert Pickus called the radical analysis "so much pure crap."[46] Through this dialectic of mutual abuse between its left and right wings, the hope of building a unified movement rapidly receded from view.

In any case, Vietnam Day led to the creation of the Vietnam Day Committee, which ensured that henceforth any major demonstration on the East Coast would be matched by one on the West Coast. By and large, events in California were a few degrees wilder and farther Left than eastern ones, just as Venice Beach is more colorful than Martha's Vineyard. Exactly why this was so is unclear; one guess is that Californian institutions were not as rigid or staid as eastern ones because they were newer.[47]

The third event of the spring was little noticed. The adversary culture's first political pilgrimage of the Vietnam War period took place in July, when a delegation of the Women's Strike for Peace met in Jakarta with women representing the Democratic Republic of Vietnam and the National Liberation Front. Cora Weiss, an heiress of the Helena Rubenstein cosmetic fortune, and a WSP member, was the main organizer from the American side. Also attending was Nguyen Thi Binh, who was touted as the NLF's future foreign minister once the war was won. This meeting set the stage for future trips to Hanoi and set up a direct conduit for North Vietnamese disinformation. Through this conduit, Hanoi was able to charm and use hundreds of members of the antiwar movement in coming years. It was also the remote origin of the Committees of Liaison that Hanoi later used as a way to avoid the U.S. government with respect to requests for information about American prisoners of war.

The event that took place in the Congress was barely noticed at the time but it probably had more effect in the long run on administration policy and the morale of those who made it than anything that happened in the antiwar movement. It had to do with money.

In early May, the administration asked Congress for a $700 million defense supplemental to finance the war. President Johnson did not have to do this; he could have moved other monies around. But he wanted a reaffirmation that the Congress was still with him after the military escalations undertaken earlier in the year.[48] He got it: In the Senate the vote was 88 to 3 and in the House it was 408 to 7. But in the process a number of Senators voiced reservations and went out of their way to attach specific meanings to their votes. The press covered the vote well and the administration took notice. Senator Gaylord Nelson voted against along with Morse and Gruening. Equally important, Senators Fulbright, Jacob Javits, and George McGovern voiced reservations and made a point of telling their former Senatorial colleague, Vice President Hubert Humphrey, about them.

## CREATING THE NATIONAL
## COORDINATING COMMITTEE

As the year proceeded, the Marxist Left and the new pacifists found themselves increasingly in mutual, if occasionally uneasy, cooperation against the liberals. To their ranks was added a radical segment of the black movement. As Watts burned from August 11 to August 16, about 300 radical activists met in Washington at the Assembly of Unrepresented Peoples with the express purpose of fusing the cutting edges of the "black struggle movement" and the antiwar movement. Instrumental in the assembly's creation were Robert Moses of SNCC, David Dellinger, and Staughton Lynd. Thirty-three organizations were involved, including those of the old Left. The aim was to use discontent over the war and the widespread sympathy for the civil rights movement to radicalize as much of the American population as possible. Stopping the war was a secondary consideration.

The meeting began on August 6, Hiroshima Day. Buoyed by the success of the April rally, new demonstrations were planned as an adjunct to the formal, organizational meetings. One of them prompted a counterdemonstration by the American Nazi Party, whose members hurled red paint at Dellinger, Lynd, and Moses at the head of the march; a fracas ensued, and more than 350 people were arrested. Dellinger refused to pay his fine and spent a month in jail. *Life* magazine ran a picture of the paint-spattered trio in its August 16, 1965, issue next to a photograph of a demonstrator burning his draft card—an increasingly popular activity among militant pacifists. An encounter with Nazis and colorful photos landing in *Life*—now this was *really* newsworthy.

The riots in Watts, where 14,000 national guardsmen fought snipers and looters for a week on national television just months after the most important civil rights legislation in American history had been passed, were counterproductive to the civil rights movement. Similarly, the photogenic arrests of radicals in *Life,* and the growing association of images of radical antiwar protest with ghetto rioters and looters, were counterproductive to the antiwar movement as they almost completely overshadowed SANE's moderately toned newspaper advertisements.

The most important thing about the Assembly of Unrepresented Peoples was not the marches or the arrests or the press coverage, however. That weekend, the assembly formed from among its 33 constituent groups the National Coordinating Committee to End the War in Vietnam (NCCEWV), the crucial umbrella organization of the antiwar movement for the next two years. Its main offices were in New York City, the heart of the adversary culture; its student auxiliary was housed near the University of Wisconsin campus.

In light of its radical political agenda and the fact that numerous local antiwar organizations, many on college campuses, had sprung up more or less spontaneously in 1965, the NCCEWV had two immediate goals. First, it sought to radicalize and direct as many local organizations as possible, and second, it sought to join together white and black radicals across the country. It had good success in both endeavors, at least for a while. In its first project, on October 15 and 16, 1965, the NCCEWV helped to stimulate more than 50 protests in what it called the International Days of Protest. These protests featured draft card burnings, mass street mobilizations, and localized acts of violence.

Contrary to what one might have expected, SDS was not part of the assembly. It was invited to participate but declined. Some first-generation SDSers declined partly because of obvious old Left participation. They favored nonexclusion in principle but their antipathy to the old Left grew with every successive attempt at infiltration. But there was a deeper issue too.

At its June 1965 meeting SDS had elected Carl Oglesby—a 30-year-old sometime novelist and playwright, sometime graduate student, and former technical writer for the Bendix Corporation—to be its president on the basis of his "expertise" about Vietnam. He had written a 60-page pamphlet on the topic based in part on what he had learned at Bendix, and it became SDS's essential text on the war. Otherwise, Oglesby was not "political"; in his own words, he did not "know the difference between Lenin and Trotsky" at the time and did not care.[49]

Despite Oglesby's election, which clearly reflected SDS's concern with Vietnam, the organization as a whole could not make up its mind about how important the war was compared to its efforts to transform America and bring about true "participatory democracy," an essentially anarchist notion about how to make authority as egalitarian as possible. By the time SDS received the assembly's invitation, factional division between those who thought Vietnam should be a vanguard issue and those who thought otherwise had so confused and paralyzed the organization that it could not, and did not, respond. Only in September, a few weeks before the October International Days of Protest, did SDS agree to be a sponsoring organization despite having had virtually no input into the activities' planning and promotion.

Thus, after having shown its strength in the April rally, SDS declined to accept its new mandate and take the organizational lead of the antiwar movement—at least at this point. The same meeting that elected Oglesby refused to authorize a strong, centralized national campus organization. It refused to organize or support a national campaign of draft resistance. It insisted on the autonomy of local chapters and failed even to specify what its National Office was for. Among other things, this showed that as of 1965, SDS retained a strong residual anti-Communist, anti-authoritarian, and anti-centralization bias. Its program was as diffuse as it was maximalist and idealistic. As a consequence, SDS radicalism became more a collection of individual acts, unlimited intentions, and high hopes than a revolutionary movement or party in any serious sense of the words.

## COMPETITION AND ESCALATION

The International Days of Protest in October 1965 represented another successful escalation of antiwar protest organized by the core groups of the adversary culture. They also represented a further outflanking and overtaking of liberal protest, which in turn led to the increasingly bitter division of the movement as a whole.

By autumn, the divisions of spring were much more sharply defined. The October 1965 NCCEWV demonstrations were the first to openly break the law. They were the first to indicate the violence to come and to suggest the guerrilla theatrics of future protest. During the Fifth Avenue Parade protest in New York, which was affiliated with the NCCEWV protest even though organizationally distinct, puppets of a bloodstained Uncle Sam and of ghostlike creatures carrying stretchers with dead children caught the eye. In New York too, draft cards were burned while television cameras whirred away. In Oakland, demonstrators tried to obstruct activities at the Oakland Army Base, a main embarkation point for troops headed to Vietnam.

Left-Liberals in SANE and Americans for Democratic Action strove to match the organizing progress of the Left. In November 1965 SANE sponsored a rally in Washington that strove to involve as many clergymen as it could, Jewish, Catholic, and Protestant, black and white, alike. This effort gave birth to Clergy and Laity Concerned Over the War in Vietnam. The rally, dubbed "A Call to Mobilize the Conscience of America," drew about 25,000, compared to the roughly 100,000 altogether who had been involved in the International Days of Protest demonstrations.

As usual, SANE sought an image of moderation and evenhandedness. It even sent a cable to North Vietnamese leader Ho Chi Minh demanding that he stop his side of the war and warning him that demonstrations such as the one planned would not by themselves stop the American war effort.[50] It was a tactful gesture for, on this particular occasion, SANE had a very special problem with which to deal. The NCCEWV decided to have its annual meeting in Washington at the same time as the scheduled SANE rally; it was merely "lending support" from its roughly 1,500 delegates and their associates. SANE members interpreted the timing coincidence differently: They saw the NCCEWV presence as a challenge and a problem. They knew that radical activists would want to speak, they knew they would show up with unauthorized signs and would try to usurp the media attention drawn by the stars and headliners SANE had invited. They were also worried about violence and counterviolence. (In the meantime, as the NCCEWV was trying to take over SANE's rally, the Trotskyite Young Socialist Alliance was trying to take over the National Coordinating Committee and nearly succeeded.[51])

In the end, compromises were reached, some of which worked out and some of which did not. Sanford Gottlieb of SANE was the organizer of the march. He refused to allow NCCEWV affiliates to have their signs and slogans as an official part of the rally. But he agreed not to have rally marshals remove the signs physically; he was afraid of providing a pretext to deliberate violence. Gottlieb also tried to stack the list of speakers with as many household names as possible. In addition to Spock, Mrs. King, and Norman Thomas, also speaking were cartoonist Jules Feiffer, playwright Arthur Miller, actor Tony Randall, novelist Saul Bellow, and polio fighter Dr. Albert Sabin. SANE also tried to exclude radicals from the speaker's rostrum, refusing permission to Lynd, Dellinger, Robert Moses, and Linus Pauling.[52] Only one radical, SDS president Carl Oglesby, was allowed to appear. This was meant both as a tactical concession and as a ploy to give the march a greater appeal to young people. It was also an effort to try to wean an irresolute SDS away from the NCCEWV radicals. It was a concession that backfired badly.

After several tedious speeches, Oglesby took the podium to attack "corporate liberalism" and imperialism. He declared the "Liberal Left" to be the enemy and, to the chagrin of SANE's leadership, drew by far the loudest applause of any speaker. He said:

> The original commitment in Vietnam was made by President Truman, a mainstream liberal. It was seconded by President Eisenhower, a moderate liberal. It was intensified by the late President Kennedy, a flaming liberal. Think of the men who now engineer that war—those who study the maps, give the commands, push the buttons and tally the dead: Bundy, McNamara, Lodge, Goldberg, the President himself. They are not moral monsters. They are all honorable men. They are all liberals. . . . We have become a nation of young, bright-eyed, hard-hearted, slim-waisted, bullet-headed make-out artists, a nation—may I say it?—of beardless liberals.[53]

As Ogelsby spoke, a political entrepreneur of the Left, one Walter Teague, was selling Vietcong banners for $10 each, and a fair number appeared waving away over the heads of the vast crowd. Worse, the National Liberation Front sent a telegram to SANE expressing best wishes for a successful march and released two American prisoners of war to demonstrate its solidarity with the rally. This embarrassment was a joint scheme of the WRL and the WSP, aided by the contacts established at the Jakarta meeting. Luckily for SANE, the press coverage of the rally stressed the patriotic, middle-class, nonsubversive nature of the crowd as a whole, excepting "a few fired-up youth."[54] Inside the antiwar movement, however, no one needed a weather vane to see which way the wind was blowing.

After the Washington rally, the radical Left opened a full attack on the Left-Liberal parts of the movement through its journals, *Radical America, Studies on the Left, New Left Review, Socialist Revolution* (later *Socialist Review*), *Liberation,* and *Ramparts.* Representative was the charge of Robert Wolfe, editor of *Studies on the Left:* "It is already clear to everyone except SANE and its allies that one cannot protest the war in Vietnam in the name of a more sophisticated version of anti-Communism without lending credence to the very myth which has produced the war."[55] Descriptions of the war in antiwar rhetoric sounded increasingly like caricatured sloganeered criticisms of capitalism, a vulgarization of the Leninist theory of imperialism, to wit: Dow Chemical Corporation runs U.S. Vietnam policy, and so forth.

One key to the difference between liberals and radicals was what to do about the draft. Radicals were now prepared to counsel draft resistance as a key to their program. This was, of course, against the law because it presumed civil disobedience of one kind or another. Not to be set too far aside is the fact that radicals were younger as a group than liberals and therefore tended to have a greater personal stake in the draft issue. At least some radicals well understood that the draft was a touchstone issue in the dispute within the movement. Indeed, it was exploited partly to drive this polarization wider.[56]

The music changed too. Nineteen sixty-five was the year the "theme song" of the antiwar movement, the "I Feel Like I'm Fixin' to Die Rag," was written. In it Country Joe and the Fish sang: "Come on Wall Street let's move fast, / your big chance has come at last; / there's lots of good money to be made, / supplying the Army with the tools of the trade."[57] Country Joe and the Fish's music was almost universally banned from the radio along with albums by The Fugs, Ed Sanders's wild and bizarre group. It was underground material, therefore extremely hip and extremely popular, so much so that radio play did not matter. Other songs about draft evasion, another increasingly popular theme of "resistance," were also penned, recorded, and enthusiastically received, often by folk lyricists who had begun singing for integration and who now were singing for antiwar demonstrations. For the first time too, bands such as the Jefferson Airplane, the Grateful Dead, and the Byrds rose to fame by pioneering politicized rock and roll mainly on the West Coast.[58] This musical development, in turn, had roots in the folk phenomenon of the early 1960s, championed by Vanguard Records with artists such as Peter, Paul and Mary, Odetta, and a variety of black blues musicians such as Elizabeth Cotton and Mississippi John Hurt. Before them, the political folk tradition went back through Woodie Guthrie, The Weavers (with Pete Seeger), Paul Robeson, and more recently, Phil Ochs, who wrote "Draft Dodger Rag" and other explicitly political songs, many having to do with civil rights.[59] The Byrds's Jim McGuinn (who changed his name to Roger in 1968) got his start with the New Christy Minstrels, a group, like the Brothers Four, the Kingston Trio, Burl Ives, Harry Belafonte, and Peter, Paul, and Mary, that had popularized folk music for general audiences in the late 1950s and early 1960s.

The changes in music were quite striking in those years. In 1964, all the top AM-radio hits were fluffy, apolitical songs, like "Little Old Lady from Pasadena" by Jan and Dean. In 1965 Barry McGuire's "Eve of Destruction" began a new trend in "heavy" and even macabre lyrics. "Eve of Destruction" came from the folk genre and it showed, even before Bob Dylan's first chart hit, "Like a Rolling Stone," that there was a market for "serious" lyrics linked to a "badboy" attitude. Todd Gitlin suggests that the Rolling Stones's big hit "Satisfaction," and the whole Stones image for that matter, picked up on and rode the market for badboyism into stardom.[60] As another sign of the times, in 1965 the top song on the pop charts was explicitly political and about Vietnam; but it was not antiwar, it was pro-war. As noted in passing earlier, it was Barry Sadler's "Ballad of the Green Beret," which spoke of "fighting soldiers from the sky, fearless men who jump and die." The "Ballad of the Green Beret" was probably an explicit answer to "Eve of Destruction"—at least that's how many saw it at the time. Indeed, one New York radio station staged a "battle of the Barrys" in 1965, a sort of mini-election of social inclinations. McGuire won by one vote.[61]

Finally, it is worth noting that the politicization of youth music created a counterpoliticization, just as the movement itself created a backlash. Merle Haggard's "I'm Proud to be an Okie from Muskogee" was probably the most famous of the counterballads, and it was such a good song that even hippies in time came to appreciate it by way of their tongue-in-cheek interpretation of it. Haggard, however, was serious, and so were most of the truck drivers, hard-hats, steel workers, farmers, clerks, and housewives who listened to it. After all, the southern barroom favorite of the day, "There Stands the Flag," was nearly as popular, and no tongue-in-cheek interpretation of that number is possible.

## POLITICAL PILGRIMAGE: FIRE AND BACKFIRE

To round out a remarkable year, Herbert Aptheker, a leading American Communist and head of the American Institute for Marxist Studies in New York, arranged a trip for himself, Staughton Lynd, and SDSer Tom Hayden to Hanoi. This was the first time that prominent antiwar activists had gone to North Vietnam. A number of activists had tried to go previously but were prevented, not because the U.S. government opposed it, but because the North Vietnamese government had. Now that Hanoi had changed its mind, a steady stream made the political pilgrimage, starting with radicals Hayden and Lynd in December 1965 and continuing with political personalities of an entirely different character, such as actress Jane Fonda and former U.S. Attorney General Ramsey Clark a few years later.

As a rule, antiwar leaders who traveled to Hanoi fell hook, line, and sinker for everything they were told. They felt themselves afire with revolutionary zeal, confirmed in their radicalism, and made special by their opportunity to visit a socialist country. Most reported on returning that they were buoyed by their visits, during which they were told how much their activism was appreciated by the North Vietnamese. As David Wells has written, Cornell University professor Douglass Dowd reported himself "so high on these people. To walk down the streets of Hanoi and see those little kids . . . Jesus Christ, it makes you weep with joy for the species."[62] He and others also burned with hatred for what the United States was doing to the Vietnamese people, who had such "strong commitments to building a decent society." Donna Allen, another pilgrim, said about traveling to North Vietnam: "When you come back, you've dedicated your life."[63]

The reaction of American labor to activists' trips to North Vietnam was immediate, bitter, and very instructive—or should have been. When Hayden got back from North Vietnam in early 1966, several building trade unions called for stronger support for South Vietnam and compared antiwar leaders who went to Hanoi to scabs and strikebreakers.[64] This, in turn, enraged New Leftists, who were so persuaded that they knew what was best for labor that they accused laborers of being middle-class sellouts to the struggle. Wrote Marvin Garson, an FSM leader at Berkeley: "The next time some $3.90 an hour AFL-type workers go on strike for a 50 cent raise, I'll remember the day they chanted 'Burn Hanoi, not our flag,' and so help me I'll cross their fucking picket line."[65]

The right wing of the antiwar movement took a totally different attitude. In early 1966 SANE established a special trade union division, using some older Leftist labor leaders in New York as organizers.[66] By May 1966 more than 30 unions were affiliated, and labor representation in all of SANE's antiwar activities persisted throughout the entire period of the war. They were simply overwhelmed, however, by the radical protest and could not prevent the sharp turn of the "hard-hats" against the antiwar movement and, by indirection at least, *for* the war policy.[67]

In retrospect, 1965 was a key year in both the Vietnam War and the antiwar movement. By February the Johnson administration had Americanized the war, and by April the adversary culture had climbed to the top of opposition to it. One sort of escalation begot another. This remained the pattern of the next three years, in Vietnam and at home.

# Groundswell

*Our American people, when we get in a contest of any kind—*
*whether it is in a war, an election, a football game, or whatever*
*it is—want it decided and decided quickly; get in or get out.*
—Lyndon Johnson, November 1967 press conference

The main source of rising antiwar sentiment in the country at large in 1966 and 1967 did not come from the increased activism of the antiwar movement but from the war itself. As body counts mounted, Pentagon double-talk accelerated, and important officials defected from the Johnson administration, it took either an indefatigable optimist or a full-fledged moron to conclude that the war was going well. By the end of 1966, 6,644 Americans had been killed in action, about 6,000 of them in 1966 alone. There were 385,300 U.S. soldiers in Vietnam, 200,000 more than the previous year. Yet no creditable predictions of victory were heard.

However quickly antiwar sentiment spread in the country, the radicalization of the antiwar movement, and especially its diffuse leadership, spread even faster. This had two effects. First, an inevitable element of duplicity and bad faith arose on the part of the antiwar leadership toward its rank and file. As antiwar activist Sam Brown put it: "Virtually all the antiwar leadership was of the 'inevitably by-product' school, while most of the participants in marches and campaigns were of the 'aberrational-occurrence' school."[1] Second and more important, the expansion of radical tactics in antiwar protests left many Americans in a kind of limbo— inclined to oppose the war but not wanting to be associated with what they viewed as an unpatriotic movement.

## FROZEN ADMINISTRATION, FLUID MOVEMENT

Both the war and various forms of opposition to it continued in 1966. In retrospect it is clear that the Johnson administration and the movement became locked in a strange embrace. The administration made efforts to appear "fair" and open in 1965; Secretary McNamara and his aides saw antiwar delegations at the Pentagon, sent speakers to teach-ins, and dispatched "truth squads" to college campuses. In 1966, as the war became more frustrating and internal debates more protracted, and as the protests became more radical and the accusations more personal, the administration turned decidedly hostile to the movement. There were fewer meetings and more curt statements. The best illustration of the change, perhaps, was a tense episode in November between McNamara and the Harvard SDS in Cambridge, in which McNamara's car was surrounded and pounded on by angry young men who seemed to have a penchant for very personal violence.[2]

The administration's cold shoulder to public dissent was undoubtedly a mistake that helped the radical wing of the antiwar movement in its internal battles with the liberals. In the earlier phase, liberals could argue with some credibility that its lines of communication and influence inside the government were having an impact; some evidence could be, and was, put forward by SANE, Americans for Democratic Action, and the other groups to this effect. But to the extent that the administration stopped talking to the antiwar movement, this argument was undermined. Many liberal protestors of the 1964-65 period reacted to this treatment by moving farther Left, although for most no doubt this was caused by other factors as well. The radical wing of the movement reacted to the administration's hostility with increased hostility of its own, now ever more personalized against President Johnson himself. With the added hostility the movement's sense of its own nobility and importance grew too. It was better to be snubbed than not to be noticed at all, just as bad publicity is often said to be better than none at all.

Johnson's public demeanor also contributed to the disdain with which antiwar protestors regarded him. Some of it was simply the result of the public's missing President Kennedy's charm. Some of it was anti-Southern prejudice, magnified by the civil rights movement's having drawn attention to the "white South." But it was also a function of Johnson's strained speech and rigid appearance on television and at press conferences. Lyndon Johnson was a witty man not reluctant to use colorful language in private, but in Camelot's White House he bent over backward to appear urbane and serious before the court of Ivy League easterners. Such a demeanor was unnatural for him, and those inclined to distrust or hate him wrongly interpreted it as evidence of disingenuousness.

Clearly, the antiwar movement contributed to a growing defensiveness on the part of the administration—a defensiveness that was sensed keenly in the Congress—but it was not the main cause. Rather, the administration's defensiveness mainly reflected its own internal doubts and forebodings of policy drift. Administration policies simply appeared fossilized. Despite the increased military effort there were no negotiations in sight despite earnest secret efforts to arrange talks. The administration's *apparent* lack of interest in a negotiated settlement, in turn, fueled the sense of drift—the war was not being won or lost, no end was in sight, and young men continued to die in ever greater numbers. It is no wonder that ever greater numbers of people grew distraught. The widening of antiwar sentiment, then, and the lengthening of the exposure time of the middle class to the proselytizations of the radical Left, was a direct result of the Johnson administration's unfortunate conduct of the war, both on the battlefield and politically at home. Although the administration knew it was failing, as *The Pentagon Papers* were to show so vividly, it could not bring itself to change course one way or the other.

The antiwar movement had become as fluid as the Johnson administration had become paralyzed. On the Left, sectarian radicals and the new pacifists continued organizing and protesting, but their cooperation was never easy or consistent. On the one hand, the size of the problem confronting the antiwar movement—the war itself, its continuing if declining general popularity, and the administration's political power to pursue it within the political base of the Democratic Party—argued in favor of cooperation and collaboration. On the other hand, the more diverse the radical constituency of the NCCEWV became, the less able it was to agree on anything tactically or ideologically. As to tactics, some groups, mainly the militant pacifist ones, stressed civil disobedience. But old Left groups, notably the Trotskyite Socialist Workers Party, objected to getting arrested for symbolic purposes. Still other groups, including many blacks, preferred active "resistance," and not only of the nonviolent sort.

When it came to ideological dispute, no subject was too minute to give rise to spleen-spilling displays of anger and accusation. As long as A. J. Muste was still active, such disputes in the leadership were manageable. From his days as a Trotskyite, Muste had a knack for patching up arcane arguments. He managed to keep the New York Fifth Avenue Parade section of the NCCEWV together long after the NCCEWV itself exhibited the characteristic, telltale signs of Leftist sectarianism, which began to surface in January 1966.

The NCCEWV met that month in Milwaukee. It could not decide on anything except to sponsor a second International Days of Protest in March. Some groups wanted to create a new unitary national organization to end the war out of the loose umbrella coalition of the NCCEWV. Some wanted to create a third political party. A few spoke of creating a guerrilla war behind enemy lines in "Amerika." There were endless arguments about tactics and slogans and much personal bitterness among group leaderships. Looking at the sectarianism of the NCCEWV in 1966 and 1967, and of SDS in 1968 and 1969, it is not hard to understand why successful Leftist putsches, such as the original Bolshevik one, first turned their guns on their erstwhile Leftist associates. In dealing with the bourgeoisie, one can expect quaint manners and even a stodgy standing on principle. But from other believing Leftists one could expect only what any vanguard party would do were it to find itself in an analogous position: an attempt to take power by any means, including calumny and deceit. The only thing that kept some NCCEWV radicals from physically assaulting one another was fear of detection and prosecution by local police and the FBI.

In March 1966, the second NCCEWV International Days of Protest drew 50,000 demonstrators to New York City and 150,000 more to dozens of simultaneous protests across the country. The New York rally was centered around the Fifth Avenue Peace Parade Committee. The committee was chaired nominally by Muste, but the real work, this year as in 1965, was done by Norma Becker, a WRL radical from New York City who had been active in the civil rights movement. The parade was a success by most measures, but the NCCEWV was not. After the International Days of Protest, the NCCEWV could not regain a focus for continued cooperation. It died partly from inanition, partly from the fatigue brought on by a perpetual failure to agree on direction or tactics, and partly by the unwillingness of constituent groups to provide either decision-making authority or significant amounts of money to the center.

Liberals, meanwhile, though better organized and financed, were having troubles of their own. SANE de-emphasized mass rallies and instead organized the "Voter's Pledge Peace Campaign," an effort to politicize the American mainstream against the war. It supported dozens of peace candidates in primaries in the 1966 midterm election, all of whom lost, including the most glamorous candidate of all: Robert Scheer, running in Berkeley with the help of campaign manager Jerry Rubin.[3]

In the meantime, Allard K. Lowenstein and Curtis Gans at ADA started a Dump Johnson movement, the forerunner to the Eugene McCarthy and Robert Kennedy presidential campaigns of 1968. The Democrats did poorly in the 1966 midterm elections; Lowenstein and Gans believed Vietnam was the reason. They also feared that the country would polarize over the war. According to an associate, Fred Craig, Lowenstein "thought the dialogue on the war would be captured by the crazies or the left, and a whole generation would have to choose between Staughton Lynd and Lyndon Johnson."[4] The rank and file of ADA, however, feared a rupture with the labor movement and eventually voted to support Johnson. Lowenstein and Gans searched for support elsewhere and managed to find some, formally announcing the Dump Johnson campaign in August 1967, but they had to chase the antiwar movement as it lurched ever farther leftward.

## WILLIAM FULBRIGHT, STOKELY CARMICHAEL, AND JOHN Q. HIPPIE

The year 1966 was notable in three other ways, as well: Opposition to the war rose steadily within the Congress and within the president's own party; SNCC entered the antiwar movement in a major way; and the counterculture encountered the antiwar movement in earnest. The first development augured for de-escalation in Vietnam, but the latter two augured for just the reverse. While the antiwar movement may well have extended the reach of the counterculture, the counter-cultural aura of the antiwar movement helped it not one iota.

Public Senate hearings, led by Senator William Fulbright, were held on Vietnam for the first time in 1966. The hearings projected to the American people the message that dissent could be politically moderate and responsible.[5] SANE and other Left-Liberal groups had tried to foster a respectable, patriotic image for opposing the war. It is not clear to what extent they had failed or succeeded by 1966 but the Fulbright hearings certainly helped the effort. Millions of Americans saw the nation's elected representatives publicly asking tough and logical questions in measured tones in the venerable and tradition-bedecked Senate caucus room. They heard the estimable George Kennan express his doubts about future escalation and about what the human and moral costs of winning the war were likely to be. They heard Senator Fulbright himself, the sponsor of the Tonkin Gulf Resolution, say publicly that he regretted having even voted for it, not to mention having sponsored it on President Johnson's behalf.[6]

The hearings not only altered the image of opposition to the war, they also got the administration's attention. One result was that, soon after the announcement that Senator Fulbright would hold hearings, the administration mounted a public relations campaign centered on the famed Honolulu Conference, a summit between the U.S. and South Vietnamese leaderships. More important, the hearings forced an inter-agency effort inside the administration to develop a coherent public defense of the war. But this effort instead brought out contradictions and disagreements that, in time, undermined morale and set the stage for major policy reversals in 1968.

The public demonstrations against the war no doubt bothered Johnson too, not necessarily for what they said about him or his administration's policies, but for what they seem to have represented in his mind. Once, in 1966, a contingent of Secretary McNamara's whiz kids tried to persuade the president with statistics and computer printouts that a massive conventional bombing of Hanoi might be effective militarily. Johnson reportedly answered: "I have one more problem for your computer: How long will it take five hundred thousand angry young Americans to climb that White House wall out there and lynch their President if he does something like that?"[7] One cannot judge from a single statement—in this case Johnson probably used the image of antiwar protest to argue against a policy he opposed on other grounds—but it is at least possible that antiwar protests reinforced certain parameters for escalation already in the president's head.

But clearly, of all the factors bearing on the administration's disinclination to escalate militarily at various stages in the war, the antiwar movement in the street was the least of them, if it figured at all. Certainly dissent in the Senate was taken more seriously for both its content and its political implications. It was that dissent that moved the administration to act, or react, particularly since it came from within the president's own party. When Johnson said in private counsel in September 1967 that "The major threat we have is from the doves," opposition from senior Democratic Party figures is certainly what he meant.[8]

Some administration principals, perhaps President Johnson himself, may have eventually changed their views about Vietnam because of worries about the domestic political implications of pressing on. During the period when the Democrats would have suffered from withdrawal—remember, before 1968 the administration felt, rightly, that it had more to worry about from opposition to its Right that wanted to escalate militarily—the administration's view of the global and regional political consequences of failure in Vietnam coincided with what made sense in terms of domestic politics. Both told Johnson to soldier on. But when the two elements began to diverge—and the Fulbright hearings were really the beginnings of that divergence—real problems emerged. By the time domestic political considerations also seemed to auger for doing less in Vietnam than more, some officials may also have rethought the security rationale for the war, judging the consequences of U.S. retrenchment to be less serious.

To keep watch on establishment opinion after the Fulbright hearings, President Johnson began convening the Wise Men, trusted advisors who were mainly party elders out of government service. They included: former Secretary of State Dean Acheson, George Ball, General Omar Bradley, McGeorge Bundy, Douglas Dillon, Cyrus Vance, Arthur Dean, John J. McCloy, General Mathew Ridgeway, General Maxwell Taylor, Robert Murphy, Henry Cabot Lodge, Abe Fortas, and Arthur Goldberg.[9] In the end, in March 1968, it was the change of heart among the Wise Men conjoined to the changed views of a new secretary of defense, Clark Clifford, that persuaded Johnson to change course in Vietnam. Though perhaps not entirely unrelated to the antiwar movement, the views of such men were much more influential than any number of demonstrations and symbolic acts of civil disobedience could have been.[10]

A third kind of dissent also arose in 1966, and it was the kind President Johnson loathed most: the defection from the inner team of his closest aides. The first to leave the administration was McGeorge Bundy, Johnson's National Security Council director. Robert McNamara followed in 1967. As with the street demonstrators, Johnson did not hear the contents of Bundy's dissent until his anger dissipated, if then—for Johnson, this was disloyalty pure and simple.

As for Senator Fulbright, his reversal was also deeply painful on a personal level. Fulbright was not a White House advisor or cabinet member but he had been one of Lyndon Johnson's closest colleagues in the Senate in the old days and, as noted, led the way for the Tonkin Gulf Resolution at the president's request. The families were friends; Lyndon and Lady Bird used to sit on the Fulbright's porch discussing books with the senator and his wife. But not in 1967. In August 1967 Lady Bird wrote in her diary:

> I think the most frustrated I've been lately is reading a speech that Senator
> Fulbright made in which he indicated that the country is damned because we

are spending so much in Vietnam instead of spending it here to take care of the poor and the underprivileged—this from a man who has never voted for any Civil Rights measure and who even voted against Medicare in 1964.[11]

Finally in this regard, the results of the 1966 elections were not an insignificant message to the president. The Democrats got pasted, losing 47 seats in the House, the exact number gained in 1964.[12] The war might not have been responsible for all of the damage—some of it was a natural falling off of Johnson's 1964 coattails in a midterm election—but Johnson suspected that it was responsible for much of it.

So much for the developments that tended toward limiting American participation in the war. Now for those that tended in the opposite direction.

First, 1966 was the year when Stokely Carmichael and SNCC entered the antiwar picture in a big way, forcing the center of the civil rights movement led by Martin Luther King, Jr., headlong toward an antiwar position.[13] The war in Vietnam had not yet hurt the War on Poverty, nor had it diminished the administration's commitment to civil rights and social justice; the Johnson administration was prepared to borrow money to pay for both, and it did. SNCC's main impact in joining the radical antiwar movement and in displacing the Southern Christian Leadership Conference was twofold: it pushed the antiwar movement toward political irresponsibility, and, more critically—and precisely as Dr. King had feared—it undermined the broad sympathy for black grievances that had been built up in the country over the last decade and a half.[14]

Second, it was toward the end of 1966 that the term "hippie" first entered the public lexicon. The flower children, with their drugs and acid rock, did as much to hurt the image of the antiwar movement in the country at large as Senator Fulbright's hearings had done to help it.[15] Most Americans seemed confused about Vietnam; not surprising, really, since it was an extremely complicated matter. Practically everyone harbored doubts about the war, particularly as it continued to go badly. But now many began to dislike the antiwar movement as much or more than they disliked the war, and they associated the nascent counterculture—and particularly the associated drug culture—with the antiwar movement even though, as of yet, the connections were neither formal nor extensive. In fact, the counterculture and the New Left as of 1966 were in most respects opposite poles of youth culture. SDS was political; the counterculture, represented by LSD experimenter and author Ken Kesey, Harvard professor Timothy Leary, and a strange if creative group of cultural anarchists known as the Diggers, was antipolitical. In a famous incident in Berkeley in 1965, Kesey told a crowd of protestors that politics, any politics, was just a dead end. "You're not gonna stop this war with this rally," he shouted at the crowd. "Look at the war, turn your backs on it and say fuck it."[16]

The feeling was totally mutual. The Trotskyite Young Socialist Alliance liked to refer to the counterculture as a "sick escapist milieu."[17] As far as most Port Huron SDSers were concerned, hippies were too apolitical and those who soon became Yippies[18] were simply lunatics—psychedelic Bolsheviks and Marxist acidheads. The real political types may have grown their hair long, but they did not lose their lives in drugs. Tom Hayden, for one, was the movement's straight man for years, or so he claimed.[19] Todd Gitlin too tried to explain to his colleagues that the "free love" and "free lunches" they enjoyed were luxuries based on American "theft" of Third World resources.[20]

The sharp differences between the antiwar movement and the counterculture did not prevent the proliferation of connections between the two. Such connections were in a sense forced on SDS and the New Left because the inroads the counterculture was making in American society simply outran SDS's efforts to politicize the campuses. It is hard to say just when and why it happened, but sometime in 1966 and 1967 marijuana hit American university campuses in a big way. There is no question that the spirit of rebellion, romanticism, and moral energy associated with the counterculture was enhanced by getting stoned, particularly in small, sexually heterogeneous groups. The apparent lucidity that occurs under the influence of marijuana—not to speak of LSD[21]—also allowed many to accept shallow political thinking as sublime wisdom. Not that interesting things do not happen to a mind under the influence of hallucinogenic drugs; it's just that they rarely seem as interesting the next morning, if they can be remembered at all.

Drug use was also vaguely associated with the aura of the civil rights movement in the distorted and attenuated sense that marijuana was long a part of urban black subculture. For white antiwar activists, everything black was "cool" to one extent or another, a matter we will return to later. Marijuana and, to a lesser extent, cocaine, fit this imitative pattern. The reason the country at large suddenly became concerned about drug use was not because it was so concerned about the welfare of heretofore socially marginal groups, but because young, middle-class whites were imitating them, not only in drug use but in attacking other aspects of middle-class moral styles.[22]

Popular music, again, played a role in this. It accelerated the merger of the drug culture with antiwar politics. Even the seemingly innocuous duo of Simon & Garfunkel illustrates the point. A 1966 song, "The Sounds of Silence," produced in both a folksy, without-drums version and an AM-radio folk-rock version, swept the charts. The lyric was vaguely political, railing against something, and sincerely so, only against what was never quite clear; it certainly had nothing explicitly to do with Vietnam or with drugs. It was in that sense—at the same time intense but diffuse—a true symbol of the era. Two other songs on the album, however, did have to do—by way of sarcasm at least—with politics and drugs. One, called "A Simple Desultory Philippic (Or How I Was Robert McNamara'ed Into Submission)," made no sense at all but contained a string of pop cultural referents, including ones to Norman Mailer, General Maxwell Taylor, Robert McNamara, Ayn Rand, Bob Dylan, Dylan Thomas, and Barry Sadler just for starters, and quoted a Dylan lyric about getting stoned.[23]

The other song, the album's last tune, was "Silent Night," in which the music was overlaid with a news broadcast fabricated by Paul Simon. In the beginning of the song, the music is loud and the radio is soft. As the song proceeds, the volume of the first track decreases as that of the second increases. The news narrative mixes mention of comedian and social critic Lenny Bruce's death from a drug overdose with civil rights themes, random violence, Vietnam War items, and antiwar protests. (Recall, this was issued in 1966, before the March on the Pentagon.) The last part of the "news" went as follows:

> In Washington the atmosphere was tense today as a special subcommittee of the House Committee on Un-American Activities continued its probe into anti-Vietnam war protests. Demonstrators were forcibly evicted from the hearings when they began shouting antiwar slogans. . . . Former Vice President Richard Nixon says that unless there is a substantial increase in the present war effort in Vietnam, the U.S. should look forward to 5 more years of war. In a speech before the convention of Veterans of Foreign Wars in New York, Nixon also said opposition to the war in this country is the "greatest single weapon working against the U.S."[24]

Very quickly after 1966 some rock music tuned itself to the rhythms of the counterculture and the drug culture within it. Most popular songs that one heard day and in and day out had nothing to do with either, but dozens falling in the countercultural category easily come to mind: the Jefferson Airplane's "White Rabbit," Procol Harem's "Whiter Shade of Pale," the Byrds's cover of Dylan's "Mister Tamborine Man" and their own "Eight Miles High," the Beatles's "Strawberry Fields" and "Lucy in the Sky with Diamonds" (whose initials read LSD), the Grateful Dead's "Truckin'," and the Doors's "Light My Fire," the title of which was taken from an Aldous Huxley essay in praise of mescaline.[25] Less well known but more explicit was the song "Panama Red," which celebrated the virtues of a certain strain of marijuana.

As social critic Louis Menard has pointed out, not only was the music more than occasionally about drugs, and performed by performers who were on drugs, but it was designed to be listened to by people on drugs.[26] Anyone who has never experienced listening to this genre of music while high on marijuana, LSD, or other hallucinogens can only guess what this statement means. If, on the other hand, one has experienced this phenomenon, nothing more need be said.

At the same time, it is important to recognize that the joining of music with the drug culture was not an invention of the counterculture. Odes to mind-altering substances are nearly as old as mind-altering substances, as any Native American from the Southwest can tell you. But more proximate origins can be found in the jazz subculture of the interwar years, especially its predominantly black parts. Literally dozens of jazz songs that praised cocaine and "reefer" exist; and the counterculture's adulation of black culture helped propel this music and the drug experience into the counterculture, which was made up of white, middle-class kids. The consciousness-expansion experiments of the Beat Generation formed another connective tissue to the combination of music and drugs. This comes out in full force in a number of Jack Kerouac's novels and appears in the poetry of Allen Ginsberg and Alan Watts. Besides, it was no secret how Ken Kesey and the Merry Pranksters got so merry.[27]

Mention of the Beat Generation reminds us that not only was music transformed by the political environment of the counterculture, but so were other forms of entertainment. Humor stands out as an example. Lenny Bruce closed the distance between social criticism and humor. Before Bruce, the model was Will Rogers—homespun, gentle, and satirical more than sarcastic. Bruce was daringly obscene, biting, and bitter. Without Bruce there could have been no Dick Gregory of Vietnam antiwar-era notoriety, whose work mixed in the same combination as Bruce's humor and sense of hurt. Jerry Rubin, too, used to listen to Lenny Bruce tapes before delivering his own Yippie speeches, trying to emulate his cadence and tone.[28]

As suggested earlier, the spread of the drug subculture had tremendous relevance to the antiwar movement. Before 1967, SDS was a sober, highly idealistic, albeit increasingly extreme group of young people. Countercultural hippies, whose existence and numbers were enlarged by the antiwar movement, but who existed independently of it, were initially an occasional and colorful adjunct to the New Left. Like the New Left too, they were more anarchist in spirit than proto-Marxist (though not anarchists by way of political philosophy, for most hippies had never heard of Mikhail Bakunin, Peter Kropotkin, or Emma Goldman for that matter). Beyond the natural anarchistic affinity between SDS and hippiedom, drugs clearly brought SDS closer to the counterculture and the counterculture closer to SDS.

SDS had never been exclusionist or doctrinaire about membership. But its membership grew so fast after 1966 that inner-SDS factionalism, a phenomenon natural to "anti-elitist" organizations, grew beyond control. According to former SDSer Kirkpatrick Sale, SDS grew from 2,500 members in 41 chapters in December 1964 to at least 40,000, and perhaps as many as 100,000 members in 350 to 400 chapters by November 1968.[29] In the early days, SDS had to compete with the old Left Du Bois Clubs, the Maoist May 2nd Movement, and the Trotskyite Young Socialist Alliance. But SDS's ranks swelled due to its leading role in opposing the draft just as draft quotas soared upward.[30] The Du Bois Clubs went out of business and the M2M movement dissolved. YSA disappeared, too, but in a different way;

it became the Progressive Labor caucus within SDS, secretly considering itself as a vanguard Bolshevik faction within the Left. In any case, YSA had attracted only a small number of romantic cultists.

As often happens in a suddenly popular movement, the old core cadres of SDS now had to pay attention to its new membership to keep them from slipping away into other groups. Seeking to ingratiate themselves to the hordes of new would-be radicals and themselves swayed by the romantic arguments of the counterculture, many SDSers began to adopt countercultural fashions and mores—including drugs. Some true, original SDS ascetics argued against joining the counterculture or allowing the counterculture to join them. The typical red diaper baby and "straight" radical simply could not grasp how the best way to organize certain people could be to get them stoned. They understood the difference between a political idealist and a romantic, a distinction put well by novelist Tom Robbins, who clearly takes the latter's side. "No matter how fervently a romantic might support a movement," he wrote,

> he or she eventually must withdraw from active participation in that move-
> ment because the group ethic—the supremacy of the organization over the
> individual—is an affront to intimacy. Intimacy is the principal source of the
> sugars with which life is sweetened. It is absolutely vital to the essential
> insanities. Without the essential (intimate) insanities, humor becomes inof-
> fensive and therefore pap, poetry becomes exoteric and therefore prose,
> eroticism becomes mechanical and therefore pornography, behavior becomes
> predictable and therefore easy to control. As for magic, there's none at all
> because the aim of any social activist is power over others, whereas a magician
> seeks power over only himself. . . . [E]very cause, no matter how worthy,
> eventually falls prey to the tyranny of the dull mind. In the movement, as in
> the bee house or the white ant's hill of clay, there is no place for idiosyncrasy,
> let alone mischief.[31]

Jerry Rubin said essentially the same thing, not in a novel, but in Chicago in 1968: "Marijuana makes each person God. . . . Marijuana is destroying the schools. Education is conditioning. Pot deconditions. School makes us cynics. Pot makes us dreamers. Education polarizes our brains into subjects, categories, divisions, concepts. Pot scrambles our brains into a perfect mess."[32] And we mustn't forget musician John Sinclair, who claimed that LSD brought "everything into focus for the first times in our lives. . . . Until we started eating all that acid we couldn't figure out what was happening—we knew things were all wrong the way they were but we didn't know how they could be different. . . . LSD cleared all that up."[33]

Ascetic SDSers were soon in the minority when confronted with this general view of how drugs clarified the mind and allowed political and other truths to pour forth. The old SDSers could not successfully fight the appeal of drugs, especially when advertised by Jerry Rubin and his friends. Moreover, the hippies were useful to SDS in other ways. The attacks against the educational prerogatives of the university could never have succeeded to the extent they did without the hippie and later the Yippie students. This battlefront became increasingly important to SDSers for several reasons. Its successes could generate visible proof of SDS's clout; it enabled SDS to compete for student loyalty over competing campus organizations; and some believed that for students and intellectuals to become a revolutionary vanguard, it was necessary to seize control of one's home turf—in this case the university.

Eventually, the argument within SDS to adopt and adapt to the countercul-ture received powerful endorsement from none other than Carl Oglesby. Oglesby believed that cultural rebellion and political opposition could be made compatible. "Rock music and long hair and dope," he later said, "the damned socialist organi-zations couldn't stand that stuff. They had no conception at all, it seemed, of the relationship between political and cultural rebellion. Our approach always was to make the connection happen, to bring the cultural and the political into the most intimate interplay."[34]

Oglesby got sympathy and also some help from David Dellinger, who thought the same. New pacifist thinking had always emphasized the individual more than the group, the spiritual more than the rational, and the aesthetic over the ascetic. Dellinger devoted the April 1967 issue of Liberation to the debate between the counterculture and the political types. Elder SDSer Henry Anderson laid out the anticounterculture position, while Allen Ginsberg, already a legend, wrote for the counterculture in the sense of urging a form of transpolitics rather than the antipolitics of Kesey and Leary.[35] By the end of 1967, the counterculture and the New Left had become almost indistinguishable to the naked eye.

But what goes around comes around. The undermining of educational standards and the intellectual laxness that spread on campus infected everything it touched, including SDS. Victories against the university, if not against the Johnson administration, also encouraged a kind of headiness, and the drugs and the countercultural romanticism and the headiness all fed on one another until, by the end of 1967, there were not many sober souls left in SDS. This combination of New Left politics and countercultural styles, incubated in the university, was about to explode onto the country and the antiwar movement in the March on the Pentagon. But we are getting ahead of ourselves; we must first meet Sidney Peck.

## SIDNEY PECK PICKS UP THE PIECES

The surge of radicalism that overtook the antiwar movement after 1965 was not the doing of sublime leadership in the adversary culture, and before 1967 it certainly had nothing much to do with students or the New Left; indeed, what is striking in retrospect is how little real sustained coordination and control came from the Left. Liberals were far better organized than Leftists, and far better fixed financially to advocate their more moderate views. Still they failed, largely because the trajectory of an idea, once set in motion, is not easily reversed. There is a logic to ideological escalation wherein perceived failure leads not to the abandonment of a course of action but to further commitment to it.[36] That is how the left-wing parts of the antiwar movement outflanked the liberals—indeed, it converted droves of them into Leftists—despite mediocre organization and minimal planning. Liberals and liberal organizations were frustrated that their moderate tonalities, addressed to people in the administration who dressed, spoke, and acted like they did, had gotten them nowhere, and they fell one after the other into the radical camp. For a time, what little organization there was on the Left to cope with this surge of new support was provided mainly by one man—Sidney Peck.

Within the radical core of the antiwar movement, both fatigue and querulousness overtook it precisely at the moment of its greatest opportunity to politicize "the masses." The Second International Days of Protest had been a success despite the subsequent crumbling of the NCCEWV; but the antiwar movement had developed a life of its own even without a working umbrella organization. Much had changed: The Congress was aroused, the press was sizzling with trouble for the administration, and the movement seemed to be able to raise protests and demonstrations more or less at will. The radical core had overwhelmed the liberal protest, which was now split and on the defensive. It could do all these things, but it could not organize itself or, more important, stop or even slow down the war.

Although the NCCEWV fractured after the March events, the constituent groups remained. As before, too, there was still an "objective" reason for continued cooperation. A. J. Muste set out to build a new organization. Sensing that the only way to give a new coalition the coherence that the NCCEWV lacked, Muste turned to the stalwarts of the old Left. First he sought out Sidney Lens, an old Left Marxist of the Trotskyite persuasion whom Muste knew from his labor organizing days in the 1930s. Lens had founded the Chicago Peace Council in 1965 as an auxiliary of the World Peace Council, which was a product of the Soviet government's agitprop efforts. Lens demurred, so Muste turned to another Peace Council founder, this time in Cleveland, a certain Sidney Peck, who taught sociology at Case Western Reserve University. Muste wanted Peck to assume the nuts-and-bolts job of coordinating what radical organizations were doing, to provide a sort of clearinghouse for tactics. Peck agreed.

Peck had gotten involved in the antiwar cause through the teach-in movement, but he was no newcomer to radical politics. Some years earlier he had played the somewhat odd role of a Communist conservative in the early New Left. From the beginning, it seems, he viewed New Left deviationism as, in Lenin's words, "an infantile disorder." In the first issue of *Studies on the Left,* then published in Madison, Wisconsin, where Peck received his Ph.D. in 1959 at the age of 33, Peck reviewed C. Wright Mills's famous *The Sociological Imagination.* He liked the book well enough but he took Mills to task for questioning the continued applicability of classical Marxian analysis. This was brave because Mills was already a hero unparalleled among Leftists in general. When Mills died in 1962 at the age of 45, he was richly eulogized in the pages of *Studies on the Left,* and his death, without question, enhanced his general influence.

Another example of Peck's more "conservative" old Left inclinations can be found in volume 2, number 1 (1960) of the same journal, where he published an article, based on his dissertation, entitled "The Political Consciousness of Rank and File Labor Leaders." Peck argued that U.S. laborers *had* to have a class consciousness; if they did not, then Marx would have been wrong about substructure and superstructure. In those early days of *Studies on the Left,* most of those who wrote articles were either on the editorial board or were invited to be on it. Not Peck, and as the journal moved more toward what Mills had dubbed the New Left in its pages, Peck's name dropped from the journal altogether.

In the 1960s too—long after the Nazi-Soviet Non-Aggression Pact, the McCarthy period, and Nikita Khrushchev's famous "secret" anti-Stalin speech of 1956 had depleted the ranks of the U.S. Communist Party to near zero—Peck was a party member in Wisconsin, where he had for a time held a teaching job at the University of Wisconsin. Reportedly, Peck did not leave the party but was expelled. In 1966 he was probably not a formal party member or associate, but he was and considered himself to be an "independent" Marxist-Leninist of orthodox hue. It is also clear that Peck's views led him to enthusiastically favor a North Vietnamese victory and an American defeat in Southeast Asia.

Peck devoted himself to rebuilding the antiwar coalition.[37] As he did so, partly due to his own efforts and partly due to the tilt of the times, the ideological focus of the movement moved toward the older sectarian Left. Basically, Peck's model was Stalinist in the sense that he favored what amounted to "democratic centralism" in the core leadership, sought "openings to the right" without compromising the leadership, and argued vehemently against New Left-style "gimmicks or theatrics."[38]

Three meetings were held in Cleveland, in May, October, and November of 1966, all aiming toward major demonstrations in New York and San Francisco in April of the next year. SDS and SANE both refused to have anything to do with the meetings, the latter because of the obvious Communist Party participation in them. The SWP attended these meetings, the CP was there, the Youth Against War and Fascism was represented, and a coterie of obscure black nationalist/Marxist groups were there as well. As for SDS, it resented the old Left "borers," as they called them in double entendre parlance; but, in addition, it was still undecided about the centrality of the war in its program for the revolutionary remaking of America. Applying its anti-elitist ethos and "participatory democracy" credo to itself, SDS could not decide about anything.

As Peck's planning proceeded, it was decided to name the group the Spring Mobilization Committee to End the War in Vietnam (SMCEWV). For purposes of general consumption, Muste became chairman. The four vice-chairmen were Peck, Robert Greenblatt of Cornell University, Edward Keating of *Ramparts,* and David Dellinger. A more radical antiwar movement core quartet had never before been assembled. But the stroke of genius at the November meeting was the eventually successful decision to woo Dr. Benjamin Spock away from SANE and into the radical nest.

Before long, the SMCEWV had at its side a student replica called the Student Mobilization Committee to End the War in Vietnam. It was founded in December of 1966 at the University of Chicago. The moving spirit was Bettina Aptheker who, like her father Herbert, was a Communist Party member.[39] Just as Muste and Peck sought through the senior circuit to leverage SANE and the liberal protest toward the Left, so through the junior circuit did a younger generation of radicals trained in vanguard party methods seek to outflank a still "anti-elitist," and hence disorganized and thoroughly outmatched, SDS on campus.

Thanks to Peck, the early months of 1967 marked a high watermark of old Left influence in the antiwar movement. It was not absolute influence, control, or anything close to it, but neither was it negligible. Marxist influence was not apparent to most at the time in part because it was deliberately concealed in order to maximize the size and power of the evolving public protest. As Fred Halstead of the Trotskyite SWP later wrote, slogans such as "Victory to the Vietnamese Revolution" were inopportune from the point of view of mobilizing the mass of Americans; the "central task . . . was to put maximum pressure on the U.S. to get out of Vietnam. That would help the Vietnamese revolution more than anything else we could possibly do."[40] The aim of the core leadership of the SMCEWV was clear: to assemble the broadest possible support for a rally dedicated sotto voce to the most radical of causes, namely, the complete withdrawal of U.S. forces from Southeast Asia, which would clearly mean the victory of the Vietnamese Communists against the United States. This would, it was hoped, accelerate the revolutionary process in the United States itself.

Yet even within the newly radicalized core of the antiwar movement there was little harmony over aims and tactics. Peck's organizing committee considered itself a vanguard for the purposes of the April rally, but, within that core, groups such as the SWP considered themselves the vanguard within the vanguard. The closer to the old Left a SMCEWV representative was, the more he was inclined to put longer term and organizationally parochial interests ahead of the issue at hand. Halstead, for example, worked for the ultimate revolution on one extreme and for the institutional strength of the Socialist Workers Party on the other. Lost in this set of priorities was stopping the war. For the less self-consciously vanguardish groups such as the AFSC, SCLC, and Clergy and Laity Concerned, the antiwar issue took precedence over parochial organizational interests. It was not that these latter groups were unaware that others were trying to use them to varying degrees— usually they were very much aware of it. But most concluded that the dangers of being used successfully were small and were less than the damage that would be done by fractionalizing the antiwar movement.

Muste and Peck determined that two human symbols were critical for achieving the diverse aims of the SMCEWV constituent groups involved in planning the April rally. One was Spock and the other was Martin Luther King, Jr. Spock came of his own accord, a great windfall for the Left. King's participation took some doing.

The WRL's David Dellinger was the architect of King's association with the April rally. He arranged it by persuading the Reverend James Bevel of the Southern Christian Leadership Conference to assume major responsibilities for coordinating the rally's nuts and bolts. Still, Dr. King was reluctant to come. He had been stung by the press earlier in 1967 for speaking out against the war, and some of his liberal white sponsors threatened to abandon him financially at just the time when Stokely Carmichael and SNCC were becoming a serious threat to his leadership. As King wavered in the days before the rally, Dellinger appealed to King through his assistant, Andrew Young, telling Young that blacks were going to come anyway, King or no King, and did he want the crowd to hear only Carmichael? Young was persuaded and brought the argument to King, who thought it over and agreed to address the rally under the condition that Carmichael not be allowed to speak, a promise made and subsequently broken.[41]

The April rally brought about a general escalation of rhetoric, "trashings," and evidence of the new presence of Black Power radicals in the movement. Seeing King and Carmichael on the same dais, with King appearing on the defensive, reduced the reservoir of sympathy for black grievances among many white Americans. Polarization was what the radical Left ultimately sought, and that is what it was starting to get, certainly in regard to race relations. Television showed it to the whole country—now in living color as well as black and white.

## AND NOW, BACK TO THE WAR

By the early spring of 1967, added to the persistence of a sense of policy drift were damaging questions about the credibility of the Johnson administration's reporting of the war. The administration had deceived itself for so long that it now could not help but deceive the American people as well. In July, the Joint Economic Committee determined that the war, in 1967, would cost between $4 and $6 billion more than the $20.3 billion the administration had requested—this, it will be recalled, just a few years after Robert McNamara had told the Congress that the U.S. could afford to fight a limited war in Vietnam "forever." On August 3, 1967, President Johnson asked for a 10 percent tax surcharge to pay for the war. If it was true, as Secretary McNamara had said repeatedly, that the war was not a serious financial strain, then why the surcharge? That is what the network commentators began to ask, in prime time, when the war first hit the pocketbook of the American taxpayer. Now this was news.

Clearly, one reason for the alienation of American opinion, in the broadest sense of the term, was television. It has been said many times, but it is worth saying again: Vietnam was the first television war. What that means is not so clear, however. Some on the Right have long argued that the press was against the war, and they deliberately tried to turn the majority of patriotic Americans against it too.[42] In fact, the press was, on the whole, pro-administration until 1968, and press coverage probably lagged behind the American people's own suspicions of incompetence and incipient failure during most of the Johnson administration. What the press did from 1964 through 1968 at the least was simply to report what it learned, just as it showed the antiwar movement as it was, with the somewhat surprising impact noted earlier. That, however, was more than enough for the American people to sense that something wrong was going on. The press did not set out to be adversarial; but it became so simply from trying to tell the truth.

In this simple portrayal of the press's role during the war, one of the most stunning effects of television news comes clear: Television viewing is, as the scholar Richard Wightman Fox put it, "one of our culture's key methods of creating folk traditions." It is "an indispensable means of feeling solidarity with masses of our fellows, especially in moments of crisis or terror."[43] Certainly a war qualifies as a crisis, and it was not the blood and gore being shown that mattered most for, in fact, before the Tet offensive, rather little of it was shown. Tet was the occasion for the first live television coverage of the war because a satellite had been lofted above the Pacific Ocean just weeks earlier. Before Tet, film footage of the war was edited and in the editing process most sharp images of injury and death were expunged.[44]

No, to focus on the blood and gore is to miss the point. Rather, as a ritual vehicle of the secular American religion, television was the medium through which Americans were knit together as a community of faith and hope by common concern over the war. Walter Cronkite and his colleagues Howard K. Smith and Eric Severeid were the officiating priests, and the body count displayed on the wall behind the news anchor, there every day and every week for years, was the stark and riveting altar of collective sacrifice. In a time of trouble for any community, it is natural—or at least historically consistent—for its members to seek means of collective expression. Television news took on that role as tens of millions of Americans watched the same images, saw the same numbers, and confided in the same faces.

Radicals whooping it up in the streets could not hope to match the power of the nightly ritual. Indeed, the whooping was televised too. To carry the religious metaphor one step further, antiwar antics appeared to many viewers as impiety, even heresy, before the solemn ceremony of joint concern. Even the postal service reinforced the message. The most common definitive stamp of the day was a somber gray, five-cent George Washington, looking upward with less martial strength and more soft reverence than in other portraits. It was also common in the days after 1965 for stamps to be cancelled with the message "Pray for Peace." Antiwar demonstrators, especially ones who waved Vietcong flags, struck the typical participant in this extended service of the American civil religion as downright satanic.

The credibility gap and the financial gap together, and television's creating socially powerful collective knowledge of them, led in time to a sharp erosion of support for the administration's policies in the Senate. Senators watch television too. This erosion of support resulted from and fed a broadening of unease about the war, if not outright antiwar sentiment, in the country at large. It may be distressing to acknowledge the social power of television even to the point of shaping the views of the national leadership, but it is true just the same. A constant topic of conversation in the Senate dining room in those days was how the national news anchors were presenting the Vietnam story.[45] Elected officials paid close attention to how the news was told and to how it was received, not just to detect bias, but to learn a certain form of truth as it was being produced.

## SANE UNHINGED AND VIETNAM SUMMER

The passage of time without progress toward negotiations further strengthened both the national organization and the radicalization of the antiwar movement. It resulted in a closer ad hoc coordination among radical groups, and more important, it stoked increasing disaffection among members of Left-Liberal antiwar groups like SANE and drove them to the Left. The net result was to contribute to the influence of Marxist and new pacifist radicals within the movement as a whole.

As suggested earlier, this was not really a case of radical penetration of middle-class, mild-mannered organizations as such. Rather, frustrated by their impotence to affect U.S. policy, many members of liberal, mainly middle-class groups ceased acting like mild-mannered liberals. Internal ideological escalation was fueled by the programmatic failure of more moderate aims and tactics, and, in effect, the movement as a whole was brought closer ideologically to radical positions. The former Left-Liberal center of the antiwar movement was not pene-trated so much as self-propelled to the Left with the help of the Johnson adminis-tration. When it arrived, radical pacifists and Marxists young and old, arrayed in Sidney Peck's new antiwar coalition, were ready and waiting for them.

This process was vividly illustrated in the internal disputes that wracked SANE's leadership throughout 1967. In the winter, the heir to the NCCEWV was busy organizing its Spring Mobilization to End the War campaign to be held April 15. Based on past successes with the International Days of Protest, and coordinated again by Norma Becker, the SMCEWV aimed at both the further development of a radical antiwar coalition and, through its nonexclusionary bait, the co-optation and overwhelming of what remained of liberal protest. It worked.

Instrumental in this success was the fact that both Martin Luther King, Jr., and Dr. Spock agreed to serve as chairmen. Stunned by SNCC's sudden success and notoriety, King agreed to join the SMCEWV project in order to weaken Carmichael, but his decision had the unintended effect of legitimizing Carmichael and his Black Power demagoguery among young blacks nationwide. SANE suffered a similar fate thanks to Dr. Spock.

Spock's joining the SMCEWV had the effect of importing the movement's deepest fissure into SANE's own leadership struggles. Norman Thomas and Norman Cousins, the elder statesmen of the organization, were very upset at Spock. Acting for SANE, they refused to endorse the April 15 march. Several important local chapter leaders were enraged at this, however, and supported Spock. After the April 15 march, the divisions within SANE worsened. Although as an organization SANE stuck to its moderate course, sponsoring the "Negotiations Now" campaign in 1967, it had been weakened internally and was losing adherents— including Spock—money, and national media attention to the radical Left.

Evidence of the SMCEWV's organizing power was manifested in the April 15, 1967, demonstrations in New York City, which drew over 100,000 people. This simply would have been impossible to pull off a year earlier. Although not everyone was happy with what happened at the rally—some objected to some of the speakers (such as Carmichael) and some of the slogans (such as Carmichael's "No Vietnamese ever called me nigger")—none of the organizing groups felt it could afford to let go of what it had helped set in motion, whether for moral, practical, or tactical reasons. The success of the April rally also had the effect of subsequently enlarging the list of associated organizations, including many groups identified with the right wing of the movement, which now found they had nowhere else to go.

These developments whetted the appetite of the core of Leftists and pacifists who now dominated the group and raised the stakes for the soft utopians as well, some of whom now came to realize, at least privately, that they were easily replaced and hence expendable. This provided additional incentive for some liberal activists to become more radical, quite aside from what was happening in Southeast Asia; one either went with the general flow of the loosely connected leadership, or one washed up on shore. The radicals' growing command over the movement was demonstrated in May when 700 activists met to plan another mass rally for late October. Sponsored by the newly named National Mobilization to End the War in Vietnam (heir to the Spring Mobilization), it was to be called the "March on the Pentagon to Confront the Warmakers." The choice of name and the choice of site gave clear indications of the basic direction within the antiwar movement.

Another sign of the shift in the center of gravity was Vietnam Summer 1967. Vietnam Summer started as a liberal project modeled on the successful Freedom

Summer of 1964. Although assembled by liberals (notably Chester Hartman of Harvard), pacifists, and "straight," middle-class, faculty radicals, the activity was open to all. Some 20,000 people participated in its various workshops and activities. Before long, power was flowing from the bottom up; the New Left had joined and then stolen the activity for itself.[46] Perhaps more important, SDS stole Vietnam Summer's image. SDS President Greg Calvert took the opportunity to praise Che Guevara and Fidel Castro and to say at a Vietnam Summer event: "We are working to build a guerrilla force in an urban environment. We are actively organizing sedition."[47] Even though SDS had not organized the Vietnam Summer, the dominant participation of youth, combined with SDS's provocative interpretation of what its membership was doing, doomed the project's liberal aims. For about two years after the summer of 1967, there was not much point in the right wing of the peace movement trying to compete with the Left, especially the New Left, in forms of mass organizing and mass protest. For the most part they left off trying.

The escalation of the movement's demands matched the evolving consolidation of radical dominance within the core leadership. Neither development led to the other in any simple fashion—it was truly a dance of the dialectic. This is not to say, again, that what was happening in Southeast Asia was not the key factor in the general expansion of antiwar feeling—it was. But an inner dynamic was also partly responsible for movement's sharp drift to the Left and its increasingly strident public demands for complete U.S. withdrawal from Southeast Asia.

## THE LITERARY LEFT AND THE MOVEMENT

To the Left's rising chorus was added, slowly but surely, a segment of the New York literati. The year 1967 witnessed the growing merger of antiwar activism with other streams of social criticism from many sources, including the literary Left.[48] This merger broadened the antiwar movement's agenda and in turn helped radicalize or reradicalize social criticism itself. The literary Left gave student radicals, in particular, the confidence that what they were doing dwelt at a high level of political sophistication. The sudden and rapt attention paid to their writings, in turn, helped the literati feel as if they, too, were living life on a heroic scale, as if they mattered. Indeed, the alienation of many intellectuals from fundamental American institutions—of which sociologist David Riesman's widely read *The Lonely Crowd*[49] was as much a personal projection as a picture—was the stored powder that further fueled the antiwar explosion in its most radical phase.

The role of the American intelligentsia in the antiwar movement is a peculiar story. The fact that we have so far not needed to mention it indicates its very modest relevance. The real significance of the collision between the radical Left and the literati during the Vietnam War was that, while the war and the antiwar movement eventually ended, the reradicalization of the literati has not. It migrated instead to other subjects—human rights, El Salvador, race relations, South Africa, the Palestinians, the Kurds, and so forth—and it still migrates today.

Moreover, what was written at the time remains an important legacy; today's graduate students cannot "read" an antiwar demonstration or an SDS meeting, but they can read Mary McCarthy's old articles in the *New York Review of Books*. The literary Left did not start the antiwar movement or even play a major role in it. Nevertheless, as the movement's booster, chronicler, and interpreter, the literary Left assumed a significance that transcended its initial minor role.

In the 1960s, the intellectuals of the literary Left fell into two echelons corresponding roughly to generational experience and status within the intellectual world. The somewhat older generation, whose luminaries included I. F. Stone, Irving Howe, Mary McCarthy, Dwight Macdonald, Paul Goodman, Norman Thomas, Norman Mailer, and Herbert Marcuse, among others, had cut their teeth on the Marxist radicalism of the 1920s and 1930s. Even those who had themselves never been Marxists could nevertheless not escape the political culture of their intellectual crowd, which was shaped by those conflicts and idioms of thought.

But over the years, with the "good war" and the age of affluence, many radical intellectuals from the 1920s and 1930s had turned away from explicitly political concerns and busied themselves with the peculiar, insular life of the New York literary establishment. Particularly in the Eisenhower period, the Leftist intelligentsia that had displayed so much energy in the interwar years seemed tamed and largely uninterested in the political landscape. Dwight Macdonald, the literary critic and writer who died in 1982, is perhaps the best example; from having been an argumentative and schism-causing radical in the 1930s and the 1940s, he settled down in the 1950s and 1960s to write rather placidly—for him—for *The New Yorker* and *Esquire*. Of those who spoke up about politics at all, most had become liberals by default, and their disillusionment with the Communism of their youth had turned many of them into anti-Communists, anti-Stalinists to be sure. Most had come to accept the necessity of containment; some were downright avid about it even if they felt uncomfortable with the Cold War rhetoric of John Foster Dulles and slightly squeamish about the political company that they were keeping.

There were exceptions, of course. In 1957, Norman Mailer wrote *The White Negro* in which he justified black violence against whites, including robbery and assault. He believed such violence to be cathartic and liberating, much in the tradition of Georges Sorel. It may well be that were it not for Mailer, James Baldwin's *The Fire Next Time,* which made similar points, either would never have been written or would never have been accepted as it was. Mailer's continued glorification of violence is well known; this, rather than the plight of blacks in the 1950s, could well have been his main interest.

The second echelon of the literati was either somewhat younger or less plugged into the New York literary crowd; it included Arthur Waskow, Marcus Raskin, Noam Chomsky, Andrew Kopkind, Ronald Steel, Theodore Roszak,

Christopher Lasch, and others. Most had not been involved in the arcane Trotskyite-Stalinist controversies of the 1930s; many were instead indebted culturally to the Beat Generation and had been active in the civil rights movement, which most of the older generation had watched from the sidelines.[50] Although many members of the second echelon in the late 1950s and 1960s would have called themselves liberals, they were not as seemingly tired and quiescent as liberals of the older generation. Many had never inured themselves to containment, nor was there engraved upon their political souls the anti-communism of experience of those who had waged the intellectual battles of the interwar era.[51]

The immediate effect of the antiwar movement on the literary Left was the repoliticization, reradicalization, and especially the rejuvenation of the older generation. Many intellectuals who had been radical youths experienced a second youth through their involvement in the antiwar movement. As Lasky put it, somewhat tartly, the New Left and the counterculture were avidly "cheered on by ageing intellectuals and poets longing for lost puberty."[52] Dwight Macdonald provided a vivid example. In 1968 he was invited to Morningside Heights, where Columbia University radicals prepared a hero's welcome for him. There he saw the students waving red flags and heard them intoning nonnegotiable demands at the university administration. Macdonald, who admired the Abraham Lincoln Brigade in the 1936 Civil War, exclaimed: "It's just like Spain."[53] (He had apparently forgotten that lots of people actually got killed in Spain.)

This is not to say that many members of the literary Left were not alienated and hostile to American institutions and society before the antiwar movement, or that seeking the fountain of youth was their only or main motive. To take one vignette, at a 1960 conference on "American Writing Today," a youthful John Cheever said that "life in the United States in 1960 is Hell. . . . [The] only possible position for a writer now is negation." The young Philip Roth too, in his inimicable style, said that America "stupefies, it sickens, it infuriates."[54] However, despite having had such practice, the antiwar movement influenced the literary Left, young and old alike, far more than the literary Left influenced the antiwar movement. The real significance of the literati is that they have provided over time more of the connective tissue through which the beliefs of the adversary culture have been communicated to a widening strata of Americans.

While sociologically interesting, too much ought not be made of the generational division just drawn. Some members of the older group assumed as radical a posture as possible—Mary McCarthy, for example—while some members of the younger echelon remained relatively moderate throughout—Bayard Rustin, Michael Walzer, and Michael Harrington. Moreover, the general trajectory of the antiwar movement as it escalated toward radical rhetorical heights affected intellectuals as a group more uniformly than the diversity of their backgrounds might imply. As Sandy Vogelgesang, a former State Department official turned social analyst has suggested, this trajectory can be aptly described as one that moved from a view of the war as a lapse in judgment, to a view of the war as immoral, and finally to a view of the war as an expression of illegitimate authority.[55]

In looking at the literary Left's record on Vietnam, three things stand out. The first is, again, its decidedly ancillary role in the movement as a whole at the time. The second concerns the romanticism of its politics and the increasingly conformist views of the war held by the literary Left as time passed. The third is the emotional and antipolitical reactions that its political impotence occasioned.

First, while the split in the intelligentsia between Left-Liberal and radical mirrored that of the core political activists and followed the movement's same general escalatory trajectory, the literary Left was always one or two pulses behind the core of the movement. Even at the most radical phase of the movement there were relative moderates and liberals, grouped around *The New Republic, Commentary,* and, to a lesser extent, *Saturday Review.* As with the movement as a whole, there was even an in-between crowd, radical with respect to social vision and political conclusions but milder tactically and anti-Communist exclusionist throughout. Here Irving Howe's journal *Dissent* comes to mind as does *Partisan Review.*[56] As with the movement as a whole too, there were increasingly fewer liberals and tactical moderates as time passed. Self-styled maximalists and radicals grouped around the *New York Review of Books* and *The Nation* as their views became more extreme. Like the radical wing of the antiwar movement, they reserved some of their sharpest barbs for liberals. Said Norman Mailer, for example: "We may be living in the shadow of the biggest hype of them all, our last con game: red-neck dynamics; liberal rhetoric. There is the eradicable suspicion that liberal rhetoric was conceived by Satan to kiss the behind of something unspeakable."[57]

But again, the main point is that one is hard-pressed to find many new or original ideas coming out of the literary Left that had not already been expressed or anticipated by the New Left or the counterculture. The intelligentsia did not lead, it followed; it did not create, it reworded; it did not do, it chronicled. As Mitchell Goodman, a novelist and one of the Boston Five, admitted: "The kids invented the 'Resistance' movement, we came along behind."[58]

Of course, the reference to "kids" was palpably false—Muste (born 1885), Lens (born 1912), Dellinger (born 1915), Peck (born 1926), McReynolds (born 1929), and Lynd (born 1929) were hardly kids. Goodman's off-the-cuff remark demonstrated the literary Left's ignorance of real cause and effect in the antiwar movement, even as it accurately described its own *arriviste* status. As Lasky put it, answering his own question of what came first, the chicken or the egghead, the literati were "camp-followers of the children's crusade."[59] Mary McCarthy and Susan Sontag went to Hanoi, true, but Tom Hayden went first.

This does not mean that the intelligentsia played no role in the antiwar movement even at the time. One can detail at least two functions it did fulfill. For the most part, radical university faculty members had more to do with the 1965 "teach-in" movement than the New York literary set, whose affiliations with universities were usually not central to their professional lives. People such as Kenneth Boulding and Anatol Rapoport (Michigan), Gabriel Kolko (Pennsylvania), Seymour Melman (Columbia), Howard Zinn (Boston University),[60] Sheldon Wolin (Berkeley), Douglas Dowd and George Kahin (Cornell), and the like were behind the teach-ins. But the literary Left applauded the teach-in movement, joined it as it proceeded, and tried to develop an overarching intellectual architecture that tied racial violence and capitalist economics at home to the violence in Southeast Asia and the "Cold War mentality" writ large. Susan Sontag put it best: Vietnam was, she said, "the key to a systematic criticism of America."[61]

The literary Left never did develop a serious systematic critique, but it believed it had done so and this reinforced the confidence that New Left radicals had in their own thinking. Many had been brought to their radicalism by people well over thirty—Herbert Marcuse, I. F. Stone, Paul Goodman, C. Wright Mills, Erich Fromm, among others. Now others well over 30 were reinforcing it. A good example was Robert Jay Lifton, a psychiatrist, who urged students to go on replacing history with experience, to express "their Protean selves," and to revel in uncontrolled spontaneity as the means to create the New History.[62]

Even more important, whereas few students rushed to read the latest copy of the *New York Review of Books,* faculty members often did. Truth be told, the difference between a typical radical faculty member of the 1960s and a member of the literary Left, located mainly in New York City, was one of degree. The latter simply had more influence, success, and stature, which, naturally, those younger or less imposing wished to emulate. So, for radical or alienated faculty members, who were in many ways the center and sine qua non of campus protest, the literary Left functioned as a sort of oracle.[63]

The Left intelligentsia, then, reinforced and gave added confidence to the radical movement. Of less importance, they also denied their support to President Johnson and to the war. The debacle of the 1965 White House Festival of the Arts, where the literary and artistic Left, led by the irascible poet Robert Lowell, first openly protested the war, was the model of the relationship between the administration and the intelligentsia for the duration.[64] All in all, this development led to the increased estrangement of the intelligentsia from the public at large and thus to its even more extreme political marginality.

Second, the antiwar reaction of the literary Left became increasingly self-indulgent, to the point of being essentially antipolitical to a much greater extent than the antiwar movement as a whole. This was not true of everyone, but it was of most. The need to express moral outrage, to be a conscience to the nation, to be literarily evocative and metaphorically extreme—this is what the intelligentsia was best at and what it saw as its natural calling. Yet the sort of combative language and logic it displayed made the literary Left close to programmatically useless. A good deal of its expression, Norman Mailer being the best example, was for purposes of ego gratification and symbolic catharsis—not to change anyone's mind.[65] The literati never answered Staughton Lynd's probing question: "Is what's intended a moral gesture only, or a determined attempt to transform the American power structure?"[66] Certainly, Susan Sontag's remark that "the white race is the cancer of human history," or Mary McCarthy's assertion that to prevent "America from being taken in by itself" she could countenance the "worldwide triumph of Communism," were not calculated to have a politically positive effect on middle America.[67]

In fact, as Lynd implied, having an effect was never the point for most members of the literary Left. Some fantasized about the power of intellectuals as a class à la Italian Marxist Antonio Gramsci, but at the same time they revelled in their own marginality.[68] Most seemed to imagine themselves in a kind of self-imposed metaphysical exile, as if they were like Pablo Picasso and Pablo Casals who stayed away from Spain under General Francisco Franco. They were also a kind of secular priesthood to many. For most self-styled progressives of the day, it was as if God had departed when the streets were paved. Their fuller secular notions of modernity pigeonholed traditional ways—religious or political—as social backwardness encrusted with superstition and a relentless antimodern bias. To them, form was regressive and God was ignorance.

One may speculate that the self-imposed social marginality of the literary Left followed from their parents' actual experience of social marginality in American society. The literary Left was very much disproportionately Jewish and first-generation native born. (Even those who were not Jewish, such as Mary McCarthy, had special reason for marginality—she was orphaned in 1918 at the age of six when both of her parents died of influenza.) Their parents suffered from their own marginality; most had fled from an alien land to a new land that was alien too, albeit in a more benign way. The literary Left of the Vietnam era, it seems, *wanted* to suffer; it wanted a life as gigantically mythapoetically tragic as that of their parents. When reality proved recalcitrant, imagination filled the gaps. The literary Left may have come so alive in the Vietnam War period because of the general surplus of angst in the air. The easier it was to suffer—vicariously if possible—and the more they suffered, the better they felt.

The reradicalization and rejuvenation that the antiwar movement provided the literary Left also helps to explain its general fondness for the counterculture, closely associated as it was with the youth culture, as it grew into prominence. While the old Left hated it, and the New Left divided over it, the literary Left was overwhelmingly enthusiastic about it. The counterculture too was inclined to extremes; it too was emotional; it too was enthralled by magic and fantasy. It was a kind of living social poetry for the intelligentsia to gaze upon, and in so gazing see its ideal self. The counterculture, like the endpoint of the literary Left, ended up as a form of antipolitics. No wonder that the literary Left felt more comfortable inviting people to "piss on the White House lawn" along with Jerry Rubin than it did joining with those interested in day-to-day political work and an analytical critique of American foreign policy.

There were those in the Left who counseled the literary Left away from narcissism and antipolitics. Michael Walzer, for example, pointed out that "no one can be morally justified in acting (however heroically) in ways that defeat his own purposes." Michael Harrington decried the "middle-class tantrums" of both the New Left and the literary Left. The journalist Theodore Draper warned intellectuals in general, and Norman Mailer in particular, that their antics were turning the antiwar movement into "a morally self-satisfied but ultimately impotent cult." It did no good. An answer of sorts came from linguistics professor Noam Chomsky, who argued that having spoken the truth and having exposed the lies, he found that "the truth does no good."[69] In her uniquely pandemonic style, Mary McCarthy added, "If the opposition wants to make itself felt politically, it ought to be acting so as to provoke intolerance."[70]

The degree of conformity of views was also striking. Despite some disagreement about tactics, and some modest differences as to what the war "really" represented and reflected about a sick American society, there was a remarkable consensus within the intelligentsia that was totally hostile to the war. So uniform was the hostility that, since everyone believed more or less the same thing, competition ensued mainly over who could express it most vividly. The nearly automatic response of most intellectuals to each new development in the war should have raised a question about the extent to which the intelligentsia, by its own definition, was properly performing its duty. For if intellectuals react automatically either for or against the establishment or the government, they renounce their critical function. Instead of claiming that President Johnson was wrong because his ideas were bad, the literary Left essentially claimed instead that his ideas were bad because they were his.[71] No real introspection can be discerned in such a posture.

This is ironic because the literary Left, although it essentially spoke to itself and argued with itself with a general disregard for the rest of the country, was acutely self-conscious about its role as an intelligentsia, and a specifically American intelligentsia.[72] Its members saw themselves as the natural and legitimate repository of the moral conscience of the nation, a mid-twentieth-century composite of Thomas Paine, Henry Thoreau,[73] and labor anarchist of legend and song, Joe Hill. When the government and the American people refused to grant the intelligentsia such a mandate, the literary Left turned condescendingly elitist. The anger brought out different reactions in different people, and the range of responses reflected the ambiguous relationship that intellectuals of all sorts, and American intellectuals in particular, have had with the idea of real power and responsibility. Some became very elitist, as is suggested by Mary McCarthy's call to provoke intolerance. When Paul Goodman was criticized for invoking a minority's assumption of the majority's prerogatives, he answered that "some of us think we are living in a pre-revolutionary period if only because the unique problems of modern times are not susceptible to old formulas."[74]

In yet another link to the counterculture and its essentially antipolitical ethos, some members of the literary Left came to hate power itself and to disavow conventional politics altogether. Theodore Roszak, the greatest impresario of the counterculture among the intellectuals, wrote that: "Politics is the organization of power and power is the enemy of life."[75] This too was a kind of elitism, only turned inward. It expressed the view that power always corrupts and that the lot of the intellectual who seeks power is to be corrupted by it. This was an especially influential view in light of the fact that the Camelot of the Kennedy administration had been celebrated in earlier times as a kind of political triumph of the intellectuals; never before had so many been so close to power—although, ironically, it took Richard Nixon's empowerment of Henry Kissinger to boost an intellectual into a position of real authority. The rejection of political responsibility went hand in hand with a rejection of conventional liberalism because, aside from being an intellectual's administration, the Kennedy administration represented the new liberalism as well. Many intellectuals took solace in the view that their genius in sensing the futility of conventional politics was before its time and that they would be vindicated eventually. But, then, anything may happen eventually.

For a few others, political impotence led neither to elitism and antidemocratic delusions nor to countercultural escapism, but to a kind of radical individualism focused on a concern with the loss of their personal American dream. Norman Mailer became self-avowedly patriotic and even religious in the bizarre sense of turning his own idiosyncratic visions into an impossible, but literarily evocative, social scheme. *Armies of the Night,* his personal tale of marching on the Pentagon in October 1967, is a perfect symbol of the fusion of the literary Left and the antiwar movement. It helped Mailer to create an image of himself as both the writer/philosopher and man of action; significantly, the book's subtitle was *History as a Novel, the Novel as History.* No doubt this helped Mailer feel better about himself, and American literature may be the better for it. But the antiwar movement was not.

## THE ANTIWAR MOVEMENT IN BLACK AND WHITE

Radical behavior often has a way of reinforcing radical thinking, as well as the other way around. By the end of 1967, a cycle of ideological-tactical escalation was spinning out in full spiral. Pushing the radicalization process along was the emergence of black separatist radicalism in the person of Malcolm X, who, before his murder in 1965, had referred to Dr. King's "I Have a Dream" speech as "the farce on Washington." Stokely Carmichael and H. Rapp Brown of SNCC, and especially Eldridge Cleaver, Huey Newton, and Bobby Seale, founders of the Black Panther Party, an avowedly Marxist-Leninist organization, gained prominence after Malcolm X's death. This was black activism at its most violent, unrepresentative, and extreme. One SNCC song, "Hell, No! I Ain't Gonna Go!" went like this: "I ain't goin' to Vietnam / I ain't burning my brothers to serve the man / I ain't goin' to Vietnam / The Vietcong's just like I am." The refrain called the U.S. Army the Ku Klux Klan.[76]

Nevertheless, for many white radicals the addition of black nationalists to the antiwar brew added an attractive and, for some, even nostalgic touch of the civil rights past. There were also a few important figures who linked the civil rights movement to the new black nationalism, or at least so it seemed. There were Bayard Rustin and John Lewis. There were the ambiguous figures of Martin Luther King, Jr., Roy Wilkins, and A. Phillip Randolph, associated with the old civil rights movement but invocable for multiple purposes. Also very important was the black wing of the literary movement, especially James Baldwin's writings. His *The Fire Next Time* had a major impact when serialized in *The New Yorker*. So did Cleaver's *Soul on Ice*,[77] and Ralph Ellison's *Invisible Man*.[78] Somehow, and it was not a long distance to travel in those days, Baldwin's "the fire next time" turned into "burn baby burn," the taunt of black radicals as ghettos went up in flames in the mid-1960s. Meanwhile, the literary Left, enthusiastically led by Mailer, followed the transition from Baldwin's nuance to SNCC's rapture with violence without missing a beat.

This was thought natural. In the view of the white part of the movement, black nationalism expressed the civil rights struggle coming of age, having now evolved into its "true revolutionary phase." Repeatedly over the years, white radicals looked to the civil rights movement for models. To give just one example, Staughton Lynd saw draft resistance as the moral equivalent of Mississippi Summer, "something white radicals could do which would have the same spirit, ask as much of us, and challenge the system as fundamentally, as had our work in Mississippi."[79]

With the emergence of the Black Panthers, the linking of the white and black parts of the revolutionary movement became an obsession for many white radicals. But as white radicals sought to embrace the most radical parts of the black movement, they encouraged the black movement's irresponsibility by endowing Carmichael, Brown, Newton, and Seale with an importance and a bargaining power that the young black leaders had probably never dreamed of attaining.[80] The romantic view taken by many young white radicals of the Black Panther Party became an enduring theme in the next few years and ultimately played a role in the self-destruction of SDS.

SDS had developed a cult of the urban guerilla, featuring American blacks as a romantic vanguard. The importation of scenarios from abroad—Cuba, Algeria, and especially North Vietnam—was churned into a view of revolution in America that saw black revolutionaries as agents of polarization that would lead to the revolution. This is what led many white revolutionaries, including Tom Hayden, but especially the Maoist Progressive Labor caucus members, to believe that the summer's urban violence in the ghettos would lead to the revolutionary mobilization of the black masses by physically worsening their situation. Hayden wrote in *Rebellion in Newark*: "Men are now appearing in the ghettoes who might turn the energy of the riot into more organized and continuous revolutionary direction."[81] It was this theory of black revolutionary vanguardism that later led others to attribute to Hayden the phrase: "Get a nigger to pull the trigger."

But clearly, with or without Hayden, the neocolonial analogy, taken largely from Franz Fanón, author of *Wretched of the Earth,* became very popular among black radicals, and remains so today.[82] In this theory, black America was occupied territory, just like South Vietnam. It stood to reason, therefore, as Cleaver put it, that "if white America is the mother country and black America the colony, the white police are occupation troops."[83] Robert Williams epitomized this view even before Malcolm X came along.

Williams helped start the idea of black self-defense as revolutionary action in North Carolina in the period from 1957 to 1959. In the 1960s he became a Maoist, and speaking against Martin Luther King, Jr., and the non-violence of the civil rights movement, Williams argued that violence was cathartic and liberating. He saw himself as a vehicle of black polarization and revolutionism in the North, hoping that once the match was lit, Progressive Labor could control the fire. In the Harlem riots of 1964, Williams, Bill Epton, and other PL activists openly displayed themselves as Communists and tried to take political advantage of the riots as best they could, even though they did not start them. Epton called for the smashing of the state, urging rioters to "kill a lot of these cops, these judges, and we'll have to go up against their army. We'll organize our own militias and army."[84] Williams and Epton also tried to provoke black attacks against Dr. King in the South as well.

The early existence of even a small number of black Communist radicals clearly influenced SNCC and Stokely Carmichael. The radicalization of the SNCC eventually led it to the positions of Williams and Epton, and their positions served as templates and guideposts along the way. Carmichael moved from predicting violence to advocating it in early 1967: "More and more people are now beginning to plan seriously for major urban guerilla war . . . where we can move seriously within this country to bring it to its knees." Carmichael also embraced the polarization theory: "You create disturbances, you keep pushing the system. You keep drawing up contradictions, until they have to hit back; once your enemy hits back, then your revolution starts. If your enemy does not hit back, then you do not have a revolution."[85]

White radicals believed that most white people were afraid of blacks. They saw black urban violence as a path to a revolution they would ultimately control, however. But, of course, very little could outdo black urban violence as a general source of white backlash against radicalism and against the antiwar movement, with which it came to be indelibly associated.

A taste of what was to come took place in September 1967, when the National Conference for a New Politics (NCNP) met in Chicago at Palmer House. The conference took place just a few weeks after an outburst of ghetto riots the likes of which had never before been seen in America. The violence expressed the wishes of many white radicals who wanted to "connect black rage with white radical militancy" in order to create a new radical force in American politics. To some delegates, that meant forming a third party, which was the driving concept behind the original notion of the NCNP the previous year, and which had first arisen in the context of the NCCEWV. Such attitudes initially led SDS to boycott the NCNP, charging that its desire to work within the system evidenced a "Left-Liberal delusion." But things had changed by 1967. SDS was not there as a member organization but many SDS members did attend. Although organized by professional Left activists, most of the 2,000 delegates were under 30 years of age.

The blacks, sensing the deference of the audience, took advantage of an unexpected opportunity. During Martin Luther King's keynote address to the conference, black militants drowned him out by chanting "Kill whitey, kill whitey."[86] The black caucus, having terrified the gathering with loud voices and displays of weaponry, presented a list of 13 demands. Included among them was a demand for 50 percent black representation on all committees, even though less than one fifth of the delegates were black. To this the blacks added a demand for the condemnation of the "imperialistic, Zionist war in the Middle East," and another for efforts to be taken in white communities to humanize their "savage and beastlike" character. Some white delegates objected to these demands but then, as one conference organizer put it, "the walls of Palmer House began to drip with guilt." The 13 points carried by a margin of three to one.

Even this did not satisfy many black delegates, some of whom were on an enormous power trip. James Forman of SNCC took the stage surrounded by colorfully dressed bodyguards. He commenced to insult all the whites in the room. This was generous of Forman in that context; H. Rapp Brown refused even to address an integrated audience. Forman then demanded that the blacks be given 50 percent of the conference vote as a whole. This was quickly granted. While many of the white delegates slipped quietly and carefully out of the room, others remained and, according to participant Walter Goodman, "they fairly tingled with pleasure under the lash of [Forman's] demagogy."[87] One white delegate said: "We are just a little tail on the end of a very powerful black panther, and I want to be on that tail—if they'll let me."[88] SDS radicals would later refer to such phenomena as "shedding one's white skin privilege."

As the original organizers of the NCNP looked on in shock and disgust, white delegates ended up accepting black demands insisting that "liberation" could come only through violence, and actually endorsed specific preprogrammed violence. The reason was summed up by Columbia University radical leader Mark Rudd: "Confrontation politics puts the enemy up against the wall and forces him to define himself" as the fascist he is.[89] The Chicago meeting led to "Stop the Draft Week" in early October, which was meant to precede the March on the Pentagon.[90] This coordination was not difficult to accomplish for many participants in the NCNP conference also were involved in Peck's National Mobilization campaign.

The disaster at Palmer House, as the conference was familiarly called, in turn spilled over and soon affected the cohesiveness of the Spring Mobilization, whose inner divisions were only slightly less daunting. Those divisions in turn were exacerbated by SDS's renewed interest in the antiwar movement after nearly two years of intellectual wandering and organizational foundering, and, with SDS's return, the antiwar movement was truly launched to its highest trajectory. But before charting this trajectory, let us examine more closely what made SDSers and other young radicals tick.

# Sources of Sixties Radicalism

*Everything starts in mysticism
and ends in politics.*
—Charles Péguy

Sixties youth radicalism is inexplicable without understanding the proto-religious, festive, anti-ascetic, anti-intellectual character of the "mature" New Left and the times it influenced. Even in the calmer present, the aging Vietnam generation lives life under the influence of its remembered youth. What motivated this generation then—threats to its authenticity, the need for personal autonomy, a desire to fill life's expectations with results and to do the right thing—still motivates it today, decades after Vietnam. Before the radicalism of the antiwar movement can make much sense at a remove of more than a quarter century, some discussion of its nature and inner logic is necessary. That is the purpose of this chapter.

If anything is clear from looking back on the 1960s and the antiwar movement, it is that the Vietnam War catalyzed and accelerated, but did not create, powerful collective feelings in the Vietnam generation. The expression of these feelings tended sometimes to the irrational, but, underneath, young people were striving to gather together and examine what was bothering so many of them, and perhaps to do something about it. Much of 1960s radicalism reflected a deep discontinuity in normal socialization patterns in the postwar period and led to a search for inner anchors of authority. As SDSer Robb Burlage said at the time, probably without recognizing the significance of his own remark: "We are spiritually unemployed."[1] Finding employment of this special sort was what the New Left was really all about.

## NEW LEFT/OLD LEFT

The New Left radicalism that had emerged on campuses was of an entirely new sort.[2] Its links to the youth culture, its openness, ideological eclecticism, emotional volatility, and thoroughly homegrown qualities confounded most, charmed some, irritated many. Many conservative anti-Communists who supported American policy in Vietnam simply assumed that the New Left was a Communist front influenced, if not controlled, from abroad. Had this been so, the New Left would have been a much less serious and interesting phenomenon. Clearly, there were some connections between old and new versions of the Left, especially through the vehicle of red diaper babies,[3] but the differences were more significant. No one understood this better than the denizens of the old Left.

By 1967 the New Left had stolen the show, at least as far as the antiwar movement's basic image in the country was concerned.[4] This did not cheer the veterans of the old Left with whom younger New Left firebrands had great arguments. The differences between the old and New Left, with Communists and their fronts at the core of the former and SDS sometimes more and sometimes less firmly at the core of the latter, were many. The most important differences had less to do with the content of the two groups' respective ideologies, though many disagreements existed on that score too, than with style and attitude. Six major differences may be noted.[5]

First, the old Left was intellectually serious. Its ideas may have been wrong but they were at least complex ones that had emerged from a century and a half of European intellectual thought. Its members read political literature, not posters and underground comics; they wrote essays and books, not slogans and graffiti. They were emotionally committed but also disciplined; most knew a tautology when they saw one. Despite the inherent simplifications of Marxism, which have contributed much to its appeal, old Leftists were interested in problems, complexities, contradictions, and texts.

Most members of the New Left developed a peculiar form of instant ideological wisdom instead. They spoke in short paragraphs speckled with invented vocabulary. Indeed, one thing that is striking about the 1960s is the degeneration of expression, in the sense of the loss of interest in making analytical distinctions.[6] With considerable help from the drug culture, noted Paul Berman, New Left theories turned into "put-ons or jokes, or fictions that claimed to be non-fictions. They elevated puns into a literary genre. Even to understand certain of these theories, you had to be a little out of your mind."[7] But that was just the point: To be out of your mind was to be in it. The psychiatrist of the counterculture, R. D. Laing, even suggested in his popular book *The Politics of Experience* that schizophrenia was a normal, logical, and healthy reaction to living in a sick society.[8]

The New Left's views were also emotional and mostly undisciplined. The movement took on an anti-intellectual tone, with enraged antipatriotism the order of the day. Radical activist David Cooper provided an example in July 1967: "A year or two ago I witnessed a happening in which an obsessively arranged pile of books was burnt—it was, I think, a German philosophical dictionary in twenty volumes. This was a perfectly reasonable protest against institutionalized pseudo-scholarship."[9] Raymond Mungo put it more colorfully: "From Vietnam I learned to despise my countrymen, my government, and the entire English speaking world, with its history of genocide and international conquest. I was a normal kid."[10]

If what was said felt right, that was more important than whether it made sense. Texts did not matter as much as touch; like Susan Sontag, the New Left was "against interpretation." It was, in fact, dogmatically anti-dogmatic, a notion captured succinctly by Jerry Rubin when he wrote that "ideology is a brain disease."[11] Novelist Tom Robbins put it this way:

> In terms of hazardous vectors released, the transformation of ideas into dogma rivals the transformation of hydrogen into helium, uranium into lead, or innocence into corruption. And it is nearly as relentless. The problem starts at the secondary level, not with the originator or developer of the idea but with the people who are attracted to it, who adopt it, who cling to it until their last nail breaks, and who invariably lack the overview, flexibility, imagination, and, more importantly, sense of humor, to maintain it in the spirit with which it was hatched. Ideas are made by masters, dogma by disciples, and the Buddha is always killed on the road.[12]

New Left radicals wanted to be masters, not one another's disciples. This trait helps explain the movement's intellectual volatility and its incapacity to organize itself to actually do anything coherently political. This is why one writer could aptly characterize New Left politics as a "banzai charge into nowhere,"[13] and why another could describe the New Left's radically decentralized, very un-Marxist views on economic matters as "like Robinson Crusoe's island writ exceedingly large."[14] One Leftist more inclined to old Left rigor wrote of this tendency: "Marxism was generally used so loosely that its insights were often mechanically linked with those of other epistemologically incompatible theories which, in turn, helped create the theoretical chaos so prevalent among much of the contemporary Left."[15] To which a genuine New Leftist would have rejoined: "Right; so what?"

Thus it was that during its active lifetime an uncontrolled, constantly accelerating ideological escalation, based on feeling rather than thought, took place within the New Left. The more intense the feeling, the more radical was the thought; the more radical the thought, the more heroic the act; the more heroic the act, the more defiant the image; and the more defiant the image, the better. The theories were not theories so much as "illegal thoughts," deliberately subversive provocations heaped one on top of the other.

The second difference between the old Left and the New Left was that old Leftists often ran in families. It was the garment worker on the Lower East Side who bore the radical child. Brothers and sisters went to party meetings together. The social camaraderie of the meeting hall replaced that of the church or synagogue. The labor movement was not a symbol of somebody else's struggle—it was real life. But overwhelmingly in the case of the New Left, the young radical had difficult relations with parents and family.[16] Radicalism marked social discontinuity in the homes from which New Left activists came.[17] This discontinuity sometimes became a dominant reinforcement for radicalism, a student becoming a radical in order to hurt his parents by rejecting all they had tried to teach and give him. The Vietnam generation reacted with fury to the bursting of its middle-class suburban bubble, and many blamed their parents for it. This may also explain why the disproportionately Jewish memberships of radical leftist organizations were often in the forefront of anti-Zionist, anti-Israel, and sometimes even anti-Semitic New Left tendencies. The pains of social discontinuity were frequently a more important underlying motive for student radicalism than anything going on in Southeast Asia. For most, the war in Vietnam was the occasion for rage, but not the reason for it.

Third, and closely related, was the fact that whereas the old Left actually had included many authentic members of the proletariat, and whereas many of its intellectuals came from proletariat and immigrant backgrounds—people who knew poverty firsthand and needed no help imagining exploitation—the New Left was made up primarily of not just middle-class but disproportionately upper middle-class students.[18] Campuses whose students were of more humble parentage were the least radical; the campuses of the rich were the epicenters of antiwar activism. As has frequently been the case in other circumstances, there was an inverse proportion between the invocation of proletariat internationalism and the proletariat backgrounds of those invoking it.[19]

Fourth, the old Left's original model of emulation was the Soviet Union. After the Nazi-Soviet Non-Aggression Pact of 1939, the romance subsided but it never disappeared. The end of the Stalinist era revived it and the old Left came to believe that Soviet reformers had rescued the revolution for all time. By the mid to late 1960s, the old Left—Trotskyite cultists excluded—had a mixed but generally positive view of Soviet Communism. China also was favored, at least before the Cultural Revolution.

When the New Left began in the early 1960s, it reveled in being an authentic American movement, not an echo of a foreign cabal. Moreover, without an orthodox model it was also without an orthodox doctrine. It took pride in that too. As noted earlier, from Port Huron onward the New Left was always vaguely Marxoid, but owing in part to its initial patriotic desires and the general influence of the new pacifism, it was not officially Marxist-Leninist until 1969—a year after its de facto disintegration.[20] The New Left developed instead its own hybrid model of revolutionary purity. The Soviet Union was a spent force; even Herbert Marcuse, a German Marxist of the Frankfurt school and the New Left's somewhat misappropriated patron saint, had said so. China, especially with the onset of the Cultural Revolution, appealed to many. But it was Third World revolutionism—including most prominently the Vietnamese and Cuban types[21]—that really captured imaginations. Franz Fanón became a best-selling author, as did French Marxist Régis Debray.[22] The "Che syndrome" appeared as an obsession with romantic loner revolutionism.

Not only was the New Left not pro-Soviet, it was on balance antistatist despite its infatuation with Havana and Hanoi. It was veritably obsessed with tearing down what it took to be large, impersonal social structures of all kinds, paralleling Dorothy Day's and Peter Maurin's personalism doctrine of the 1930s. Social leveling was thought synonymous with social justice and required institutional and bureaucratic leveling too. Mario Savio of Free Speech Movement fame put it this way:

> That "respectable" bureaucracy masks the financial plutocrats; that impersonal bureaucracy is the efficient enemy in a "Brave New World." . . . [B]ureaucracies begin as tools, means to legitimate goals, and end up feeding their own existence. The conceptions bureaucrats have is that history has in fact come to an end. No event can occur now that the Second World War is over which can change American society substantially. We proceed by standard procedure. . . . America is becoming ever more the utopia of sterilized, automated contentment. . . . This chrome-plated consumers' paradise would have us grow up to be well-behaved children. But an important minority of men and women coming to the front today have shown that they will die rather than be standardized, replaceable and irrelevant.[23]

A related Rousseauean impulse in the New Left was strong too: belief in the ascendance of the noble savage—in this case, the student revolutionary—the pure and noble intellect unadulterated by the falsities of class thinking and not yet pounded into submission by the bureaucratic mentality. Some even imagined that, since they had earned a special view of exploitation and repression from the perspective of the child of the exploiter and repressor, they therefore had both special insight and a special responsibility to fight against them.

Fifth, the old Left was capable of tactical pragmatism. It could form united fronts and it could compromise. It could be coldly devious and secretive, and it often was both. Communists hid their true affiliations and their real views when they devised front organizations and infiltrated still other organizations in order to become the controlling but more or less invisible Communist faction inside of them. The old Left understood protracted struggle and patience. It is even fair to say that it sometimes recognized that revolutions had costs as well as benefits. Old Leftists were also ascetics in their personal habits, following the recognition that the arduous work ahead demanded personal sacrifice. And they hated jazz.

The contrast with the New Left is almost complete. Tactical pragmatism meant selling out; talk of protracted struggle illustrated a lack of self-confidence; talk of patience was an excuse for timidity. The New Left had no time for deception;

it flew its radical banner openly for all to see. It detested and ridiculed the old Leftists who were regularly to be found skulking around New Left gatherings trying to turn them into an "innocents' club."[24] Revolutions had no costs to the pure of heart; "liberation" was a form of secular messianism, a convulsion of truth and purification. The old Left displayed the tactical conservatism born of the experience of war, poverty, the Great Depression, and disappointment. The New Left displayed the tactical extravagance of utopianism, fantasies of invincibility born of opulence, and the boredoms of material security. This is what led older Leftists to complain that the New Left was not political at all. Said Erich Fromm: The New Left is ultimately not "concerned with politics; for if one is not concerned with steps between the present and the future, one does not deal with politics, radical or otherwise."[25]

As for asceticism, what is one to think of a student revolutionary with the diary of Che Guevara in one hand and *Mr. Natural* comic books and the mescaline-induced sayings of Carlos Castaneda's *Don Juan* in the other, with an admiration for the ultimate ascetic, Lenin, in the heart, and a joint in the mouth? Perhaps some vintage graffiti, circa 1968, says it best: "Never work," "The more I make love the more I want to make revolution," "All power to the imagination," and perhaps most interestingly of all, "Life without dead times!" Emma Goldman's famous remark, "If there's no dancing at the revolution, I don't want to be there," became something of a theme for many, decorating T-shirts, buttons, and Day-Glo wall posters by the score.

The anti-asceticism of the New Left, though present from the beginning in mild form, grew uncontrollably when the New Left and the proto-anarchistic counterculture flowed into each other after 1966. The New Left never had much chance to politicize the American working class using the war as a vanguard issue, as it had hoped, in its campaign for participatory democracy. In fact, New Leftists knew little about real labor or real laborers and they never really tried to organize workers until late in the day. A quote from Tom Hayden (in 1971!) illustrates both points: "My idea was to go to the mainstream, but . . . the Movement had gotten itself isolated at the very moment that large numbers of people were ready to be mobilized."[26]

Yet there was considerable working-class opposition to the war, not least because it was the children of the working class who were represented disproportionately in the U.S. military fighting in Vietnam—this on account of the II-S student deferment. Had the New Left been capable of pragmatism, it might have noticed.[27] Working-class opposition grew steadily as the war became deadlier and more protracted—even some Teamsters Union and United Auto Workers locals were denouncing it by 1970[28]—and student radicals had their best chance of finding common cause with the proletariat. Their chances of recruiting workers grew too, because of the subordination and general fatigue of the old Left in the labor movement. But the irreverent countercultural style adopted by the movement destroyed that chance forever. Working-class men and women hated the movement as much or more than they hated the war; Eric Hoffer, the longshoreman philosopher, stood for "traditional values" and "against absurdist America . . . LSD and happenings."[29] Labor organizer Harry Bridges, who opposed the war, hated both hippies and the New Left with equal fervor.[30] Eugene D. Genovese, a self-described old Leftist, wrote that he could not bear "the drugs, obscenity, contempt for traditional styles of dress and deportment . . . flaunted sexuality [and] self-indulgence marketed as self-expression."[31] The New Left in its latter days, he went on, "apparently without reflection [promoted] an extreme individualism that has been the historic contribution of the bourgeoisie and the target of all serious socialism."[32]

It was not, of course, the first time that middle- and upper-middle-class radicals had attracted a flaky entourage. Long before the New Left existed, George Orwell lamented, in a truly prophetic remark, about "the horrible—the really disquieting—prevalence of cranks wherever Socialists are gathered together. One sometimes gets the impression that the mere words 'Socialism' and 'Communism' draw towards them with magnetic force every fruit-juice drinker, nudist, sandal-wearer, sex-maniac, Quaker, 'Nature Cure' quack, pacifist and feminist in England."[33] The New Left would answer Fromm, Genovese, Orwell and the rest—again to use Tom Robbins as spokesman—only that "dullards can put a pox on the most glorious moral enterprise by using that enterprise as a substitute for spiritual and sexual unfolding. . . . [I]t is dullness and not evil that begets totalitarianism."[34]

This leads to the sixth significant difference between the old and New Left. Old Leftists always spoke, wrote, and thought in terms of "we," in terms of a radical community. The power of this first-person-plural attitude was so strong as to eclipse individual personalities. Indeed, the yearning of some people to melt into the group helps explain the cultist power of old Left sectarian groups. In the end, the New Left tilted toward a similar pattern, but for most of its life, and certainly that part where its most creative energies were set loose upon the country, New Left members spoke not in terms of "we" but of "I." Again, Robbins captures the sense of things: "A romantic . . . recognizes that the movement, the organization, the institution, the revolution, if it comes to that, is merely a backdrop for his or her own personal drama and that to pretend otherwise is to surrender freedom and will to the totalitarian impulse, to replace psychological reality with sociological illusion." But, he continues, "such truth never penetrates the Glo-coat of righteous conviction that surrounds the social idealist when he or she is identifying with the poor or the exploited."[35]

Social analyst Christopher Lasch recognized the first-person character of the New Left early on, observing that the point of having a political position was mainly "to get the self going."[36] Richard Flacks, a founding member of SDS and a red diaper baby, also warned against the excessive emphasis on "personal salvation and gratification," "the effort to reach levels of intimacy and directness with others . . . to be self-expressive, to be free."[37] Novelist Tom Wolfe also took aim at counter-cultural narcissism, coining the term "radical chic."[38]

More than "free," however, the New Left watchword of the day was "authenticity;" authenticity was thought of as a secret lodestone or magical formula that would extract the pure Rosseauean native from the hard patina of the impersonal technetronic age.[39] It is not hard to see where the slang phrase "Get real" came from.

Criticism of New Left essentialism and narcissism did little good. New Left revolutionaries were so firmly products of the middle class and the new suburbs that, while they could change the content of their thought, they could not as easily change its style or social context. The personal directedness of many New Left members was not revolutionary at all; it was just the narcissism that had been programmed into the baby boomers of the flush 1950s, now dressed up as political selflessness and hallowed with the label of participatory democracy. The confusion was wider even than that; it infected the elders too, so that some sociologists such as David Riesman could complain about anomie and alienation and still urge their students to be inner-directed, a formula for nothing more than more anomie and alienation.[40] With such talk in the air from the elders, it is no wonder that Franz Kafka (in translation) became a literary titan of the era.

The search for personal fulfillment obviated any possibility of achieving or even formulating organizational purposes. Everyone's revolution was personal and private; revolution was in the heart and everywhere in the air but there never was a serious revolutionary organization or program. As historian Alan Brinkley concluded, the New Left "ultimately did not betray its commitments to 'participatory democracy' and 'personal authenticity' as succumb to them."[41] And the reason, ironically, that pure democracy could provide the motivating energies that it did is that, since democracy is an ideal that has never been perfected in society, it necessarily retains a revolutionary aspect.

So, the New Left was not like the old Left or the new pacifism. As it developed, it took freely from both, as well as from the liberal academic critique of American society from the 1950s and early 1960s, picking the most evocative slogans it could find and assuming their internal logical agreement. To this intellectual mélange was later added the styles, or antistyles, of the counterculture, and the result was a unique phenomenon. "The SDS vision was neither Marxist nor libertarian," wrote sociologist Michael Kimmel, "neither mainstream liberal nor social democrat; it was irreducibly democratic."[42]

More than that, the New Left represented the collective spasm of a generation thrown naked and unprepared into postwar reality. As such it came to be more than a form of political idealism, with all of idealism's foibles. It became a form of political escapism into an idealized and impossible future. And, as with other kinds of revolutionary escapism, a certain festive—and religious—atmosphere came to be associated with the protests.[43] Sometimes, as French poet Charles Péguy puts it in the epigraph beginning this chapter, things start in mysticism and end in politics. Other times, however, it's the other way around.

With the coming of the carnival came the fuzzing of distinctions between normal social exchange and the up-for-grabs character of life in the throes of revolution. Revolution became a kind of self-conscious theater, although not for the first time. While unique in the particulars of each of its manifestations, the general phenomenon of youth revolution, complete with its religiosity and festival, its sexuality and theater, is well known; indeed, the phrase "the theatre of revolution" is Alexis de Tocqueville's, who was speaking of the failed revolutions of 1848 only a few years after they took place.[44] This is crucial, for it links the antiwar movement's inner energies to something larger and deeper than the distempers of the moment. It links them to religion.

## THE DOGMATISM OF THE NONJUDGMENTAL

The student radicalism of the 1960s, however political it may have looked, bore resemblance to a religious movement. It was therefore about culture in the fundamental, not the superficial, sense because culture—even counterculture—is, after all is said and done, mainly about meaning making. That is also why 1960s radicalism's principal contemporary intellectual heir, eco-anarchism, is infused with a spiritual side that amounts in its extreme forms to worship—in this case worship of nature.

A strong hint of the religious passion of the antiwar movement at its radical height was the unmistakable tendency for arguments and assumptions to become unambiguous and unassailable from within—to become dogma. For example, one of the underlying sources of concern over the war touched on the moral raw nerve of using force against a small, backward country. For the Left, America's very soul was at stake in the perpetuation of such barbarities. Antiwar activists believed that if the U.S. involvement in the war was not ended, crimes of unimaginable proportions would ensue, such as nuclear genocide, for which no atonement would be possible. Radical activists did their utmost to persuade those less committed to this view—perhaps as a way of persuading themselves further—even though it was a wild exaggeration. To discuss the war in anything but morally and politically apocalyptical terms was to be cavalier about the issues. To do so in front of an audience of true believers in the saving power of the revolution to come was to invite accusations of heresy. True believers in the movement raced to closure on analytically open and complicated issues, propelled headlong by their most cherished beliefs. Whether in religion or politics, this is how dogmatic styles of belief always operate.

Many radical antiwar activists seemed to need the belief in the equivalent of a moral apocalypse for reasons of personal commitment; the more portentous and dramatic the stake, the more praiseworthy one's dedication becomes and the more unequivocal one's commitment must be. After all, few activists devote themselves unrestrictedly to an issue with more gray area than black or white, with real complications and genuine open-endedness. Simple Manichean metaphors offering the clarity of moral certainty work much better. An internal escalation of commitment can take place among true believers of all stripes, wherein uncertainties and ambiguities are assuaged only by increased psychological investment. As philosopher Robert Nisbet observed: "Zeal and passion feed on themselves in political-moral causes, as in revolutions."[45]

There is a Janus-like social aspect to such zeal. On the one hand, many of the members of adversary culture groups, then and now, are impelled to be politically organized and active around some unconventional or controversial cause, and demonstrate a need to express moral sentiments together with others through politics.[46] This amounts to a form of secular worship. Social bonds reinforce personal faith and commitment, commitment in turn forges social bonds with new strength. This is a powerful magnet, as are other forms of communal worship.[47] Dissent from the prevailing views that tie together any community of activists is thus not an intellectual problem alone; it entails social and even personal costs. This dissuades many not only from dissenting but from even allowing the intellectual basis of dissent to gather in consciousness.[48] Former activist Jeffrey Herf tellingly described the interpersonal dynamics of SDS's 1969 national convention: "By 1969 the New Left had developed an intense and oppressive sense of community. It is impossible to exaggerate the degree of sheer fear, fear of isolation, of being thought cowardly, of losing one's friends, and not being in on the action when the revolution took place, that I and many other veterans of the new left felt at that convention."[49]

But on the other hand, the psychological attractiveness of nonconformity—the different drummer phenomenon—points to the exaggeration of the individual. This, too, seems an important part of many activists' psychological constitution. Small, tight-knit protest or countercultural groups offer the best of both worlds; one can be a nonconformist relative to the culture at large and at the same time enjoy the psychological safety of a mutually devoted support group. Arthur M. Schlesinger, Jr., speaking of the multiculturalism of the 1990s, wrote: "It is ironic that the celebration of diversity concludes in a demand for conformity."[50] Ironic yes, surprising or unusual, no. The same irony was hard at work in the New Left in the momentous collision between participatory democracy, which celebrated the individual, and the programmatic implications of radical Leftist ideology, which effaced the individual.

The emotional backdrop of the antiwar movement, the personal catharsis it provided its adherents, and the peer support it could generate go far toward explaining why many second-echelon activists, young and old, often seemed impervious to rational arguments about the Vietnam War or other aspects of U.S. foreign policy. It was not only or primarily that many were ignorant of the subject, it is rather that knowledge was subordinated to feelings. When people have a strong need to believe something, mere facts are powerless to stop them. Even the waning of the Vietnam antiwar movement did not put an end to such needs for many; other issues—ecology, antinuclear power and nuclear-freeze movements, antiapartheid causes, Central American sanctuary protests, protests against hunger, among others—managed to take up the slack.

As time passed, some 1960s-era protestors grew out of the desire to be part of an anti-establishment cause; their lives filled with other challenges and activities—though whether such changes happen out of maturity, exhaustion, or cynicism rests in the eye of the beholder. But everyone except perhaps the dullest of dullards needs something beyond the self in which to believe, and for those who did not discover it in family, profession, or the other traditional sources of spiritual stamina, the flow of antiestablishment activism remains today their religion.

The powerful proto-religious aspect of the antiwar movement is also important for another reason: it destroyed the capacity of the true Marxian Left to control the movement or define its spirit. As social historian Eugene Genovese has admitted, the historical failure of the Left was caused by "a deep flaw in our very understanding of human nature—its frailties and possibilities—and by our inability to replace the moral and ethical baseline long provided by the religion we have dismissed with indifference, not to say contempt."[51] The counterculture sensed this, and its antipositivist, antimaterialist, anti-"scientific", anti-ascetic attitudes in the end overwhelmed and silenced the power of the conventional Left. The religious impulse was irrepressible.

## THE LOGIC OF SEX AND REVOLUTION

Speaking of the anti-ascetic, it is striking how many New Left radicals and counterculture figures used sexual metaphors to describe the mutual attraction of politics and revolution. One recalls the famous Joan Baez anti-draft poster from around 1968, which read: "Girls say yes to boys who say no. . . ." Susan Sontag, famous for coining several provocative 1960s phrases, hit the nail on the head by referring to "a promiscuous idea of revolution."[52] Other unpublished (and largely unpublishable) connections between revolution and sex abounded as well.

Moreover, descriptions of antiwar protests at the time and since veritably spill over with sexually suggestive language. "From the numbers," wrote Zaroulis and Sullivan, for example, in a 1984 book that perhaps recalled personal experiences, "flowed an electric current of pleasurable excitement, anticipation, and existentially created fellowship."[53] If one did not know otherwise, would not reference to flowing electric currents of pleasurable excitement, anticipation, and existentially created fellowship suggest sex? This is not accidental; it is part of the broader dynamic that sustained the radical core of the antiwar movement until the end.

But why was this? It isn't easy to say, but some observations may be made.

First, there has always been a relationship between religion and sex. On the one hand, celebratory and plaintive religious rites have long concerned themselves with fertility and procreation, partly because they were seen as the magical domain of the gods. On the other, religion has also engaged itself in the control and limitation of sexual relations to ensure the stability of society itself. Both aspects of the relationship have always had a political dimension as well.

More obviously, sex happens most frequently among young people, and the antiwar movement was overstuffed with young people. Antiwar demonstration and meetings replaced the cotillions and house parties of earlier days; they were the places one met members of the opposite sex, and the commitment to the movement was a great sexual accelerator because most people assumed a natural affinity on the basis of the peace culture.

Besides, the antiwar movement was a great party in many ways; antiwar demonstrations were fun. If one wanted to get stoned on someone else's dope, or end up at day's end having sex with someone who had been a total stranger 24 hours earlier, or hear live music with stirring lyrics, or avoid reading or studying (or teaching), antiwar demonstrations were ideal. All one had to do was sit through the speeches, and they were usually not especially taxing on the intellect.

Many demonstrators were impelled by precisely such motives, but this was not, it must be understood, cynicism or irresponsibility of any simple sort. It was part and parcel of an attitude about the true revolutionary personality in which sexuality played no small role. The revolution to come, of which Vietnam was the vanguard issue, would tear down "false constraints" and "artificial restrictions and inhibitions" of all sorts.[54] Being "free" was being a good revolutionary, as was the essentially religious impulse to do what was right. There was a widespread assumption that establishment society had corrupted sex and made it seem dirty and vulgar, encrusting it with bourgeois legalities such as marriage. Moreover, many young people saw a good deal of hypocrisy about sexual matters all around them. They claimed that they were condemned for their own sexual freedom by parents and elders to whom adultery had become a way of life because they had failed to use their freedoms when they were young.[55] Having sex free of legal attachment and hypocrisy was being a cultural revolutionary—or so many young men liked to think.[56]

The general male attitude toward sex fit in with the individualistic ethos of the counterculture, the "do your own thing" mantra of the day, the "I" focus of the revolution. Again, as with the popularity of drugs, some older SDS ascetics had a hard time understanding "how fucking your brains out would bring the revolution," as one such individual put it to me. But it was an irresistible temptation for most young men, and it is not hard to see why.

Women's attitudes were harder to gauge. The bra burnings of the time may well have been a form of liberation for many, but it also made women more sexually arousing to most men. Perhaps most women knew this. Their male ideal becoming mixed with politics, some women sought out political heroes. Chances are that some men in turn knew and used this knowledge to bed down their woman of choice. Todd Gitlin, quoting Al Haber's wife, Barbara, noted in a remark that suggestively combined politics, sex, and religion that at the top of this heap "there were a few dozen men who stood out as incarnations of the Revolution, so that to sleep with them was the equivalent of taking political communion."[57]

The logic of sex in the New Left and the counterculture, understood in this way, illustrates the strange and scintillating interplay among sex, religion, and the politics of the New Left, the connection, in 1960s vernacular, between the "love-in," the "be-in," and the "sit-in." It also throws light on the inner assumptions that sustained much of the political radicalism and cultural experimentation that went on.

Put a bit differently, it seems that many students and younger activists had inherited an attenuated and narcissistically reinterpreted version of an old civil rights tactic—"creative disorder."[58] Creative disorder involved the deliberate sabotage of the normal so that people could see the attitudes and assumptions underlying the structure of taken-for-granted social behavior. When this behavior involved the systematic racism of segregation, creative disorder no doubt fulfilled a positive purpose. But introduced into an intellectual milieu in which Muste-like definitions of violence and Savio-like definitions of victimization ran without limit, creative disorder was another thing altogether. This is the kind of thinking that brought the hippies—and later the Yippie Party—into public consciousness and into the center of the antiwar movement with the clownish and magical antics of Jerry Rubin and Abbie Hoffman, both of whom not incidentally often used sexual metaphors and highly explicit sexual language in their efforts.

There is also evidence of the connection between sex and radical politics when things broke down at the end of the decade. Many movement activists deeply missed the excitement, the sense of engagement, the communal ties, and the sexual life that typically went with it. Therefore, it is not surprising that a number of former (mainly male) radicals became obsessed with sex after the denouement of the antiwar movement, as though it were a substitute for former political activism. One vivid, if saddening, example concerns Sidney Peck.

While chairman of the sociology department at Clark University during the 1970s, Peck was accused of sexual harassment by a colleague, a charge that was echoed by not one but four other women, mostly graduate students, who had their own complaints against him. Peck claimed that the women had misinterpreted his form of "sensitivity therapy" and he filed suit against them for defamation of character to the tune of $23 million. Students began referring to Peck as "the Pecker" and the whole affair became very embarrassing. Peck even described the faculty member in question—a Leftist refugee from Pinochet's Chile—as a hysterical female, which did not endear him to campus feminists. Even some of his left-of-center colleagues who at first flocked to support him soon urged him to drop his suit.[59]

The larger point here, however, has nothing to do with Sidney Peck or the occasional sexual frustrations and indiscretions of middle age. It is rather that the logic of sex in the revolution during the movement's radical heyday provides a window on the logic of the revolution itself, not as it was understood through books and pamphlets but as it was understood in the hearts and minds of those most committed to it. Young people, if not also others, frequently confuse the relationship between sex and love, which boils down more or less to the difference between an act and an intention. Intention comes first—or certainly it should—and gives meaning to the act. This goes for revolutionary politics too. Before one "makes" a revolution one has to know what for, or the act displaces intention, and as with sex and love, the result is ephemeral gratification for some, heartbreak for others, and little or no lasting positive effect for anyone.

## GENERATIONAL POLITICS AND 1960S RADICALISM

Antiwar radicalism, in short, consisted of a powerful psychological parallax that united politics, sex, and religion, all organized around a general assault on the presumed hypocrisy of existing social mores. But why? Why such a broad attack over a limited war thousands of miles away, and why then? It was not because of the Vietnam War, but something much more fundamental, much deeper. What was it? Conventional political analysis cannot account for the essence of 1960s-style radicalism, which reached its apex in 1968, but a social-psychological perspective on student radicalism can shed some light.

Every generation of youth thinks its own time represents a special moment in history and, in a sense, every generation is correct. No two ages are the same; new times are formed from old times. Yet if every age is special, then no age is special. Certainly, generational conflict is nothing new, or else Malachi would not have spoken 2,500 years ago of generational reconciliation in the context of messianic hope.[60] Nor would Plato and Aristotle have identified generational cleavages as central to the evolution of the political process if this conflict were such a small matter.[61]

It is clear that student protest was not just about Vietnam. Moreover, not all student protest was radical, and not all student radicalism was expressed in overt protest. Standing more than a quarter century away from it, what can we say about the inner origins of 1960s radicalism?

One of the main reasons for the youthful upheavals of the 1960s was the sense of tension between the optimistic moralism of liberal internationalism at home and abroad, epitomized by John F. Kennedy, and the value-shorn managerial technocracy designed, somehow, to bring it all into being.[62] The marriage of moral impulse and pragmatic style was the very signature of postwar liberalism. President Kennedy himself was a historical hinge, separating the old and tired from the new and energetic.

The youth of the period identified closely with this energy and idealism because both the opportunity for idealism was at hand and because their parents usually encouraged it. Movie and television images encouraged it too, from *Mighty Mouse* and *Tom Terrific* cartoons to those most dashing and popular of outlaws, Zorro and Robin Hood. Sam Brown said it well: "A generation came of age at a time of immense prosperity. Demographically we broke the charts. Economically, our feeding, housing, and need to be educated made work for almost everybody in America. . . . We had the luxury to be idealistic. . . . We were encouraged to be idealistic. And so we were . . . young men and women of good intentions who wanted to make America better."[63] Baby boom generation political humorist P. J. O'Rourke made the same point this way:

> When we came of age in the 1960s, we found the world wasn't as perfect as Mr. Greenjeans and Mrs. Cleaver said it would be, and we threw a decade-long tantrum. We screamed at our parents, teachers, police, the president, Congress, and the Pentagon. We threatened to hold our breath (as long as the reefer stayed lit) and not cut our hair until poverty, war and injustice were ended.[64]

The first test at home of the marriage between idealism and the technocratic style was civil rights, and it was here that the tension between moral pretense and the managerial style emerged. As far as youth was concerned, the elders were failing the test. Memory is selective. Today the Kennedy administration is generally viewed as a crusading pioneer in improving race relations. In fact, it was cautious about civil rights and the Justice Department run by Robert F. Kennedy was hardly more than sheepishly incrementalist when it came to implementing old laws and urging new ones against Jim Crow in the South.[65] When Tom Hayden and other SDS members traveled south during the Kennedy administration to help voter registration drives, they were shocked to find the FBI and the Justice Department, in effect, on the wrong side despite the image and rhetoric emanating from Washington. To young SDSers, this was not tactical prudence but cynical hypocrisy.

The New Left was known for its hatred of liberals, as SDS president Carl Oglesby's speech at a 1965 SANE antiwar rally, described earlier, attests. Civil rights was a major reason for this hatred; liberals had been disgustingly slow about caring for equal rights in the post–World War II period as far as young radicals were concerned. Vietnam soon became another reason to despise liberals. The same game-theoretical pragmatism, cost-benefit rationalism, and social engineering mentality that came to dominate the war on poverty also dominated the war in Vietnam.

It was all bound up in a medical or, better, a psychiatric metaphor that came to have a curious power in American popular culture in the 1950s.[66] This metaphor held that society could be construed as a neurotic individual and treated as such. As banker and insightful social analyst Charles Morris has recalled, in 1957 Congress established a Joint Commission on Mental Health to find out how "well or badly adjusted" Americans were, and in 1962 it passed the Mental Health Act mandating the establishment of federal services to solve all problems of maladjustment and unhappiness—marriage counseling, alcohol treatment, programs for unwed mothers, services to reclaim juvenile delinquents.[67] In popular culture and language too, one began to "use psychology" to outwit another person. The juvenile delinquent, by the wisdom of the day, was the victim; his parents were the oppressors, and the nastier the victim the worse the crimes of the oppressors. The therapy: behavior modification.

The application to politics of this medical analogy, particularly with the appearance of psychological and psychiatric metaphors to explain political maladies, was linked to the bias toward positivism and pragmatism that has long been the hallmark of American philosophy from Charles Sanders Peirce, William James and John Dewey to Richard Rorty.[68] Apparently following political sociologist Daniel Bell's famous pronouncements on "the end of ideology," President Kennedy said that the problems of the 1960s were those of managing a modern economy, not problems having to do with ideology.[69] Poverty, delinquency, and crime were social *diseases,* not moral or political problems. They were to be solved by paramedical *technology,* in this case applied social science, not a consort of value and justice. The war on poverty was social engineering designed in essence as one huge behavior modification scheme. These were days when psychologist B. F. Skinner's behaviorism was not only taken seriously but elicited little criticism. So, giving poor people money was not the way to cure poverty; rather government had to skew marginal inputs of education and income, like so much penicillin, and socially healthy and constructive attitudes toward work and community would emerge as outputs.

It was inevitable that these metaphors would eventually influence American conceptions of foreign and military policy. Liberals approached the world and the Cold War with a social worker mentality, imagining that the entire globe was, as conservative critic James Burnham wrote in 1964, "a gigantic slum eagerly awaiting the visit of an international legion of case workers."[70] The strategy used to fight the war in Vietnam—graduated response—was similarly crafted: a cost-benefit, analysis-inspired bargaining, game-theoretical strategy, in which force was employed not to win or to hurt the enemy but to persuade him to do (negotiate) or not do (escalate) certain things. Note, too, the simultaneous American effort to reform Vietnamese politics, society, and economy all in the context of fighting a war. This did indeed look like a foreign policy experiment performed by America-as-social worker. It had effects roughly similar to such experiments at home—failure.

The 1960s critique of American society was, as Morris pointed out, united around a kind of warmed-over French existentialism, defined very loosely as "against rationalism" and a "revolt against pragmatism."[71] Nevertheless, many students sensed that there was something deeply wrong with technical, rationalist approaches to what were at base political and moral problems. Not only problems with the war on poverty and disaster in Vietnam evoked discomfort with the managerial style; there was also something about the passionlessness of the language that gave off a foul odor. As children, members of the 1960s generation were encouraged to be idealistic, and that idealism carried a certain tone: Again we are reminded of Peter Pan, Mighty Mouse, Zorro, and the rest flying easily over the bad guys and carving innocent Zs in Sergeant Garcia's buttocks. But when they tried to do what they were taught, they ran into the gray suits and the gray minds of uniformity and spiritual pallor. The music stopped.

It was no coincidence, therefore, that Randolph Bourne was eventually rediscovered in the 1960s and reissued in paperback for university course use.[72] Bourne, a radical journalist during World War I, noted the centralizing tendencies of the war and identified a new class of experts who were more interested in the technical than the moral or political side of war. Bourne, in a sense, anticipated the *Brave New World* themes that Mills, Stone, Riesman, Fromm, Marcuse, and Goodman as well as Norman O. Brown,[73] Lewis Mumford, Edgar Z. Freidenberg, and others were writing about in the decades before the 1960s, warning of a world in which a managerial class wielded extraordinary power through impersonal technologically driven institutions outside of any philosophical, moral, or ideological discourse.[74] More popular expositions of similar themes included William H. Whyte, Jr.'s *The Organization Man* (1956) and the 1955 novel by Sloan Wilson, *The Man in the Gray Flannel Suit*. The same fears aided the popularity of certain European writers—Albert Camus, Herman Hesse, and the aforementioned Kafka—who had earlier plied similar emotional and literary waters.

Of course, American writers of the 1960s and social critics of the 1950s were not the first to calculate the costs of modernity in this sense. "With the progress of science and technology," wrote German sociologist Max Weber, man "has lost his sense of prophecy and, above all, his sense of the sacred. Reality has become dreary, flat and utilitarian, leaving a great void in the souls of men which they seek to fill by furious activity and through various devices and substitutes."[75] Nor was it the case that no elder during the 1960s saw the philosophical resonances of the counterculture and the antiwar movement as complaints against the conditions of modernity itself in that most pioneeringly modern country, the United States. "There is a growing number among the young of our day," wrote British philosopher Isaiah Berlin in 1972,

> who see their future as a process of being fitted into some scientifically well-constructed program . . . of producing the greatest happiness for the greatest number. . . . This moves them to gloom and fury or despair. They wish to be and do something, and not merely be acted upon, or for, or on behalf of. They demand recognition of their dignity as human beings. They do not wish to be reduced to human material, to be counters in a game played by others, even when it is played, at least in part, for the benefit of these counters themselves. A revolt breaks out on all levels.
>
> The dissident young opt out or attack universities, intellectual activities, organized education, because they identify them with this huge and dehumanizing machinery. Whether they know it or not, what they are appealing to is some species of Natural Law, or Kantian absolutism, which forbids the treatment of human beings as means to ends. . . . It is the very triumph of scientific rationalism everywhere, the great eighteenth century movement for the liberation of men . . . that, by a curious paradox, has imposed a yoke that, in its turn, evoked an all-too-human cry for independence from its rule.[76]

Other observers have linked the American technical class, the supposedly faceless liberals and experts of the technocracy, with John Dewey's and William James's dreams of rational social management in the World War I epoch and especially with Frederick Taylor's influential 1911 book, *Principles of Scientific Management.* They have drawn an intellectual lineage leading from Presidents Wilson to Kennedy, from Dewey and James to John Maynard Keynes and B. F. Skinner, and from Bourne to the New Left and the counterculture.[77]

Of the unprecedented aggrandizement of authority by the U.S. government during World War I, for example, social analyst Henry Fairlie wrote: "There was no conspiracy. There was merely the unchecked sway of a propelling idea."[78] In 1971 Robert Nisbet explicitly linked the lineage of American positivists, Wilsonian idealists, and technocratic war makers of 1916 with those who ran the Vietnam War. Democrats led the country into war, he argued, because the intellectuals who dominate the party's upper echelon were seized by a crisis mentality. "Among modern intellectuals," he wrote, "there is frequently observed a fondness for the uses of power, especially centralized bureaucratic power in service to large scale moral objectives." This is precisely what happened in Vietnam after the Diem coup, argued Nisbet.

> The Washington intellectuals, having in effect destroyed a government many thousands of miles away, were honor-bound, not to say politically delighted,

to govern South Vietnam themselves. Once again political intellectuals were in the delicious position of being able, through centralization of command, through computer-rationalism, through large scale undertaking, with crisis-mentality regnant, to take charge. This was the real, and very nearly irreversible beginning of the American war in Vietnam. . . . Kennedy and his intellectuals, not Johnson and his Texas intimates, are the real architects of Vietnam.[79]

This was the same "unchecked sway" of more or less the same "propelling idea" that Fairlie spoke of in the context of World War I, but back then they had neither the computers nor the hubris to be found in McNamara's Pentagon. The repeated failures of rational social management on a grand scale flowed from a form of hubris uniquely applicable to those Americans, whether in Dewey's age or in McNamara's, who believed that the application of social science-based management styles could revolutionize public policy without worry or major cost.

But just as economic planners can never be as intelligent as the market, so the simultaneous American effort to reform Vietnam administratively, politically, and economically, all while fighting a war, stretched administrative capacity to and beyond the limit. As political scientist Patrick Lloyd Hacker argued: "It was impossible to accomplish the three-fold intervention in the midst of the war; and, in large measure, the war's outcome can be explained in terms of the attempt to do so."[80]

The anti-technetronic critique of American society in the 1950s and 1960s was so pervasive that it was argued from both Left and Right. It was also connected firmly to American philosophical traditions, particularly the egalitarian Jeffersonianism that has remained such a strong impulse in American history that it marginalized intellectuals in the nineteenth century just as it marginalized and delegitimated intellectuals and other "experts" in the 1960s.[81]

Just as important, perhaps, the Leftist expression of this criticism had a new social base in the 1960s: the university. The social criticism of the 1950s, the key to the New Left's early intellectual life, gained enormous power from the rise of the university as an institution in American life. For the first time ever, in the early 1960s there were more university students than farmers in the United States. The emergence of the university as a key social institution, and the fact that radicalism had always lived well within the university, was a demographic contribution of sorts to student radicalism. So was the elitism of intellectuals' social criticism; intellectuals both Left and Right have often been contemptuous of the supposed cultural mediocrity of the bourgeoisie, epitomized by Nietzsche's famous "last man." What is the significance of this intellectual elitism? Just this: Most members of the New Left came from elitist strata of American society to that society's elite universities.[82] So for all the talk about the common man's liberation and equality, the match of elitist intellectual theories to the youth of elite segments of society is much too coincidental to ignore. The New Left was a generational revolt within the establishment, not part of a class war. The radicalism of the 1960s had nothing to do with class except for its belief that there was a class basis to American racism, and here again we see the special importance of blacks and images of black liberation in the antiwar movement.

The generational impulse toward the arational was not entirely unjustified, although its excesses were of course legion. How do you defeat the desiccation of the spirit except by recourse to feelings? Morris saw a cycle at work in which the creative period of pragmatism and empiricism had given way to bursts "of irrationalism and intellectual experimentation," largely because the civil rights movement "had thrown questions of morality and values into sharp relief, questions that the incremental style of the technocrats was particularly ill-equipped to deal with." Morris argued that the

> anti-ideological bias that had been so conducive to technological progress was
> now undercutting the consensus that the technocratic state needed to func-
> tion smoothly. And if the radicals displayed an overweening arrogance, it was
> matched by the hubris of the technocrats. Marcuse's vision of a pervasive and
> totalitarian state . . . was certainly an exaggeration, but it was not altogether
> implausible. B. F. Skinner's psychological writings provided a text, and the
> adventure in Vietnam a living example.[83]

This line of reasoning recalls other interpretations suggesting that the 1960s were a kind of compensation for the suffocating social and political narrowness of the 1950s.[84] Morris Dickstein, for example, argued a *traison de clercs* theory in reverse: namely that 1950s' intellectuals were not doing their job as marginal men, as inherent critics of the status quo, and that this negligence led to excess in the 1960s. Morris took an even broader view of social action and reaction, postulating a dialectic that swings back and forth from epoch to epoch, between a dour Puritan view of man and an optimistic, progressive one, the 1950s in this instance being an example of the former, and the 1960s of the latter.[85]

Maybe; this is, anyway, what many people thought during the 1960s. But there are problems with such macrosocial interpretations. The idea of corrective cycles smacks of homeostatic metaphors that, however appealing, make for weak analysis. What does it really mean to say that the energies of empiricism and pragmatism had run their course? How does this connect us to the hearts and minds of alienated young people in universities in the 1960s?

It doesn't directly, but Morris speculated further, looking at the stratification of value among different groups of Americans in the 1960s:

> There is an odd and inverse symmetry between personal and abstract systems
> of morality. The greater the stress on concrete values of family, hard work,
> sexual morality, and conventional religious ethics, the greater, it seems, the

acceptance of an amoral, *realpolitik* posture in international relations. . . . On
the other hand, the most fervent advocates of morality between nations and
racial groups are often the most ready to derogate long-standing personal
values. When breaking with tradition, perhaps, the tendency is to break with
it across the board.[86]

This makes a certain amount of sense and helps explain why, if the New Left felt
ill at ease with Cold War *realpolitik,* they elected to attack the family, authority
figures, and traditional religion as a consequence. It would have been just as logical
to assert that U.S. foreign policy required correction *according to* essential domestic
political values and not in opposition to them.[87] Instead, the Left operated on a
contamination-by-association rule, concluding that a foreign policy that could
produce such immorality must be based on a domestic system that was itself
immoral. In other words, it broke with the moral system across the board.

Some blame this all-encompassing social attack on the prevalence of Marxist
analysis on the Left, in which notions of a military-industrial complex and corporate
capitalism were at the center of the critique of American society. But it was not so,
at least not for most. The attack against authority was not only broad but far too
intimately familial to be explained by the popularity of Marxism. Its roots go deeper
into the psychological sources of 1960s youth alienation.

## OUTER AUTHORITY, INNER AUTHORITY

Student radicalism of the 1960s was not a monocausal phenomenon; it had both
extrinsic sociopolitical dimensions, of which Vietnam was but one, and intrinsic
psychological dimensions. As the political philosopher Michael Walzer wrote in
1965, bringing us back to the interwoven themes of politics and religion:

> All forms of radical politics make their appearance at moments of rapid and
> decisive change, moments when customary status is in doubt and character
> (or "identity") is itself a problem. . . . There is a point in the modernization
> process when large numbers of men, suddenly masterless, seek a rigid
> self-control; when they discover new purposes, dream of a new order,
> organize their lives for disciplined and methodical activity. These men are
> prospective saints and citizens . . . [88]

Walzer was writing about Puritans, Jacobins, and Bolsheviks. He might just as well
have been writing about those original SDS members who met at Port Huron in
June 1962.

On the extrinsic level, the connection between the civil rights crisis at home
and the foreign policy crisis in Vietnam was a function of experience; it was what
the Vietnam generation saw and felt, and it was wildly at variance with expectations

accumulated during the optimistic and affluent 1950s. Marxist temptations and labels such as racism and imperialism followed on this experience; they did not define or create it. As American society and government absorbed and assimilated these shock waves of dissent, both with respect to civil rights and Vietnam, the experience became less vivid and more ambiguous and the Marxist critique crumbled before contrary experience. More important, the connection between the undermining of extrinsic authority—that of government, organized religion, and the social hierarchy broadly construed—and the undermining of intrinsic authority—that of parents and of conscience itself—had nothing to do with Marxism. So what did it have to do with?

Several observers have tried to correlate personal, psychic, and family disorder or anxiety with a propensity to radicalism and violence among students.[89] Such theses, long popular on the Right, argue that the kids were screwed up and imply that there was nothing necessarily wrong with the country or the Vietnam War. In other words, student radicals became radical because dysfunctional personal and family lives led them to take revenge on society.

The guiding metaphor of this theory is half Freudian and half Skinnerian. It is Freudian in the sense that preconscious—and thus unresearchable—anxieties of, for example, the social marginality of Jews led to displacement—or sublimation perhaps—into politics. It is Skinnerian in the sense that an essentially deterministic input-output, frustration-aggression model gives the theory its main structure. It is true that a large proportion of early New Left activists were both Jewish and came from broken or troubled homes.[90] Tom Hayden, twice divorced today, is himself the product of a broken home; his (Catholic) parents divorced when he was 10.[91] Psychic displacements probably did account for at least some of the radical impulse in almost every radical and for most of it in a few radicals. But this argument intimates that radicalism was wholly a function of intrinsic disorders in the family and subsequently in the minds of youth. But to get something like the 1960s, there has to be both an intrinsic propensity or latency toward alienation and an extrinsic catalyst, a reason for the latency to be actualized. It is no good denying either.

Social psychologist Lewis Feuer threw some light on the relationship between intrinsic and extrinsic authority.[92] He also took a psychological approach with strong Freudian elements to student radicalism, defining the idealism and utopianism characteristic of student movements in Oedipal terms as a function of coming to grips with parents and with the development of broad social competence. He argued that all student movements are examples of "*projective politics* in the sense that they have largely been dominated by unconscious drives; the will to revolt against the deauthoritized father has evolved into a variety of patterns of political action."[93] In Melvin Lasky's words, "sons, as so often in the past, were revolting against their fathers; the Oedipal psychodrama" had returned, this time en masse and in public.[94]

Feuer's study ranged cross-culturally over student movements for 150 years, and, although he wrote in 1967 and 1968, his work lacks both 1960s content and temperament. However, Feuer related in his introduction that he pleaded with students and faculty at Berkeley to understand the antinomian character of student movements, to see that they have always possessed dark sides of arationality, suicidalism, and terrorism. No one listened, but this is not surprising, especially if Feuer is right to contend that "the conflict of generations . . . derives from deep, unconscious sources."[95] If so, then by definition how could people relate to and deal with them?

Nevertheless, there's no denying a prophet his due; Feuer predicted terrorism and he was right. He pointed to a trajectory of self-hate and isolation, and, while it did not develop into classic suicidalism, the drug culture and the "premature aging" syndrome confirm the basic insight.[96] Moreover, by concentrating on the intrinsic sources of alienation—and by citing other cases of generational transition yielding political difficulty—Feuer made it impossible to explain 1960s student radicalism on the level of high politics alone, whether concerning Vietnam, civil rights, or any other discrete issue.

Feuer's effort to contain all student protest across generations and cultures did miss some important differences about more modern times. Modern student radicalism contained stark programmatic differences from its forebears. The core of the protest, as political scientist Suzanne Berger pointed out, was "not against the failure of the state and society to provide for economic growth and material prosperity, but against their all-too-considerable success in having done so, and against the price of this success."[97] There were three new elements in 1960s protest argued Berger: the rejection of affluence as an adequate justification for existing social arrangements; the revolt against economic or technological or social determinisms and their technocratic blush; and the rejection of the state as the principal agent of change. This stood against a past radicalism that was essentially materialist, determinist in the form of nineteenth-century positivisms, and statecentric. In other words, 1960s radicalism in Western countries was a postindustrial radicalism befitting a postindustrial milieu.[98]

Berger was wrong about youthful radicalism's never having cared before about non-material questions and she missed the real engine of alienation that fueled 1960s youth radicalism. Israeli social analyst S. D. Eisenstadt and anthropologist David Gutmann came closer. Eisenstadt argued in 1971 that then current student radicalism should be seen as the convergence and mutual reinforcement of two major sets of conditions and processes: extreme intellectual antinomianism and unprecedented generational discontinuity.[99] He pointed intriguingly to an interplay between extrinsic and intrinsic influences in student radicalism, combining the alienation of the intellectuals with the revolt against the managerial ethos and the conflict of generations. Eisenstadt emphasized the alienation of intellectuals

from governmental authority and noted the important role of radical young faculty
in shaping the alienation of the 1960s generation. Many students took studies of
their own alienation so seriously, he wrote, that alienation became self-fulfilling. It
became fashionable among the young elite to brood over social questions as if this
were a sign of profundity.

Eisenstadt did not really explain the discontinuity of the generations,
however. He spoke of a breakdown in historical awareness and suggested that
parents had not communicated the significance of recent events still undergoing
the process of historical interpretation and consolidation—the Great Depression,
the New Deal, World War II. It was almost in passing that Eisenstadt hit on a crucial
element of American generational discontinuity; he wrote that "the discrepancy
between the permissive premises of family and educational life and the realities of
adult life . . . have tended to create their feelings of frustration and disappointment."[100] Eisenstadt did not state the half of it.

The very consciousness of what child-rearing was had changed. Suburbia
had undermined the power of the extended family and social and religious
traditions. The popularization—really the vulgarization—of the Dr. Spock method
of childcare led to the notion of sparing the rod and approaching one's child as a
psychiatrist would approach a patient.[101] The children of the 1960s, when they
complained to their parents that they needed to "do their own thing," were often
accommodated by parents fearful of creating "maladjusted" or "repressed" progeny.
Here one recalls the then popular understanding of juvenile delinquency, replete
with its medical and psychiatric metaphors.[102]

David Gutmann has also argued that subjective projective processes help
explain student radicalism.[103] He, like Eisenstadt, looked at a range of social and
psychological discontinuities keying on the socialization process itself. He argued
that a healthy process of generational transition requires parents to mediate
between the child on the one hand and the Godhead on the other—whether that
actually be God or, more common in modern times, the secularly sacralized
constellation of social values deemed good. The parent, particularly the father,
paves the child's way into the adult world, the father's authority in the family
working as a microcosm of authority relations in general. It is important that
children respect the parent as having power, as having what children want
eventually for themselves. The development of a conscience—the internalization
of society's core values—cannot be understood except in terms of the transitive,
mediative character of parental authority.

According to Gutmann, this process was undermined for the Vietnam
generation for all the reasons discussed earlier. The implications he sees, however,
are stunning. His fuller argument is worth review, for it connects us back to our
chronological narrative circa October 1967.

The urge to political power, Gutmann argued, often masks various forms of inner emptiness. Alluding to the drug culture, he argued that Vietnam generation elitists had

> rediscovered the remedies of the aristocrat. They hunger for sharp, vivid experience—the bad trip as well as the good trip—to temporarily allay some inner dullness. . . . The inner malaise is politicized, rephrased into a plausible attack against social injustice. . . . A fullness of rage against the establishment and a sense of unity with other activists are partial substitutes for the absent morale, the missing inner core.[104]

What caused the missing inner core? Deficient superego formation in Freudian language, a weak, poorly defined conscience in plainer English. How did this happen? The answer lives at two levels: what parents did, and why they did it.

The deepest source of the generational conflict of the postwar era—the truest source of deficient superego formation—and the pivot of the banishment of the sacred was the breakdown of the socialization process starting with an irresolute parent delegitimized in the child's eyes by the parent's refusal to exert authority. Gutmann wrote:

> The loss of legitimacy has its most direct and severe consequences at the point where society, in the person of the parents, confronts the yet unsocialized child. The legitimated parent can speak with authority and is therefore enviable. He can propose to the child the ancient contract: "Conform to my legitimate authority and you will thereby acquire it for yourself." But the delegitimated parent has no mythic, sanctified base for his authority. If he still insists on it, he appears either hypocritical or arbitrary. More frequently, the delegitimated parent looks *to his own child* for love and validation; he refuses to be authoritative, because he thereby risks the loss of his child's love, which he needs to assuage his own emptiness. Parents so needful of supplies from their child signal clearly that they have none of their own; and the basis for the ancient socialization contract breaks down.[105]

And most critical of all:

> The parents' overriding need for the child's love will not provoke an answering love in him, but rather his rage and contempt: "If they need me, then they have no supplies of their own; and if they have no supplies of their own, then what can they give me and why should I try to be like them, or even bother to fight for what they have?"[106]

Feuer's description of the surrender of the authorities at Berkeley in 1964 reads as though it were excerpted from Gutmann's text:

> A psychological parricide had taken place . . . ; the fathers were in debacle, defeat, de-authoritized, floundering; the fathers confessed that their values were wrong. . . . What were the consequences? Not guilt . . . but a loss of standards, a collapse of all conceptions of right and wrong. Was there anything valuable which the elder generation could transmit [if it conspired in its] . . . own abdication?[107]

The rage of student radicals against society was indeed often a projection; the real target was their vacillating parents, or if not their parents then the moral vacancies that vitiated their spirits. As often as not, sad to say, parents deserved what they got and so, in a way, did a society that let youth down so hard.

This insight helps us to answer, partly at least, two other oft-noted questions. Why were Jews so disproportionately involved in student radicalism?[108] Because that group of mostly urban, acculturated Jews was fated to gather the bitter harvest of two generations of sometimes obsessive materialism and assimilation, the casting off of tradition and piety for the salve of liberalism and its assumed powers of protection against anti-Semitism. One of the best examples is Abbie Hoffman himself, whose upbringing stranded him between knowledge of tradition and assimilationist parents:

> My parents got sucked into the social melting pot where they were to simmer uncomfortably for the next thirty years. Having opted for life in mainstream America it became very difficult, even hypocritical for them to try to push any strict code of tradition down our throats. . . . Deep down, I'm sure we felt our parents' generation was a bunch of cop outs. Six million dead and except for the Warsaw ghetto, hardly a bullet fired in resistance. . . . I was shuffled back and forth between Orthodox yeshiva after school on weekdays and the reform Temple Emanuel on weekends. It was getting me pretty mixed up. Eventually tefillin and Torah lessons gave way to dancing classes and discourses (in English) on the nature of life and how good things were in America.[109]

And second, why did the New Left openly flaunt its Leftism at the height of the Cold War? Because it was poison to the delegitimated fathers. It was the cruelest punishment that could be inflicted by the children on the parents, and therefore it was chosen.

So much for what the parents did. Why did they do it? Here we must go back to the broader trends described earlier. Reminiscent of Morris's description of prostrate liberalism and Weber's reference to the desacralization of modern life, Gutmann suggested that the demythologization and rationalization of Western culture had simply gone too far too fast. "If the superego is the internal outpost of society's morality," he wrote,

> that morality must finally be upheld by myths, for moral behavior is the working out within the normal, everyday life of the mythic principles that were originally

set down and required by the gods. Moral behavior . . . pays off with the sense of meaning [but] . . . in a secular postindustrial society the basic contract that transforms the superego into a working or tolerable mental institution is compromised. The skeptical, secular spirit of the times portrays all life ways as being potentially ridiculous if not actually corrupt. . . . As he demythified and secularized the world, post-superego man reduced the credibility of the mythic domain and of its arbiter, the superego, within his own head.[110]

In other words, the uncompromising rationalism of secular society undermines itself by vitiating the very base for moral behavior, which in turn vitiates the basis for any meaningful community or social contract.[111] Or, in the case of young people, it vitiates the basis of belief in a purposeful relationship between themselves and the larger society.

Students may not have understood exactly what was happening to them but—eventually at least—some of their professors did get an inkling. The moral crisis evoked by the civil rights struggle was for the Vietnam generation sharpened and deepened not only by the ensuing Vietnam War, but also by the almost total skepticism characteristic of modern Western universities—the spearheads of the desacralization of everyday life in our times. Belatedly in most cases, some professors rued the way they had consistently criticized almost every political, religious, and moral theory of Western civilization, and had failed to provide any positive philosophy of life in the place of, as Califano put it, "the gods whose feet of clay they had smashed."[112]

## MAGIC, MYTH, AND RELIGION

Those without working superegos, without the beliefs that make up a conscience, are by definition alienated. Meaning comes hard for the alienated because meaning exists only in relation to value, and the structure of values, ultimately, is mythic. Alienation, in turn, invariably gives rise to attempts to reconnect with the Godhead or to find a new one. Gutmann cited anthropological evidence that certain psychopathologies are desperate attempts "to contact the external sources of power when the superego has either failed to develop or when it can no longer function as an internal regulator of self-esteem. . . . Individual failures in superego formation would lead to driven, regressive, and magical attempts to eat up or blend into the outer forms of power."[113] Like trying to levitate the Pentagon, perhaps?

Gutmann's references to magic are especially significant. The counterculture was suffused with magic, and radicalism's utopianism represented a form of magic as well. Alienation, in short, did lead to the psychological atavisms predicted.

Examples were everywhere. The Diggers, a group of self-described cultural anarchists, defined countercultural politics as "making magic on a daily basis."[114]

The popularity of tarot cards and the *I Ching,* the infatuation with Herman Hesse and Carlos Castaneda, the cult of LSD—all this reflected the allure of the magical. Related to the allure of the magical was the hallmark of the counterculture: the merging of the comedic impulse with political activism. Today as ever before, magic goes hand in hand with clowning. Because comedy deliberately sabotages the boundaries between normal relational understandings in order to generate the tensions that make humor, it is in a way a kind of magic.

Jerry Rubin and Abbie Hoffman were masters of political comedy as well as expositors of political magic. They are the ones who put Marxism—Groucho's, not Karl's—into guerrilla theater by throwing dollar bills from the balcony of the New York Stock Exchange and running a pig as the Yippie presidential candidate in 1968. At a break in the 1969 Chicago Seven trial (for the 1968 violence outside the Democratic National Convention) Hoffman ran over to Mayor Richard J. Daley, wearing boxing gloves, and drawled: "Why don't we settle this thing here and now—just you and me? To hell with all these lawyers." Hoffman also once proclaimed: "There are seven million laws in this country, and we aim to break every single one of them, including the law of gravity."[115]

This referred, of course, to the famous attempt to levitate the Pentagon in October 1967, which Hoffman led while SDS members were busy defacing the building with pig blood.[116] Hoffmann had asked Paul Krassner to buy some cornmeal, with which he planned to encircle the Pentagon in a pre-levitation rite. "The novelist Robert Stone drove me to a farm in Iowa, where I duly requested some cornmeal to go. The farmer asked 'Coarse or fine?' I looked at Stone. He shrugged. 'Since it's for a magic ritual,' he said, 'I would definitely recommend coarse'."[117] Was the levitation attempt supposed to be real magic, or just funny? Under the circumstances, both.

Only in a carnival atmosphere could such antics get as much attention as they did. It was *surrealpolitik,* a kind of political dadaism. It persisted for many years. At Woodstock, it may be recalled, when the rains began for the second or third time the crowd began to chant "No rain, no rain" in a mantra. Many were actually expecting this to do some good. Later on, this same impulse to magic led former radicals, notably Rennie Davis, into transcendental meditation and pseudo-religious cults of many sorts.

Related to magic and comedy were efforts to invent and capture new taboos—particularly those having to do with the sexual and the obscene. Hoffman once imagined a sexual equivalent to MACE that he called LACE, a combination of LSD and the "transmission agent" DMSO. LACE would be absorbed through the skin and become an instant aphrodisiac. Hoffman invited the press to his apartment and connived Paul Krassner to be sprayed "accidentally" with LACE, whereupon he was to act strangely and remove his clothes. "I was then," wrote Krassner, "to start making out with a lovely redhead who had also been 'inadvertently' sprayed, along with another, deliberately sprayed couple, right there in the living room while the journalists took notes."[118] Was it supposed to be mainly a magic gag, a comedy skit, or an excuse for sex? Such distinctions made little sense at the time.

Sixties radicalism, as a search for the lost anchor of a mythic, meaning-giving world, may also explain the conspiratorial nature of New Left theorizing, especially when directed against the liberal humanism of their elders. Conspiracy theories, at least grand ones, go in and out of style historically and across cultures. The common thread that knits them together is that they occur after long-standing central beliefs about society and self are broken asunder in one way or another. Because they allow no ambiguities, conspiracy theories rebatten a drifting world for those who adhere to them, giving a sense of purposefulness to what is otherwise painfully chaotic.

In a sense, conspiracy theories are a kind of magic too. They astound, they create cognitive parsimony, and they are not real in the sense that they do not correspond to anything objective. They also share this in common: Anyone who truly believes in either will believe in practically anything.

Indeed, the attraction of conspiracy theories also suggests why the power of New Left and counterculture groups was so strong. No one likes to be alone for too long, but it is easier with a sense of self-esteem and a sense of general orientation in the moral and social world. Without it, one seeks shelter not just through conspiracy theories about capitalism and imperialism but also through like-minded companionship. This is why post-superego man is easy prey for the totalitarian temptation. The galloping authoritarianism within student radicalism, particularly as it approached the 1970s, was bolstered by its strident moralism, which, as sociologist Irving Louis Horowitz put it, was always "a ready handmaiden to the 'totalitarian democracy' that the historian Jacob Talmon spoke of."[119]

## SIXTIES RADICALISM AS A
## SEARCH FOR THE SACRED

The concern with radical community and conformity of belief illustrated the drive both to build a system of value as a basis of inner authority and to create a means of communal worship to share and reinforce those values. Antiwar rallies, whatever else they were, were a form of communal worship and adversary culture gatherings today still are; that is partly the source of attraction to them, often as a substitute for more conventional forms of communal prayer.

Having accomplished this construction of values and community made many people much happier, particularly if one could set aside the real problems— in the ghettoes or in Southeast Asia—that gave rise to the movement in the first place. This in turn accounts for the celebratory, festive character of student radicalism in the last few years of the 1960s and into the beginning of the 1970s. Even as napalm was falling by the ton in Vietnam, antiwar rallies became less angry and more inclined to celebrate the dawning of the countercultural Age of Aquarius. The music was upbeat and hopeful, the sense of purposefulness palpable. What one informant said of participating in the Paris riots of May 1968 easily fits the sense of what was happening in the United States:

> It's a moment I shall never forget. Suddenly, spontaneously, barricades were being thrown up in the streets. People were building up the cobblestones because they wanted—many of them for the first time—to throw themselves into a collective spontaneous activity. People were releasing all their repressed feelings, expressing them in a new festive spirit. Thousands felt the need to communicate with each other, to love one another.[120]

This describes the powerful social intimacy of a communion of believers more than it does a political protest. It describes, in short, a religious experience, of which Woodstock was probably the zenith.[121] As Louis Menard put it, speaking of the countercultural dimension to the antiwar movement: "The counterculture looked to many people like simple hedonism. . . . But the counterculture wasn't hedonistic; it was puritanical. It was, in fact, virtually Hebraic: the parents were worshipping false gods, and the students who tore up (or dropped out of) the university in an apparent frenzy of self-destructiveness . . . were, in effect, smashing the golden calf."[122] Indeed, its superficial Marxism notwithstanding, it was neither a positivist nor a rationalist phenomenon, but an energetically idealist one in both the philosophical and commonsense meaning of the term. It was—it sounds strange but it is nevertheless true—quite conservative in some ways.

Finally, as Michael Walzer pointed out long ago, whether one speaks of Puritans, Jacobins, Bolsheviks, or New Leftists (who did not yet exist when he wrote the following), there is a common psychological dynamic that invariably produces the soldier-saint, the religiously, morally motivated militant. "The saint is a soldier whose battles are fought out in the self before they are fought out in society. Revolution follows from Puritan sainthood—that is, from triumph over Satanic lusts. . . . [I]t is the acting out of a new identity."[123] For 1960s radicals, the triumph over materialism, technocracy, and dullness, and the revolt against the impersonal served this very purpose. This is why, while the antiwar movement appears to have come before the counterculture, in a more fundamental sense the counterculture was the source of it all.

Student radicalism of the 1960s was a product of the undermining not just of certain values, and not just of the code of liberal humanism as taught by parents and teachers, but of the very grounds of value itself on both an extrinsic and intrinsic level. The tension between expectations and reality, between moral pretense and the cold managerialism of technocracy, between liberal platitudes and liberal passionlessness, drove young idealists from their faith in outer authority to seek inner authority. But when they arrived inside, they found little to sustain them, and so they went looking for God, many of them in all the wrong places. Their parents had largely abdicated their traditional roles as value giver and power bringer. Traditional religious establishments—one would think the last refuge of a stable nonrelativist value structure—had for the most part joined the enemy in a visionless enthusiasm for the new modernity. The liberal theologians of the 1950s and 1960s who catered to the upper strata of American society, who introduced popular psychological relativisms into their theological discussions, and who talked about the death of God, were not just describing a condition in metaphor or, as they claimed, just making statements about society after the enormity of World War II.[124] They did not understand or intend it but, for the children of the 1960s, they were all too often accomplices in killing God. The harm such people have done is almost incalculable.

In retrospect, one can see evidence of the search for the sacred even in seemingly inconsequential events. John Lennon once boasted famously that the Beatles were more popular than Jesus and in so doing created a tremendous uproar. But the real reason for the uproar was that, among most youth at least, he was perfectly correct.[125] Lennon missed his own point, that he *was* a god and his fans were his disciples, in an era when the God of their forefathers had gotten lost on His way to the suburbs. Nor is it coincidental that toward the end of the 1960s, after the commercial arts eventually came around to mimic real life, that we were witness to popular musicals such as *Jesus Christ Superstar* and *Joseph and the Technicolor Dreamcoat.*

The mixture of religion and politics grew to be potent too in the protest music of the period. Christmas was an particularly popular theme. Aside from Simon and Garfunkel's merger of "Silent Night" with the "Seven O'Clock News" mentioned earlier, Laura Nyro's 1970 recording of "Christmas In My Soul" is a stellar, if obscure, example. After describing America as a dying country and making reference to both the sins of politics and the politics of sin, Nyro wrote of weeping Madonnas extinguishing noel candles. This was followed by a reference to Black Panther "brothers bound in jail" and homeless Manhattan Indians. Having summoned the properly bitter tone, Nyro incongruously implored her listeners that now the time "has come to fight" for peace and love. The song ends with the classical phrase "joy to the world."[126]

It was not obvious then, but what were such lyrics and how were they heard, except as religious verse? Like antiwar rallies, playing and listening to such music were deeply moving experiences; they too were a kind of prayer. Often awkward or incongruous contents notwithstanding, they filled youth's need for religion, a need neglected by their elders.

In short, there *were* reasons, powerful ones, why so many of the middle-class, pleasure-principled, idealistic youth of the 1960s became alienated, angry, and even violent. It is hard to place blame for all the anger, disappointment, and sadness of love lost that this caused. It seems wrong to absolve irresponsible youth entirely, but it seems even less fair to blame the Vietnam generation for what was a multi-generational erosion of the transmission of social values over which it could exercise no control and which it could not possibly have understood. This erosion led to strange episodes such as tens of thousands of youths trying to levitate the Pentagon.

# 6

# Best of Times, Worst of Times

*The end had come, but it is not yet in sight.*
—John Kenneth Galbraith

U nderstanding the Vietnam antiwar movement at any given time in its history requires two foci, one on the war and the sitting administration's handling of it, the other on the internal dynamics of the movement itself. As we return to our chronicle, in mid-1967 we find the Johnson administration staggering against failure. It dared not lose the war but could not win it either, and it could not credibly explain why to the American people. It had allowed the war to become protracted, and its own internal doubts about how to prosecute the war successfully were baldly illustrated by key personnel abdications from the administration and by a widening credibility gap that was less a consequence of willful distortion than of deep, abject confusion.

Action in the antiwar movement arena, meanwhile, was increasingly dominated by SDS and the New Left, whose meteoric rise was about to reach its height. As it rose, SDS ran into the core of the adversary culture—now composed of Sidney Peck and his colleagues—which had been serving as the leadership of the movement, such as it was, since late 1965. This was almost as momentous a collision as that between the movement and the Johnson administration.

We start our tale of these strange times focused on the movement's epochal March on the Pentagon, switch back to the war at the time of the Tet offensive, then behold the cacophonous self-destruction of SDS in 1968, and finally track the movement as it encountered internal and national political change in 1969 with the inauguration of Richard Nixon as president.

## FROM NONVIOLENCE TO RESISTANCE

The October 1967 March on the Pentagon was the first major public manifestation of the full radicalization of the antiwar movement's ideology and protest tactics, and it also was the moment when the New Left truly brought its power and imagination to bear within the core of radical organizers of the new pacifism and the sectarian Left. Much of that imagination rose in the head of Jerry Rubin.

It was Rubin who, in the planning stages of the October 1967 demonstration, suggested that the rally focus on the Pentagon and not Capitol Hill. It was also Rubin, in a conversation with Allen Cohen, editor of the psychedelic San Francisco *Oracle,* who first thought of the idea of magically levitating the Pentagon, which, with its five sides, looked to him like a Satanic star symbol—even though Abbie Hoffman was later to become responsible for the "operation" itself. It was also Rubin who printed up a wild, obscene, and really quite crazy version of *The Mobilizer,* which was the Mobilization to End the War's (Mobe) generally staid newsletter, and in so doing he angered many an old stalwart of the Fifth Avenue Parade organizing committee. Sidney Peck tried to have Rubin's edition of the *Mobilizer* squelched, but Rubin leaked it to the press, which made it perhaps the most famous and widely read edition of the *Mobilizer* ever published.[1]

Along with its free-flowing countercultural antics, the New Left also was ready to introduce new and more violent tactics at the March on the Pentagon, going beyond the mere collection and burning of draft cards, occasional "trashings," which amounted mainly to turning over garbage cans and randomly spreading their contents around, and heaving bottles and bricks through storefront windows to help "liberate" their contents.[2] More violent methods—including assaults with intent to injure police and draftboard officials and arson aimed at public property (mainly buildings and vehicles)—had already begun to emerge during Stop the Draft Week.

Stop the Draft Week, planned for the week of October 16, 1967, was, as advertised and intended, filled with violence. Oakland, California was the key case in point. Radical activists surrounded and literally attacked the local draft board with bricks, bottles, and metal bars for four days running. At one point, violence wracked a 20-square-block area; street fighting with the police was a permanent feature of the "battle." There was also considerable violence at the University of Wisconsin campus near the original student headquarters of the NCCEWV.

As a prelude to both Stop the Draft Week and the planned march on the Pentagon, the literary Left tried to lend a helping hand. Led by Institute for Policy Studies principals Marcus Raskin and Arthur Waskow, 158 members of the literary and professional Left came together to sign "A Call to Resist Illegitimate Authority," which was first published in the *New York Review of Books* in late September, just before Stop the Draft Week. This "Call" was a final version of a statement that had been circulating in various drafts for several months, during which it was titled "A Call to Confrontation with Illegitimate Authority." Waskow and Raskin toned down some parts of the statement, but sharpened others, especially those related to the draft. It called for "open resistance to the war and the draft" as a means to strengthen the country's moral resolve to oppose and stop the war. At a press conference announcing the call, spokesmen for the 158 signers also pledged their own acts of civil disobedience during the week of October 16, and several clergymen among the signers promised their churches and synagogues as sanctuaries from the police should draft resisters wish to avail themselves of them.[3] This was, in point of fact, the origin of "sanctuary" movements that later had as their main focus the provision of sanctuary for Nicaraguan and Salvadoran leftists in the 1970s and early 1980s.

At the same time, too, the movement's radical core was reaching out to improve relations with Hanoi and the Vietcong. A delegation of antiwar activists met with a high-ranking Vietnamese Communist delegation in Bratislava in early October. The movement now had, in effect, an active foreign policy.

But all of this was just prologue to the big event: The new violence came to full life in the "March on the Pentagon to Confront the Warmakers," Sidney Peck's would-be organizational triumph, which soon leaped well beyond his or anyone else's control.

Tom Hayden put the New Left's core aim perfectly at the time: The movement, he said, had moved from "Bring the Troops Home" to "Bring the War Home." Peaceful, passive marches filled with song and ringing declarations were not enough anymore. The movement ineluctably moved, or was moved by its increasingly radical leadership, from protest to resistance. When, on October 21, 1967, a late arriving group of SDS antiwar demonstrators storming the Pentagon poured pig blood all over the building, the rest of the movement—even that part not attending or giving explicit support—generally approved of the escalatory tactics. Gone from sight or mind was the model of Gandhian Satygraha, the nonviolent tactics of the civil rights struggle, and gone was A. J. Muste, too, who had passed away on February 11, 1967, at the age of 82. Instead came a "guerrilla protest," "guerrilla theater," and David Dellinger's eclectic forms of "active resistance."[4]

Evidence of ideological radicalization in the movement as a whole was also easy to find toward the end of 1967. Pragmatic *realpolitik* arguments against the war faded away, abandoned less for their rightness or wrongness than for their perceived ineffectualness. Arguments that the Vietnam war was a "mere" civil war acquired a critically important corollary: It was a civil war that the National Liberation Front deserved to win. Such a view was buttressed both by an increasingly positive affection for Vietnamese revolutionary socialism, which was greatly accelerated by the accumulation of political pilgrims who had gone to Hanoi and by a caricature of the South Vietnamese regime as venal, sadistic, and authoritarian. So the Vietcong banner flew at rallies in large numbers for the first time.

Opposition to U.S. involvement in Southeast Asia also became unambiguously total; the demand was not for modifications of policy but for the overthrow of the policy as a whole and, for most, the overthrow of those who had made and were still making it. What had been a minority position in the movement 18 months earlier was now by far the dominant position. The right wing of the movement had been decisively isolated and enfeebled, its personnel raided and its treasury stagnated.

The March on the Pentagon proved to be quite an affair. As had happened often before, arguments developed at the eleventh hour within the organizing coalition. The SWP wanted a legal mass march with a minimum of opportunity for the police to make arrests; Trotskyites always opposed jail time as being counter-productive to organizing the workers. Radical pacifists insisted on nonviolent civil disobedience; the more arrests the better as far as they were concerned. SDS leaders, who had given little support to the project because they believed that doing so would only "delude people into thinking they were having an effect," now decided secretly to mount a "vanguard action." Also, in the meantime, thanks to Dellinger's invitation, Jerry Rubin was busy calling on people to "come piss on the White House lawn" through the *Mobilizer* and other methods.

As a result of all this, Sidney Peck feared that he would lose his cherished opening to the Right, and that the attempt to hold together as wide a coalition under an actual radical aegis as possible would fail. Under his leadership, NCCEWV principals decided that the March on the Pentagon would be a three-part project: a rally at the Lincoln Memorial with no shenanigans whatsoever; a lawful march to the Pentagon along the indicated government-approved route; and, finally, a second rally at the Pentagon, complete with civil disobedience for those who wished to engage in it.

The rally began at the Lincoln Memorial as planned. There were speeches and songs, much as usual. Noteworthy among them—and indicative of how the movement was now tilting—was John Lewis of SNCC asking for a moment's silence for Che Guevara, killed earlier in the year by the Bolivian army. Then Dellinger took the microphone and announced the end of peaceful protest and the beginning of "confrontation." "This is the beginning," he said, "of a new stage in the American peace movement in which the cutting edge becomes active resistance."[5] Whether he knew what SDS was about to do is not clear and was debated long afterwards by activists friendly to Dellinger, and those not so friendly. He probably did know.

As the rally marched to the Pentagon along a circuitous route marked out by the Washington Park Police, a group of a few hundred SDSers broke away and tried to storm the building. About two dozen got inside the building, whence they proceeded to "trash the place." They were arrested rather physically. This in turn set off the rest of the SDS contingent; bottles, cans, rocks, and obscenities were hurled at the military police. A little while later, after attempts at going ahead with the speechmaking and the rest of the set program had been abandoned by Peck, Dellinger and his horde of counterculturals hacked a hole in the wire fence that had been erected outside the perimeter of the door leading to Defense Department principals' offices and ambled off toward Secretary McNamara's suite. Before they got there they were all arrested in a cloud of tear gas.

Peck was left in the parking lot, virtually alone, with the job of controlling and organizing the crowd, as the rest of the organizing committee had gone off to get arrested without having warned him of their plans. At this point, many people left as confusion and boredom took hold. Others proceeded through the hole in the fence so that they could get arrested, too. And still others hung around for several hours, and some even bedded down for the night in the parking lot, where the marijuana haze was thick and pungent.

The next morning, a few hundred people still remained, and some of the speeches planned for the previous day finally were given. That night the march permit expired and most protestors, many of them out of food, left for home. But others decided to avail themselves of their last chance to get arrested in a group at the Pentagon. The grand total of arrests for the two days came to 683—a new movement record. Dellinger took special pride in the fact that, for the first time, federal troops and national guard officers were called out to deal with the crowds. For Dellinger, these more serious police counted as evidence that the movement was succeeding in "provoking intolerance," in Mary McCarthy's words, and unmasking the sinister face of American fascism.

The March on the Pentagon was an epochal experience for those who attended. Despite the almost total breakdown of coordination and loss of direction, it represented an escalation of protest tactics, and it made most of those present feel very heroic and moral. It also made them feel like veterans of a struggle, proud pioneers of brave protest in an evolving hierarchy of movement achievements. Particularly for the young, it was an emboldening experience and one from which the level of enthusiasm for spreading the movement of protest radiated brightly.

The antiwar movement drew much confidence from the March on the Pentagon and also from what seemed to be the rapid spread of antiwar sentiment, for which it more often than not (wrongly) took credit. Even mass-media magazines such as *Life* and *Newsweek*, public figures such as Walter Cronkite, and a coterie of assorted celebrities were suddenly questioning aspects of the administration's war policies in Vietnam that they had heretofore avoided.[6] Nothing could have been more natural, and it did not take a march on the Pentagon to produce new expressions of doubt and dissent. By the end of 1967, 16,021 U.S. soldiers had been killed in the war, 10,000 in 1967 alone. There were now 485,600 U.S. soldiers in South Vietnam, and there was no end in sight to the fighting and the dying.

Meanwhile, in the movement itself—inner public opinion, as it were—the burgeoning minions on the penumbra of the increasingly radicalized center had not all had their "political consciousness" raised, but many had. As suggested earlier, the radicalism of the antiwar movement's leadership moved faster than the expansion of overt antiwar sentiment in the country at large, and probably played a role in limiting it. Nevertheless, opposition expanded at all levels. By the end of 1967, according to a Harris poll, about 19 percent of American college students believed in the need for a mass revolutionary party. That amounted to over a million students. Listen to how Sam Brown described his own journey from patriotic dissenter to radical protester:

> I remember attending a march in 1965 in which both Norman Thomas and Carl Oglesby spoke. Thomas spoke in terms of moral outrage, about rescuing the national soul. As the son of a religious, Midwestern family, I could identify easily with ministerial pleas. Oglesby talked about U.S. imperialism with language that set my teeth on edge. Within a year, I read Oglesby's speech in essay form and found myself agreeing with it. Within two years, I found it hard to restrain myself from using his language.[7]

And if many were not yet radicalized by the end of 1967, there was always next year. And what a year 1968 turned out to be.

## TET AND THE WISE MEN

Unlike 1966 and 1967, which were only incrementally different from 1965 in terms of the conduct of the war, 1968 brought a big change. The key event of the year, which shaped the rest of the war, was the Tet offensive launched by the Vietcong, and the Johnson administration's military and political reactions to it.

On January 31, 1968, the Vietcong launched a coordinated attack against the South Vietnamese government with the aim of actually bringing it down. Heretofore, the Vietcong had concentrated on denying the South Vietnamese government control over rural areas of the country, this according to the maxim of Asian Communist tactics derived from the Chinese revolution that the countryside would surround the cities. This is done by assassinating rural chiefs, engaging in random murders for purposes of intimidation, ambushing traffic on roads, forcing expropriation of food, and making mandatory political indoctrination of villages under Vietcong control.

Cities, meanwhile, were thought to be the natural quarters of class enemies—intellectuals, parasites, foreigners, corpulent bureaucrats—while the countryside was the domain of the peasant, Asian communism's substitute of necessity for a nonexistent revolutionary vanguard composed of an industrial proletariat. This theme persisted elsewhere in Asia, as well; it was just this sort of revolutionary bias that led the Khmer Rouge in Cambodia to destroy its own cities and murder millions of such "class enemies" with bullets, rocks, pitchforks, and hammers.

While seeking control of the countryside, the Vietcong had infiltrated urban areas of South Vietnam, placing sympathizers secretly in as many positions of authority and power as possible. But they rarely if ever engaged in overt military activity in urban areas—until Tet. Tet was designed to be a two-pronged uprising: Much-larger-than-usual units of Vietcong soldiers would attack urban areas, including Saigon and Hue, in concert with the sudden "coming out" of the thousands of planted urban agents. While regime forces were pulled away from their barracks and the center of town, this urban uprising was designed to disrupt central communications, transport, intelligence coordination, medical services, and also kill as many high officials and members of their families in their homes as possible. The combined result was expected to be the collapse of order, the Vietcong's seizure of munitions, radio stations, and power-generating facilities— and the subsequent prostration and surrender of the regime.[8]

It didn't turn out that way. As has become clear, the Tet offensive was a huge military mistake from the Vietcong's point of view, a mistake from which it never fully recovered.[9] Its conventional assaults were defeated, though in some cases, such as in Hue, it took weeks to do it and the price was high for the army of the Republic of Vietnam (ARVN), for U.S. forces, and for Hue's civilian population. During their reign in Hue, the Vietcong murdered thousands of local leaders, officials, and businessmen (in particular, ethnic Chinese). As many as 3,000 bodies were found in one mass grave.

Nevertheless, the exposure of the Vietcong's urban agents in Hue and elsewhere led to their wholesale slaughter, the most famous (thanks to a photograph captured by Associated Press photographer Eddie Adams) single episode being the public summary execution, by a pistol shot to the head, of a Vietcong agent by Saigon's police chief, General Nguyen Loc Loan. The agent, a Vietcong lieutenant, together with a small squad of associates, had reportedly just murdered several of the police chief's closest aides, including an aide's wife and all his children in their own home.[10]

Notwithstanding its literal defeat, Tet gave lie to the American military's analysis of the war and its recently proclaimed projections of eventual victory.[11] Tet proved that if the U.S. definition of victory carried with it limited cost, then the United States was nowhere near victory, contrary to what General Westmoreland had told the Congress just weeks before.[12]

Initially, the president's closest military and White House advisors had told him that Tet was a victory for the United States. Judging by how many of the enemy were killed, and the frustration of their evident intention, indeed it was. This pleased the president, partly because he interpreted it as evidence that Bundy and McNamara's doubts had been unfounded. It also partly offset the depressed public reaction to the blood and death of Tet, which Johnson could have interpreted as transient. But President Johnson was a savvy politician. He was well aware of the broader psychological and political impact of Tet. He was also sensitive to his subordinates' reluctance to be frank with him. Contrary to many received myths about Johnson's insularity, he frequently reached outside of his administration's inner circle for advice. One of the reasons Johnson chose long-time Washington insider Clark Clifford to replace McNamara as secretary of defense turned on Clifford's generally supportive but still critical advice in earlier years.

And so, after Tet, Johnson called upon Harry Truman's secretary of state, Dean Acheson, whose judgment he trusted most of all, to give his opinion of developments in the war. Acheson pleaded ignorance of the war's detail and so Johnson told him to go and talk to midlevel officials of his own choosing until he was satisfied that he could report effectively. Acheson went to Clifford, and Clifford sent him on to William Bundy of the State Department, George Carver of the Central Intelligence Agency, and a few well-placed others.

In the meantime, Clifford had been conducting his own review of Vietnam policy when Tet occurred. He did not at all like what he found; in particular, he discovered that the Joint Chiefs of Staff had a program for not losing the war, but no program for winning it or even ending it in a tolerably acceptable manner. Clifford had entered the Pentagon as a cautious hawk, but his Vietnam Task Force findings soon tempered his views.[13]

Instrumental, it seems, in Clifford's change of heart was Paul Warnke, then assistant secretary of defense for international security affairs (ISA), who had had a major influence, as well, on Robert McNamara's change of heart. Warnke, who became director of the Arms Control and Disarmament Agency and chief U.S. strategic arms control negotiator in March 1977, believed that without a fundamental political improvement in Saigon, the war was unwinnable save through the essential destruction of North Vietnam, something that no one was seriously contemplating. He believed this fundamental improvement in Saigon to be unlikely and that, therefore, while U.S. troops might kill many more of the enemy than the enemy killed of U.S. troops, the war would be essentially endless. It is worth pointing out that, while Warnke had many an ally in the State Department, his views were not widely shared in the Pentagon. For example, Warnke was the only one at his level in the government who thought that the North Vietnamese had fulfilled their part of the San Antonio Formula for a cessation of the U.S. bombing.[14]

When Clifford talked to Warnke, Warnke told him that favorable kill ratios aside, in 12 months the United States would be no closer to winning the war than it was right now; the only difference would be that another 10,000 Americans would probably be dead. Warnke helped see to it that others of similar view in Defense and in other agencies got Clifford's ear. Once Clifford was converted to this view, he made sure that Acheson met the same people. Therefore, it was no surprise that when Acheson reported to the president on March 15, three days after the New Hampshire primary, which had boosted Senator Eugene McCarthy's candidacy for the Democratic presidential nomination to new heights, he told Johnson that, in Vietnam scholar Herbert Schandler's words, "the time and resources necessary to accomplish our military objectives in South Vietnam were no longer available. The American public would support neither an increased effort nor even the present level of effort over an extended period. Acheson concluded that the ground war had to be changed, the bombing stopped or greatly reduced, and the war brought to a halt as soon as possible in keeping with the American commitment to South Vietnam."[15]

Acheson's advice accorded in part with that of another trusted advisor, Supreme Court Justice Arthur Goldberg, who had earlier suggested a bombing pause. Five days after meeting with Acheson, Johnson called Goldberg in for a conference. Johnson told him that in a few days, at Clifford's suggestion, the Wise Men would meet again and when they did, Goldberg was to present for their consideration the view he had expressed in his memorandum to the president. On March 25, the President again convened the Wise Men: Acheson, Ball, Bradley, McGeorge Bundy, Dillon, Vance, Dean, McCloy, Ridgeway, Taylor, Murphy, Lodge, Fortas, and Goldberg. Later in the day, they met at dinner with Secretary of State Rusk, W. Averell Harriman, Walt Rostow, Richard Helms, General Earl Wheeler, Paul Nitze, Nicholas Katzenbach, and William Bundy. There the Wise Men questioned the group of officials about various aspects of the war.

After dinner, all of the government officials left and the Wise Men received three briefings on the war, one each from Philip Habib of the State Department, Major General William E. DuPuy from the office of the Joint Chiefs, and George Carver from the CIA. In retrospect, some observers have argued that these briefings were "cooked" by Warnke and Clifford to convey a pessimistic appraisal. Others, including Rusk, have reasoned that the briefings were unbalanced but not deliberately so, because these officials did not want to come across as rosy-eyed and therefore not credible.[16] However it happened, when the Wise Men reported to the president the next day at the White House, they were as pessimistic or more so than Acheson had been a few days earlier. Johnson was stunned. He demanded to hear the three briefings himself. (He heard only two; Habib elected not to return to the White House.) Most of the group recommended vast changes in strategy; dissenting from the new consensus were Fortas, Murphy, and Taylor. In the end, the Wise Men's views, now added on to Acheson's, persuaded Johnson to change course.

Central to many of the arguments the Wise Men made were pained references to divisions in the United States over the war and the erosion of public support. Goldberg, in particular, restated his view that Tet was a serious and not a transient defeat as far as public opinion was concerned, and that the president "could not press on" without wide public support. In *The Vantage Point,* if his own recollections can be taken as valid, Johnson wrote of that meeting that "all the advisors expressed deep concern about the divisions in our country. Some of them felt that those divisions were growing rapidly and might soon force our withdrawal from Vietnam."[17] He may well have been speaking in particular about Cyrus Vance, later Jimmy Carter's secretary of state, who said: "Unless we do something quick, the mood in the country may lead us to withdrawal."[18] It also seems that Johnson was greatly affected by Walter Cronkite's televised remark on the war after Tet, on

February 27, in which he for the first time suggested that pressing on with the war was no longer justified by its costs. After watching the broadcast, Johnson reportedly said: "Cronkite was it."[19]

Cronkite or no Cronkite, President Johnson was deeply impressed at how affected the Wise Men had been by Tet. He later wrote: "They were intelligent, experienced men. I had always regarded the majority of them as very steady and balanced. If they had been so deeply influenced by the reports of the Tet offensive, what must the average citizen in the country be thinking?"[20]

Not, evidently, what Johnson thought they were thinking. In retrospect, the Wise Men's judgments—and by extension the president's as well—about public opinion seem to have been mistaken. The data indicate that public opinion against the war was not stronger after Tet than the opinion that favored staying the course; and, of course, whatever public opinion might have been, it begs the question of how much of a constraint on policy that opinion really was at various periods in the electoral cycle.[21] A pre-Tet Gallup poll (January 3, 1968) put President Johnson's approval rating at 39 percent, with 49 percent disapproving. The first post-Tet poll, on February 14, came out at 35 percent to 50 percent—hardly a striking difference. In February 1968, when Gallup asked whether individuals considered themselves hawks or doves on Vietnam, 61 percent said hawk and only 23 percent said dove. So what happened?

The Wise Men were probably misled by the short-term fluctuation in the polls on the "mistake" question. The Tet offensive itself, in fact, had generated more support for the war, in a manifestation of the well-known rally-round-the-flag effect.[22] It was not until February 1968 that opinion sampling began to show a shift of opinion against the war, and it showed a particularly sharp one because the numbers were, in a sense, correcting themselves back to the median from the upward blip at the time of Tet. Additionally, the public shift in Cronkite's views after Tet and the airing of dramatic prime-time special reports on national television probably sharpened the opinion blip a few degrees. The Wise Men apparently mistook this correction for a sharp shift in basic opinion, which in fact did not occur.

Additionally, there was no chance that the Congress might force a withdrawal nor, at the time, were there easy means for it to do so even had it wanted to. The president had at least until the November 1968 election to stay the course, and if the people of the United States really opposed the war, they would say so at the polls. Even the success of Eugene McCarthy in New Hampshire, which weighed heavily on Johnson's mind and those of the Wise Men, we now know, was based largely on an irritation with irresolute war policies. In other words, many Democratic "hawks" voted for McCarthy to send a message to Lyndon Johnson, which said, in effect, get tough in Vietnam or we'll inflict McCarthy on the country.[23] In light of all this, why did so many of the Wise Men seem to hold the views they did about public opinion and the base of domestic support for the war? And how did they persuade, or apparently persuade, the president of the importance of supposed shifts in opinion?

As noted earlier, it is clear that the Wise Men and the president were concerned about opinion polls and dissent in the Congress in the aftermath of Tet, and some of the changes in the polling percentages were quite sharp, albeit temporary as it turned out. But then, by late March, Johnson's approval rating did a nosedive. His handling of the war was rated at 39 percent in January but only 26 percent by the third week in March. His overall approval rating as president sunk from 48 percent in February to 36 percent in late March, and while the reason may not have been related directly to Vietnam, the Wise Men could not have but thought otherwise.[24]

On balance, as Schandler as well as Gelb and Betts make clear, the change of course in early 1968 was an internal governmental affair. Key defections in the Defense and State Departments, as well as in the White House in 1966 and 1967, new personnel with different views, the rise of economic pressures, distress within the military and at the U.S. Embassy in Saigon, accumulating domestic political injury to the Democratic Party—all played out against the context of what all saw from the start to be a *limited* engagement for *limited* purposes—led to a shift in policy. These dynamics are quite sufficient to explain the president's March 31 speech, in which he announced a search for negotiations to end the war, a halt in the bombing, and that he would not seek or accept the Democratic nomination for president in 1968. No "help" from the angry street was necessary to persuade Johnson to make this speech. Indeed, many believe that the president's awareness of his own health problems contributed much to his decision not to stand again for office (he died on January 22, 1973, so he would have barely finished another term had he won reelection). It is thus probably doubly wrong to argue, as Small and Hoover do, that "the movement's activities *directly* influenced Johnson's decision not to run for the presidency in 1968."[25]

What is not so clear, on the other hand, is the role antiwar demonstrations may have played in the Wise Men's assessments of the public mood. It is at least possible that while antiwar demonstrations actually served to reinforce support for the war effort in the country at large, it may have had a different effect on that elite group of largely eastern liberals. The Wise Men, after all, held a deep cultural kinship with the social and intellectual points of origin of the antiwar movement, and may have been moved by the emotional engagement of the antiwar cause. If this was the case, then the antiwar movement may have had an effect on the conduct of the war at a crucial moment, not through public opinion as such but through images and interpretations of public opinion mediated through and within the political and moral calculations of a small but very important elite group.

Moreover, while the "domestic division" they had spoken of to President Johnson may have meant to them mainly opposition in Congress, in the Democratic

Party, and in the elite press, images of tens of thousands of America's youth protesting in the streets cannot have been entirely absent from their mind. Indeed, some of their own children were out there as they sat thinking and talking on March 25 and 26, 1968. In their counsel to the president, the Wise Men, therefore, may have functioned as connective tissue between the antiwar movement and U.S. policy in Southeast Asia. Even this cannot be proven, however, and it is still more likely that Johnson's Wise Men seized on domestic divisions, ill-defined at that, as a pretext to change course; a change whose real reasons were more substantive.[26]

In any case, President Johnson's speech of March 31 changed the basic terms of reference for both the war and the antiwar movement. As for the public at large, the March 31 speech triggered dramatic shifts in opinion, as noted in Chapter 1. For example, by April 28, 1968, those who called themselves hawks on Vietnam stood at 41 percent; doves were at 41 percent, and those with no opinion had risen to 18 percent. President Johnson's "disapproval" rating rose to 52 percent in the September 4 Gallup poll. The data show, simply and plainly, that the American people followed their leaders—away from war in 1968 just as they had followed President Johnson toward war in 1964 and 1965. Whatever the Wise Men or Lyndon Johnson were thinking and saying to one another throughout February and March 1968, it was the president's decision that decisively changed the flow of public opinion, *not the other way around*. Certainly, the word from the White House was far more important than anything going on in the streets, which brings us to the second half of our 1968 portrait: developments in the antiwar movement.

## THE MOVEMENT GOES CRAZY:
## MOTHERFUCKERS AND MAYHEM IN BOULDER

By 1968, the inner escalatory logic of the New Left–led antiwar movement drove it to a spasm of nihilism and braggadocio. The specter of open dissent, evident confusion, and ultimately retrenchment in the Johnson administration in the aftermath of the Tet offensive was a key development. Johnson's reversal of course reshaped definitively the coming presidential election in November, but the emergence of new political possibilities fed the antiwar movement's frothing imagination and hence also its tendency toward self-destruction. As noted earlier, the presidential campaigns of first Eugene McCarthy and later of Robert F. Kennedy were very important in this latter regard. The McCarthy and Kennedy candidacies had their sources in the increasingly immoderate but still not fully radicalized Left-Liberal establishment, not in the seemingly burgeoning minions of the New Left. Despite Tom Hayden's appearance at Robert Kennedy's funeral, a gesture that struck many observers as a bit bizarre, the New Left vociferously opposed both candidacies.[27]

New Left tactics adopted in 1968 were politically nihilistic, increasingly violent, and overwhelmingly counterproductive both to the New Left and to stopping the war. The year 1968 represented the beginning of the self-destruction of the New Left, even though it appeared at the time to those within and those without to have reached a new zenith of influence and growth. In that year the New Left was a sparkling meteor, bright and astonishing, and its leadership was convinced that it stood on the cusp of revolution. But like all meteors made brilliant to the eye by crashing to earth, it did not last long.[28]

The tactics adopted by the New Left were directed less against the administration or the Democratic Party as such than against those parts of the antiwar movement that preached, practiced, or contemplated moderation. As far as the New Left was concerned, that was pretty much all of the antiwar movement, both hated liberals and detested sectarian Leftists. After the renegade SDS action at the Pentagon, old hands within the movement were anxious about future SDS participation. SWP leader Fred Halstead and the other Trotskyites were particularly alarmed: They saw the agitated state of the country as an opportunity to create a national front on a fully nationwide basis, and they knew that civil disobedience, planned violence, and open obscenity would hurt the effort. Sidney Peck was of a similar view.

The only real ally that SDS had in the core leadership was David Dellinger, who did his best to bring SDS and the counterculture along with him. "This was one of the most uphill fights I had to make," Dellinger later said. "All the traditional people, the ones who had been in the longest, were saying we shouldn't do it, and I went the other way with a lot of the younger, newer people. And to get there and find all those people confirmed my feeling that the older people were wrong in their prediction."[29] As David Farber put it, Dellinger "consciously tried to move the Mobe into a closer alliance with increasing numbers of young radicals who were using drugs and looking to the counterculture for insights into everyday life and changing consciousness."[30]

Dellinger was right about one thing at least: The rest of the Mobe tried to isolate him and his contingent of hippies. Abbie Hoffman once commented about being at a 1968 Mobe meeting: "We were treated like niggers, you know; we were irrelevant."[31] And isolated they became. As a result, SDS took itself out of the Mobe and essentially directed its own movement during 1968. Partly as a result, too, the pacifist organizations formed their own caucus on October 22, 1968, which they called the National Action Group (NAG). The results of what the New Left did that year dwarfed anything the old Mobe or new pacifist types could have thought of, and the damage it did to stopping the war was enormous.

What SDS and the New Left, led by Tom Hayden and colleague Rennie Davis and abetted by David Dellinger, tried to do at the Democratic National Convention in Chicago is well known and need not be repeated in detail here.[32] What is noteworthy is that Chicago was chosen as a site of mayhem by the radical side of the antiwar movement not to influence the convention to dump Hubert Humphrey and choose Eugene McCarthy, but to mock the entire affair. On the eve of the Chicago fiasco, Hayden said: "We are coming to Chicago to vomit on the 'politics of joy,' to expose the secret decisions, upset the night-club orgies, and face the Democratic Party with its illegitimacy and criminality. . . . The government of the United States is an outlaw institution under the control of war criminals."[33] Or, as Paul Krassner put it, "In the summer of 1968 a group of us went to Chicago to try to get a police permit for a revolution. . . . We didn't get a permit."[34]

As to what in fact happened in Chicago, it is true that the Chicago Police Department overreacted, but they would not have had a reason to act at all had Hayden and Davis not believed that they stood on the edge of a revolutionary upheaval and promoted the violence—something Hayden has always denied doing, but not very convincingly. Moreover, there had been ample warmups for Chicago: In the first half of 1968, there were over 200 major demonstrations on campuses, most accompanied by preplanned violence.

Other things had gone crazy too, besides New Left political tactics. As broader countercultural themes butted up against the more specific albeit illusory agenda of the New Left, they fed on each other to the point that no political program capable of discipline, inner stability, or even reason was possible. Paul Goodman, who wrote *Growing Up Absurd* in 1960,[35] was an anarchist and a patron saint of the counterculture, but by 1968 even he realized that something had gone terribly wrong. While trying to distinguish for his graduate students between careerism and a true professional calling, Goodman was astonished to hear his students tell him that there was no such thing as a true profession in a capitalist culture, that the "power structure made all the decisions," and the professional classes were merely well-paid lackeys of the ruling class. There was no need for experts, it was only important to be "human," and all good would follow. Wrote Goodman, in a paragraph that, not coincidentally, anticipated current deconstructionist fads:

> Suddenly I realized that they did not really believe that there was a nature of things. Somehow all functions could be reduced to interpersonal relations and power. There was no knowledge, only the sociology of knowledge. They had so well learned that physical and sociological research is subsidized and controlled for the benefit of the ruling class that they did not believe there was such a thing as the simple truth. To be required to learn something was a trap by which the young were put down and co-opted. Then I knew that I could not get through to them.[36]

Goodman had given his students his idealism and his ideas, but not his learning or his discipline. He had given them energy but no way to guide or control it. He told them that they had grown up absurd, and, in the end, they reacted by proving the point. By the time of his death in 1972, Goodman had become a critic of the counterculture and of the erosion of academic standards it generated.

The October 1968 national SDS convention illustrated vividly the distance that SDS and the student movement as a whole had traveled. The convention took place shortly after the upheavals that had rocked Columbia University earlier in the year—sit-ins, strikes, and demands against the university having largely to do with "neighborhood projects." SDS had been at the center of the Columbia events with Mark Rudd its charismatic spokesman, and the national attention SDS received from the Columbia events had buoyed its status on campuses across the country. But as before, increased notoriety, bringing with it a growing and increasingly diverse membership, was the victory that led to defeat.

The joining together of SDS and the counterculture produced some unusual products, so much so that the 1968 SDS convention was beyond control and almost beyond imagination to anyone not inured to the peculiarities of the youth political subculture. Factionalism, countercultural chemicals and obscenities, and countless other manias released in train were superabundant. Almost as soon as the convention began in Boulder, Colorado, the circus started. Two splinter groups, the Progressive Labor caucus and Up Against the Wall, Motherfuckers, or just Motherfuckers for short, went at each other with a vengeance.

Up Against the Wall, Motherfuckers was a small but strange group of self-styled anarchists mostly from the Lower East Side of New York City who advocated "armed love." They named themselves after a line taken from a LeRoi Jones poem.[37] (The next line, incidentally, is "This is a stick-up," and both were used in Mark Rudd's open letter to Columbia University president Grayson Kirk on April 22, 1968.) In proper anarchist jargon, the Motherfuckers described themselves as an affinity group, and in proper counterculture lingo as "a street gang with an analysis." Their aim, as self-described artists, was to destroy one-dimensional society and to prevent the use of art as a reinforcement of the status quo. Their heroes were Herbert Marcuse and that strand of European anarchists who held that there is no higher principle of social or intellectual organization than free association. Their official self-description included the following: "We defy law and order with our bricks, bottles, garbage, long hair, filth, obscenity, drugs, games, guns, bikes, fire, fun, and fucking."[38]

The Progressive Labor caucus, though nominally Maoists, was actually about as close to Stalinist as could then be found within SDS. Its members wore short hair, they did not "do" drugs, and they hoped to bring SDS as a whole more in line with a formal Marxist-Leninist platform—they succeeded the next year, as related later, but only to inherit the wind. They were very dogmatic about their revolutionary analysis; when reality did not fit their views, then it was so much the worse for reality. They were not Stalinist only in the sense that they were not loyal to the Soviet Union.

As the Progressive Labor caucus made its early move to grab the platform in Boulder, the Motherfuckers virtually tore the place apart. One of its members characterized the Progressive Labor position as "less exciting than a lukewarm fart in August." Headier language followed. Strange and obscene though they were, the Motherfuckers at least saw through the creeping authoritarian spirit within SDS. Reacting against the Progressive Labor "robots," one Motherfucker argued: "What I'm saying is it's bullshit, dig it, bullshit, to support repression anywhere. Dig. Look at Cuba, China. The German SDS had its conference in Yugoslavia—that's freedom? That's bullshit, man; you're all fucked up if you can support that in the name of internationalism." The "speech" went on for some time, ending with the suggestion that the PL caucus members go "get laid," "cool out," and "live, man."[39]

Again, in somewhat more temperate language, let us draw one last time from Tom Robbins. What the Motherfuckers were warning against was tunnel vision,

> a disease in which perception is restricted by ignorance and distorted by vested interest. Tunnel vision is caused by an optic fungus that multiplies when the brain is less energetic than the ego. It is complicated by exposure to politics. When a good idea is run through the filters and compressors of ordinary tunnel vision, it not only comes out reduced in scale and value but in its new dogmatic configuration produces effects the opposite of those for which it originally was intended. That is how the loving ideas of Jesus Christ became the sinister clichés of Christianity. That is why virtually every revolution in history has failed: the oppressed, as soon as they seize power, turn into oppressors, resorting to totalitarian tactics to "protect the revolution." That is why minorities seeking the abolition of prejudice become intolerant, minorities seeking peace become militant, minorities seeking equality become self-righteous, and minorities seeking liberation become hostile (a tight asshole being the first symptom of self-repression).[40]

Allowing for the natural excesses of fiction, this is really a pretty good description of what happened to SDS between about 1964 and 1969.

## THE 1968 ELECTION AND BEYOND

The shift in the Johnson administration's position after Tet did not effect directly the central ideological cleavages within the antiwar movement itself, but Eugene McCarthy's peace candidacy did stir things up quite a bit. The antiwar movement as a whole divided over whether to support McCarthy. Left-Liberals were supportive, if not of McCarthy, then of Robert Kennedy who soon joined the fray after McCarthy successfully tested the water. The core of the New Left and the other more radical segments of the movement, recently emboldened by what it took to be its toppling of Lyndon Johnson, argued that opposing the war through the mechanism of the Democratic Party would bring about the bourgeoisization of the revolution and ultimate capitulation.[41] They were now very far indeed from SDS's 1964 election slogan: "Part of the way with LBJ." But many people who had been drifting toward the Left were enticed by McCarthy. The McCarthy phenomenon clearly acted as a brake on the leftward trajectory of the antiwar movement as a whole, although not on that of the inner core or SDS. In short, the McCarthy and Kennedy candidacies had the effect of polarizing the movement by forcing a choice between an inside-the-system and an against-the-system tactic.

Partly to blunt the McCarthy challenge inside the movement, radical tactics in 1968 increased in intensity with each passing day. The Democratic National Convention in Chicago was only the most dramatic event of the year, but from Tet to the November election, escalating radical protest tactics became the norm. Destroying draft records was a favorite activity, as the notoriety of the Catonsville 9 and the Milwaukee 14 showed.[42] Tom Hayden also had come to believe that the sheer nuisance value of radical actions might be a way to actually stop the war, but in addition he wanted to create a mass-based revolutionary party. But this was an election year and its results proved Hayden flat wrong about the utility of radical tactics. Rather, radical protest helped put Richard Nixon into the White House over Hubert Humphrey by delivering to Nixon, the 1950s symbol of anti–New Deal policies, the backlash vote of the those who had been the major beneficiaries and supporters of New Deal legislation, the white middle- and lower-middle class.

This came about partly because Nixon and Humphrey were not the only ones running. Governor George Wallace of Alabama was in the race too, and in retrospect, the Wallace vote clearly hurt Humphrey in southern states that at that time traditionally voted Democratic. Wallace prospered from the antiblack and anti-desegregationist backlash in the South and also from antiradical sentiment with which it had become associated in voters' minds. At every whistle stop on his campaign, Wallace used to say things such as: "If any long-haired hippie gets down in front of my presidential limo to protest, that'll be the last car he ever gets down in front of, I can promise you that." Most of the time, the applause for such statements was vigorous and spirited. The Republicans sent out vice presidential nominee Spiro Agnew, governor of Maryland, to steal Wallace's thunder, and the competition between the Nixon and Wallace camps for the so-called hard-hat vote gave the presidential race a decidedly mean spirit.

There is really no room for doubt that the backlash against the antiwar movement contributed to Nixon's victory. Gitlin's observation about the Chicago riots is worth repeating in part: "As unpopular as the war had become, the antiwar movement was detested still more—the most hated political group in America, *disliked even by most of the people who supported immediate withdrawal from Vietnam.*"[43]

Yes, the New Left helped put Richard Nixon in the White House. It thwarted the election of a member of a Democratic Party already three-quarters turned against staying the course in Vietnam, but still determined to seek an honorable exit with the least amount of general damage to U.S. foreign policy. The New Left, by systematically trashing Humphrey's campaign, thus helped to prolong the war and prolong the killing, for a Humphrey administration almost surely would have effected a faster withdrawal than the Nixon administration did.

Moreover, not only would a Humphrey administration have wound down the war quicker, it also would have stood a better chance of preventing the fall of Saigon in March 1975. Given the natural interests of a Democratic administration dealing with a Democratic majority in the Congress, Humphrey probably would have found it much easier than Nixon to persuade the Congress to back South Vietnam. As president, Humphrey would have come to the task without having invaded Cambodia and without Watergate too. Had Humphrey been elected, it is likely that not only would the U.S. role in the war have ended sooner, but that South Vietnam would not have been ripe for the plucking in 1975 and thus would not have fallen.

The 1968 election results should have made it clear that radical antiwar activism was not increasingly effective even though antiwar sentiment in the country was becoming larger and potentially more effective, and part of the reason clearly was the excesses of the countercultural New Left. Not only did Richard Nixon win the White House, not only did George Wallace's successes outside the South stun northern liberals, but the two earliest and most vocal opponents of the war in the Senate, Ernst Gruening and Wayne Morse, both lost their seats. But some antiwar radicals and their supporters among the literati just did not get the message. Norman Mailer, for one, thought everything was fine in the fall of 1968, lauding what he called "the new Nixon." As a result of thinking like this, the 1968 Democratic Party convention fiasco and the subsequent disarray in the party after Humphrey's defeat opened forever wide the rift in the antiwar movement.

The "masses" of the antiwar movement, as opposed to the core of radicals in SDS, had looked kindly on Senator McCarthy's candidacy. Many who had gone "clean for Gene" subsequently expressed their activism through the defeated and newly reconstituted Democratic Party.[44] The core of Left-Liberal establishment support that had stood behind the antiwar movement from the beginning also applauded and greatly aided this direction. But the radical inner core of SDS turned to yet *increased* radicalism and some turned all the way to terrorism in the form of the Weather Underground. Still others took a scenic para-religious course, dropping out of politics for cults or personal hedonism. The scene was set, in other words, for a breakup, and then a breakdown of the New Left.

## SDS'S LAST GASP

The split in the antiwar movement precipitated by the McCarthy campaign and the relative radicalization of the defeated Democratic Party were both evident by early 1969. The Democrats lost the election but the McCarthy candidacy had turned the tide against the increasing radicalization of the antiwar movement. Indeed, initially many SDSers had opposed coming to Chicago for fear that the hated Clean for Gene movement might co-opt many fringe members of the radical camp. In a way, their fears proved justified. The radicals argued over what was going wrong; numerous new factions emerged as infighting wracked organizational capacities on various levels. The movement was particularly ill-prepared for the new Nixon administration's assault on the Left that led to the famous Chicago Seven (eight, if one includes Bobby Seale) conspiracy trial. When the Justice Department indicted David Dellinger, Tom Hayden, and the others, initially there were no organized protests.

The advanced decay and radicalization of SDS was illustrated particularly well by what happened at the 1969 SDS national convention. The 1968 SDS convention was wild but also somewhat humorous, the humor partly a function of a diffuse optimism and headiness about the movement and its influence. The 1969 SDS convention was wild too, but wild and sad. Idealism generally dies a painful death; SDS's was no exception.

By June of 1969, when an SDS convention convened in, of all places, Chicago, factionalism had proliferated almost beyond imagination. To the Motherfuckers were now added the Crazies and the Mad Dogs; both were arrayed against the grim-faced "straights" of the Progressive Labor caucus. But in 1969, unlike in 1968, the "center" of SDS also had collapsed and was divided against itself. The so-called National Office faction was divided into "groupuscles" such as the Klonsky-Coleman. There was also the San Francisco Bay Area Revolutionary Union and other regional groupings that did not appear to have a clear ideological point of view. Black nationalists were also present; so, for the first time, were independently grouped feminist caucuses.

After a day and a half of general lunacy and vitriolic speeches, the main battle lines finally emerged. On the one side was the Progressive Labor caucus, and on the other was a National Office faction led by Bernadine Dohrn and fronting a document entitled "You Don't Need a Weathervane to Know Which Way the Wind Blows" after a Bob Dylan lyric. (While this was going on, most of the Motherfuckers and the Crazies were reportedly too stoned to move.) It called, essentially, for the creation of urban guerrilla lines behind the "front" with the Black Panther Party as the revolutionary vanguard force. Dohrn's views were no secret. On hearing of the murders of actress Sharon Tate and her friends by Charles Manson and his "family," this is what Dohrn had to say: "Dig! First they killed those pigs, then they ate dinner in the same room with them, and they even shoved a fork into a victim's stomach. Wild!"[45] Manson himself was much subtler: "Death is psychosomatic," he said.[46]

A struggle for the platform ensued; Progressive Labor won, marshalling its discipline and making best use of its democratic centralist tendencies. In other words, it organized ruthlessly and it lied shamelessly. PL spoke insincerely of participatory democracy and tried to steal New Left slogans for vanguardish uses, just as the Bolsheviks stole anarchist slogans in 1917 for similar purposes.[47]

Ironically, it was precisely this kind of internal putsch that SDS believers in participatory democracy thought had been made impossible by the organization's decentralization. Oglesby had said that "it is hard to see how a group could be 'taken over' unless it has handles of power that can be seized, some 'central apparatus' that can enforce order."[48] He was wrong.

PL's victory was aided, ironically considering Dohrn's role, by some especially maladroit remarks made by her Black Panther allies about women. After a day of backroom meetings, Dohrn led the majority of the delegates out of the hall to form their own new convention. They called themselves the Revolutionary Youth Movement (RYM), a term originating with SDS president Michael Klonsky. But the ultra-left Weatherman National Office faction led by Dohrn soon broke away from the RYM and turned immediately to experiments in high explosives and bank robbery.[49] This was, after all, the year in which Warren Beatty and Fay Dunaway rose to countercultural fame in *Bonnie and Clyde,* an extremely violent film in which the most memorable line was: "We rob banks."

Dohrn's walkout prompted in turn a reorganization of the more conventional left-wing groups, who went on to form RYM-II.[50] After that, things really got complicated. But the simple point is nevertheless clear: SDS had committed suicide. The original founders, those from Port Huron days, could hardly believe their eyes. As Gitlin put it: "How could the organization that began by echoing Albert Camus and C. Wright Mills end with one faction chanting 'Ho Ho Ho Chi Minh, Dare to Struggle, Dare to Win' while members of the other waved their Little Red Books in the air and chanted 'Mao, Mao, Mao Tse-tung'? The comic-book crudeness of the sloganeering . . . was self-evident to anyone with a residual hold on reality."[51] The trouble was that there were not many people with a residual hold on reality left: the idealistic, anarchistic, and broadly cultural approach of the early New Left had turned into the dogmatic, statist, and narrowly political latter-day New Left. What were the reasons?

Some argue that the failure to stop the war is mainly what led to the increasing frustrations that turned youthful radicalism in more organizationally pointed directions. While this was perhaps true to some degree, this explanation fails to account for why the majority of young radicals did not become Marxist-Leninists or Weathermen. Some believe that such latter-day views were inherent in the original ideas of the Port Huron statement. There is doubtless some truth to this too; what Hayden wrought in June 1962 was grab-bag anti-establishmentarianism that evolved to the Left in ways that could not have been entirely predictable.

But another less often noted reason is that participatory democracy, and the generally non-judgmental ethos of the original New Left, did not provide a sound defense against vanguardist sectarian Leftists like those in PL and the SWP. It is really too much to expect that tens of thousands of hours of meetings over the years between fuzzy and impressionable young New Left radicals and sectarian Marxist-Leninists, who argued from a far more practiced viewpoint, had no cumulative effect. The headiness of the times and the increasingly "hip" quality of radical sectarian ideas as time went on all took their toll, and this is not to speak of the additional organizational influence of members of the old Left such as Sidney Peck, Fred Halstead, Sidney Lens, and others. This does not mean that the old Left "used" young radicals of the mid-1960s SDS. Rather, the formlessness of their ideas and their organization led at least a substantial minority toward generally kindred ideas with more shape, and ideas advanced by disciplined believers who had always demonstrated more patience and tactical subtlety than had SDSers. In a way, it was a function of attrition.

Sometimes, admittedly, it also worked the other way, with the counterculture stealing the serious Leftist. Jerry Rubin was a prime example. In 1964 Rubin toured Cuba for two months courtesy of the Progressive Labor Party. He later said: "This was the final step for me. . . . I started to see things the way the Cubans did."[52] Rubin's plunge into the bizarre ways of the Yippies came later after his encounter with drugs; Rubin did not smoke marijuana until he was 28 years old, and first took LSD even later on, in 1967.[53]

Thus SDS officially became a Marxist-Leninist party only after it no longer mattered, after SDS had imploded and after the larger Left movement of which it was a part had fractured and dissipated as well. In this sense one might say that while PL inherited SDS, the counterculture in the end absorbed and then suffocated the New Left. The anarchist elements in 1960s radicalism were always more appealing to the majority than the ascetic, statist dimensions of the sectarian Left.[54] The personal roots of New Left radicalism, the "I" focus of the revolution, made what there was of a programmatic dimension of the New Left unsustainable. As Jimi Hendrix put it in "The Wind Cries Mary"—undoubtedly with something else in mind—castles made out of sand do fall into the sea, and it usually doesn't take long.

After the implosion, many radical movement members were now moving toward new lifestyles rather than new political constituencies, toward political communes and collectives rather than parties and coalitions.[55] The eclipsed right wing of the movement, on the other hand, less burnt out and less manic than the radical Left, stayed around and, in time, picked up what remained of the movement. This didn't happen all at once, of course, and at the time is was not clear that it was happening at all—it never is. As John Kenneth Galbraith once put it with regard to the onset of the Great Depression, the end had come but it is not yet in sight. Just as the lines of left and right wings of the movement crossed toward the Left in 1965, so they crossed back again in 1969. It is to that year, and the entrance in earnest of Richard Nixon, that we now turn.

## ANTIWAR CLASS OF '69: MORATORIUM AND MOBE

Nineteen sixty-eight had been a terrible year in more ways than one. Given what went on in the United States—the assassinations of Martin Luther King, Jr., and Robert F. Kennedy, the disaster in Chicago, and the rest—it was almost easy to forget that things had not gone well in Vietnam either. In the end, the Tet offensive was indeed a military disaster for the Vietcong, but the price to Americans seemed so large that few seemed to care.

By the end of 1968, nearly another 15,000 Americans had been killed in action, the largest yearly figure yet, bringing the grand total by the time of Richard Nixon's inauguration to more than 30,700 dead. Increasingly, too, draftees, as opposed to regular army troops, were doing most of the dying, speeding the flow of dissent against the war back home in the most direct and emotionally taxing way imaginable.[56] There were 536,000 U.S. soldiers in South Vietnam by year's end. By these measures, at least—and they were hardly insignificant ones—the antiwar movement had stopped nothing.

After Lyndon Johnson's March 31 speech, what amounted to a lame duck Johnson administration did not fight the rising flow of opposition very hard; it was caught up in a general sense of exhaustion, frustration, and drift. Partly as a consequence, popular sentiment against the war grew rapidly, as was reflected in popular culture, once again, in the music.

The greatest musical heroes of the era, the Beatles, moved through all the stages of politicization from apolitical adolescence to the counterculture to cultural revolution. John Lennon led the way and along with him were pulled many millions of young fans via the deliberately psychedelic *Sgt. Pepper's* album. "Give Peace a Chance," a later Lennon composition, quickly became a kind of general antiwar anthem, replacing the more folky standards of earlier years. By 1968, then, even the Beatles had gotten political but, suggestively, only *after* they had gotten stoned.

So widespread was antiwar sentiment that genres of music other than rock were also now expressing antiwar views. Motown Records artists were also dabbling with political lyrics. "We don't need to escalate" sang Marvin Gaye in his song "What's Goin' On." "War, uh! What is it good for? Absolutely nothin'" sang Edwin Starr in a widely played AM-radio hit.

The quintessence of rock music as a combination of instant community, instant political wisdom, and drugs was, of course, the famous Woodstock rock festival in the summer of 1969. Woodstock has acquired an almost deified status among much of the 1960s generation and those that came after too, an attenuated modern equivalent of the Exodus from Egypt or the Immaculate Conception. Country Joe and the Fish were there for starters, but even Crosby, Stills, and Nash, at that point not yet a particularly political band,[57] joined the fracas, with Graham Nash, a British national formerly from the band The Hollies, urging the crowd in the song "Chicago" to go to Chicago in support of the Conspiracy—the trial of the Chicago Seven—and advising them further and more generally to throw "rules and regulations . . . out the door."

Meanwhile, as the New Left lay dying of its self-inflicted wounds while the Woodstock Nation sang along, both older hands and new tried to pick up the pieces of the antiwar movement. On the Left the old guard of professional adversary culture activists, Trotskyites, new pacifists hyperradicalized by the antiwar movement experience, and former liberals enthralled by the seeming heroism of radical action went back to work. The New Mobilization Committee to End the War in Vietnam, heir to the National Mobilization Committee, fell into the hands of David Dellinger and Rennie Davis, one of many SDS refugees in the New Mobe.

They first planned the "Counterinaugural," meant to coincide with Richard Nixon's inauguration as president on January 19, 1969. It was a countercultural fest punctuated by modest violence and proportionately modest arrests. It planned deliberate outrage with upside-down American flags and greased squealing pigs named "Richard Nixon." It was a failure, however. Fewer than 10,000 people came and many just watched, not knowing quite what to make of the spectacle. A few months later the Student Mobe, having been seized by the Trotskyite YSA, the vanguard within the vanguard, planned a national student strike for April 5-6. It too flopped.

Times were suddenly much harder for antiwar movement radicals. The siege of Chicago and the McCarthy campaign, each in their own way, had isolated the left-wing of the movement. Moreover, the new Nixon administration's Justice Department soon busied itself irritating the movement's leadership with arrest, surveillance, and, in the case of the Black Panthers, direct attack. Assistant Attorney General Will R. Wilson announced that by December 1969, draft resisters were being prosecuted at 12 times the rate that occurred during the Johnson administration.[58]

Despite the doldrums of the radical movement in its post-Chicago phase, David Dellinger began the process of planning its next major national protests. But as an organizer, Dellinger was no A. J. Muste or Sidney Peck, and his efforts languished. Dellinger thought that the Mobe should organize itself around the Conspiracy, a deliberately ambiguous term referring simultaneously to the upcoming trial of the Chicago Seven, who had been indicted in March, and to what they viewed as the nature of the U.S. government. Rennie Davis, one of the indicted, thought the same.[59] In other words, at a time when the Mobe needed to reduce its isolation to be effective after Chicago, Dellinger and his increasingly famous "kids" were glorifying what happened there: "the will of the people was so overwhelmingly nonviolent, I couldn't believe it," said Dellinger. "It was absolutely inspiring."[60] Even many longtime fellow activists wondered what planet Dellinger had been on lately.

The end of Dellinger's brief organizational stewardship came in the early spring of 1969 at the annual Fifth Avenue Peace Parade in New York. At that parade Dellinger broke his word to the other Mobe principals by allowing Jerry Rubin and Abbie Hoffman to address the crowd. Both tried to incite the Crazies to attack the police. Dellinger claimed that he had not known about this beforehand and averred that it had bothered him quite a lot, but few of the other organizers believed him given his long and checkered track record on such matters. So in May, after the Easter debacle, the Mobe turned once again to Sidney Peck, who called for a meeting in Cleveland in July.

As the radicals fell into a funk, the liberal right wing of the antiwar movement was beginning to reemerge, not so much through SANE or other established organizations of the Left-Liberal pantheon, but more through a new project of the Clean for Gene organizers and their youthful cohorts. In the early spring, the youth coordinators of the McCarthy campaign, assisted by SANE, the ADA, and especially Allard K. Lowenstein, formed the Vietnam Moratorium Committee.[61] The Moratorium Committee was based initially on the idea of a national strike, which was the brainchild of Jerome Grossman of MassPax—since evolved into the Council for a Liveable World. The idea was fairly simple: Grossman called for a one day national strike on October 8, 1969, if all U.S. troops were not withdrawn by then. Then, in early November, there would be another strike, this one for two days. And so on, adding one day of strike per month until either the war ended or the economy stopped.

Grossman's own group thought that a general strike was too radical an idea. Besides, some observed, if the strike died before the Nixon administration buckled, as was thought likely, that would prove the administration's case that a majority of Americans was not opposed to the war after all. Grossman did not give up, however, and decided to shop the idea to people he knew from the McCarthy campaign. One of those he called was Lowenstein.

Lowenstein had been instrumental in keeping the McCarthy workers together, even without McCarthy, after the 1968 campaign. Still working from the Dump Johnson premise of November 1966—namely, that unless liberals opposed the war, opposition to it would drift toward counterproductive political extremism—he had put together a group of 253 college newspaper editors to support nonradical opposition to the war. By April 1969, with the help of Sam Brown and David Hawk of the McCarthy campaign, Lowenstein arranged a meeting between these editors and National Security Advisor Henry Kissinger. The meeting did not go very well; Kissinger was collegial but not persuasive. Remarks made to the group by John Erlichman, Nixon's domestic affairs advisor, left most of them with an eerie feeling. But Hawk and Brown left the meeting determined to use the network Lowenstein had put together. A few days later, at Lowenstein's suggestion, Jerome Grossman called Brown, whom he had met through the McCarthy campaign, to ask him what he thought of the idea of a national strike.[62] Brown was noncommittal until MassPax dangled $25,000 in front of him. Hawk changed "National Strike" to "Vietnam Moratorium" and within a few weeks the two opened an office on Vermont Avenue. They picked October 15, 1969, as a target date.[63]

The Moratorium Committee and the New Mobe represented the two basic wings of the antiwar movement as of 1969. Their activities early in the year epitomized their essential differences.

The Moratorium sought an opening toward broad establishment opinion and to Nixon's "silent majority" and the Congress. The Mobe, while it remained under Dellinger's hand, sought conspiracy and fronted the counterculture. The two groups nevertheless soon found themselves in a sometimes congenial, sometimes cold embrace. Unlike the period after 1965, when no cooperation on the planning level between the liberal and radical wings of the movement occurred, this time the two organizations agreed to work together. The cooperation was uneasy but it endured because there were pragmatic reasons for it, the main one being that Sidney Peck, once he returned to his central leadership position, saw the Moratorium as a "way back" for the weakened Mobe. He saw it as yet another opening to the Right, albeit of a different, more limited sort. The professional old Left radicals—as opposed to Dellinger and his delusions—had been chastened by the experience of 1968 and understood that they were no longer the majority force in the movement. Also, with SDS practically out of business, Peck hoped that the way was clear for the reassertion of calmer and more orthodox hands.

Also very important, the Left-Liberal groups were now far more radical than they had been before the Vietnam experience. Indeed, SANE's agreement to go along with the cooperative arrangement between Moratorium and Mobe reflected its leadership's acknowledgment that its rank and file was now more radical than the leadership. Thus, while the radical core could not hold itself together, it had succeeded in winning over ideologically much of the right wing of the movement. Specifically with regard to Vietnam, by early 1969 young liberals were pushing for complete and immediate U.S. military withdrawal, a position beyond that adopted by congressional opinion in years to come, even in its more adamant, anti-Nixon mood. Yet, organizationally speaking, it was the Mobe that sought the organizing shelter of the Moratorium.

The October Moratorium, it was decided, would be a series of nationally coordinated local events. The essential idea—really its genius—was to develop a way that allowed and encouraged ordinary people all over the country to participate in an "action" against the war without having to travel anywhere, without having to break the law, and without having to be seen in the company of others who were breaking the law, waving Vietcong banners, or shouting obscenities at police. The Moratorium turned out to be a tremendous success; it truly was an opening to the Right. The reasons for its success are worth reviewing.

First, the Moratorium clearly played on the tension that ordinary people felt at the time about Vietnam. Increasing numbers of Americans had resigned themselves to withdrawal, largely on account of the "follower" mentality discussed earlier.[64] On March 31, 1968, a decision had been made that—while it technically meant only a halt in military escalation and not a withdrawal—communicated to the American people that winning the war was no longer the principal U.S. purpose in Southeast Asia.

That decision too, was essentially confirmed as far as most people were concerned by the rhetoric and early policies of the Nixon administration. This rhetoric did exactly what it was intended to do: salve the public mood. A March 30, 1969, Gallup poll gave Richard Nixon an approval rating of 65 percent, to only 9 percent opposed (and 26 percent undecided). Even more dramatic, Nixon gave a major speech on Vietnam on November 3, 1969, emphasizing Vietnamization and negotiations—his "secret plan." The next day Gallup tried to find out what those who watched the speech thought. Nixon's approval to disapproval rating had climbed to 77 percent to 6 percent, with 17 percent undecided. Even though doves now outnumbered hawks in Gallup surveys (55 percent to 31 percent on November 13, 1969), Richard Nixon was a popular president. This could only be because the majority somehow identified Nixon as a dove on Vietnam relative to what had come before. It certainly was not because the American people believed that Vietnamization could save South Vietnam. At no time from 1966 to 1972 does any polling data whatsoever exhibit confidence that the South Vietnamese could defend themselves alone or produce a stable government if left to their own devices.[65]

But from the right wing of the antiwar movement there came the clarion warning: If the United States was planning to withdraw most of its forces and turn matters over to the South Vietnamese, then why were so many young Americans still dying? This point tapped into a growing sentiment in the population at large, which asked: If the United States was going to get out of Vietnam, why not get out now? If victory was not the goal, why spend lives on something less?

This point cannot be emphasized too much. The new pervasiveness of antiwar attitudes in the country at large *followed* President Johnson's speech of March 31, 1968, as the data presented earlier show. In early 1970, for example, given a choice between withdrawal now or at a more gradual pace, Gallup counted 35 percent in favor of immediate withdrawal and 55 percent in favor of a more gradual process. The larger percentage willing to countenance slower withdrawal probably reflected the judgment that a government that admitted to having made a mistake was again to be trusted at least a little, and if that penitent government believed that winning the peace if not the war would take more time, then so be it.

The more important point, however, is that together those in favor of withdrawal added to 90 percent. "The swing of opinion against the war," wrote historian Godfrey Hodgson, "did not mean that the peace movement had succeeded in achieving its dream of mass conversion. It reflected the cannily realistic judgment that winning the war didn't seem to be worth the price,"[66] precisely what the nation understood from Lyndon Johnson's March 31 speech.[67] The right wing of the antiwar movement capitalized on this transformation of attitude about the war, and tried now to speed withdrawal by changing the ratio between those who favored immediate withdrawal and those who elected a slower pace with more conditions. That is what the Moratorium was all about.

Normal politics helped advance this aim too. Nixon's initial popularity was vulnerable to a new constellation of partisan politics. Once the war had become a Republican war, the liberal Democratic center that had declined to oppose a sitting president from its own party went after Richard Nixon with a hearty partisan passion.[68] Humphrey, Senator Edmund Muskie, Averell Harriman, Congressman Stewart Udall, Arthur Goldburg, and dozens of others who had served the Johnson administration in positions of confidence supported and even sponsored the Moratorium. With such big names on board, others who had been reluctant heretofore to criticize the war publicly—businessmen, union officials, newspaper editors—were now encouraged to do so. Money therefore began to roll in, allowing that little office on Vermont Avenue to spend over $700,000 in six months and still end up with a positive balance in the bank.

The Mobe helped too. By persuading its far-flung network of local radicals to mainstream their protests, the Mobe was instrumental in helping build a grass-roots level of support for the Moratorium. Indeed, the Mobe took out office space in the same building on Vermont Avenue to be near the action and the "smell of the money," as one Moratorium worker subsequently put it. The groups worked so closely that on October 5, the *New York Times* stated that the Mobe and the Moratorium had "joined forces."[69]

The liaison between the Moratorium and the Mobe was epitomized by what David Hawk called the Stewart Meacham Express. Meacham had been the American Friends Service Committee representative within the Mobe since the middle of 1966; his title there was "national peace secretary." More important than Meacham's title was his role within the antiwar movement as the representative of the National Action Group (NAG), the pacifist caucus formed in October 1968. Meacham organized joint Moratorium-Mobe teams to visit a number of cities to bring to life antiwar groups and knit together their radical and Left-Liberal wings. On occasion, the team brought money with them, which helped their efforts a great deal. As Sidney Lens subsequently put it, in many smaller cities "the Mobe *was* the moratorium."[70]

While the Mobe took an interest in the Moratorium, the Moratorium also took an interest of sorts in the Mobe, which still pressed on in planning its own separate calendar for 1969. When Peck accepted the Mobe's organizational burden once more, it was not only Dellinger's behavior that concerned him, but also the man who had asked him to do so: Fred Halstead of the Socialist Workers Party.

Peck was very much aware of what the PL caucus had done to SDS and of what YSA had done to the Student Mobe. SWP tactics led Peck to claim subsequently that he preferred dealing with old Left "straight" Communists than to dealing with either the Maoist or the Troskyite variety because the latter were both permanently and pathologically organized. They always said the same thing in unison and voted in a bloc; they stayed later at meetings than any of the other groups and by doing so often inherited a greater share of decision power.

Peck decided that the Cleveland meeting would not be "open," lest the SWP "stack and pack" the proceedings, but invitational. Peck assembled a "steering committee" that reflected his concern, giving as little ground to Halstead as he thought necessary. It included: Norma Becker, representing the Fifth Avenue Parade Committee and also, in effect, the WRL; Barbara Bick, WSP; Rennie Davis, SDS; Dellinger, *Liberation* magazine and the Conspiracy; Douglas Dowd from Cornell University; Al Evanoff, representing District 65 of the Retail, Wholesale, and Department Store Workers; Richard Fernandez of Clergy and Laity Concerned; Jerry Gordon, co-chair with Peck of the Cleveland Area Peace Action Council and a SWP ally of Halstead; Halstead himself; Arnold Johnson of the U.S. Communist Party; Donald Kalish of UCLA; Sidney Lens representing the Chicago Peace Council; John McAuliff of the Committee of Returned Volunteers (Peace Corps); Stewart Meacham; Peck; Maxwell Primack of the Chicago Peace Council; Carl Rogers of the Committee for the Presidio 27; Irving Sarnoff of the Los Angeles Peace Council; and Cora Weiss from WSP.

Having developed some confidence in this group, which clearly tilted more toward old Left directions than New Left ones, Peck agreed to allow others to come, not as delegates, but as observers. Very quickly, the YSA-dominated Student Mobe decided to hold a meeting in Cleveland at the same time to "crash" Peck's invitation-only party. They demanded delegate status but were refused save for one additional steering committee member, Carol Lipman.

There were heated arguments as to what the Mobe should plan to do. The first major dispute started with Dellinger, who brought Mark Rudd and Kathy Boudin of the Weathermen to a meeting, demanding that the Mobe line up behind what amounted to a civil insurrection in Chicago to coincide with the opening of the Chicago Seven conspiracy trial. Peck disagreed as did, of course, Halstead and his friends. The SWP proposed instead a mass demonstration without civil disobedience or preplanned violence. There was no agreement; eventually, after hours of bickering, the steering committee ended up accepting Lens's suggestion that the Mobe do both.

Peck had expected trouble from Dellinger and had taken the precaution of inviting David Hawk to Cleveland as an observer, just in case. Hawk became, in effect, an additional member of the steering committee as the arguments became protracted. In the end, the conference agreed to support the October 15 Moratorium, a November 15 Mobilization demonstration in Washington and San Francisco, as well as a Chicago "action," provided that the groups that had already commenced their preparation would "collaborate on tactics" with the steering committee. This meant essentially submitting to Peck's authority and scrapping deliberate plans to break the law.

The battle was not over, however; chairmen had to be chosen to manage each of the three actions. This occasioned more infighting, with the SWP trying to isolate Peck by getting him to work on the Chicago action, thus throwing Peck and

Dellinger together and leaving the other two actions open for easier penetration. But Halstead ultimately failed when at the last minute Peck traded Chicago to hometowner Sidney Lens for Washington, so to speak.[71]

In any event, despite the divisiveness of the renamed "New" Mobe, it did at least hang together, while SDS had not. More impressive than that, it managed simultaneously to maintain its nonexclusionary policies and still find an opening to the Right, and to control if not defeat the Trotskyites and the New Left/new pacifism alliance of Dellinger and Rennie Davis. It was testimony to the skill of cool old Left heads among the likes of new style radicals like Dellinger and Davis that it could do this. By no account was it easy.

## VANGUARDISM, VEXATION, AND VIOLENCE

The first of the three events to take place was the Chicago "action" on October 8, 1969—the infamous Days of Rage. Not surprisingly, SDS, which was now in the process of being reduced more or less to the Weathermen, had refused Peck's conditions for the Mobe's endorsement. Essentially, the Weathermen rump of SDS had wanted to do what it wanted to do, and wanted the Mobe to pay for it. Peck refused and the Weathermen wrote a derisive letter in response, calling the Mobe the "twice-yearly Sunday afternoon antiwar movement" and stating sarcastically that it "declined their offer of support."[72]

Only a few hundred people showed up for the Days of Rage, not the thousands that Mark Rudd had predicted. Tom Hayden and Bernadine Dohrn spoke briefly, after which the crowd went on a rampage smashing windows, assaulting bystanders, attacking police, and, of course, getting arrested. The Weathermen had expected much help from their Black Panther allies but the Panthers stayed away. A Panther leader in Chicago, Fred Hampton, later referred to the action as "Custeristic." They nevertheless took the opportunity to seek out and beat up Rudd, still famous from Columbia student revolt days, who had run away. It was hard to claim that Rudd did not deserve it; he had told a December 1969 Weathermen gathering in Flint, Michigan, that: "It's a wonderful feeling to hit a pig. It must be a really wonderful feeling to kill a pig or blow up a building."[73]

Next came the Moratorium on October 15. Estimates of participation in mass demonstrations always vary, but over a million people probably participated in the Moratorium in one way or another. The largest crowds, interestingly enough, formed in places that had not become accustomed to demonstrations, while in New York, Berkeley, and Washington, the crowds were a bit thinner. Even so, they were more socially diverse than ever. Again, some of the music in Washington that day illustrates the point.

Earl Scruggs is a legendary five-string banjo player born in North Carolina in January 1924. Scruggs revolutionized bluegrass music in the company of its founder, Bill Monroe, in the late 1940s with his new style of playing. In the 1950s, after Scruggs and guitar player and vocalist Lester Flatt left Monroe's Bluegrass Boys to form Flatt & Scruggs, they helped popularize bluegrass nationwide through several national television appearances. Then Scruggs's theme song, "Foggy Mountain Breakdown," became the title track to the movie *Bonnie and Clyde,* and the group also provided the theme music for the television show *The Beverly Hillbillies.*

Southern folk music was associated in the minds of most young northern Americans with stock southern political attitudes: racism, patriotism, and passivity in the face of foreign policy issues. This is why it was so striking when Scruggs showed up with his son, Randy, at the Moratorium in Washington to play for the crowd. Few in the audience recognized who was ascending the stage that afternoon, but when the band broke into "Foggy Mountain Breakdown," the crowd roared with enthusiasm. It seemed to many that whereas the war was tearing the country apart, the antiwar movement was bringing it all together. After his part of the music was over, Scruggs was interviewed. He said: "I think the people in the South is just as concerned as the people that's walkin' the streets here today. . . . I'm sincere about bringin' our boys back home. I'm disgusted and in sorrow about the boys that we've lost over there. And if I could see a good reason to continue, I wouldn't be here today."[74]

Even more important than diverse crowds and surprising music were efforts set afoot by legislators in the Congress to support the Moratorium. Charles Goodell of New York, who had taken Robert Kennedy's seat after his assassination, for example, sponsored a resolution to cut off funds for the war. The Nixon administration pretended not to notice but it went out of its way to create countersymbols. On October 15, the White House announced that the president would make a major speech on Vietnam on November 3, and developments in the negotiations with North Vietnam were featured in the day's press briefing. In the end, the Moratorium did not deflect the administration's attempt to speed the negotiations by bringing military pressure onto North Vietnam. Its main effect, and a very important one, was to speed and spread the flow of antiwar sentiment into the mainstream of American society, which, in turn, eventually gave the Congress a sense of popular mandate to attack the war from Capitol Hill sooner rather than later.

The third event of the season, the Mobe's demonstrations, took place the next month in Washington and San Francisco. Before it happened, however, two battles raged. The first was between the organizers, led by Bradford Lyttle, a pacifist and veteran Mobe organizer, and the Nixon administration, which argued over the parade route, over toilets, over everything that could conceivably be argued about. Local FBI agents employed disinformation techniques to sow dissension between the Mobe organizers and Washington's black community; predictions of violence were voiced in hopes of keeping the crowd small. The Nixon administration's dirty tricks had begun.

The other battle was between the Mobe and Moratorium organizers. While the Mobe had endorsed the Moratorium, the Moratorium had never endorsed the Mobe. Having made a successful opening to the Right, most Moratorium organizers did not want to jeopardize it by supporting demonstrations whose tone and effect were at best unpredictable. One proponent of not endorsing the Mobe was Martin Peretz, later editor-in-chief of *The New Republic*. At a MassPax meeting in his home, the decision was taken neither to endorse nor denounce the Mobe but instead to sponsor more local Moratorium activities on November 14 and 15.

At the bottom of this argument was the persisting philosophical divide between the radical and Left-Liberal sections of the movement. Sidney Lens explained the 1969 divide: "The Moratorium kids aren't all that conservative. The difference . . . between us is that in their thinking everything goes back to ballot boxes. In our thinking, everything goes back to the streets." Sam Brown reflected on Lens's view: "If we're in a prerevolutionary state, then screw the great middle class [and] put together the coalition that over the next thirty years will change the country." But we are not in a prerevolutionary state, thought Brown; the war was an aberration, not a "natural" consequence of capitalism, and therefore it was both wrong and cynical to use the war "as an organizing tactic to complete some other agenda."[75] Political activity should be directed toward the ballot box, even if one used the street to do so.

Then came President Nixon's infamous November 3 speech in which he called upon the "silent majority" for support and attacked the antiwar movement more directly and more vigorously than ever before. Whether Nixon's challenge had much of an effect one way or the other in the long run is hard to say. Nixon himself thought it won over public opinion. Mobe organizers thought it the perfect appetizer to a reradicalized antiwar movement. What it did in the short run, however, is indisputable; at the last minute it persuaded the Moratorium to endorse the Mobe.

Thanks in large part to Stewart Meacham, the Washington Mobe demonstration was not designed to be a reprise of the Counterinaugural or the Days of Rage, but more like that of the Moratorium. And it was, at least at the beginning. The March Against Death, which Meacham had proposed and organized, was deliberately somber, orderly, and even quiet. It was designed as a religious ceremony, specifically a funeral march. The first marchers, leaving from Arlington National Cemetery to cross Memorial Bridge, were made up of family members of soldiers killed in Vietnam. Benjamin Spock and William Sloane Coffin, former chaplain at Yale University and leader of the Riverside Church Disarmament group, were the "clergy" in attendance.[76] Each of roughly 45,000 marchers stopped in front of the White House and spoke the name of an American soldier killed in the war. Each protestor then deposited a card bearing the soldier's name into one of 40 coffins waiting near the Navy Civil War Memorial on Pennsylvania Avenue. A few hours later the coffins were carried to the Washington Monument to take their place at the head of the mass demonstration planned for that day. This was very effective political theater.

All was peaceful at the subsequent demonstration, but not in keeping with the solemn tone of the March Against Death. There also were a few supposedly "renegade" actions that got out of hand late in the day. One took place near DuPont Circle, which at the time was a center of the drug trade and counterculture in Washington. Another, an unauthorized "Mass for Peace," took place at the Pentagon; 186 people were arrested, including Senator Philip Hart's wife. On the Washington Monument grounds, meanwhile, Senators McCarthy, McGovern, and Goodell spoke, or tried to anyway. They were hooted down by SDS radicals waving Vietcong flags. Sidney Lens called on the crowd to stop the American death machine the world over, and made one of the most explicitly Marxist speeches ever heard at a major rally. In the end, the music made everyone feel better, from Lennon's "Give Peace a Chance" to the standard Peter, Paul, and Mary repertoire.

Then the trouble started, and if there really was a silent majority, its support for the administration and the war could only have been reinforced by the Mobe's performance that day. Although SDS and the Weathermen had parted company with the Mobe, having become its opposition to the Left, the Conspiracy had not. Dellinger had gotten a permit to march from the rally to the Justice Department. The Moratorium people, who thought it their duty to protect the image of the Mobe by preventing violence and obscene countercultural antics, were horrified when they found out very late in the day what was about to happen. Dellinger took the microphone and, flanked by Rubin and Hoffman, both of whom had been denied the right to speak by the old Left organizing core, announced a march on the Justice Department. Behind dozens of NLF banners, the group of a few thousand approached the building. When they arrived, a Vietcong flag was raised on the flagpole, red paint bombs were thrown along with rocks and bottles, and groups of Yippies, Mad Dogs, Crazies, and Weathermen generally went wild. The police responded with so much tear gas that it eventually spread over more than 20 square blocks of downtown Washington.

And the effect of all this? Richard Nixon's public approval rating rose.[77] Sam Brown concluded at the time that the Mobe demonstrations produced a strong backlash in public opinion. He was absolutely correct.[78] This had been the basic pattern all along.

# 7

# Denouement:
# Tin Soldiers and
# Nixon Coming

*When I hear a man applauded by the mob I always feel a pang of*
*pity for him. All he has to do to be hissed is to live long enough.*
—H. L. Mencken

Richard Nixon's winning of the White House in November 1968 has to rank as one of the most improbable events in American political history. Nixon made his reputation as an implacable anti-Communist, a supporter of Senator Joseph McCarthy, and an unscrupulous mean-spirited campaigner. As Eisenhower's vice president, Nixon languished except during the periods of Eisenhower's illnesses, and even then Secretary of State John Foster Dulles was more visible than Nixon. Nixon won the 1960 Republican presidential nomination to succeed Eisenhower's two terms, but Eisenhower's endorsement was weak, to say the least. At a famous pre-election press conference, when asked what ideas Nixon had contributed over the eight years of his tenure, Eisenhower responded glibly that he could not think of a single one. Nixon lost not only the 1960 presidential election to John F. Kennedy, but also lost the race for the governorship of California in 1962. At his concession speech, he bitterly told the press that they wouldn't have Richard Nixon "to kick around anymore." Virtually everyone, Democrat and Republican alike, concluded that Nixon's political career was finished. President Johnson said in 1964, with an air of happy finality: "I just knew in my heart that it was not right for Dick Nixon to ever be president of this country."[1]

But Nixon wasn't done yet. Barry Goldwater's unsuccessful 1964 campaign had the effect of moving the Republican Party temporarily away from doctrinaire conservatism. A growing national consensus about the legitimacy of civil rights and the evil of segregation made it politically unwise for the Republicans to strand themselves outside that consensus, but at the same time a backlash against the speed and social implications of change in many parts of the country opened the way for populist candidates to utilize burgeoning fears and insecurities. Nixon stood somewhere in between the conservative and moderate wings of the Republican Party, an uncompromising anti-Communist in world affairs, but, like Eisenhower, less hard-edged in domestic matters.

Most important, Nixon represented a reversal of the common image of a Republican as a wealthy and well-born elitist. Nixon, born neither rich nor well-placed, resented the eastern liberal establishment all his life, and most of that establishment had been Democratic at least since Franklin Roosevelt's time. Nixon's capacity for personal resentment meshed well with the populist sentiment rising in the South and among the white working class. These developments revived Nixon's political chances as time passed but they alone would never have been enough to put him in the White House. That took two other things: George Wallace and the Vietnam War.

At first glance, it seems that Wallace should have caused Nixon more problems in the election than he caused Hubert Humphrey, because they were in competition for the populist vote in the South and for the votes of white, blue-collar workers. But because of the tradition of Democratic power in both those domains, Wallace ended up hurting Humphrey more when the electoral votes were counted.

The war helped Nixon in a different way. Nixon was considered an expert in foreign policy, an interest he worked on and cultivated in his years out of public office. And a foreign affairs expert was precisely what many frustrated and disillusioned voters thought the country needed after watching the debacle in Vietnam develop. He was also considered anti-Communist enough to satisfy many Democrats who wondered whether irresolution in Vietnam indicated a softness in the overall U.S. position in the Cold War. The antiwar movement helped him too, as noted earlier, by adding to the backlash against the Democrats. If Norman Mailer hated Lyndon Johnson enough to think that there really was a "new Nixon," then perhaps others did too.

In one sense at least, there was a new Nixon—in domestic policy. "We are all Keynesians now," he once stated, apparently with sincerity.[2] But Nixon's vaunted secret plan to end the Vietnam War, which arguably was the factor that boosted him to victory over Hubert Humphrey in 1968 in a very close election, was never anything more than a de-emphasis on land action and an added emphasis on air power and negotiation from strength—a combination that U.S. military policy and diplomacy had already hit upon in the latter half of 1968. Nixon just packaged it for politics.

There was another sense in which Nixon was not new. He had a keen sense of his enemies—he even listed them, after all—and the radical antiwar movement was made up of the kinds of people Nixon hated most: the children of liberal establishment elitists, wealthy Jews, and violence-preaching blacks. If that hatred was not fairly clear at the time—and it really was—it has become clear since.[3] At the president's behest, in ways both legal and illegal, the administration went after antiwar radicals with a vengeance. Compared to the principals of the Johnson administration, those in the Nixon administration thought about their opposition— of all sorts—in a more concentrated way.

This had everything to do with the personality of Richard Nixon, not any increased effectiveness on the part of the antiwar movement. Similarly, the kinds of attitudes that motivated the Watergate break-in owed little to Democratic prospects in 1972 and everything to the personality of the administration, formed from the very top.

Unlike the Democrats, who ultimately managed to use Watergate and subsequent related sins to unseat Nixon, the antiwar movement helped the new president out quite a lot in the early months of the administration. Even as the movement as a whole was gravitating back toward the center, the extremely photogenic activities of the hyperradical Left made it seem otherwise. Just as there are certain people who love the excitement and danger of storms, so Richard Nixon was a man who thrived on adversity. Thanks to the Black Panthers, the Weather Underground, and Rennie Davis's May Day Tribes, Richard Nixon could truly relish the storm.

### BAD WEATHER

The November 1969 Mobilization, retaining its militant image and agenda despite its broader endorsement, had roused as many as half a million protestors in Washington and 350,000 in San Francisco, together constituting the largest political demonstration in the history of the United States at the time. Yet the November demonstrations could not revive the radical domination of the antiwar movement as their steering committee had hoped. Not only that, the steering committee itself could not hold together. At a meeting in December 1969 in Cleveland, the loose coalition of Conspiracy supporters around Dellinger attacked Peck and Meacham, pronouncing the Mobe rally a failure and the Moratorium a disgrace. With this, the Conspiracy took over the Mobe, or what was left of it. Peck, Meacham, and a few other of the older organizers were disgusted; they quit. The sectarian disease of the Left—factionalism—had struck yet again. And this did not even take into account the hyperradical Left that had never been part of the New Mobe, notably the Weathermen.

The Weather Underground was a natural consequence of the antiwar movement's inner dynamic of schism, frustration, and escalation. As a result, the discrediting of the radical antiwar movement in the eyes of most Americans continued throughout 1969 as its more youthful associates were implicated in bank robberies, murders, bombings, and indiscriminate street violence. Between September 1969 and May 1970, there were more than 250 antiwar movement–related bombings, mostly the work of the Weather Underground. Publicity from the trial of the Catonsville 9, which made the Berrigan brothers famous nationwide, did not play well in Peoria. After the Mobe demonstration the Weathermen's October "Days of Rage," which were so filled with violence that only the innermost core of SDS took part in them, were followed by a meeting in December in which John Jacobs, one of Bernadine Dohrn's associates, intoned: "We're against all that's 'good and decent' in honkey America. We will burn and loot and destroy. We are the incubation of your mother's nightmare."[4] The movement's association with the Black Panther Party, which had by now turned into a group of violent self-possessed nihilists, did not help.

On campus, 1969 was a year that felt like afterburn, exhaustion, and frustration. SDS, splintered into half a dozen pieces, was far too bizarre and cultish for most students. One of its most prominent oldsters, Carl Oglesby, was busy traveling to Cuba and starting a project that, finished by others, came to be known as the Venceremos Brigade—a Marxist project vaguely modeled after the Lincoln Brigade of Spanish Civil War fame—that, whatever it did in Cuba, was not very useful for mobilizing a campus majority. SDS on campus was virtually dead. The hippie penumbra of the New Left quickly lost whatever modest interest it had ever had in real political work and turned increasingly to drugs, head-shop commerce, "instant communism" (otherwise known as theft), and assorted countercultural religious callings.[5] In time, hippiedom-lost furnished "straight" cults such as the Unification Church with a reservoir of burned-out personalities looking for the first anchor of questionless stability they could find.

As for the merely Left as opposed to the ultra-New Left parts of the movement, the New Mobe, now in the control of the Conspiracy caucus, concentrated on promoting dissent and protest within the military. But its efforts fizzled when the Nixon administration marshaled the Justice Department to prosecute draft resistance and evasion with a passion unknown in the Johnson years. More important still, however, to the movement's failure was its inability to calmly assess its circumstances. The truth was that the events of 1969 were really the last collective gasp of the radical movement, but the radical caucus badly misread the state of the nation and the state of the antiwar movement. They believed they stood on the cusp of revolution. They did not see the unraveling of the movement for what it was; instead they fantasized that the true vanguard groups that would lead the revolution had finally emerged. These groups, now finally separated from the chaff of pretend revolutionaries, were believed to bear the seeds of future power and success. In fact, to the extent that the November demonstrations were successful, they were so because they followed the Moratorium so closely and because the Nixon administration's attack on the movement as a whole had produced a late endorsement of the Mobe by the Moratorium.

Moreover, insofar as youth was mobilized in the movement, it was really mobilized more along Sam Brown's line than it was along Sidney Lens's.

Even among the most radical too, there were differences of opinion about tactics. As far as the Weathermen were concerned, every other part of the movement was worthless; they were certain too that the war would not stop until the government was overthrown by their small bolshevik clique. The Dellinger caucus, as noted earlier, also believed that the nation stood near revolution but they put their faith not in vanguard para-militarism but in a broad radical explosion across American society. With the counterculturals on board, and with the headiness inspired by the strange and bizarre Chicago conspiracy trial, many believed that a mass *and radical* antiwar movement had finally congealed—this not despite the 1968 elections and the movement of the country as a whole to the Right, but because of them. They believed that the necessary precondition of polarization having been accomplished, a revolutionary explosion was just around the corner. Dellinger was ready, eager, and willing to light the match. "Unless the movement becomes more dangerous," he said, "it will become irrelevant."[6]

Peck, Meacham, and others of more moderate temperament, if not moderate politics, reasoned that the demonstrations of 1969 had on balance been a success despite the organizational problems they revealed. They had shown that, despite the disaster of the siege of Chicago, the movement was still alive, and that despite the deft public diplomacy of the Nixon administration, not all the people were hoodwinked. They also believed that the movement represented at least some restraining power on what the administration wanted to do militarily in Southeast Asia. Zaroulis and Sullivan, clearly identifying with Peck against Dellinger, make a claim that approximates the wishful delight of Peck à la 1970. It is worth quoting because it repeats what has become common knowledge among former antiwar movement activists and "peace studies" academics. "The leaders of the Moratorium and the New Mobilization," they wrote:

> had no way to know how great was their success, how real was their achievement. Not until several years later did word leak out that Nixon and Kissinger had been seriously and secretly contemplating at that time a fierce escalation of the war, possibly to include the use of nuclear weapons. The antiwar sentiment generated and aired in the fall of 1969 made it politically impossible for the President to proceed with his plan.[7]

Zaroulis and Sullivan do not reveal the source of this "leak."

In fact, the supposition that the antiwar demonstrations of 1969 prevented the Nixon administration politically from escalating the war makes little sense in light of two facts: first, the administration was far more popular than the antiwar movement and could have done whatever it wished on the battlefield, provided it was willing to pay the price in the court of broad public opinion; and second, the administration *did* escalate the war a few short months thereafter—by invading Cambodia.

The additional claim that the use of nuclear weapons was seriously contemplated is completely insupportable, as is suggested by even a casual reading of *The Pentagon Papers*—and given the selectivity with which *The Pentagon Papers* were edited, it is very far-fetched to think that any reference to the possible use of nuclear weapons would have been omitted. Way back in 1954 the Joint Chiefs did propose that if the United States became engaged in Vietnam, consideration be given to using tactical nuclear weapons. But with the significant changes in U.S. thinking about nuclear weapons in the ensuing years, the Joint Chiefs conspicuously ignored the possible use of nuclear weapons after U.S. intervention in 1965.[8] Claiming that nuclear weapons might have been used in 1970 or 1971 means that it had to have been an initiative of the Nixon White House over and above the sensibilities of the uniformed military. But there is simply no evidence for such a supposition.

Another curious part of the Zaroulis and Sullivan analysis, and of most other sympathetic treatments of the antiwar movement, is that they agree with Peck's then-current assessment that the "fall actions of 1969 were a high point for the antiwar movement, the time of its greatest success."[9] But they then quickly add that "the Movement's success belied its true condition," which was one of nearly total organizational disintegration, deep personal bitterness, and debilitating sectarian rivalry. They explain how both of these things could be true simultaneously by simply saying that the movement's time of "greatest success was also its moment of greatest peril."[10]

Actually, the reverse was the case. The antiwar movement as construed in the broadest sense benefited from the organizational incompetence of its adversary cultural core. As the vacuum created by that incompetence was increasingly filled by liberals and Left-Liberals in the early 1970s, the waxing right wing of the movement, working through the community and through the Congress, achieved eventually its greatest influence. In truth, 1969 was not a good year for the antiwar movement either programmatically or institutionally; it only appeared so because 1968 had been such a catastrophe. Indeed, the ultimate failure of the radical core to hold together despite its 1969 "comeback" presaged a few years later a truly effective phase of the movement as it integrated itself more closely into mainstream political institutions.

The transformation of the movement back toward a liberal and Left-Liberal center of gravity took some time. Even the McCarthyite peace liberals lost energy after the fall of 1969. Alas, the Woodstock Nation had no government. Part of the reason, no doubt, was that despite the president's November 3 speech, the Nixon administration had a more clever approach to dealing with opposition to the war than its predecessor: It dissimulated, saying one thing and doing another. It was just harder to get people excited about protesting a war that they thought was coming to an end anyway. And that is what many people thought. Nixon and his aides spoke of winding down the American share of the fighting and negotiating an end to the war altogether. The body counts were getting smaller, escalation of the air war was not common knowledge, and the average American thought that within a year—two years at the most—the fighting would be over, or virtually over.

So when the Moratorium Committee disbanded in mid-April of 1970, a victim of exhaustion and division, there was no sense of panic, no sense of a need for a new mobilization of energy to reconstitute the movement, and no expectation of the great military drama to come. Just days later President Nixon ordered the invasion of Cambodia.

## CAMBODIA AND KENT STATE

The invasion of Cambodia and the shootings at the Kent State and Jackson State universities in early May 1970 shut down college campuses across the United States in greater numbers than ever before. The reason had to do with the dramatic nature of events overseas: a pre-planned U.S. invasion of "yet another" country coming suddenly, and seemingly contradicting the de-escalatory tendencies of the Nixon administration. Another major part of the reason, clearly, was the deaths of university students; it was only *after* Kent State that the May 1970 demonstrations took on their vast scale.

The former participants of the Mobe saw the Cambodian invasion as a great opportunity. As luck would have it, at the very moment of the invasion, about three dozen members of what it is fair to call the rump of the Mobe from the previous few years were meeting in Cora Weiss's apartment in New York City. With the single exception of the Trotskyites, all those assembled agreed to sponsor a rally in Lafayette Park, across from the White House, on May 9. At the last minute, the government granted a permit, adding another divisive element to an already fractious organizing group. Without a permit, Dellinger had said, anyone who came would be involved in de facto civil disobedience. Dellinger would have preferred it this way, which is of course why the government issued the permit.

This was pretty much beside the point however; the truth is that a lot of unaffiliated, unorganized, and politically nonradical students, their universities on strike, headed to Washington expecting to be involved in much more than civil disobedience. Many were willing to be tear-gassed, beaten up, and even shot at as their peers had been at Kent State. It was an unusual, if brief and rare, moment of student solidarity in the face of what was seen as brutal and criminal authority.

Again the music of the times expressed something of the emotions. By 1969-70, Crosby, Stills, Nash, and Young had taken up the mantle of musical spokesmen, making hits out of the incident at Kent State. These were embodied in two songs—anthems really—"Ohio" and "Find the Cost of Freedom," a line from the former giving this chapter its name. "Ohio" warns of "tin soldiers and Nixon coming" to shoot students, and then it asks the students to "get down to it," which most people took as a recommendation to steel oneself for battles to come, both literal and metaphoric. Then sang Stephen Stills and company:

> Find the cost of freedom
> buried in the ground.
> Mother Earth will swallow you,
> lay your body down.[11]

It is a slow song, beautiful and soft, sung with soaring, choirlike harmonies. The last few bars are sung a capella to deepen the haunting impression.[12]

With the atmosphere of religious martyrdom in the air, and the music to go along with it, the spring 1970 Washington demonstration was one that no organizers could ever have put together—more than 130,000 people showed up on very short notice. Indeed, the Mobe was always rushing to catch up with the spontaneous activism of individuals and small groups, all the more so because time was short. Beside that, old divisions resurfaced—Peck against Dellinger, with Rubin and Hoffman against Halstead, and so on during a week of frenetic and futile attempts at consensus and organization.

In the end, there was no agreed-upon plan for nonviolent action, and, clearly, speeches and singing were not going to be enough for many protestors on May 9. The main reason for the failure to agree was that, as usual, the SWP opposed civil disobedience because it believed it to be counterproductive to maximizing public support for anti-establishment causes, and the counterculture representatives, especially Chicago Conspiracy celebrities Hoffman and Rubin, opposed nonviolence. Unlike in 1969, there was no steering committee to broker a compromise and there was no time. By 1:00 in the afternoon on May 9, about 120,000 people had assembled on the Ellipse and all around the reflecting pool, a good number of them mad as hell. And although there was an excellent sound system, there was no set program and no real leadership to make use of it to mold the crowd or encourage it to perform acts of civil disobedience. According to Bradford Lyttle, "about 120,000 morally outraged people were assembled at the Ellipse, at least 20,000 of whom were prepared for the risks of a determined civil disobedience action." But, as activist George Hopkins put it, "no call for such action came because of lack of consensus among the Mobe Steering Committee and disagreement among civil disobedience advocates about the type of action to undertake."[13]

So instead, there were several speeches, a lot of milling about, and a lot of marijuana smoke in the air. As the day wore on, there were some sporadic skirmishes with federal Park Police and a few tear-gas canisters were fired. About 300 people were arrested but no one got hurt. Had it not been for the good sense of the rally marshals, the restraint of the administration, and particularly the skill of the Park Police and the Washington police department, practically anything could have happened on May 9. That nothing did is doubtless why many New Mobe would-be organizers thought the day did not correspond to the mood of anger and militancy. Clearly, many would have felt much better if there had been more violence, more tear-gas, and lots more arrests. Many militants blamed the Socialist Workers Party, which had supplied the marshals for the rally, for preventing them from engaging in civil disobedience.[14]

The important thing about the 1970 demonstrations is that they really were spontaneous outbursts. A 1970 Harris poll indicated demonstrations on 80 percent of American college campuses, well up from all previous years and probably triple the yearly average. Moreover, 58 percent of students were found to have participated, and 75 percent said they agreed with the goals of the protest—a similarly huge increase, if true, from previous years. A similar 75 percent favored "basic changes in the system," 11 percent described themselves as "radical" or "far Left," and 44 percent agreed that social progress was most likely to come from pressures "outside the system."[15]

Public opinion generally also turned sharply against the Nixon administration in the second half of 1970. After the rhetoric of withdrawal, people felt as if they had been duped, more or less the way liberals felt about Lyndon Johnson after the 1964 election. Nixon's approval rating fell below 50 percent for the first time according to Gallup polls; only 38 percent thought he was doing a good job in Vietnam compared to 46 percent who now favored immediate withdrawal.[16] But the Cambodia-related protests occurred, as noted earlier, precisely at a moment when neither radicals nor liberals were organized to take advantage of the welling up of emotion and activism to mold it into something that would endure beyond the passions of the moment. Thus, as it turned out, the 1970 demonstrations were the denouement of the-masses-in-the-streets phase of the antiwar movement. They were a sort of spontaneous conditioned reflex to an extraordinarily crisp and clear escalation of the war in Southeast Asia and on campus. With a single exception, there was not much in the way of large, nationally organized public protest thereafter, and it was not because of students' fear of getting shot.

Rather, the Nixon administration was winding down the ground war, the main killing machine—of Americans at least—in Vietnam; "only" 4,200 U.S. soldiers were killed in Vietnam in 1970, fewer than half the number killed in the previous year, and troop levels were headed down, resting at 334,600 by the end of the year. By the end of 1971, troop strength was down to 156,800—back to 1965 levels—and only about 1,200 were killed during that year. The sensitivity of public opinion to casualties seems to be logarithmic in nature, so that even steady increases in casualties lose their ability to turn people against a war or increase their level of mobilization against it, other factors being equal.[17] How much more unlikely is effective antiwar activism, then, when the casualty rate is decreasing absolutely?

Moreover, the administration's rhetoric was calming. Specifically, on November 12 President Nixon stated publicly that U.S. troops were now limited to a defensive role. More important by far, the pot (bad) luck draft was replaced by a lottery system in early 1970, which eased the psychological strain for many, and in December 1972 President Nixon ended the draft altogether.

As a result of first changing and then ending the draft, Nixon was able to manipulate public opinion about the increased bombing of North Vietnam, which the administration was employing as pressure against Hanoi to negotiate an end to U.S. participation in the war. An April 25, 1972, Gallup poll showed that respondents favored stepped-up bombing by 47 percent against 41 percent, this majority support coming in response partly to a recent North Vietnamese offensive. Clearly, most people did not care as much about how many Asians died in Southeast Asia as they did about the level of U.S. ground combat participation and how many Americans died.

Ending the draft and punching the wind out of the antiwar movement on the one hand, and escalating the air war on the other, was a clever and effective White House tactic. Mike Royko, at the time a pro-war columnist, put it baldly years later:

> . . . in an instant it was over. It was as if someone had flicked a lightswitch. Presto, the throbbing social conscience that had spread across America went limp. The anti-war, pro-peace signs went into the trash bins. Even if you offered free beer and marijuana, you couldn't get enough students together to hold a sit-in. That amazing transformation happened on the day the President signed into law the end of the draft. At that moment, about 99.9% of those who had sobbed over napalm, Christmas bombings and man's inhumanity to man suddenly began looking for jobs on Wall Street.[18]

Sam Brown put it with more modest candor: "Unfortunately, the end of the draft probably had a substantial impact on the anti-war movement. . . . A lot of high-minded idealists turned out, at least in part, to be interested in self-protection."[19] Which brings us back to campus.

## BACK IN THE U.S.S.-ERSITY

A popular Beatles song of 1969-70, "Back in the U.S.S.R.," seemed to suggest—it was never really clear—that the United States and the Soviet Union had become interchangeable for most purposes. If that is what John Lennon and Paul McCartney meant, they were wrong, but many university students, with the same lack of clarity of thought, seemed to believe it. In any case, the 1970 Washington rally ended but the mobilization on campuses did not.

The defunct Moratorium managed to rouse itself sufficiently to issue a call for a national university strike against the Cambodian incursion, but by the time it did, dozens of campuses had already gone on strike under the leadership of independent, more or less spontaneous, student-faculty committees. The action was on campus, not in Washington, and thus the anticlimactic nature of the Washington rally really did not matter very much.

The New Left, and particularly the still-functioning local chapters of SDS, desperately tried to lead the 1970 upheavals on campus but they were no longer in a good position to do so.[20] They had competition; SDS was probably involved in less than a quarter of the student demonstrations of that period. This was very ironic: In 1965, 1966, and even 1967, when the leadership of the antiwar movement was there for the taking, the SDS leadership for one reason or another chose not to take it. Now when it wished to seize the movement, it found that it could not do so thanks to its hyperradical and organizationally incoherent condition. Its brand of radicalism was already passé; Rubin and Hoffman were kings on campus because of the publicity that had flowed from the Chicago trial, and they were definitely not SDS-like anymore except in the most superficial ways. It was circus time, not time for crypto-Marxist revolutionary slogans. The campus rhetoric of 1970 was not less bombastic than that of 1968 but it was much less coherent politically and much less programmatically oriented. The war demands were ostensibly the same—total and immediate American withdrawal from Southeast Asia—but the systematic social criticism of American society, of which Vietnam was the supposed catalyst and cause, was more muted. The speeches were shorter; indignant hippies far outnumbered hardened SDS firebrands. One heard more about the university needing to cancel final examinations than anything about the immorality and decay of capitalist society.

By 1970 student protest had become an institution without a specific political agenda, an imitation of itself, a social form into which virtually any cause or content, large or small, could be poured. Many of the campus protests of 1970-71 retained antiwar themes, but most now took aim at university policies, ROTC programs, military and corporate job interviewing on campus, and other such matters. Also, whereas the festive aspects of protest and demonstration in the period from 1966 to 1968 had been ancillary to the political point of the protest, by 1970-71 the festive aspects had become their own point. In almost every sense, form had overwhelmed and displaced content. The streaking phenomenon, wherein students ran naked through selected parts of campus and nearby neighborhood streets, was the quintessential expression of the lack of serious content to the student protest in this period. If anything marked the end of student political activism, it was streaking.

Many university administrators recognized this, some quickly, some not so quickly. When they did, they were greatly relieved by the realization that they now had to deal with matters of roughly equal magnitude to the phone-booth stuffing and goldfish swallowing of earlier times. Historian L. William O'Neill relates the following illustration:

> In the fall of 1969 the most important radical student group at New York University was called Transcendental Students. At a time when SDS could barely muster twenty-five members, five hundred or more belonged to TS. It began the previous semester when a group protesting overcrowding in the classroom staged a series of freak-outs in classrooms. This proved so attractive a custom that it was institutionalized. Rock, pot, and wine parties had obvious advantages over political action. The administration shrewdly made a former restaurant available to TS for a counter-cultural center. The students welcomed it as a haven for "guerrilla intellect" where the human spirit could breathe free. The administration saw it as just another recreational facility, which, of course, it was. And what dean would not rather have the kids singing out in a restaurant than locking him in his office?[21]

Similarly, at the University of Pennsylvania, the TEP fraternity at the very center of campus, looking out on College Hall, the statue of founder Benjamin Franklin, and the main library, and whose 25-by-40-foot side wall was the main political broadside on campus, was abandoned by the national fraternity organization in 1970 for lack of interest. The university purchased the building and turned it over to students to do with more or less as they pleased, suggesting that it would be off limits to campus police. A group of students tried to clean up the building in preparation for such uses. This effort did not progress very far, however; more interest was expressed in personal and chemical indulgence. Suddenly the university administration proposed setting up a peace symbol nearby just outside the main library, only about 50 yards from the TEP house wall. Most students were charmed by this gesture, which was in fact a near-naked effort at co-optation. In a solemn ceremony, the sculpture was unveiled; it remains in place today. The co-optation seemed to work because, soon thereafter, during spring break, the old frat house was demolished. When students returned after break, there was general surprise, but no protest as the general revelry found other quarters. Thanks to the peace symbol, the university administration remained more or less safe from protest for many months.

## MOVEMENT MELTDOWN

One way to think about the radical core of the antiwar movement, in a metaphor sure to resonate well among many college students today, has to do with the proportions of beer and foam in a quart glass. A little beer in the bottom of the glass, when shaken violently, quickly produces a glass filled with foam. In time, the foam dissipates and one is left again with the original, placid liquid at the bottom of the glass, only with less chemical energy than before. In a way, campus and professional radicals were the beer, the antiwar movement at its popular height was the foam (and the beer itself seemed to disappear), and the violent shaking was provided by the war itself and Washington's mismanagement of it. By 1971, to follow the metaphor to its conclusion, the foam was gone and the beer was back, but it was stale and unappetizing.

By 1971 the antiwar movement seen as a whole was again becoming irreversibly "domesticated." Sensing the shift, and despite the campus upheavals of that spring, SANE and other Left-Liberal groups turned their attention to encouraging the Congress to cut off funds for the war and in other ways limit the government's power to pursue it. Operation Pursestrings, set up by SANE in May of 1970, was a case in point. This was followed, very successfully after the 1972 elections, by other similar drives.

Radicals did not leave off trying to organize and reorganize, but their efforts were fitful. As they tried, the center of gravity within the deteriorating radical core of the movement shifted from the New Left to the new pacifism with its now indelible countercultural aura. Sidney Peck, along with Dave Dellinger, Bradford Lyttle, Ron Young—also of the AFSC—and others, tried to reform a version of the Mobe by organizing the National Coalition Against War, Racism, and Repression (NCAWRR)—later mercifully renamed the Peoples Coalition for Peace and Justice (PCPJ). Other offshoots of the New Mobe broke away to found the National Peace Action Coalition (NPAC), led by the Socialist Workers Party. Just as the Progressive Labor vanguard had "inherited" SDS after helping to destroy it, the SWP ultimately "inherited" the Mobe in much the same way—an object lesson close to home of the vicissitudes of popular fronts and what eventually happens to them.

As for SDS, the Weathermen were underground, making bombs, and the rest of its mantle fell to Rennie Davis. In the latter part of 1970, Davis organized what became known as the May Day Tribes to stop the government. The effort was most colorful, but it was not a great success.

Meanwhile, the NPAC and the PCPJ differed over many things, just as their principals had disagreed for years under the umbrella of the various Mobe organizations. The NPAC favored a single-issue focus on Vietnam, the avoidance of the Democratic Party, and a massive campaign of civil disobedience. The PCPJ favored broad coalition building and a multi-issue approach. It accepted working through the mainstream parties as a front tactic and it favored not just civil disobedience but more active and violent confrontation as well. Neither of these two efforts got very far, and, aside from their own failure to work together, one major reason was the balkanization of radicalism.

The balkanization of the radical movement followed logically, even ineluctably, from the very character of the New Left as it moved through the 1960s. As described earlier, the New Left was from the start a first-person form of radicalism, not the "we" radicalism of sectarian Marxism. Once the counterculture's essential narcissism was added to the mix, the future of 1960s radicalism was sealed.

The New Left pioneered what became known as identity politics, the secret of which, observed Paul Berman, "was simply to invent alternative personalities and encourage people to adopt them."[22] The radical Left fell apart largely because it could not sustain the upward spiral of its radicalism in one movement, and the fissiparous tendencies took the form of the personalisms that motivated a good deal of the radicalism to begin with. But identity-politics movements remained because they became useful, even indispensable, to their adherents as a means of sustaining the high emotions of radicalism after the war could no longer do so. Indeed, even the original founders of the Liberation News Service, which had been a key clearinghouse in the antiwar movement, decided to set up a rural commune in Massachusetts in—of all times—the fall of 1968.[23]

Not that the war was gone. In 1970, as noted, another 4,200 American soldiers were killed, bringing the total to 40,024 by year's end. Nevertheless, gay rights, radical feminism, Puerto Rican independence, welfare rights, environmental issues, various ethnic revivalisms (black, Jewish, American Indian)—all of the more parochial issues that had matured in the atmosphere created by the protracted antiwar movement—began to take precedence over radicalism as an integrated political philosophy, or the war as an issue. Radicalism's core had largely self-destructed in 1968, and the larger pieces had stopped smoldering in 1969. What was left by the end of 1970 was a collection of self-appointed cultist vanguard groups uninterested in the old tactics of public protest and exhausted or bored with the war. They chose instead to follow their own parochialisms, whether political, cultural, or personal.

The emergence of radical feminism is a case in point. A common view is that radical feminism discovered itself intellectually through the basic analysis that radical politics provided during the 1960s.[24] This is partly true; certainly, there are examples of radical SDS women becoming radical feminists without ever losing the hybrid Marxism that inhered in both.[25] But feminism developed not always *with* the analyses of radicals but *at the same time against* the sociology of radicalism.[26] Male Leftists were no less chauvinistic than male non-Leftists, and sometimes a good bit more so. A self-styled White Panthers Party had included in its 1968 manifesto the following imperative: "Fuck your woman so hard till she can't stand up."[27] Needless to say, with such truly revolting attitudes on the loose, there were very few young women at the head of New Left organizations.[28] At the 1969 Counterinaugural, when young feminist Marilyn Webb tried to speak, all hell broke loose. A number of men in the crowed shouted "Take it off!" and "Take her off the stage and fuck her!" Even more stunning, Webb later got a call—she thinks it was from future Weather Underground leader, Cathy Wilkerson—threatening: "If you ever give a speech like that again, we're going to beat the shit out of you wherever you are."[29] Some black males, in particular, used to refer derisively to early expressions of feminism as "pussy power."

Just as significant, perhaps, were the countercultural earth-mother images of women as pedestaled, child-bearing cornucopias of sexuality, beauty, and sustenance. The occasional vulgarity, constant obscenity, and overt sexuality of the counterculture aided the emergence of feminism only by its *negative* example—mature and secure women, after all, tend not to be exhibitionist or promiscuous. Feminist anger may have defined itself initially in terms of the radical critique of capitalism and other class-minded concepts, but its development as a distinctive consciousness and radical community had at least as much to do with radical experience as with radical ideas.

Nevertheless, balkanization or not, the early months of 1971 did not go so badly for the radical antiwar movement, or so it seemed. On April 24, 1971, the last large antiwar demonstration took place in Washington. Featuring Vietnam veterans discarding their medals, it drew as many as 300,000 people. In San Francisco, 150,000 turned out in support.[30] But the advanced balkanization of radicalism was evident in the demonstrations of the spring of 1971, and in the planning for them as well. The PCPJ, cooperating with the May Day Tribes, decided on a mass rally in Washington on April 24 and on nonviolent actions on May 3 designed to bottle up office buildings and traffic so that the government would have to shut down, choking from the congestion. The NPAC supported the April 24 action but did not help plan it. It wanted nothing to do with the May 3 plans, which were the brainchild of Rennie Davis and some of his friends.[31] Dellinger, as usual, was also supportive, and proved to be the link between Davis and the PCPJ. Dellinger argued for "open, disciplined, carefully focused nonviolent resistance." Such activities "as work stoppages, draft-board disruptions, and other organized attempts to paralyze the war machine," Dellinger argued, would "add power and variety to the movement's assortment of tactics."[32]

As things turned out, it was the speakers' platform on April 24 that was really congested, packed full with the splinters of radicalism, and not traffic in downtown Washington—which, before the subway system was built, was always horribly congested even without the aid of antiwar protestors. The speeches, from radical groups of every description, went on for hours and hours, constituting a veritable smorgasbord of demands and accusations. Aside from an occasional humorous incident (as when a young man got his penis stuck in an empty wine bottle while trying to urinate in it), it was probably the most boring antiwar rally ever held. But it was also one of the most peaceful; in a way, it was a throwback to 1965. There were a few "independent actions" that resulted in arrests, and members of the May Day Tribes did tie up the New Jersey Turnpike for hours on their way home—again, something that happens often enough all by itself—but it was a relatively uneventful day.

Not so the May 3 activities. By the end of that week, over 12,000 people had been arrested for a variety of petty inconveniences and "trashings"—easily an antiwar movement record. Some of those arrested were held at a Washington Redskins' practice field, others were later taken to the Washington Coliseum. A demonstration in support of those arrested took place on May 5 at the east front of the Capitol. Four congressmen spoke to the crowd: Bella Abzug, Parren Mitchell, Ronald Dellums, and Charles Rangel. Thanks partly to Dellums's incendiary rhetoric, more violence occurred, and by the time the rally had ended, another 1,000 protesters had been arrested.

These demonstrations did not shut down the government, partly because the government was ready for the plans. It did disrupt some people's schedules however. The president was in San Clemente, whether by design or coincidence is still a matter of dispute. But a few hundred key administration officials were ordered to be at their offices before 6 A.M. lest the government in fact be disrupted. The May Day actions did reinforce the image of the antiwar movement as a radical and irresponsible force and actually hastened the movement toward the reliberalization of protest. It also shed none too soft a light on those members of the literary Left, such as Noam Chomsky, who so avidly supported them.[33] Even columnist Mary McGrory, no supporter of the war or Mr. Nixon, wrote in the *Washington Post* that May Day was "the worst planned, worst executed, most slovenly, strident and obnoxious peace action ever committed."[34]

Moreover, by now, after Tet, after Cambodia and Kent State, most people who opposed the war had well-defined reasons of their own for so doing, and those who did not oppose it were unlikely to be swayed by the likes of Rennie Davis's May Day Tribes. The lack of impact of street demonstrations and the divisions within the movement combined to essentially put it out of business. After 1971 there were no more mass public demonstrations against the war, even though the war still went on. There were, of course, many smaller demonstrations, with the level of violence and extent of radical organization proportionately greater within them.[35] But they did not garner much attention; the press and the rest of the country had grown tired and inured to such actions. They were no longer newsworthy unless really spectacular.

The most influential demonstrations of that spring were not the violent ones, however, but those organized independently by the Vietnam Veterans Against the War (VVAW) as a part of the April 24 demonstrations. They were small but poignant occasions; they included the turning in of war medals and the laying of wreaths with Gold Star Mothers at Arlington National Cemetery. With John F. Kerry, later a U.S. senator from Massachusetts, as their spokesman, the VVAW made a powerful impression on the Congress and, through the media, on the American people.[36] The reason is simple: veterans were by definition patriotic. They were not draft-dodgers. They did not and never had rooted for the enemy. They were not spoiled students on elite college campuses. They did not have long hair, wear beads, or openly smoke pot. In short, the very fact that they appeared respectable helped earn their views respect.

On balance, however, the movement's meltdown after mid-1971 still remains to be explained. After all, after 1971 several things took place that, one would have thought, might have reignited mass public protest. The March 1971 the trial of Lieutenant William Calley and public review of the My Lai massacre, however, brought few into the street. Neither did the most massive leakage in U.S. history—the publication of *The Pentagon Papers* after a former Defense Department official turned protestor, Daniel Ellsberg, leaked them to the press a few weeks after the My Lai story broke. For both the average person and the intellectual, there was plenty of new material at which to become furious. But relatively few did. Even throughout 1973-74, during the height of the Watergate crisis—perhaps the most serious Constitutional crisis in American history short of the Civil War—not a single major student demonstration aimed at Richard Nixon took place. Why?

The balkanization of radicalism explains part of the astonishing quiet of the period from 1972 to 1975; in other words, there was a broad organizational reason for it. There were also specific reasons for quiet at times when something different might have been expected. The White House deliberately planned the December 1971 Christmas bombings, we now know, to coincide with a time when colleges across the country were not in session. More generally, the winding down of U.S. participation in the war, along with the end of the draft, accounted for much of the quietism in one way or another.[37] But there were two other less obvious reasons, too, one having to do with the ideological superficiality of most antiwar radicalism, another having to do with class interests.

One might have thought that if the antiwar movement's systematic radical critique of American society was as strong as many believed it to be at the time, then a cascade of angry protest would have continued over virtually every salient public issue. The New Left did succeed for a time in capturing the broad generational perturbation of the 1960s; it then expanded this perturbation beyond politics into proto-religious countercultural realms and, ultimately, bore antipolitics and general collapse. Initially, its sheer energy was the New Left's principal attractiveness to many—it sounded like the authentic voice of a generation of desperate social pioneers in tone and decibel level, the actual content of its ideology being decidedly secondary. It was an emotional expression, especially after the counterculture joined it, and it is the nature of strong emotion to soon subside.

The radical critique of American society never captured the antiwar movement as a whole, and that was mainly because events vividly demonstrated its falsity to anyone who would look. Its successful openings to the Right from time to time did not result, as Dellinger, Peck, Halstead, and others hoped they would, in the permanent mass radical politicization of an entire generation of new revolutionary cadres. Again, aside from a very small core of genuine radicals, radical social criticism was for most an idealistically grounded emotional outburst, not an intellectually integrated paradigm of radical politics. It was more like yelling at one's parents over their supposed hypocrisy than it was lecturing the proletariat and trying to raise its consciousness. As Jeffrey Herf put it: "Only a very small minority of 1960s students were radical leftists. Our greatest successes took place when we were able to link our radicalism to a more generally shared idealism."[38]

As for class interests, the early 1970s were sudden hard times for the U.S. economy, or so it seemed in comparison to the times gone just before. The economic troubles of this period have left only faded impressions after so long a time, largely because the troubles that came after were of an even more serious magnitude. But it is hard to overstate the psychological shock that wage and price controls, inflation, and the abandonment of the convertibility of the dollar into gold caused at the time. The Vietnam generation had grown up in times of unparalleled economic expansion. Its members took it for granted that such growth would never end. It took it for granted that the U.S. economy would forever generate sufficient wealth both for private consumption and public investment. It was an entitlement of history, so to speak, that each generation would live better and have more opportunity than the one before. When all of this was suddenly thrown into doubt, the middle class, including its younger college-dwelling generation, would not in the end commit personal financial suicide. While earlier college classes tended to pursue their interests without close regard to what could be done with a history, or a political science, or a sociology degree, later ones were more narrowly pragmatic. With the end of the draft and the winding down of the war, students became less concerned about rarefied moral issues and more concerned with getting a good job.

Finally, added to the ephemeral nature of radicalism and the downturn in the economy, the subculture of protest on campus had changed. The college classes of the 1965-69 period had graduated; they had passed through that remarkable bastion of carefree irresponsibility—the college campus—and were gone. Those who followed were not there "at the creation," to borrow a phrase from Dean Acheson's autobiography, and their sense of sharing a community of anger and idealism grew narrower as drugs and worry about their personal career futures both limited their energy for political causes. All this taken together—movement incoherence caused by sectarians and balkanization, administration tactics of winding down the war and ending the draft, the painful prick of a less happy economic reality, and the evolution of campus subcultures—but none of it in isolation, explains the meltdown of the street-protesting antiwar movement and the curious calm at war's end.

## THE NEW DEMOCRATS AND
## THE CONGRESSIONAL PHASE

It was just as well. The less that angry students and well-practiced radicals did in
the streets, the less press they got, and the fewer the antiwar antics there were, the
less the American people proved reluctant to state their opposition to the war. Also,
the longer the Nixon administration continued the war despite the expectations of
an end its rhetoric had raised, the more upset the American people became. In
December 1971 a Gallup poll showed that now 73 percent of the American people
favored the expeditious withdrawal of all U.S. ground troops from Vietnam.[39]

Slowly but surely, the antiwar movement's center of gravity moved away from
radical pacifists and the radical Left, back toward the political center, toward positions
held by SANE and the Friends Committee on National Legislation. The Friends
Committee was adept, for example, at creating and distributing packets of information
to college students—one was called "Don't Stop Now"—that were essentially how-to
manuals for lobbying mainstream politicians. The main target of this effort, and the
hoped-for vehicle of reform, was the defeated Democratic Party.

The 1972 elections, and especially the 1974 midterm elections, brought into
the Congress scores of Democrats (and some Republicans) opposed to the war,
many of whom—like Al Gore, Jr., and Stephen Solarz—had been involved in years
past in the antiwar movement. It is important to understand, however, that antiwar
protest in the streets is not what changed the political complexion of the Congress;
it was instead the seeming illogic of withdrawing so slowly that so many Americans
were still getting killed, and a sharp decline in Nixon's popularity and truthworthi-
ness after the invasion of Cambodia and the increased bombing of North Vietnam.

In any case, the level of congressional activism with respect to the war
increased yearly, particularly as it became ever clearer that the Nixon
administration's program for quitting Southeast Asia was much slower than most
congressmen desired. The precedent had been set on December 22, 1970, when
the Congress voted to cut off all funds for U.S. operations in Cambodia and Laos.
Before the Watergate break-in of June 22, 1972, however, no other major congressional action occurred despite a great deal of talk and effort. Several attempts to
cut off funds for the war introduced as amendments to various bills failed to pass
muster. The most important of these efforts, clearly, was the McGovern-Hatfield
amendment, which is discussed later in more detail.

The truth was, too, that over time an anti-antiwar movement had gained
steam in reaction to radical Left provocations, and congressmen had to pay
attention to not one but two groups of angry constituents—those against the war,
and those against those against the war, the latter becoming better organized and
less inhibited about vocalizing their views with each passing day. They knew that
after Lieutenant Calley's conviction, for example, mail to the White House and to

individual lawmakers ran at least ten-to-one in Calley's favor. This was not just because many felt Calley to have been scapegoated for the sins of higher-ups, but because many people were simply disgusted with attacks on the U.S. military as an institution and wanted them to stop.

Strong as this reaction was, it was not strong enough to stop the New Democrats. The capturing of the Democratic Party by what were then called New Politics forces was clearly of significance with regard to how the Vietnam War ended. Some antiwar activists turned to the Democratic Party in order to restore liberalism and humanism as they understood it to a party that had been corrupted by right-wing labor groups, Dixiecrats, and monied classes. Others, surely a minority, saw the party as a Trojan horse, as a vehicle to legitimate not liberalism but radicalism. As the founder of gonzo journalism, Hunter S. Thompson, said in his classic on the 1972 campaign, *Fear and Loathing on the Campaign Trail*, "the only way to save the Democratic Party is to destroy it."[40]

Whatever the motives, there can be little doubt that with Senator George McGovern's winning of the nomination in 1972 and the changes undertaken in the rules committee just prior to that to allow greater minority participation, the Democratic Party became simultaneously more open in terms of its processes and much farther to the Left in terms of the attitudes of its political activists. It also became more than a little flaky at times, and, in so doing, fulfilled George Orwell's insight into the sorts of people Left movements tend to attract. Clearly, with a heavy dose of countercultural atmospherics, the Democrats went beyond what the 1948 Henry Wallace wing of the party had hoped for, and was then also well beyond what the Jesse Jackson Rainbow Coalition aspired to in the 1980s. Indeed, between 1972 and 1976 the Democratic Party was as close to a major national party of the Left as the United States has ever had, this despite the fact that its rank and file remained fairly centrist or even socially conservative.

After the November 1972 elections, and especially after American prisoners of war had been returned, the Congress became much more active in trying to limit and stop U.S. participation in the war. On June 24, 1973, the Congress voted to prohibit all bombing in Cambodia. On November 7, 1973, it passed the War Powers Resolution over a presidential veto. On August 20, 1974, Congress reduced aid to South Vietnam from $1 billion to $700 million; even the original figure was much less than the administration had wanted and had promised the South Vietnamese.

With such attitudes regnant among significant numbers of Democrats in the Congress, it is not surprising that there were major battles between the Congress and the White House. Aside from those just mentioned, all of which the Nixon administration and later the Ford administration opposed, one such battle led in 1974 to the Clark Amendment and, ultimately, to the cutting off of funds for the last act of the Vietnam war. The War Powers Resolution and the Clark Amendment both restricted the Executive Branch's prerogative in foreign policy. The former is almost certainly unconstitutional. The latter, which may be unconstitutional too, notably restricted U.S. foreign policy in Africa after the Portuguese Revolution in 1974; indeed, it was designed to prevent U.S. involvement of any kind in the Angolan Civil War. As a result, Marxist-Leninists backed by the Soviet Union succeeded in Angola. This brought Cuban forces to Africa, protracted the civil war in Angola, emboldened Soviet proxy expansionism elsewhere in Africa (Ethiopia, Mozambique), contributed in turn to the hardening of South African regional and domestic policies, and, not incidentally, led to the deaths of several tens of thousands of people in the process. The cutoff of funds for South Vietnam, of course, led to a North Vietnamese conventional military victory in March 1975—not, admittedly, for objective military reasons, but rather for equally important psychological ones.

The truth of the matter was that while the Nixon-Ford administration did not have to contend with crowds in the streets after 1971, its hands were tied much more firmly by antiwar activism in the Congress than those of the Johnson administration ever were. It is impossible to assign a particular date to the shift from an antiwar movement whose tactical and programmatic center of gravity was radical to one whose center was again more liberal. As noted, the seeds went back to the Moratorium in 1969; and the right wing of the antiwar movement, while eclipsed and outflanked, was never completely destroyed even before that time. The May 9, 1970, rally, described earlier, is probably as good a starting date as any other for the shift back to the Right of the movement's center of gravity.

Not only was a very angry crowd uncharacteristically orderly on that day, not only were more senators and congressmen to be found on the Ellipse than ever before, but also—hardly noticed at the time—parts of the federal bureaucracy itself had begun to express public misgivings about the war. In the crowd on May 9 were several hundred federal employees marching behind banners whose message mocked President Nixon's characterizations of antiwar protestors. Their signs read: "Federal Bums Against the War" and "Federal Employees for Peace." Fifty foreign service officers also signed and made public a letter to Secretary of State William Rogers urging "reconsideration" of current policy. Also extremely important, hundreds of protestors took the time to knock on the doors of their congressmen and senators, a gesture that would have been frowned upon and almost universally derided only two years earlier.[41]

The 1970 events—the invasion of Cambodia and the explosion of protest it evoked—also had served to generate the amendments in the Congress designed to stop or limit the war, an idea whose origins were to be found in modest congressional support for the October 1969 Moratorium. The most prominent was the McGovern-Hatfield end-the-war amendment, around which Operation Pursestrings had been designed. As noted earlier, Operation Pursestrings was SANE's idea to engage college students in lobbying for the amendment. It was a way for the liberal and Left-Liberal right wing of the antiwar movement to move back onto campus in the wake of the demise of SDS and the Student Mobe. There was some Operation Pursestrings activity on about 100 campuses, but it never caught on in a big way. Too many campuses were remote from urban areas for the idea to be very practicable, and, besides, canvassing took more time and was not nearly as much fun as antiwar demonstrations. The amendment was defeated on September 1, 1970, by a vote of 55 to 39.

Nevertheless, the Congress-oriented antiwar activities of 1969 and 1970 were the harbingers of the kinds of tactics that ultimately proved to be very effective after 1970. Aside from Operation Pursestrings, a number of other projects, many organized and run by veterans of the McCarthy campaign, had taken root. The Princeton Plan, which also became known as the Movement for a New Congress, was similar to SANE's 1966 Voter Peace Pledge Campaign. The idea was to get college students to work for peace candidates at the level of primary campaigns. A National Petition Committee, centered at the University of Rochester, had started collecting signatures and money simultaneously, continuing its activities into 1971. Also, many university faculties had organized lobbying trips and campaigns, including, on occasion, the participation of university presidents. Last, an important sign of the times was that a number of labor unions had managed to creep out from under AFL-CIO leader George Meany's tight pro-war policy grip and express themselves against the war. Of these "defections" by the far the most important was that of Walter Reuther of the United Auto Workers. Two days before he was killed in an air crash, he telegrammed President Nixon expressing his deep concern and distress about the war.

The most vivid evidence of the transformation of the antiwar movement, beyond the continuing disintegration of the Mobe, was the Senate passage of the Cooper-Church amendment for cutting off funds for the Cambodia operation on June 30, 1970, although final congressional passage did not occur until mid-February of the next year. This was the first in a very long series of tussles between the administration and the Congress over financing the war; at first most of them were won by the administration, but, as indicated earlier, most were later won by the Congress. The first major victory was not in an authorization or an appropriation bill, but rather the passage of the Mansfield "sense of the Senate" resolution in June 1971, which called upon the administration to set a date for the final withdrawal from Vietnam.

The pace of congressional pressure on the administration, and the administration's reluctance to fight it, increased markedly as the 1972 Presidential elections approached. McGovern's early candidacy, announced in January 1971, helped to focus much of the pressure and led each Democratic candidate to move to the Left in an attempt to undermine his bid. In the meantime, the Republican Party's recollection that it had run in 1968 on a promise to end the war, and its knowledge that the war had still not ended, led it to accelerate its own timetable for withdrawal in order to make sure to beat McGovern in November.

McGovern lost the election, of course, but both the fact that he ran and the efforts undertaken by the Nixon administration to defeat him accelerated the withdrawal of U.S. forces and of the U.S. commitment to South Vietnam. Moreover, despite Nixon's re-election, the complexion of the Congress changed markedly in the direction of stopping the war. It was in the Congress, after 1972, that the redomesticated antiwar movement had its clearest effect by denying, *in extremis,* the Government of South Vietnam the weapons it needed (and that it had been promised repeatedly) to fend off a *conventional* North Vietnamese attack in March 1975.[42] Unquestionably, too, the escalation of the air war, revelations of the illegal 1969-70 bombing of Cambodia, the My Lai massacre trial popularized by Seymour Hersh's first two shock-journalism books,[43] and the availability of *The Pentagon Papers*[44] all contributed mightily to the congressional mood. All of it, however, was produced directly and indirectly by the war itself, not by the residue of an antiwar movement in the streets.

## VIETNAM AND NIXON'S DÉTENTE

The congressional phase of the antiwar movement affected not only U.S. policy in Vietnam but also U.S. foreign policy in general. How could it be otherwise, when Vietnam had become *the* consuming and orienting issue within U.S. foreign policy? Generally, the liberal and Left-Liberal critique of U.S. foreign policy held increasingly that containment had not been misapplied to Southeast Asia, as had been Morganthau's argument back in 1965 and 1966, but that containment was, in effect, morally wrong. American power in the world, said these new liberals, was too often antiprogressive, and the United States was getting itself "on the wrong side of history"—as it was said in those days—not just in Vietnam but throughout the Third World. America was, they argued too, overcommitted and prone to broadly misread nationalism as Communism. The Cold War and the arms race were both dangerous anachronisms; rather, "human rights" and development in the Third World should be America's vocation, not military adventures and exhibitions of destruction against Third World peoples.

The Nixon administration, too, came into office with its own new design, but one quite different from that which Congressional supporters of the antiwar movement had in mind. Nixon and Henry Kissinger wished the United States to play the role of power balancer on a global scale and by so doing to reinvent containment according to other means. To achieve this, a de facto U.S.-Chinese alliance against the Soviet Union was the key to eventually normalizing the U.S.-Soviet relationship, which, to Kissinger, meant transforming the Soviet Union from a revolutionary to a status quo power. Aside from developing the China card as leverage against the Soviets, arms control, and the relaxation of tension in Berlin, the rest of Germany, and beyond that the rest of Europe (in that order), U.S.-Soviet trade and other exchanges were all part of the formula for success.

But Vietnam stood in the way of all of this. The war, it was believed, made developing the China card virtually impossible. It threatened to eviscerate the defense budget both at the hands of the Congress and, by diverting funds away from strategic programs, to put sound arms control at risk. It was a point of contention with America's European allies. It encouraged isolationism too, making any active internationalist U.S. foreign policy more difficult to maintain. The war, therefore, had to go.

But for Nixon and Kissinger Vietnam could not be quit under dishonorable and humiliating terms. Hence the demand for "peace with honor." A precipitous withdrawal, it was felt, would undermine American credibility with allies and potential partners alike, all but ruining any hope of an activist and successful American foreign policy. Also, Nixon and Kissinger hoped that the beginnings of the new foreign policy would facilitate an honorable exit from Vietnam. They believed that the road to Hanoi lay through Moscow and Peking. The fact that the December 1971 bombing of Hanoi and Haiphong Harbor, where Soviet ships were damaged and Soviet crewmen killed, did not prevent Soviet premier Leonid Brezhnev from greeting Nixon in Moscow in June 1972 and going through with the SALT treaty, seemed to Nixon to validate the point. Moscow would be made to choose: a better relationship with the United States or help Hanoi, but not both.

Taken together, Nixon and Kissinger's scheme was called détente. It was called détente because that is what Nixon and Kissinger wished it to be called, a gentle word from an earlier day that connoted reasonableness, moderation, arms control, and general safety. There was a good reason for using such a word. Vietnam was not the only thing that stood in the way of policy success. The American people and the Congress also had to support such a plan. But just telling the truth about what was supposed to be achieved was not enough; it was never enough for the Nixon administration in any sphere of activity. Instead, Nixon and Kissinger used the vocabulary and rhetoric of their critics in the service of a *realpolitik* and very unsentimental notion of how to deal with the Soviets in the coming post-Vietnam period.

Doing so was politically astute: to embrace arms control and to articulate limits to American commitments (as did the Guam Doctrine first and then the full-fledged Nixon Doctrine shortly thereafter) was to invade, so to speak, the American political middle, all in the service of traditional Cold War geopolitical ends. In other words, if you can't beat them, pretend to join them. This stratagem effectively undercut McGovern's appeal in 1972, and having George Wallace around as opposition to the Right allowed Nixon to appear utterly centrist. All this occurred, of course, even as the ground war in Vietnam continued and the air war escalated.

Still, smoke and mirrors aside, the Nixon administration actually absorbed much of the liberal critique of U.S. foreign policy penned in the early to mid-1960s. When Nixon remarked that "we are all Keynesians now" he might as well have spoken more broadly about the conservative embrace of liberal attitudes. Nixon administration principals were not just tactical manipulators; many if not most of them were really sucked into the intellectual currents of the time. After all, the war in Vietnam *did* shatter the postwar foreign policy consensus based around containment, even among many Republicans. Listen to Secretary of Defense Melvin S. Laird's statement kicking off the administration's Defense Department budget proposal for fiscal year 1973:

> Our objective . . . is a generation of peace and a better quality of life for all Americans. The Nixon Administration has devoted three years of constant effort to moving us toward that objective. . . . These have been years of *transition:*
>     —From War to Peace.
>     —From a wartime economy to a peacetime economy.
>     —From a federal budget dominated by defense expenditures to one dominated by human resource programs.
>     —From an era of confrontation to an era of negotiation.
>     —From arms competition toward arms limitation.[45]

These were not the words of old-fashioned, pre-Vietnam Cold War Republicans.

Clearly, then, although the main vehicle of the antiwar movement's influence was its influence in the Democratic Party, Republicans also had to acknowledge, one way or another, that a new era was at hand, and that even a Republican secretary of defense had to speak to it in new language. After all, containment was not just Truman's legacy, it was Eisenhower's as well. Something was needed to take its place as a schemata for U.S. policy in the future, not just something to tell the American people, but really something in the minds of decision makers. This task would have confronted any administration in the post-Vietnam era, Democratic or Republican; it just so happened that a Republican won the 1968 election.

In any event, the concepts chosen by the Nixon administration did not sound like "containment by other means." Multipolarity, strategic "sufficiency," the movement from "confrontation to negotiation" (especially arms control negotiations) in U.S.-Soviet relations, the partial devolution of U.S. military responsibilities overseas as in the Guam Doctrine, and all this coupled with the planned reduction of U.S. military capacity from a two-and-a-half- to a one-and-a-half-theater war capability—sounded more like liberal Democratic notions of the pre-Vietnam or early Vietnam period as expressed in the writings of such critics as Edmund Stillman and William Pfaff, Ronald Steel, Stanley Hoffmann, and George Ball.[46] But by 1969, such notions could be considered centrist because, thanks to the antiwar movement, the entire political spectrum had shifted to the Left in the intervening years.

Thanks to the Nixon administration, such ideas became very popular in the United States in the 1970s among relevant interested publics. They must have been popular in Moscow too—albeit in a different way. The fact that a Republican administration was espousing such convenient ideas in order to create its "new majority"—to once again recall Patrick Buchanan's phrase when he worked in the Nixon White House—made opposition from the Right that much more difficult. It was not until Ronald Reagan's challenge to President Ford in 1976 that such opposition emerged at all, and then unsuccessfully.

Whether Nixon administration principals really believed such notions, or whether they were merely protecting the nation from the post-Vietnam backlash, as its principals have subsequently claimed, the result was to make, or to allow others to make, and believe, very extravagant claims for the policies of détente. The Nixon administration's devotion to its own pollsters and its now well-appreciated political rapacity also contributed to the distension of expectations that were bound in time to be frustrated by the hard reality of U.S.-Soviet differences.

Indeed, while the heisting of the language of the 1960s liberal critique of American foreign policy worked politically for Richard Nixon, it ultimately failed as foreign policy. The atmospherics of U.S.-Soviet relations improved from 1969 to 1973, but the substance did not. Nor did Soviet aid to Hanoi diminish significantly. Indeed, Soviet military power and global expansionism was not contained between 1969 and 1975; instead it grew. As it did, the reality of a changing military balance made it nearly inevitable that SALT I would give a far greater advantage to the Soviets than to the United States and its allies. The Soviets did cooperate in reducing tensions in Europe, most notably through the Quadripartite Agreement on Berlin in 1971, but the effect of this was to encourage West European neutralism and left-wing political successes. As for trade, it was modest and poorly managed, the "great grain robbery" of 1972 being a case in point. And, of course, South Vietnam fell anyway, most ignominiously, and with the help of ample Soviet arms. In addition to poor performance on the merits, and despite every attempt to make it appear otherwise, Nixon's own political weakness as the Watergate scandal widened tolled the death knell to his foreign policy.

The political souring of détente, especially after the October 1973 Middle East War and the accompanying oil shocks, left a bottomless void. With the defense budget falling each year head over heels before congressional cuts, a return to the pre-Vietnam version of containment was physically impossible, and this was not to speak of the near-total intellectual discrediting of the policy itself thanks to the debacle in Vietnam. American weakness in general and Richard Nixon's political weakness specifically, however, made his reinvented version of containment unsustainable too. Under Gerald Ford, Henry Kissinger's Middle East pyrotechnics, and atavistic spasms such as the Mayaguez incident, took the place of an overall foreign policy strategy. By the beginning of 1976, U.S. foreign policy was weakened to the point that many critics argued that there was none.

This can hardly be said to have been the antiwar movement's doing, either directly or otherwise. It was, to say it plainly, the Nixon administration's own fault. Still, the antiwar movement's entry into the Congress, especially after 1972, inclined the administration to choose language and to make claims about what it was doing that international realities could and would not sustain. Détente was oversold in part so that the anti-Hanoi pressures of the administration's Vietnam policies could be sustained politically. In the end, both policies failed, one in October 1973 at the Suez Canal, and the other, finally, in March and April 1975 in Saigon.

# Vietnam as Metaphor, 1975–92

*Aussitôt dit, aussitôt fait.*

The Vietnam War ended ambiguously. The U.S. military withdrawal, which may be said to have started on March 31, 1968, and ended on January 11, 1973, was very slow and punctuated by sharp escalations of violence, such as the late April 1970 invasion of Cambodia and the December 1971 Christmas bombing of Hanoi and Haiphong Harbor. American participation ended by negotiation, but the war itself ended militarily in a way that violated and negated those negotiations. This unsavory conclusion to the war raised several questions that persist even today. Did the United States do all it could, only to lose South Vietnam anyway, or did it abandon Saigon, searching only for, as former U.S. intelligence official Frank Snepp put it, a "decent interval"?[1] Were more than 58,000 American lives lost in vain, or not? If those lives were spent in vain, who was to blame?

As a nation, America did not achieve consensus on these questions in the first 15 years after the war. The war stayed with us long after the guns fell silent, and in a less vivid and inclusive form it does so still.[2] The war was with us in the revival of the Great Debate over American foreign policy in the Carter and Reagan administrations,[3] the last acts of the Cold War. It has also inhabited the writings of the adversary culture and academia, television and the movies, art and popular culture generally—all of it in turn influencing American political culture itself, slowly, quietly, but still significantly. And wherever images of the war went, images of the antiwar movement went with them as Vietnam cum "afterimage" embedded itself into American political discourse.

The story of what has happened to the image of the Vietnam War and the antiwar movement in American society is, of course, quite different from the story of the war and the antiwar movement themselves. There is an important connection, however. After the war, acts and writings about the war and the antiwar movement entered into a new dialectic. The "lessons" of Vietnam became an autonomous influence on policy, and policy drawn under such conditions in turn influenced subsequent writings. Establishing causality in history is never easy, and when memories and interpretations themselves become acts—as they invariably do—it becomes harder still.

As important, because central arguments about the war and the antiwar movement were never settled, Vietnam's symbolic life has not condensed, explained, or healed but simply ferried the quarrels of one era over the waters to be fought again in another. The Vietnam parable was picked up and vaulted into consecutive new milieus, old puzzles and anxieties rolled together with new ones. While some have sought to expiate the demonic spirits of a lost war, others have carried Vietnam from Managua to Sarajevo. This is no surprise, for how the past is remembered is always a product of competing visions and interests that are *about* the past but *for* the future.[4]

The inevitable tangle of the historical process with the process of writing history makes it hard to know what happens to our opportunity to grasp the integrity of a time and place as we move away from it. Do we see fundamental patterns of the Vietnam War and the antiwar movement more clearly, gaining perspective as we gain distance? Or do we interpose so many subjectivities that we mistake the inchoate shapes of the present for the texture of the past? In their many seemingly prosaic forms, these are the questions addressed in this chapter.

## JIMMY CARTER,
## RONALD REAGAN, AND THEIR CRITICS

The foreign policy of both the Carter and Reagan administrations was modeled partly on lessons its principals learned about Vietnam, while criticism of both presidents and their policies flowed from different lessons others had learned from the same events.[5] The essence of the argument between Carterite and Reaganite thinkers on foreign policy issues was very much an argument about the true meaning of Vietnam. Was Vietnam a symptom of all that was wrong with U.S. foreign policy, as most Democrats seemed to think, or was it a symbol of a noble policy gone awry precisely because of such thinking, as most Republicans believed? Even arguments within the confused and politically weakened Democratic Party, such as those between candidates Gary Hart and Walter Mondale in the 1984 Democratic primary campaign, turned on "lessons" of Vietnam.[6]

The terms "hawks" and "doves" were born in the Vietnam War, and back then everyone knew what they meant because the terms pertained to a single issue: the war. But as these terms lived on, their meanings expanded and became less precise. Hawks and doves became more mature birds—birds with general attitudes about policy instead of specific disagreements about tactics in a particular Southeast Asian war. Here, too, old arguments took on new life.[7] This is why still-Leftists and "second-thoughts" no-longer-Leftists could argue vociferously about who wrote and said what about the Sandinistas in terms of what had been said about the Vietcong 20 years earlier.[8]

Such analogizing is both distortive and inevitable. It is distortive because history doesn't really repeat itself. It is inevitable because reasoning by analogy is sometimes the only kind of reasoning available in ambiguous situations. Moreover, the argument over U.S. foreign policy, at its core, is a difficult, interesting, and portentous one. The central question in this century has always been the same: Under what circumstances and for what purposes is it wise and justifiable to project American military power abroad?

In the two decades before Vietnam, the consensual answer to that question was described under the rubric of containment, which was in practice a vigorous internationalism grafted onto America's unique blend of moralism and often cavalier naivete about other cultures. The Great Debate that had dominated U.S. foreign policy discourse between the Spanish-American War and Pearl Harbor was reduced uncharacteristically to quibbles over tactics. This broad consensus ended in Vietnam. In the second half of the 1970s, America was inclined to retreat from this central question into a new isolationism, an inclination reinforced by the Carter administration, whose version of détente stressed selective U.S. strategic disengagement.[9] This inclination was supported by much of the post-Vietnam constituency in the Congress and also by spinoffs from the right wing of the antiwar movement, which had metastasized into organizations such as the Coalition for a New Foreign and Military Policy.

The Democratic Party elite's views on most issues concerning U.S. foreign policy departed sharply from pre-Vietnam assumptions. Its international orientation, formed with explicit reference to the Vietnam trauma, contained ten axiomatic elements.[10]

First, physical survival is the preeminent goal of foreign policy just as fairly distributed material opulence is the preeminent goal of domestic policy; the purpose of foreign policy, ultimately, is that there be one. Second, since peace is the highest political good, ideology should never be allowed to undermine it. Third, the Soviet threat to world peace is exaggerated by the U.S. military–industrial complex's never-ending need to generate and maintain profits. Fourth, nuclear weapons and nuclear deterrence are immoral, and because of the possibility that such weapons might be used, the employment of force on any level involved escalatory dangers exceeding any possible benefit. Fifth, the use of force can be justified in self-defense, but its use for purposes of intervention is not only wrong but always counterproductive. Sixth, political structures are culturally relative and judgmentally equal; socialism may constrain liberty but capitalism has its costs in social injustice, and one cannot judge which debilities are worse. Seventh, the reason for world poverty and for many nations' failure to develop economically is a system of neocolonialism driven by U.S.-based multinational corporations and abetted by the U.S. government. Eighth, the United States's greatest power is the power of its example; coercion of any kind—military, economic, diplomatic—produces only animosity, and since U.S. policy is generally coercive, most anti-Americanism is America's own fault. Ninth, U.S. economic and military aid is designed to prop up local cliques that support U.S. economic and military interests and should be redirected to meet "human needs." Tenth, since the U.S. government cannot be trusted to accommodate itself to any of these policy reforms, critics must assume adversarial postures to force change.

But outside advocacy, or even what left-wing Democrats believed was advocacy, was not the key factor in U.S. foreign policy in the Carter years. The inside of Jimmy Carter's head, and of Secretary of State Cyrus Vance's and others, was the key factor. The Carter administration's general antipathy to force and its fears of overextension were clearly functions of bad memories of Vietnam. Import-ant members of the administration had been scarred—aside from Vance they included Anthony Lake and Richard Holbrooke, who were, respectively, director of policy planning in the State Department and assistant secretary of state for the Far East. And, of course, President Carter himself had strong feelings about the lessons of Vietnam. During the 1976 presidential campaign he said, in what could only be read as a repudiation of traditional containment policies:

> We have learned that never again should our country become militarily involved in the affairs of another nation unless there is a direct and obvious military threat to the security of the United States or its people. We must not use the CIA or other covert means to effect violent change in any government or government policy. Such involvements are not in the best interests of world peace, and they are almost inherently doomed to failure. . . . We must never again keep secret the evolution of our foreign policy from the Congress and the American people. They should never again be misled about our options, our commitments, our progress, or our failures.[11]

There is no question that whenever the Carter administration contemplated activism in international affairs, and especially whenever the possibility of using force arose, ghosts of Vietnam stalked the White House from root cellar to roof.[12] Of the key principals, only National Security Advisor Zbigniew Brzezinski, who had supported the war from his hawk's roost at Columbia University, and Secretary of Defense Harold Brown, who had been secretary of the air force during the war, ever seriously contemplated the use of force, whether against Khomeini's Iran or Sandinista Nicaragua. Secretary of State Vance, whose Pentagon experience during the Vietnam War had convinced him that the United States should *never* use force abroad, is perhaps the best example ever of the Vietnam syndrome in power. When Vance resigned after the botched 1980 raid into the Iranian desert to rescue U.S.

diplomats taken hostage by the Iranian regime in November 1979, it was not because he had been overruled on the matter; it was because as a matter of principle he could not serve a president who would use force.

The effect of Vietnam on the Carter administration's attitude toward Latin America was even more vivid. In the 1950s and 1960s, U.S. political leaders in both parties worried about Communist expansion into the Western Hemisphere, and especially the Caribbean basin. Presidents Eisenhower, Kennedy, and Johnson all determined to prevent, forestall, or overthrow regimes in which Communists played or were thought to have played major roles. In all instances—Cuba, the Dominican Republic, Guatemala, Surinam—there was a bipartisan consensus both in the Congress and outside of it that the United States should use every available means, including military force and covert operations, to prevent the establishment or expansion of Communism in the Caribbean basin.

By the mid-1970s, this consensus had been eroded deeply by the travails of Vietnam and Watergate. A new generation of liberal-isolationist politicians, journalists, clergymen, and academics, influenced by the adversary culture of the Vietnam War era, became hostile to all U.S. force projection and tolerant of Marxist and Marxist-Leninist regimes such as those in Salvador Allende's Chile and Fidel Castro's Cuba. This new political voice quickly acquired influence over American public opinion, parts of the foreign affairs bureaucracy, and especially the Democratic Party. Some who had learned to rail against nondemocratic allies of the United States by attacking the government in Saigon now actively sought the weakening of U.S. "hegemony" in Latin America by curtailing U.S. military assistance and foreign investment there. The idea gained ground that the United States could live with any Latin American regime, even a Communist one, as long as it did not become a Soviet military base. Such ideas had been around for years on the Left; the Institute for Policy Studies was especially fond of Latin Leftism thanks to Saul Landau, one of its resident scholars. But suddenly, after Vietnam, notions that seemed extreme in 1965 found a growing audience after 1975.

This new attitude toward Latin American politics as part of the U.S. political spectrum was joined to the ageless American contempt for repressive, antidemocratic regimes and yielded in the Carter administration a morally grounded impulse to hurt such regimes on principle. Since the Central American–Caribbean region was assumed to be of only modest strategic importance, such an impulse was more widely indulged than it might otherwise have been. It was widely believed that small and vulnerable countries such as Nicaragua could not pose any serious threat to U.S. security. These notions were strongly represented in the Carter administration and shaped U.S. policies toward the Somoza regime. Old priorities were abandoned in favor of a policy that sought rapid domestic reform in Nicaragua and assumed that U.S. pressure to that end could not redound to the strategic disadvantage of the United States.

Beyond new Latin leanings came a general upsurge of concern for human rights, another of the many consequences of the Vietnam antiwar movement. Concentration on human rights themes was for many a means of expiation for the sins committed against Vietnam; penance was to be achieved by experiencing and expressing revulsion against repressive regimes worldwide and punishing them, particularly those regimes friendly to the United States. Many young anti–Vietnam War activists joined the adversary culture, enlisting in the human rights crusade as the next logical step in fighting U.S. imperialism.[13] New human rights groups thus sprang up in the 1970s and established groups became larger and more active, lobbying the media, the Congress, and the State Department against repressive right-wing, but seldom left-wing, dictatorships.[14]

There was also a parallel explosion of congressional interest in human rights in the mid-1970s led by a small group of liberals within the Ninety-fourth Congress in 1974—sometimes called the Watergate class—notably Tom Harkin, Toby Moffett, and Stephen Solarz.[15] This produced an effort to redirect policy through legislative amendments to foreign aid bills and security assistance programs and in the congressional hearings process. In 1976 congressional legislation passed a mandate that "the principal goal of the foreign policy of the United States should be to promote the increased observance of internationally recognized human rights by all countries."[16] President Carter's own moralistic tone on foreign policy issues promoted this general focus. Both democratic and nondemocratic Leftist opponents of pro-Western authoritarian regimes took advantage of new U.S. attitudes to pursue their own efforts to weaken, discredit, and, if possible, overthrow those governments.

This general climate, plus Carter's hesitancy over crises in Nicaragua and Iran in 1978-79, energized critics into action. In both instances, pro-U.S. authoritarians had been replaced by anti-U.S. totalitarians, just as in Vietnam. In both cases the Soviet Union benefited and in one the victors were in ideological sympathy with Moscow. Thus was born in 1979 the Kirkpatrick Doctrine, the vanguard of the conservative attack against Carter and the flagship of the early Reagan administration's foreign policy.[17]

Jeanne Kirkpatrick, a political scientist soon to become U.S. Ambassador to the United Nation in the Reagan administration, argued—as had prominent political scientists in the 1950s—that there were important differences between authoritarian and totalitarian regimes. The former, Kirkpatrick pointed out, were interested in political power narrowly construed while the latter strove to take total social power in order to create "the new man" of some intellectual's fetid imagination. This made mere authoritarians more responsive to pressures for incremental reform than true totalitarians. If a choice had to be made between them, said Kirkpatrick, U.S. policy should favor the former as a lesser evil.

It is hard to say how much the vigorous conservative challenge to Carter's foreign policy led to his defeat in 1980. Certainly, failures in Central America,

Southwest Asia, and worsening relations with the Soviet Union were impossible to keep secret from the American people. The indignities of the Iranian hostage dilemma, in particular, did not help him. And Ronald Reagan and his supporters, having seized the Republican Party from relative moderates, were not shy in expressing their view of the lessons of Vietnam. Reagan stated during the 1980 campaign that the "Vietnam Syndrome had to go," defining it in more or less the same terms as had Jimmy Carter, only with the opposite valence. Reagan told a veterans' audience that: "It is time we recognized that ours was, in truth, a noble cause."[18]

Nor were Reagan administration principals, once in office, reluctant to claim that President Carter had mislearned the lessons of Vietnam. America must not shirk its responsibilities but stand tall: that meant rearming and reinvigorating foreign policy with an array of military options and, to be blunt, armed threats. One of the Reagan administration's first acts was to issue a White Paper on El Salvador detailing Nicaraguan and Cuban intrigues. Secretary of State Alexander Haig, Jr., spoke ominously about "going to the source" of the aggression. With this tack and this language it was impossible not to invoke images of Vietnam: State Department White Papers in 1964 and 1965 had been the lightning rods of debate back then, and talk about going to the source of aggression raised the same fears of a spreading conflict, then into China, now into all of Latin America and the Caribbean. In 1983 the administration "took a piece from the board" in the invasion of Grenada to demonstrate its seriousness.

Yet the Reagan administration did not turn the clock back to 1964, even though it often spoke as if it wished to. Its foreign policies sounded much tougher than they really were.[19] Even veteran Vietnam-era journalist, and no friend of the Republicans, Jonathan Schell, noted that in the Reagan years "the world of words and the world of deeds drifted apart," with the administration using force only where it was very easy—Grenada and Libya—and shrinking from pressing on where costs mounted—Lebanon—or where they promised to mount, as in Syria and Nicaragua.[20] Such caution could be hidden beneath cute phrases such as "constructive engagement," but it was virtual timidity all the same.

Schell also argued that Reagan captured perfectly the ambivalence of the American people about intervention, and insisted—quite correctly—that the un- digested lessons of Vietnam were the font of this ambivalence. "The public," he wrote, "was philosophically in favor of intervention but viscerally opposed. . . . The public was left in a state of unresolved ambivalence—repelled by the tangible prospect of any more Vietnams yet still attracted to the policies that had led the United States into Vietnam." Moreover, while, in Schell's view, McGovern and Carter lost the presidency, in 1972 and 1980, respectively, because they recognized only one side of this ambivalence, "Reagan was politically wiser. He followed to the letter the public preferences revealed in the latter days of the Vietnam War: he gave the public McGovernite decisions accompanied by Nixonian talk, and the public returned him to office in a landslide."[21] Schell oversimplified—Nixon himself, it will be recalled, gave the public McGovernite talk but Johnsonian decisions—but there is a basic truth to his analysis.

In another way, too, the Reagan administration's bark was more noticeable than its bite. Only once since 1973 has the invocation of the War Powers Act been a major political issue, and that was over the U.S. Marine deployment in Lebanon in 1983-84. The linkage to Vietnam was explicit; said Congressman Gene Snyder of Kentucky, for example:

> Obviously, even after he [Lyndon Johnson] had the Gulf of Tonkin resolution in his pocket, it was not the President's intention to use it to expand the American presence in Vietnam. . . . I contend that these limitations and restrictions are nothing more than good intentions—like the ones we heard from the administration in 1964—and we must recognize that a war in the Mideast can be just as hard on good intentions as a war in Southeast Asia was.[22]

Snyder asked the Congress to reject President Reagan's request to extend his authority to keep the Marines in Lebanon, a request the president had tried to sell by implausibly invoking a Soviet threat in the conflict there—another dissonant echo of Vietnam, bouncing in the opposite direction.

The Reagan administration could have had its way for a long time had it decided to keep or increase the U.S. deployment in Lebanon. It also could have challenged the constitutionality of the War Powers Resolution, as many conservatives urged it to do. But the administration did not challenge the resolution, and it decided to withdraw from Lebanon. The dynamics of that particular affair, and dispute over it within the administration, were the key factors in the decision, but the death of Marines far away, the imprecision of American purpose, the absence of reliable local allies, the dissension of many European friends, bad press, and public pressure enabled through the War Powers Resolution all smacked of the combination that had made Vietnam such an ugly affair from the perspective of at least two White House staffs. While things may have turned out the same in Lebanon, Vietnam or no Vietnam, there is no doubt that its shadow glowered over the Reagan White House as the principals worked the matter through.

But the Reagan administration's foreign policy did have its bold side, and conservatives' lessons of the Vietnam War speak directly to its origins and logic. The understanding that the president and his advisors had of the Vietnam War led, in inverted form, to the Reagan Doctrine. To track this process properly, we must retrace once again the tangled subjective history of détente.

As noted earlier, the Nixon administration hid one foreign policy in the language of another in order to sell it to a wounded and skeptical American public:

It put the body of containment in the clothing of "détente." The problem was that the policy failed thanks to Soviet determination to prey upon American political and military weakness. The rhetoric of détente bought the Nixon administration more time domestically, which, while it contributed to Nixon's reelection in 1972, could not save the policy itself. After the October 1973 Middle East War, the gap between what it promised and what it delivered became too large to ignore. One should not judge too harshly; American fatigue, self-doubt, and internal recriminations put the revival of robust containment in the period from 1969 to 1973 beyond all but the most charismatic of leaderships. Nevertheless, fail it did, and with the fall of Saigon in 1975, the idea of "détente" failed with it.

But this can be confusing. What had failed was a policy, not the name for it. Détente as a name for what Nixon was trying to do was in truth somewhat misappropriated; as a French wag said at the time: Détente was the continuation of containment by the advent of other means, and sometimes the same means.

The Nixonian détente, which may be called Détente I to distinguish it from future versions, was clearly designed with Vietnam in mind. So was Détente II, that of Jimmy Carter. Détente had always sounded like a good idea to most Democrats, but the situation after 1976 required that they redefine what it meant. That was difficult to do, however, under circumstances of weakened American military power, dispirited national will, and a divided Democratic Party. In any event, the foreign policy of the Carter administration, described earlier, also took the name détente and, like the first version, it failed too.

So by the time Ronald Reagan came to office, détente in two different versions had been discredited. The Nixon-Kissinger détente became the first negative blueprint from which conservative Republicans began working after 1976, and the Carter administration's version became the second as they rose to national prominence thereafter. Neither indirect containment nor its virtual abandonment would do. Reagan rejected both Détente I and Détente II, the word itself becoming close to unspeakable in the White House.

Instead, the Reagan administration sought the offensive, striving indirectly to undermine Soviet imperial overextension. The Vietnam metaphor became fully inverted and thus was born the Reagan Doctrine. If Soviet aid to Hanoi helped make U.S. commitments too heavy for its resources to bear in Vietnam, then U.S. aid to the Afghan *mujahideen,* to UNITA in Angola, to the Nicaraguan Contras, to those fighting the Soviet-supported Vietnamese occupation of Cambodia, could do the same to the Soviet balance between commitments and resources.[23] There was considerable enthusiasm in the bureaucracy for this approach; it seemed poetic justice. According to authors Mohammed Yousaf and Mark Adkin, many CIA officials openly regarded the war in Afghanistan "as a heaven-sent opportunity to avenge Vietnam by shedding other people's blood rather than American."[24] Said

Congressman Charles Wilson along similar lines: "There were 58,000 dead in Vietnam and we owe the Russians one. . . . I have a slight obsession with it because of Vietnam. I thought the Soviets ought to get a dose of it."[25] So did Ronald Reagan. The Reagan Doctrine, then, had much more to do with the lessons of Vietnam than first met the eye.

In the end, ironically, the Reagan administration's anti-détentism ended up being called détente—Détente III. The twice-fought battle over détente had become so deeply embedded in the vocabulary of the U.S. foreign policy debate that not even the Reagan administration could ignore it. Critics, including prominent Carter administration officials turned out of office in 1981, constantly attacked the Reagan administration for jettisoning the chances for détente—still as ill-defined, and therefore useful, as ever. Reagan buckled and, in his second term, allowed the word into the White House lexicon. Thanks largely to its liberal critics—those who believed diametrically opposite lessons about Vietnam—the Reagan administration's chief foreign policy success will go down in history as nothing less than the success of détente. Heaven help future historians as they try to sort this one out.

Nevertheless, the Reagan presidency did indeed achieve détente, and more besides. It did so by means of strength and resolve that was unavailable to the Nixon and Ford administrations during the post-Vietnam malaise, and that was deemed undesirable by the Carter administration.[26] Fair and equal arms control agreements were consummated, real reductions in nuclear weapons were achieved for the first time in the Intermediate Nuclear Forces Treaty of December 1987, Soviet opportunism was checked in the world's peripheries, the agenda of U.S.-Soviet summitry was broadened, trade increased, and a better mutual understanding of limits and interests was established in both Washington and Moscow. The stage was then set for an American foreign policy less "obsessed with communism," to use Carter's term, less military in emphasis, and more concerned with development, democracy, and human rights—all of which the Reagan administration turned to in its second term to one degree or another.

The Western victory in the Cold War transcended détente, of course. Yet, in a way, the Cold War still might not be over had it not been for the Vietnam antiwar movement. How so? The antiwar movement helped elect Richard Nixon twice and this, together with the ascendancy of the New Politics in the Democratic Party, paved the way for Ronald Reagan's entry into the White House in 1981. In turn, thanks to the Reagan-Bush foreign policy, the Cold War ended on basically American terms, and without a shot being fired.[27] Could it even be, in a roundabout way at least, that American defeat in the Vietnam War, through the train of consequences it unleashed, helped bring about the destruction of the Soviet Union? And if indeed the antiwar movement contributed at least a little to American defeat, doesn't it follow that it deserves some of the credit?

## FAMINE AND FEAST IN THE ACADEMY

While all this was going on, the use of Vietnam as a metaphor also enjoyed a career in the academy, where the writing vaguely paralleled what was happening in Washington. But this career began slowly and the reason is interesting.

It is a truism of the philosophy of history that a book written in, say, 1885 about events in 1812 necessarily reveals something about both eras. The readers of that book in 1995 had better understand this if they are to appreciate what is before them. Although the process is greatly telescoped in consideration of literature about Vietnam and the antiwar movement—we are measuring by decades instead of centuries—this insight is still seminal. One can stand at any point in the triangle of years and "see" the other two points. This is why Joseph Epstein, editor of *American Scholar,* can say of current assessments of the 1960s: "Tell me what you think of that period, and I'll tell you what your politics are."[28] This triangle of the philosophy of history explains several otherwise mysterious curiosities concerning the academic literature about the Vietnam War.

The American intelligentsia was strangely silent about the American experience in Vietnam for the first half-dozen years after the fall of Saigon. With only a few exceptions, most historians, social critics, and political scientists avoided serious thinking or writing on the subject.[29] In the second half-dozen years after the fall of Saigon however, which was coterminous with the Reagan presidency, there was an avalanche of analytical literature as well as much fiction and filmmaking about almost every aspect of the war.[30] Setting aside for a moment the contents of this production, what accounts for the juxtaposition of the quiescent and the frenetic?

The first and probably the most important reason was psychological fatigue; after having lived anxiously with Vietnam for more than a decade, ignoring it seemed broadly therapeutic. A second reason was a humility born of either shame or abashed reminiscences of youth, particularly as the sense of embarrassment grew over the character of Hanoi's rule. This did not stop antiwar veterans young and old from involving themselves in human rights crusades the world over or in ecological activism, but in polite liberal circles Vietnam became a something like the mad uncle in the sanatorium whom no one ever mentions.[31]

What then accounted for the frenzy of publishing, filmmaking, and media docu-glare that went on for the next decade and a half? As silence is sometimes therapeutic, so is cathartic release. But a more interesting possibility is less clinical than political, and it is this: Only with the coming to office of the Reagan administration, with its seemingly globe-spanning interventionary inclinations, and with the fears of atavistic Cold Warriorism that some of its early rhetoric inspired, did the Great Debate over American foreign policy revive with any intensity. One Leftist with antiwar movement experience put it directly: "Nostalgia for the 1960s has only grown with the triumph of Reagan and Bush, the rise of 'neoconservativism' and the 'New Right,' the rollback of the welfare state, and the continuation of imperialist policies in Central America and elsewhere."[32]

While Reagan administration principals did believe that the American posture, military and diplomatic, had shrunk too much, its policies were, as noted, far more circumspect than its rhetoric. But opponents on the Left, who believed the Cold War was already over in 1981, as many had believed it to be over in 1955, 1963, and 1972, were nevertheless frightened. In consequence, a new form of Jules Feiffer's rocket rattle was soon produced by the adversary culture; it was called the nuclear-freeze movement, marshaled by its organizers as a broadly partisan effort to injure the Reagan administration and bring down the conservative ascendancy.[33] The majority of those who favored the freeze, of course, did not put partisan political motives ahead of moral commitment, but, as with the Vietnam antiwar movement, that did not change the organizers' motives.

Along with the freeze movement came dozens of academic books attacking the idea of deterrence itself along with the Republican administration. Another sign of the times was the plethora of contending "doctrines" in the early to mid-1980s that sought to make some sense out of the need to pursue containment as a policy after Vietnam had discredited it as an idea. Aside from Reagan's own doctrine, perhaps the best known was that of Secretary of Defense Caspar Weinberger, which, reflecting the deep scars of Vietnam within the professional military, specified five conditions for military intervention that were unlikely ever to be met, it seemed, under any circumstances.[34]

It was the return of the Great Debate that caused the outpouring of books about Vietnam. Wittingly or not, honestly or not, such books were as much about then-current intellectual and political confrontations as they were about past military ones. To defend a view of the war's origins or an explanation for American failure was often only a small step from advocating a line of reasoning or a policy pattern with respect to disputes over Central America, Angola, Afghanistan, or southern Africa. In short, Vietnam became the key part of the metaphorical currency of the still-divided American foreign policy discourse. If the essential instinct that led to U.S. involvement in Vietnam was sound, then Reagan's suspicions about détente and his interventionary inclinations were sound too—if not, then not.

It never was true, as the bumper stickers claimed in the early and mid-1980s, that El Salvador is Spanish for Vietnam. But it was true—and remains true—that many people simply cannot discuss questions about the use of American power abroad except in reference to the idiom of assumptions and images at whose center lie the nation's divided memory of Vietnam.[35] Despite the almost total lack of true analogy—historical, strategic, or moral—we saw this kind of analogizing in the academic literature in discussions of U.S. policy in Central America throughout the

1980s, at the outset of the Kuwait crisis in 1990, and, with perhaps greater justification, during the Bosnian crisis of 1993-95.

Some of the literary confrontations waged over these years were over broad political and philosophical questions.[36] Other confrontations were less broad, as for example the arguments over American military performance in Southeast Asia.[37] Still others found their source in lighter writing about lighter products, as the tiny tempest critics made over the film *Hanoi Hilton* in 1987 attested.[38] Conclusions stretched from the sublime to the absurd.[39] One book, cowritten by professors at the U.S. Military Academy, concluded that since the war and the antiwar movement did not destroy the constitutional structure of the United States, it was not very important.[40] Another, by Marilyn B. Young, was a history of the war exactly as every 1960s radical would want it told.[41] But, characteristically, its purpose was not directed only to the past; toward the end, Young implores all Americans "to accept responsibility" for the war, and she calls U.S. actions in Lebanon, Libya, Grenada, Panama, El Salvador, Nicaragua, and Angola part of the "whole Orwellian world" for which Washington has been responsible since the end of the Vietnam War. Young even managed to place most of the blame for post-1975 violence in Southeast Asia, even that between China and Vietnam in 1979, on the United States.[42]

Beyond the books written both by and for the intellectual elite, there was also an outpouring of textbook literature on the war and the antiwar movement. College professors and even high school teachers had finally discovered Vietnam as a topic for history and politics discussions by the early 1980s.[43] Such literature also followed a pattern of first famine and then feast—or gluttony. University of Pennsylvania students who had been in high school during the Carter administration complained that their high school history texts had stopped cold in 1965; they knew nothing about Vietnam. Most college freshmen five years later however, had been exposed at least glancingly to Vietnam, the antiwar movement, and the counterculture. Not surprisingly, what some had learned in high school did not square with what others had learned. The teaching of the lessons of Vietnam to high school students and university undergraduates has exhibited the same schizophrenia exhibited by the battle between latter-day hawks and doves over the meaning of the war. Virtually all "readers" and teaching units claim to seek balance, but few have achieved it.[44] One can hardly blame pedagogues and textbook writers however, for not agreeing on a subject that now five consecutive presidents of the United States have never straightened out among themselves.

Finally in this regard, books specifically about the antiwar movement present something of a problem. Unlike nearly every other aspects of the war, the movement has not been subject to a synoptic analytical critique.[45] Instead of normal sociopolitical analysis we have had mainly variations on chest-thumping or breast-beating. The chest-thumping, while a good source of sometimes reliable information, is mainly hagiographic self-justification of modest analytical value.[46] "Eyewitness" accounts abound, some dating from the late 1960s or early 1970s, others more recent.[47] Some are superficial,[48] others unflinchingly radical,[49] some distorted by lesser ideological fixations,[50] and a few are quite good.[51] There are also several "oral histories."[52] Beyond the memoirish, some works join themselves to the self-conscious field of "peace history," and while their bias is clear, the anecdotal data they have amassed and preserved is invaluable.[53]

The breast-beating school is small but interesting, falling into a respected tradition of writings by intellectuals who embraced and then rejected Communism over the years.[54] While the tone of this writing has tended toward the shrill, the insights have often been sharp, certainly more so than those of former foes of the movement who wrote as if the "hippies and bombthrowers" were demons to be exorcised rather than parts of a social movement to be studied.[55]

Virtually all these works shared one similarity: an insistence that the 1960s were unique. This insistence seemed to parallel the obsessive self-consciousness of the era for, even while it was happening, the 1960s was chronicling, criticizing, and celebrating itself in streams of print, film, and song.[56] It was a paradoxical time too: Many young people believed they were living for the moment and making history simultaneously, the former implying a lack of reflexive interest and the latter presuming lots of it.

Social life always freezes into itself the conceptions we have of it, but the process is not usually so self-conscious or rapid. In a way that few previous decades had, the 1960s rolled back on itself, its introspectiveness creating a keen sense of accelerated experience.[57] One piece of evidence may be found in changes in common language that occurred between roughly 1963 and 1973, as certain an indicator of novel social experience as the rings on a tree stump are a guide to its age.[58]

This self-consciousness never ended and may even have expanded in the last 25 years as edited memory confronted the cognitive frontier of the present.[59] The outpouring of books about the 1960s from those who spent their youth within it has probably had a kind of multiplier effect on how radical a time we imagine it to have been. Life does imitate representations, even representations claiming to be drawn directly from life.

Perhaps the greatest problem with the existing literature on the movement is not a general ideological bias but its inability to separate analysis from both moral judgment and personal location. It fails to examine seriously fundamental questions about the war itself and, by assuming a two-dimensional understanding of the war, judgments of the antiwar movement come out flat as well. Thus have old myths about the war flowed unreflectively into new "knowledge" about the antiwar movement. The literary genre that has emerged is best characterized as political folklore for, like all folklore, it has aimed at capturing and conveying personal and emotional truths, not objective historical ones.

## USING THE MOVEMENT, SELLING THE MOVEMENT

Still other symbolic uses of Vietnam, the antiwar movement, and the 1960s generally have been constructed. As a symbol, Vietnam stands for things it should not stand for, but it stands nonetheless. As is generally the case when metaphors are cast so widely, a dilution process takes place over time that distorts original content. A kind of inversion occurs; every time "Vietnam" gets slapped on to another topic or product, that new attachment moves the content of the metaphor farther away from its original construction. It is then no longer the same metaphor. For those who were not adults during the war and the antiwar movement, the potential for miscommunication through these attenuated uses of Vietnam is very great indeed.

Sometimes this attenuation is deliberate. The adversary culture has employed Vietnam as a metaphor in several ways, all keyed around the unshakable belief that the antiwar movement, child of the adversary culture, was instrumental in bringing about the end of the U.S. commitment to South Vietnam. On that basis, the adversary culture grew and planned for the future in the years immediately after the fall of Saigon. Its groups still believe today that they have been responsible for a whole host of other "victories"—defeat of Contra aid, sanctions against South Africa, the Intermediate-range Nuclear Forces Treaty, and others besides. They sometimes explicitly compare these "victories" to the one in Vietnam.[60]

This raises a problem for contemporary adversary culture members. Everyone knows by now what happened in Vietnam; it is not possible to claim plausibly that the lot of most people there has been better under Communist rule than it was under the government of South Vietnam. This problem is parried in one of three ways. Some, such as the irrepressible David Dellinger, still claim (as of 1986, in any case) that things *were* better, even before Hanoi's version of perestroika began.[61] Most argue that the verdict was inevitable, that the United States could not have won, and that the antiwar movement thus served to cut America's losses in blood, treasure, and integrity. This means, in effect, that what actually happened in Vietnam is not an issue. A few, such as Joan Baez, have admitted that they were wrong about the likely consequences of a Communist victory.

Still, the adversary culture has marketed images of Vietnam that have nothing to do with what happened to the Vietnamese. The War Resisters League has fought against all deployments of U.S. nuclear weapons using Vietnam in its solicitations. How? To the WRL, U.S. involvement in the Vietnam War always held forth the possibility of the use of nuclear weapons. To sell the nuclear-freeze movement in the 1980s, actor Martin Sheen fronted a WRL solicitation that joined together Central America and the nuclear freeze as the WRL had formerly joined together Vietnam and the prospect of nuclear war. Sheen told readers that tax dollars are financing "atrocities" in Central America that are "as horrifying as the

ones you and I remember from Vietnam—the napalm, the wanton destruction of
whole villages, the incredible loss of life." Next we discover the basis for Sheen's
expertise: "I learned a lot about the evil of war when I starred in a movie about
Vietnam—*Apocalypse Now.*" The solicitation was geared to bring the supposed
analogy between Vietnam and El Salvador into high relief. Sheen wrote: "I believe
it is not too late to prevent this nation from committing another Vietnam—or
worse." (The phrase "*committing* another Vietnam" suggests semantically that
Vietnam was not a strategic miscalculation or even a deed of shame, but a crime.)
Sheen's reference to some still "worse" crime is clarified later:

> I am deeply concerned that President Reagan—totally committed to a "Holy
> Crusade" against an "Evil Empire," but unwilling to risk another Vietnam-style
> defeat of American troops in a foreign jungle—might be prepared to launch
> a "limited" nuclear war rather than lose in Central America.

Sheen then switches to capital letters:

> THAT IS WHY IT IS URGENTLY IMPORTANT . . . TO STOP THE U.S. WAR
> IN EL SALVADOR, BEFORE SOMETHING EVEN MORE UNTHINKABLE
> THAN ANOTHER VIETNAM TURNS OUR WORLD INTO A SMOKING RUIN.

There have been parochial political uses of Vietnam as well. For example,
many American Jewish Leftists invoke Vietnam to justify their association with
Peace Now, the Israeli peace movement—even though the situations (the United
States in Vietnam, Israel in the West Bank) bear no resemblance to each other.[62]
Even some Israelis do this. On June 6, 1992, at Tel Aviv University a small group
of protestors held signs reading: "25 years of Israel's Vietnam."[63] Other Jews ridicule
such borrowing but sometimes use Vietnam metaphors themselves to do so. Thus
Ze'ev Chafets, a Detroit-born Israeli journalist, criticized a planned gathering of
Jewish Leftists with the title "An Invitation to Tikkunstock," a compound reference
to the liberal Jewish journal *Tikkun* and Woodstock.[64]

On occasion, too, what various salesmen of Vietnam want is not hearts or
minds, but something much simpler: money. Reference to Vietnam can sell books,
for example. Handsome bulk-mail solicitations from Time-Life books trying to sell
*The Vietnam Experience* show how marketers have thought through the divided
image of Vietnam. They sell it by raising emotion and remaining ambiguous about
judgments. "Which was your Vietnam Experience?" a brochure asks, as Jimi
Hendrix–like images coexist with offers for a free battle map of Vietnam and a book
entitled *Combat Photographer.* "Whether you fought in it . . . or for it . . . or against
it. . . . It's time to make peace with the past," the reader is told. "Whether you
supported or opposed it, there's no denying that we're all still feeling the effects of
the Vietnam War. Only by understanding how and why it happened, can we put
it in perspective and learn from it." The reader can make peace with the past, it

turns out, just by buying four books at $14.99 each (plus ubiquitous shipping and handling fees).

In case the reader doesn't get the idea from the core contents of the solicitation, the back page of the letter carries two photos, one of a soldier carrying an M-16 with bullets flying all around him, the other of a student wearing a University of Ohio sweatshirt, his right hand raised in a victory signal. Both captions are vast exaggerations of most personal experiences. Next to the protester, for example, is this copy:

> You risked being spat on and accused of being a traitor or a coward. Your
> family turned against you. You were arrested and beaten by the police. Even
> in the sanctuary of your college campus you were subject to FBI surveillance.

Clearly, the aim of this solicitation is to raise emotions and summon memories of youth in order to loosen billfolds. It reinforces the "us against them" image of the times, which, while perhaps good for selling books, may not be as healthy for the country. But business is business, and to work the solicitation must induce or capitalize on memories edited to maximum emotional pull. What Time-Life seems to really be selling is youth—selling it back to its original owners.

There are other uses of Vietnam that stand out even more dramatically as abuses in pursuit of money. One was perpetrated by ABC News in the *New York Times* on April 26, 1990, where an advertisement for a Peter Jennings special report called "From the Killing Field" used the famous and still deeply moving picture of Vietnamese children fleeing a napalm attack. Beneath the photograph were words to the effect that the United States was still at war against Vietnam through its support for anti-Vietnamese forces in Cambodia.[65] Given what Vietnamese military forces were doing to their own people at the time, not to speak of the Cambodians, this has to rank as one of the most outrageous manipulations of Vietnam as metaphor ever witnessed.

The music business, too, has been forever changed by the 1960s. As many have noted, 1960s music first joined song and politics in a mass cultural medium. Political music had always existed in the United States, notably in patriotic songs and labor movement ballads, but before radio and record players relatively few people could be reached, and the frequency of repetition and the pace of producing new material was modest. The 1960s changed all that forever.

The music business in this country today is truly big business, but it retains symbolic vestiges of political baptism in the 1960s. This gives rise to strange incongruities. It is common, for example, for rock celebrities to associate themselves with political causes, whether Farm Aid concerts or Paul Simon's *Graceland* album, and doing so recalls the nobility of music's roll in fighting the Vietnam War. The politics are still at least vaguely left wing too; when *Rolling Stone* editor Jann Wenner endorsed Jerry Brown for president in 1992 it was hardly a surprise,[66] nor were the magazine's featured interviews with Noam Chomsky, perhaps America's most charismatic antiestablishment radical.[67] Nor is it surprising to see coverage of any and all efforts to legalize marijuana, a latter-day joining of drugs and politics.[68] On the other hand, when Neil Young, famous member of Crosby, Stills, Nash and Young, decided to vote for Ronald Reagan in 1980, it *was* a surprise; the rock music world could barely believe its ears.

In fact, the image of 1960s music as having been devoted to causes is mostly false. Some musicians were consciously political but most were just trying to sell records—not that there is anything wrong with that, and not that musicians should all have felt obligated to be political activists just because their music was popular. Roger McGuinn, the leader of the Byrds, revealed in 1990 that the band's members spent a great deal of time on drugs and were mainly interested in making records people would buy.

> *Fricke*: Was there much organized political activity in the rock community on issues like civil rights and the Vietnam War?
>
> *McGuinn*: Not that I can remember. I was political in that I didn't like inhumanity to man. But I really didn't get involved. I didn't vote either. I didn't do anything. I was tied up in my own little world.
>
> *Fricke*: Yet the Byrds were writing and recording songs that fueled the civil-rights and antiwar movements.
>
> *McGuinn*: We figured that was our contribution. Actually, we were just doing songs. We really meant them when we did them. But that was the end of it. When I was off the road, I was at my house, playing with my gadgets. And staying stoned a lot. That was my life. I mean, we were hedonists.[69]

Rock's left-wing "bad boy" bias inherited from the antiwar movement remains in the sense that rock is supposed to be a form of antiestablishment expression. Its "bad boy" rebelliousness helped make it popular in the first place and that remains crucial to its appeal, especially for "acid" rockers. (The term is *not* coincidental.) But there is virtually nothing antiestablishment about the record business or about *Rolling Stone* magazine for that matter. Just as Madison Avenue successfully marketed the attenuated language of the counterculture, so big business has long since harnessed rock for profit, and those businessmen are not outsiders in gray suits but people who are part of "the generation" and who espouse superficially the ethos of the 1960s even as they stuff cash in their pockets. For anyone who had been languishing in doubt about this, the staging of Woodstock '94 should have put all doubt to rest.

True, some rock musicians resist and still write songs like "You Bowed Down" (Elvis Costello) and "The Money-Go-Round" (Ray Davies of the Kinks), but most don't. This makes some of them feel guilty and no doubt fuels the desire to lend their names and occasional talents to "causes." If this sounds like a formula for inauthentic authenticity, that's because it is.

But this was a problem in the 1960s too. While authenticity was the ideal of both the counterculture and its music, few young people knew what authenticity was. When Joe Cocker sang the Beatles's song "With a Little Help from My Friends" at Woodstock on August 17, 1969, it was, as Louis Menard put it, "an imitation British music hall number performed in upstate New York by a white man from Sheffield pretending to be Ray Charles. On that day, probably nothing could have sounded more genuine."[70]

## HERE, THERE, EVERYWHERE

While many policy debates over the years referenced Vietnam in so many ways, and while its image was marketed in countless ways, the war and antiwar movement also seeped into cultural consciousness from local newspapers, television and radio talk shows, barber shop and beauty parlor banter, the paperback section at Woolworths, and in the dozens of veterans' projects and hard-luck stories of redemption and deprivation all around us.[71] Vietnam can be summoned to consciousness just by looking through the magazines at any airport or train station bookstore.[72] Why? Because stories that recall the war and the antiwar movement seem never to disappear for long.

The bizarre 1974 episode in which Patricia Hearst and her fiancé were kidnapped but then joined the Symbionese Liberation Army evoked the Weathermen. The tragedy of the Vietnamese boat people, which began months after the fall of South Vietnam in 1975, evoked U.S. failure, as did the killing fields of Pol Pot's Cambodia. For years, too, seemingly open questions about American prisoners of war and soldiers missing in action (POWs/MIAs) remaining in Indochina churned up strong emotion and much news copy; in the 1992 presidential election, in particular, the coincidence of Ross Perot's interest in the matter and the assertion by Russian president Boris Yeltsin that American servicemen may have been turned over by the North Vietnamese to Soviet interrogators brought the issue back once again.[73]

Over time, the prisoner of war question became entwined with U.S. diplomatic decisions about whether and under what conditions to engage in diplomacy with the Vietnamese government. So persistent has this theme been in the news that the *Washington Post* could entitle an editorial headline "The End of the Vietnam War" in May 1992.[74] But it still wasn't over. Senator John F. Kerry, sponsoring a bill in January 1994 to lift the economic embargo against Vietnam, pleaded with his colleagues that it was "time to put the war behind us."[75] The resolution, in a breathtaking example of the circular logic of political reality, also called on Vietnam to improve its human rights record. Of course, it was the antiwar movement's anguish over *South* Vietnam's human rights record that introduced the contemporary version of the human rights plank into U.S. foreign policy pronouncements in the first place.

In mid-1994, Vietnam was back in the Senate. When President Clinton nominated Sam Brown to be U.S. Ambassador to the Conference on Security and Cooperation in Europe, Republican Senator Robert C. Smith of New Hampshire denounced Brown as a "radical war protestor," adding that "many" of Clinton's "national security nominees" were "unabashed anti-war activists or radical extremists. . . . The President continues to surround himself with the type of people he protested with in the golden years of the anti-war movement. And it is having a devastating effect of the quality and effectiveness of our national security policy." Inaccurate though Senator Smith's remarks were, they were popular enough to twice deny administration supporters the 60 votes they needed to end the filibuster against Brown.[76] If that were not enough, Newt Gingrich, the new Speaker of the House of Representatives following the 1994 midterm elections, pledged to attack "McGovernicks" and "the counterculture" in order to restore American virtue—two symbols pointing obviously to the antiwar movement environment.

On a less political level, human interest stories about burned-out vets surface regularly.[77] The best-seller list has been bedecked from time to time by books whose focus is Vietnam. Neil Sheehan's *A Bright Shining Lie,* the tale of John Vann, the outspoken American military advisor in South Vietnam, won a Pulitzer Prize, and made book news for months in 1988 and 1989.[78]

The antiwar movement and the counterculture return now and again as nostalgia merchandise for worried yuppies. The mounting of Woodstock '94 at Saugerties, New York, in August 1994 was a prime example—not that John Sebastian, formerly of the Lovin' Spoonful, had not already been trying to resell Woodstock many times over on late-night TV for several years. We have also seen generationally displaced uses of the counterculture in youth fashion, where the daily items of 1960s youth culture have been turned into artifacts: sandalwood, peace signs, bongs, Indian hash pipes, and all the rest. "So saturated has the culture become with the icons of the era," wrote journalist Katherine Bishop, "that teen-agers wear their mothers' old peace-symbol jewelry without understanding how it was connected to the Vietnam War."[79]

Recollections of the movement also return regularly through the occasional obituary, of Abbie Hoffman, Jerry Rubin, or Huey Newton,[80] and in news of the sixth, seventh, or eight rejection by the parole board of Charles Manson's freedom.

Speaking of Manson, the national press carried a small item in November 1993 about two brothers in California—where else?—making money selling Manson T-shirts, with a dark—what else?—likeness of Manson on the front and the words "Charlie Don't Surf" on the back. "Charlie don't surf" is a famous line uttered about the Vietcong by actor Robert Duvall in the film *Apocalypse Now,* here meant simply to note—humorously one supposes—that it is hard to surf while doing life in prison. As with many other "double meaning" takes on the period, the younger set probably misses the full blast of wit. Manson, anyway, earned royalties from the sales, enough for "smokes and Cokes" according to a prison guard.[81] A month later it came out that rock star Axl Rose (William Bruce Bailey, as named at birth) included one of Manson's old songs secretly on a Guns n' Roses album, something that might have earned him much more money. The outrage was so great however, that new pressings of the CD were to exclude the Manson cut, and monies earned from the original pressing were to go to the homeless instead. Rose tried to deny he knew it was Manson's song, saying he thought it was written by a member of the Beach Boys. But he ends the song with a sigh, saying quietly, "Thanks, Chas." Said Doris Tate, Sharon Tate's sister: "Doesn't Axl Rose realize what this man did to my family?"[82] Not really, Doris; he was only six-years-old when it happened.

Moving from the sinister to the silly, every so often recollections of Jane Fonda's broadcasting from Hanoi evokes strong memories. Vietnam veterans, in particular, seem to still have it in for Fonda, referring to her derisively as "Barbarella" after her early airhead sex-kitten role in the space fantasy movie of the same name, and even displaying bumper stickers saying: "Nuke Jane Fonda."[83]

Even the business section of the newspaper occasionally alludes to Vietnam. When the Federal Reserve raised interest rates in November 1994, the *New York Times* subtitled a commentary: "Aim Heavy Weapons At Hard-to-See Foe."[84] Even if one did not recall Walter Lippmann's famous remark, that in Vietnam the U.S. Army was trying to kill a cloud of mosquitoes with an elephant gun, it was clear to anyone older than 30 years that the metaphor referred to Vietnam—and was not complimentary to Alan Greenspan, the Federal Reserve's erstwhile chairman.

Both thoughtful and ridiculous recollections of the counterculture are also frequent reminders of the antiwar movement atmosphere, as is the occasional offbeat story about the counter-counterculture.[85] In May 1991, for example, there was a brief flurry of interest about a proposal by several conservatives who wanted to erect a bust of Spiro Agnew in the Capitol.[86]

No event is exempt: When American diplomat hostages returned from Iran in January 1981, *Playboy* noted the difference between how they were received and how Vietnam vets had been welcomed home. This touched off a cascade of letters, of which three were published. One veteran bitter about how the antiwar movement spoiled his homecoming wrote:

> I was drafted; they were all volunteers.
>
> I was sent against my will; they took their families.
>
> I saw brutality, injustice, and waste; they endured.
>
> I had no support from students; students held them hostage.
>
> I got letters only from my family; the whole world became their family.
>
> I had marches and demonstrations against my being there; they had marches and demonstrations to help them come home.[87]

The letter went on for another four or five couplets, ending with a plaintive "Thank you, America." The author's point seems to have been that the return of the hostages bore little resemblance to the return of Vietnam vets. But why should it have? What did one thing have to do with the other? All that needed to happen to evoke these comparisons was for some Americans who had suffered a tough time overseas to come back home, and what it showed was not injustice to Vietnam vets—that had happened long before—but how psychologically present Vietnam remained.

Images of Vietnam and the antiwar movement have also proliferated widely in popular culture, especially through film.[88] Many people much too young to have watched television news during the war have seen *Alice's Restaurant, Easy Rider, Apocalypse Now, The Deer Hunter,* and *Hair,* to name only the best known. They have also seen Sylvester Stallone as *Rambo,* drawing first, second, and third blood. They have seen *The Killing Fields,* whose Cambodian gore is accurate enough but whose political context is largely absent. They have seen *The Big Chill,* which most probably associate with their parents. They have watched the television series *M\*A\*S\*H* and the original film too, both of which were really about Vietnam even though they were set in Korea. Similarly, Kurt Vonnegut's book *Slaughterhouse Five,* and the film made after it, while set during World War II, aimed to illustrate the absurdity of war and was obviously written with Vietnam in mind. One can only imagine what these films communicate to 18-year old college freshmen nowadays.

More recent Vietnam-related films include *Good Morning Vietnam, Full Metal Jacket, Platoon, Casualties of War,* and *Born on the Fourth of July*; all give diverse but highly truncated images of the war and the antiwar movement, many of them aiming to comment as much on the present as on the 1960s. Much of this truncation is deliberate, Hollywood being one of the last remaining bastions of chic Leftism in America, a development itself accelerated by the antiwar movement and the counterculture.[89] For example, Brian De Palma said of *Casualties of War,* which is about a gang rape of a Vietnamese woman by a group of American soldiers, that his movie "encapsulated" American involvement in Vietnam. He actually had even grander ambitions. Said George Szamuely of De Palma's intended message:

> The American presence there was a crime visited on the Vietnamese, but it is part of the larger crime of aggressive masculinity. Redemption comes belatedly by way of a conditional exoneration that exacts as its price the imprisonment of macho swagger. Thus the politics of the 60s and 80s join hands.[90]

Exactly right, which is why the news that movie rights to Neil Sheehan's *A Bright Shining Lie* were purchased by Jane Fonda did not cheer the heart of many a Vietnam veteran.[91]

There has been, however, some inadvertent entertainment value to come out of the politicization of Hollywood, thanks to the astonishing ignorance of some entertainers. Since 1976, would-be presidents have taken their cash-seeking campaigns to Hollywood. In 1976, singer Diana Ross asked Jimmy Carter what he was going to do about Vietnam. Carter answered tartly: "The war is over."[92]

Some images of the era, at least, have been portrayed in fairly subtle ways. To return to the movies for a moment, in Woody Allen's film *Bananas* there is a scene in which Allen, playing Fielding Melish, stands trial for sedition because he has become the dictator of a fictional Latin American republic called San Marcos. Acting as his own counsel, his behavior in the court leads the judge, who looks very much like Chicago Seven trial judge Julius Hoffmann, to have him bound and gagged. In this state, mumbling incomprehensibly, Melish, still defending himself, comically breaks down a hostile witness into an admission of lying. But anyone who did not remember what actually happened to Bobby Seale in a Chicago courtroom in 1970 could not possibly have sensed the serious undertone to the humor, and could not have understood it fully.

Similarly, in the animated television program *The Simpsons,* an episode about the family's runaway dog shows Homer Simpson's demonic boss "conditioning" the lost pooch into a ferocious watchdog. The method, where the dog's head is held still in metal and leather braces while his eyes are propped open before horrific scenes (for a dog), obviously parodies actor Malcolm McDowell's ordeal in *A Clockwork Orange,* based on Anthony Burgess's strange but powerful tale of revolt against the diabolical technocracy of the police state. Few of the younger set, it may be assumed, caught the reference.

But other references are hard to avoid. No one, young or old, can escape Vietnam and 1960s metaphors in certain major news stories. The Los Angeles riots of May 1992 touched off by the trial verdict of the policemen accused of beating Rodney King, for example, evoked many Vietnam-era references. One of the more provocative called attention to the fact that Los Angeles police, by regularly abusing their mandates, were really doing what the majority of white suburbanites wanted them to do: keep the pathologies of the inner city at bay by any means necessary. The uses of Vietnam, however, in commentator Ira Socol's version of this argument, left much to be desired: "Only when the collateral damage ends up on TV do we worry. Then our conscience takes over, and we are stunned and shocked. Like Vietnam, we have sent people to do our dirty work, but, please, don't let any of the blood splatter on us."[93]—as if managing the daily problems of the American underclass had something to do with fighting Vietnamese Communism, or as if we all agree that American soldiers in Vietnam were doing "dirty work."

One dubious reference per 1,000 words was evidently not enough, however. Socol then proceeded to contradict his own image of Vietnam veterans, moving from implying that they did "dirty work" to saying that they are victims of stereotyping. Cops, he says, "may be among the few Americans who really know whose war this is and what Americans *want* them to do. . . . They know that at times like this society will see every urban cop as a violent racist, just as American soldiers in Vietnam were portrayed as baby killers."[94]

The effort to draw a parallel rankles. That there are unflattering caricatures of both urban police and American soldiers in Vietnam based on the behavior of small minorities is an allowable comparison, but American soldiers in Vietnam were not trying to protect American citizens from direct personal jeopardy. Only the wildest denizens of the Right believed that a Communist victory in Indochina would lead willy-nilly to hand-to-hand combat with Communist soldiers on American beaches. And the members of the LAPD are not poorly trained draftees sent to a foreign land for ill-defined purposes; there are no Vietcong in Los Angeles or anything remotely like them.

Another Vietnam recollection evoked by the Los Angeles riots concerned the Black Panther Party, that vaunted vanguard of the radical antiwar movement. The *Philadelphia Inquirer* took the opportunity of the riots to interview Bobby Ware, Bobby Rush, and Bobby Seale, the first two former founding members of the Student Non-Violent Coordinating Committee (SNCC) and the latter a founder of the Black Panther Party. (Rush was also a member of the Illinois Panther Party.) Ware noted correctly that the riots this time were different from those in Watts in 1965; these were not just about race, but also the supposed failure of the judicial system. Rush urged people to think in terms of economic, and not political, solutions. Seale, it was noted, was working on the screenplay version of his memoir *Seize the Time*. This was moderate stuff from former avowed Marxist-Leninist revolutionaries implicated in several bombings and murders—an inconvenient fact unknown, forgotten, or left strategically unmentioned by the interviewing journalist. Instead, the Panthers are described as having set up "free breakfast programs and health-care clinics, including the nation's first mass sickle-cell anemia testing programs."[95]

Yet another 1960s metaphor arose out of Los Angeles when then-White House spokesman, Marlin Fitzwater, blamed the Los Angeles riots on the Great Society programs of the 1960s. This evoked a spirited response from Joseph A. Califano, Jr., who had been President Johnson's special assistant for domestic affairs, pointing out which of a great many programs Fitzwater could not possibly have been talking about.[96] There was, perhaps, a fleck of truth in both Fitzwater's accusation, if he was referring to welfare's role in creating a dependency syndrome, and in Califano's, if he was referring to the initial self-help design of most Great Society programs. But a fleck is only a fleck: Blaming something that happened in 1992 on something that was done in 1964, while skipping everything in between, is absurd. Pretending that the Great Society did not misfire in major ways is equally implausible. Thank heaven, anyway, that neither came right out and mentioned the war in Vietnam.

Even AIDS activists have invoked Vietnam and the antiwar movement. ACT-UP (AIDS Coalition to Unleash Power) is an organization dedicated to staging militant demonstrations to pressure the government to do more to deal with the

AIDS problem. Robert Rafsky, dying of AIDS, described his gradually growing support for ACT-UP. Though he went as a skeptic to his first ACT-UP meeting: "It didn't take long to hear their sincerity and confusion. They were trying to use the protest tactics of the civil rights movement and the Vietnam War to save their lives."[97]

Of course, the differences between civil disobedience in the three cases—the civil rights movement, the Vietnam War, and AIDS—are absolutely stunning. The civil rights movement was not about saving lives in a literal sense but about changing laws and practices that were fundamentally un-American in letter and spirit. The Vietnam antiwar movement was about saving the lives of a special group only if one agrees that much radical activism was merely a fancy method of draft evasion; but neither Rafsky nor most of those still sympathetic to the antiwar movement will likely agree to that. ACT-UP, on the other hand, cannot justifiably claim that it demonstrates to change unjust laws, or to uphold the equality principle, or to affect American foreign policy. It demonstrates because it believes that American society is "homophobic" and that government deliberately slows medical research because it wants "undesirable sexual deviants" and intravenous drug users to perish. The civil rights movement and the antiwar movement were both about America at large, about everybody; ACT-UP, whatever it may claim, is about a self-selected group paranoid about society in general and concerned about medical problems pertaining mainly, though not exclusively, to themselves.

But such differences, knowledge of which requires a moment's reflection, matter little in this context. To the sympathetic reader the Vietnam metaphor works well simply translated as: a noble, heroic, lifesaving thing to do. Yet just as the radical phrase of the antiwar movement was counterproductive to stopping the war, ACT-UP's militancy and barely veiled disdain for non-homosexuals almost certainly reduces general sympathy for AIDS victims among the public at large.

## VIETNAM AND THE 1992 ELECTION

There were major uses of Vietnam in the 1992 presidential campaign too, focused primarily around Governor Bill Clinton's method of avoiding military service. Clinton avoided service by creating an artificial time warp between private life and the National Guard. When this became known, opinion about it split like a tree hit by lightning.

On the one hand were those who had been part of the antiwar movement who saw what Clinton did as sensible and natural. It may have been cowardly in 1965 or 1966 to do what Clinton did, some opined, but by 1969 any fool could see that the war was a mistake if not a crime, and who wants a president who would take a chance on throwing his life away for nothing?[98] "Mr. Bush miscalculates," asserted columnist Anna Quindlen in the *New York Times,* "and miscalculates again.

With his attacks on Mr. Clinton's dissent during the Vietnam era, he insults a huge group of Americans who believed the policy in Southeast Asia was ill conceived."[99] Besides, there soon came the chorus that "everybody did it," including the then–vice president of the United States, Dan Quayle.

But on the other hand were those arguing that Clinton was selfish, and selfish people should not be president. Walter A. McDougall, a Vietnam combat veteran and professor at the University of Pennsylvania, argued that Clinton "wanted to have it both ways: to make no sacrifice and pay no future price." Worse, said McDougall, Clinton

> rejected all authority until such time as *he* decided America's government had ceased to be "dangerous and inadequate." At the same time he plotted to advance his own career so that someday America must bow to *his* authority. But according to his own logic, we citizens today would have no more obligation to respect the authority of a Clinton Administration than he showed our Government then.[100]

McDougall was not defending the war or trying to equate draft dodging with adultery or other private matters as other observers inclined to do. Honor is more important in a president than fidelity in his marriage. But because Clinton chose himself over his honor, said McDougall, he had no right to ask others to sacrifice for their country.

Fearing the fallout from this argument and other, much cruder forms of it, Clinton's supporters carried the argument back. Michael Mandelbaum, an old friend and political advisor to Clinton, defended him in *The New Republic* almost to the point making Clinton's youthful errors look saintly.[101]

Other 1960s issues soon dogged Clinton. The candidate admitted, for example, that he had smoked marijuana once "but didn't inhale." This is like saying you gargled a beer but didn't swallow. Clinton no doubt wanted to avoid lying but feared that admitting marijuana use would be politically harmful; hence the ridiculous response. His personal ambivalence, however, reflected a more general one: American society still has not come to terms with what it thinks about the 1960s, and among antiwar-movement types, drug use and draft-dodging are two of the principal symbols of that ambivalence. A cartoon by Jim Morin of the *Miami Herald* captured this perfectly. In box one, one candidate proclaims that during the 1960s he opposed the war and did everything possible within the law to avoid being drafted, to which an old woman replies: "Self-centered unpatriotic gutless wimp!!" In the second box, a different candidate proclaims that he fought in and supported with pride a just war against the Vietnamese Communists. To which the same old woman replies: "Are you nuts?"[102]

Clinton was not the only candidate with a Vietnam problem, but the ambiguity of the situation was such that Vietnam veterans were almost equally ill at ease over what to make of their service. Presidential contender Bob Kerrey, senator from Nebraska, even said that "being a Vietnam veteran is more of a liability than an asset." This was probably untrue on balance, but reminding voters of unresolved issues that they would rather forget can have its costs.[103] Another cost is that pretending that an entire generation or two of Americans did not do the things they almost all did—such as smoke marijuana—risks disenfranchising nearly all of them from public service. There is more than a little hypocrisy in 60-year-old bourbon and gin swillers looking down on 40-year-olds who smoked pot in college.

As it turned out, the Clinton-Gore ticket was born in the Vietnam War like no other could have been. Clinton's first job after leaving college was working for Senator William Fulbright, and since Fulbright's obsession at the time was Vietnam, it became the young Clinton's too. As for Gore, his father's antiwar position was probably responsible for his losing his 1970 bid for reelection to the Senate. In trying to help his father, the younger Gore joined the military.[104] In a way, Gore's wartime record "saved" Clinton's even though it too was motivated by antiwar sentiment.

On a sillier note, a former and still-radical radical evoked the counterculture on behalf of Ross Perot. Warren Hinckle, editor of *Ramparts* between 1964 and 1969, argued that Perot understood that the system was the enemy—just as 1960s radicals said it was—and that the two-party establishment was conspiring to smear him just as it smeared the antiwar movement when the latter was in its "most creative" phase.[105]

In the end, what the 1992 election showed about Vietnam was that the generational wheel is turning fast. Clinton's Vietnam record did not hurt him as much as George Bush had hoped. Nor did it help him as much as some supporters wished. Other issues—the economy, education, health care—mattered more, and the election was fought over the issues of 1992 more than over the images of 1968.

Now that the Vietnam generation is in office, however, we shall see where the spinning wheel takes us all next. At the midway point through the Clinton administration, the influences of the past have been real but muted. Hillary Clinton's left-wing biases, in particular, have shown to be stronger than the president's, but to what general effect is hard to say. Not only have the effects seemed fuzzy, sometimes so have the sources. In a *Newsweek* interview, Mrs. Clinton called herself "an old-fashioned Methodist." She recounted that while at Wellesley she read the Methodist magazine *Motive,* where she said she recalled being impressed by an anti–Vietnam War "article by a Methodist theologian, Carl Oglesby, called 'Change or Containment.'"[106] Methodist theologian Carl Oglesby?! Did SDS perform baptisms too?

# Back in the Street: Vietnam and the Kuwait War

*It's like déjà vu all over again.*
—Yogi Berra

The use of Vietnam as metaphor in the Kuwait crisis of 1990-91 rests in a class all its own. That war was the first since Vietnam to produce anything like an antiwar movement for the simple reason that, unlike U.S. military actions in Lebanon, Grenada, and Panama, fighting Saddam Hussein's Iraq at least seemed to have the potential to be long, bloody, and possibly unsuccessful.

Studying the Kuwait War antiwar movement is a little like a physicist studying a subatomic particle: Neither lasts long enough for the observer to get a good fix on it. Nevertheless, analysis is in order if only because in the history of American social criticism and political dissent, there seems to be a law close to that in evolutionary biology holding that ontogeny recapitulates phylogeny. Just as every animal fetus is said to repeat as embryo the evolutionary pathways of preceding millennia, so the Kuwait antiwar movement followed similar, if suddenly truncated, terrain traversed by abolitionists, suffragettes, labor agitators, ban-the-bomb pacifists, and Vietnam antiwar protestors before them.

The reasons for the similarities between the Vietnam antiwar movement and the truncated Kuwait antiwar movement include, of course, the living memory and model of Vietnam itself. The debate over how the United States should respond to Iraqi aggression against Kuwait was awash in references to Vietnam. Many tactics, slogans, and theories from the Vietnam era were recovered, dusted off, and adjusted for reuse. A few of the "Make Love, Not War" signs may even have been 1960s originals. We know that life imitates art; in 1990-91 we learned that adversarial politics imitates itself.

The White House, the Defense Department, the print and electronic media, and the adversary culture all participated in applications of Vietnam to the Kuwait crisis. So did the Congress, for 24 senators and 76 congressmen served in the armed forces during the Vietnam War, about half in the reserves or National Guard.[1] Ordinary Americans at every level perceived supposed parallels too. Outside of the government and in the new antiwar movement, comment seemed congenitally unable to let Vietnam cum metaphor alone.[2] Whether used in a sophisticated manner or not, mention of Vietnam had the general effect of raising an already portentous matter into an even more intense one, as all the unfinished emotional business from Vietnam was dragged alongside events in the Persian Gulf. In a way, the United States fought not one war but two in January and February 1991, one physically in the Persian Gulf and the other metaphorically over a war finished for nearly a quarter century.

On balance, an examination of the Kuwait antiwar movement reveals more parallels with Vietnam than differences, but differences are striking too. The most important one is that radicalism never became ascendant in the Kuwait War movement. The most significant opposition to war came from within the Senate and the Democratic Party. The fact that this was so only strengthens the observation that the intellectual descendants of the Vietnam antiwar movement, while many years aged and changed, still claimed a strong hold on that party.

Another very important difference is that, in the case of Vietnam, the antiwar movement started after the war and grew as the fighting grew, while in the Kuwait crisis it started before the war and virtually disappeared when the fighting started.[3] Thus, the 1990-91 movement resembled not the radical 1966 to 1969 phase of Vietnam antiwar movement or the redomesticated phase of the 1970 to 1974 period, but the first phase, 1961 to 1964.

Important differences notwithstanding, comparisons between the two movements are worth making both to examine a special use of Vietnam as metaphor and to learn more about the American tradition of political dissent and self-scrutiny.

## DRAMATIS PERSONAE:
## INDIVIDUALS AND ORGANIZATIONS

The distance in time between Vietnam and the Kuwait crisis was about the same as that between the end of World War II and Vietnam. Just as some of the few conscientious objectors and labor agitators of the 1930s and 1940s were around to help kick off the Vietnam antiwar movement, so some from the 1960s tried to start an antiwar movement in 1990. Many an old adversary culture face was in evidence.

The Reverend Philip Berrigan made certain that he was among the first to be arrested. On December 30, 1990, he and 11 other protestors poured red dye into a fountain on the White House grounds to symbolize the blood that would flow in a Middle East war.[4] David Cortright was back too, as executive director of SANE, which had lately absorbed institutionally the nuclear-freeze movement. Cortright was the author of *Soldiers in Revolt,* written at the Institute for Policy Studies in 1972—"a product," he said then, "of the struggle within the American military against repression and the Indochina intervention."[5] In 1990 Cortright emphasized the peace movement's need to educate Americans about the costs of a militarized foreign policy: "During the Vietnam War, the teach-in movement was a valuable tool to raise public awareness and build opposition to U.S. policy. We need a similar effort now."[6] To Cortright in 1990 as well as in 1965, "education" was presumed to always result in opposition to U.S. policy.

One of the reasons this was so in the 1960s was that speakers not opposed to U.S. policy were usually shouted down at teach-ins. This used to be called "positive intolerance." Whatever it was called in 1990-91, it was back. Page 11 of the January 11, 1991, *New York Times* carried a photograph of a teach-in at the University of Michigan—where it had all started in 1965—with the following caption: "As the deadline for war in the Persian Gulf draws nearer, an antiwar movement is building in the United States. A teach-in at the University of Michigan on Wednesday discussed the possibility of the military draft being re-enacted. A student, above, in favor of the draft, was shouted down."

Bella Abzug was not to be denied either. The former congresswoman told a New York City rally in February 1991—about a month after the air war started on January 16—that President Bush had missed a chance for peace when he dismissed Saddam Hussein's eleventh-hour offer as a "cruel hoax." It was Bush who was responsible for a cruel hoax, she said. "No sooner did George Bush hear there was an opening for the first time, instead of saying we would have to see if more progress could be made, they launched 3,000 more sorties."[7]

Ron Kovic—the Vietnam veteran made famous by the movie *Born on the Fourth of July,* based on his book of the same name—added his voice as well, specifically and not surprisingly invoking Vietnam. Referring to the U.S. bombing of a shelter in Baghdad that housed the families of the Ba'ath Party elite, he said: "There were 347 civilians killed in My Lai," he said, "and over 300 bodies have already been recovered from the bomb shelter in Baghdad. This has pushed most of us in the antiwar movement to redouble our commitment to end this war. We're sickened by the insensitivity and callous disregard for life by this Administration."[8] Referring to the wounds he had sustained in Vietnam, which have confined him to a wheelchair ever since, he also told churchgoers: "My life is a living example of the devastation and loss that can result from a miscalculated, deceptive and secret foreign policy."[9]

David McReynolds of the War Resisters League was active again, as well, and again give the war-as-natural-outcome radical argument as opposed to the war-as-aberration argument: "Just as the U.S. war in Indochina was not an accident but the logical consequence of twenty-five years of Cold War ideology . . . the U.S. intervention in the Gulf is the logical consequence of the repeated commitments of successive presidents."[10] Most astonishing of all, perhaps, was George McGovern's declaration that he was "ready," if called upon, to run again for president.[11]

Country Joe McDonald was back too. Although his newest record was not political, he found himself and his guitar in the middle of a San Francisco antiwar rally, which was beamed across the country courtesy of CNN. Country Joe told an interviewer that he didn't feel like parodying war as he once did: "I don't feel any of that stuff anymore around the Gulf. I just feel a very strong conviction that we shouldn't be at war, and we have to do all we can to stop it. I don't feel like writing any clever songs about it."[12] The Rolling Stones, meanwhile, one of the least political of all major 1960s rock bands, suddenly decided to write a political lyric. In "Highwire," the Stones criticized Western countries for arming Middle Eastern dictators.[13]

Vietnam antiwar movement academics were also active. These were not the original prominent participants from the 1960s, but as their hagiographers, carrying word of A. J. Muste and Norman Thomas, they were the next best thing. Charles Chatfield, friend, aide and co-author with the late "peace science" professor Charles DeBenedetti, predicted—wrongly—that the United States could become sharply polarized if war broke out. He was quoted in the *New York Times* partly as scholar, partly as embodiment of what he had written about with DeBenedetti.[14]

The movement gained not just from the presence of individuals who were well known 20 years earlier, and not just from the continuing organizational energies of the Vietnam era, but also from the growth of the Vietnam generation into professional and community life, taking their sacred if edited memories of heroic days and energetic times with them. As Todd Gitlin put it: "In part the anti-war effort reflects the numbers of anti-Vietnam campaigners who now hold positions of power in mainstream institutions. In part it is an artifact of antiwar positions that the institutions themselves eventually adopted during the Vietnam War."[15]

No one should have been surprised by the rapid development of an opposition to U.S. policy in the Persian Gulf. Ample institutional linkages enabled the rapid growth of a more or less coordinated antiwar movement. These institutions had been in readiness for years, nurtured through the human rights focus against America's authoritarian allies in the 1970s, and the nuclear freeze, antiapartheid, antinuclear power, and pro-Sandinista and FMLN campaigns of the 1980s.

Of course, not everyone was satisfied with the movement's rapid coalescence. Complained one man at a February 18 rally in New York City: "The problem is we're only at Day 30 of the war. It's hard to generate a peace movement on the scale of Vietnam after only 30 days."[16] At the same rally, another participant added that the lack of American bodies was hurting the movement: "What we really need to get people out here is boys coming home in body bags."[17] Indeed, movement activists made much over news of the large number of bodybags the Pentagon had ordered; it was like cash in the bank.

## LEFT- AND RIGHT-WING AGAIN

As had been the case during the Vietnam War, divisions on strategy and tactics between left-wing and right-wing factions within the movement were soon to be found. Led by Ramsey Clark,[18] the radicals formed the National Coalition to Stop U.S. Intervention in the Middle East, which held a January 19 rally in Washington. The more centrist Campaign for Peace in the Middle East held a January 26 rally. Parallels with the April and June 1965 rallies were almost eerie.

The radicals were suitably extreme, believing (again) that the war was just the face of a demonic capitalist America set to ravage the whole world. Said radical activist Sahu Barron during the June Washington victory parade: "We do not want the media to portray the picture that there was universal consent about this genocidal war or this fascist military spectacle taking place out here."[19] The *City Lights Review* too, was busy publishing poetry and analysis during the crisis and war, eventually resulting in the volume *War After War: The New Corporate/Military Order, the Middle East, and Insurgencies on the Home Front.*[20] Does the language sound familiar?

The organizations involved in the radical shard of the movement were familiar too. The January 18, 1991 edition of *Workers Vanguard* proclaimed: "Defeat U.S. Imperialism! Defend Iraq!"[21] The *Workers Vanguard* is the paper of the Sparticist League, which is the U.S. section of the International Communist League (Fourth International)—in other words, the Trotskyites again. Their position was as clear as ever: Use the war there to bring revolution here.

> The Sparticist League . . . calls for a new, class-struggle leadership of the workers movement, for a revolutionary workers party to link the factory to the ghetto and fight for the liberation of all the oppressed. Down with the capitalist system of exploitation, of poverty amid wealth, of racism and war! Imperialist war can be the mother of socialist revolution![22]

The Progressive Labor Party's newspaper, *Rebellion,* took a similar line, directing itself particularly toward black and Hispanic soldiers. "Turning imperialist war into class war," it said, "will smash these murderers once and for all. We shouldn't fear imperialist war; we should use the guns they have put in our hands to kill our real enemies, the brass and the bosses."[23] Yes, the PL caucus of SDS had survived into the 1990s, and their analysis was the same:

> El Salvador, Colombia, Angola, Somalia, Northern Ireland, Lebanon, Cambodia, etc. Wars are being fought for control of profits. . . . Bush and Hussein

are business men. They are both trying to grab profits from the oilfields. So what's the difference between business men and mass murderers? Nothing. Imperialist war and capitalism go hand in hand.[24]

The remnants of sectarian Communism were not, of course, the only or the main forces behind the left wing of the new antiwar movement. As radicals eventually coalesced into the Coalition Against Intervention, along the way came the Action Network, a mélange of New York City radicals. It was, in a way, a new version of the Fifth Avenue Parade Committee, and, like that one, it included sectarian Communist participation. One of its advertisements, "Statement of Unity of the Stop the U.S. War Machine," shows this influence clearly.

The sheet argued that while Saddam Hussein was a tyrant, the United States and its allies built him up and have no right to intervene in the region. Action Network called for broad resistance, and especially for GI resistance; this sounded rather a lot like the PL position. The slogans were familiar too. In bold letters, there were three: "Hell No! We Won't Go!"; "U.S. Out of the Gulf!"; and "Stop the U.S. War Machine, No Matter What It Takes!" Farther down the sheet we find a statement on "diversity": "The Action Network includes students, movement activists, war veterans, professionals and punks, artists and G.I. resisters. We have diverse politics and philosophies: religious, anti-racist, pacifism, revolutionary communism, environmentalism, anti-interventionism, and beyond." We are then told that a national office in New York was preparing posters, kits, speakers' bureaus, and resource literature. A "Travelling Troublemakers Tour" was in the works too. It emphasized however, that "local actions are decided by the people in local chapters"—shades of participatory democracy.

Then came the "credentials" list:

> We've organized people's blockades at military bases and recruiting stations, campus demonstrations, and forums, programs and rallies. On the day of the U.N. vote, the Action Network was at the U.N. with its banners, dipping the flags of the U.S. and U.N. in "blood" to denounce the vote for the war. Since last fall, the Action Network played a major role in the successful campaign to free Jeff Patterson (the first active duty G.I. to refuse orders to Saudi Arabia).

The long "partial list of signatories" included a number of familiar organizations, among them: Vietnam Veterans Against the War; ACT-UP; Progressive Student Alliance; Revolutionary Communist Brigades; Revolutionary Communist Party, U.S.A.; Pledge of Resistance; and many more besides. Some familiar names showed up as well: the lawyers William Kunstler, Leonard Weinglass, and Ron Ruby, who had defended Vietnam antiwar protestors twenty years earlier; Joe Stork of the generally anti-U.S. and anti-Israel *MERIP Reports;*[25] Eqbal Ahmed, formerly of the Institute for Policy Studies; Howard Zinn of Vietnam antiwar fame; and Joey Johnson, described as "a notorious flag burner."

While the radicals were organizing, so were liberals, Left-Liberals, and pacifists. As always, the American Friends Service Committee[26] and the War Resisters League were instrumental in initial organizing.[27] As in the early 1960s, SANE was a prime mover in the campaign. There too was the Fellowship of Reconciliation, the Women's International League for Peace and Freedom, Women's Strike for Peace, Physicians for Social Responsibility, Greenpeace, Pax Christi, and Democratic Socialists of America.

But, as was the case years ago, they had a hard time keeping those who were even more radical out of their organizing committees. This again proves that when popular fronting by radical groups is juxtaposed against the liberality of liberals, the former demonstrates greater strength. By the time the endorsements were offered and accepted for the January 26 affair, they also included, to mention but a sampling, all of the following radical groups and Communist fronts: ACT-UP; the Brandywine Peace Community; CISPES (Committee in Solidarity with the People of El Salvador); the Hands Off Cuba Coalition; Fourth Internationalist Tendency; the Lawyers Committee on Nuclear Policy; the Lesbian/Gay Labor Alliance; the National Alliance Against Political and Racist Oppression; the Palestine Human Rights Committee; Nicaragua National Network; the Palestine Solidarity Committee; Progressive Student Network; the Revolutionary Workers League; the Socialist Workers Party; *The Guardian*; the U.S. Peace Council; the War Resisters League; the Young Communist League; and Young Socialist Alliance.[28] Individual signatories on the sponsorship list included former SDS President Carl Davidson, William Kunstler, Herbert Daugherty, Gus Newport (socialist mayor of Berkeley), author Studs Terkel, and Howard Zinn.

Obviously, radical attempts to penetrate the organizing committee had been successful beyond the wildest dreams radicals would have entertained in 1965. The main reason was that "liberal" groups in 1990 were much farther to the Left to start with than they were in 1965. But the radicals, not yet satisfied, made a further effort to infiltrate the movement's right wing. Just as the National Coordinating Committee succeeded in infiltrating SANE's November 1965 rally, that is what the coalition tried to do to the campaign in late 1990. Another widely distributed broadside illustrated the effort.

Called "An Open Letter to the Movement Against U.S. Intervention in the Middle East," dated December 17, 1990, it declared: "We Need Unity in the Fight Against the War." It began:

> Since late November and early December the movement against U.S. intervention in the Middle East has been confronted with a serious division in our ranks. Two dates are being presented for marches in Washington, D.C. and San Francisco—January 19 and January 26—by two different national coalitions. Their political slogans are virtually identical. This is a tragic and unnecessary development.

The sheet goes on to argue that it was too late to unite for one rally, so therefore the January 26 rally should build on the January 19 one. The signatories, none of them well known, ask both national coalitions to cooperate in this endeavor.[29] In other words, the liberals should, at their January 26 rally, allow the full sponsorship and participation of the groups that sponsored the January 19 rally.

As in 1965, the right wing of the movement was moved by pleas for unity, thus opening the door wide for the radicals. The January 26 affair proved the success of radical tactics. Given its size and the attendance of true moderates, it also showed once again how radicalism in a mass movement can become all but invisible to oblivious participants on the fringes.

Protestors assembled near the Capitol in contingents of veterans, labor groups, and students. Politicized black groups too, as had SNCC and especially the Black Panthers years ago, were determined to use the war to vent their hatred of white people. As in Vietnam, they associated themselves with the left wing of protest. Blacks involved in the January 26 march however, segregated themselves from the rest of the group—shades of H. Rapp Brown at Palmer House. Danu Smith's National African-American Network Against U.S. Intervention in the Gulf led the way; its signs read "No civil rights; we won't fight" and "Down With Racist Poverty Draft."[30] Others demanded "reparations" for racism. The most astonishing example of black opposition to the war appeared in *The Prism*, the Amherst College newspaper. An anonymous black student wrote, in language not entirely dissimilar from that of the Palmer House debacle:

> I believe that this escapade was merely another attack on the darker-skinned peoples of the world by the United States of Amerikkka. . . . Any leader that refuses to be one of Amerikkka's bitches is either wiped out or has his country attacked. Hussein got tired of sucking Amerikkka's dick and look what you did. . . . The New World Order is merely a euphemism for an Old Dixie Plantation. . . . Let me tell you, one day the people of this world are going to wake up and find out what kind of Devils you are. You are going to be asleep in your big soft beds, and we are going to creep up on you and slit your fucking throats. . . . That is what the Communists did in Vietnam. . . . They told whitey to get the fuck off their land, and when whitey did not go, he got himself killed.[31]

As for the Kuwait War, the author's position was clear: "I hope you die. He he he! I cannot wait to watch your Devilish blood run down the streets of Amerikkka. Die, whitey. Die! You have to die because you are trying to kill me."[32]

The January 26 rally also featured groups of radical Koreans, Filipinos, and Palestinians along and their U.S. supporters. A Palestine Liberation Organization contingent waved the PLO flag. The Communists and their banners were true throwbacks to the 1960s. The Revolutionary Workers League banners read "Victory to Iraq; Defeat U.S. Imperialism" and "My Blood for Your Oil? Piss Off Fascist Swine." The Communist Party, U.S.A. and its Young Communist League were there handing out copies of *People's Weekly World*. Actually, the CPUSA was there "twice" because the U.S. Peace Council, one of its fronts, was also in evidence. The Trotskyites were represented by the Socialist Workers Party and its Young Socialist Alliance.[33] They held a familiar sign, bearing their slogan from Vietnam days and the title of Fred Halstead's book: *Out Now!*[34]

There was also an anarchist contingent, waving the traditional black flags with a white A in the center. Their slogans, reminiscent of those of the 1968 Diggers and Motherfuckers, were the most riotous of all: "Dictators Here, Dictators There, Smash Authority Everywhere," and "Fight the State, not its wars." The best was "Kick the ass of the ruling class." The anarchists led no violence, contenting themselves with burning American flags and draft registration cards.

The Revolutionary Communist Brigades and Revolutionary Communist Party too, excelled at revising the old Vietnam-era custom of "trashings" and "breakouts," which is when small groups of people leave the parade route and head toward the sidewalk with mayhem in mind. On January 26 breakout tactics mainly involved pounding on mailboxes with sticks and knocking over trash receptacles, trying to stir police action and arrests. Washington police, however, arrested no one all day. Civil disobedience was planned as well, as a "die-in," which would have protestors falling into the street in front of the White House to block traffic. It did not come off very successfully; police blocked the access to the site and the cold eventually persuaded most demonstrators to leave.

And the speakers? The masters of ceremonies included Gus Newport and Jack O'Dell, both associated with the Communist Party, U.S.A and its front, the World Peace Council, U.S.A.[35] One speaker was Angela Sanburo, director of CISPES; another was Jeanne Butterfield, representing the Palestine Solidarity Committee. (The PSC is not just any Palestinian group, but a front of George Habash's Popular Front for the Liberation of Palestine, a Marxist-Leninist organization that opposes Yasir Arafat's al-Fatah from the secular Left.) Aside from the Marxist-Leninists, there was also James Forbes of the Riverside Church, who had replaced William Sloane Coffin of Vietnam antiwar and nuclear-freeze movement fame. There was Charles Rangel, Democratic congressman of New York. There were a pair of U.S. Army physicians, Yolanda Huet-Vaugh and Harlow Ballard, David Cline of Vietnam Veterans Against the War, and actor Tim Robbins.[36] Actress Susan Sarandon spoke on behalf of the Military Families Support Network. Molly Yard of the National Organization for Women spoke and so did Jesse Jackson and many others.

The point is: All this happened at the so-called liberal, centrist, right-wing movement rally. And when it was over what stood forth, somehow, was the "moderate" character of it all. This was partly because there had been no violence and no arrests among the roughly 150,000 in attendance. Eight out of ten attendees described themselves as "liberal." Of those, half said they were "very liberal." Only one of five described themselves as pacifist, and only one in six said they had marched against the war in Vietnam.

But even of those only a few had any idea who started organizing the rally and who finished organizing it. January 26, 1991, was like November 18, 1965, in the sense that radicals trying to use public concern to advance a broader revolutionary agenda managed to make use of, but not control, what started as a Left-Liberal project with a primarily liberal audience base.

## TACTICS, SYMBOLS, LANGUAGE

Outside of public demonstrations, movement tactics followed similar left-wing and right-wing dispositions from Vietnam days. The left wing mounted an International War Crimes Tribunal during which anti-American radicals tried to haul the U.S. government before the court of world public opinion; in the 1960s it was Bertrand Russell's doing, in 1991 it was Ramsey Clark's with help from Michael Parenti.[37] Sponsored by the Los Angeles Coalition Against U.S. Intervention in the Middle East, the tribunal finished its deliberations on February 29, 1992, finding President Bush, Defense Secretary Dick Cheney, and others guilty of 19 counts of mass murder (of 250,000 Iraqis no less, probably at least 10 times the number actually killed) and other assorted "crimes." They sent a letter to U.N. General Secretary Boutros Boutros-Ghali telling of their findings, and international press coverage of the event was fairly extensive in some quarters. *Kayhan International,* an Iranian paper, listed the 19 charges, reprinted the letter to Boutros-Ghali in its entirety and lavishly described the "trial" scene in New York.[38]

In addition to war crimes tribunals, antiwar organizations used lawsuits in an attempt to put government on the defensive. Formerly a "liberal" tactic in the Vietnam era, it was now more broadly employed. For example, the Proposition One Committee sued the federal government in March 1991 on First Amendment grounds over a Lafayette Park antiwar protest. In the park, which is directly across from the White House, Peace Park had maintained a 24-hour vigil "for peace, justice and disarmament" since 1981. According to the War Resisters League, the protestors "share the park at night with the homeless" and pose for pictures with tourists during the day. During the Kuwait War, cartoonist Garry Trudeau put Peace Park in his *Doonesbury* comic strip, after which they were joined by Minnesota Peace Drum, another protest group that included five Native Americans. They beat drums for peace. With this, the federal Park Police determined that 60 decibels was the noise limit that should be tolerated—which is fairly loud. Also, drums were silenced at 7 P.M. each evening. In retaliation for these limitations, suit was brought.[39]

Other protest tactics, just like some of the slogans, were carbon copies of Vietnam-era demonstrations, too. As mentioned earlier, Philip Berrigan was ready with red dye to simulate blood—at least he did not use real blood this time around, as he did when he poured animal blood on draft records in 1968. Guerrilla theater was back too. In Chicago, protestors wore paper masks in the form of television sets to protest the media's coverage of the war. A human chain across Lakeshore Drive stopped traffic for miles, reminiscent of Washington traffic jams caused by Rennie Davis's May Day Tribes and New Yorkers tying up the New Jersey Turnpike on their way home from Washington rallies. In Olympia, Washington, protestors dug mock graves on the lawn of the state capitol. Others staged mock funeral processions—echos of Stewart Meacham's funeral march tactics in 1969—with white-faced pallbearers carrying wooden coffins.

More seriously, two individuals committed suicide by setting themselves on fire, a method first brought to the attention of Americans by Vietnamese Buddhist priests and then copied by a small number of Vietnam-era protestors. On December 9, 1991, a 48-year-old Vietnam veteran died after setting himself on fire in Isleton, California. On February 18 at Amherst College, a man in his 20s, not a student, did the same. He carried a peace sign, on the back of which was pasted his driver's license. After the Amherst suicide, more than 1,200 people gathered to pay homage; one woman was arrested for trying to put a wreath on the corpse. Within two hours of the incident, 30 local peace activists held a candlelight vigil—yet another religious ceremony popular in the Vietnam era—while some held signs saying "Stop this crazy war."[40]

Additionally, a few military personnel suddenly had second thoughts about their chosen calling. Recalling how important military dissent was in the Vietnam period, the War Resisters League went out of its way to encourage such "resistance."[41]

As always, a national crisis is an opportunity for adversary culture organizations to raise money. The Kuwait War was no exception, and using memories of Vietnam to raise this money seemed the preferred tactic. *The Nation,* the only significant hard Left publication remaining in the United States today, was quick with a mass-mail solicitation crowing with its anti-establishment credentials. As part of its pitch, the solicitation reads as follows:

> For starters, in which of the following invasions did the mainstream media
> serve as anything gutsier than a cheering section for American intervention?
>> Vietnam, in 1965
>> Grenada, in 1983
>> Panama, in 1989
>> The Persian Gulf, in 1991
>> NONE OF THE ABOVE

In some cases even the music was the same. Asked by a reporter what she would do on the evening of January 15 as the deadline for Iraqi compliance with U.N. ultimata passed, Mirella Wong, a student at St. Francis College in Brooklyn said: "I'm going to stay up and wait past the deadline . . . and I'm going to play Joan Baez records."[42] This was not surprising for 1960s folk and rock songs represented the easiest way for young people of the early 1990s to connect to the themes of the 1960s and be politically socialized through them—even if they sometimes missed the songs' occasional political references.

Commentator Francis Shor quickly drew the lesson of Vietnam toward the shores of Kuwait: We should negotiate and not bomb because otherwise we will introduce "a cycle of violence," and more, "the myopic politics that got us into Vietnam and now into a war with Iraq show the contradictions of an imperial America."[43] Tom Wicker compared the failure of the American and Iraqi governments to work out a prewar venue for a summit, which was eventually overcome in part when Tariq Aziz met James Baker in Geneva, as a "shape of the table" disagreement like the one "that so long delayed negotiations in Paris to end the war in Vietnam."[44] This was an astonishing remark: How could anyone hanker for a repeat of ignominious Paris Accords in 1991? Those accords did not "end the war" on the agreed terms; they turned out to be a precondition to North Vietnam's conquering and subjugation of South Vietnam. If Henry Kissinger, who won a Nobel Peace Prize for this "achieve-ment" can admit as much,[45] why couldn't Tom Wicker?

Jesse Jackson, meanwhile, challenged President Bush "to stop the bombing and start talking," precisely the language used by the right wing of the antiwar movement from 1965 to 1968.[46] Greenpeace published in effect a body-count sheet: If the Pentagon would not comment on the number of dead—"we already had enough of that in Vietnam," said General Thomas Kelly to the press corps in Saudi Arabia—the antiwar movement would go out of its way to do so.[47] Greenpeace totals exceeded 224,000, a figure way beyond reality as later determined.

There was a reprise of righteous indignation against aerial bombardment of technologically less developed people. Columnist Colman McCarthy of the *Wash-ington Post* called it the cowards' air war.[48] Others demanded an answer from Secretary Cheney as to why civilians were not off-limits entirely in the air war; shades of Vietnam's rules of engagement controversy.[49] Accusations of technowar were voiced as well.[50] Six Harvard students went to Iraq to look for evidence of war crimes.[51] Referring to Vietnam, one M.I.T. student complained in Luddite-like countercultural overtones: "What we're doing in the Gulf is barbaric. As we get higher and higher technology, we get a lower and lower form of humanity."[52]

Conversely, the question of when to leave off the air war and go to the ground was also discussed in accord with Vietnam metaphors. *The Wall Street Journal,* for example, worried about letting the air war become a form of graduated response:

> The air war in Vietnam, and later the ground campaigns as well, were run
> under the doctrine of "graduated response." The notion was that we would
> use our superior firepower to gradually turn up the heat until Ho Chi Minh

cried uncle. This proved to be a strategic disaster. . . . A modern example of graduated response would be letting the sanctions work for 18 months, followed by six months of aerial attacks, followed—maybe—by a ground war. Is this likely to work any better with Saddam Hussein than it did with Ho Chi Minh?[53]

Thus, not only were some of the banners, slogans, and symbols the same, but the use of Vietnam-era language and catch-phrases was ubiquitous. R. W. Apple, Jr., of the *New York Times* thought this was inevitable; perhaps, but his own writing relished it all the same.[54] So did Jim Miller, author of *Democracy Is in the Streets,* judging by a contemporary *New York Times* article.[55]

There were still other similarities between 1960s and 1990s movements. As before, protestors accused the sitting administration of lying, deception, and conspiracy. Of special interest was the view, widespread on the Left, that consolidation of ownership in the media made it impossible for the press to report the war truthfully. Other versions held that Bush the oil man was going to war for oil companies' profits. Stories of secret meetings and huge political and financial payoffs abounded.

Political pilgrimage took place as well. Some of it was to be expected: Louis Farrakhan, leader of the Nation of Islam, happily went to Baghdad. So did Sandinista leader Daniel Saavedra Ortega—for all that it mattered.[56] But so did an economist with the U.S. Treasury Department named Anthony Lawrence. He went with 150 others from 16 countries as the Gulf Peace Team to protest American imperialism. His claim to fame was that his remarks were carried via CNN and Peter Arnett live from Baghdad.[57] Otherwise, political pilgrims to Baghdad were rather shocked at their treatment. They also failed to find much internal dissent, which upset their desire to create a form of people's moral equivalence. Rather, reported members of an American Fellowship of Reconciliation pilgrimage, Iraqi schoolchildren, speaking of Americans and Israelis, were gleefully singing and shouting "yes, kill them, slaughter them all."[58]

Ecologically oriented arguments against war were invoked, just as they were toward the end of the Vietnam period, after Earth Day in 1970. This may seem hard to understand since Saddam Hussein was the ecoterrorist, and not allied forces. But one report managed to blame coalition forces for drinking up all of Saudi Arabia's fresh water and polluting the country.[59] Guilt was promoted, too, and children were used as objects to expiate adult angst. According to a short item in *The New Republic,* the National Childhood Grief Institute published *My Desert Storm Workbook: First Aid for Feelings.*[60] The book was designed to "help children cope" with the violence and destruction of the war.

As in the 1960s, protest and mobilization in the United States heard at least a faint echo in Western Europe and the Third World. Anti-American sentiment abroad weighed in as best it could against American policy. *Al-Fajr,* a pro-PLO paper published in Jerusalem, tried to convince its English-language readership that the war for Kuwait was "just another Vietnam."[61] It also gave prominent coverage to antiwar activities.[62] Interestingly, this had the effect of persuading a good many people—Palestinians in Jordan as well as Iraqis—that America would not go to war. The general effect, therefore, was to make war more likely by convincing the Iraqi leadership and the Palestinian "street" that they need not back down.[63] In Germany, there were rallies against American policy, but also concern with Germany's having financed Iraq's war machine and provided unconventional weapons technology.[64] Some East European intellectuals, newly freed from Communist shackles, managed to attack American policy too. Ivan Klima, in Prague, wrote a popular anti-U.S. play called *No Blood for Oil.*[65]

## STUDENTS, CELEBRITIES, LITERATI

As expected, college campuses bubbled in 1990-91 as they did back in the 1960s. But back then they bubbled to the boiling point and beyond; in 1990 they did not.

By January 27 students had managed to create a national organization based on six principles of unity—not bad considering how little time had passed since the beginning of the air war on January 16.[66] They chose February 21 as their day of national protest in Washington, which turned out to be just two days before the beginning of the ground war. Since a sense of drama was in the air, and since no one knew how easily and quickly a ground war would go, fear aided organization and commitment.[67] But the rally was not a great success; the weather was bad and attendance was disappointing.

Things were fairly placid on the local level too. At Kent State University, scene of the May 1970 tragedy, there were a few rallies but most students were disinclined to protest.[68] Even at Quaker colleges such as Haverford, student opinion was widely scattered.[69] Most faculty there were disappointed in the lack of antiwar enthusiasm.[70]

Nevertheless, almost unbelievably, there was antidraft agitation in 1990-91 despite the obvious fact that there was no draft.[71] Undergraduate college students of the 1980s were accused of being a "me" generation. If so, then students of the 1990s would have to be called the "me, me, and only me" generation. Knowing little about either the Persian Gulf or Vietnam, the first thing many students worried about was not their country, not Kuwait, and not moral or economic questions—but about themselves. University of Pennsylvania student organizers asked me to address a group on the "crisis." I asked them: "What exactly did you have in mind?" Three of them answered immediately and almost in unison: "We want to know if there'll be a draft." I showed them out of my office with the suggestion that they read a newspaper once in a while.

Hollywood celebrities were active as well in the antiwar movement, a phenomenon institutionalized in the Vietnam era. They were represented in both left-wing and right-wing antiwar camps. Aside from Susan Sarandon and Tim Robbins, mentioned earlier, Martin Sheen and Kris Kristofferson stood out. Kristofferson said that the war against Iraq had shown that the U.S. government was just like Nazi Germany and that George Bush and his advisors were the "party of death," murdering innocent babies and children in the name of freedom.[72] Filmmaker Oliver Stone was not to be outdone, however. He said: "I see a parallel reality. There is a major time warp going on here. The quickening of the American pulse. We all feel the '60s are coming back," he said hopefully.[73] He wasn't the only one longing for the 1960s. A 24-year-old woman complained to Joan Baez that the new generation was disadvantaged: "In the Sixties, you guys had it all. You had a cause. You had the music. You had the momentum, and you had each other. We don't have any glue."[74] Clearly, a lot of people hoped the Kuwait crisis would furnish exactly such glue.

Meanwhile, the literary Left weighed in again. E. L. Doctorow used *The Nation* to write an open letter to President Bush opposing the use of force.[75] Virtually every liberal publication accused the administration of actually *wanting* war. The *New Yorker* proclaimed: "Our policy in the Gulf—purportedly based on the theory that only if Hussein is convinced war is imminent can war be avoided—is in fact moving us toward war. . . . Our policy in the Persian Gulf offers little evidence that American officials are making any effort to find" a stopping point short of war.[76] Kurt Vonnegut chimed in, too, saying a year after the war: "The atmosphere in this country since the Persian Gulf War is like that at a party in a beautiful home, with everybody being polite and bubbly. And then there is this stink coming from somewhere, getting worse all the time, and nobody wants to be the first to mention it."[77]

## CONTRIBUTIONS FROM WASHINGTON

The Bush administration furnished a few Vietnam parallels of its own. For example, Vice President Quayle was sent out as a stalker of protest, just as Richard Nixon had used Spiro Agnew in well-known and oft-recalled ways. Quayle told reporters that antiwar protests were among "the least inspiring sights" he had seen, and complained that the press had exaggerated their size and importance. He also proclaimed: "Operation Desert Storm will not be another Vietnam. . . . They will not be asked to fight with one arm tied behind their back."[78] The president also wrote the heads of 460 college newspapers in what seemed like a reprise of the early truth-squad efforts of the Johnson administration.[79]

Relatedly, there were the same arguments over the patriotism of dissent. Quayle did not accuse protestors of risking American lives overseas. But he did not have to. Polls showed that most Americans thought it was wrong for demonstrations to take place while U.S. troops were in a combat zone. A Gallup poll published on

January 31 asked: "Is it good that Americans who disagree with the government are speaking out on what they believe, or is it a bad thing for Americans to be demonstrating against the war when U.S. troops are overseas?" The answer was illuminating but, judging from Vietnam-era data presented earlier, hardly surprising. Fully 63 percent said it was a bad thing; only 34 percent said it was good.[80] Some of both groups explicitly invoked Vietnam to support their view.[81]

More important, President Bush was determined not to let the war become protracted, not to let antiwar sentiment have time to develop, not to let the press gain easy access to the war zone,[82] and not to let body counts and returning coffins become central points of reporting about the war. The president also tried to bypass Vietnam by drawing heavily on "lessons" of World War II.[83] These decisions flowed from Bush's own practical lessons of Vietnam, and all were applied strongly in the Kuwait War. John Kerry, of Vietnam Veterans Against the War fame in the 1960s and a senator from Massachusetts in 1991, put it accurately: "There is a general sense left over from Vietnam that they don't want the media telling an independent story for fear of what the repercussions might be."[84]

As a result of administration precautions, new but predictable arguments about press coverage of the Vietnam war arose. Those opposed to the war parodied Pentagon restrictions and bitterly denounced the view that the press had been responsible in any way for the loss of the Vietnam War.[85] Those who favored the Kuwait War were in sympathy with the Pentagon's attention to the subject, if not happy with its meat-ax bureaucratic approach to it.

Meanwhile, the epicenter of the discourse over the press was clear: It was Peter Arnett, broadcasting for CNN from Baghdad. Many Americans accused him of aiding and abetting the enemy. Said conservative critic K. L. Billingsley: "In effect, Arnett served as an anchorman, producer, and reporter. He checked no sources, provided no balance, and offered no alternative theories. What he was doing was not journalism but public relations ventriloquism" for the Iraqi side.[86] Senator Alan Simpson's public comments to the same effect raised eyebrows, but there was more than a little truth to the accusation. On one occasion, Arnett reported that a bombed building was not a military target, and that it had no such markings: no perimeter fence, no rooftop indications of military-related activity. The very next day (February 13) the New York Times carried a photo of the building on page 1 clearly showing a perimeter fence and roof vents.

This was no surprise to those who remembered Vietnam, where Arnett made his professional reputation. There in 1968 Arnett reported that a Vietcong squad had occupied part of the U.S. embassy compound in Saigon during the Tet offensive, an exaggeration that became and remains common knowledge.[87] In addition, the infamous quote: "It became necessary to destroy the village in order to save it," was reportedly invented by Arnett on February 7, 1968, and attributed to U.S. Air Force Major Chester L. Brown in Arnett's story about the fight for Ben Tre.[88]

The administration contributed to another Vietnam-Kuwait parallax by helping the formation of a constitutional question. Constitutional issues were raised about the executive branch's power to send American soldiers into battle and keep them there. Before the January 1991 congressional debate, President Bush averred that he alone had sufficient constitutional authority to commit U.S. troops. Fifty-four Democrats objected and brought suit.[89] For a while, in the latter part of 1990, it looked as if the White House did not want a congressional debate; and it looked as if the Congress did not want to commit itself through debate and vote either. Eventually, the Congress did vote the president his authority, even though everyone in the room heard echoes of the Tonkin Gulf Resolution reverberating in their heads.

And when the authority was granted, it happened oddly. The 1964 vote was very lopsided; the 1991 vote was close. This was partly because the dangers of open-ended presidential authority were not as clear in 1964 as they were after Vietnam. And it was despite the fact the rationale for using force to repel aggression in 1991 in the Persian Gulf was much clearer than it was in the Tonkin Gulf, where we still do not know for certain and do not agree on exactly what happened.

## CHANGES IN THE CHURCHES

Some of the differences between the 1960s antiwar movement and that of the early 1990s was to be found in the churches. Activism in the Vietnam era and in the series of causes that followed helped politicize America's liberal church organizations to unprecedented levels.[90] This occurred at a time when the sectarian Left was in significant overall decline, and the result was to turn the liberal churches into one of the main repositories of adversary culture activism.

At the same time, however, liberals as a group were becoming ever less inclined to invoke religious rhetoric in the service of a political agenda. This was partly because politics replaced religion, or rather became religion, in the lives of many activists, and they therefore felt no need for traditional religion. But the main reason, perhaps, was *Roe v. Wade,* and the electrifying impact it had on the marshaling of religious rhetoric by social and political conservatives. By the time of the Kuwait War, as Stephen L. Carter put it, "public religious appeals are generally associated with conservative causes, which might explain why liberals often seem over-enthusiastic in the rush to register their distaste for religion."[91] In any event, the result of these two vectors crossing in time was to make the churches of the late 1980s far more predictably antiwar but also far less influential among the broader liberal constituency on whose behalf they claimed to speak.

Every major Christian religious denomination in the country opposed the use of force against Iraq to liberate Kuwait, aligning in their tactical pronouncements with the majority of Democrats who urged that sanctions and diplomacy be given time to work. On December 28, 1990, the National Council of Churches called for a day of prayer and fasting on January 6 to stop the impending war.[92] On January 7, 1991, 18 church leaders published "A Message to the American People" in the *New York Times* in which they stated: "Our nation must not submit to the inevitability of war. By acting now on a very broad scale, we as a people of faith will mobilize on behalf of a peaceful alternative."[93] A key signatory of the message was Thomas Gumbleton, auxiliary bishop of the Roman Catholic Archdiocese of Detroit, a member of Pax Christi, and a former leader in the nuclear-freeze movement. On January 12 Unitarian Universalist ministers took out another full-page ad in the *New York Times*. It featured grave markers.[94]

The role of the churches was a clear turnabout from Vietnam times. By the end of the Vietnam War, the churches were actively engaged against the war, but they were not in the beginning. Richard John Neuhaus, who helped found Clergy and Laity Concerned about the War in Vietnam, put well the shift in attitudes over the years: "At that time there was a perception that what we were doing was a daring thing to do. Today, what was then deemed the normal thing would require considerable daring, that is, to say that military intervention in the Gulf is a reasoned moral policy."[95]

In fact, religious leaders were again split on the war; the difference was that the proportions were reversed. While the majority of Christian organizations opposed the use of force, not all did. Just as there were Catholic and Protestant supporters of the Vietnam War, and just as the administration in Washington used them to show that religious people were not all to one side, the same thing happened again during the Kuwait crisis. Bernard Cardinal Law of Boston said on January 25, 1991, that prompt military action in the Gulf had become a necessity; the White House happily took note of his remark. At the same time, Bishop Gumbleton urged mass conscientious objection within the military.[96]

The role played by the Jews underwent an even greater turnaround than the role played by the churches, but in the opposite direction. During the Vietnam War, Jews were prominent in all parts of the antiwar movement. In the Kuwait War context they were not. Not even all of those Jews who once might have expected to oppose the Bush administration did so. Arthur Waskow, perhaps the most prominent Jewish veteran of the Vietnam period—the inventor of "creative disorder" and Rennie Davis's senior May Day Tribes advisor from 1971—wrote candidly:

> I supported not only worldwide sanctions against Iraq but also the presence of U.S. troops in a defensive posture in the Gulf and in Saudi Arabia. In those ways I disagreed not only with the left factions that called the January 19 march against the war but also with the much larger and more centrist January 26 coalition that insisted on the slogan, "Bring the troops home now."[97]

One obvious reason for the shift in Jewish attitude was the clear and present danger to Israeli security represented by Iraq. The June Middle East War took place smack in the middle of the Vietnam War—in 1967—and was an event of very considerable importance for Jews of nearly every political description, but only radicals took the trouble to force a common explanatory paradigm on the Middle East and Southeast Asia. In the Kuwait War, a different common paradigm of thought was imposed by obvious circumstances: Israel was a de facto member of the coalition whose fate it was to absorb attacks but not respond to them. Certainly, Israel was as much Iraq's enemy as Kuwait, and, of course, Iraq actually attacked Israel while the Vietcong did not. In 1990-91, in short, the United States and Israel had a common enemy in Iraq and that changed everything for American Jews otherwise inclined to protest. Waskow grasped this but was shocked to find that others in the peace movement did not: "Perhaps most distressing of all to me and other antiwar Jews was that some in the major antiwar groups were so one-dimensionally committed to support of the Palestinian struggle for self-determination that they were unable to feel any empathy for Israel at the same time, even when its civilians came under fire from Iraq."[98]

Waskow went on to relate how, in Philadelphia on January 17, he and others were starting to plan the next day's activities when news came of the first Iraqi Scud missile attacks on Israel. The meeting became a gathering of tears, prayers, and frantic telephone calls to friends and family in Israel. When Waskow tried to explain what had happened to non-Jews in the new "movement," he related: "'Many American Jews have "non-soldier" family under fire in the Gulf,' I said, 'and we can't even "bring them home" because they already are home. Can you have the same empathy for them and for us as you do for U.S. soldiers and their families, who are after all carrying out the war we oppose?' From all but one person, I got blank stares."[99]

Similarly, said Betsy Tessler of the Philadelphia chapter of New Jewish Agenda, a left-wing group with origins in the Vietnam era through an earlier organization called Breira (Alternative): "The safety of Israel is not a concern to them. . . . They don't want to take the time to even talk about it." Tessler took part in the January 26 Washington rally but said she would not go to another. Her group's inclusion of the slogan "Security for Israel" provoked sharp hostility from other marchers. "I didn't feel comfortable or safe outside the Jewish contingent," she said.[100]

This and related phenomena changed the minds of many Jews away from the assumptions they had taken from the Vietnam era. At the Lincoln Square Synagogue on Manhattan's Upper West Side, a place one would expect to find antiwar Jews, one former Vietnam antiwar protestor said: "It's strange for me because years ago I marched against the Vietnam War when it was so clear that violence is bad, that war is bad. But now I see that violence can suck you in to the point where you have no choice but to fight."[101]

Outside of the churches and synagogues, another difference involved companies largely run by Vietnam generation businessmen advertising their opposition to the war. One ad, appearing in the *New York Times* of December 24, 1990, was entitled

"An unnecessary war." It stated: "The price of gasoline should never be a reason to send our sons and daughters off to die in a foreign war." The ad was signed by representatives of 19 companies, among them Ben & Jerry's Ice Cream, Gardener's Supply Company, *Utne Reader,* Paul Newman/Kayso Productions, Hemmings Motor News, and Earth Care Paper Company. In addition, a coalition of American environmentalists largely drawn from the Vietnam generation declared opposition too.[102] In the pre–Earth Day 1960s, of course, such a thing would have been impossible.

Another striking and happy difference was that even radical antiwar protestors took the trouble to distinguish the war policy from the soldiers who were about to fight it. This was, of course, ironic, for today's military is a volunteer army, while many a "baby killer" who returned from Vietnam had, as a draftee, never wanted to fight in the first place. The reception given to returning servicemen and women was different as night and day.

Yet another difference is that the Vietnam antiwar movement started during a Democratic administration, which meant that partisan opposition to the Left of the administration was limited to radical and Left-Liberal groups. Republicans were Lyndon Johnson's "objective ally" against them. In 1990-91 however, the Republican Bush administration was more vulnerable on partisan grounds to strong political attack for, all else being equal, one would expect Democrats to rally against a Republican president. Bush had no "objective ally" outside his own party. And yet he had his way with a Democratic-dominated Congress because that Congress was itself mightily impressed with the public outrage and arousal against Saddam Hussein's aggression. Antiwar protest, from whatever quarter, was a decidedly minority phenomenon. In a sense, then, George Bush had the majority of the American people for his "objective ally."

Indeed, Americans were not much inclined to the no-blood-for-oil slogans of the antiwar movement. While pro-war rallies occurred throughout the Vietnam War, they never compared in frequency or size with the antiwar movement. In the Kuwait War, however, support for the war was widespread, if shallow, across every strata of American society. More anti-antiwar press commentary was to be found than antiwar commentary.[103] The Washington victory parade drew 200,000 people, considerably larger than the largest antiwar demonstration.[104] Antiwar protestors attended this rally to mock it, but "they were quickly lost in a sea of American flags waved by the thousands of spectators and emblazoned on thousands more T-shirts and posters."[105]

Anti-antiwar demonstrations were also quicker to develop than in the Vietnam era, and probably did so partly because the model of Vietnam-era protest had become so much a part of the American menu of public behavior that it could be adopted by activists of any political persuasion. The Coalition for America at Risk, for example, took to the streets in opposition to antiwar protests. They also prepared T-shirts and related paraphernalia that used to be the province of antiwar protestors.[106] Other support groups included the American Security Council[107] and the ad hoc Committee for Peace and Security in the Gulf, made up largely of former Reagan administration officials.

The most significant change for our purposes was simply that many of those who had protested in the Vietnam era thought differently about the Kuwait crisis. Whether it was because the situation was different or because they had changed basic views is difficult to say. Some of both seems to have taken place. One former Vietnam era protestor, the inimicable Sam Brown, said: "It's a real odd thing for an old antiwar person to be thinking, but there are wars and there are wars. Every time I hear a parallel to Vietnam, I blanch. I see the movement people gearing up, the same familiar faces, and I want to say 'Hold on, hold on.' It's a whole different situation that needs to be examined on its own merits."[108] Another, Congressman Stephen Solarz, was even more direct:

> Ironies can sometimes be painful. I began my political career in 1966 as the campaign manager for one of the first anti-war congressional candidates in the country. Now, a quarter century later, I find myself supporting a policy in the Persian Gulf that might well lead to a war that many people believe could become another Vietnam. Such a position is more and more anomalous, I know, in the Democratic Party. And yet I cannot accept, or be dissuaded by, the analogy with Vietnam.[109]

Even movement sympathizers later admitted that they were outgunned, although many were reluctant to say why. Historian Paul Boyer complained:

> [Barbara] Epstein boasts of how quickly her campus mobilized against the Persian Gulf War. "UCSC faculty are so progressive," she says; "they were able to organize themselves more quickly than faculty on other campuses." With the benefit of hindsight, what strikes one is not how rapidly an antiwar movement surfaced, but how quickly it was buried in a blizzard of flags, yellow ribbons, media images of high-tech weaponry, and "welcome home" parades heavy with military hardware.[110]

Of course, had the war dragged on inconclusively as bodies were delivered home, public opinion probably would have changed despite the apparent lack of ambiguity about who were the good guys and who were the bad.[111] We must not forget that to the majority of Americans in 1965 and 1966 a nearly equivalent clarity existed. But—and this final difference is worth repeating—President Bush was determined not to let that happen. This is part of what he had in mind when he contemplated ending the Vietnam syndrome.

No one should have been surprised at President Bush's deliberately going out of his way to mention Vietnam after the Kuwait War was over. He had made much of it in his inaugural address in 1989:

We need compromise; we've had dissensus. We need harmony; we've had a chorus of discordant voices. . . . And our great Parties have too often been far apart and untrusting of each other. It's been this way since Vietnam. That war cleaves us still. But friends, that war began in earnest a quarter century ago; and surely the statute of limitations has been reached. This is a fact: The final lesson of Vietnam is that no great nation can long afford to be sundered by a memory.[112]

## LESSONS WITHIN LESSONS

Given this view, it was natural that President Bush triumphantly proclaimed the Vietnam syndrome to be dead once the Kuwait War was won. But was he right? Did his conduct of the war put it to rest? Or is it still thumping away beneath the floorboards?

One thing is certain: There was no shortage of instant interpreters of the meaning of the war. After the dust had settled, antiwar agitators and pro-war proponents began interpreting the results in such a way as to vindicate prior judgments. Opposing sides also foretold the future impact of the war by extending forth their fears or their hopes. Thus the pro-war camp was certain, along with the president, that stability in the Persian Gulf would improve, and many hoped for other spillover effects, from the deterrence of other aggression to boosting the Arab-Israeli peace process. The antiwar camp, on the other hand, was sure that several terrible consequences lay ahead. Many were bitter that the United States and its coalition partners won so easily and feared that, as a result, a New World Order would be forced upon the globe, an order good for rich white people and terrible for everyone else.[113] Others believed, less expansively, that victory would persuade the elite that force was the easiest answer to nearly every foreign policy problem, and that cheap oil was good for us when in fact, they believed, it was not.[114] Activist Margaret Hummel wrote: "Now I fear that war will be more and more accepted as a way to solve our problems and that we'll spend more and more on the military instead of on problems at home that are more pressing."[115]

More temperate views held that while the war was a success, it did not prove that sanctions and waiting would not have eventually accomplished the same thing at lower cost. Some also exaggerated the downside of the war, especially the aftermath in Kurdistan, while ignoring the probable consequences of either waiting or failing to oust Iraq from Kuwait.[116] In particular, the suffering of Iraqis, the overkill air power used by the allies, the burying of Iraqi soldiers alive in their sand berms, bombing "the highway of death"—all these and other unpleasantries of the war were emphasized, and the achievements ignored.[117]

Most interesting—and what concerns us most here—is that judgment about the Kuwait War doubled back to include judgment about Vietnam. Not only were the lessons of the Kuwait War the subject of debate, but the lessons of the Kuwait War for the Vietnam War were too—as if arguments that could not be closed on their own terms could be closed on the basis of another war, as if the Kuwait War was a palimpsest whose secrets could be discovered by examining the vellum.

The main argument was over whether the Kuwait War had destroyed the Vietnam syndrome or not. Some said yes.[118] Others said no.[119] Still others argued that those on the Right were trying to "prove" things from the Kuwait War that never were true to begin with: for example, that the press or the rules of the air war lost the Vietnam War.[120] It was the sort of discussion made confusing by the fact that there was no common definition of what the Vietnam syndrome actually was.

At least one man of the Left, Richard Falk of Princeton University, agreed ruefully that the Kuwait War had vanquished the Vietnam syndrome. But he saw it this way: "Ever since Vietnam American leaders have been looking for a formula that would permit the use of force in the Third World but avoid the semblance of war."[121] With the Kuwait War, Falk wrote, they succeeded. But there were also some on the Right who argued, also ruefully, that it had not. Joshua Muravchik, defining the syndrome differently, argued that the Vietnam paradigm was fully embedded in the warnings and criticism of the war, so much so that mere victory could not vanquish them.[122] Michael Klare of the Institute for Policy Studies made a similar argument from the Left, emphasizing still another aspect of the so-called syndrome: "The way we fought this war was as much a response to the Vietnam Syndrome as it was to the nature of the enemy. There was going to be no quagmire this time, there was no graduated buildup, there was no chance the military would have to fight with one hand tied behind its back."[123]

While the Kuwait War definitely ended the Vietnam syndrome for some, including many Vietnam veterans,[124] both Klare and Muravchik were right to assert that the Kuwait War did not vanquish the syndrome altogether. Indeed, there was much irony in President Bush's proclamation of its death. If it was dead, why was the president so worried about overextending American commitments in Southwest Asia? Why did he hesitate to help the Iraqi Kurds and Shiites? Why did he rule out tracking down and "arresting" Saddam Hussein? Why did he not consider, as some thought he should, a protracted occupation of Iraq? Why did the administration not press for more vigorous enforcement of U.N. resolutions that Iraq violated at every opportunity after March 1, 1991? The best answer is that the cost in lives and treasure might have soon violated the still-low threshold of the American people for sustaining such costs. If that is not the Vietnam syndrome, then it has never existed.

Even that is not the end of this story. In the final hours of the Bush administration in January 1993, the president had to decide how to respond to repeated Iraqi violations of U.N. Security Council resolutions. When it was finally decided that a military response was required, what form did it take? Graduated response. Wrote Michael Gordon of the *New York Times*:

> Despite repeated threats of broad retaliation by Washington, the air strike against Iraq today was a minimal military action, intended not to produce a decisive military outcome but to send the political signal that Washington and its allies were determined to enforce the restrictions imposed on Baghdad at the end of the Gulf War. The raid . . . had more in common with the philosophy of gradual escalation in the Vietnam war than the day-and-night blitz of the Gulf War. . . . As in Vietnam, the United States struck, ordered a pause in the bombing to evaluate the response, and suggested it would expand the attack if Baghdad did not get the message.[125]

How was it that the man who believed he had destroyed the Vietnam syndrome in early 1991 again fell victim to it in early 1993? No, the Vietnam syndrome is not dead, certainly not by the hand of George Bush.

It is wounded, however. Every democracy has a threshold for risking military adventures overseas and, as de Tocqueville saw, the American one is high when it comes to spending money and lives on foreign adventures not directly germane to American security or the promotion of American values. The bitter legacy of Vietnam had the effect of raising that threshold still higher. It had happened before: The meager results of American sacrifice in World War I, once they came clear, contributed mightily to the isolationism of the 1930s. Clearly, the American propensity for international activism is a function of its presumed price. When price is uppermost in the public mind, the country inclines to caution. When it is not, it is less cautious. All the Kuwait War did was to lower that threshold a few notches, for the price paid was low. Certainly, the notion that the U.S. military could not be used effectively abroad in a major effort was shattered hither and yon.

The real question, then, is *how much* did the Kuwait War lower the American threshold for foreign military intervention? Some thought a lot, as noted earlier, but that was not clear. George Bush's caution in late February 1991 and thereafter in the Persian Gulf, and in the early stages of the Bosnian crisis, can be read as evidence of the Vietnam syndrome at work. At that time, in another explicit example of links between Vietnam and Bosnia, Strobe Talbott wrote that he favored "an all-out [NATO] peacemaking effort" as a way for the United States to "truly cure itself of the Vietnam syndrome."[126]

But that hasn't happened despite Talbott's coming to a high State Department position under Clinton. The very restrictive attitude of the Clinton administration on the use of force shows that the Vietnam syndrome is alive and well again. This is hardly surprising considering the intellectual pedigree of key Clinton administration figures. The appointments of Les Aspin, Anthony Lake, Peter Tarnoff, and Frank Wisner to senior foreign policy positions make the point: The group first met in Vietnam thirty years earlier, and Lake resigned his government post to protest the U.S. invasion of Cambodia in 1970.[127] Talbott was also an antiwar activist whose first college editorial at Yale during his senior year called for the decriminalization of marijuana. This was an administration that could not forget Vietnam even if it wanted to—not that many people were inclined to let them forget it: On May 31, 1993, the president was heckled and booed during a visit to the Vietnam War Memorial in Washington. Even the words the administration has used to describe American tactics invoke the ghosts of Vietnam, including the ghosts of graduated response. On March 22, 1994, in reference to dealing with North Korea's rush to achieve nuclear weapons capability, Secretary of State Warren Christopher spoke of "progressively stronger measures" against them.[128]

But in Bosnia at least, Tabott's 1992 plea notwithstanding, President Clinton's reluctance to commit U.S. forces makes sense. President Bush, former Republican secretaries of state Henry Kissinger, Alexander M. Haig, Jr., and Lawrence Eagleburger, and most other experienced American statesmen believe that the dangers of American military intervention in the former Yugoslavia outweigh any likely benefits. Talbott was wrong: Bosnia is not a place to cure ourselves of a Vietnam syndrome. Rather, as President Clinton has had the good grace to sense, it is the first important instance since Vietnam where applying its cautionary lessons make sense.

The Vietnam syndrome is best described as a tendency rather than as a reflex of what to do when faced with a choice. One cannot expect crisp lessons from past wars, for such lessons can never be specific enough to navigate the present, and presidents, however attentive they may be to analogy, either know that from the start or soon come to know it, and often the hard way.[129] Besides, we shouldn't want to get rid of the Vietnam syndrome if that means making ourselves deliberately obtuse to Vietnam's broader lessons.

As for the antiwar movement's lessons, many aging hippies would have been surprised to learn in 1990 that the Vietnam antiwar movement actually had been counterproductive to stopping the war in Vietnam. Whether such knowledge would have stopped a new movement from developing is unknown because motives differ when people take to the streets, and sometimes the motives have little to do with the issue at hand. Some 40-something-year-olds were no doubt trying to reclaim the youthful exuberance they knew in the 1960s. Some 20-year-olds felt cheated for being born too late, for missing the music when it was hot, the drugs when they were easy to get, and the sex when it was still safe.

Engined by such sources, antiwar sentiment might indeed have made an impact had the crisis become protracted. If, after 60 days of air assaults and only limited ground action, Iraqi forces had not been removed from Kuwait and American casualties had started coming home on the 6 o'clock news, the Bush administration would not have stopped the war, but it might have worried about the home front, and with good reason. Its worry, in turn, probably would have convinced it to hasten the end by risking more American lives in heavier ground assaults. What a tragedy it would have been if, once again, well-intentioned people had let their emotions lead American soldiers to unnecessary death. What a blessing it was that it didn't happen.

Thus, as was the case a quarter century ago, the movement to oppose the Kuwait War was diverse, emotional, and photogenic to the electronic media. Even more than was the case then, most protestors were well-intended and patriotic beyond doubt. But just as was the case in the 1960s, this movement, to the extent it might have waxed strong in the context of a protracted war, would likely have gotten more, not fewer, American soldiers killed as a consequence.

## MOVEMENTS WITHIN MOVEMENTS

Not only was the Kuwait War used to judge the Vietnam War, the Kuwait War antiwar movement has been used to judge the Vietnam antiwar movement. As a subset of Vietnam syndrome analysis, there was also commentary on how well or poorly the antiwar movement itself had done. Many observers believed that the movement had done well considering the constraints, and many activists and sympathizers looked forward to their next chance.[130] Some saw hope and reinforcement. Sandy Close, executive director of Pacifica News Service, wrote that "the big 'NO' of the left in the 1960s . . . today finds an echo even on the podiums of Washington's Kuwait War victory celebrants: 'No one hates war more than me,' [General Norman] Schwarzkopf told flag-waving crowds."[131]

This was wishful thinking, as the high levels of atavistic pride unleashed by the war made clear.[132] Other protestors agreed and vowed to continue protesting even though the war was over. One tactic was to follow General Schwarzkopf around and interrupt his speeches.[133] Defense Secretary Cheney was also the object of a few minor protests.[134] And the politicized Quakers and their sympathizers now had a new reason not to pay federal taxes.[135]

Other movement sympathizers argued that divisions and misconceptions had led to a poor movement performance and that the weakness of the movement would be the main reason that more bad things would happen in the future. Failure did not often stir a rethinking; most of those who thought they had been right to protest in the 1960s also thought they were right to do the same in the 1990s. In their view, what had changed was that the country was more conservative and more militaristic than it had been before; any other differences between Vietnam and Kuwait, in their view, were insignificant.

It was precisely this assumption that touched off some of the most effective critiques of the movement. Michael Lerner of Seattle 8 and May Day Tribes fame, now editor of *Tikkun,* said that "the movement exhibited '60s nostalgia at its worst."[136] Similarly, Jacob Weisberg claimed that antiwar forces "remain emotionally and intellectually stuck in a '60s rut. What has been striking about the protest movement to date is the extent to which its arguments, slogans, sources of support, and techniques—even its style and sensibility—are dominated by memories of the Vietnam era."[137] Again Lerner complained: "The general problem is that it's attempting to squeeze the complex reality of the '90s Mideast into the more simple realities of the '60s and Vietnam."[138]

More eloquent to this effect than Lerner or Weisberg was the analysis of Paul Berman. Berman noted the oft-remarked fact that statesmen and diplomats often try to prevent future wars by acting as though the dangers faced are analogous to the past, particularly to the most seminal or proximate past experience believed analogous to the one at hand. This gets them in deep trouble—like the deep trouble of World War II, for example, which was caused by statesmen trying to prevent another World War I. Berman extended this reasoning and argued that antiwar movements also can oppose "the wrong war." He called this the Norman Thomas syndrome, for it was Thomas who erroneously opposed U.S. participation in World War II on the basis of what he thought he had learned about World War I. (It should be added for the sake of fairness that Thomas ultimately came around.) This, Berman argued, was exactly what the Kuwait antiwar movement was doing.

As a man of the Left, Berman granted that it was right to oppose the Vietnam War, but the Kuwait War, he argued, was a war against fascism on the march. It was a "progressive" war. Writing in late January 1991, he warned that if the antiwar movement was successful, the result would be to "have a progressive war under conservative auspices—while the nation's best progressives go on mobilizing against the war in Vietnam."[139] Of this kind of mistaken analogizing, social critic George Weigel noted: "Our policy meets every one of the criteria these people have urged on us. It's a just cause, defending Arabs, under the authority of the United Nations, an act of collective security against a guy condemned by Amnesty International who kills cormorants. And they're still against it."[140]

Former radicals who were no longer men of the Left took keen notice of the Vietnamization of the Kuwait antiwar movement. Peter Collier, struck by how often Vietnam was mentioned by the new generation of protesters, argued that the new movement had bet on the hallowed memories of the Vietnam movement era and lost.

> The stakes were clear from the onset. This would be a parallax war in which
> the fighting might be done in Kuwait and Iraq but the ground to be contested
> was Vietnam. Bush knew it: he had said that he wanted to cut off the Vietnam
> experience and kill it. The Left was equally determined to protect Vietnam as
> its holy ground, the once and future war in which America would be

repeatedly humiliated. For the Left, it was a meal ticket and ace-in-the-hole, the double bind with which it had whiplashed this country for 20 years. *No more Vietnams* was the sanction that kept this country impotent and unsure, and made sure that it did not act in its own interests.

The Left bet heavy and lost heavy, said Collier:

> The Left not only lost the war, but it lost Vietnam as well, its Camelot and its Holy Grail. Now Vietnam is once again what it actually always was—the aberration, not the norm.[141]

The only way to really find out if the Left lost the use of Vietnam in opposing the Kuwait War is to wait for the next major war and antiwar movement and then observe how Vietnam as metaphor is used, by whom, for what purposes, and to what effect. Most likely, the Kuwait War does not represent a major superseding experience to Vietnam. It did not displace Vietnam as the key metaphorical currency that gets traded whenever discussions of the projection of American military power arise.

The way Bosnia has been seen from the start by the Clinton administration has been a case in point. Ronald Steel put the basic parallel well: "Like Bosnia, Vietnam was a war that Johnson was wary of getting involved in at the time," largely for fear that it would divert attention and money from domestic issues.

> But the pundits said, "How can we just stand by and let this happen?" And columnists like Joe Alsop questioned Johnson's manhood. And so he acted. In Vietnam, we acted as leader of the free world. In Bosnia, we are told we must act as leader of the whole world. . . . In the end, the same pundits who drove him into the war abandoned him.[142]

According to *New York Times* writer Thomas Friedman, Clinton aides admitted that this analogy was "very much on the President's mind" and that he feared his entire presidency could be swallowed by Bosnia just as Johnson's was swallowed by Vietnam.[143] That may not be the Vietnam syndrome defined as "one hand tied behind the back," but it is a lesson reasonably chosen and learned just the same, in this case a wise one.

# 10

# Truths and Consequences

*The knowledge of death, of the implacable limits*
*placed on a man's existence, severed us from our youth*
*as irrevocably as a surgeon's scissors had once severed us from*
*the womb. . . . We left Vietnam peculiar creatures, with*
*young shoulders that bore rather old heads.*
—Philip Caputo, *A Rumor of War*

A main argument of this book is that the major effects of the Vietnam antiwar movement have been and continue to be felt more in the United States than in Southeast Asia. We nevertheless begin this final chapter with one last visit to Vietnam, then return home to survey the continuing consequences of the war and the antiwar movement.

## SOUTHEAST ASIA:
## HOW MUCH DID THE MOVEMENT MATTER?

To evaluate the effect of the antiwar movement on the prosecution of the war and its final outcome is difficult business. We can sum up our argument as follows: To the modest extent that the antiwar movement ever worked to limit U.S. involvement in Vietnam, it did so *before* the election of Lyndon Johnson and *after* the election of Richard Nixon, particularly after U.S. ground troops had been withdrawn and U.S. prisoners of war returned in early 1973. In between, and particularly in the period between 1965 and 1970—and possibly up to the 1972 election—the movement achieved nothing concrete according to its own measure and probably helped the sitting administrations to manage the broadest segments of American public opinion into relative quiescence. Its counterproductive impact may have been modest—as modest as its limiting impact before and after this core period—but that was its direction.

It is clear that the Johnson administration was *self-restrained* from sharp escalation, not restrained because of public opinion, which was more hawkish than the administration much of the time, or because of the antiwar movement, which was marginal to the decision-making process throughout. Antiwar demonstrations mounted and populated by radicals stifled at least as much if not more nonradical dissent against the war than they stimulated. Most Americans, while concerned about a war seemingly without end or prospect of clearcut victory, were more prepared to suffer in silence than to associate themselves with lurid leftists and yelping Yippies.

And when the Johnson administration changed course in March 1968, it did so through a calculation of various costs and benefits in which the antiwar movement counted as only one of several factors and certainly not as a major one. Nor can the changed views of the Wise Men, as they revisited the problem in February and March of that year, be ascribed to the antiwar movement in any simple way. Their changed views appear to have been predicated not only on erroneous assumptions about public opinion after the Tet offensive, but also on account of a confluence of other, more fundamental factors than what they referred to euphemistically as divisions in the nation. Even then, to the Wise Men, those divisions probably meant divisions in establishment opinion, division among Democratic politicians and opinion leaders, not the dissent represented by radicals in the streets.

The antiwar movement succeeded eventually in limiting U.S. military involvement only to the extent that antiwar sentiment became reliberalized through the Democratic Party and its post-1969 Moratorium youth contingent. At that point, only after the fizzled incandescence of the New Left in the 1968-69 period, the movement affected marginally the timing and perhaps the tone of the decision to negotiate withdrawal, and this was done in consort with the Congress—hardly an extra-parliamentary phenomenon over all. The movement was not responsible for the overthrow of policy itself; that rested first with Lyndon Johnson's decision to change U.S. policy aims and then with Richard Nixon's decision to limit them further in deference to broader foreign and domestic policy goals.

We mustn't forget, too, that while the movement moved back toward and into the Democratic Party between 1970 and 1974, that party never had a chance to freely pursue its own plans for withdrawal from Vietnam. This is because the Republicans won the White House in the 1968 election. In other words, another layer, or filter—a Republican White House—interposed itself between the flow of antiwar sentiment into mainstream politics and actual executive branch decisions about the war. President Nixon did shape his administration's diplomatic and military policies over Vietnam to what he thought domestic political traffic would bear, but that isn't the same as claiming that the movement had a direct restraining influence on administration policy. Rather, the deradicalized movement merged with growing broad public antiwar sentiment, which pushed the Democrats, and the Democrats pushed the Republicans, who, as practicing politicians, were already looking toward the next midterm and presidential elections. Such dynamics describe what radical movement activists used to refer to derisively as "working through the system." It is hardly heroic, and hardly the stuff of which many antiwar radicals were proud then and are still proud of today.

As antiwar sentiment became more firmly ensconced in the Congress, it contributed to the cutoff of U.S. aid to South Vietnam, undermined Saigon's confidence, and contributed to its fall to the Communist regime in Hanoi. This might not have happened had the Nixon administration taken a different approach to the Paris Accords and to foreign policy priorities generally. That is to say: The White House made the essential decision to disengage using the Paris Accords as a means to create a "decent interval." It was a decision not to find out if Vietnamization would work if it took 10 or 12 years instead of 2 or 3. There was nothing inevitable about this decision, but, with a new global foreign policy to unfurl and an election to win in 1972, Richard Nixon made it. To blame the Congress entirely for the fall of South Vietnam is unfair.[1] To blame—or credit—the antiwar movement isn't justified in the least.

The antiwar movement neither lost the war nor caused the subsequent bloodbath in Southeast Asia. In the broadest sense, the war was lost because the American ship of state itself had lost its bearings. The expansion of containment to Asia and its post–Korean War militarization merged with a rapidly expanding economic base to produce a level of American hubris that was bound to send its ship of state onto the rocks sooner or later. However morally motivated, the U.S. commitment to Vietnam was strategically unsound; thus, even had the war been won the costs might well have exceeded any strategic benefits. But the war was not won because U.S. administrative, diplomatic, and especially military strategies failed. In other words, even beyond a flawed decision to commit itself, which flowed from the lack of a realistic strategy for containing polycentric Communism in the geostrategic peripheries of the Cold War, the Vietnam War was lost by some combination of the U.S. military's inability to adapt to politico-military counterinsurgency warfare, ill-advised micromanagement of the war by Pentagon civilians, and maladroit meddling in South Vietnam's stygian political system. None of these sources of American defeat was set in motion or significantly worsened either by antiwar activism or by fear of it in Washington.

What happened to the Vietnamese and Cambodian people happened because the war was lost, but, again, the antiwar movement did not play a major role in that. The only way to argue otherwise is to assume that the movement bolstered Hanoi's morale to a decisive degree as it contemplated the "correlation of forces." No doubt the antiwar movement did boost morale in Hanoi to some degree—how could it not?—but no evidence suggests it was decisive.

Even if we assume the war was unwinnable, it still does not follow that the antiwar movement can take credit for driving that point home. The Wise Men and their bureaucratic allies made their decisions after the Tet offensive in light of their own sense of limits. After all, by March 1968 the United States had already gone beyond its self-imposed restrictions and still not won, and it had to contemplate the possibility of causing still greater damage to American life and squandering still more of its treasure without victory. Such a specter was quite sufficient to generate a change of view; it required no help from the street.

About the essential decision to fight in Vietnam, the antiwar movement was right but for the wrong reasons. The war's sources had nothing to do with the sinister face of corporate capitalism, but the war *was* a mistake. The Johnson administration *was* pursuing policies that, even though well-intended, were incoherent and unwise. Public dissent against those policies was a reasonable response to such unwisdom. There is, after all, nothing sinister about protesting either a futile war or the steely hubris of a government that cannot recognize or admit that it has erred.

The antiwar movement was not responsible for the basic flow of American government judgments about Vietnam, and what minor influence it did have tended to reinforce policy stasis during the Johnson period and to quicken modestly the reduction of military activity during the Nixon period. How does this affect common arguments about the merit, the guilt, and the responsibility that the antiwar movement should bear for what happened in Southeast Asia after 1975?

Few can doubt that a horrific bloodbath took place in Southeast Asia after 1975, and that millions of people who suddenly wanted desperately to escape their homeland did so for good reason.[2] Doves have tended to argue that the antiwar movement saved American lives but did not sacrifice Asian ones because the war was unwinnable, and what was going to happen was going to happen eventually anyway. American participation in the war made what happened worse, they claim, especially in Cambodia,[3] but it never could have made anything better. Most hawks have claimed the reverse, blaming what happened directly on the loss of the war, and the loss of the war on the antiwar movement and other related maladies on the home front. What are we to make of these judgments in light of the analysis brought here?

One way to answer this question is to divide our thinking into consideration of intentions and consequences. Judging intentions alone is often fruitless because the world rarely abets the simple transformation of intentions, whether good or evil, into intended consequences. Judging consequences alone, however, can suggest the premise that history proclaims its own meaning—that what happened was meant to happen—but it doesn't.

What goes for the antiwar movement goes for the war itself. Even if we discount the impact of the movement, it is still no simple matter to determine how much of what happened in Southeast Asia after 1975 was the fault of the United States. Would South Vietnam have survived without American intervention in 1964-65? If not, did all the United States achieve amount to a delay of a decade? Was that worth 58,000 American lives? Would Cambodia have been spared Pol Pot and then a Vietnamese occupation had the Nixon administration not bombed and invaded the country? Or doesn't it follow instead that a quicker Communist victory in Vietnam would have brought the Khmer Rouge to power sooner rather than later? So in consideration of intentions and consequences it is best to consider those of the antiwar movement and the government it opposed together.

As to intentions, the great majority of those active in the antiwar movement clearly felt themselves to be patriotic Americans. The movement cannot be fairly characterized as having been made up of primarily individuals who were self-hating, psychologically aberrant, or sociopathic. Acts of self-sacrifice, powerful idealism, and a deep love of country characterized the antiwar movement at least in part throughout its existence.

The U.S. government was also well-intended. It wished to stop Communism because it believed it to be wrong, and it wanted to help the Vietnamese achieve self-determination because it believed that to be right. There was no hidden agenda of economic exploitation, of seeking bases in order to wage aggressive war against China, of fighting mainly to generate profits for a military-industrial complex.

But good intentions are not always useful measures for judgment because everyone except the pathologically ill is well-intended at least on an abstract level. When parts of the antiwar movement came to believe that love for country required destroying all existing social structures and norms, it adopted the same dubious logic (dubiously) attributed to a U.S. military commander who said that a certain Vietnamese village had to be destroyed in order to be saved. When the Johnson administration went to war, it did almost everything wrong, from undermining the Saigon government instead of building it up to pushing peasants and intellectuals both into the arms of the Vietcong instead of the other way around. Instead of being flexible enough to recognize error, the U.S. military pursued its counterproductive behavior to a virtual point of no return, politically if not literally, on the battlefield. So much for good intentions.

When one speaks of consequences, on the other hand, the first thing to remember is that ethics is a serious discipline. Several popular but blithe judgments that have been made about Vietnam slide off the low end of the logic scale. Some have argued, for example, that the war effort was worth it, despite the loss of South Vietnam, because it bought a decade's worth of time for the rest of Southeast Asia to mobilize and develop, and for ASEAN (the Association of Southeast Asian Nations) to consolidate.[4] Is this really what 58,000 Americans died for?

Others have argued that since Communism is dead anyway, and since Vietnam is a basket case, it proves that even bothering to stop Communism in Southeast Asia was a stupid thing to do in the first place. Mickey Kaus of *The New Republic* argued that the best case against Communism in the area is Vietnam's economic failure, a case that never could have been made had the United States won the war: "Vietnam may even (in the long run) be better off for the Communists' victory. In power they discredited themselves in a way that never would have been possible if they'd remained a Philippine-like guerrilla opposition."[5]

This is a worthwhile line of reasoning if only because it makes nonsense of Frances Fitzgerald's prophecies about the "cleansing effects" of the Vietnamese revolution.[6] The only thing that the Vietnamese revolution cleansed, or should have cleansed, was the foolish idea that Third World revolutions are cleansing. But Kaus never mentions costs: the re-education camps; the boat people who left, risking or giving their lives in the process; and the millions living in deepening poverty and fear under Hanoi's iron fist since 1975. Is scoring a rarefied debating point about Asian Communism worth it to those who have paid the price? Too bad Kaus never bothered to ask them.

Clearly, justifying the war post hoc on the basis of "results" that were neither primary nor explicit is not very compelling. Neither is justifying opposition to the war based on information no one could possibly have had at the time; obviously, it isn't much of an achievement to conclude that the war was unwinnable after one already knows the outcome. Just because something is hard to do—such as bringing ethics to bear on a war after the fact—is no reason to be satisfied with arguments like these.

Moral judgment is always a problem but always a necessity. So I make mine: Both the government and the antiwar movement were well-intentioned, and both failed to translate good intentions into good consequences. The same can probably be said for both South and North Vietnamese leaders. Simply put, what happened both here and in Southeast Asia is that the mistakes of the powerful overwhelmed the mistakes of the weak. Is it so, as Nietzsche said, that "the errors of great men are venerable because they are more fruitful than the truths of little men"? No, they are only more horrible. The antiwar movement never came close to doing the sort of harm that the failed policies of the U.S. government did. Unfortunately, it seems fairly clear that neither movement nor government did anybody in Vietnam any good at all.

## THE VIETNAM GENERATION REVISITED

More than a quarter century has passed since the great tumult of 1968. For many of those who were students at the time, that anniversary carried ambiguous implications. In popular culture, the 1960s are an iconic time, imagined to have been full of heroism and great fun. But for those who were there and can still remember anything about it, there are embarrassments amid the glory. As N. R. Kleinfield predicted early in 1993: "This will be a year of considerable personal revisionism." "It will be necessary," he added, "to respond to interminable questions about where you were when, and to formulate droll responses if the facts don't sound so good anymore. Many who had a quiet year in Chicopee will proudly assert that, yes, they were Abbie Hoffman's right-hand man in Chicago, absolutely they were gassed. Yes, it was indeed they who took the admissions office. Free love? You better believe it."[7] And, as Landon Jones quipped, while the actual attendance at

Woodstock was less than half a million, "twice that many later claimed they had been there, and three times as many thought they had."[8]

For most, the truth was a lot less dramatic. "Okay," concluded Kleinfield, "for a while, I thought the apocalypse was hovering somewhere out there. But I kept a level head. When I read those radical leaflets urging, 'Burn your money,' I balked. I bought more bell-bottoms."[9]

There is a serious point lurking in this wit. Whatever anyone young was thinking or doing in 1968, everyone who survived has since grown up. That is always an ambiguous task that leaves an ambiguous legacy, whether it happens in the late twentieth century or the late twelfth. As a result, it is impossible to say exactly how and how much the Vietnam generation was affected by the war and the antiwar movement. The data we have on the subject are at best impressionistic and even less reliable than Vietnam-era polling data. But they are worth a brief look.

Consider the fact, for example, that between 1959 and 1975—the first and last years that there were U.S. casualties in Vietnam—about 60 million Americans turned 18 years of age. In 2020 these generational cohorts will be at the height of their social power. At least four presidential elections may be influenced decisively by them, the first one having been in 1992. What they learned from their seminal political experience—the Vietnam War and the antiwar movement—is therefore of more than marginal importance.

One group within the Vietnam generation deserves special note: those who fought the war and those who fought fighting the war by various legal and illegal means of draft resistance. During the Vietnam era, about 29 million American men came of draft age, and of those, over half found some legal or illegal way to avoid military service. About 2 million men were drafted during the period, but only about 10 percent of all those who entered military service by draft or by volunteering went to Vietnam. (It is a misconception that draftees did most of the fighting and dying in Vietnam; regular, professional military troops did so for all but a few years.) Additionally, about 450,000 young men violated draft laws, but only about 3,000 were punished with jail sentences. Also, while there were only 24 proven cases of battlefield desertion, at least 20,000 men left their units once they returned stateside. All this adds up, in varying ways to be sure, to intense personal experiences that many carry with them today.

Beyond that, the rest of the Vietnam generation, even those who never went to Vietnam, was buffeted by two kinds of crises, one political and one social. The political crisis was defined by civil rights and Vietnam, the social crisis by major changes in socialization and family structure decades in the making. The antiwar movement erupted from the former, the counterculture from the latter, but the eruptions were sufficiently simultaneous to render the distinction theoretical for most purposes.

Despite this novel experience, the sociopolitical profile of the baby-boomers exhibits much continuity with that of previous generations. As political sociologist

Paul Light observed: "Just because an age group grows up at the same time does not mean it will become a social generation. . . . Not every one will share the zeitgeist. Moreover, just because a zeitgeist existed in the 1960s does not mean it is preserved today." And yet, Light concludes that "the baby boom as a whole remains more liberal than older and younger generations alike. The zeitgeist may be fading with time, but it still exists at some level of political consciousness, and such differences may last a lifetime."[10]

Light is correct but unspecific. Ideally, it would be nice to be able to specify the differences and then determine which can be traced to the antiwar movement and the counterculture, and to what degree. Unfortunately, it is hard to do the former, and impossible to do the latter. One cannot easily show that Vietnam and the antiwar movement were responsible for certain attitudes of the Vietnam generation but not others. It is one thing to call the Vietnam generation "haunted," as did Myra MacPherson, quite another to identify the ghosts.[11]

Such uncertainty bothers most social scientists to the point that they refuse to speculate about it in print. That has left the field to the emotions of partisans. As Menard put it:

> [T]he change that the counterculture made in American life has become nearly impossible to calculate—thanks partly to the exaggerations of people who hate the '60s, and partly to the exaggerations of people who hate the people who hate the '60s. The subject could use the attention of some people who really don't care.[12]

It's not that I don't care, it's that the uncertainty strikes me as a challenge instead of a deterrent. So let's start by looking briefly at some representative data, and move on to humble interpretation.

However fragile it may be, one of the only ways we know to get answers to questions about how events and experiences affect attitudes is to ask people. One poll taken in 1987 was based on the question: How much would you say you have been affected by the Vietnam War? (1) A great deal, (2) quite a bit, (3) only some, (4) not much, (5) not at all?[13] Not surprisingly, answers showed that the closer to the generational epicenter of the Vietnam War–era cohorts one was, the more Vietnam was said to have had an impact. That is neither surprising nor particularly interesting.

Somewhat more interesting is how individuals say they were affected. Six main overlapping categories emerge from survey data. Most respondents, about 35 percent, cited personal and family involvement. Typical responses included references to knowing friends or relatives who served in Vietnam, fear of the draft, and knowledge of friends still working through problems stemming from their being in Vietnam. Next was the effect of casualties, cited by 28 percent. About 10 percent believed that people died for no good reason, and 10 percent remembered being repulsed by hearing the death tolls and body counts.

The third category concerned foreign policy: About 21 percent "learned" from Vietnam that—in a typical response—"America should stay out of other countries' problems." But some learned that "we should have fought harder or not fought at all." Still others learned that governments mismanage military operations.

The fourth category concerned veterans' health problems (18 percent), especially the lingering of depression and drug addiction. The fifth concerned politicization/activism, where 14 percent said that the war and the antiwar movement shaped their views of the U.S. government and society, generally in a negative fashion. Of these, however, there was a split between those who became and have remained politically active and those who lost interest in politics after the war was over. And the sixth concerned government credibility (12 percent), where the overwhelming majority expressed a loss of faith in government and authority in general. Typical comments were that from the war, "I learned that we were not the good guys"; "We lost face"; and "My view that America always fights for right was destroyed."[14] Thus, as these data and others suggest, what is generally true about American attitudes toward war, peace, and the projection of American power overseas tends to be systematically more pronounced in the attitudes of the Vietnam generation.

Adding up the number of those who say they were affected, and looking at how they were affected, in the three nonpersonal categories—foreign policy, politicization/activism, and government credibility—it is clear that well over half of all respondents born between 1943 and 1969 say they were affected either a great deal or quite a bit. This is not everyone, and not everyone who was affected was affected in the same way, even at the time.[15] But the Vietnam generation and the generations just after it do mistrust the military more, favor American intervention overseas less, and doubt the credibility and integrity of their government more than those who came before or who have come two generations and more after. Other research has also indicated that protestors within the generation, compared to their cohorts who were not protestors, favor Republican presidential candidates less by major margins, support extra-parliamentary political activity, oppose prayer in public schools, support federal intervention to support school desegregation, and believe that poor people, women, and minorities are greatly underrepresented in the political process.[16]

Beyond that, research suggests strongly that the relevant generational cohorts as a whole see political activism as a personal option for dissent in far greater numbers than previous generations. Moreover, Vietnam and Watergate led to a sudden and sustained reduction in voting levels in the United States. In the period between the end of World War II and the denouement over Vietnam between 1968 and 1970, about half the electorate voted in midterm elections. By 1972 that number had dropped to around 36 percent, and it has stayed there ever since except for a slight upward blip in 1982. That it has stayed low suggests that new levels of electoral nonparticipation reside within certain age cohorts, and they do: the Vietnam generations. Taken together, support for extra-parliamentary activity combined with reduced voting means that a substantial part of the generation is alienated from the core institutions of American democracy.

As suggested earlier, this attitude applies not only to the Vietnam generation but also to the one or two generations after it. Why? Nicholas Lemann, born in 1954, has explained his own experience in an illuminating way. As to the military, for example, Lemann noted: "I grew up with a complete ignorance of and hostility toward the American military. When I was a teenager I assumed without even thinking about it that there was something wrong, even pathological, with anyone who was in the service." On government credibility, he added:

> Mostly because of Vietnam, I grew up regarding every American president in my lifetime as a pathological war criminal. . . . I also believed, as did my friends, that America could do nothing right; that it was a force for evil in the world; that, therefore, the country's leadership was also stupid and venal . . . and that the whole idea of order and authority was probably wrong, too.[17]

He added: "I can remember two political events in college that caused people to go out in the streets on warm nights, whooping and yelling with joy: the resignation of President Nixon and the fall of the government of South Vietnam to the Communists."[18] The Vietnam generation began in idealism and ended in cynicism; the generation after it caught just the cynicism, and has had a hard time shaking it ever since.

Of all the changes in public attitudes in the Vietnam generation, the one with the broadest impact is probably that concerning confidence in the political community and its institutions. Few Americans today between the ages of 38 and 48 take anything a politician says at face value. Even many of those who always rejected antiwar radicalism cannot rid themselves of many of the enduring images of that period. When the Dow Chemical Corporation runs television commercials typifying itself as the company for which idealistic young chemists and scientists want to work for the betterment of humanity, as it did in the period between 1988 and 1990, people who had nothing in particular against Dow Chemical, who have no knowledge of any maleficence on its part then or now, and who have never seen napalm in action, recoiled involuntarily in horror.

Perhaps we should never have taken any politician at face value; perhaps no myth about community and country is ever fully benign. But cynicism in a democracy is a dangerous thing if it exceeds certain limits. A government that is supposed to be of, by, and for the people cannot function very well for very long if large numbers of people are persuaded, for whatever reason, that the reverse is really true. The experience of the war and the antiwar movement does seem to have deepened that cynicism—but of course, so did Watergate and, to a lesser degree, other scandals in high places since.

Cynicism has another face too. One major consequence of the Vietnam War on the Vietnam generation is that the belief in American exceptionalism was dealt a severe blow. Perhaps also as a result, instilling pride in the basic institutions of government is no longer a major focus of elementary and secondary school education. Those who went to elementary, junior high, and high school before Vietnam were taught a heroic version of American history but they also really learned something; they read the Declaration of Independence, studied the Constitution and the Bill of Rights, and pondered parts of *The Federalist Papers*. After Vietnam, many children were no longer taught civics the same way, if they were taught civics at all. A pervasive guilt about racism and Vietnam led to a widespread reluctance of teachers to convey a positive image of American political institutions, and, in some cases, an overweening reluctance to make judgments at all. The reluctance to make moral judgments or even to discuss such matters in public school classrooms, the guilt some educators feel about saying anything positive about American history, and the zeal with which mea culpa versions of that history are presented in many textbooks and classrooms, leads to a socialization process wherein government comes to represent the "other." The socialization of the Vietnam generation and particularly those immediately after it is probably a major source of such attitudes. Listen again to Lemann:

> I am not someone to whom the idea that our country and its dominant institutions were deeply and fundamentally flawed was a dramatic revelation. It was what I grew up on. . . . Most of my childhood friends are now businessmen and housewives, radical by no stretch of the imagination. What makes us all enormously different from our parents is not the way we live our lives, but the assumptions that lie behind the way we live: not patriotism but cynicism. . . . How could anyone have actually believed in Vietnam? In a president? In the idea that the nation occupied some moral higher ground? Those who did certainly looked silly to us.[19]

Though hard to measure, then, the Vietnam War and the antiwar movement politicized and pushed an entire generation vaguely to the Left. The Vietnam generation was never seized by radical revolutionary thinking, and today, after the dissolution of European Communism, it is certainly not so inclined. Neither what goes on in the academy or the adversary culture has direct impact on what the Vietnam generation thinks and believes today. But neither is the Vietnam generation the same politically as those that came before it. Without thinking of themselves as socialists or Marxists, and certainly without *being* socialists or Marxists, many of its members nevertheless think about politics in implicitly Marxist categories bound together by their vulgar materialism: interest group politics, military-industrial complexes, and the like. Journalist Morton Kondracke wrote disparagingly, but accurately, that "From C. Wright Mills through Oliver Stone, it's been gospel on the far left that the military-industrial complex runs America and that the U.S. economy can't function without huge defense budgets. The claim is hogwash, of course."[20]

Kondracke is right that the claim is hogwash, wrong to think it resides only on the far Left. Marxoid schemes of interpretation have become second nature to much of the Vietnam generation, especially to those who went to elite colleges in the 1960s and 1970s. One can see the attitudinal effects in everything from grass-roots "peace" organizations, feminism, alternative media groups like Pacifica News, identity-ethnic political groups, the gay rights movements, the Rainbow Coalition, and the politicization of the churches.[21]

More serious Leftists take heart from such changes. Richard Flacks, for example, is not bothered by the absence of a mass-based party of the Left in America because he believes that leftism is overcoming its isolation. He takes special interest in the Left's entrenchment in academia, where its influence is felt on the "dominant outlooks of the social sciences and humanities." Flacks argues that, in America, social movements do what left-wing parties did and still do in Europe.[22] By that criterion, Flacks and others would agree, the Left is doing well in society despite the fact that American politics has moved in the other direction.

Nor are most American Leftists worried that the ideology is not often strict and explicit, even in the academy, the one place one might expect rigorous ideological positions to flourish. Ideology is usually more powerful when its possessor is not aware of it; what results is that it is the ideology that possesses the thinker rather than the other way around. Thus Marxian social analyst Stephen Eric Bonner views Madison Avenue's theft of the 1960s countercultural vocabulary to sell everything from cars to Coke as an antithesis undermining capitalism itself:

> It is irrelevant that many of the cultural gains [of the 1960s] were ultimately integrated into the commodity structure of capitalism. The fact that they are now *taken for granted* does not deny their progressive character; expanding the responsibility of young people; freeing sexuality from petty-bourgeois norms; attacking racism in personal life; emphasizing commitment and the political element in artistic expression; seeking new forms of experience and bringing the repressed cultures of minorities and nonwestern peoples into the public eye were valuable contributions.[23]

So, for example, while the themes in the musical *Hair* or the early New Age sentiments in *Joseph and the Technicolor Dreamcoat* did not hit the mainstream until long after they were passé in the movement, this kind of "trickle-down effect" simply works that way. By this measure, the attitudinal changes of the counter-culture are just starting to make a social impact, as this generation's fathers and mothers pass on new values to their children.

Bonner reminds us of an important point here, even if one may disagree about how valuable such contributions as he mentions really have been. It is that

1960s radicalism was not conventionally political in expression, but cultural. It identified a cultural system as a means of social control, not just the workings of the political class, which is why groups like the Yippies were simultaneously political and cultural. Bonner overreaches in claiming that 1960s radicalism was "a cultural avant-garde with a mass following" because he downplays the role of the old Left and exaggerates its following, but the general analysis is accurate enough.[24] The counterculture did generate a cultural critique with far-ranging consequences. The question really is: Were those consequences benign in the main, or not?

Many observers assume that just because these consequences have been so vast the critique must have been justified. Others demur.[25] One critic, Andrew Schmookler, has argued that countercultural critiques, though correct and necessary at the time, have led to excesses by way of the denigration of family values, the abnegation of patriotism, and the error of seeing rights as inhering to groups as opposed to individuals. But, he noted, such excesses have stimulated a conservative social critique with clarity and depth that "progressives," he pleads, should pay attention to.[26] Writing seven months before the November 1994 midterm election, Schmookler's observation comes about as close to political prophecy as we are likely to see.

Besides, the notion of excesses and cycles rings at least partly true, and this is why it makes sense to say that the impact of the counterculture has been mixed. The opposition to technocracy was probably healthy; the assault against family values probably not. But this is largely a matter of taste and temperament, not analysis.

Then there are drugs. Many argue that the drug epidemic in American society is a product of the 1960s counterculture and the atmosphere generated by the antiwar movement. Some of the drugs themselves, at least in the beginning, came from Vietnam with returning servicemen. But cocaine, heroin, and crack are not the same, argue many 1960s folk, as marijuana, hashish, and even LSD, and they are not a result, direct or indirect, of the antiwar movement or the counterculture. As with other aspects of tracing the impact of the antiwar movement and the counterculture, such linear unifactorial extrapolations designed to get us from the 1960s to the 1990s usually end up being fairly ridiculous.

The counterculture's drug habits have calmed down quite a bit if only because few of those who were young in 1968 have had the physical stamina to maintain such a punishing chemical regime into adulthood. But the ideals linger. In fact, some of the more vigorous pro-drug songs were not written in the 1960s, but in the 1970s and beyond. Songwriter Peter Rowen's "Free Mexican Airforce," for example, deftly combined the drug culture with social protest, and many of those who were part of the drug scene a quarter century ago would agree with most of the sentiments expressed in the lyrics, even if they won't always admit it. The line "It is not marijuana destroying the minds of the young," but rather "confusion continued for power and greed in all forms" comes most easily to mind.[27]

The sentiment echoed by 28-year-old Matt Beckley at the Clinton inauguration festivities is clearer still: "Bill Clinton is one of us. He grew up in an age when you knew what a hippie was and what pot smokers were."[28] Beckley, selling "Inhale to the Chief" bumper stickers, was representing the National Organization for the Reform of Marijuana Laws. Did Beckley believe Clinton's assertion that he "didn't inhale"? Did you?

## WAR, PEACE,
## AND FOREIGN POLICY IN PUBLIC OPINION

As suggested earlier, the Vietnam War deepened the almost reflexive American distaste of things military. Together with the end of the draft and the absence of any other form of mandatory national service, a discontinuity between society and the military has arisen in American political culture. Today's military is more conservative, more Republican, more traditionally minded by far than the norm of American society.[29]

The military subculture was deeply affected by the Vietnam War and the antiwar movement in other ways too. One of the main redoubts of the Vietnam syndrome today lies within the officer corps of the U.S. military. U.S. military officers today who came of age during the Vietnam War are overwhelmingly opposed to doing battle on ambiguous operational and military turf. They are deeply suspicious and sometimes plainly hostile to civilian judgment with respect to the use of force, and they are sensitive to the reality that if civilian strategists and politicians lack public support for a military campaign, it is they, soldiers in combat, who will end up paying the price for vacillation and error. This made up the essence of the Weinberger Doctrine mentioned earlier. As one officer summed it up: "Mr. President, don't send us to war again unless you have clear-cut political goals and attainable military objectives. Sir, don't send us unless you give us sufficient forces and the freedom of action to use them according to the principles of war. And, Mr. President, *you'd better have a hell of a lot of public support*."[30]

Such remarks have Vietnam and the presumed power of the antiwar movement written all over them. The nearly reflexive opposition on the part of many to U.S. military intervention abroad is the "lesson" of the Vietnam War most directly applicable to opinion about foreign policy. The Kuwait crisis notwithstanding, it is a certainty that after the Cold War, antimilitary and isolationist themes will vie to dominate the future as the Vietnam generation inherits its share of political and social power. Thinking of themselves in large part as heirs of the anti-interventionist antiwar movement, the Vietnam generation is less inclined to internationalism than any generation since those that followed World War I. And that is not just because the world is confusing, or because we can't afford the money intervention requires, it is because of attitudes rooted in the Vietnam era.

Some impressionistic polling data are suggestive in this regard. A 1988 poll revealed that only 27 percent of young men surveyed could think of any reason that would lead them to enlist in the armed services, and another 22 percent said they would enlist only if America was directly threatened by invasion. Voluntary enlistment is drastic, true, but another statistic from the survey is more revealing: When asked what the United States should do if faced with another situation like Vietnam (not further defined), 55 percent said that we should under all circumstances stay out, and another 15 percent said it would depend on the circumstances. The group most inclined toward intervention, interestingly, consisted of Vietnam veterans and families of veterans, but even there an absolute majority—52 percent—opposed intervention.[31]

Interestingly, such themes are present in both liberal anti-interventionists and conservative isolationists alike, just as in the 1930s. In the aforementioned survey, while Republicans were less inclined against intervention than others, those in young age cohorts were still very disinclined. Asked whether American involvement in Vietnam was right, only 16 percent said yes; the number for Republicans was only 25 percent for such age cohorts.[32]

Also noteworthy is that the antiwar movement, through its successful stigmatization of the South Vietnamese government, also had an important effect on the concept of U.S. alliance relationships. Rather than accept imperfect but strategically significant regimes as lesser evils in a global struggle, the antiwar movement, by casting South Vietnam as a vicious tyranny, exacerbated American difficulties in sustaining relations with other anti-Soviet authoritarian regimes.[33] By the early 1970s the antiwar movement's argument that the government of South Vietnam was a tyranny, complete with murderous police chiefs and tiger cages, had filtered down to the liberal middle of American society and even into the bureaucracy. In its original incarnation, that argument was part willful misrepresentation and part ignorance. At the end, it functioned as a way to make the majority of Americans feel less guilty about dumping the South Vietnamese.

It still does. In the introduction to *The Bad War,* Kim Willenson, hardly a radical or an expert on Vietnam, intoned what has become common knowledge about South Vietnam: "We knew the corruption was endemic not just to the civil government but to the police and the military as well. . . . [M]any [officers] spent their time plotting how to turn a dollar by selling their supplies, or how to get themselves back to safe and lucrative positions in Saigon."[34] Again, this became true thanks to the character of U.S. intervention. It didn't start out that way and didn't have to become that way.

In milder versions too, this "lesson" of Vietnam will just not go away. Writing in opposition to U.S. policy in the aftermath of the April 1992 coup d'état in Peru, one observer noted: "Vietnam taught us—I would hope—that military governments cannot command the popular allegiance needed to defeat a peasant-based revolution."[35] That is not at all what Vietnam should have taught us. Only if Peru's Shining Path movement bordered giant Communist countries that armed it and helped it diplomatically, and if the United States took full administrative and military control of the Peruvian war effort, would this argument even begin to make sense. Indeed, the Salvadoran army, armed and trained by the United States, did very well against a peasant-based revolution, well enough to force a political settlement on at least halfway fair terms.

It is hard to escape the conclusion that the long-standing indeterminacy of U.S. purposes and military strategy and the erosion of its willpower out of ignorance, misperception, and political rapacity in Washington all contributed more to the result of the Vietnam War than any sins of authoritarian commission or democratic omission by the South Vietnamese government. Moreover, failed American policies contributed to the replacement of a weak, modernizing proto-authoritarian government in Saigon with one in Hanoi that still ranks among the world's preeminent tyrannies. When the management of relations with authoritarian allies goes really wrong, as it later did in Iran and Nicaragua, this is precisely what happens. Vietnam was the main model: The real lesson is that just when some people think things cannot get worse in some foreign capital, their own advocacy against that capital can help make them worse.

But this is not the lesson that most Americans have learned from Vietnam. Instead, most believe now, as the Left-Liberal antiwar movement believed then, that the U.S. government should not expect to be able to save a government from attempts to overthrow it if that government tyrannizes its own people. The Vietnamese case does not disprove that assertion, which generally makes sense, but it does not prove it either. Of course the United States should not defend a villainous regime against its own people except under truly extraordinary circumstances, but the American commitment to Vietnam was not to an especially tyrannical regime and its government's failings had little to do with the reality of U.S. failure in Vietnam. That said, "Vietnam" has become part of the currency of the U.S. debate over how to deal with non-democratic states inclined to cooperate with the United States. As a symbol, it stands for things it should not stand for, but it stands nonetheless.

## THE DEMOCRATS AND THE ELUSIVE MAJORITY

Another important consequence of the war and the antiwar movement concerns the health of the Democratic Party, half of the formula that has traditionally given the American two-party system its creative tension.

The antiwar movement aided the disintegration of the Democratic Party and transformed its critical base, the coalition of Franklin Roosevelt and the liberal internationalists that followed him. It did this by influencing presidential politics, internal party dynamics, and the nature of the party's constituency.

As mentioned, the antiwar movement helped elect Richard Nixon twice, once by hurting Hubert Humphrey and once by abetting the nomination of George McGovern. In 1968 it was not only the trashing of the Democratic National Convention and the McCarthy candidacy that hurt the party, it was the antiwar movement's personal dislike of the individuals who were responsible for the war policies. That meant President Johnson above all, but it also tarred Vice President Humphrey.

This was unfortunate because Humphrey was an early doubter and an early, though quiet, in-house dissenter from the Johnson administration's war policies. This led to his virtual exclusion from the president's inner circle by 1967. Besides, an honest observer in 1968 could easily have concluded that, after all that had happened, a Democratic administration was far more likely to effect a rapid de-escalation of the war than a Republican one led by Richard Nixon. Yet many in the antiwar movement strongly denied this, and still others, mainly the intellectual Left, voted for Nixon not because they trusted him, but because their personal animus for the liberal betrayers of Camelot knew no limits. Aside from Norman Mailer's sudden enthusiasm for the new Nixon, even Dick Gregory, himself a presidential candidate in 1968, said: "But if Humphrey becomes President, you got that thug [Mayor Richard Daley] running the White House, and when I think of that, I could almost love Dick Nixon. Anyone can talk about Tricky Dick, but when you saw the Democratic Convention. . . . we all know."[36]

By 1972 the war was still not over, but the Democratic Party that had presided over the war from 1961 on *was* over. The antiwar movement had taken over the party, dismantled its traditional hierarchy, disenfranchised professional politicians, and turned the party apparatus over to young parvenus. Not only did these new managers nominate George McGovern, they also helped focus in the common mind the connection between the antiwar movement and the "new" Democrats. After McGovern was trounced and the vibrations of victory over the old politicians had worn off, the party successfully turned to Jimmy Carter in 1976. Carter's election was largely a fluke, for he ran against Gerald Ford, an unelected president in the aftermath of a major national scandal laid squarely at the feet of the Republican Party. But Carter, as self-styled outsider, never really got hold of the party, and so its internal re-reform was only partial. That is why the 1984 and 1988 elections, which provided chances never taken for the Democrats to recapture the coalition that had made it the majority party in the postwar period, were lost. The Democrats nominated candidates seen to be soft on national defense—Michael Dukakis, in particular—and flamed downward to easy defeat.

Most important, thanks in part to the image of the antiwar movement and in part to what new party activists did upon assuming control, the party's constituency was vitiated. It may sound strange, but the rank and file of the Democratic Party before Vietnam was at least as socially conservative as the Republican Party—maybe more so. Why? Simply because working-class people tend to be more conservative in their morals, not to mention their actual behavior, than business and professional classes. When New Politics antiwar veterans walked in the front door of the Democratic Party, huge numbers of others left by the back door and never returned. And this has nothing to do with race: After the

Southern segregationists in the party were discredited in the 1960s, the way was wide open for a nonracist yet still socially conservative Democratic leadership in the Congress. That this did not occur, despite the strenuous efforts of the minority of conservatives in the party, was partly the fault of the Vietnam War and antiwar movement—to the (so far) everlasting benefit of the Republican Party.

That the Democrats' recovery as a party was only partial before 1992 was borne out by the contradiction between how well it did in the Congress—in 1986 it won control of both houses—and how poorly it did running for the White House. Before the end of the Cold War, the Democrats never recovered a shared and persuasive view of national purpose, foreign policy approach, or national security policy. Most party activists throughout the 1980s and into the 1990s, politically teethed in the antiwar movement, were still well Left of the party rank and file. That is why pro-defense Democrats in the Democratic Leadership Conference— Sam Nunn, Charles Robb, and others—could have won a national election, but not their party's nomination to stand in one.

It took the end of the Cold War to put the Democrats in the White House. With the Cold War over, the image of presidential toughness lost much of its salience, giving centrist Democrats a better chance. Indeed, President Bush's status as a president better suited to deal with foreign affairs than domestic ones, thought initially to improve his chances in 1992, actually played against him. With the Cold War over, the average voter was inclined to think: Now that the main problems to solve are here at home, who needs George Bush?

In short, the end of the Cold War turned on its head the political value of the Democrats' image as isolationists disinclined to project power abroad. Former Carter White House advisor Stuart Eizenstat had said in 1987 that: "A decade after Vietnam, the party is at risk of being perceived as today's neo-isolationist party—a reversal of role from its internationalist attitude, which dates from the days of Woodrow Wilson."[37] He was right, but a political liability in 1987 became an asset in 1992, and Bill Clinton, a rank novice in foreign and security policy, won the election. In this regard, clearly, changes in the world did more to revivify the prospect of a Democratic presidency than anything the party did for itself.

This raises a perplexing question. During the second half of the Cold War, when security and foreign policy questions had very high salience, the United States had a Republican president and a Democratic Congress. Now, when domestic policy questions have very high salience, the United States has a Democratic President and a Republican Congress. Broadly speaking too, the president operates in foreign affairs more freely and authoritatively than the Congress, which only has the power to obstruct, not to act in foreign policy. The Congress, on the other hand, has far more freedom to act and maneuver with respect to domestic policy. It would seem, therefore, that wherever the Democrats win out, the main action is someplace else. Is this just a coincidence, or is vox populi more subtle than most of us suspect?

## CONGRESSIONAL PREROGATIVE,
## POLLSTERISM, AND THE IMPERIAL PRESS

The Vietnam War, and Watergate on top of it, was also the occasion for the invasion of the executive branch's prerogative by the Congress. And the antiwar movement, as it percolated into the Congress after 1968, was a motivating factor.

Of course, executive-legislative tussles over foreign policy are nothing new, and, throughout American history—and not only American history—war has greatly increased the power of the executive branch. The Vietnam War, in particular, vastly increased the power of the National Security Council.[38] The proper balance between the executive and legislative branches in foreign policy has been under dispute at least since Thomas Jefferson bought Louisiana without congressional approval. The effect of Vietnam can fairly be likened to an oscillation that nearly knocked the whole pendulum over.

The War Powers Act was a direct result of the Left-Liberal recapturing of the antiwar movement after 1968, and the success of its passage was a direct result of Richard Nixon's political weakness. Less noted but equally consequential, the Budget Reform Act of 1974 allowed the Congress expanded power over the purse and facilitated the explosive expansion of its own staffs, both having proved themselves to be of dubious value to effective government or the welfare of the American people.[39] For more than a decade, the United States appeared incapable of pursuing any protracted policy around the world that involved the use of force beyond our shores, or the threat thereof, in part because the Congress would not allow it.

Having hamstrung the conduct of American foreign policy did not bother those who believed that the United States did too much—of the wrong things, anyway—overseas in the first place. But it did bother others. Some members of the Reagan administration were tempted beyond prudence to build workarounds to congressional constraint, epitomized by the series of Boland amendments limiting U.S. activities in and around Nicaragua. One such workaround gave us the Iran-Contra scandal. It would be too much to blame the antiwar movement and its legacy for the limited self-destructive tendencies of the Reagan administration, but it is not to much to say that the structural paralysis the administration inherited was a factor.

Since 1989 matters have leveled out considerably. President Bush took the United States to war twice in three years, in Panama and in the Persian Gulf, and while War Powers–related constitutional issues were raised, the War Powers Act was not invoked, American policy was not hamstrung, and foreign dictators and tyrants could not take comfort that American law would serve their interests as opposed to those of the United States. But history does not end and the War Powers Act is still on the books. The fact that Clinton administration principals have considered effectively scrapping important sections of it is testimony to the War Powers Act's origins and to its dubious legality and practicality.

The antiwar movement's presumed successes also encouraged the reification of "public opinion" as a force in American political life, and probably raised the significance of political consultants and pollsters in government. The antiwar movement, to be sure, was not the only factor here, but it was probably a seminal one. After all, it was over Vietnam that dissent on foreign policy first came to really matter politically in the postwar period, and in the wake of defeat it was widely believed that the United States was beaten in Vietnam by antiwar activism of various hues. Most people believed and still believe that America left the field of battle in Southeast Asia because of the moral opprobrium of an aroused population.[40] More important, it was clear to politicians on the earthiest of levels that, in essence, the people "fired the boss" twice—first Lyndon Johnson, then Richard Nixon—in a display of uncharacteristic arousal. This is a lesson no president since 1975 has ignored, but it is arguably a lesson that has had a pernicious effect on presidential leadership. Presidents ought to be concerned with doing what is right, not with their approval ratings; they should be concerned with the mastery of power for proper purposes, not with spinning images and creating photo opportunities.

It is odd how the reluctance to lead, which sometimes means being frank with the American people, can circle the block. The Reagan administration in the period between 1986 and 1988 was unwilling to admit that there were high stakes and risks worth running to secure the Persian Gulf from locally generated chaos and possible Soviet designs. Fears of public opposition too, helped lead the administration to below-the-table stealth—sending arms to Iran, facilitating the diversion of weapons from Saudi Arabia to Iraq, and providing satellite intelligence to Saddam Hussein's murderous regime. This, in turn, played a role in convincing Saddam Hussein that America lacked backbone. Many times he invoked American defeat in Vietnam as a reason for believing that the United States would not fight to evict Iraqi forces from Kuwait. In a roundabout way, then, presidential fear of public opinion contributed to a weakness in U.S. public diplomacy that, in this case, encouraged aggression and got the United States into a war.

Then there is the so-called imperial press. It is standard conservative rhetoric that the U.S. press opposed U.S. government policies in Vietnam.[41] This is just not so. While there were exceptions, the doubts and anxieties expressed by the press were not different in kind or degree from the common fare at home. Nor did field reporting from Southeast Asia lead to special doubts and anxieties among the attentive population or within the Johnson administration that were not already present. The data do show that unfavorable commentary about South Vietnam and its attempts at democracy, particularly after the Tet offensive, was strong, but it does not reveal special oppositional attitudes toward either the Johnson or the Nixon administrations before 1973, when Watergate clouds the picture.[42]

In other words, press views followed public and government views to a considerable extent; before Tet, the press—especially correspondents in Southeast Asia—were in general supportive of policy. The exceptions—David Halberstam, Jonathan Schell, Neil Sheehan, Seymour Hersh, Michael Herr, Peter Arnett—were just that, exceptions. And of these, Halberstam and Sheehan, at least, started out being sympathetic to the war effort. To blame these people for reporting what they saw is a little like the old custom of shooting the messenger when you do not like the news he brings. As Colonel Harry Summers put it in praise of William M. Hammond's *The Military and the Media:*[43] "After supporting the American troop commitment for more than two years, by late 1967 public sentiment was either win the damn war or get the hell out. And when the government seemed to be unable to do either, public support went down the tubes. To blame the media for this switch displays a fundamental ignorance of what America is all about."[44] Clark Clifford's observations are similar. Most of the reporting from the war zone, he wrote, "reflected the official position. Contrary to right-wing revisionism, reporters and the anti-war movement did not defeat America in Vietnam. Our policy failed because it was based on false premises and false promises."[45]

All true. But there is another point to be made about the media and Vietnam. The mass media developed a morbid fascination with the very worst of what the antiwar movement had to offer.[46] Obviously, the national media did not create the movement or the counterculture but it exaggerated both. One reason was that both were very picturesque. Another was that the national media dwells in the Northeast, as did most of the movement, and was especially attentive to the intellectual environment from which it arose.[47]

Thus everyone knew that "students were rebellious" in the 1960s because the popular press never ceased telling us. Antiwar protests were so much exaggerated as special movements of the young that many high school and college students persuaded themselves that they therefore should take part, not because they opposed the war, but simply because they were young.[48] But many of those who went to college in the large state universities of the Midwest, for example, rather than in the schools of the elite, have had to rearrange their memories retrospectively in order not to be left out of the market for nostalgic recollections of righteous heresy. In fact, most college campuses were fairly quiet most of the time (May 1970 being the major exception)—whatever people thought privately—and even on elite campuses true radical activists never amounted to more than a few percent of the graduate and undergraduate populations.[49] In short, the so-called generation gap was not very big, not nearly so big as the media portrayed it.[50] It could be also that the media's fishbowl characterizations of the movement encouraged other Americans to exaggerate its importance. If so, this only strengthened its role as a negative follower group.

## POLITICAL CORRECTNESS
## AND THE COUNTERCULTURE

One of the most important residual effects of 1960s radicalism is felt today in faculty appointments in American universities. While the country as a whole has become more conservative, college faculties may well have moved farther Left—although there doesn't seem to be any easy empirical means to determine just exactly how far. Oddly enough, the end of the Soviet Union may have accelerated movement to the Left, as if the Soviet Union had to die in order for "real" socialism to be born.

Intellectuals, of course, are critics by nature, even by definition. Every society living beyond bare subsistence needs them. But in the last two decades, a gap has arisen between faculty views and those of the ordinary Americans largely because of the entrance and advancement of the Vietnam generation in the academy. The academy's self-marginalization, in turn, makes it harder for it to perform its role as social critic and isolates campus life too much from the life of the country.

Not only that, but since the antiwar movement, Marxist and Marxoid thinking has embedded itself in particular disciplines, which, when turned and tossed sufficiently, produce highly questionable approaches and conclusions. Examples of Marxoid thinking are ubiquitous nowadays and hold a respectable, if sometimes exaggerated, place in the academy. Black studies, woman's studies, deconstructionist fads in history and literature departments, the lit-crit approach to teaching law, the urge to "multiculturalism" and the banishment of "Dead White Males" from undergraduate curricula—all of this is led by academics who came of intellectual age during the Vietnam War and who were affected by the environment of the antiwar movement and the counterculture. University administrators who have taken to defining racism and rape in absurdly broad ways, and who urge mandatory "sensitivity training" for incoming freshmen, are part of the same phenomenon.

Broadly defined, this is what has become known as political correctness—PC. There is no doubt that the Vietnam War and the antiwar movement was *the* seedbed for PC.[51] Academics do most of the spade work in this garden today. While many have exaggerated the broad influence of political correctness, it has served to insulate certain dubious forms of scholarship from criticism because they have the right politics.

Some Marxoid academics, for example—many of Vietnam generation age—have applied special admixtures of their own interests to the basic Marxoid formula and have ended up producing hybrids of all sorts.[52] The process of creating such hybrids is reminiscent of nothing so much as the ideological stream-of-consciousness methodology of the New Left and the counterculture. As Tzvetan Todorov put it, purveyors of political correctness seriously believe "that there is no difference between fact and interpretation, between reason and belief, between justice and self-interest. . . ."[53] Indeed, the skepticism with which the Vietnam generation was educated, the smashing of the gods' clay feet it experienced, has led 30 years later to a cynicism so deep that it not only denies the existence of objective truths, but even denies the existence of objectivity altogether. Deconstructionist, or postmodernist, thinking is a form of intellectual nihilism; it is even worse than cynicism.[54]

It should not be surprising that the Vietnam era was the origin of the deconstructionist surge. Was it not, after all, the hallmark of 1960s thinking to efface distinctions instead of sharpen them, to degrade the specificity of language, to destroy formalisms, even ones that make sense, and to emphasize feeling over thinking? The tone of political correctness fits the description to a tee. Paul Berman put it this way: "Race/class/gender-ism is, in short, a bit of the old ultra-radicalism. It is '68 Philosophy, American-style, with certain virtues of the French original, too—the impiety carried to eye-opening extremes, sometimes the wit, though the American version tends to be more earnest and less clever than the French."[55]

Another important carryover from the antiwar movement to modern PC multiculturalism is its visceral anti-Americanism. Richard Rorty said it well:

> The mythic America is a great country, and the insecure and divided one is a pretty good one. As racist, sexist, and homophobic as the United States is, it is also a two-hundred-year-old functioning democracy—one that has overcome divisions and mitigated inequalities in the past and may still have the capacity to do so. But by proclaiming the myth a fraud, multiculturalism cuts the ground out from under its own feet, quickly devolving into anti-Americanism, into the idea that 'the dominant culture' of America, that of the WASPs, is so inherently oppressive that it would be better for its victims to turn their backs on the country than to claim a share in its history and future.[56]

The one important way that political correctness departs dramatically from the spirit of the 1960s is in the tone, which, somehow, has gotten reversed. Purveyors of PC are really quite humorless. Since jokes are usually at the expense of something or someone, and since the perfect equality of all people—and animals, and even things?—is sacred, most jokes have to be expressions of disrespect, and by definition disrespect cannot be funny. "The humorless ethos of the politically correct humanities departments could not be more antithetical to the spirit of the 1960s," wrote Menard. "Even the most callow radicalism of that era had nothing to do with the sort of doctrinaire political attitudes critics of the contemporary academy complain about."[57] Indeed, in this regard they are far more like *old* Leftists than New. Even Todd Gitlin sees it: "A bitter intolerance emanates from much of the academic left."[58]

PC thus combines the worst of both Leftist worlds. From the old Left it takes a falsely heroic and witless seriousness, and from the New Left it takes an irrational emotionalism and a veritable abhorrence for common sense. It has also taken something from the counterculture: irrationality and no small dollop of mysticism.

Just as 1960s radicalism ended up being counterproductive to its own stated objectives—ending the war, democratizing America, and all the rest—so PC's supposed devotion to liberal humanism is spited by a conspiratorial approach to the traditions of the academy and by its obsession with "multiculturalism," which, looked at closely, resembles in its theoretical assumptions centuries-old racial theories about the ideational implications of biological essences that used to find expression only on the far Right.[59]

Even more telling in this regard is the academic Left's abandonment of the central idea of traditional Leftist thinking: the notion of a universal spirit and the interest of mankind. Identity politics from the early 1970s seems to have overwhelmed anything universal. Again we have the worst of two worlds: the petty eccentricities of academic life and the parochial motivations of identity politics. In a remark bordering on contrition, Gitlin noted the curious reversal of traditional Left and Right attitudes:

> In the nineteenth century, the right was the property of aristocracies who stood unabashedly for the privileges of the few. Today, the aspiring aristocrats of the academic right tend to speak the language of universals—canon, merit, reason, individual rights, transpolitical virtue. For its part seized by the logic of identity politics, committed to pleasing disparate constituencies, the academic left has lost interest in the commonalities that undergird its obsession with difference.[60]

What Gitlin—a man who still thinks, as quoted in Chapter 1, that "America's political and cultural space would probably not have opened up as much as it did without the movement's divine delirium"—does *not* say is that the antiwar movement experience contributed much to the birth of notions of multiculturalism that exalt the parochial in our society, that deepen the attraction of identity politics, and that undermine the sense of community without which America ceases to exist as an idea and becomes merely a place.

## THE ADVERSARY CULTURE REVISITED

The Vietnam War is long over but the adversary culture that formed the core of the antiwar movement is with us still. On occasion, its critical voice may help keep us honest. On other occasions, it misleads gullible cynics and impressionable idealists with eccentric analysis and artful posturing. Furthermore, because emotional allure remains its main currency, it feeds the emotionalism that can disfigure policy debates from South African sanctions to dealing with Haiti, Iraq's Saddam Hussein, or the war in Bosnia. One consequence of the antiwar movement is that by radicalizing formerly liberal organizations, the web of synapses through which the agenda and the vocabulary of the adversary culture reaches the muscle and sinew of the American body politic has been widened and quickened. That this exists amid a seemingly conservative shift either means that much of the ideological middle has dropped out of American politics and there is more polarization than ever, or that many analysts are confusing anger and disorientation over rapid change with conservative views. Perhaps it means both.

Whatever may be the case with respect to domestic issues, there is no doubt that influential political lobbying by radical groups and their now often church-based liberal sympathizers has become a permanent feature of the U.S. foreign policy landscape. The antiwar movement was without question the midwife of this development, which began even before the war was lost.

When Saigon fell, the radical core of the antiwar movement was jubilant, for a Communist victory was what it had hoped for all along. It remained jubilant for a surprisingly long time; even in the mid-1980s a CISPES slogan read: "Vietnam has won; El Salvador will win." When a minority of former activists—mainly pacifists—tried to call attention to North Vietnam's perfidy toward the National Liberation Front and cruelty toward its own people, they were shouted down.[61] The successors of the radical antiwar movement that make up the adversary culture today are not reluctant to claim that Vietnam "won" and they are not ashamed to claim part of the credit. For most nonradical movement veterans, the fall of Saigon was a curious denouement begetting a lapse of attention and little more.

The adversary culture's enthusiasm for Vietnamese Communism did not focus much attention for long. Instead, the radical inclination veered off in new directions. As noted, some developed enthusiasms for Latin American Marxist revolutions, having learned nothing from the failure of the Vietnamese form. Others devoted themselves to a politicized form of human rights advocacy. Others balkanized. But withal, the antiwar movement led to the temporary restocking of the old Left, on campus and off.

But before leaping to the present, a coming to terms with the past seems in order. Twenty-five years is long enough for us to try to know the shape and significance of the adversary culture as a result of the antiwar movement. What can we say about the colliding interests, agendas, and personalities within the movement, and what can we learn from them for our own time and for the future? Did radical sectarian agendas advance because of the antiwar movement? Were liberals and other politically ill-defined protesters and petition-signers manipulated as so many "useful idiots" to promote communism in Southeast Asia and deliberate social chaos in the United States toward the same ultimate end?

There is no question that "useful idiots" were sought out, and that sectarian Leftists achieved some discrete victories. They eventually captured SDS in 1968-69, for example, for all the good it did them. In a general sense, too, the political environment shifted to the Left during the 1960s and 1970s, and, more important, it is not so easy to distinguish between "the agitation of the intellectual Left," as Mueller dubbed it and dismissed it, and a mass movement.[62] By itself, the Left was neither a mass movement nor a controlling directorate behind one, at least not in any simple or direct way. Still, after reviewing the role of the Fifth Avenue Parade Committee and Sidney Peck's organizing labors, and noting that these small ad hoc hard Left committees called most of the rallies, staged most of the demonstrations, designed most of the civil disobedience, and even ordered some of the violence, it is difficult to argue that the Left was *that* peripheral.

In the end, however, no one used anyone effectively for long.[63] To the extent that people were used, they lent themselves to it, usually not blindly but within the context of ideological and organizational competitions more or less understood by all the principals. There were three basic reasons why revolutionary vanguard organizations did not manage to guide the antiwar movement, directed ostensibly at Southeast Asia, into a revolutionary one directed inward. First, the movement was too large and diverse for any group to control or shape. Second, even the radical elements within the movement were divided and the New Left, to the extent that it had influence, opposed precisely the subterfugic tactics that would have facilitated widely successful popular front strategies. In a sense, then, given the depth and breadth of genuine opposition to the war, the government was lucky that the New Left was so prominent in the antiwar movement at least between 1967 and 1969. Third, even the non–New Left radical core of the antiwar movement was divided. This division was exacerbated, in particular, by the SWP within the movement as a whole, by PL within SDS, and by YSA within the movement's youth section.

Taken together, these divisions, and the size and seamlessness of the movement, were so daunting that not even the passivity of the Johnson administration or the bombast of the Nixon administration could drive it together for long. Not only was the radical movement divided, but its basic ideological pitch never sunk in very far, except in a small minority who went on to rob banks, set off bombs, and "be underground." It probably did not penetrate as deeply as radical ideas penetrated many strata of American society in the 1930s. The speed with which apparently radical youthful convictions dissipated with the end of the draft was a wonder to behold.

But if the range of acceptance of the radical, revolutionary critique of American society was really that modest between, say, 1964 and 1974,[64] then how does one explain the apparent power of this social critique at the time? Aside from the role played by the mass media, noted earlier, part of the answer may have something to do with the self-doubts of the liberal American political class of that time. Many government leaders—including some of the Wise Men—privately accepted the criticisms of their most pernicious adversaries, or were emotionally influenced by their passion if not their content. Most likely, their generally liberal sensitivities connected them more firmly to the protestors' fierce emotions than to the "silent majority" that supported staying the course or escalating the war as a means of disengagement. This was true of some prominent individuals within the Nixon administration, too. And all this is notwithstanding the fact that the overwhelming majority of Americans have no trouble with and experience no alienation toward fundamental American social values, which helps explain the vanquishing of "centrist" Republicans, the losing record of "soft" Democratic presidential candidates, and the lengthy popularity and political strength of Ronald Reagan.

Nevertheless, the impact of the antiwar movement even on the non-elite segment of the American political milieu was not inconsequential. The adversary culture aside, the movement embraced more diverse segments of American society than any previous anti-establishmentarian movement had. Also, the adversary culture and its arguments were at the core of the movement, and, as a result, liberal participants got a heavy dose of radical medicine in heady times. Generations of Americans just now making their mark on American society, who were never part of the adversary culture itself, live in a changed cultural milieu. The countercultural ethos is communicated widely in popular music, film, and television. Through such media many traditional American values have been disparaged; Dan Quayle might have been unwise in 1992 to take on Murphy Brown—a.k.a. Candice Bergen—but the general point was not far-fetched. So whereas the impact and effectiveness of the radical impulses of the antiwar movement were limited *at the time,* what has become of them as they have incubated over the years is another matter. The number of people who will listen sympathetically to radical critiques of American society and take them seriously is far larger today than it was in 1963. As one observer put it:

> The popular view would have us believe that 60's radicals have accommodated, perhaps even embraced the 80's life style. For those who climbed aboard the 60's wave late or whose commitment to it was not particularly strong, there may be some truth to this view. However, when applied to [Freedom Summer] volunteers, the popular account is demonstrably false. . . . The New Left lives on in contemporary America in the lives and involvements of people like the Freedom Summer veterans. They are the keepers of the Leftist flame, nurturing the ideological and organizational remnants of what was once a proud and thriving movement.[65]

How many people does this involve? Recall the datum that by early 1968, more than a million U.S. university students hoped for a mass-based revolutionary party. The number of radical Leftists in America today does not approach the levels of the late 1930s, to be sure, but it may be double the level of the late 1950s—although no one really knows. The inner core of the student radicals of the 1960s have indeed become the professional radicals of the 1990s. The numbers were small relative to the masses of people involved in the antiwar movement, but they are large relative to the cadres of radicals left over from the 1950s. Interestingly, many—like Richard Flacks— are of the New Left minority who came not from middle-class "bourgeois" families but from old Left "revolutionary" families. New Leftism was for some a phase between old Left origins and "new" old Left destinations.

Additionally, social gospelers are with us still; now they are called liberation theologians. In some ways, the situation of the adversary culture today resembles the situation in the 1920s, when pacifists seized the center of gravity from Marxists and Left-Liberals alike. Pacifist groups today are liable to be more radical on practically every issue than non-pacifist adversary culture groups.[66] Perhaps this points to a general rule, that varieties of pacifism and anarchism carry the smoldering torch of the adversary culture in quieter times, only to be eclipsed in headier hours by whichever vanguard party of the Left can manage to seize the moment. This seems to be the view of some of the members of the Left as well. Michael Ferber, one of the original Boston 5, wrote in *The Nation* in 1987 that: "The religious Left is the only Left we've got."[67]

Just as important, the adversary culture's constituent liberal organizations have moved sharply away from the mainstream liberalism of the 1950s and 1960s. That sort of liberalism today is probably found in the *Republican* Party in its Eastern and Northeastern redoubts. Before Vietnam, it was fair to describe SANE, WILFE, the AFSC, and other antiwar activist organizations as liberal either in ideology or in tactical tone. Not today. The antiwar movement was a form of accelerated experience for the cadres of these groups, the general effect of which was to move them farther toward radical postures. SANE is a good example.

In the late 1960s, SANE was still led by moderates such as Donald Keys, Norman Cousins, and Norman Thomas. But Keys and others resigned as the flow of power toward the Left became irresistible, and, in 1972, David Cortright became SANE's executive director. Cortright is no liberal. In his *Soldiers in Revolt,* he acknowledged his debt to Marcus Raskin of the Institute for Policy Studies in his foreword; Raskin, in turn, wrote the book's introduction where he praised Cortright for teaching us that "the struggle was not only against the war, but against an authoritarian military machine oiled for world imperialism."[68] Seymour Melman, another SANE board member, was, in the early stages of the Vietnam War, a typical Left-Liberal, a respectable academic at an Ivy League university. But by 1970, in *Pentagon Capitalism: The Political Economy of War,* Melman wrote: "The Government of the United States now includes a self-expanding war machine that uses military power for diverse political operations . . . . To the older pattern of exploitative imperialism abroad, there is now an institutional network that is parasitic at home. This is the new imperialism."[69] These are not liberal statements.

Finally in this regard, before Vietnam, SANE opposed non-exclusionary tactics. It no longer does. It digested the nuclear-freeze movement, a prime opening to the Right, and generally seeks coalitions with groups to the Left as well. SANE's leadership today does not remember the Communist tactics of the 1930s; they remember Vietnam and they think of the antiwar movement as having been a victory over the demonic forces of American capitalism and imperialism.

Taken together, what are these changes liable to lead to? It's hard to say. On the one hand, academic radicalism and adversary culture activism could together seize on some future national crisis and challenge the "system" once again. They could make the nuclear-freeze movement of the early 1980s look like afternoon tea. On the other hand, the relative demographic decline of youth and the country's sharp turn toward conservative views may point in a different direction. No one can say what the intersection of these trends will bring except to point out, again, that it suggests a polarization of American politics. Both radicals and conservatives in the 1960s opposed liberals, as that term was understood before Vietnam. By November 1994 it seemed clear that the liberalism of that era has been devastated—it almost no longer exists at all. It is also clear that given the right circumstances—of which political polarization is one—a little radicalism can go a long way.

That this is so is not necessarily a bad thing. Whatever the excesses and failures of its radical side, the antiwar movement as a whole shows that there are limits as to what the executive branch can do in the face of public opposition. In America, when the emperor has no clothes, we get rid of him. In the 1980s, days of congressional intrusion into the prerogatives of the executive branch, this seemed a shallow or even irrelevant observation. But the way the Bush administration spoke about its own privileges and the Congress's lack of them when it came to the Kuwait War reminded us that the future is stretched long before us.

There may be another positive consequence of the antiwar movement, but it is up to us to bring it about. The eruption of popular revulsion against the war—misguided or not—and the essentially integrative response of the political system to protest, no matter how slow and painful, illustrated the essential health of American democracy. Radicals failed to reveal the sinister, oppressive, unresponsive face of capitalist "Amerika" because there was no such face.

At the time, it seemed to many that America was coming apart. Perhaps it was, but if so, it was not the first time and it probably will not be the last. Below the then-apparent wildness and trouble was an underlying rhythm of balance and control. The greatest strength of a political system is not that it is forever quiet but forever adaptable. Some on the Left believe that American adaptability is demonic, which is a true measure of their alienation. Thus academics John Carlos Rowe and Rick Berg state: "American ideology is itself an extraordinarily canny artist, capable of accommodating the most vigorous criticism and for that very reason powerfully resistant to significant social and political changes."[70] What they see as demonic should instead inspire self-confidence, that while we make mistakes, we also have a system that can correct them. De Tocqueville's remark on this count still rings true: "The great privilege enjoyed by the Americans is not only to be more enlightened than other nations but also to have the chance to make mistakes that can be retrieved."[71]

The learning of that simple lesson could be the most positive consequence of the antiwar movement. People should speak their minds even if in retrospect what they say looks foolish. As for the political culture as a whole, such pulses of emotionalism, even if hurtful in the short term, are a small price to pay for our liberty.

There is a final, related pedagogical point to be made about the adversary culture and its role. Failure to see adversary culture activity sociologically can lead to a simplistic understanding of contemporary protest movements. Some on the Left have indulged the myth of romantic populism even as they have pursued vanguard tactics: CISPES was a good example from the 1980s. But some on the Right have too quickly seen manipulation and deceit where popular concern and grass-roots organization has been real: The nuclear-freeze movement was an example of that. It takes both organizers and a legitimate raison d'être to produce anything like the antiwar or the nuclear-freeze movement. Serious analysis must get beyond images of democratic romanticism and conspiracy theories; the real questions have to do with political socialization and organization. In this light, the antiwar movement was an important event in the evolution of American political life. To study such a thing we don't need dueling demonologies, but dispassion and data.

## ECO-ANARCHISM AND THE COUNTERCULTURE

Of all the new frontiers discovered or invented by the adversarial subculture in the late 1960s none was more potentially significant than Earth Day and the development of a new version of an old type of American radicalism—anarchism. Even Lasky agrees that here, at least, was an idea: "The so-called 'friends of the earth,' with their tender-minded concern for the eco-environmentalist ('green') problems turned up with the only 'idea of '68' that proved to be lasting and constructive."[72]

The New Left radicalism of the late 1960s may turn out to be much less significant than the eco-anarchist radicalism that the New Left in its countercultural phase helped to propel into being. The latter is becoming the center of the adversary culture in the United States and in Europe. Anarchist radicalism also fits much better with the American character and historical experience than Marxist radicalism ever did.[73] Evidence for this is all around us, from the popularity of tax revolts to the resurgence of libertarian ideology and the fascination with "mountain men," hermits, hobos, and eccentric loners of every description.

Eco-anarchism owes much to the continuing evolution of the new pacifism, as well. The new pacifism of the 1930s entered the anti-Vietnam war movement still looking like the blue-blooded church-related movements of its origin. But a sizable part of it, propelled ahead by the energy crisis, exited the antiwar movement looking like the small-is-beautiful, appropriate technology, antinuclear power, Greenpeace–Rainbow Warrior movement we recognize so well today.[74] Many areas of social criticism developed by the new pacifism and adopted by the New Left—the malevolence of advanced technology, the socially corrosive effects of "economies of scale," the inherently "violent" nature of capitalist economic organization, the spiritual vacuity of materialism, the immorality of the consume-and-throw-away economy—became the banner concepts of ecological anarchism.[75] Ralph White-head, a Democratic Party consultant, was correct to assert that "the 'civil religion' of the baby boom generation is at least light green."[76] And it is getting greener every day with fears of ozone depletion, greenhouse effects, rain forest spoilation, and species/genetic depletion.

Some ecology enthusiasts have aligned with the full range of existing anti-establishment notions and institutions. Some of these include extreme expressions of contemporary narcissism: transcendental meditation, EST, and the rest of the avant-garde therapeuticalism of the 1960s and 1970s.[77] This is escapist antipolitics, much like the escapism of the New Left revolutionary vision, only it is an escapism privatized, turned inward rather than outward.

But other eco-anarchists have generated serious radical critiques of advanced industrial society—capitalist and noncapitalist—some with alluring populist overtones.[78] Just as their influence ought not to be exaggerated, it would be a mistake to dismiss them. Such ideas may become more popular not least because a few of them actually make some sense. They also cross the ideological curve between what is conventionally seen as far Left and extreme conservatism. The eco-anarchists have inherited and are reshaping the remains of the counterculture—the part left over from Madison Avenue's "pucker power" and "join the Dodge rebellion" rape of the counterculture's vocabulary. They are turning it from romantic slogans and personal protest into small but real institutions. All the hippie communes are bust, but the anarchist Committees of Correspondence and alternative economy cooperatives are not.

Moreover, the anger that many American voters feel lately, as illustrated by the 1992 presidential election and the 1994 midterm election as well, shares many points of contact with an eco-anarchist critique. The points of connection back to counterculture themes of the 1960s are many and unmistakable. When Americans hear eco-anarchist themes, to the extent they do, many, if they are of the right generation, have already heard these ideas before during the days of the antiwar movement and the counterculture.

The eco-anarchist critique keys on the role of modernity run amok in the form of social gigantism: too much bureaucracy, conformity, advertising, noise, pollution, drugs licit and illicit—and all of it too fast. We do not need to build and buy more widgets, but to learn how to appreciate and nurture what we already have. Eco-anarchism relatedly displays an almost mystical love of the land, of small-scale farming, of linking oneself to the cycles of nature. The fundamental problems of modern society include the evisceration of individual and family autonomy at the hands of mammoth concentrations of power and money, both driven by the inner logic—the technologic—of modern production and communications technologies. The source of social malaise and the resulting economic inefficiencies stems from violating the minimum requisites of human scale and from flooding daily life with artificial images of self and society—shades of Marcuse's *One-Dimensional Man*.

Eco-anarchists see a social revolution in America's future. It will be, they suggest, a popular revolt against the bureaucratization of life, the routinization of work, the undermining of family, the banalization of the political, the institution-alization of unearned privilege, the suppression of genuine choice—in short, against the suffocation of the spirit. Most argue that our lives are diminished in quality because our senses are bombarded by a relentless, numbing, and ultimately befuddling sameness. Advertising, commercialism, materialism, and television are the Molochs of our Technopolis. Clearly, the intellectual roots of such a view can be traced to the pre-counterculture 1960s and even the 1950s: to Marshall McLuhan, Paul Goodman, Theodore Roszak, and the beatniks.[79] Anyone who doesn't recognize this sort of language from the 1960s just wasn't there.

Eco-anarchists also believe that just as American democracy needed a push from outside establishment circles to bring it back to basics before—by Jacksonians in the 1820s, abolitionists in the 1850s, progressives and populists in the 1890s, labor agitators in the 1920s, and counterculturalists in the 1960s—so it needs a push today to return the country to its values. The push has to come from below, they say, and it has to be popular and spontaneous to really make a revolution. It is, in short, a recycling of participatory democracy. Indeed, as argued earlier, the New Left featured much that resembled native American anarchist inclinations; of the residue of the 1960s, this is the element that is the most prominent. The focus on the individual remains; this is why eco-anarchists believe that every individual should fight techno-gigantism, and that it will only be defeated by individuals who together build parallel institutions from the ground up that suit human needs.

In short, today's eco-anarchism is green counterculturalism 25 years later. This is the adversary culture's radical thesis today after the collapse of the sectarian Left.[80] If history is any guide, it will mingle with mainstream views—as it already has—and when the next major political crisis strikes the United States, it could well explode into prominence—it could even launch a successful third party bid for national office if the two main parties cannot find a way to co-opt it first. To think this cannot happen is to misread a central dynamic of American social history.

Also important, eco-anarchism is a proto-religious movement with a heavy adumbration of antimaterialism. Like its precursors, it too is a search for the sacred.

## THE POLITICS OF MEMORY:
## BEYOND FAITH AND REASON

The telltale heart beats loudest within the breasts of those who were there at the creation of the antiwar movement and who lived through its intense, unstuck times. This is the font of the politics of memory, elusive and unfathomable, yet indelible and ineradicable. The movement's consequences for the Vietnam generation, and through it for America itself, have been felt already for a decade or more. They can never be wholly undone. As Lemann and so many others have come to realize:

> Everything is pretty much the same on the surface. Underneath, everything is different. We have no center. Our parents did. . . . People like me assumed the [American] enterprise was not noble, rebelled against it for a time, and then joined it, not out of the sincere belief of our parents, but because there was no other choice. That's why today, although we're better educated than they were, we vote less. It's why . . . we feel no loyalty to our employers. It's why marriage and children scare us. . . . When that is the way you are, how do you conduct your life?[81]

It's a tough question.

Whether the revolt of the 1960s, excesses and all, helped move America back to its original spiritual career remains to be seen. Even most 1960s apologists seem unaware of what it is that the youth revolt of the 1960s was trying to teach us. It needs to teach us this: The centrality of value, as communicated and sacralized within the most deeply rooted of family processes, is the core of any healthy society. Without it, we are lost. It comes down to knowing the difference between right and wrong and being able to teach this to our children with sincerity and confidence.

The fact that this issue was raised by the tumult of the 1960s, even if inchoately, is what redeems the entire epoch if nothing else does. This key point, too, has a way of suggesting whether and if the ideas of the 1960s are still meaningful. It is a simple thing really: If the problems that evoked the 1960s have been solved, then the ideas lose force and interest. "Ideas perish from inanition far more frequently than as a result of being refuted by argument," said Isaiah Berlin, because the problems they were designed to confront are no longer pressing. "Philosophy comes from the collision of ideas which create problems. Life changes, so do the ideas, so do the collisions."[82]

But the cultural critique made in the 1960s has not gone away; the strong attraction to the 1960s is *not* mere nostalgia. The French have a phrase that may explain this attraction: *jolie laide*. This literally translates as "good-looking ugly woman." What it means is a woman who is somehow attractive despite not being conventionally pretty. This phrase well describes the 1960s. The reason so many remain fascinated with these difficult and even embarrassing times is that the deeper issues that gave rise to the revolt are with us still. We have not solved the riddle of how to live meaningful and happy lives beyond the ages of both faith and reason. Until we do, the 1960s and other molten times like them will tantalize us with visions of a better world, even amid the miseries of generational warfare and the inevitable anxieties of social change.

# Epilogue: McNamara's Lament

As we have taken pains to show, now some 25 years after the fact, a mild (at least) schizophrenia can still be seen in American images of the Vietnam War and the antiwar movement. Old battles have been re-fought hundreds of times in films and documentaries, in classrooms and barrooms, on op-ed pages and in letters to the editor, at dining room tables and over superheated telephone lines.

Over time the neurosis often seems to subside, less from resolution than from inanition. But it always seems to return in one way or another, whether elicited by arcane events such as Charles Manson's umpteenth parole hearing, or by more substantive issues such as the debate over whether and on what terms to normalize relations with Vietnam. It was often said by critics of American intervention in Vietnam that it was a civil war. This wasn't really true for the Vietnamese, but in an intellectual sense at least, a civil war is exactly what Vietnam became, and remains, for Americans.

The most recent event to elicit this American schizophrenia over the Vietnam War and the antiwar movement was the publication of Robert S. McNamara's *In Retrospect,* a 30-year-belated memoir of a bad time. Aside from the various comments about McNamara's motives for writing such a book, the book itself, the critics agree, doesn't tell us much that other scholarship hasn't already, and told us better. The relative poverty of the book, however, is itself quite revealing because it says something about the poverty of the man.

Robert S. McNamara has an unusual—perhaps unique—talent for error in that he has not only been ineluctably wrong in all the major policy judgments he has made in his life, but he has subsequently been wrong about how and why he was wrong. Centrally this involves Vietnam, but not only Vietnam: Consider nuclear weapons and prospects for nuclear war, for example.

Having come into the White House riding the myth of a missile gap between the Soviet Union and the United States in the 1960 election, McNamara, as President Kennedy's secretary of defense, subsequently presided over the largest sustained buildup of U.S. strategic forces in history—although he, too, knew the missile gap was a myth. With the help of RAND Corporation analysts, McNamara soon devised a theory of offense-oriented strategic stability based on notions of essential quality and numerical parity. But since the United States had built ICBMs so fast and so furiously between 1961 and 1963, it would take the Soviet Union several years to reach essential parity, and when they did, it was at levels vastly higher than if the United States had been more restrained in its own building programs.

Having created overkill, McNamara subsequently became a dove, opposing virtually every new U.S. strategic system throughout the 1970s and 1980s, and especially opposing research and development or deployment of defensive systems. This was at a time when the Soviets had already achieved parity and were instead straining for superiority. He turned to writing books; *Blundering into Disaster,* for example, was much beloved by the arms-control-as-theology crowd who, apparently, had forgotten or never known of McNamara's role as the father of overkill. The point is that McNamara has tried more than once to obscure and do penance for his own history.

But this takes us far afield from Vietnam. There, in Southeast Asia, McNamara again proves himself wrong about how he was wrong. He still doesn't really get it. He doesn't understand that it wasn't the inherent weakness of South Vietnam that was to blame for defeat, but the fact that the Americanization, first of the administration of the war and then of the war itself, robbed any South Vietnamese leadership—after we unwittingly conspired in assassinating the leadership we inherited—of the nationalist credentials it needed to win hearts and minds, and hence the war.

McNamara also doesn't seem to understand that it wasn't enemy morale as such that defeated the United States, but mammothly counterproductive U.S. military tactics. As reviewed in Chapter 1, the search-and-destroy mentality, which was popular with Pentagon civilians and brass because of the vast advantages held by the United States in sheer firepower, had the effect of creating millions of internal refugees and of pushing rural populations into the arms of the Vietcong. What started in 1964 as a wholly owned subsidiary of the North Vietnamese Communists became by mid-1966 a genuine—and well-armed with stolen U.S. weapons— South Vietnamese opposition movement.

McNamara's compounding of error upon error on the antiwar movement is also striking. At the time, McNamara refused even to listen to what moderate protestors were saying. It is telling that *In Retrospect* doesn't even mention the famous 1966 Senate hearings presided over by Senator J. William Fulbright, which had a huge effect on the country and in the Congress by legitimating patriotic dissent. McNamara confesses that within his family he had a tendency to clam up when uncomfortable subjects around the war arose. What he doesn't admit, but which is manifest, is that he took the same approach to the country at large.

The net effect of the great silent treatment orchestrated by the Johnson White House and the McNamara Pentagon after the failure of the 1965-era "truth squads" was to discredit the liberal wing of the antiwar movement and thus help accelerate the internal dynamic of the movement toward the radical Left. Liberal dissenters had been able to argue in the early going, with some merit, that their arguments deserved a hearing; when Arthur Schlesinger and Hans Morganthau expressed misgivings, it was hard for administration principals to ignore them. But once the administration insisted on ignoring all who questioned the wisdom—not the morality—of the American commitment in Vietnam, they left the field wide open to the Left and its growing countercultural entourage, who questioned not only the morality of the U.S. role in Vietnam, but also the legitimacy of established American public life altogether.

McNamara was wrong then about how to handle the protestors, and now he's wrong yet again. In *In Retrospect* McNamara wrote of the October 1967 March on the Pentagon to Confront the Warmakers:

> I could not help but think that had the protestors been more disciplined— more Gandhi-like—they could have achieved their objective of shutting us down. All they had to do was lie on the pavement around the building. We would have found it impossible to remove enough of them to keep the Pentagon open.[1]

In a sense, McNamara is right to say that the protest that day, and others, generally would have been more acceptable to American opinion, and more effective, had there not been a Students for a Democratic Society "breakout" from the planned protest,which succeeded in breaking into the Pentagon itself, where SDSers splashed pig blood all over the walls.

But who is he trying to kid about being Gandhi-like? Suppose 20,000 protestors had laid down on the pavement. That would have closed the Pentagon on Saturday, October 21, 1967? For the sake of argument, let's say it would have. But what about Monday, October 23? Or Friday, October 27? How long can thousands of protestors lie on the pavement? Can anyone imagine Robert McNamara, in the specific incarnation of error in which he resided in October 1967, turning and saying to his generals: "Well boys, they're still out there lying on the pavement after a full week; I guess we'll have to call off the war"?

To make such a remark, Gandhi and all, and pass it off as an analysis of the antiwar movement is an insult to everyone's intelligence, whether or not they were even born at the time. In any event, insult or not, the publication of *In Retrospect* has led to uncountable minions proclaiming—yet again—that since McNamara admits we were wrong about Vietnam, those who protested the war must have been right. But the fact that two plus two doesn't equal five does not prove that two plus two therefore must equal three. And never mind that such conclusions never bother to distinguish between the liberal protest, which saw Vietnam as an aberration, and the more influential radical protest, which saw the war as a natural consequence of the evils of American corporate capitalism. How does McNamara's having been wrong make Noam Chomsky, Tom Hayden, Sidney Peck, Fred Halstead, and David Dellinger right?

Such inane logic is usually safely and properly dismissed—except perhaps when the president of the United States is one of those so proclaiming, as in fact he did. Then it becomes a different sort of problem, that of historical truths being mangled publicly in high places. So then, McNamara isn't alone after all.

A. G.
Philadelphia
June 22, 1995

# Notes

---

## Introduction

1.  This view is not unique to me but it is rare. Two scholars who make this point are John E. Mueller *War, Presidents, and Public Opinion* (New York: John Wiley, 1973), pp. 164-65, and in "Reflections on the Vietnam Antiwar Movement and on the Curious Calm at the War's End," in Peter Braestrup, ed., *Vietnam as History: Ten Years After the Paris Peace Accords* (Washington: The Wilson Center and University Press of America, 1984); and George C. Herring in *America's Longest War: The United States and Vietnam, 1950-1975,* second edition, (Philadelphia: Temple University Press, 1986), p. 173. But it is not the main thesis of either gentleman and, because their interests were elsewhere, neither fleshes out the logic of the observation. The point is also argued in a very restricted context in Randall M. Fisher, *Rhetoric and American Democracy: Black Protest Through Vietnam Dissent* (Lanham, MD: University Press of America, 1985). Another obscure example is Robert Nisbet, "War, Crisis and Intellectuals," *Wall Street Journal,* January 25, 1971, p. 10. There Nisbet wrote in passing that "once the more violent and obscene of student-faculty demonstrations against Vietnam had disgusted the vast majority of Americans, few relished the thought of seeming to think along the same lines." Oddly, Nisbet took the opposite view the year before: "[H]ad it not been for the passionate attack from the Left, the curse upon America [the Vietnam War] that began substantially in the early 1960s might well have continued further into the future." "Who Killed the Student Revolution?" *Encounter* 34,2 (February 1970). Finally, Steven E. Ambrose made the point in passing—exactly one sentence—in a review of Tom Wells's, *The War Within: America's Battle Over Vietnam* (Berkeley: University of California Press, 1994), who he says, rightly, takes the conventional view. See *Foreign Affairs* 73,4 (July/August 1994), p. 170.
2.  Here see Paul Burstein and William Freudenberg, "Changing Public Policy: The Impact of Public Opinion, Antiwar Demonstrations, and War Costs on Senate Voting on Vietnam War Motions," *American Journal of Sociology* 84,3 (July 1978): 99-122.
3.  Wells, *The War Within,* p. 4.
4.  I capitalize Left and New Left as well as Right throughout the text. I do not capitalize left-wing, right-wing, pacifist, liberal, or the word "old" in front of Left. This is because Left and Right have common sense directional meanings if they are not capitalized, while left-wing, right-wing, liberal, and pacifist do not. New Left designates a phenomenon limited to a particular time and can be described as a single phenomenon, but old Left, even restricted to the American context, refers to a much more diffuse array of ideas and movements over a much longer period. Capitalizing "Old Left" would imply a coherence I do not wish to suggest.
5.  Mueller's phrase in "Reflections on the Vietnam Antiwar Movement."
6.  The fringe groups of the Left were accorded the label "adversary culture" by Lionel Trilling in the 1960s. Lionel Trilling, *Beyond Culture* (New York: Viking, 1965), pp. xii-xiii. By it he meant to group together that small but noisy and ever shifting mélange of Marxists, anarchists, pacifists, and liberal secular millenarians of various descriptions who reflexively oppose every U.S. administration, less for what it does than for what it is. "Adversary culture" is not a term accepted by all observers, especially its own members; the academic subset of the adversary culture prefers to call itself "the peace reform," for example. I use Trilling's adversary culture, which strikes me as a less evaluative term.
7.  I prefer the term "Kuwait War" to "Gulf War" for two reasons: The war was about Kuwait and fought in Kuwait more than in the Persian Gulf, and Gulf War gets confused with the Iran-Iraq

War (1980-88), which was often called the Gulf War before 1990. I have left "Gulf War" as is in quotations and citations, of course.

---

## Chapter 1

1. An example is contained in The Heritage Foundation, "Making the World Safe for America: A U.S. Foreign Policy Blueprint," April 1992, p. 9. The text reads in part: "America also learned from its mistakes in Vietnam and Lebanon that when the nation does become involved militarily in other states, the American military must be allowed to fight to win."

2. A nearly pure example of the doves' myth is the letter to the editor by Erna Gold, "Look at Vietnam Generation Now," *New York Times,* July 16, 1994, p. A15. See also Tom Wicker's use of Clark Clifford's memoir, *Counsel to the President* (New York: Anchor Books, 1991), in his column "An Unwinnable War," *New York Times,* June 12, 1991, p. A27.

3. At the time, too, to add a further irony, the nearly universal view within the antiwar movement was that it had accomplished nothing by way of stopping the war. See testimony to this effect quoted by Wells, *The War Within: America's Battle Over Vietnam* (Berkeley, CA: University of California Press, 1994), pp. 163-64.

4. Tom Hayden quoted in "An Elegy for the New Left," *Time,* August 15, 1977, p. 67.

5. Irwin Unger, *The Movement: A History of the American New Left, 1959-1972* (New York: Dodd, Mead, 1974), p. 207.

6. Joshua Muravchik, "Mississippi Burning: Airbrushing History," *The World & I* (March 1989): 178.

7. Quoted in Eric Pace, "Jerry Rubin, 56, Flashy 60's Radical, Dies; 'Yippies' Founder and Chicago 7 Defendant," *New York Times,* November 30, 1994, p. B13.

8. "In Praise of the Counterculture," *New York Times,* December 11, 1994.

9. Thomas Powers, *The War at Home: Vietnam and the American People, 1964-1968* (New York: Grossman, 1973), p. xiii.

10. David J. Horowitz, "The Anti-war Movement: Vietnam Lessons," in John Norton Moore, ed., *The Vietnam Debate: A Fresh Look at the Arguments* (Lanham, MD: University Press of America, 1990), pp. 303-4.

11. Charles Kaiser, *1968 in America: Music, Politics, Chaos, Counterculture, and the Shaping of a Generation* (New York: Weidenfeld & Nicolson, 1988), p. 222.

12. John E. Mueller, *War, Presidents, and Public Opinion* (New York: John Wiley & Sons, 1973), p. 62.

13. George McGovern, "Foreword," in Melvin Small and William D. Hoover, eds., *Give Peace a Chance* (Syracuse: Syracuse University Press, 1992), pp. xi-xii.

14. Ibid., p. xii. My emphasis.

15. David Farber, "The Counterculture and the Antiwar Movement," in Small and Hoover, eds., *Give Peace a Chance,* p. 19.

16. Todd Gitlin, *The Sixties: Years of Hope, Days of Rage* (New York: Bantam, 1987), p. 335.

17. Sam Brown, "The Defeat of the Antiwar Movement," in Anthony Lake, ed., *The Vietnam Legacy* (New York: New York University Press, 1976), p. 121.

18. Small and Hoover, "Introduction," *Give Peace a Chance,* pp. 4-5. My emphasis.

19. Melvin Small, *Johnson, Nixon and the Doves* (New Brunswick, NJ: Rutgers University Press, 1988), p. xi. See also Small, "The Impact of the Antiwar Movement on Lyndon Johnson, 1965-68: A Preliminary Report," *Peace & Change* (Spring 1984).

20. Small, *Johnson, Nixon and the Doves,* pp. 20-21. See note 25 for a listing of much of this literature.

21. Ibid., p. 21.

22. I. L. Horowitz is cited for *The Struggle Is the Message: The Organization and Ideology of the Anti-War Movement* (Berkeley: Glendessary, 1970), a book written in 1969, clearly before it made sense to have concluded anything definite. Berger is cited for "Indochina & the American Conscience," *Commentary* (February 1980), a short essay whose main focus is not even the antiwar movement, and which never pretended to strict scholarship as opposed to more general analysis.

23. Nixon is cited as *No More Vietnams* (New York: Arbor House, 1985), p. 15, where Nixon says that antiwar opinion was "a factor . . . but not the decisive factor."

24. Small, *Johnson, Nixon and the Doves,* p. 176.
25. The relative insignificance of antiwar protests in shaping public opinion was established many years ago in the professional literature. See John P. Robinson, "Public Reaction to Political Protest, Chicago 1968," *Public Opinion Quarterly* 34,1 (Spring 1970); Harlan Hahn, "Correlates of Public Sentiment about War: Local Referenda on the Vietnam Issue," *American Political Science Review* 64,4 (December 1970); E. M. Schreiber, "Anti-War Demonstrations and American Public Opinion on the War in Vietnam," *British Journal of Sociology* 27,2 (June 1976); Sidney Verba and Richard Brody, "Participation, Policy Preferences, and the War in Vietnam," *Public Opinion Quarterly* 34,3 (Fall 1970); William R. Berkowitz, "The Impact of Anti-Vietnam War Demonstrations Upon National Public Opinion and Military Indicators," *Social Science Research* 2,1 (March 1973); and especially Mueller, *War, Presidents, and Public Opinion.* Wells claims precisely the reverse: that the movement speeded broad antiwar sentiment. *The War Within,* p. 6.
26. See John P. Robinson, "Balance Theory and Vietnam-Related Attitudes," *Social Science Quarterly* 53,1 (December 1970).
27. Kenneth Heineman, "The Silent Majority Speaks: Antiwar Protest and Backlash, 1965-1972," *Peace & Change* 17,4 (October 1992): 426. The same point is made in Herbert Parmet, *Richard Nixon and His America* (Boston: Little, Brown, 1990), and see H. Edward Ransford, "Blue Collar Anger: Reaction to Student and Black Protest," *American Sociological Review* 27,3 (June 1972).
28. Robinson, "Public Reaction to Political Protest."
29. See Schreiber, "Anti-War Demonstrations and American Public Opinion on the War in Vietnam."
30. The meaning of polling data is not self-evident, but neither is it subject to infinitely variable interpretation. On such problems, including those originating with flaws in methodology, see Mueller, *War, Presidents, and Public Opinion,* chap. 1. My presentation of this data is not exhaustive, not only because it is inherently inconclusive, but because Mueller has already done what can be done with it. I refer to his work often even when I disagree with him. A sample of polling analyses of the Vietnam War, in addition to those mentioned in note 25 above, include: Seymour Martin Lipset, "The President, the Polls and Vietnam," *Transaction* (September/October 1966); Philip Converse and H. Schuman, "'Silent Majorities' and the Vietnam War," *Scientific American* (June 1970); Milton J. Rosenberg, Sidney Verba, and Philip Converse, *Vietnam and the Silent Majority: The Dove's Guide* (New York: Harper & Row, 1970); Sidney Verba, Richard Brody, Norman H. Nie, Nelson W. Polsby, Paul Erdman, and Gordon Black, "Public Opinion and the War in Vietnam," *American Political Science Review* 61,2 (June 1967); and William L. Lunch and Peter W. Sperlich, "American Public Opinion and the War in Vietnam," *Western Political Quarterly* 32,1 (March 1979).
31. Mueller, *War, Presidents, and Public Opinion.*
32. Ibid., p. 59.
33. See ibid., p. 104. A sure sign of President Johnson's declining popularity was the publication by Simon & Schuster of *Quotations from Chairman LBJ* in early 1968, an obvious takeoff of the *Sayings of Chairman Mao.* When a major commercial publisher can make money ridiculing the president of the United States, something has changed.
34. So insists, rightly, William J. Duiker, *U.S. Containment Policy and the Conflict in Indochina* (Stanford, CA: Stanford University Press, 1994), pp. 362-63.
35. Totals add to 108 percent because some people gave more than one answer.
36. Mueller argues that the speech did not have a sharp impact (*War, Presidents, and Public Opinion,* p. 57), nor did any "event." But if events don't change opinion, what does? Moreover, Mueller's chart [p. 56] does show a relatively steep decline from the speech to the Republican Convention in the summer of 1968, and he says on p. 70: ". . . because of the follower phenomenon, one finds major shifts in public opinion on questions of policy after policy changes." Certainly, the March 31 speech is an example of a policy change.
37. Arthur H. Miller, "Political Issues and Trust in the Government," *American Political Science Review* 68,3 (September 1974), p. 958. This confirms the importance of "followers," those who take their cue from the president. See Mueller, *War, Presidents, and Public Opinion,* pp. 122-36.
38. Dean Rusk, *As I Saw It* (New York: W. W. Norton, 1990), p. 500.
39. See Rosenberg, Verba, and Converse, *Vietnam and the Silent Majority.*
40. Mueller, *War, Presidents, and Public Opinion,* p. 62.

41. Ibid., p. 164. Mueller cites classic studies done on World War II by Hadley Cantrill.

42. George Herring, *America's Longest War,* p. 173

43. See Robinson, "Public Reaction to Political Protest," pp. 1-9.

44. Ibid., p. 173n, and Robinson, "Public Reaction to Political Protest."

45. Cited in John E. Mueller, "Reflections on the Vietnam Antiwar Movement and the Curious Calm at War's End," in Peter Braestrup, ed., *Vietnam as History: Ten Years After the Paris Peace Accords* (Washington: Wilson Center and University Press of America, 1984), p. 152.

46. Bundy memorandum for the President, November 10, 1967 in President's Appointment file, November 2, 1967, Lyndon B. Johnson Library, cited in Charles DeBenedetti (with Charles Chatfield), *An American Ordeal: The Antiwar Movement of the Vietnam Era* (Syracuse: Syracuse University Press, 1990), p. 211.

47. For one example, see Powers, *The War at Home,* p. 184.

48. James Reston, "Washington: The Stupidity of Intelligence," *New York Times,* October 17, 1965, p. E10.

49. We take up the nature of the academic literature in Chap. 8.

50. Melvin Lasky, "The Ideas of '68," *Encounter* (November 1988): 5, 9.

51. Joseph Conrad, "A Familiar Preface," *A Personal Record* (1912), quoted in Rhoda Thomas Tripp, *The International Thesaurus of Quotations* (New York: Thomas Y. Crowell, 1970), 813: 6.

52. Gitlin, *The Sixties,* pp. 435-36.

53. See for example Stanley Kauffmann's offhand remark in *The New Republic,* April 27, 1987, p. 26. Kauffmann was disputed by Timothy McLaughlin (May 25, 1987, p. 41). For one argument that the war was winnable, see Norman Podhoretz, *Why We Were in Vietnam* (New York: Simon & Schuster, 1983).

54. The collapse of the European communist countries after 1989 occasioned a similar silence on the part of the academic Left. See the biting commentary by Eugene D. Genovese, "The Question," *Dissent* (Summer 1994): 371-76.

55. Abbie Hoffman quoted in Andrew Cassel, "Anti-war Forces Relive '68 Democratic Meeting," *Philadelphia Inquirer,* August 29, 1988, p. 7A.

56. David Lehman, "Time for a New Generation to Shout," *Chicago Tribune,* August 30, 1993.

57. Birnbaum quoted in Ronald Radosh, "The Know-Nothing Left," *Second Thoughts* I,1 (Summer 1989).

58. Todd Gitlin, "The Radical Potential of the Poor," *Internationalist Socialist Journal* 5,24 (1966): 874.

59. Peter Collier and David Horowitz, "Panthers, Contras and Other Wars," *The New Republic,* June 26, 1989, p. 39.

60. David J. Forman, "Rules of the Protest Game," *Jerusalem Post,* May 5, 1993.

61. But see David Horowitz and Peter Collier, "Another 'Low Dishonest Decade' on the Left," *Commentary* (January 1987). The title comes from W. H. Auden, one of the few literati in the 1960s to resist the romanticism of rebellion.

62. See Paul Hollander, "The Survival of the Adversary Culture," *Partisan Review* 53,3 (Summer 1986), his book of the same name (New Brunswick, NJ: Transaction, 1987), and his *Anti-Americanism* (New York: Oxford University Press, 1992). Also consider two reviews of this last mentioned. Morton Kondracke's "Leaning on the Left," *New York Times,* March 15, 1992, wrongly accused Hollander of exaggerating the importance of the adversary culture and, worse, missed the book's thesis. That thesis is that anti-Americanism at home and especially abroad, though it parades as progressivism, is more accurately a reaction against the pioneering nature of American society. (The same point is made in Michael Howard, "Cold War, Chill Peace," *World Policy Journal* X,4 [Winter 1994]: 31.) A better review of Hollander is Paul Johnson, "The Litany of Anti-Americanism," *The National Interest,* no. 27 (Spring 1992), pp. 92-95.

63. Roger Kimball, *Tenured Radicals* (New York: Harper & Row, 1990).

64. I agree with Andrew Krepinevich, Jr., *The Army in Vietnam* (Baltimore, MD: Johns Hopkins University Press, 1985); and similarly the political/administrative critique of U.S. policy in South Vietnam offered by Guenter Lewy, *America in Vietnam* (New York: Oxford University Press, 1978). See also William Colby with James McCargar, *Lost Victory: A Firsthand Account of America's Sixteen-Year Involvement in Vietnam* (Chicago: Contemporary Books, 1989), and Larry Cable, *Unholy Grail* (New York: Routledge, 1991).

65. Gavin published his criticism in *Harper's* (February 1966). See Powers, *The War at Home*, pp. 105-13, for a description of the abuse heaped on him by Robert McNamara, Cyrus Vance, and General Earl Wheeler.
66. Kissinger interviewed in *Penthouse* (December 1986): 80. Kissinger has since detailed his views of Vietnam in *Diplomacy* (New York: Simon & Schuster, 1994).
67. Douglas Pike, "South Vietnam: Autopsy of a Compound Crisis," in Daniel Pipes and Adam Garfinkle, eds., *Friendly Tyrants: An American Dilemma* (New York: St. Martin's, 1991); and see Nguyen Tien Hung and Jerrold L. Schecter, *The Palace File* (New York: Harper & Row, 1986).
68. For an extended argument, see Adam Garfinkle et al., *The Devil and Uncle Sam* (New Brunswick, NJ: Transaction, 1992).
69. Mueller, *War, Presidents, and Public Opinion*, pp. 100-1.
70. Johnson once angrily cut off a reporter complaining about Diem, "Don't talk to me about Diem. He's the only guy we got out there." See Powers, *The War at Home*, p. 5.
71. See Pike, "South Vietnam," pp. 41-62.
72. See Edward A. Olsen, "South Korea under Military Rule: Friendly Tyrant?" in Pipes and Garfinkle, *Friendly Tyrants*.

## Chapter 2

1. Another look at the adversary culture over time is John Patrick Diggins, *The Rise and Fall of the American Left* (New York: W. W. Norton, 1992).
2. See Charles DeBenedetti's edited volume of devotionals to Jane Addams, Eugene V. Debs, Norman Thomas, Albert Einstein, A. J. Muste, Norman Cousins, Martin Luther King, Jr., and the Berrigan brothers in *Peace Heroes in Twentieth Century America* (Bloomington: University of Indiana Press, 1986).
3. Paul Johnson, "The Litany of Anti-Americanism," p. 93.
4. On the American Catholic aspect of this see George Weigel, *Tranquillitas Ordinis* (New York: Oxford University Press, 1986), pp. 107-256 in particular. See also "Paul Johnson: Artist, Poet and Author," *Crisis* 12,11 (December 1994): 46.
5. See Arthur M. Schlesinger, Jr., *The Disuniting of America* (New York: W. W. Norton, 1992), chap. 1.
6. Traditional "peace churches" in the United States were strengthened in the aftermath of the Franco-Prussian War by an influx of Hutterite pacifists. The activities of the Quaker Universal Peace Union and Peace Association of Friends in North America are also of interest. See Charles DeBenedetti, *The Peace Reform in American History* (Bloomington: Indiana University Press, 1980), pp. 59-62, and Margaret Hope Bacon, *Mothers of Feminism: The Story of Quaker Women in America* (San Francisco: Harper & Row, 1986).
7. See DeBenedetti, *The Peace Reform in American History*, pp. 71-2; E. Berkeley Tompkins, *Anti-Imperialism in the United States: The Great Debate, 1898-1920* (Philadelphia: University of Pennsylvania Press, 1970); and John Chambers, *The Eagle and the Dove: The American Peace Movement and U.S. Foreign Policy, 1900-1922* (Syracuse: Syracuse University Press, 1991).
8. Sociologist Peter Berger has noted the tendency toward alliance of activist women and clergy until the present day. See his "Religion in Post-Protestant America," *Commentary* (May 1986), p. 43.
9. See "Mark Twain on American Imperialism," *The Atlantic Monthly* (April 1992), pp. 49-65.
10. See DeBenedetti, *The Peace Reform in American History*, chap. 5, and for a period piece see William J. Hull, *The New Peace Movement* (Boston: World Peace Foundation, 1912).
11. "The Voices of Emancipation: The Jewish Anarchists," audio tape, Pacifica Productions, 1981.
12. See Marc Karson, *American Labor Unions and Politics, 1900-1918* (Boston: Beacon Press, 1958), chap. 5.
13. For a discussion of the evolution of the term "liberal," see David Green, *Shaping Political Consciousness: The Language of Politics in America from McKinley to Reagan* (Ithaca, NY: Cornell University Press, 1988), especially pp. 76-85.
14. See C. Roland Marchand, *The American Peace Movement and Social Reform* (Princeton, NJ: Princeton University Press, 1972).

15. This is a good place to be explicit about vocabulary. By my definition a liberal is someone who accepts the basic institutional arrangements of capitalism but would use government to soften the social discontinuities of a private economy. I use "Left-Liberal" to identify a socialist vision of ends coupled to inside-the-system tactics. My use of language differs from DeBenedetti's and other "peace reform" authors in important ways. In *The Peace Reform in American History* DeBenedetti labeled what emerged from World War I as a dichotomy of liberal-internationalists and liberal-pacifists. He cites differences between them but claims that both "had roots in the country's prewar liberal tradition, which blended the sensibilities of Social Gospel Christianity, a socialist mode of social analysis, and a pragmatic concern with ends and means" (p. 106). Liberal-internationalists are liberals, but the ideologically anti-capitalist socialist-pacifists that emerged from the war were not liberals just because they were anti-Communist. Perhaps DeBenedetti *only* meant by liberal someone who believes that revolutionary transformations can be accomplished by working *within* the system, whereas radical means someone who believes they cannot. That is a useful distinction but, if that is all "liberal" means, then the term is stripped of programmatic significance. Finally, "liberal" is a legitimizing inside-the-mainstream term in American political culture. DeBenedetti believed that "democratic" or anti-Communist socialists ought to fall inside the mainstream, so for him they are "liberals." That this blurring is so widespread today is a measure of how far the liberal parts of the political spectrum moved Left during the Vietnam War.

16. See Harvey Klehr, *The Heyday of American Communism* (Gainesville, FL: Basic Pub., 1984).

17. This discussion parallels my *The Politics of the Nuclear Freeze* (Philadelphia: Foreign Policy Research Institute, 1984) and uses the sources noted therein. On Muste, see Nat Hentoff, ed., *The Essays of A. J. Muste* (New York: Simon & Schuster, 1967). For an example of Muste's own writing, see *Nonviolence in an Aggressive World* (New York: J. S. Ozer, 1938).

18. See the discussion in Weigel, *Tranquillitas Ordinis,* pp. 148-53, the sympathetic biography of Day by Mel Piehl, *Breaking Bread: The Catholic Worker and the Origins of Catholic Radicalism in America* (Philadelphia: Temple University Press, 1982), and Charles A. Meconis, *With Clumsy Grace: The American Catholic Left, 1961-1977* (New York: Seabury, 1979).

19. Whereas the labor movement matured, most of the pro-labor intelligentsia did not. Intellectual Leftism made deep inroads in the 1930s into America's traditional upper classes, converting some from noblesse oblige to class conscious self-criticism and political pilgrimage. See Paul Hollander, *Political Pilgrims: Travels of Western Intellectuals to the Soviet Union, China and Cuba* (New York: Oxford University Press, 1981). Noteworthy as an example is the life of Upton Sinclair, whose 1904 book *The Jungle* was reprinted in the 1960s and widely assigned in high school and college classrooms. See Art Casciato's summary in Bernard K. Johnpoll and Harvey Klehr, eds., *Biographical Dictionary of the American Left* (Westport, CT: Greenwood, 1986), pp. 361-63.

20. Kaiser, *1968 in America,* p. 3.

21. The Louvin Brothers, *The Louvin Brothers,* Rounder Records Specialty Series No. 07, 1980.

22. For details of the new pacifism's activities from 1946 to 1956 see the sympathetic account of Lawrence S. Wittner, *Rebels Against War: The American Peace Movement, 1933-1983* (Philadelphia: Temple University Press, 1984), pp. 151-239, and for a less hagiographic view see Guenter Lewy, *Peace & Revolution: The Moral Crisis of American Pacifism* (Grand Rapids, MI: Eerdmans, 1988).

23. The split was not complete. Even into the early 1960s, Norman Cousins was a prominent member of both SANE and the United World Federalists. See Milton S. Katz, *Ban the Bomb: A History of SANE, the Committee for a Sane Nuclear Policy, 1957-1985* (Westport, CT: Greenwood, 1986), p. 86.

24. See ibid., pp. 47-56; Wittner, *Rebels Against War,* pp. 258-61, and especially Guenter Lewy, *The Cause that Failed: Communism in American Political Life* (New York: Oxford University Press, 1990). Irving Howe claimed that Cousins told him this was not so (*The New Republic,* October 15, 1990) but further investigation, courtesy of FBI documents unearthed through the Freedom of Information Act, proved that it *was* the case. See "Back to the Fifties," *The New Republic,* December 10, 1990, p. 10.

25. On Turn Toward Peace see DeBenedetti, *The Peace Reform in American History,* pp. 166-69 and Katz, *Ban the Bomb,* pp. 70-71. Wittner does not mention Turn Toward Peace in his otherwise encyclopedic narrative.

26. Katz, *Ban the Bomb,* pp. 69-70.

27. Raskin's more recent views can be read in *The Common Good: Its Politics, Policies and Philosophy* (New York: Routledge and Kegan Paul, 1986).

28. A phrase made famous by journalist David Halberstam.

29. See Irving Louis Horowitz, ed., *The Rise and Fall of Project Camelot* (Cambridge, MA: M.I.T. Press, 1974).

30. Some have referred to the U.S. military's approach in Vietnam as "scientific technowar." There's some truth to this; at the time the popularity and novelty of systems management was so wide spread that it was bound to spill over into the Pentagon. But to reify the notion and make it the centerpiece of an analysis of a failed strategy is going too far. See James William Gibson, *The Perfect War* (Boston: Atlantic Monthly Press, 1986), who goes too far.

31. The importance of affluence in the student rebellions of the 1960s has been widely noted. See Cyril Levitt, *Children of Privilege: Student Revolt in the Sixties* (Toronto: University of Toronto Press, 1984); Landon Y. Jones, *Great Expectations: America and the Baby Boom Generation* (New York: Ballantine, 1981); Joseph A. Califano, Jr., *The Student Revolution: A Global Confrontation* (New York: W. W. Norton, 1970), pp. 46-48; and Edward Shils, "Dreams of Plentitude, Nightmares of Scarcity," in Seymour M. Lipset and Philip Altbach, eds., *Students in Revolt* (Boston: Houghton Mifflin, 1969).

32. If the television series *M\*A\*S\*H* had a slightly corrosive effect on a generation, consider the impact of an image of the army conveyed to the youth of the 1950s as a bunch of conniving card-playing knuckleheads never seen with a weapon.

33. Gitlin quoted in Katherine Bishop, "The 60's Legacy: From the Inside Out," *New York Times Education Section*, January 8, 1989, p. 22.

34. Here see Leo Marx, *The Machine in the Garden: Technology and the Pastoral Idea in America* (New York: Oxford University Press, 1964).

35. A point developed in Klaus Mehnert, *Twilight of the Young: The Radical Movements of the 1960s and Their Legacy* (New York: Holt, Rinehart and Winston, 1976), chap. 1.

36. See the interview of Hayden in *Rolling Stone,* October 26, 1972, and the account in Gitlin, *The Sixties,* p. 54.

37. See Kenneth Keniston, *The Uncommitted: Alienated Youth in American Society* (New York: Harcourt, Brace and World, 1965) and *Youth and Dissent* (New York: Harcourt Brace Jovanovich, 1971).

38. Daniel Yankelovich et al., "Trend Reference Book" (New York: Yankelovich Monitor, 1985), p. 26, quoted in Paul C. Light, *Baby Boomers* (New York: W. W. Norton, 1988), p. 246.

39. I have used the label that African-Americans used for themselves at various periods rather than revocalize the past at the behest of the present.

40. This point is detailed in Maurice Isserman, "You Don't Need a Weathervane but a Postman Can Be Helpful," in Small and Hoover, eds., *Give Peace a Chance.*

41. This "pendular" phenomenon in cognitive processes has been much studied. For a discussion attuned to politics, see Robert Jervis, *The Logic of Images in International Relations* (Princeton, NJ: Princeton University Press, 1969), pp. 102-110.

42. Califano, *The Student Revolution,* p. 44.

43. Francis Bacon, *The Essays or Counsels, Civil and Moral, of Francis Ld. Verulam, Viscount St. Albans* (Mount Vernon, NY: Peter Pauper Press, n.d.), p. 59.

44. DeBenedetti, *The Peace Reform in American History*, p. 170. Katz's work on SANE does not mention this.

45. For an analysis of the impact of the encyclical, see Weigel, *Tranquillas Ordinis,* pp. 137-46. Emphasis in original.

46. See Nancy Zaroulis and Gerald Sullivan, *Who Spoke Up? American Protest Against the War in Vietnam* (New York: Doubleday, 1984), p. 8.

47. For details on the origins of the SPU and SDS, see James Miller, *"Democracy Is in the Streets": From Port Huron to the Siege of Chicago* (New York: Simon & Schuster, 1987), chaps. 2-4; DeBenedetti, *The Peace Reform in American History,* pp. 166-69; William L. O'Neill, *Coming Apart* (Chicago: Quadrangle, 1971), pp. 277-78; and George R. Vickers, *The Formation of the New Left: The Early Years* (Lexington, MA: D.C. Heath, 1975). Vickers was a participant in the early New Left.

48. Luce's story is a strange one. By 1965 he had broken with the Progressive Labor Party and turned to the Right. See his *The New Left Today: America's Trojan Horse* (Washington: The Capitol Hill Press, 1971).

49. DeBenedetti, *The Peace Reform in American History,* pp. 170-71, and interview with Robert Schleifer, one of the original leaders of M2M, Philadelphia, July 1987.

50. For a participant's account see Joan Baez, *And a Song to Sing With: A Memoir* (New York: Summit, 1987).

51. See Zaroulis and Sullivan, *Who Spoke Up?* p. 20.

52. See William P. Bundy, "The Path to Viet Nam: Ten Decisions," *Orbis* (Fall 1967): 647-63.

53. For example, K. O'Donnell, who claims to have heard this firsthand from President Kennedy and offers direct quotes to this effect. "LBJ and the Kennedys," *Life,* August 7, 1970.

54. Gary Wills, *The Kennedy Imprisonment: A Meditation on Power* (New York: Pocket Books, 1982), p. 283.

55. For details, see Wittner, *Rebels Against War,* pp. 281-82; DeBenedetti, *Peace Reform in American History,* pp. 170-75; and Fred Halstead, *"Out Now": A Participant's Account of the American Movement Against the Vietnam War* (New York: Monad Press, 1978).

56. SANE's role in the period from 1963 to 1965 is instructive here. See Katz, *Ban the Bomb,* pp. 93-99.

57. See Leslie Gelb and Richard K. Betts, *The Irony of Vietnam: The System Worked* (Washington: Brookings Institute, 1979), pp. 69-86.

58. Hanoi had reason to be buoyed by the neutralization of Laos. See Norman Hannah, *The Key to Failure: Laos and the Vietnam War* (Lanham, MD: Madison Books, 1987).

59. See Roger Hilsman, "Vietnam: The Decision to Intervene," in Jonathan R. Adelman, ed., *Superpowers and Revolution* (New York: Praeger, 1986), pp. 119-21, 125-36, and 139-40.

60. On Morse and Gruening, see Zaroulis and Sullivan, *Who Spoke Up?* pp. 16-44 and Townsend Hoopes, *The Limits of Intervention* (New York: McKay, 1969).

---

## Chapter 3

1. The reference is to the popular *First Family* comedy albums of Vaughn Mearder.

2. Quoted in Powers, *The War at Home,* p. 15.

3. Ibid., p. 9.

4. That President Johnson was still considering all options before finally deciding to escalate in 1965 is demonstrated in David M. Barrett, *Uncertain Warriors: Lyndon Johnson and his Vietnam Advisors* (Lawrence: University of Kansas Press, 1993).

5. Reported in the *New York Times,* February 4, 1965, p. 3.

6. On his deathbed, Douglas MacArthur warned Johnson against U.S. involvement in an Asian land war. See William Manchester, *American Caesar* (Boston: Little, Brown, 1978), p. 10.

7. Indeed he was adamant about it. See Johnson's remarks quoted in Doris Kearns, *Lyndon Johnson and the American Dream* (New York: Harper & Row, 1976), pp. 251-52.

8. Bundy quoted in Henry Brandon, *Special Relationships* (New York: Atheneum, 1988), p. 224. This memo was excluded from *The Pentagon Papers,* although an earlier Bundy memo of February 7, 1965, which supported a policy of limited retaliation, is included. This and other cases of omission suggest that the editors of *The Pentagon Papers* strove to make a particular impression on the country.

9. Bundy quoted in Henry Brandon, *Special Relationships,* p. 224.

10. For the text, see Miller, *"Democracy Is in the Streets."*

11. Mills's most influential work was *The Power Elite* (New York: Oxford University Press, 1956).

12. See David Horowitz, "A Letter to a Political Friend," in John H. Bunzel, ed., *Political Passages: Journeys of Change Through Two Decades, 1968-1988* (New York: Free Press, 1988), pp. 187-212.

13. See Maurice Isserman, *If I Had a Hammer* (New York: Basic Books, 1987).

14. One of Kirkpatrick Sale's points in *SDS* (New York: Random House, 1973).

15. Zaroulis and Sullivan, *Who Spoke Up?* p. 27.

16. Personal communication, David Horowitz, January 1987.

17. Humphrey quoted in *Life,* July 30, 1965, cited in Powers, *The War at Home,* p. 48.

18. On what happened at Berkeley with the Free Speech Movement, see Zaroulis and Sullivan, *Who Spoke Up?* p. 27, and better, see Powers, *The War at Home,* pp. 30-34. DeBenedetti (with Chatfield)

barely mentions the Free Speech Movement, and does not mention Mario Savio once in nearly 500 pages of *An American Ordeal.*

19. Powers, *The War at Home,* p. xvi. It might be an edited memory because few young people, even from Yale, knew or thought much about the Vietcong before 1964.

20. Doar is quoted in Sally Belfrage, *Freedom Summer* (New York: Viking Press, 1965), p. 22. Other anecdotal material can be gleaned from Mary King, *Freedom Song* (New York: William Morrow, 1987).

21. Some of the earliest demonstrations were at the University of Pennsylvania, where students and faculty protested chemical/biological warfare research being done for the government. See Jonathan Goldstein, "Vietnam Research on Campus: The Summit/Spicerack Controversy at the University of Pennsylvania 1965-67," *Peace & Change* 11,2 (Spring 1986).

22. See the sympathetic history by Mitchell K. Hall, *Because of Their Faith: CALCAV and Religious Opposition to the Vietnam War* (New York: Columbia University Press, 1990).

23. Potter quoted in Zaroulis and Sullivan, *Who Spoke Up?* p. 41.

24. For exposition of this view, see David J. Horowitz, *Empire and Revolution* (New York: Random House, 1969).

25. Paul Berman, "The Fog of Political Correctness," *Tikkun* 7,1 (January/February 1992): 53.

26. Ibid., p. 53.

27. Gregory Calvert, "In White America: Radical Consciousness and Social Change," in M. Teodori, ed., *The New Left: A Documentary Record* (Indianapolis: Bobbs-Merrill, 1969), pp. 414-15. Emphasis in original.

28. For an example, see the AFSC's *Peace in Vietnam: A New Approach in Southeast Asia* (New York: Hill & Wang, 1966).

29. Reinhold Niebuhr, "Two Forms of Utopianism," *Christianity and Society* 12,4 (Autumn 1947).

30. Brown, "The Defeat of the Antiwar Movement," p. 122.

31. Noted in Powers, *The War at Home,* p. 56.

32. I. F. Stone, "A Reply to the White Paper," *I.F. Stone's Weekly,* March 8, 1965.

33. Powers, *War at Home,* pp. 54-56, and DeBenedetti with Chatfield, *An American Ordeal,* pp. 107-9.

34. Quoted in Zaroulis and Sullivan, *Who Spoke Up?* p. 40.

35. Also see David McReynolds, "Pacifists and the Movement," in Small and Hoover, eds., *Give Peace a Chance.*

36. At the time SDS argued that the liberals tried to steal *their* rally. See "The Student's March on Washington," *The Left,* reprinted in full in Matthew Stolz, ed., *Politics of the New Left* (Beverly Hills, CA: Glencoe Press, 1971), pp. 88-99.

37. Robert Moses later changed his name to Robert Parris. I refer to him by the name he was using contemporaneously.

38. Potter quoted in *Liberation* (May & June/July 1965).

39. Dylan himself, however, was absent. While many tried to claim Dylan for the antiwar movement, he really never showed up. He had written many civil rights-related songs, including "Chimes of Freedom," and several antiwar songs such as "With God on Our Side," recorded famously by Joan Baez. But by the mid-1960s, Dylan was either out of or simply beyond politics, as his "My Back Pages" strongly suggests. The refrain in that song, made into a hit by the Byrds, is that "I was so much older then," but "I'm younger than that now."

40. This meeting is reported in Richard Walton, *The Remnants of Power* (New York: Coward McCann, 1968), p. 178.

41. Rustin quoted in Nat Hentoff, "Review of the Press," *The Village Voice,* June 24, 1965.

42. Later, on June 21, 1965, Bundy did debate Morgenthau on television; Eric Severeid was the moderator. Bundy ambushed and destroyed Morgenthau according to all accounts. See Powers, *The War at Home,* pp. 67-68.

43. Schlesinger quoted in Louis Menashe and Ronald Radosh, eds., *Teach-ins: U.S.A.* (New York: Praeger, 1967), p. 170.

44. Lynd's speech can be found in James Petras et al., eds., *We Accuse* (Berkeley: Diablo Press, 1965), pp. 153-58, also cited in Powers, *The War at Home,* p. 323-24.

45. Compare Lynd in *Liberation* (June-July 1965) with Rustin's "From Protest to Politics," *Commentary* (February 1965).

46. Pickus quoted in DeBenedetti with Chatwick, *An American Ordeal,* p. 116.

47. On Berkeley in the 1960s, see William Rorabaugh, *Berkeley at War: The 1960s* (New York: Oxford University Press, 1989).

48. Zaroulis and Sullivan, *Who Spoke Up?* pp. 42-43.

49. Ibid., p. 48.

50. The *New York Times* printed the text on October 29, 1965.

51. See Powers, *The War at Home,* pp. 90-92.

52. For details, see Katz, *Ban the Bomb,* pp. 97-99. Gottlieb was no fuzzy liberal; see his "State Within a State: What Is the Military-Industrial Complex?" in Michael Harrington and Irving Howe, eds., *The Seventies: Problems and Proposals* (New York: Harper & Row, 1972), pp. 184-201.

53. Oglesby's speech can be found in Paul Jacobs and Saul Landau, eds., *The New Radicals: A Report with Documents* (New York: Vintage, 1966), and in Mitchell Cohen and Dennis Hale, eds., *The New Student Left* (Boston: Beacon, 1967).

54. Quoted in Zaroulis and Sullivan, *Who Spoke Up?* p. 59.

55. Wolfe quoted in Katz, *Ban the Bomb,* pp. 99-100. See also Paul Boyer, "From Activism to Apathy: The American People and Nuclear Weapons, 1963-1980," *Journal of American History* (March 1984), pp. 821-44.

56. Here see Tom Bell, "We Won't Go—A Case Study," *New Left Notes,* March 27, 1967, pp. 6, 8-9. This is reprinted in Alice Lind, ed., *We Won't Go: Personal Accounts of War Objectors* (Boston: Beacon Press, 1968).

57. This song was recorded on Vanguard Records, No. 79266, 1967. For the full lyrics see John Ketwig, ". . . and a hard rain fell," in Reese Williams, ed., *Unwinding the Vietnam War from War into Peace* (Seattle, WA: Real Comet Press, 1987), pp. 19-20. There were more than just songs about the draft; Arlo Tatum and Joseph S. Tuchinsky's *Guide to the Draft* (Boston: Beacon Press, 1967) went through four editions. It was a guide to *avoiding* the draft, of course.

58. For one review of the music, see Terry H. Anderson, "Pop Music and the Vietnam War," *Peace and Change* 11,2 (Spring 1986). Kaiser's *1968 in America* also makes much of the music.

59. Ochs's "In the Heat of the Summer" is an outstanding example of the latter. See generally R. Serge Denisoff, *Great Day Coming: Folk Music and the American Left* (Urbana: University of Illinois Press, 1971).

60. Gitlin, *The Sixties,* pp. 195-97.

61. Related in ibid., p. 197.

62. Dowd quoted in Wells, *The War Within,* p. 162.

63. Allen quoted in ibid., p. 162. Wells's sympathy for this and other remarks is obvious; see also pages 163-64.

64. Noted in Peter B. Levy, "The New Left, Labor and the Vietnam War," *Peace & Change* 15,1 (January 1990): 50. See also Heineman, "The Silent Majority Speaks: Antiwar Protest and Backlash, 1965-1972."

65. *The Berkeley Barb,* May 19-25, 1967, quoted in Levy, "The New Left, Labor and the Vietnam War," p. 54, and identically in Powers, *The War at Home,* p. 200. Powers cites the original, Levy does not.

66. See Levy, "The New Left, Labor and the Vietnam War," p. 57 and sources noted therein.

67. Ransford, "Blue Collar Anger: Reaction to Student and Black Protest."

## Chapter 4

1. Brown, "The Defeat of the Antiwar Movement," p. 123.

2. See Powers, *The War at Home,* pp. 135-37.

3. See Katz, *Ban the Bomb,* pp. 100-1; the contemporary account by Andrew Kopkind, "Anti-Vietnam Politics: Peace Candidates in Oregon, California," *The New Republic,* June 4, 1966; Powers, *The War at Home,* pp. 124-28; and DeBenedetti with Chatwick, *An American Ordeal,* p. 147.

4. Craig quoted in Richard Cummings, *The Pied Piper: Allard K. Lowenstein and the Liberal Dream* (New York: Farrar, Straus & Giroux, 1973), p. 341.

5. See Mueller, *Wars, Presidents and Public Opinion,* p. 129, for evidence.

6. These hearings were published as *The Vietnam Hearings* (New York: Random House, 1966). Fulbright's own *The Arrogance of Power,* published in 1967 (New York: Random House), contributed as well to legitimating dissent against the war.

7. Johnson quoted in Zaroulis and Sullivan, *Who Spoke Up?* p. 92.

8. Notes by Jim Jones, September 5 and 12, 1967, Appointment File, Diary backup, box 75, LBJ Library, cited in Barrett, *Uncertain Warriors,* p. 107.

9. See Walter Isaacson and Evan Thomas, *The Wise Men* (New York: Simon & Schuster, 1986).

10. See Herbert Schandler, *Lyndon Johnson and Vietnam: The Unmaking of a President* (Princeton, NJ: Princeton University Press, 1977), chaps. 5 and 9.

11. Lady Bird Johnson, *A White House Diary* (New York: Holt, Rinehart, and Winston, 1970), p. 549.

12. They gained four Republican seats so the net loss was 43.

13. See David J. Garrow, *Bearing the Cross* (New York: Morrow, 1987), and the review essay by C. Vann Woodward, "The Dreams of Martin Luther King," *New York Review of Books,* January 15, 1987, pp. 8-9. See also Adam Fairclough, "Martin Luther King, Jr., and the War in Vietnam," *Phylon* 45 (March 1984).

14. See Herbert Shapiro, "The Vietnam War and the American Civil Rights Movement," *Journal of Ethnic Studies,* 16 (Winter 1989), and Aaron Wildavsky, "The Empty-head Blues: Black Rebellion and White Reaction," *The Public Interest* (Spring 1968). More generally, see William L. Van Deburg, *New Day in Babylon* (Chicago: University of Chicago Press, 1992).

15. "Hippie" came from "hipster," a term of the Beat Generation. This came from the adjective "hip," which applied to both being in the know generally and to jazz music if it was the "right" sort. "Hip" came from "hep," as in "hep cat," having the same meaning from earlier decades of jazz. But "hep" came from the military cadence of calling out left-right, left-right from sometime around the turn of the century, "hep" being a gutturalized form of "left." How hep made the transition from the military left to the equivalent of jazz "cool" before World War I is not clear.

16. Kesey is quoted in many places, including David Farber, "The Counterculture and the Antiwar Movement," in Small and Hoover, eds., *Give Peace a Chance,* p. 9.

17. Ibid., p. 11.

18. The Yippies (Youth International Party) did not formally exist until January 16, 1968, when brought into being by Abbie Hoffmann, Paul Krassner, Ed Sanders, and Jerry Rubin. But like many things back then, Yippies existed before they were named. The name did not really start as an acronym for Youth International Party; that came later. According to Jack Hoffman and Daniel Simon in *Run, Run, Run: The Lives of Abbie Hoffman* (New York: Tarcher/Putnam, 1994), someone asked Hoffman what was Yiddish for hippie, and Abbie said "yippie." But Paul Krassner also takes credit for the name. See Krassner, "Jerry Rubin," *The Nation,* December 19, 1994, p. 749.

19. Tom Hayden, *Reunion: A Memoir* (New York: Random House, 1988), pp. 204-5.

20. Todd Gitlin, "What Are We Doing to Dismantle the System and What to Decorate It," *Liberation News Service,* 1968, cited in Farber, "The Counterculture and the Antiwar Movement," p. 12. As Farber notes, Gitlin mentions none of this in his book *The Sixties.*

21. An entire literature grew up around LSD. For an early harbinger of it, see Timothy Leary, Richard Alpert, and Ralph Metzner, "Rationale of the Mexican Psychedelic Training Center," in Richard Blum and Associates, *Utopiates: The Use and Users of LSD* (New York: Atherton Press, 1965). For an analytical account, see Jay Stevens, *Storming Heaven* (New York: Harper & Row, 1988).

22. See Joseph R. Gusfield, "The (F)utility of Knowledge? The Relation of Social Science to Public Policy toward Drugs," *Annals of the American Academy of Political and Social Sciences,* no. 417 (January 1975), especially pp. 6-11.

23. Simon and Garfunkel, *Parsley, Sage, Rosemary and Thyme,* Columbia CS 9363, 1966. "Everybody must get stoned" was a line from Bob Dylan's first pop radio hit and also its title.

24. Ibid.

25. Louis Menard, "Life in the Stone Age," *The New Republic,* January 7 & 14, 1991, p. 41.

26. Ibid., p. 41.

27. Tom Wolfe's famous 1968 novel, *The Electric Kool-Aid Acid Test* (New York: Farrar, Straus & Giroux, 1968) spread word of such goings on.

28. Krassner, "Jerry Rubin," p. 749.

29.  Sale, *SDS*, pp. 663-64. Seymour Martin Lipset estimated that at its height, SDS had no more than 6,000 dues paying members to the national organization, and only 30,000 other locally affiliated members nationwide. Lipset, *Rebellion in the University* (Chicago: University of Chicago Press, 1971), p. 75. These figures may be technically accurate but they underestimate SDS's spontaneous membership during times of accelerated experience. Paying dues is a good indicator of organizational affiliation in most cases, but this was not one of them. See Helen Lefkowitz Horowitz, "The 1960s and the Transformation of Campus Cultures," *History of Education Quarterly* 26 (Spring 1986).

30.  At least one study dating from 1968 claimed that draft status had no effect on student opinions about the Vietnam War, but this conclusion is not convincing. See Allen H. Barton, "The Columbia Crisis: Campus, Vietnam, and the Ghetto," *Public Opinion Quarterly* 32,3 (Fall 1968), pp. 348-50.

31.  Tom Robbins, *Still Life with Woodpecker* (New York: Bantam, 1980), p. 150.

32.  Rubin quoted in Jeffrey Herf, "Reliving the Sixties," *Partisan Review* 57,2 (Spring 1990): 253.

33.  Sinclair quoted in ibid., p. 252.

34.  Oglesby quoted in Farber, "Counterculture and the Antiwar Movement," p. 12.

35.  Ibid., p. 13.

36.  See Leon Festinger et al., *When Prophecy Fails* (Minneapolis: University of Minnesota Press, 1956).

37.  Peck revealed his views on the matter in "Notes on the Strategy and Tactics of the Movement Against the War," *New Politics* (August 1968).

38.  Ibid. But to say, as Peter Levy does ("The New Left, Labor, and the Vietnam War," p. 60), that this means that Peck, along with Sidney Lens and Fred Halstead, steered the antiwar movement "in a more conciliatory direction" is wrong. Conciliation hardly describes what they were trying to do, which was to foment a mass-based Communist revolution in the United States.

39.  Zaroulis and Sullivan, *Who Spoke Up?* pp. 97-98.

40.  Halstead, *"Out Now,"* p. 80.

41.  Zaroulis and Sullivan, *Who Spoke Up?* pp. 110-11.

42.  Arnaud de Borchgrave, "The Role of the Media in the Vietnam War," in Moore, ed., *The Vietnam Debate* (Lanham, MD: University Press of America).

43.  Richard Wightman Fox, "The Reality Box," *New York Times Book Review,* May 4, 1992, p. 7.

44.  See Don Oberdorfer, *Tet!* (Garden City, NJ: Doubleday, 1971). See also Peter Braestrup's two volume *Big Story* (Boulder, CO: Westview, 1977).

45.  Conversation with Senator Henry M. Jackson, Washington, May 21, 1979.

46.  Kenneth Keniston, *Young Radicals: Notes on Committed Youth* (New York: Harcourt, Brace and World, 1968).

47.  Calvert quoted in Zaroulis and Sullivan, *Who Spoke Up?* p. 118.

48.  Examples of social criticism include those collected in David Cooper, ed., *To Free a Generation* (New York: Collier Books, 1968). See also Alexander Cockburn and Robin Blackburn, eds., *Student Power: Problems, Diagnosis, Action* (Harmondsworth: Penguin/New Left Review, 1969). See also Theodore Roszak's *The Making of a Counter Culture: Reflections on the Technocratic Society and Its Youthful Opposition* (Garden City, NY: Doubleday-Anchor, 1969), and its copious notes.

49.  David Riesman, *The Lonely Crowd: A Study of the Changing American Character* (New Haven: Yale University Press, 1961). The book was first published in 1955 by Doubleday, with coauthors Nathan Glazer and Reuel Denny.

50.  The failure of the older intelligentsia to care much about race relations while it debated fine points of Marxist philosophy in Manhattan up through the early 1960s is noteworthy. As Elizabeth Hardwick wrote, "the intellectual life in New York and the radical life of the Thirties" were "the worst possible preparation for our participation in the civil rights struggle. Looking back, it is curious to remember how small a part the Negro's existence played in left-wing movements." "Curious" is one way to put it; less charitable phrases also come to mind. See Hardwick's "Selma, Alabama: The Charms of Goodness," *New York Review of Books,* April 22, 1965.

51.  There were a few members of the literati who did not go the way of the crowd: W. H. Auden, James Michener, and John Updike are the most prominent examples. See Updike's retrospective "On Not Being a Dove," *Commentary* (March 1989).

52.  Lasky, "The Ideas of '68," p. 3.

53.  Macdonald quoted in ibid., p. 3.

54. Cheever and Roth quoted in Jeffrey Hart, *The American Dissent* (Garden City, NY: Doubleday, 1966), p. 247f. Little has changed; the intellectual Left is still antipatriotic. See Richard Rorty, "The Unpatriotic Academy," *New York Times,* February 13, 1994.

55. Sandy Vogelgesang, *The Long Dark Night of the Soul: The American Intellectual Left and the Vietnam War* (New York: Harper & Row, 1974), p. 5. Much of what follows in this section is indebted to this excellent book.

56. Ibid., pp. 27-31.

57. Norman Mailer, "Statement on Vietnam," *Partisan Review* 32,4 (Fall 1965): 642.

58. Mitchell Goodman quoted in Vogelgesang, *Long Dark Night,* p. 137. The "Boston Five" were Goodman, Benjamin Spock, William Sloane Coffin, Michael Ferber, and Marcus Raskin; they were arrested and charged with conspiracy over their effort to aid draft resistance.

59. Lasky, "The Ideas of '68," p. 4.

60. Zinn was especially creative in trying to reconcile the New Left's anti-Marxist aspects with Marxism. See his "Marxism and the New Left," reprinted in Stolz, ed., *Politics of the New Left,* pp. 36-48.

61. Susan Sontag, *Styles of Radical Will* (New York: Dell, 1969), p. 271.

62. See Robert Jay Lifton, *Boundaries* (New York: Random House, 1969), especially pp. 99-106.

63. For a flavor of this, see the essays in Theodore Roszak, ed., *The Dissenting Academy* (New York: Pantheon, 1968). Anyone familiar with campus orthodoxies today will notice how tame and reasonable most of these essays sound compared to current politically correct literary criticism and "praxis-directed" social science teaching. Mueller wrote that the activism of faculties in the 1960s, as opposed to their passivity in the Korean War era, had something to do with a more secure job market. Perhaps. See Mueller, *War, Presidents, and Public Opinion,* p. 160.

64. See Powers, *War at Home,* pp. 65-66, and DeBenedetti with Chatwick, *An American Ordeal,* pp. 115-16. On Lowell, see Sarah Payne Stuart, "'Bobby Was a Difficult Child': My Cousin Robert Lowell," *New York Times Book Review,* November 20, 1994, pp. 3, 40-42. Lowell was a conscientious objector during World War II and was imprisoned as a result, but this was after he was twice turned down trying to enlist.

65. On Mailer, James Baldwin, and Noam Chomsky see Paul Johnson, *Intellectuals* (New York: Harper & Row, 1988), pp. 305-41.

66. Lynd quoted in Vogelgesang, *Long Dark Night,* p. 170.

67. Cited in ibid., pp. 138, 175.

68. See Christopher Lasch, *The New Radicalism in America, 1889-1963* (New York: Knopf, 1965), which outlines the development of a self-consciousness among American intellectuals. See also Alvin W. Gouldner, *Against Fragmentation* (New York: Oxford University Press, 1985).

69. Walzer, Harrington, Draper, and Chomsky quoted in Vogelgesang, *Long Dark Night,* pp. 169, 136, 127.

70. McCarthy quoted in Vogelgesang, *Long Dark Night,* p. 125. In McCarthy's defense, she was always acerbic and never let ideology dull her sense of right and wrong, or else she would not have called Lillian Hellman a liar and gone to court over it. See Michiko Kakutani, "Our Woman of Letters," *New York Times Magazine,* March 29, 1987 for a glowing pocket biography. For a review of Hellman's pathology of lying, see Hilton Kramer, "The Life and Death of Lillan Hellman," *The New Criterion* 3,2 (October 1984): 1-6.

71. See Tzvetan Todorov, "Stalled Thinkers," *The New Republic,* April 13, 1987, p. 26.

72. No one was more self-obsessed than Noam Chomsky. See his "The Responsibility of the Intellectuals," *New York Review of Books,* February 23, 1967 and *American Power and the New Mandarins* (New York: Random House, 1969).

73. It was no surprise, incidentally, that Thoreau's writings became widely available in the 1960s. I have a dog-eared paperback called *Essays on The Duty of Civil Disobedience and Walden* (New York: Lancer, 1968).

74. Goodman quoted in Vogelgesang, *Long Dark Night,* pp. 136-37.

75. Theodore Roszak, "The Disease Called Politics," in Paul Goodman, ed., *Seeds of Liberation* (New York: Braziller, 1965), p. 450. Whatever one thinks of his views, Roszak was the most creative thinker in the literary/academic Left of the time.

76. The implied notion that blacks and Vietnamese were somehow racially alike did not survive black-Asian encounters in American cities in the 1970s and 1980s.

77. Much less noted was Cleaver's *Soul on Fire* (Waco, TX: Word Books, 1978), written after Cleaver had returned a changed man from exile in Algeria and elsewhere.

78. Ralph Ellison, *Invisible Man* (New York: Random House, 1972).

79. Lynd quoted in Isserman, "You Don't Need a Weatherman . . . ," in Small and Hoover, eds., *Give Peace a Chance.*

80. See the recent biography of Newton by Hugh Pearson, *The Shadow of the Panther* (New York: Addison-Wesley, 1994), which is not very flattering to the Panthers or Newton. The book underplays the role of white radicals in the Panthers' rise.

81. Hayden quoted in Nigel Young, *An Infantile Disorder? The Crisis and Decline of the New Left* (Boulder, CO: Westview, 1977), p. 455.

82. Franz Fanón, *Wretched of the Earth* (New York: Grove Press, 1968).

83. Eldridge Cleaver quoted in quoted in Young, *An Infantile Disorder?* p. 260.

84. Epton quoted in Young, *An Infantile Disorder?* p. 261.

85. Carmichael quoted in ibid., pp. 262, 283.

86. This description is based on O'Neill, *Coming Apart,* pp. 288-89.

87. Goodman quoted in ibid., p. 295. See also Renata Adler, "Letter From Palmer House," *The New Yorker,* September 23, 1967, pp. 56-88, reprinted in William P. Greenberg and Duane E. Smith, eds., *The Radical Left: The Abuse of Discontent* (Boston: Houghton Mifflin, 1970), pp. 31-53.

88. Quoted in Zaroulis and Sullivan, *Who Spoke Up?* p. 128. See also Isserman, "You Don't Need a Weatherman . . . ," in Small and Hoover, eds., *Give Peace a Chance,* pp. 32-33.

89. Mark Rudd, "University in Revolt," in Jerry Avorn, *Up Against the Ivy Wall* (New York: Atheneum, 1968), p. 33.

90. Some observers fix the origins of the Weathermen in Stop the Draft Week, especially as enacted in Oakland, California. See Young, *An Infantile Disorder?* p. 276.

---

## Chapter 5

1. Burlage quoted in Todd Gitlin, "Reflections on 1968," *Dissent* (Fall 1993): p. 487.

2. It was new to the American scene, but Irving Louis Horowitz saw several similarities between New Left radicalism of the 1960s and *fin de siècle* French Leftism. See the introduction to the second edition of *Radicalism and the Revolt Against Reason* (Carbondale, IL: Southern Illinois University Press, 1968), pp. v-xviii.

3. These red diaper babies showed up in unexpected places. Take Country Joe McDonald: His mother was Florence Plotnick, child of Russian Jewish immigrants. Her mother was a Communist, her father an anarchist Zionist. Florence joined the Young Communist League at the age of 12 and had been arrested 24 times by the age of 18. This is the woman on whose lap sat "Country Joe." See "Florence McDonald, 73, Berkeley Radical," *New York Times,* July 1, 1989, p. A10. Another example is Sally Belfrage, a civil rights activist whose father, she said later, "was a Red and so in trouble all of the time." Eric Pace, "Sally Belfrage Dies; Writer Specializing in Memoirs Was 57," *New York Times,* March 15, 1994.

4. The literature on the New Left is extensive but scholarly and dispassionate approaches are uncommon. The first account, written before the New Left exhibited its worst features, is Jack Newfield, *A Prophetic Minority* (New York: New American Library, 1966). Two of the best are Nigel Young's *An Infantile Disorder?* and Irving Louis Horowitz's *The Struggle Is the Message.* Others not already mentioned include Wini Breins, *The Great Refusal: Community and Organization in the New Left: 1962-1969* (New York: Praeger, 1982); Milton Cantor, *The Divided Left* (New York: Hill and Wang, 1978); Edward J. Bacciocco, Jr., *The New Left in America: Reform to Revolution, 1950-1970* (Stanford, CA: Hoover Institution, 1974); James Weinstein, *Ambiguous Legacy: The Left in American Politics* (New York: New Viewpoints, 1975); William J. McGill, *The Year of the Monkey: Revolt on Campus, 1968-69* (New York: McGraw-Hill, 1982); and Irwin Unger, *The Movement.* For contemporary or near contemporary works, see James Simon Kunen, *The Strawberry Statement: Notes of A College Revolutionary* (New York: Avon, 1970); Michael Cohen and Dennis Hale, eds., *The New Student Left;* Alan Adelson, *SDS* (New York: Scribners, 1972); M. Miles, *The Radical Probe:*

*The Logic of Student Rebellion* (New York: Atheneum, 1971); and Kirkpatrick Sale, *SDS*. An extensive bibliography of empirical work as of 1970 can be found in the special issue, "Student Protest," *Annals of the American Academy of Political and Social Science* (May 1971).

5. For another typology differentiating New and old Left, see Young, *An Infantile Disorder?* p. 310. Mueller argued that "the 'new Left' of the late 1960s seems . . . to be the old Left with new methods of expression, a new vocabulary." *War, Presidents, and Public Opinion*, p. 158. While an excellent analyst of public opinion, on this point Mueller was wrong.

6. For a striking example of the degeneration of expression, see Eldridge Cleaver's introduction to Jerry Rubin, *Do It! Scenarios of the Revolution* (New York: Simon & Schuster, 1970), pp. 6-11.

7. Berman, "Fog of Political Correctness," p. 54.

8. R. D. Laing, *The Politics of Experience* (New York: Pantheon, 1967).

9. David Cooper, "Beyond Words," in his *To Free a Generation*, p. 201.

10. Raymond Mungo, *Famous Long Ago: My Life and Hard Times with the Liberation News Service* (New York: Pocket Books, 1971), p. 5. See also Abe Peck, *Uncovering the Sixties: The Life and Times of the Underground Press* (New York: Pantheon, 1985).

11. Rubin, *Do It!* p. 113.

12. Robbins, *Still Life with Woodpecker*, pp. 85-86.

13. Kim McQuaid, *The Anxious Years: America in the Vietnam-Watergate Era* (New York: Basic Books, 1989), p. 163.

14. Assar Lindbeck, *The Political Economy of the New Left: An Outsider's View* (New York: Harper & Row, 1971), pp. 36-37.

15. Stephen Eric Bonner, *Moments of Decision: Political History and the Crisis of Radicalism* (New York: Routledge, 1992), p. 110.

16. See Stanley Rothman and S. Robert Lichter, *Roots of Radicalism: Jews, Christians and the New Left* (New York: Oxford University Press, 1982).

17. Breaking with parents was a "bridge-burning" experience said by some to be a prerequisite to membership in a social transformation movement. See Luther Gerlich and Virginia Hine, *People, Power, Change: Movements of Social Transformation* (Indianapolis: Bobbs-Merrill Company, 1979).

18. An extreme example is that of Silas Bissell. See Wallace Turner, "Tip Leads to Arrest of Radical Sought in 1970 Case," *New York Times*, January 22, 1987.

19. Of course, virtually all American protest movements have an upper-middle class center of gravity. Reliable data on the particulars of this phenomenon are virtually non-existent.

20. "Marxoid" refers to someone who has absorbed the general categories of Marxist thinking (class struggle, imperialism, exploitation of labor) but has never actually studied Marxism or thought critically about it.

21. See David J. Horowitz, "Nicaragua: A Speech to My Former Colleagues on the Left," *Commentary* (June 1986), and Steve Wasserman, "Cuba and the Panacea of Revolution," *Tikkun* 2,2 (March/April 1987), pp. 99-103.

22. I refer to Fanón's *The Wretched of the Earth* and Debray's *Revolution in the Revolution.* (New York: MR Press, 1967). A good description of the New Left canon is found in Jeffrey Herf, "The New Left and Its Fading Aura," *Partisan Review* 53,2 (Spring 1986): 243.

23. Mario Savio, "An End to History," in Stolz, ed., *Politics of the New Left*, pp. 130-34. A note for the curious: Frank Fukuyama's 1992 book on "the end of history" does not mention Savio. A further note: In this way at least, New Left views were akin to Burkean conservativism, so much so that they sound like Herbert Hoover's warnings against the power of bureaucracy in the 1920s.

24. The words of the German Communist Willi Muezenberg. See R. N. Carew Hunt, "Willi Muezenberg," in David Footman, ed., *International Communism*, St. Anthony's Paper, no. 9 (Carbondale: Southern Illinois University, 1960), p. 87, cited in Guenter Lewy, "Does America Need a *Verfassungsschutzbericht?*" *Orbis* (Fall 1987): 278.

25. Erich Fromm, *The Philosophy of Hope: Toward a Humanized Technology* (New York: Harper & Row, 1968), p. 8.

26. Hayden quoted in Levy, "The New Left, Labor, and the Vietnam War," p. 65.

27. See H. Hahn, "Dove Sentiments among Blue-collar Workers," *Dissent* (May/June 1970): 202-5, and Levy, "The New Left, Labor, and the Vietnam War," pp. 46-69, and the many contemporary citations therein.

28. Hahn, "Dove Sentiments among Blue-collar Workers," p. 62.
29. Eric Hoffer, *The Temper of Our Time* (New York: Harper & Row, 1966).
30. Charles P. Larrowe, *Harry Bridges: The Rise and Fall of Radical Labor in the United States* (New York: Lawrence Hill, 1987), especially pp. 376-78.
31. Personal communication from Eugene Genovese, letter dated March 2, 1987.
32. Ibid.
33. From *The Road to Wigan Pier,* quoted by Charles Krauthammer in "Stretch Marx," *The New Republic,* August 16-23, 1982; also in Krauthammer's *Cutting Edges* (New York: Random House, 1985), p. 48.
34. Robbins, *Still Life with Woodpecker,* p. 151.
35. Ibid., p. 151.
36. Christopher Lasch, *The Agony of the Left* (New York: Knopf, 1968), p. 180. Another early recognition of this trait is Horowitz, *Radicalism and the Revolt Against Reason,* pp. v-vi, and see Nicholas von Hoffman, *We Are the People Our Parents Warned Us Against* (Chicago: Quadrangle, 1968).
37. Flacks quoted in Alan Brinkley, "Dreams of the Sixties," *New York Review of Books,* October 22, 1987, p. 16.
38. Thomas Wolfe, *Radical Chic and Mau Mau-ing the Flak Catchers* (New York: Farrar, Straus & Giroux, 1970).
39. Here see Lionel Trilling, *Sincerity and Authenticity* (Cambridge, MA: Harvard University Press, 1972), and Marshall Berman, *The Politics of Authenticity* (New York: Atheneum, 1970). This goes on still; see Henry S. Kariel's critique *The Desperate Politics of Postmodernism* (Amherst: University of Massachusetts Press, 1992).
40. A point made by Allan Bloom in *The Closing of the American Mind* (New York: Simon & Schuster, 1987), p. 155.
41. Brinkley, "Dreams of the Sixties," p. 16.
42. Michael S. Kimmel, "The Sixties without Metaphor," *Society* 26,3 (March/April 1989): 80.
43. Here see S. R. Turkle, "Symbol and Festival in the French Student Uprising," in Sally Falk Moore and Barbara Meyerhoff, eds., *Symbol and Politics in Communal Ideology: Cases in Question* (Ithaca, NY: Cornell University Press, 1975).
44. Pointed out in Lasky, "The Ideas of '68," p. 7, who cites Raymond Aron, *Le Révolution Introuvable* (Paris: Fayard, 1968).
45. Robert Nisbet, *Prejudices: A Philosophical Dictionary* (Cambridge, MA: Harvard University Press, 1983), p. 6.
46. See Kim Solomon, "The Peace Movement: An Anti-Establishment Movement," *Journal of Peace Research* 23,2 (June 1986).
47. See generally Peter L. Berger, *The Sacred Canopy* (New York: Doubleday-Anchor, 1969).
48. Social psychologists have studied such phenomena. See the classical experiments by Solomon Asch, "Effects of Group Pressures in the Modification and Position of Judgments," in Harold Guetzkow, ed., *Groups, Leadership and Man* (Pittsburgh: Carnegie Press, 1951), and Irving Janis, *Victims of Groupthink* (Boston: Houghton-Mifflin, 1967).
49. Herf, "Reliving the Sixties," p. 246.
50. Schlesinger quoted in William H. Honan, "Schlesinger Sees Free Speech in Peril," *New York Times,* May 27, 1994.
51. Genovese, "The Question," p. 375.
52. Quoted in Lasky, "The Ideas of '68," p. 4.
53. Zaroulis and Sullivan, *Who Spoke Up?* p. 79.
54. The social criticism of the 1950s, itself radicalized by the late 1960s, made this one of its standards. Paul Goodman, Jules Henry, R. D. Laing, Herbert Marcuse, and many others plied this theme as, for example, in Jules Henry, *Culture Against Man* (New York: Vintage, 1963).
55. See Califano, *The Student Revolution,* p. 44.
56. Again the music is relevant: David Crosby's song "Triad," the last recording he made with the Byrds, and popularized by the Jefferson Airplane, is about a man asking his two girlfriends why they can't "go on as three."
57. Gitlin, *The Sixties,* p. 372.
58. See Arthur Waskow, "The Meaning of Creative Disorder," in *From Race Riot to Sit-in* (New York: Doubleday, 1966), pp. 276-90.

59. See Anne Field, "Harassment on Campus: Sex in a Tenured Position," *Ms.* (September 1981).

60. Malachi 3:24.

61. See Aristotle, *Rhetoric,* tr. W. R. Roberts (New York: Modern Library, 1955), pp. 123-24, and *Plato's Epistles,* tr. G. R. Morrow (Indianapolis: Bobbs-Merrill, 1962), p. 220.

62. See Charles Morris, *A Time of Passion* (New York: Harper & Row, 1984).

63. Sam Brown, "The Legacy of Choices," in Grace Sevy, ed., *The American Experience in Vietnam: A Reader* (Norman: University of Oklahoma Press, 1989), p. 199.

64. P. J. O'Rourke, "What Went Wrong?" *Wilson Quarterly* (Autumn 1988): 163.

65. See Powers, *The War at Home,* chap. 3, and Morris, *A Time of Passion,* pp. 48-69.

66. See especially Philip Reiff, *The Triumph of the Therapeutic: The Uses of Faith After Freud* (New York: Harper & Row, 1966).

67. Morris, *A Time of Passion,* pp. 96-98. Morris is literally an amateur; he makes his living in the business world, not in academia. That does not make him less an interesting or insightful writer.

68. Dewey was anti-1960s because he championed notions of social reform that smacked of behaviorism and condoned the use of force to make minorities accept majority choices. On the other hand, he saw democracy as an absolute value, leading Robert B. Westbrook to say that Dewey's ideas echo resoundingly in the Port Huron statement, and that he is most relevant precisely for the American generation that stopped reading him. Robert B. Westbrook, *John Dewey and American Democracy* (Ithaca, NY: Cornell University Press, 1992).

69. See President Kennedy's Yale University commencement speech, June 11, 1962, printed in the *New York Times,* June 12, 1962, p. 20. Many became familiar with these remarks because they were quoted prominently in Roszak's *The Making of a Counter Culture,* p. 11. Daniel Bell's *The End of Ideology* (Cambridge, MA: Harvard University Press) was first published in 1960.

70. James Burnham, *Suicide of the West* (New York: John Day, 1964), p. 11.

71. Several analyses of the 1960s stress the poor health of American liberalism. See Allen J. Matusow, *The Unravelling of America* (New York: Harper & Row, 1984) and Godfrey Hodgson, *America in Our Time: From World War II to Nixon—What Happened and Why* (Garden City, NY: Doubleday, 1976).

72. See Randolph S. Bourne, *War and the Intellectuals, Collected Essays 1915-1919* (New York: Harper & Row, 1964).

73. See Norman O. Brown, *Life Against Death* (Middletown, CT: Wesleyan University Press, 1959).

74. One observer considers Bourne a prophet of sorts. See Bruce Clayton, *Forgotten Prophet: The Life of Randolph Bourne* (Baton Rouge: Louisiana State University Press, 1984). See also the essays by Edgar Z. Friedenberg, Lewis Mumford, Murray Bookchin, Seymour Melman, Ira Einhorn, Nat Hentoff, and Seymour Martin Lipset, in Charles A. Thrall and Jerold M. Starr, eds., *Technology, Power, and Social Change* (Carbondale: Southern Illinois University Press, 1972). A recent book that sketches many of the main personalities of the period is Andrew Jamison and Ron Eyerman, *Seeds of the Sixties* (Berkeley, CA: University of California Press, 1994).

75. Julien Freund, *The Sociology of Max Weber* (New York: Pantheon, 1969), p. 24.

76. Isaiah Berlin, "The Bent Twig," *Foreign Affairs* 51,1 (October 1972): 26-28.

77. See Henry Fairlie, "War Against Reason," *The New Republic,* November 6, 1989.

78. Ibid., p. 61.

79. Nisbet, "War, Crisis and Intellectuals," *Wall Street Journal,* January 25, 1971. Nisbet is a conservative, but the radical critique of the 1960s shared the conservative opposition to managerialism. This pointed to the anti-authoritarian, anti-statist, and proto-anarchist side of 1960s radicalism. See also Loren Baritz, *Backfire: A History of How American Culture Led Us Into Vietnam and Made Us Fight the Way We Did* (New York: Morrow, 1985).

80. Patrick Lloyd Hacker, *Suicide of an Elite: American Internationalists and Vietnam* (Stanford: Stanford University Press, 1990), p. viii. While the point is strong, I do not think this made the war unwinnable in the sense explained in chap. 1.

81. See Liah Greenfeld, "Transcending the Nation's Worth," *Daedelus* 122,3 (Summer 1993): 54-55.

82. Some have argued, amazingly, that antiwar protest was centered at the best universities because that was "where students had the most knowledge and understanding of American history." Gold, "Look at Vietnam Generation Now."

83. Morris, *A Time of Passion,* p. 88.

84. Morris Dickstein, *Gates of Eden* (New York: Basic Books, 1977).
85. Morris, *A Time of Passion*, p. 133.
86. Ibid., p. 136.
87. See Richard John Neuhaus, "The War, the Churches, and Civil Religion," *Annals of the American Academy of Political and Social Science* 387 (January 1970): 139-40.
88. Michael Walzer, *The Revolution of the Saints* (Cambridge, MA: Harvard University Press, 1965), p. 317.
89. Rothman and Lichter, *Roots of Radicalism*.
90. Gitlin says as much in *The Sixties*, p. 107.
91. See the pop psychological portrait of Hayden by Craig Unger, "Tom Hayden's Original Sin: Looking for Absolution in All the Wrong Places," *Esquire* (June 1989).
92. Louis Feuer, *The Conflict of Generations: The Character and Significance of Student Movements* (New York: Basic Books, 1969).
93. Ibid., p. 529.
94. Lasky, "The Ideas of '68," p. 13.
95. Feuer, *The Conflict of Generations*, pp. 8, 10, 480, and 528-29 most vividly.
96. On premature aging see David Gutmann, "The New Mythologies and Premature Aging in the Youth Culture," *Social Research* 40,2 (Summer 1973): 248-68.
97. Suzanne Berger, "Politics and Antipolitics in Western Europe," *Daedelus* 108,1 (Winter 1979): 32.
98. Horowitz, *Radicalism and the Revolt Against Reason*, p. vi.
99. S. N. Eisenstadt, "Generational Conflict and Intellectual Antinomianism," *Annals of the American Academy of Political and Social Science* 395 (May 1971). See also Edward Shils, "Totalitarians and Antinomians," in Bunzel, ed., *Political Passages*, pp. 1-31, and Eisenstadt's *From Generation to Generation* (New York: Free Press, 1956).
100. Eisenstadt, "Generational Conflict and Intellectual Antinomianism," p. 74.
101. See Reiff and Christopher Lasch, *The Culture of Narcissism* (New York: W. W. Norton, 1979).
102. Note also Midge Decter, *Liberal Parents, Radical Children* (New York: Coward, McCann and Geoghegan, 1975).
103. See David Gutmann, "The Subjective Politics of Power: The Dilemma of Postsuperego Man," *Social Research* 40,4 (Winter 1973).
104. Ibid., p. 571.
105. Ibid., pp. 603-4. For discussions of morality and the early stages of the socialization process, see Jerome Kagan and Sharon Lamb, eds., *The Emergence of Morality in Young Children* (Chicago: University of Chicago Press, 1987).
106. Gutmann, "The Subjective Politics of Power," p. 604. Breakdown in the socialization process is also behind Robert S. Laufer's views in "Sources of Generational Consciousness and Conflict," *Annals of the American Academy of Political and Social Science,* (May 1971): 80-94. Also see Shils, "Dreams of Plentitude, Nightmares of Scarcity," pp. 1-35, and especially Thomas Molnar, *Authority and Its Enemies* (New Rochelle, NY: Arlington House, 1976), chap. 3.
107. Feuer, *Conflict of Generations*, p. 480.
108. See Rothman and Lichter, *Roots of Radicalism*; Arthur Liebman, *Jews and the Left* (New York: John Wiley, 1979); and Mueller, *Wars, Presidents, and Public Opinion*, pp. 166-67.
109. Abbie Hoffman, *Soon to be a Major Motion Picture* (New York: G.P. Putnam and Sons, 1980), pp. 15-16. This theme is elaborated in Hoffman and Simon, *Run, Run, Run: The Lives of Abbie Hoffman*.
110. Gutmann, "Subjective Politics of Power," pp. 602-3.
111. A similar analysis has been applied to the collapse of the Soviet Union, where the attempt to sacralize the profane failed miserably, destroying community and social bonds both. See Ernest Gellner, "Homeland of the Unrevolution," *Daedelus* 122,3 (Summer 1993): 146-47.
112. Califano, *The Student Revolution*, p. 45.
113. Gutmann, "Subjective Politics of Power," p. 602.
114. Quoted in Farber, "Counterculture and the Antiwar Movement," in Small and Hoover, eds., *Give Peace a Chance*, p. 9.
115. Quoted in Howard Goodman, "Echoes of Abbie," *Philadelphia Inquirer,* November 17, 1994, p. G3.
116. On the comedic side to the Yippies, see Joseph R. Urgo, "Comedic Impulses and Society Propriety: The Yippie Carnival," *Studies in Popular Culture* 10,1 (1987).

117. Paul Krassner, "Abbie," p. 616.

118. Ibid. Krassner is still at it; see his account of taking LSD before appearing as a witness in the Chicago Seven trial: "Disorder in Judge Hoffman's Court," *The Nation,* October 11, 1993, pp. 389-91. The article is an excerpt from the then forthcoming *Confessions of a Raving, Unconfined Nut: Misadventures in the Counterculture* (New York: Simon & Schuster, 1994.)

119. Horowitz, *Radicalism and the Revolt Against Reason,* p. vi. The reference to Jacob Talmon is to his *The Origins of Totalitarian Democracy* (London: Secker & Warburg, 1952).

120. Ronald Fraser, ed., *1968: A Student Generation in Revolt* (New York: Pantheon, 1969), p. 74.

121. Some still intone praises to Woodstock. See Steven Doloff, "Woodstock's Message Is Still True," *Philadelphia Inquirer,* August 8, 1991, p. 27-A.

122. Menard, "Life in the Stone Age," p. 38, and see Daniel Bell, "A Search for the Sacred," in *The Winding Passage* (Cambridge, MA: Abt Books, 1980).

123. Walzer, *The Revolution of the Saints,* p. 318.

124. For example Richard Rubenstein, *After Auschwitz* (Indianapolis: Bobbs-Merrill, 1966), pp. 151-52.

125. For a radical's appreciation of Lennon, see Jon Wiener, *Come Together: John Lennon in His Times* (New York: Random House, 1984).

126. Laura Nyro, *Christmas and the Beads of Sweat,* Columbia KC30259, 1970.

## Chapter 6

1. Farber, "The Counterculture and the Antiwar Movement," p. 16.

2. Powers chronicled this evolution well; see *The War at Home,* pp. 186-95.

3. See Zaroulis and Sullivan, *Who Spoke Up?* pp. 139-40.

4. David Dellinger's account of this is found in his book *More Power Than We Know: The People's Movement Toward Democracy* (New York: Doubleday, 1975).

5. Quoted in Zaroulis and Sullivan, *Who Spoke Up?* pp. 136-37.

6. Walter Cronkite did not explicitly oppose the war until after the Tet offensive: the February 27, 1968 CBS evening news to be exact. But his tone had changed before that. The role of celebrities in the antiwar movement deserves a volume unto itself. For one essay that wants to bless the heroine but cannot help damning her, see Jeanne Zeidler, "Speaking Out, Selling Out, Working Out: The Changing Politics of Jane Fonda," in Edward Crapol, ed., *Women and American Foreign Policy: Lobbyists, Critics, and Insiders* (Westport, CT: Greenwood Press, 1987), pp. 119-36.

7. Brown, "The Defeat of the Antiwar Movement," p. 124.

8. The origins of Tet seem to have much to do with an argument between pro-Soviet and pro-Chinese factions with the North Vietnamese Politburo and military staff. North Vietnam's Russian advisors, through whom it was getting most of its military supplies, counselled against such an uprising, judging it premature and tactically unsound. The Chinese advisors were for it, and they eventually won out.

9. The North Vietnamese, and even General Giap himself, have admitted this. See Keith B. Richburg, "Historians From U.S., Vietnam Confer on War," *Washington Post,* December 11, 1988, p. 27; and Stanley Karnow, "Giap Remembers," *New York Times Magazine,* June 24, 1990.

10. See Stanley Karnow, *Vietnam: A History* (New York: Viking, 1983), p. 542; better, see Eddie Adams's own account in Kim Willenson, *The Bad War: An Oral History of the Vietnam War* (New York: New American Library, 1987), pp. 185-86.

11. Even humorists took failure for granted. See Art Buchwald, "'We Have the Enemy on the Run' Says Gen. Custer at Big Horn," *Washington Post,* February 6, 1968.

12. This point has been made often but never more succinctly or authoritatively than in Clifford, *Counsel to the President,* p. 474.

13. See Clifford's influential account of this episode, "A Viet Nam Reappraisal: The Personal History of One Man's View and How It Evolved," *Foreign Affairs* 47,4 (July 1969).

14. The San Antonio Formula amounted to an indirect negotiation in which the United States stated publicly its conditions for halting the bombing of North Vietnam, and then decided for itself if

the North Vietnamese met those conditions. The best accounts of Clifford's policy review and Warnke's role in it are Schandler, *Lyndon Johnson and Vietnam* and Larry Berman, *Lyndon Johnson's War* (New York: W. W. Norton, 1989). See also Barrett, *Uncertain Warriors* and Townsend Hoopes, "The Fight for the President's Mind—and the Men Who Won It," *The Atlantic Monthly* (October 1969). Hoopes was himself involved in the decision-making process.

15. Schandler, *Lyndon Johnson and Vietnam*, p. 258.
16. Ibid., p. 261.
17. Lyndon Baines Johnson, *The Vantage Point* (New York: Holt, Rinehart and Winston, 1971), p. 418.
18. Vance quoted in Berman, *Lyndon Johnson's War*, p. 197.
19. Daniel C. Hallin, *The Uncensored War: The Media and Vietnam* (New York: Oxford University Press, 1986), pp. 169-70.
20. Johnson, *The Vantage Point*, pp. 408-9.
21. See Bruce Andrews, "Public Constraint and American Policy in Vietnam," *International Studies Series*, Sage Publications, Series 02-042, 4 (May 1976).
22. Mueller, *War, Presidents, and Public Opinion*, p. 106.
23. Much has been written about the 1969 McCarthy presidential campaign. See McCarthy's *The Year of the People* (Garden City, NY: Doubleday, 1969); Ben Stavis, *We Were the Campaign: New Hampshire to Chicago for McCarthy* (Boston: Beacon, 1970); and Jeremy Larner, *Nobody Knows: Reflections on the McCarthy Campaign of 1968* (New York: Macmillan, 1978).
24. See George Gallup, "Public Opinion and the Vietnam War," *Gallup Opinion Index*, Report 52 (October 1969): 9-11.
25. Small and Hoover in "Preface," Small and Hoover, eds., *Give Peace a Chance*, p. xv. My emphasis.
26. It cannot be proven for methodological reasons. First, the transcripts of the crucial meetings are only partial and their reliability is unknown. More generally, most of the Wise Men are dead and several left no papers or memoirs. Even talking to those yet alive is problematic, for memory is not always reliable a quarter of a century after the fact. The same problem attends memoirs.
27. See, for example, Carl Oglesby, "An Open Letter to McCarthy Supporters," in Stolz, *Politics of the New Left*, pp. 74-81.
28. The expansive moods of that year were not limited to the United States; what happened in Paris and in Germany had similar festive-escapist features. See Bernard Brown, *Protest in Paris: Anatomy of a Revolt* (Morristown, NJ: General Learning, 1974).
29. Dellinger quoted in Zaroulis and Sullivan, *Who Spoke Up?* p. 139.
30. Farber, "Counterculture and the Antiwar Movement," p. 17.
31. Hoffman quoted in ibid., p. 17.
32. Much has been written about what happened in Chicago. For accounts of various sorts and levels of detail, see the relevant sections of Zaroulis and Sullivan, *Who Spoke Up?*; Gitlin, *The Sixties*; Fraser, ed., *1968*; Irwin and Debi Unger, *Turning Point, 1968* (New York: Scribner's, 1989); and David Farber, *Chicago '68* (Chicago: University of Chicago Press, 1988).
33. Hayden quoted in Farber, *Chicago '68*, p. 114. The "politics of joy" was a reference to Hubert Humphrey's main campaign slogan.
34. Krassner, "Jerry Rubin," p. 749.
35. Paul Goodman, *Growing Up Absurd* (New York: Vintage, 1960).
36. Goodman quoted in O'Neill, *Coming Apart*, p. 257. O'Neill does not identify the original source.
37. Gitlin, *The Sixties*, p. 239. See also "Affinity Group: A Street Gang with an Analysis," Motherfucker leaflet, 1968, reprinted in Peter Stansill and David Zane Mairowitz, eds., *BAMN (By Any Means Necessary): Outlaw Manifestos and Ephemera* (Hammondsworth, UK: Penguin, 1971).
38. Quoted in Farber, "Counterculture and the Antiwar Movement, p. 19. The Motherfuckers, or some evolved subgroup of them, made quite a scene at Woodstock, too. Having no money, they threatened to "liberate" all the food concession stands to distribute the food "to the needy." Violence ensued and, in the end, 12 stands of Jeffrey Joerger's Food for Love group were burned to the ground. For this and other tales of Woodstock, see Robert Steven Spitz, *Barefoot in Babylon: The Creation of the Woodstock Music Festival, 1969* (New York: Viking, 1979).
39. See O'Neill, *Coming Apart*, p. 292.
40. Robbins, *Still Life with Woodpecker*, p. 86.

41. See David Halberstam, "McCarthy and the Divided Left," *Harper's* (March 1968): 32-44, and Walter Goodman, "Liberals vs. Radicals—War in the Peace Camp," *New York Times Magazine,* December 3, 1967, p. 48. There is, by the by, an uncanny similarity between Goodman's analysis of problems in a leftist movement and David Lindorff's "War in Peace," *The Village Voice,* April 20, 1982, about the chaos in the nuclear-freeze movement some 16 years later.

42. See here William O'Rourke, *The Harrisburg Seven and the New Catholic Left* (New York: Crowell, 1972); and Daniel Berrigan, *The Trial of the Catonsville Nine* (Boston: Beacon, 1970).

43. Gitlin, *The Sixties,* p. 335. My emphasis.

44. For some details on SANE and Allard Lowenstein's role here, see Katz, *Ban the Bomb,* pp. 108-11. Wittner ascribes to Lowenstein and to Dr. King a more active role in persuading Senator McCarthy to run for president; *Rebels Against War,* p. 288. For Senator McCarthy's somewhat surprising retrospective evaluation of the affair, see his *Up 'Til Now* (San Diego: Harcourt Brace Jovanovich, 1987). McCarthy rued much of what his 1968 followers did to the Democratic Party once they got hold of it.

45. Dohrn quoted in David Caute, *The Year of the Barricades: A Journey Through 1968* (New York: Harper & Row, 1988), p. 443.

46. Manson quoted in Michael Andre Bernstein, "Murder and the Utopian Moment," *American Scholar* (Spring 1992): 213.

47. See Murray Bookchin's "Listen Marxist" in his *Post-Scarcity Anarchism* (San Francisco: Ramparts Press, 1971), pp. 171-220.

48. Oglesby quoted in Sale, *SDS,* p. 237.

49. See Frederick D. Miller, "The End of SDS and the Emergence of the Weathermen," in Jo Freeman, ed., *Social Movements of the Sixties and Seventies* (New York: Longman, 1983).

50. The most detailed account of the New Left as an organizational/ideological phenomenon is Young, *An Infantile Disorder?* Young wrote nearly 500 pages just on this topic, with more than 80 pages of notes and references.

51. Gitlin, *The Sixties,* p. 381. See also Dotson Rader, "The Day the Movement Died," *Esquire* (June 1983): 304-20.

52. Rubin quoted in David Lewis Stein, *Living the Revolution: The Yippies in Chicago* (Indianapolis: Bobbs-Merrill, 1969), p. 5.

53. Jerry Rubin, *Growing Up (at 37)* (New York: M. Evans and Company, 1976), p. 79. On Rubin, see also Anthony Lukas, *Don't Shoot: We Are Your Children* (New York: Dell, 1972), pp. 323-69.

54. Califano saw this early on; see *The Student Revolution,* p. 43.

55. David Horowitz, "Revolutionary Kharma versus Revolutionary Politics," *Ramparts* 9,8 (March 1971): 27-29, 33.

56. See Andrew J. Glass, "Defense Report/Draftees Shoulder Burden of Fighting and Dying in Vietnam," *National Journal* 2,33 (August 15, 1970): 1747-55.

57. Stephen Stills, as a member of the Buffalo Springfield, had made hits of vaguely political songs, notably "For What It's Worth." A complete list of the acts at Woodstock can be found in Spitz, *Barefoot in Babylon,* pp. xvii-xviii.

58. Jessica Mitford, *The Trial of Doctor Spock* (New York: Vintage, 1970), p. xi.

59. See Rennie Davis, "Facing Up to Repression," *Liberation* (June 1969).

60. Dellinger quoted in Zaroulis and Sullivan, *Who Spoke Up?* p. 255.

61. Details can be culled from Cummings, *The Pied Piper*; Steven M. Gillon, *Politics and Vision: The ADA and American Liberalism, 1947-1985* (New York: Oxford University Press, 1987); David Harris, *Dreams Die Hard: Three Men's Journey Through the Sixties* (New York: St. Martin's, 1982); Gregory Stone and Douglas Lowenstein, eds., *Lowenstein: Acts of Courage and Belief* (New York: Harcourt Brace Jovanovich, 1983); and Paul Hoffman, *Moratorium: An American Protest* (New York: Tower, 1970).

62. Lowenstein was murdered on March 15, 1980 by Dennis Sweeney, a former protégé turned radical. In a way, Sweeney's killing of Lowenstein works as a perfect metaphor for what the radical section of the antiwar movement did to the liberal section between 1966 and 1968.

63. Zaroulis and Sullivan, *Who Spoke Up?* p. 247.

64. Not, of course, withdrawal on any terms. A 1971 poll found that only 11 percent favored withdrawal if it jeopardized the safety of U.S. prisoners of war in North Vietnam. But then, the

POW issue was extremely emotional and the wording of polling questions, as always, was very fungible.

65. Relevant major Gallup polls were taken on December 18, 1966, September 3, 1967, and November 26, 1972.

66. Godfrey Hodgson, *America in Our Time*, p. 393.

67. Some argue that Johnson intended only to change tactics, but the simultaneous announcement that the bombing would stop, that negotiations would start, and that he was stepping down could not but give a starker impression.

68. In *War, Presidents, and Public Opinion*, pp. 116-21, Mueller emphasizes the "partisan" mentality, those who take their cue from the position of the political party with which they identify.

69. *New York Times*, October 5, 1969.

70. Lens quoted in Zaroulis and Sullivan, *Who Spoke Up?* p. 265.

71. Zaroulis and Sullivan, *Who Spoke Up?* p. 258; and for colorful detail on this meeting, see Wells, *The War Within*, pp. 332-34.

72. Zaroulis and Sullivan, *Who Spoke Up?* p. 261.

73. Rudd quoted in Caute, *Year of the Barricades*, p. 443.

74. Recorded in part on *Earl Scruggs, Family and Friends*, Columbia C30584, 1970.

75. Brown quoted in Zaroulis and Sullivan, *Who Spoke Up?* pp. 278-79.

76. See generally William Sloane Coffin, *Once to Every Man: A Memoir* (New York: Atheneum, 1977), and Lynn Z. Bloom, *Doctor Spock: Biography of a Conservative Radical* (Indianapolis: Bobbs-Merrill, 1972).

77. So reported Berkowitz, "Impact of Anti-Vietnam War Demonstrations Upon National Public Opinion and Military Indicators."

78. Sam Brown, "The Politics of Peace," *Washington Monthly* 2,6 (August 1970).

## Chapter 7

1. *Quotations from Chairman LBJ*, p. 28.

2. A recent account bearing a similar conclusion is Joan Hoff, *Nixon Reconsidered* (New York: Basic Books, 1994).

3. See H. R. Haldeman, *The Haldeman Diaries: Inside the Nixon White House* (New York: Putnam, 1994).

4. Jacobs quoted in Zaroulis and Sullivan, *Who Spoke Up?* p. 262.

5. On hippies and religion see O'Neill, *Coming Apart*, pp. 254-58.

6. David Dellinger, "April 15: Telling off the Taxman," *WIN* 6 (May 15, 1970): 24.

7. Zaroulis and Sullivan, *Who Spoke Up?* p. 296.

8. See Neil Sheehan et al., *The Pentagon Papers* (New York: Bantam, 1970), pp. 44, 330.

9. Zaroulis and Sullivan, *Who Spoke Up?* p. 299.

10. Ibid., p. 299.

11. On Crosby, Stills, Nash and Young, *Four Way Street*, Atlantic SD 2-902, 1971.

12. Nixon was haunted by the deaths at Kent State too. That night he made or received 51 telephone calls between 9 P.M. and about 4:30 the next morning. Then he suddenly ordered a car to go to the Lincoln Memorial, where he spoke with a small group of protestors until sunrise. See William Safire, *Before the Fall* (Garden City, NY: Doubleday, 1975), pp. 202-8.

13. Bradford Lyttle is quoted in George W. Hopkins, "'May Day' 1971: Civil Disobedience and the Vietnam Antiwar Movement," in Small and Hoover, eds., *Give Peace a Chance*, p. 72.

14. So claimed in David McReynolds, "Pacifists and the Movement," in Small and Hoover, eds., *Give Peace a Chance*, p. 67.

15. Harris poll, June 15, 1970.

16. Cited in DeBenedetti with Chatfield, *An American Ordeal*, p. 271.

17. Mueller, *Wars, Presidents, and Public Opinion*, p. 60.

18. Mike Royko, "Threat of a Draft Wouldn't be Worth the Effort," *Philadelphia Daily News*, October 11, 1990.

19. Brown is quoted in Willenson, *The Bad War,* p. 253. See also James Fallows, "What Did You Do in the Class War, Daddy," *The Atlantic Monthly* (October 1975): 5-19. A sympathetic oral history of draft resistance is Sherry Gershon Gottlieb, *Hell No We Won't Go: Resisting the Draft During the Vietnam War* (New York: Viking, 1991). And see Michael Useem, *Conscription, Protest and Social Conflict: The Life and Death of a Draft Resistance Movement* (New York: John Wiley, 1973).

20. See Adelson, *SDS,* pp. 48-67.

21. O'Neill, *Coming Apart,* p. 659.

22. Berman, "Fog of Political Correctness," p. 55.

23. Farber, "Counterculture and the Antiwar Movement," p. 20.

24. See for example Sarah Evans, *Personal Politics: The Roots of Women's Liberation in the Civil Rights Movement and the New Left* (New York: Knopf, 1979). As mistaken as this book is about feminism and the New Left, it is right in its analysis of the role of the civil rights struggle and broader currents in American society on the development of the women's rights movement.

25. The best and most obvious example is Shulamith Firestone. See her *The Dialectic of Sex: The Case for Feminist Revolution* (New York: William Morrow, 1970).

26. Well illustrated in Alice Echols, "'Women Power' and Women's Liberation: Exploring the Relationship between the Antiwar Movement and the Women's Liberation Movement," in Small and Hoover, eds., *Give Peace a Chance,* pp. 171-81.

27. Quoted in Gitlin, *The Sixties,* p. 372.

28. Here see Nina S. Adams, "The Women Who Left Them Behind," in Small and Hoover, eds., *Give Peace a Chance,* p. 188 especially.

29. Quotes are from Echols, "'Women Power' and Women's Liberation," pp. 179, 180.

30. See DeBenedetti, *The Peace Reform in American History,* p. 189, and Zaroulis and Sullivan, *Who Spoke Up?* pp. 358-360.

31. Detail on PCPJ and NPAC wrangling over the 1971 actions can be found in Hopkins, "'May Day' 1971," in Small and Hoover, eds., *Give Peace a Chance.*

32. Dellinger quoted in ibid., p. 73.

33. See Noam Chomsky, "Mayday: The Case for Civil Disobedience," *New York Review of Books,* June 17, 1971.

34. McGrory quoted in Hopkins, "'May Day' 1971," in Small and Hoover, eds., *Give Peace a Chance,* p. 84.

35. A good summary can be found in Wells, *The War Within,* pp. 533-55, 563-67.

36. On the GI movement generally see James R. Hayes, "The Dialectics of Resistance: An Analysis of the GI Movement," *Journal of Social Issues* 31,1 (Fall 1975): 125-39.

37. Mueller, "Reflections on the Vietnam Antiwar Movement," p. 151.

38. Herf, "New Left and Its Fading Aura," p. 244.

39. Cited in Zaroulis and Sullivan, *Who Spoke Up?* p. 348.

40. Hunter S. Thompson, *Fear and Loathing on the Campaign Trail, 1972* (New York: Fawcett, 1973), p. 8. Thompson was paraphrasing the famous remark supposedly made by a U.S. soldier referring to a Vietnamese village, but that was reportedly invented by another journalist, Peter Arnett. See Chap. 9, p. 252.

41. See Zaroulis and Sullivan, *Who Spoke Up?* p. 329.

42. The failure of the Paris Peace Accords to prevent the destruction of South Vietnam is also subject to different interpretations. A nuanced account that basically blames the South Vietnamese government (but fails to reckon U.S. responsibility for that government) is Alan E. Goodman, *The Lost Peace* (Stanford: Hoover Institute, 1978). Gareth Porter blames the United States for everything in *A Peace Denied: The United States, Vietnam, and the Paris Agreement* (Bloomington: Indiana University Press, 1975).

43. Seymour Hersh, *My Lai 4: A Report on the Massacre and Its Aftermath* (New York: Random House, 1970), and *Cover Up: The Army's Secret Investigation of the Massacre at My Lai 4* (New York: Random House, 1972).

44. A paperback edited by Senator Mike Gravel of Alaska was soon available.

45. Melvin S. Laird, "The Secretary's Summary," *Defense Department Report, FY-1973: The Foundation of a Strategy for Peace,* February 15, 1972, p. 1.

46. Stillman and Pfaff authored two widely read books: *Power and Impotence: The Failure of American Foreign Policy* (New York: Random House, 1966) and *The Politics of Hysteria* (New York: Harper & Row, 1964). George Ball also helped popularize "multipolarity" in his *The Discipline of Power: Essentials of a Modern World Structure* (Boston: Atlantic, Little-Brown, 1968). Finally, see Stanley Hoffmann's influential *Gulliver's Troubles, or the Setting of American Foreign Policy* (Boston: McGraw-Hill, 1968). Such literature was not the sole source for Nixon's "structure of peace." Nixon's lengthy vice-presidential experience and the striking similarities of many of his approaches to policy issues to those of President Eisenhower have been overlooked; but that is another subject.

## Chapter 8

1. Frank Snepp, *Decent Interval: An Insider's Account of Saigon's Indecent End* (New York: Random House, 1977).

2. As illustration, see Leslie Gelb, "Kissinger vs. Kerry," *New York Times,* September 27, 1992.

3. Even one of Richard Nixon's post-presidential books was *No More Vietnams* (New York: Arbor House, 1985).

4. John Bodnar studied how events are officially commemorated in America, including the design of the Vietnam memorial. See *Remaking America: Public Memory, Commemoration, and Patriotism in the Twentieth Century* (Princeton, NJ: Princeton University Press, 1992).

5. Examples of efforts to draw lessons from Vietnam include: Berger, "Indochina & the American Conscience"; W. Scott Thompson and Donaldson D. Frizzell, eds., *The Lessons of Vietnam* (London: Macdonald and Jane's, 1977); Harrison Salisbury, ed., *Vietnam Reconsidered: Lessons From a War* (New York: Harper & Row, 1984); John Wheeler, "Coming to Grips with Vietnam," *Foreign Affairs* 63,4 (Spring 1985); David Fromkin and James Chace, "What *Are* the Lessons of Vietnam?" *Foreign Affairs* 63,4 (Spring 1985); Mark Falcoff, "Let's Be Honest About Vietnam," *The American Spectator* (December 1987); and Walter H. Capps, *The Unfinished War: Vietnam, and the American Conscience* (Boston: Beacon, 1982).

6. They argued specifically over the application of Vietnam to Central America. See Fromkin and Chace, "What *Are* the Lessons of Vietnam?" pp. 734-41.

7. The same made be said of the Cold War and its ending. One might have thought that the way it ended would settle many old arguments, and in an antirevisionist way. But revisionists have refused to be persuaded: see the essays by Walter LeFeber, Noam Chomsky, and Richard Barnett in Michael J. Hogan, ed., *The End of the Cold War* (New York: Cambridge University Press, 1992). Jacob Heilbrunn argues that revisionism will be eclipsed by the light of truth coming out of the former Soviet Union ("The Revision Thing," *The New Republic,* August 15, 1994, p. 39). He is naive.

8. See the exchange between Peter Collier and David Horowitz on the one hand and Paul Berman on the other, "Panthers, Contras and Other Wars: 'Destructive Generation': An Exchange," *The New Republic,* June 26, 1989, pp. 38-42.

9. Argued in Richard C. Thornton, *The Carter Years: Toward a New Global Order* (Washington: Paragon, 1991).

10. Following David Gress, "Neutralism and World Order," in William R. Kintner, ed., *Arms Control: The American Dilemma* (Washington: Washington Institute Press, 1987), pp. 58-59.

11. Jimmy Carter, "New Approach to Foreign Policy," American Chamber of Commerce, Tokyo, May 28, 1975, in *The Presidential Campaign 1976, Volume One, Part One, Jimmy Carter* (Washington: U.S. Government Printing Office, 1978), p. 67. The themes of this speech were repeated throughout the campaign and the Carter presidency until the Soviet invasion of Afghanistan in December 1979.

12. See Carl Gershman, "The Rise and Fall of the New Foreign Policy Establishment," *Commentary* (July 1980).

13. See Lars Schoultz, *Human Rights and United States Policy Towards Latin America* (Princeton, NJ: Princeton University Press, 1981), p. 371.

14. Especially the Washington Office on Latin America, Amnesty International, the Council on Hemispheric Affairs, and the Institute for Policy Studies.

15. Mark Falcoff, "Uncomfortable Allies: U.S. Relations with Pinochet's Chile," in Pipes and Garfinkle, eds., *Friendly Tyrants*, p. 276.

16. Section 502 B of the 1961 Foreign Assistance Act, as amended in 1976.

17. See Jeanne Kirkpatrick, "Dictatorships and Double Standards," *Commentary* (November 1979).

18. Quoted in Howell Raines, "Reagan Calls Arms Race Essential to Avoid a 'Surrender' or 'Defeat,'" *New York Times,* August 19, 1980, pp. A1, D17.

19. See Coral Bell, *The Reagan Paradox* (New Brunswick, NJ: Rutgers University Press, 1989).

20. Jonathan Schell, "Speak Loudly, Carry a Small Stick," *Harper's* (March 1989), p. 46.

21. Ibid., p. 47.

22. Snyder quoted in Fromkin and Chace, "What *Are* the Lessons of Vietnam?" p. 726.

23. The decision to aid the *mujahideen* was taken in the Carter administration but Carter did not systematize it into a proto-Reagan Doctrine, nor was the purpose and extent of the aid the same. The key decision to change the aid mission was National Security Decision Directive 166 (NSDD-166) of 1985.

24. Mohammed Yousaf and Mark Adkin, *The Bear Trap: Afghanistan's Untold Story* (London: Leo Cooper, 1992), p. 4.

25. Wilson quoted in ibid., p. 116.

26. The confusion about the many roads over which the word détente has been hauled since 1969 is deep. William Hyland argued in 1987 that the "return to détente" is an inevitable conclusion that all men of responsibility must reach. But what he took to be the inevitability of détente did not distinguish its forms, thus vitiating the meaning of the statement. See Hyland, *Mortal Rivals: Superpower Relations from Nixon to Reagan* (New York: Random House, 1987). See also Michael B. Froman, *The Development of the Idea of Détente* (New York: St. Martin's, 1992).

27. I am aware of the arguments that U.S. foreign policy had nothing to do with the collapse of the Soviet Union. See Ronald Steel, "The End and the Beginning," in Hogan, ed., *The End of the Cold War*; and Abraham Brumburg, "Changes in Russia and the American Right," *Dissent* (Winter 1992): 21. I regard these arguments as procrustean attempts to rescue erroneous past judgments. Some are clever, but all are wrong.

28. Epstein quoted in Charles Paul Freund, "The View from Over 30," *New York Times Book Review,* August 14, 1988, p. 7.

29. The earliest example is Anthony Lake, ed., *The Vietnam Legacy: The War, American Society and the Future of American Foreign Policy* (New York: Council on Foreign Relations. 1976). Other exceptions were Lewy, *America in Vietnam*; Schandler, *Lyndon Johnson and Vietnam*; and Gelb and Betts, *The Irony of Vietnam: The System Worked.* See also David Halberstam, *The Best and the Brightest* (New York: Random House, 1972), even though written before the fall of Saigon. Of the other books published between 1975 and 1981, many were on military matters by military men. See William Westmoreland, *A Soldier Reports* (Garden City, NY: Doubleday, 1976) and D. R. Palmer, *Summons of the Trumpet: U.S.-Vietnam in Perspective* (San Rafael, CA: Presidio, 1978). There was also much fiction set in Vietnam. See Tim O'Brien, *If I Die In a Combat Zone* (New York: Delacorte, 1973), and Philip Caputo, *A Rumor of War* (New York: Holt, Rinehart and Winston, 1977). There is also fiction about war veterans set in the United States after their return home. See Thomas B. Morgan, *Snyder's Walk* (Garden City, NJ: Doubleday, 1987) and especially William Ryan, *Dr. Excitement's Elixir of Longevity* (New York: Dell, 1987). Two collections of short stories are Jerome Klinkowitz and John Somer, eds., *Writing Under Fire: Stories of the Vietnam War* (New York: Dell, 1978) and Jeanne Van Buren Dann and Jack Dann, eds., *In the Field of Fire* (New York: St. Martin's, 1986). English professors are also at work analyzing this literature; see Tobey C. Herzog, *Vietnam War Stories: Innocence Lost* (New York: Routledge, 1992).

30. Except the antiwar movement. The only notable exception, subsequently made into a movie, was Ron Kovic, *Born on the Fourth of July* (New York: Simon & Schuster, 1976).

31. Not all authors were deterred; see Alexander Kendrick, *The Wound Within* (Boston: Little, Brown, 1974) and Milton Viorst, *Fire in the Streets: America in the 1960s* (New York: Simon & Schuster, 1979). Almost half of Kendrick's *The Wound Within* is about the period before 1965, and there is little about the antiwar movement as such in what follows. There are also no notes.

32.  Bonner, *Moments of Decision*, p. 104.

33.  I traced the adversary culture origins of the freeze in Garfinkle, *The Politics of the Nuclear Freeze*, especially Chaps. 2 and 3.

34.  There were also lesser doctrines such as those of Senator Gary Hart and columnist Charles Krauthammer. All oozed Vietnam one way or another. See Krauthammer's "Morality and the Reagan Doctrine," *The New Republic*, September 8, 1986, pp. 17-24.

35.  An example from the Left is Michael T. Klare, *Beyond the Vietnam Syndrome: U.S. Intervention in the 1980s* (Washington: Institute for Policy Studies, 1981).

36.  Compare books by Stanley Karnow, Gabriel Kolko, George McT. Kahin, and R. B. Smith, as well as in conflicting reviews by supporters and detractors. See Karnow, *Vietnam*; Gabriel Kolko, *Anatomy of a War* (New York: Pantheon, 1985); George McT. Kahin, *Intervention* (New York: Knopf, 1986), and R. B. Smith, *An International History of the Vietnam War* (New York: St. Martin's, 1985). See the review of the latter three books by George C. Herring, "America and Vietnam: The Debate Continues," *American Historical Review* 92,2 (April 1987). A small war was also fought between Guenter Lewy and Norman Podhoretz on the one hand and Theodore Draper on the other. Draper's counter-revisionism is found in "The Ghosts of Vietnam," *Dissent* ( Winter 1979), where he attacked Lewy, and "Podhoretz's Vietnam War," *The New Republic*, March 10, 1982, where he attacked both Lewy and Podhoretz. Both are reprinted in Draper's *Present History* (New York: Random House, 1983).

37.  See Palmer, *Summons of the Trumpet*; Harry G. Summers, Jr., *On Strategy: A Critical Analysis of the Vietnam War* (Novato, CA: Presidio, 1982); Krepinevich, *The Army in Vietnam*; Gibson, *The Perfect War*; and Thomas C. Thayer, *War Without Fronts: The American Experience in Vietnam* (Boulder, CO: Westview Press, 1985). Other periodical citations may be found in Bob Buzzanco, "The American Military's Rationale Against the Vietnam War," *Political Science Quarterly* 101,4 (Winter 1986), p. 559.

38.  See, for example, Stanley Kauffmann's review in *The New Republic*, April 27, 1987, p. 26. For the conservative side to this debate, see the cover story in *Insight*, June 8, 1987 called "The Suppression of 'The Hanoi Hilton': How the Critics Killed a Politically Inconvenient Movie," and Robert K. Dornan, "Hanoi Hilton: Too True to Make It at the Box Office?" *The World & I* (August 1987), pp. 242-45.

39.  One of the more stimulating interpretations is Hatcher, *Suicide of an Elite*. Less inspired is Lawrence E. Grinter and Peter M. Dunn, eds., *The American War in Vietnam* (Westport, CT: Greenwood, 1987).

40.  George K. Osborn, Asa A. Clark IV, Daniel J. Kaufman, and Douglas E. Lute, eds., *Democracy, Strategy and Vietnam* (Lexington, MA: D.C. Heath, 1987).

41.  Marilyn B. Young, *The Vietnam Wars, 1945-1990* (New York: HarperCollins, 1991). Better is William S. Turley, *The Second Indochina War* (New York: New American Library, 1986).

42.  See Jonathan Mirsky, "Reconsidering Vietnam," *New York Review of Books*, October 10, 1991, pp. 49-51.

43.  See Robert Reinhold, "The 60's Legacy: The Past Examined," *New York Times Education Section*, January 8, 1989.

44.  A good effort is Bill McCloud, *What Should We Tell Our Children About Vietnam?* (Norman: University of Oklahoma Press, 1989). It is a collection of brief remarks from over 60 individuals, from cabinet ministers to grunts to protestors. One of least balanced is Jerald M. Starr, *The Lessons of the Vietnam War: A Modular Textbook* (Pittsburgh: Center for Social Studies Education, 1988). The Advisory Board for the book included: Sudan Alexander of Educators for Social Responsibility, Norman Cousins of SANE, David Cortright, Robert Jay Lifton, Kurt Vonnegut, and Frances Moore Lappé. See also Walter Capps, ed., *The Vietnam Reader* (New York: Routledge, 1991) the contents of which are extremely broad, and Grace Sevy, ed., *The American Experience in Vietnam: A Reader* (Norman: University of Oklahoma Press, 1989), which is admirably balanced. Then see Patrick J. Hearden, ed., *Vietnam: Four American Perspectives* (West Lafayette, IN: Purdue University Press, 1990), which is composed of four lectures by George McGovern, William Westmoreland, Edward Luttwak, and Thomas McCormick. Finally, see David W. Levy, *The Debate Over Vietnam* (Baltimore, MD: Johns Hopkins University Press, 1991), which is balanced but ducks most of the tough questions.

45.  This observation can been confirmed by perusing James S. Olson, *The Vietnam War: Handbook of the Literature and Research* (Westport, CT: Greenwood, 1993). There are however, good analyses of discrete parts of the antiwar movement. Maurice Isserman's *If I Had a Hammer* analyzes well the early connections between old line Communists from the interwar period and the origins of the New Left. James Miller's *"Democracy Is in the Streets"* provides detail about the origins of SDS. Neither effort gives a full interpretation of the antiwar movement, however, and while Isserman's scholarship impresses despite an underlying bias for the old Left, Miller's does not. A book praised on its dust jacket by Tom Hayden—who is its star—and by Marcus Raskin of the Institute for Policy Studies as "accurate and objective" leaves anyone with a more critical attitude immediately suspicious. Indeed, the book rues the natural excesses of youth but not anyone's judgment. Paul Berman's review was too kind: "Don't Follow Leaders," *The New Republic*, August 10 & 17, 1987, pp. 28-35. For a different view of Hayden see John H. Bunzel, *New Force on the Left: Tom Hayden and the Campaign Against Corporate America* (Stanford, CA: Hoover Institution Press, 1983).

46.  The best example is Tom Hayden's *Reunion*. See also Farber, *Chicago '68*; Hans Koning, *Nineteen Sixty-eight: A Personal Report* (New York: W.W. Norton, 1988); and Daniel Berrigan, *To Dwell in Peace: An Autobiography* (New York: Harper & Row, 1987).

47.  For two of the better examples see Jerome H. Skolnick, *The Politics of Protest* (New York: Ballantine, 1969) and Steven Kelman, *Push Comes to Shove: The Escalation of Student Protest* (New York: Houghton, 1970). See also chaps. 13-18 of Lawrence Lader, *Power on the Left: American Radical Movements Since 1946* (New York: W. W. Norton, 1979).

48.  Viorst's *Fire in the Streets* uses portraits of individuals as a vehicle to discuss issues, but little effort was made to connect the 14 chapters to one another.

49.  Sohnya Sayres et al., eds., *The Sixties Without Apology* (Minneapolis: University of Minnesota Press, 1984); George Katsiaficas, *The Imagination of the New Left: A Global Analysis of 1968* (Boston: South End Press, 1987); and the especially collection edited by Reese Williams, *Unwinding the Vietnam War*.

50.  Caute's *Year of the Barricades* is interesting in that it does not limit itself to America, but looks at the tumult in Europe though the lens of a single year, 1968. But Caute brings only a façade of comparability and writes with such a strong left-wing bias that he manages to confuse some basic points. He wrote that "the innovative ideas of the New Left—frequently, though not invariably, expressed with clarity and sophistication—constitute a treasury whose present dilapidation impoverishes us." Now, there is hardly a participant in SDS, even if still of the Left, who could say such a thing with a straight face. Then, trying to distinguish between the New Left and the counterculture, Caute tells us that the counterculture had its own "careerism" and "profit-taking," but then adds that "the political platoons of the New Left distrusted excessive hedonism and the vaporous notion that the world would change if each does his 'own thing.' This distrust reveals the more sober face of the New Left, its sense of social responsibility, its anchorage in the heart of socialist tradition. But such was the turmoil of 1968 that the majority of solid citizens neither knew nor cared about such distinctions." This paragraph describes SDS and the New Left reasonably well before 1967, but by 1968 if not earlier SDS was hardly sober. Recall Chap. 5.

51.  Gitlin's *The Sixties* is the best of the genre.

52.  See Jonathon Green, *Days in the Life* (London: Heinemann, 1988); Willenson, *The Bad War*; and Joan Morrison and Robert K. Morrison, *From Camelot to Kent State: The Sixties Experience in the Words of Those Who Lived It* (New York: Times Books, 1989).

53.  This applies to Zaroulis and Sullivan, *Who Spoke Up?*; Powers, *The War at Home*; Wells, *The War Within;* and DeBenedetti with Chatfield, *An American Ordeal*. Some staples of "peace history" include Wittner, *Rebels Against War* and DeBenedetti, *The Peace Reform in American History*. A hagiography of Women's Strike for Peace is Amy Swerdlow, *Women Strike for Peace* (Chicago: University of Chicago Press, 1993). *Who Spoke Up?, An American Ordeal,* and *The War Within* are all hagiographic of the antiwar movement as a whole. DeBenedetti believed that had the movement resisted its most radical impulses, it would have been an unsullied and noble influence (pp. 2-4). Wells, who was Todd Gitlin's student and whose book bears Gitlin's foreword, seems to like the whole movement, left and right wings (p. 7).

54.  Some of the literature of disillusionment is justly famous, as with Richard Crossman, ed., *The God That Failed* (New York: Harper, 1949).

55.  See David Horowitz and Peter Collier, *The Destructive Generation* (New York: Summit Books, 1989), and Bunzel, ed., *Political Passages: Journeys of Change Through Two Decades 1968-1988* (New York: Free Press, 1988). In the latter category see Arnaud de Borchgrave, "The Role of the Media in the Vietnam War," in Moore, ed., *The Vietnam Debate,* pp. 269-74, and especially William F. Gausman, *Red Stains on Vietnam Doves* (Denver, CO: Veracity, 1989). Myron Magnet, meanwhile, tried to blame the problems of the underclass on the 1960s legacy, but the argument is so stretched it would embarrass a rubber band. Myron Magnet, *The Dream and the Nightmare: The Sixties Legacy to the Underclass* (New York: William Morrow, 1993).

56.  Not even the interwar youth generation, that of F. Scott Fitzgerald and Thomas Wolfe, comes close to the 1960s in this regard although it seems to have been in many ways its predecessor. See James W. Tuttleton, "American Literary Radicalism in the Twenties, " *The New Criterion* 3,7 (March 1985), pp. 16-30. In any event, since the 1960s each decadal generation assumes that it must have some special character, goes in search of it, and in this manner creates it. The 1960s thus sired generationalism as a self-conscious social datum.

57.  Here see A. D. Horne, *The Wounded Generation* (Englewood Cliffs, NJ: Prentice-Hall, 1981).

58.  See Michael Walzer, "On the Role of Symbolism in Political Thought," *Political Science Quarterly* 82,2 (June 1967).

59.  See Daniel Goldman, "In Memory, People Re-Create Their Lives to Suit Their Images of the Present," *New York Times,* June 23, 1987, p. C1. Note too the apt subtitle of *The Village Voice*'s special issue on the Sixties (March 8, 1988): "the decade that won't die."

60.  See Pam Solo, *From Protest to Policy: Beyond the Freeze to Common Security* (Cambridge, MA: Ballinger, 1988).

61.  David Dellinger, *Vietnam Reconstructed* (Boston: South End Press, 1986). See also Dellinger's account of the antiwar movement epoch, *From Yale to Jail: The Life History of a Moral Dissenter* (New York: Pantheon, 1993).

62.  See any 1980s issue of *Shalom: Jewish Peace Letter* of the Jewish Peace Fellowship centered in Nyack, New York. The Jewish Peace Fellowship, founded in 1941, is affiliated with the Fellowship of Reconciliation.

63.  Personal observation.

64.  Ze'ev Chafets, "An Invitation to Tikkunstock," *Jerusalem Report,* June 20, 1991, p. 30.

65.  *New York Times,* April 26, 1990, p. A21.

66.  Jann S. Wenner, "Jerry Brown for President," *Rolling Stone,* April 30, 1992. Wenner, whom Abbie Hoffman once called "the Benedict Arnold of the Sixties," tried to make money off the expansion of the counterculture to the national level while others were trying to politicize it. See Farber, "The Counterculture and the Antiwar Movement," pp. 18-19, and Robert Draper, *Rolling Stone Magazine: The Uncensored History* (New York: Doubleday, 1990).

67.  See, for example, Charles M. Young's fawning interview with Chomsky, *Rolling Stone,* May 28, 1992.

68.  The May 28, 1992, issue of *Rolling Stone* has two more items of note: Rob Tannenbaum, "The Disciples of Pot," and mention in the "Random Notes" section the Third Annual Great Atlanta Pot Festival, p. 9.

69.  David Fricke, "Roger McGuinn," *Rolling Stone,* August 23, 1990, p. 146.

70.  Menard, "Life in the Stone Age," p. 40.

71.  Here too literature proliferates. See Patience H. C. Mason, *Recovering from the War: A Woman's Guide to Helping Your Vietnam Vet, Your Family, and Yourself* (New York: Viking, 1990).

72.  Colonel Harry Summers edits a magazine called *Vietnam,* published in Leesburg, Virginia. It is often found next to *Soldier of Fortune* on the rack.

73.  Here see H. Bruce Franklin, *MIA, Or Mythmaking in America* (New York: Lawrence Hill Books, 1992).

74.  "The End of the Vietnam War," *Washington Post,* May 7, 1991, p. 24. Also, POW-related hearings were held in the fall of 1992; on them, see Mark Hosenball, "Captive Minds," *The New Republic,* January 18, 1993.

75.  Kerrey quoted in Steven Greenhouse, "Senate Urges End to U.S. Embargo Against Vietnam," *New York Times,* January 28, 1994, p. 1.

76. See Anthony Lewis, "Guilt for Vietnam," *New York Times*, May 30, 1994. See also the hatchet job on Brown in *National Review*, May 16, 1994, p. 8.

77. Such as the cover story of the *Philadelphia Inquirer* Sunday magazine, "Battle Cry," by Vernon Loeb on May 27, 1990.

78. Sheehan's *After the War was Over: Hanoi and Saigon* (New York: Random House, 1992) was not so fortunate.

79. Bishop, "The 60's Legacy," p. 21.

80. "Huey Newton; Head of Black Panthers, Found Shot to Death," *New York Times*, August 23, 1989; "Jerry Rubin, Firebrand, '60s Radical and Co-Leader of Yippies, Dies at 56," *International Herald Tribune*, November 30, 1994, p. 3; and Krassner, "Abbie."

81. "Manson T-shirts Are Fad in Calif.," *Philadelphia Inquirer*, November 25, 1993.

82. Jesse McKinley, "A Song Slipped in Enriches a Killer," *New York Times*, December 11, 1993.

83. In 1988 Fonda tried to repent her sins, but not everyone was forgiving. See John Dillin, "Jane Fonda Regrets 'Hurt' Caused by Vietnam Deeds," *Christian Science Monitor*, June 17, 1988.

84. "Thinking as the Fed Thinks," *New York Times*, November 17, 1994, p. D1.

85. See Henry Allen, "C'mon Lighten Up America!" *Philadelphia Inquirer*, May 14, 1992. Allen alleged that the 1960s were a light time and were really all about having fun.

86. See "Two Decades Later, Capitol Considers a Bust of Agnew," *New York Times*, May 7, 1991, p. A19.

87. *Playboy* (June 1981): 64.

88. There are several attempts to follow this course, all from a perspective unsympathetic to what the authors call the neoconservatism of the 1980s. See John Carlos Rowe and Rick Berg, eds., *The Vietnam War and American Culture* (New York: Columbia University Press, 1991); Andrew Martin, *Receptions of War: Vietnam in American Culture* (Norman: Oklahoma University Press, 1994); and John Hellmann, *American Myth and the Legacy of Vietnam* (New York: Columbia University Press, 1986). See also the interesting but ideologized attempt to capture what television and movies have imparted about the Vietnam War in Michael Andregg, ed., *Inventing Vietnam: The War in Film and Television* (Philadelphia: Temple University Press, 1991).

89. See Desmond Ryan, "Martin Sheen: Man with a Mission," *Philadelphia Inquirer*, February 17, 1991, p. 1G; Valerie Richardson, "Tinseltown Insiders Create Forum to Shed the Right Light," *Washington Times*, November 23, 1991; and especially Richard Grenier, "Hollywood's Foreign Policy: Utopianism Tempered by Greed," *The National Interest* (Summer 1991). One of the most blatant examples of Hollywood Leftism is Tim Robbins's film *Bob Roberts* (1991), which is the movie version of the "national security state" mythology of the hard Left.

90. George Szamuely, "Casualties of War: A Review," *Second Thoughts* 1,2 (Fall 1989): 3. Harry Summers was not pleased with Brian De Palma's *Platoon* either; see his "Another Atrocity about Vietnam," *Washington Times*, August 31, 1989, p. F3.

91. Merle Linda Wolin, "Tales of the Hollyleft," *Second Thoughts* 1,3 (Spring 1991): 7.

92. Reported in Bernard Weinraub, "Hollywood Takes Politics Seriously, But Wants a Little Respect," *New York Times*, June 28, 1992, p. E7.

93. Ira Socol, "Trained to Do Our Dirty Work for Us," *New York Times*, May 2, 1992, p. 23.

94. Ibid.

95. Alexis Moore, "As L.A. Raged, '60s Activists Saw Similarities and Contrasts," *Philadelphia Inquirer*, May 24, 1992, p. A18.

96. Joseph A. Califano, Jr., "Don't Blame L.B.J.," *New York Times*, May 14, 1992, p. A25.

97. Robert Rafsky, "A Better Life for Having Acted Up," *New York Times*, April 19, 1992, p. E11.

98. An attitude expressed in a letter by Harold Fowler, *New York Times*, March 4, 1992, p. A23.

99. Anna Quindlen, "Rumor Has It," *New York Times*, October 11, 1992.

100. Walter A. McDougall, "What We Do for Our Country," *New York Times*, February 17, 1992.

101. Michael Mandelbaum, "Not So Slick," *The New Republic*, June 1, 1992.

102. *New York Times*, Week in Review, February 23, 1992.

103. Elizabeth Kolbert, "When 'the War' Means Vietnam, Politics Gets Muddy," *New York Times*, February 9, 1992.

104. Asserted in Sidney Blumenthal, "The Wonks," *The New Republic*, August 3, 1992, p. 11.

105. Warren Hinckle, "Ross Perot: Hero of the Counterculture," *New York Times*, July 10, 1992.

106. Kenneth L. Woodward, "Soulful Matters," *Newsweek*, October 31, 1994, p. 24.

## Chapter 9

1.  See R. W. Apple, Jr., "Views on the Gulf: Lawmakers Versed in Vietnam," *New York Times,* September 16, 1990.
2.  See for example Yuen Foong Khong, "Vietnam, the Gulf and U.S. Choices: a Comparison," *Security Studies* 2,1 (Autumn 1992). The same was true—to a lesser degree as befitted a lesser crisis—of the Haitian episode of September 1994. See William Claiborne, "Betrayed by a Fellow Resister?: Vietnam War Objectors Plan Protests on Haiti," *International Herald Tribune,* September 17-18, 1994, p. 3.
3.  Pointed out in John E. Mueller, *Policy and Opinion in the Gulf War* (Chicago: University of Chicago Press, 1994).
4.  Berrigan was not jailed for this act but he was jailed on July 6, 1994, for vandalizing an Air Force fighter-bomber in December 1993. See the *New York Times,* July 7, 1994, p. A20.
5.  David Cortright, *Soldiers in Revolt* (New York: Anchor Doubleday, 1975), p. vii.
6.  See David Cortright, "Responsibilities of the US Peace Movement," *Middle East Report* (November/December 1990): 28-29.
7.  Abzug quoted in David Gonzales, "Talk of Ground War Intensifies Mood at Antiwar Demonstrations," *New York Times,* February 18, 1991, p. 8
8.  Kovic quoted in ibid., p. 8.
9.  Josh Meyer, "Ron Kovic Calls for Pullout from Gulf," *Los Angeles Times,* August 23, 1990, p. B4.
10. David McReynolds, "U.S.-Iraq: More Than a Few Wild Cards," *Nonviolent Activist* (October/November 1990): 7.
11. Fox Butterworth, "'I Am Ready.' McGovern Says, Again," *New York Times,* January 25, 1991, p. A18.
12. Rip Rense, "Country Joe is Back, Without Anti-war Songs," *Philadelphia Inquirer,* February 17, 1991, p. I6.
13. A excerpt of the lyrics appeared in "The Pop Life," *New York Times,* February 22, 1991.
14. Quoted in Michael deCourcy Hinds, "Drawing on Vietnam Legacy, Antiwar Effort Buds Quickly," *New York Times,* January 11, 1991, p. 1, 11. *An American Ordeal* is cited in full.
15. Hinds, "Drawing on Vietnam Legacy." For Gitlin's own analysis, see "Jump-Start for the Peace Forces," *The Nation,* January 7/14, 1991, pp. 8-11.
16. Quoted in Gonzales, "Talk of Ground War Intensifies Mood," p. 8.
17. Ibid.
18. See John B. Judis, "The Strange Case of Ramsey Clark," *The New Republic,* April 22, 1991, pp. 23, 26-9.
19. Michael Wines, "Parade for Gulf Victory Draws 200,000 in Capital," *New York Times,* June 9, 1990, p. 20.
20. Nancy J. Peters, ed., *War After War* (San Francisco: City Lights Books, 1992). Adversary culture academics propounded several "Devil America" theses about the war. See Christopher Norris, *Uncritical Theory: Postmodernism, Intellectuals, and the Gulf War* (Amherst: University of Massachusetts Press, 1992), especially pp. 110-13.
21. "Defeat U.S. Imperialism! Defend Iraq!" *Workers Vanguard,* no. 518, January 18, 1991.
22. "Bush Goes for Mass Murder," *Workers Vanguard,* January 18, 1991, p. 3.
23. "Capitalism = Imperialist War," *Rebellion* 149 (1991): 1.
24. Ibid.
25. See also Stork's essay "New Enemies for a New World Order From Arc of Crisis to Global Intifada," ms., no date.
26. See "Final Examination: Gulf War 101," *Friends Journal* (October 1991), pp. 17, 40.
27. See the June 1991 *Nonviolent Activist,* the magazine of the War Resisters League, which covers many aspects of the Kuwait War aftermath as the antiwar movement saw it.
28. This is not the place to detail the pedigree of all of these organizations, or even to distinguish among the six or seven varieties of Communism involved in them. For the former, see Hollander's *Anti-Americanism,* and for the latter see Harvey Klehr, *Far Left of Center* (New Brunswick, NJ: Transaction, 1988).

29. This same group issued another plea after January 26 begging for unified action. Interested parties were to contact John Daniel on Charles Street in Baltimore.

30. This referred to the view that since blacks joined the military out of economic desperation, it amounted to a draft.

31. *The Prism* article is reprinted in part in "Annals of Political Correctness," *Second Thoughts* 1,3 (Spring 1991): p. 8.

32. Ibid. A slightly calmer expression of the same points can be found in the inaugural issue of *Real News* (Philadelphia), 1,1 (November 30, 1990). The issue bore a headline that covered almost the entire first page: "Hell No! Why Fight in the Persian Gulf?"

33. The SWP quit the Fourth International in the summer of 1990 after being eclipsed by the Workers World Party. It still considers itself to be the true Trotskyite organization.

34. Then again, some of the slogans were rather different. Here is a sample from the January 26 march in Washington: "Down with King George"; "Send Dan Quayle"; "Send Neil Bush"; "Bring Our Girls Home"; "Another Petit Bourgeois Against the War"; "War is just menstruation envy." Listed in the *Washington Post,* January 28, 1991, p. B3. A list of slogans from Los Angeles, more colorful, of course, can be found in *The Nation,* March 11, 1991, p. 292.

35. O'Dell was, in addition, Jesse Jackson's director of international affairs in Jackson's 1988 presidential bid.

36. In addition to *Bob Roberts,* Robbins starred in *Jacob's Ladder,* which one paper described as being about "twisted CIA mindgames and lots of nasty drugs." *Budapest Post,* September 29-October 5, 1992, p. 12.

37. To sample Parenti's view during Vietnam days, see his *The Anti-Communist Impulse* (New York: Random House, 1969), in which he argued that opposition to communism was a form of mental disease.

38. "International War Crimes Tribunal," *Kayhan International,* April 23, 1992, pp. 9, 14.

39. *Nonviolent Activist* (June 1991), pp. 20-21.

40. "A Man Burns Himself to Death in a Peace Gesture," *New York Times,* February 19, 1991, p. A12.

41. For details, see David Gonzales, "Some in Military Now Resist Combat," *New York Times,* November 26, 1990, p. 1.

42. Quoted in Alessandra Stanley, "As War Looms: Marches and Vigils, Talk and Fear," *New York Times,* January 15, 1991, p. A15.

43. Francis Shor, "We Learned the Wrong Lessons in Vietnam," *New York Times,* January 20, 1991. The earliest published attempts to apply Vietnam lessons to the Gulf I can find is Peter D. Feaver, "Vietnam's Wrong Lesson in the Gulf," *Christian Science Monitor,* November 23, 1990, p. 19.

44. Tom Wicker, "Broadening the Choice," *New York Times,* January 2, 1991, p. A17.

45. Henry Kissinger, *White House Years* (Boston: Little, Brown, 1979), pp. 52-53, 1466-67.

46. Robin Toner, "Liberals in Search of Values Run into Discord Over War," *New York Times,* January 27, 1991, p. A 17.

47. "Deaths in the Gulf War at the One Year Mark," *Greenpeace.* No date is given but the sheet says that the information is excerpted from *On Impact: Modern Warfare and the Environment: A Case Study of the Gulf War* by William M. Arkin, Damian Durrant, and Marianne Cherni (May 1991).

48. Colman McCarthy, "The Cowards' Air War," *Washington Post,* February 17, 1991.

49. Kenneth Roth, "Civilians Are Off-Limits—Right?" *Los Angeles Times,* February 4, 1991.

50. See Michael Klare, "High-Death Weapons of the Gulf War," *The Nation,* June 3, 1991.

51. Peter Canellos, "Students to Probe War Censorship," *Boston Globe,* April 25, 1991, p. 18.

52. Steven Penn quoted in Anthony DePalma, "On Campuses, Coordinated Antiwar Protests," *New York Times,* February 22, 1991, p. A10.

53. "Another Vietnam?" *Wall Street Journal,* February 6, 1991, p. A12.

54. See what amounted to an advertisement for thinking of the Kuwait War in Vietnam terms, R. W. Apple, Jr., "Devil of a War: It May Not Be Vietnam, but Parallels are Inescapable," *New York Times,* January 27, 1991, p. E1. See also Ellen Goodman, "Which 'Vietnam' Won't This War Be?" *Des Moines Register,* January 8, 1991, and Peter A. Olsson, "Media Power: The Vietnam and Gulf Wars," *Mind & Human Interaction* 3,3 (May 1992).

55. Jim Miller, "The Anti-War Movement, This Time," *New York Times,* January 18, 1991, p. A31.

56. Both are noted in Michael Kelley, "Before the Storm," *The New Republic,* February 4, 1991, p. 21.

57. Elsa Walsh, "Local Activist Finds Fame in Baghdad," *Washington Post,* January 31, 1991, p. A24.

58. Tony Horwitz, "Iraq Is a Hard Place, American Pacifists Ruefully Discover," *Wall Street Journal,* November 5, 1990.

59. Political Ecology Group, "War in the Gulf: An Environmental Perspective," Action Paper #1, January 1991, especially pp. 10-11.

60. "Notebook," *The New Republic,* March 18, 1991, p. 14.

61. Steve Sozby, "From Vietnam to Iraq: The Players are Different, All Else is the Same," *Al-Fajr,* February 4, 1991, p. 4.

62. Ghassan Bishara, "Anti-war Activists in Washington: Bring All the Troops Back Home," *Al-Fajr,* February 4, 1991, p. 7.

63. Interviews, Amman, January 1992.

64. See Marc Fisher, "Demonstrations Embody the Fear and Pride of Two Nations," *Washington Post,* January 21, 1991, p. A23.

65. Ivan Klima, "No Blood for Oil," *Index on Censorship* 4 & 5 (1991): 49-51.

66. See Kenneth J. Cooper, "Campus-Based Activists Organize Against War," *Washington Post,* January 28, 1991, p. A16; and DePalma, "On Campuses, Coordinated Antiwar Protests."

67. David Gonzales, "Talk of Ground War Intensifies Mood," p. 8.

68. Trish Hooper, "Today's Generation at Kent State," *Wall Street Journal,* February 6, 1991, p. A12. See also Sheldon Hackney, "On the War in the Persian Gulf," *Almanac* (University of Pennsylvania), January 22, 1991, p. 1. Mr. Hackney was president of the university.

69. See Victoria Stone, "From Words to Actions: Haverford Responds to War in the Persian Gulf," *Haverford* (Spring 1991): 28-34.

70. Personal observation: I was a visiting professor of politics at Haverford during the spring 1991 semester.

71. See Joan E. Rigdon, "Students Prepare to Dodge a Draft That Doesn't Exist," *Wall Street Journal,* February 8, 1991, p. 1.

72. See Wolin, "Tales of the Hollyleft," pp. 2-3, and Jess Bravin, "Star Wars: Hollywood Activists Give Pentagon Brass an Unusual Earful at Hearing," *Los Angeles Times,* March 5, 1992, p. 10.

73. Stone quoted in the *New York Times,* February 18, 1991, p. 3.

74. Quoted in Willenson, *Bad War,* p. 415.

75. E. L. Doctorow, "Open Letter to the President," *The Nation,* January 7/14, 1991, pp. 1, 6.

76. *The New Yorker,* November 19, 1990, p. 43.

77. Approvingly quoted in "Down the Memory Hole," *The Nation,* May 11, 1992, p. 613.

78. Maureen Dowd, "Quayle Aims at Protests, a la Agnew," *New York Times,* January 24, 1991, p. A13.

79. Andrew Rosenthal, "Bush Writes to College Papers In Appeal for Support on Gulf," *New York Times,* January 11, 1991, p. A9.

80. See the data in "Prayers and Protest," *Newsweek,* January 28, 1991, pp. 36-38.

81. See, for example, Kathleen Ryan Opon's letter in the *New York Times,* entitled "Dissent is Patriotic," February 3, 1991, p. 18.

82. And, with few exceptions, it did not. See John J. Fialka, *Hotel Warriors: Covering the Gulf War* (Washington: Woodrow Wilson Center, 1991).

83. R. W. Apple, Jr., "Defining the Issue: The White House Works to Evoke World War II Memory, Not Vietnam," *New York Times,* January 17, 1991, p. A16.

84. Kerry quoted in Andrew Rosenthal, "Bush's Tight Control," *New York Times,* January 23, 1991, p. A8.

85. See, for example, "Briefingspeak," *The Nation,* March 11, 1991, pp. 292-93, and Tom Englehardt, "Pentagon-Media Presents: The Gulf War as Total Television," *The Nation,* May 11, 1992, pp. 613, 630. See also Wicker, "An Unwinnable War," p. A27.

86. K. L. Billingsley, "Blood for Ink," *Second Thoughts* 1;3 (Spring 1991): 3.

87. In fact, only about 15 Vietcong managed to get in the compound; all were killed. See Karnow, *Vietnam,* pp. 538-39.

88. Billingsley, "Blood for Ink," p. 3. See also Peter Arnett and Michael Maclear, *The Ten Thousand Day War* (New York: St. Martin's, 1981).

89. See Martin Tolchin, "54 in House Sue to Bar Bush From Acting Without Congress," *New York Times,* November 21, 1990, p. A9, and Neil A. Lewis, "Lawmakers Lose a Suit on War Powers," *New York Times,* December 14, 1990, p. A15.

90. See here K. L. Billingsley, *From Mainline to Sideline: The Social Witness of the National Council of Churches* (Washington: Ethics and Public Policy Center, 1990), chap. 9.
91. Stephen L. Carter, "Conservatives' Faith, Liberals' Disdain," *New York Times*, August 15, 1993.
92. Ari L. Goldman, "Praying for Gulf Peace," *New York Times*, December 29, 1990, p. 10.
93. *New York Times*, January 7, 1991.
94. *New York Times*, January 12, 1991, p. A5. See also Steven Erlanger, "Church Convocation Calls for Cease-Fire In Persian Gulf War," *New York Times*, February 11, 1991, p. A15.
95. Neuhaus quoted in Laura Sessions Stepp and E. J. Dione, "Churches' Anti-War Effort Marks Departure," *Washington Post*, January 26, 1991, p. A13.
96. Peter Steinfels, "Cardinal Says Iraqi's Acts Prove Bush Right," *New York Times*, January 26, 1991, p. 9. See also Robert D. McFadden, "Amid Prayers for Peace, Preachers Split on War," *New York Times*, January 21, 1991, p. A11, and Peter Steinfels, "Debate on Persian Gulf Enlivens Bishops' Meeting," *New York Times*, November 13, 1990, p. A22.
97. See Arthur Waskow, "Jews and the Gulf War: The View From 'In Between,'" *The Nation*, May 27, 1991. By identifying Waskow as a "Jewish" veteran of the Vietnam antiwar movement, I wish to emphasize that his Jewishness was not coincidental but central to his motives.
98. Ibid., p. 68.
99. Ibid., p. 69.
100. Marc Kaufman, "Many Jews Shun Anti-war Movement," *Philadelphia Inquirer*, February 11, 1991, p. 1A.
101. Nathan Kruman quoted in McFadden, "Amid Prayers for Peace," p. A11.
102. See Thomas W. Lippmann, "Conservationists Oppose 'Oil War,'" *Washington Post*, November 2, 1990, p. A15.
103. See, for example, Juan Williams, "Double Talk From War Protesters," *Washington Post*, February 7, 1991, p. A19, and "The Protestors Heard," *New York Times*, January 27, 1991, p. 16.
104. Wines, "Parade for Gulf Victory Draws 200,000 in Capital," p. 20. See also Michael R. Kagay, "Public Shows Support for Land War," *New York Times*, February 26, 1991, p. A17.
105. Wines, "Parade for Gulf Victory Draws 200,000 in Capital."
106. Peter Applebome, "Backers of Policy Seize Initiative in the Streets," *New York Times*, February 6, 1991, p. A9.
107. See its full page advertisement in the *Washington Post*, February 27, 1991.
108. Brown quoted in Jane Gross, "The Vietnam Generation Surrenders its Certainty," *New York Times*, January 13, 1991, p. A14; and Chris A. Harmon, "New Saw a Protest I Didn't Like, but Not This Time," *New York Times*, February 3, 1991, p. E 18. A more extended argument to the same effect was Paul Starr, "No Vietnam," *The New Republic*, February 18, 1991, pp. 8-10.
109. Stephen J. Solarz, "The Stakes in the Gulf," *The New Republic*, January 7 & 14, 1991, p. 18.
110. Paul Boyer, "Where Have All the Sit-Ins Gone?" *Tikkun* 7,1 (January/February 1992): 88.
111. See Peter Braestrup, "Ho Chi Minh's Tricks Won't Work for Saddam," *Wall Street Journal*, February 5, 1991, p. A22. Also see John Dillin, "Public Backs Gulf War Only If Quick," *Christian Science Monitor*, January 11, 1991, p. 3, and John Mueller, "A Quick Victory? It Better Be," *New York Times*, January 19, 1991, p. A31.
112. Text in the *New York Times*, January 21, 1989, p. 10.
113. See B. Drummond Ayers, Jr., "For Foes of Gulf War, Nation's Victory Is Bitter," *New York Times*, March 12, 1991, p. 1, and "Pax Americana II," *The Nation*, February 11, 1991, pp. 148-49.
114. Short versions of this argument include Haynes Johnson, "Oh, Those 'Splendid Little Wars,'" *Washington Post*, July 26, 1991, p. A2 and William Greider, "Learning Wrong Lessons From the Gulf Crisis," *Rolling Stone*, October 4, 1990. A subtler but equally mistaken argument is Robert W. Tucker and David C. Hendrickson, *The Imperial Temptation: The New World Order and America's Purpose* (New York: Council on Foreign Relations, 1992).
115. Margaret Hummel quoted in Applebome, "Backers of Policy Seize Initiative in the Streets," p. 1.
116. Tom Wicker, "Winners and Losers," *New York Times*, March 16, 1991, p. 23, is a good example of both.
117. Two examples, one small and one larger, are: "Donors Say U.S. Confiscated Medical Aid Bound for Iraq," *New York Times*, March 24, 1991, p. 19; and Middle East Watch, *Needless Deaths in the Gulf War* (New York: Human Rights Watch, November 1991.)

118. David Shribman, "Victory in Gulf War Exorcises the Demons of the Vietnam Years," *Wall Street Journal,* March 1, 1991, p. 1. See also Dov S. Zakheim, "Is the Vietnam Syndrome Dead? Happily, It's Buried In the Gulf," *New York Times,* March 4, 1991.

119. See Eric Alterman, "Is the Vietnam Syndrome Dead? No, Hussein Was One of a Kind," *New York Times,* March 4, 1991.

120. Tom Wicker, "Ghosts of Vietnam," *New York Times,* January 26, 1991, p. 25. This time, this *rare* time, Wicker was correct.

121. Richard Falk, "What War?" *The Nation,* February 3, 1992, p. 112-13.

122. Joshua Muravchik, "The End of the Vietnam Paradigm?" *Commentary* (May 1991).

123. Klare quoted in Shribman, "Victory in Gulf War," p. A4. See also Robert D. McFadden, "General Who Planned Air Assault, with Lessons of Vietnam: Charles Albert Horner," *New York Times,* January 19, 1991, p. 10.

124. See the comment of Army 1st Sergeant Don Leftwich of the 101st Airborne, who served in both Vietnam and the Gulf, in John J. Fialka, "The Climactic Battle: Iraqis Are Stunned By Ferocious Assault," *Wall Street Journal,* March 1, 1991, p. A4.

125. Michael R. Gordon, "Hitting Hussein With a Stick, With a Sledgehammer in Reserve," *New York Times,* January 14, 1993.

126. Strobe Talbott, "Why Bosnia Is Not Vietnam," *Time,* August 24, 1992, p. 49.

127. See Leslie Gelb, "'Chris' and Aspin and Lake," *New York Times,* January 24, 1993.

128. Christopher quoted in the *Wall Street Journal,* March 23, 1994, p. 1.

129. Noted as well in Leslie Gelb, "Policy Monotheism," *New York Times,* March 17, 1991.

130. See Elsa Walsh, "Antiwar Movement Is Fighting a Losing Battle," *Washington Post,* March 5, 1991; and Michael T. Klare, "The Peace Movement's Next Steps," *The Nation,* March 25, 1991, pp. 361, 364-65.

131. *The Nation,* July 15/22, 1991, p. 81.

132. See the comments collected in Peter Applebome, "Sense of Pride Outweighs Fear of War," *New York Times,* February 24, 1991, p. E1.

133. Kate Shatzkin and Dave Birkland, "Minor Storm over Visit of Schwarzkopf," *Seattle Times,* April 10, 1991, p. E4.

134. "Cheney Speech Draws Protestors," *Washington Times,* May 14, 1991, p. 2.

135. See the May 1992 *Friends Journal,* which devotes four articles to the tax issue.

136. Quoted in Jacob Weisberg, "Means of Dissent," *The New Republic,* February 25, 1991, p. 18.

137. Ibid., p. 18

138. Lerner quoted in ibid., p. 18. One knows what Lerner was trying to say here but he was still wrong. There was nothing simple about Vietnam or the 1960s; Lerner only thought it was simple then and has yet to see things in a more sophisticated light. As for the Mideast 1990s writ large, yes they are complicated, but the Iraqi invasion of Kuwait was about the simplest affair one is ever likely to see in international politics. What is complicated about naked crossborder aggression and the equally basic removal of the aggression by force of arms?

139. Paul Berman, "Protestor Are Fighting the Last War," *New York Times,* January 31, 1991, p. A23.

140. Weigel quoted in Weisberg, "Means of Dissent," p. 20.

141. Peter Collier, "The Other War They Lost," *Second Thoughts* 1,3 (Spring 1991): 1, 12.

142. Steel quoted in Thomas L. Friedman, "Any War in Bosnia Would Carry a Domestic Price," *New York Times,* May 2, 1993.

143. Ibid.

---

## Chapter 10

1. I wrote this paragraph well before the publication of the Haldeman diaries, which contend that Nixon knew exactly what he was doing to South Vietnam. See Haldeman, *The Haldeman Diaries,* pp. 548-51. Kissinger, contrarily, still insists that he and Nixon thought South Vietnam could survive the withdrawal of U.S. ground forces beyond a mere "decent interval." See *Diplomacy,* pp. 695-96.

2. This is what many believe "preventing another Vietnam" ought to mean. See Doan Van Toai and David Chanoff, *Vietnamese Gulag* (New York: Harcourt, Brace, 1985), and the remarks of Senator Robert Kasten in the Congressional Record, 98th Congress, 1st session, April 27, 1983, p. H7587, quoted in Fromkin and Chace, "What *Are* the Lessons of Vietnam?" p. 741.

3. The debate over Cambodia reached a peak with the publication of William Shawcross's *Sideshow* (New York: Simon & Schuster, 1979), and Henry Kissinger's reply.

4. Douglas Pike and Benjamin Ward, "Korea and Vietnam: U.S. Success Stories," *Washington Quarterly* (Summer 1987), especially pp. 799-80.

5. Mickey Kaus, "Washington Diarist," *The New Republic,* September 10 & 17, 1990, p. 54.

6. The reference is to Fitzgerald's *Fire in the Lake* (New York: Random House, 1973), a multiple award-winning book whose popularity speaks volumes about the mindset of the American literati in the mid-1970s. I thank John E. Mueller for suggesting this connection.

7. N. R. Kleinfield, "Abbie, Eldridge and RFK: Heavy Flashback, Man," *New York Times,* January 3, 1993, and recall Goldman, "In Memory, People Re-Create Their Lives," p. C1.

8. Jones, *Great Expectations,* p. 4. Also see Frank Rich, "Peace and Love, '94 Style," *New York Times,* July 10, 1994.

9. Kleinfield, "Abbie, Eldridge and RFK."

10. Paul Light, *Baby Boomers* (New York: W. W. Norton, 1988) pp. 37-38, and the dozens of citations to relevant survey data within.

11. Myra MacPherson, *Long Time Passing: Vietnam and the Haunted Generation* (New York: Doubleday, 1985). The title, of course, comes from the refrain to "Where Have All the Flowers Gone?"—a Pete Seeger song popular in the 1960s.

12. Menard, "Life in the Stone Age," p. 38.

13. William Greider, "Hell, No, We Won't Go," *Rolling Stone* (April 7, 1988) p. 43.

14. Ibid., p. 44.

15. For early research, see Miller, "Political Issues and Trust in the Government" and André Modigliani, "Hawks and Doves, Isolationism and Political Distrust: An Analysis of Public Opinion on Military Policy," *American Political Science Review* 66,3 (September 1972).

16. See M. Kent Jennings, "Residues of a Movement: The Aging of the American Protest Generation," *American Political Science Review* 81,2 (June 1987): 370-79 in particular, and the confusing and confused essay by Ole K. Holsti and James Rosenau, "Does Where You Stand Depend on When You Were Born? The Impact of Generation of Post-Vietnam Foreign Policy Beliefs," *Public Opinion Quarterly* 44,1 (Spring 1980).

17. Nicholas Lemann, "The Post Vietnam Generation" in Horne, *Wounded Generation,* p. 210.

18. Ibid., p. 210.

19. Ibid., p. 210-11.

20. Morton Kondracke, "The Aspin Papers," p. 11.

21. This is chronicled for the National Council of Churches by K. L. Billingsley, "A Vietnam Memorial: The NCC and Indochina," *This World* (Fall 1988).

22. Richard Flacks, *Making History: The American Left and the American Mind* (New York: Columbia University Press, 1988), chap. 5. See also his "What Happened to the New Left," *Socialist Review* 19 (January/March 1989).

23. Bonner, *Moments of Decision,* p. 112. My emphasis.

24. Ibid., p. 112.

25. See Hilton Kramer, "Notes & Comments: April 1993," *The New Criterion* 2,8 (April 1983): 1-3.

26. Andrew Schmookler, "New Role for Progressives," *Christian Science Monitor,* April 1, 1994.

27. Peter Rowan, *Peter Rowan,* Flying Fish 071, 1978.

28. Gary Blonston and Robert Rankin, "Stars Turn Out Along with the Faithful," *Miami Herald,* January 21, 1993.

29. See Richard H. Kohn, "Out of Control," *The National Interest,* no. 35 (Spring 1994): 6-7.

30. Quoted in Richard Halloran, "Officers Shaped by Vietnam Taking Control of the Army," *New York Times,* June 28, 1987, p. E5. My emphasis.

31. Greider, "Hell, No, We Won't Go," p. 43.

32. Ibid., p. 44.

33. See my "Friendly Tyrants: Historical Reckoning," in Pipes and Garfinkle, eds., *Friendly Tyrants*, pp. 221-51; and Adam Garfinkle et al., *The Devil and Uncle Sam*, where Vietnam is brought as an example 13 times.

34. Willenson, *The Bad War*, p. 7.

35. Aaron Tovish, "The Only Winner in Peruvian President's Coup Is the Military," *New York Times*, April 26, 1992.

36. Quoted in Bill Marable, "Gregory Discusses Problems," *The Earlham Post* (Earlham College, Richmond, IN), October 8, 1968, p. 1.

37. Stuart E. Eizenstat, "Will the Democrats Go British Labor's Route?" *New York Times*, June 18, 1987, p. A31.

38. A point made by Hatcher, *Suicide of an Elite*.

39. See James P. Pfiffner, *The President, the Budget and Congress: Impoundment and the 1974 Budget Act* (Boulder, CO: Westview, 1979).

40. For example, again see David J. Horowitz, "My Vietnam Lessons."

41. See Martin Herz, *The Prestige Press and the Christmas Bombing* (Washington: Ethics and Public Policy Center, 1980).

42. See Daniel C. Hallin, "The Media, the War in Vietnam and Political Support: A Critique of the Thesis of an Oppositional Media," *Journal of Politics* 46,1 (February 1984). See especially the chart on p. 8. On the importance of Watergate, see Seymour Martin Lipset, *The Confidence Gap* (New York: Free Press, 1983).

43. William M. Hammond, *The Military and the Media, 1962-1968: The U.S. Army in Vietnam* (Washington: Center of Military History, United States Army, 1988).

44. Harry Summers, "Waging War as the Media Watches," *Washington Times*, September 7, 1989, p. F4.

45. Clifford, *Counsel to the President*, p. 613.

46. See the relevant parts of Robert Donovan and Ray Scherer, *Television News and American Public Life, 1948-1991* (New York: Cambridge University Press, 1992), and Ben Wattenberg, *The Good News Is the Bad News Is Wrong* (New York: Simon & Schuster, 1985).

47. So was the new conservative counterestablishment in the 1980s, which accounted for some conservatives' exaggeration of what they called the "dominant culture." They confused, and still confuse, the dominant *intellectual* culture with the dominant culture in the country at large because they too are intellectuals. The dominant culture in the country at large is conservative; otherwise, Ronald Reagan would never have been elected president once, less long twice, and the November 8, 1994 election would not have shifted power to the Republican Party in both houses of the Congress.

48. Mueller, *War, Presidents, and Public Opinion*, pp. 137-38.

49. Ibid., pp. 136-37. Indeed, as Mueller shows, youth tended to be in greater support of the war, as did the better educated (of which youth took up a major percentage at the time).

50. As was recognized by some at the time. See Joseph Adelson, "What Generation Gap?" *New York Times Magazine*, January 18, 1970. As far as polls can show, only with regard to methods of protest was there a gap, with youth upholding the tactics of the antiwar movement in principle even if they did not agree with the substance of the protest. See Mueller, *War, Presidents, and Public Opinion*, pp. 140, 165n.

51. Bloom, *The Closing of the American Mind*; Kimball, *Tenured Radicals*; and Dinesh D'Souza, *Illiberal Education* (New York: Macmillan, 1991). See also Ronald Radosh's entertaining thrashing of Jon Wiener in "Jon Wiener's Pop Marxism," *The New Criterion* 10,7 (March 1992), and Theodore Draper's review of Ellen Schrecker's *No Ivory Tower* in "The Class Struggle," *The New Republic*, January 26, 1987, pp. 29-36.

52. Psycholeftism is especially popular. See Robert Jay Lifton and Richard Falk, *Indefensible Weapons: The Political and Psychological Case Against Nuclearism* (New York: Basic Books, 1982); Robert Jay Lifton and Eric Markusen, *The Genocidal Mentality* (New York: Basic Books, 1990); and E. P. Thompson, "Notes on Exterminism, the Last Stage of Civilization," in *Exterminism and Cold War* (London: Verso, 1982). For a critique, see my "Psychobabble and Its Discontents," *Heterodoxy* 1,3 (June 1992).

53. Todorov, "Stalled Thinkers," p. 26.

54. For a spirited attack on postmodernism, see Ernest Gellner, *Postmodernism, Reason, and Religion* (New York: Routledge, 1992).

55. Berman, "Fog of Political Correctness," p. 56

56. Richard Rorty, "Demonizing the Academy," *Harper's* (January 1995): 15.

57. Louis Menard, "What Are Universities For?" *Harper's* (December 1991): 54.

58. Gitlin quoted in Berman, "Fog of Political Correctness," p. 95. Gitlin's bemoaning of the Left's losing the idea of a common humanity can be found in "From Universality to Difference: Notes on the Fragmentation of the Idea of the Left," *Contentions* (Winter 1993). A shorter version appears as "The Rise of 'Identity Politics,'" *Dissent* (Spring 1993), and an even shorter version is found in *Harper's* (September 1993), pp. 16-20.

59. See Berman, "Fog of Political Correctness," p. 96 and Kenneth Minogue, *Alien Powers: The Pure Theory of Ideology* (New York: St. Martin's, 1985).

60. Gitlin, "The Rise of 'Identity Politics,'" p. 177.

61. This incident has been forgotten in "peace science" accounts of the movement too. Wells, in *The War Within,* mentions Baez's activism and even her harrowing experiences in Hanoi [pp. 550, 559], but there is not a word about her later misgivings.

62. Mueller, *War, Presidents, and Public Opinion,* p. 159. Mueller holds that the "flaky" Left agitated but was not a mass movement. True, but that begs the question of the former's influence on the latter.

63. This is still being argued. See, for example, Maurice Isserman's review of Stephen Koch's *Double Lives: Spies and Writers in the Secret Soviet War of Ideas Against the West* (New York: Free Press, 1994), in the book review section of the *New York Times,* January 23, 1994, p. 21 in particular.

64. See Philip G. Altbach, "From Revolution to Apathy: American Student Activism in the 1970s," in his *Student Politics* (Metuchen, NJ: Scarecrow Press, 1981), p. 29.

65. Douglas McAdam quoted in Robert Reinhold, "The 60's Legacy," p. 17.

66. For evidence, see Sam Murallo, Alexandra Chute, and Mary Anna Colwell, "Pacific and Nonpacifist Groups in the U.S. Peace Movement of the 1980s," *Peace & Change* 16,3 (July 1991).

67. See Ferber's remark in an advertisement for *The Oxford Review* in *The Nation,* May 30, 1987, p. 725.

68. Cortright, *Soldiers in Revolt,* pp. vii, ix.

69. Seymour Melman, *Pentagon Capitalism: The Political Economy of War* (New York: McGraw-Hill, 1971), p. 34.

70. Rowe and Berg, *Vietnam War and American Culture,* p. ix.

71. Alexis de Tocqueville, *Democracy in America* (New York: Harper & Row, 1966), p. 208.

72. Lasky, "Ideas of '68," p. 8, text in note 5.

73. See Laurence Veysey, *The Communal Experience: Anarchist and Mystical Counter-Cultures in America* (New York: Harper & Row, 1973).

74. The reference is to E. F. Schumacher classic, *Small Is Beautiful: Economics as if People Mattered* (New York: Harper & Row, 1973). The book carries an introduction by Theodore Roszak.

75. See, for example, Murray Bookchin's *Post-Scarcity Anarchism* (San Francisco: Ramparts Press, 1971) and Charlene Spretnak, *The Spiritual Dimension of Green Politics* (Santa Fe, NM: Bear & Co., 1986).

76. Quoted in Alston Chase, "The Great, Green Deep-Ecology Revolution," *Rolling Stone,* April 23, 1987, p. 164.

77. Lenora Fulani's New Alliance Party is a bizarre amalgam of beliefs but at base it is a left-wing therapeutic cult with roots in the 1970s. See Bruce Shapiro, "Dr. Fulani's Snake-Oil Show," *The Nation,* May 4, 1992, pp. 585-94. On the cultural level, admixtures of unconventional therapy, magic and "paranormal" phenomenon still attract many. See, for example, the British magazine *Kindred Spirit Quarterly: The Guide to Personal & Planetary Healing.*

78. See Bookchin's *The Ecology of Freedom* (Palo Alto, CA: Cheshire Books, 1982). See also Jacques Ellul, *The Technological Bluff* (Grand Rapids, MI: Eerdmann's, 1990) and André Gorz, *Ecology as Politics* (Boston: South End Books, 1980).

79. Kirkpatrick Sale is a perfect example of the continuity of ideas from the New Left to eco-anarchism. Sale was a former president of SDS, wrote a book called *SDS,* and then in 1980 wrote *Human Scale,* a slightly hysterical eco-anarchist manifesto in which Vietnam is mentioned several times.

*Human Scale* (New York: Coward, McCann and Geoghegan, 1980). Then in 1993 he published *The Green Revolution: The American Environmental Movement 1962-1992* (New York: Hill & Wang, 1993), in which Vietnam is not mentioned at all. Thus the bridge is complete.

80. Not that the sectarian Left—what's left of it—isn't already plotting to elbow its way into the coming Green revolution; see Carl Boggs, *The Socialist Tradition: From Crisis to Decline* (New York: Routledge, 1995), chap. 7.

81. Lemann, "The Post Vietnam Generation," pp. 210, 212.

82. Ramin Jahanbegloo, "Philosophy and Life: An Interview," *New York Review of Books,* May 28, 1992, p. 50.

---

## Epilogue

1. Robert S. McNamara, *In Retrospect: The Tragedy and Lessons of Vietnam* (New York: Random House, 1995), p. 305.

# Bibliography of Cited Works

## Books

Adelson, Alan. *SDS* (New York: Scribner's, 1972).

Altbach, Philip G. *Student Politics* (Metuchen, NJ: Scarecrow Press, 1981).

American Friends Service Committee. *Peace in Vietnam: A New Approach in Southeast Asia* (New York: Hill & Wang, 1966).

Andregg, Michael, ed. *Inventing Vietnam: The War in Film and Television* (Philadelphia: Temple University Press, 1991).

Aristotle. *Rhetoric,* trans. W. R. Roberts (New York: Modern Library, 1955).

Arkin, William M., Durrant, Damian, and Chemi, Marianne. *On Impact: Modern Warfare and the Environment: A Case Study of the Gulf War* (May 1991).

Arnett, Peter, and Maclear, Michael. *The Ten Thousand Day War* (New York: St. Martin's, 1981).

Aron, Raymond. *Le Révolution Introuvable* (Paris: Fayard, 1968).

Avorn, Jerry, ed. *Up Against the Ivy Wall* (New York: Atheneum, 1968).

Bacciocco, Jr., Edward J. *The New Left in America: Reform to Revolution, 1950-1970* (Stanford, CA: Hoover Institution Press, 1974).

Bacon, Francis. *The Essays or Counsels, Civil and Moral, of Francis Ld. Verulam, Viscount St. Albans* (Mount Vernon, NY: Peter Pauper Press, n.d.).

Bacon, Margaret Hope. *Mothers of Feminism: The Story of Quaker Women in America* (San Francisco: Harper & Row, 1986).

Baez, Joan. *And a Song to Sing With: A Memoir* (New York: Summit, 1987).

Ball, George. *The Discipline of Power: Essentials of a Modern World Structure* (Boston: Atlantic, Little-Brown, 1968).

Baritz, Loren. *Backfire: A History of How American Culture Led Us Into Vietnam and Made Us Fight the Way We Did* (New York: Morrow, 1985).

Barrett, David M. *Uncertain Warriors: Lyndon Johnson and his Vietnam Advisors* (Lawrence: University of Kansas Press, 1993).

Belfrage, Sally. *Freedom Summer* (New York: Viking Press, 1965).

Bell, Coral. *The Reagan Paradox* (New Brunswick, NJ: Rutgers University Press, 1989).

Bell, Daniel. *The End of Ideology* (Cambridge, MA: Harvard University Press, 1960).

————. *The Cultural Contradictions of Capitalism.* (New York: Basic Books, 1978).

————. *The Winding Passage* (Cambridge, MA: Abt Books, 1980).

Berger, Peter L. *The Sacred Canopy* (New York: Doubleday-Anchor, 1969).

Berman, Larry. *Lyndon Johnson's War* (New York: W. W. Norton, 1989).

Berman, Marshall. *The Politics of Authenticity* (New York: Atheneum, 1970).

Berrigan, Daniel. *The Trial of the Catonsville Nine* (Boston: Beacon, 1970).

————. *To Dwell in Peace: An Autobiography* (New York: Harper & Row, 1987).

Billingsley, K. L. *From Mainline to Sideline: The Social Witness of the National Council of Churches* (Washington: Ethics and Public Policy Center, 1990).

Bloom, Allan. *The Closing of the American Mind* (New York: Simon & Schuster, 1987).

Bloom, Lynn Z. *Doctor Spock: Biography of a Conservative Radical* (Indianapolis: Bobbs-Merrill, 1972).

Bodnar, John. *Remaking America: Public Memory, Commemoration, and Patriotism in the Twentieth Century* (Princeton, NJ: Princeton University Press, 1992).

Boggs, Carl. *The Socialist Tradition: From Crisis to Decline* (New York: Routledge, 1995).

Bonner, Stephen Eric. *Moments of Decision: Political History and the Crisis of Radicalism* (New York: Routledge, 1992).

Bookchin, Murray. *Post-Scarcity Anarchism* (San Francisco: Ramparts Press, 1971).

————. *The Ecology of Freedom* (Palo Alto, CA: Cheshire Books, 1982).

Bourne, Randolph S. *War and the Intellectuals, Collected Essays 1915-1919* (New York: Harper & Row, 1964).

Braestrup, Peter. *Big Story* (Boulder: Westview, 1977).

Brandon, Henry. *Special Relationships* (New York: Atheneum, 1988).

Breins, Wini. *The Great Refusal: Community and Organization in the New Left: 1962-1969* (New York: Praeger, 1982).

Brown, Bernard. *Protest in Paris: Anatomy of a Revolt* (Morristown, NJ: General Learning, 1974).

Brown, Norman O. *Life Against Death* (Middletown, CT: Wesleyan University Press, 1959).

Bunzel, John H. *New Force on the Left: Tom Hayden and the Campaign Against Corporate America* (Stanford, CA: Hoover Institution Press, 1983).

Burnham, James. *Suicide of the West* (New York: John Day, 1964).

Cable, Larry. *Unholy Grail* (New York: Routledge, 1991).

Califano, Joseph A., Jr. *The Student Revolution: A Global Confrontation* (New York: W. W. Norton, 1970).

Cantor, Milton. *The Divided Left* (New York: Hill & Wang, 1978).

Capps, Walter H. *The Unfinished War: Vietnam, and the American Conscience* (Boston: Beacon, 1982).

————, ed. *The Vietnam Reader* (New York: Routledge, 1991).

Caputo, Philip. *A Rumor of War* (New York: Holt, Rinehart and Winston, 1977).

Caute, David. *The Year of the Barricades: A Journey Through 1968* (New York: Harper & Row, 1988).

Chambers, John. *The Eagle and the Dove: The American Peace Movement and U.S. Foreign Policy, 1900-1922* (Syracuse, NY: Syracuse University Press, 1991).

Chomsky, Noam. *American Power and the New Mandarins* (New York: Random House, 1969).

Clayton, Bruce. *Forgotten Prophet: The Life of Randolph Bourne* (Baton Rouge: Louisiana State University Press, 1984).

Cleaver, Eldridge. *Soul on Ice* (New York: Dell, 1970).

————. *Soul on Fire* (Waco, Texas: Word Books, 1978).

Clifford, Clark. *Counsel to the President* (New York: Anchor Books, 1991).

Cockburn, Alexander, and Blackburn, Robin, eds. *Student Power: Problems, Diagnosis, Action* (Harmondsworth, UK: Penguin/New Left Review, 1969).

Coffin, William Sloane. *Once to Every Man: A Memoir* (New York: Atheneum, 1977).

Cohen, Michael, and Hale, Dennis, eds. *The New Student Left* (Boston: Beacon, 1967).

Colby, William, with McCargar, James. *Lost Victory: A Firsthand Account of America's Sixteen-Year Involvement in Vietnam* (Chicago: Contemporary Books, 1989).

Cooper, David, ed. *To Free A Generation* (New York: Collier Books, 1968).

Cortright, David. *Soldiers in Revolt* (New York: Anchor Press/Doubleday, 1975).

Crossman, Richard, ed. *The God That Failed* (New York: Harper, 1949).

Cummings, Richard. *The Pied Piper: Allard K. Lowenstein and the Liberal Dream* (New York: Farrar, Straus, and Giroux, 1973).

Dann, Jeanne Van Buren, and Dann, Jack, eds. *In the Field of Fire* (New York: St. Martin's, 1986).

DeBenedetti, Charles. *The Peace Reform in American History* (Bloomington: Indiana University Press, 1980).

————, ed. *Peace Heroes in Twentieth Century America* (Bloomington: Indiana University Press, 1986).

————, with Chatfield, Charles. *An American Ordeal: The Antiwar Movement of the Vietnam Era* (Syracuse, NY: Syracuse University Press, 1990).

Debray, Regis. *Revolution in the Revolution* (New York: MR Press, 1967).

Decter, Midge. *Liberal Parents, Radical Children* (New York: Coward, McCann and Geoghegan, 1975).

Dellinger, David. *More Power Than We Know: The People's Movement Toward Democracy* (New York: Doubleday, 1975).

————. *Vietnam Reconstructed* (Boston: South End Press, 1986).

————. *From Yale to Jail: The Life History of a Moral Dissenter* (New York: Pantheon, 1993).

Denisoff, R. Serge. *Great Day Coming: Folk Music and the American Left* (Urbana: University of Illinois Press, 1971).

Dickstein, Morris. *Gates of Eden* (New York: Basic Books, 1977).

Diggins, John Patrick. *The Rise and Fall of the American Left* (New York: W. W. Norton, 1992).

Donovan, Robert, and Scherer, Ray. *Television News and American Public Life, 1948-1991* (New York: Cambridge University Press, 1992).

Draper, Robert. *Rolling Stone Magazine: The Uncensored History* (New York: Doubleday, 1990).

Draper, Theodore. *Present History* (New York: Random House, 1983).

D'Souza, Dinesh. *Illiberal Education* (New York: Macmillan, 1991).

Duiker, William J. *U.S. Containment Policy and the Conflict in Indochina* (Stanford, CA: Stanford University Press, 1994).

Eisenstadt, S. N. *From Generation to Generation* (New York: Free Press, 1956).

Ellison, Ralph. *Invisible Man* (New York: Random House, 1972).

Ellul, Jacques. *The Technological Bluff* (Grand Rapids, MI: Eerdmann's, 1990).

Evans, Sarah. *Personal Politics: The Roots of Women's Liberation in the Civil Rights Movement and the New Left* (New York: Knopf, 1979).

Fanón, Franz. *The Wretched of the Earth* (New York: Grove Press, 1968).

Farber, David. *Chicago '68* (Chicago: University of Chicago Press, 1988).

Feuer, Louis. *The Conflict of Generations: The Character and Significance of Student Movements* (New York: Basic Books, 1969).

Festinger, Leon, et al. *When Prophecy Fails* (Minneapolis: University of Minnesota Press, 1956).

Fialka, John J. *Hotel Warriors: Covering the Gulf War* (Washington: Woodrow Wilson Center, 1991).

Firestone, Shulamith. *The Dialectic of Sex: The Case for Feminist Revolution* (New York: William Morrow, 1970).

Fisher, Randall M. *Rhetoric and American Democracy: Black Protest Through Vietnam Dissent* (Lanham, MD: University Press of America, 1985).

Fitzgerald, Francis. *Fire in the Lake* (New York: Random House, 1973).

Flacks, Richard. *Making History: The American Left and the American Mind* (New York: Columbia University Press, 1988).

Franklin, L. Bruce. *MIA, Or Mythmaking in America* (New York: Lawrence Hill Books, 1992).

Fraser, Ronald, ed. *1968: A Student Generation in Revolt* (New York: Pantheon, 1988).

Freund, Julien. *The Sociology of Max Weber* (New York: Pantheon, 1969).

Froman, Michael B. *The Development of the Idea of Détente* (New York: St. Martin's, 1992).

Fromm, Erich. *The Philosophy of Hope: Toward a Humanized Technology* (New York: Harper & Row, 1968).

Fulbright, J. William. *The Arrogance of Power* (New York: Random House, 1967).

Garfinkle, Adam. *The Politics of the Nuclear Freeze* (Philadelphia: Foreign Policy Research Institute, 1984).

———, et al. *The Devil and Uncle Sam* (New Brunswick, NJ: Transaction, 1992).

Garrow, David J. *Bearing the Cross* (New York: Morrow, 1987).

Gausman, William F. *Red Stains on Vietnam Doves* (Denver, CO: Veracity, 1989).

Gelb, Leslie, and Betts, Richard K. *The Irony of Vietnam: The System Worked* (Washington, DC: Brookings Institute, 1979).

Gellner, Ernest. *Postmodernism, Reason, and Religion* (New York: Routledge, 1992).

Georgescu-Roegen, Nicholas. *The Entropy Theory of Economics* (Cambridge, MA: Harvard University Press, 1971).

Gerlich, Luther, and Hine, Virginia. *People, Power, Change: Movements of Social Transformation* (Indianapolis: Bobbs-Merrill Company, 1979).

Gibson, James William. *The Perfect War* (Boston: Atlantic Monthly Press, 1986).

Gillon, Steven M. *Politics and Vision: The ADA and American Liberalism, 1947-1985* (New York: Oxford University Press, 1987).

Gitlin, Todd. *The Sixties: Years of Hope, Days of Rage* (New York: Bantam, 1987).

Goodman, Alan E. *The Lost Peace* (Stanford: Hoover Institute, 1978).

Goodman, Paul. *Growing Up Absurd* (New York: Vintage, 1960).

Gorz, André. *Ecology as Politics* (Boston: South End Books, 1980).

Gottlieb, Sherry Gershon. *Hell No We Won't Go: Resisting the Draft During the Vietnam War* (New York: Viking, 1991).

Gouldner, Alvin W. *Against Fragmentation* (New York: Oxford University Press, 1985).

Green, David. *Shaping Political Consciousness: The Language of Politics in America from McKinley to Reagan* (Ithaca, NY: Cornell University Press, 1988).

Green, Jonathon. *Days in the Life* (London: Heinemann, 1988).

Greenberg, William P., and Smith, Duane E., eds. *The Radical Left: The Abuse of Discontent* (Boston: Houghton Mifflin, 1970).

Grinter, Lawrence E., and Dunn, Peter M., eds. *The American War in Vietnam* (Westport, CT: Greenwood, 1987).

Halberstam, David. *The Best and the Brightest* (New York: Random House, 1972).

Haldeman, H. R. *The Haldeman Diaries: Inside the Nixon White House* (New York: Putnam, 1994).

Hall, Mitchell K. *Because of Their Faith: CALCAV and Religious Opposition to the Vietnam War* (New York: Columbia University Press, 1990).

Hallin, Daniel C. *The Uncensored War: The Media and Vietnam* (New York: Oxford University Press, 1986).

Halstead, Fred. *"Out Now": A Participant's Account of the American Movement Against the Vietnam War* (New York: Monad Press, 1978).

Hammond, William M. *The Military and the Media, 1962-1968: The U.S. Army in Vietnam* (Washington: Center of Military History, United States Army, 1988).

Hannah, Norman. *The Key to Failure: Laos and the Vietnam War* (Lanham, MD: Madison Books, 1987).

Harris, David. *Dreams Die Hard: Three Men's Journey Through the Sixties* (New York: St. Martin's, 1992).

Hart, Jeffrey. *The American Dissent* (Garden City, NY: Doubleday, 1966).

Hatcher, Patrick Lloyd. *Suicide of an Elite: American Internationalists and Vietnam* (Stanford, CA: Stanford University Press, 1990).

Hayden, Tom. *Reunion: A Memoir* (New York: Random House, 1988).

Hearden, Patrick J., ed. *Vietnam: Four American Perspectives* (West Lafayette, Indiana: Purdue University Press, 1990).

Hellmann, John. *American Myth and the Legacy of Vietnam* (New York: Columbia University Press, 1986).

Henry, Jules. *Culture Against Man* (New York: Vintage, 1963).

Hentoff, Nat, ed. *The Essays of A. J. Muste* (New York: Simon & Schuster, 1967).

Herring, George C. *America's Longest War: The United States and Vietnam, 1950-1975,* second edition (Philadelphia: Temple University Press, 1986).

Hersh, Seymour. *My Lai 4: A Report on the Massacre and its Aftermath* (New York: Random House, 1970).

————. *Cover Up: The Army's Secret Investigation of the Massacre at My Lai 4* (New York: Random House, 1972).

Herz, Martin. *The Prestige Press and the Christmas Bombing* (Washington: Ethics and Public Policy Center, 1980).

Herzog, Tobey C. *Vietnam War Stories: Innocence Lost* (New York: Routledge, 1992).

Hodgson, Godfrey. *America in Our Time: From World War II to Nixon—What Happened and Why* (Garden City, NY: Doubleday, 1976).

Hoff, Joan. *Nixon Reconsidered* (New York: Basic Books, 1994).

Hoffer, Eric. *The Temper of Our Time* (New York: Harper & Row, 1966).

Hoffman, Abbie. *Soon to Be a Major Motion Picture* (New York: G.P. Putnam and Sons, 1980).

Hoffman, Jack, and Simon, Daniel. *Run, Run, Run: The Lives of Abbie Hoffman* (New York: Tarcher/Putnam, 1994).

Hoffman, Nicholas von. *We Are the People Our Parents Warned Us Against* (Chicago: Quadrangle, 1968).

Hoffman, Paul. *Moratorium: An American Protest* (New York: Tower, 1970).

Hoffmann, Stanley. *Gulliver's Troubles, or the Setting of American Foreign Policy* (Boston: McGraw-Hill, 1968).

Hogan, Michael J., ed. *The End of the Cold War: Its Meaning and Implications* (New York: Cambridge University Press, 1992).

Hollander, Paul. *Political Pilgrims: Travels of Western Intellectuals to the Soviet Union, China and Cuba* (New York: Oxford University Press, 1981).

————. *The Survival of the Adversary Culture* (New Brunswick, NJ: Transaction, 1987).

————. *Anti-Americanism* (New York: Oxford University Press, 1992).

Hoopes, Townsend. *The Limits of Intervention* (New York: McKay, 1969).

Horne, A. D. *The Wounded Generation* (Englewood Cliffs, NJ: Prentice-Hall, 1981).

Horowitz, David J. *Empire and Revolution* (New York: Random House, 1969).

Horowitz, David, and Collier, Peter. *The Destructive Generation* (New York: Summit Books, 1989).

Horowitz, Irving Louis. *Radicalism and the Revolt Against Reason* 2nd ed. (Carbondale: Southern Illinois University Press, 1968).

————. *The Struggle Is the Message: The Organization and Ideology of the Anti-War Movement* (Berkeley: Glendessary, 1970).

Horowitz, Irving Louis, ed. *The Rise and Fall of Project Camelot* (Cambridge, MA: M.I.T. Press, 1974).

Hull, William J. *The New Peace Movement* (Boston: World Peace Foundation, 1912).

Hung, Nguyen Tien, and Schecter, Jerrold L. *The Palace File* (New York: Harper & Row, 1986).

Hyland, William. *Mortal Rivals: Superpower Relations from Nixon to Reagan* (New York: Random House, 1987).

Isaacson, Walter, and Thomas, Evan. *The Wise Men* (New York: Simon & Schuster, 1986).

Isserman, Maurice. *If I Had a Hammer* (New York: Basic Books, 1987).

Jacobs, Paul, and Landau, Saul. *The New Radicals: A Report with Documents* (New York: Vintage, 1966).

Jamison, Andrew, and Eyerman, Ron. *Seeds of the Sixties* (Berkeley, CA: University of California Press, 1994).

Janis, Irving. *Victims of Groupthink* (Boston: Houghton-Mifflin, 1967).

Jervis, Robert. *The Logic of Images in International Relations* (Princeton, NJ: Princeton University Press, 1969).

Johnson, Lady Bird. *A White House Diary* (New York: Holt, Rinehart, and Winston, 1970).

Johnson, Lyndon Baines. *The Vantage Point* (New York: Holt, Rinehart, and Winston, 1971).

Johnson, Paul. *Intellectuals* (New York: Harper & Row, 1988).

Jones, Landon. *Great Expectations: America and the Baby Boom Generation* (New York: Ballantine, 1981).

Kagan, Jerome, and Lamb, Sharon, eds. *The Emergence of Morality in Young Children* (Chicago: University of Chicago Press, 1987).

Kahin, George McT. *Intervention* (New York: Knopf, 1986).

Kaiser, Charles. *1968 in America: Music, Politics, Chaos, Counterculture, and the Shaping of a Generation* (New York: Weidenfeld & Nicolson, 1988).

Kariel, Henry S. *The Desperate Politics of Postmodernism* (Amherst: University of Massachusetts Press, 1992).

Karnow, Stanley. *Vietnam: A History* (New York: Viking, 1983).

Karson, Marc. *American Labor Unions and Politics, 1900-1918* (Boston: Beacon Press, 1958).

Katsiaficas, George. *The Imagination of the New Left: A Global Analysis of 1968* (Boston: South End Press, 1987).

Katz, Milton S. *Ban the Bomb: A History of SANE, the Committee for a Sane Nuclear Policy, 1957-1985* (Westport, CT: Greenwood, 1986).

Kearns, Doris. *Lyndon Johnson and the American Dream* (New York: Harper & Row, 1976).

Kelman, Steven. *Push Comes to Shove: The Escalation of Student Protest* (New York: Houghton, 1970).

Kendrick, Alexander. *The Wound Within* (Boston: Little, Brown, 1974).

Keniston, Kenneth. *The Uncommitted: Alienated Youth in American Society* (New York: Harcourt, Brace, and World, 1965).

———. *Young Radicals: Notes on Committed Youth* (New York: Harcourt, Brace and World, 1968).

———. *Youth and Dissent* (New York: Harcourt Brace Jovanovich, 1971).

Kimball, Roger. *Tenured Radicals* (New York: Harper & Row, 1990).

King, Mary. *Freedom Song* (New York: William Morrow, 1987).

Kissinger, Henry A. *White House Years* (Boston: Little, Brown, 1979).

———. *Years of Upheaval* (Boston: Little, Brown, 1982).

———. *Diplomacy* (New York: Simon & Schuster, 1994).

Klare, Michael T. *Beyond the Vietnam Syndrome: U.S. Intervention in the 1980s* (Washington: Institute for Policy Studies, 1981).

Klehr, Harvey. *The Heyday of American Communism* (Gainesville, FL: Basic Pub., Inc., 1984).

———. *Far Left of Center* (New Brunswick, NJ: Transaction, 1988).

Klinkowitz, Jerome, and Somer, John, eds. *Writing Under Fire: Stories of the Vietnam War* (New York: Dell, 1978).

Koch, Stephen. *Double Lives: Spies and Writers in the Secret Soviet War of Ideas Against the West* (New York: Free Press, 1994),

Kolko, Gabriel. *Anatomy of a War* (New York: Pantheon, 1985).

Koning, Hans. *Nineteen Sixty-eight: A Personal Report* (New York: W. W. Norton, 1988).

Kovic, Ron. *Born on the Fourth of July* (New York: Simon & Schuster, 1976).

Krassner, Paul. *Confessions of a Raving, Unconfined Nut: Misadventures in the Counterculture* (New York: Simon & Schuster, 1994).

Krauthammer, Charles. *Cutting Edges* (New York: Random House, 1985).

Krepinevich, Jr., Andrew. *The Army in Vietnam* (Baltimore, MD: Johns Hopkins University Press, 1985).

Kunen, James Simon. *The Strawberry Statement: Notes of a College Revolutionary* (New York: Avon reprint, 1970).

Lader, Lawrence. *Power on the Left: American Radical Movements since 1946* (New York: W. W. Norton, 1979).

Laing, R. D. *The Politics of Experience* (New York: Pantheon, 1967).

Laqueur, Walter. *Neo-Isolationism and the World of the Seventies* Washington Papers, no. 5 (Washington: CSIS, 1974).

Larner, Jeremy. *Nobody Knows: Reflections on the McCarthy Campaign of 1968* (New York: Macmillan, 1978).

Larrowe, Charles P. *Harry Bridges: The Rise and Fall of Radical Labor in the United States* (New York: Lawrence Hill, 1987).

Lasch, Christopher. *The New Radicalism in America, 1889-1963* (New York: Knopf, 1965).

————. *The Agony of the Left* (New York: Knopf, 1968).

————. *The Culture of Narcissism* (New York: W. W. Norton, 1979).

Levitt, Cyril. *Children of Privilege: Student Revolt in the Sixties* (Toronto: University of Toronto Press, 1984).

Levy, David W. *The Debate Over Vietnam* (Baltimore, MD: Johns Hopkins University Press, 1991).

Lewy, Guenter. *America in Vietnam* (New York: Oxford University Press, 1978).

————. *Peace & Revolution: The Moral Crisis of American Pacifism* (Grand Rapids, MI: Eerdmans, 1988).

————. *The Cause that Failed: Communism in American Political Life* (New York: Oxford University Press, 1990).

Liebman, Arthur. *Jews and the Left* (New York: John Wiley & Sons, 1979).

Lifton, Robert Jay. *Boundaries* (New York: Random House, 1969).

Lifton, Robert Jay, and Falk, Richard. *Indefensible Weapons: The Political and Psychological Case Against Nuclearism* (New York: Basic Books, 1982).

Light, Paul C. *Baby Boomers* (New York: W. W. Norton, 1988).

Lind, Alice, ed. *We Won't Go: Personal Accounts of War Objectors* (Boston: Beacon Press, 1968).

Lindbeck, Assar. *The Political Economy of the New Left: An Outsider's View* (New York: Harper & Row, 1971).

Lippard, Lucy R. *A Different War: Vietnam in Art* (Seattle, WA: The Real Comet Press, 1990).

Lipset, Seymour Martin. *Rebellion in the University* (Chicago: University of Chicago Press, 1971).

————. *The Confidence Gap* (New York: Free Press, 1983).

Luce, Phillip. *The New Left Today: America's Trojan Horse* (Washington: Capitol Hill Press, 1971).

Lukas, Anthony. *Don't Shoot: We Are Your Children* (New York: Dell, 1972).

MacLaine, Shirley. *You Can Get There From Here* (New York: W. W. Norton, 1975).

MacPherson, Myra. *Long Time Passing: Vietnam and the Haunted Generation* (New York: Doubleday, 1985).

Magnet, Myron. *The Dream and the Nightmare: The Sixties Legacy to the Underclass* (New York: William Morrow, 1993).

Manchester, William. *American Caesar* (Boston: Little, Brown, 1978).

Marchand, C. Roland. *The American Peace Movement and Social Reform* (Princeton, NJ: Princeton University Press, 1972).

Martin, Andrew. *Receptions of War: Vietnam in American Culture* (Norman: Oklahoma University Press, 1994).

Marx, Leo. *The Machine in the Garden: Technology and the Pastoral Idea in America* (New York: Oxford University Press, 1964).

Mason, Patience H. C. *Recovering from the War: A Woman's Guide to Helping Your Vietnam Vet, Your Family, and Yourself* (New York: Viking, 1990).

Matusow, Allen J. *The Unravelling of America* (New York: Harper & Row, 1984).

May, Elaine Tyler. *Homeward Bound* (New York: Harper & Row, 1988).

McCarthy, Eugene. *The Year of the People* (Garden City, NY: Doubleday, 1969).

————. *Up 'Til Now* (San Diego, CA: Harcourt Brace Jovanovich, 1987).

McCloud, Bill. *What Should We Tell Our Children About Vietnam?* (Norman: University of Oklahoma Press, 1989).

McGill, William J. *The Year of the Monkey: Revolt on Campus, 1968-69* (New York: McGraw-Hill, 1982).

McQuaid, Kim. *The Anxious Years: America in the Vietnam-Watergate Era* (New York: Basic Books, 1989).

Meconis, Charles A. *With Clumsy Grace: The American Catholic Left, 1961-1977* (New York: Seabury, 1979).

Mehnert, Klaus. *Twilight of the Young: The Radical Movements of the 1960s and Their Legacy* (New York: Holt, Rinehart and Winston, 1976).

Melman, Seymour. *Pentagon Capitalism: The Political Economy of War* (New York: McGraw-Hill, 1971).

Menashe, Louis, and Radosh, Ronald, eds. *Teach-ins: U.S.A.* (New York: Praeger, 1967).

Middle East Watch. *Needless Deaths in the Gulf War* (New York: Human Rights Watch, November 1991).

Miles, M. *The Radical Probe: The Logic of Student Rebellion* (New York: Atheneum, 1971).

Miller, James. *"Democracy Is in the Streets": From Port Huron to the Siege of Chicago* (New York: Simon & Schuster, 1987).

Mills, C. Wright. *The Power Elite* (New York: Oxford University Press, 1956).

Minogue, Kenneth. *Alien Powers: The Pure Theory of Ideology* (New York: St. Martin's, 1985).

Mitford, Jessica. *The Trial of Doctor Spock* (New York: Vintage, 1970).

Molnar, Thomas. *Authority and Its Enemies* (New Rochelle, NY: Arlington House, 1976).

Moore, John Norton, ed. *The Vietnam Debate: A Fresh Look at the Arguments* (Lanham, MD: University Press of America, 1990).

Moore, Sally Falk, and Meyerhoff, Barbara, eds. *Symbol and Politics in Communal Ideology: Cases in Question* (Ithaca, NY: Cornell University Press, 1975).

Morgan, Thomas B. *Snyder's Walk* (Garden City, NY: Doubleday, 1987).

Morris, Charles. *A Time of Passion* (New York: Harper & Row, 1984).

Morrison, Joan, and Morrison, Robert K. *From Camelot to Kent State: The Sixties Experience in the Words of Those Who Lived It* (New York: Times Books, 1989).

Mueller, John E. *War, Presidents, and Public Opinion* (New York: John Wiley & Sons, 1973).

————. *Policy and Opinion in the Gulf War* (Chicago: University of Chicago Press, 1994).

Mungo, Raymond. *Famous Long Ago: My Life and Hard Times with the Liberation News Service* (New York: Pocket Books, 1971).

Muste, A. J. *Nonviolence in an Aggressive World* (New York: J.S. Ozer, 1938).

Newfield, Jack. *A Prophetic Minority* (New York: New American Library, 1966).

Nisbet, Robert. *Prejudices: A Philosophical Dictionary* (Cambridge, MA: Harvard University Press, 1983).

Nixon, Richard M. *No More Vietnams* (New York: Arbor House, 1985).

Oberdorfer, Don. *Tet!* (Garden City, NJ: Doubleday, 1971).

O'Brien, Tim. *If I Die in a Combat Zone* (New York: Delacorte, 1973).

Olson, James S. *The Vietnam War: Handbook of the Literature and Research* (Westport, CT: Greenwood, 1993).

O'Neill, William L. *Coming Apart* (Chicago: Quadrangle, 1971).

O'Rourke, William. *The Harrisburg Seven and the New Catholic Left* (New York: Crowell, 1972).

Osborn, George K., Clark, Asa A. IV, Kaufman, Daniel J., and Lute, Douglas E., eds. *Democracy, Strategy and Vietnam* (Lexington, MA: D.C. Heath, 1987).

Palmer, D. R. *Summons of the Trumpet: U.S.-Vietnam in Perspective* (San Rafael, CA: Presidio, 1978).

Parenti, Michael. *The Anti-Communist Impulse* (New York: Random House, 1969).

Parmet, Herbert. *Richard Nixon and His America* (Boston: Little, Brown, 1990).

Pearson, Hugh. *The Shadow of the Panther* (New York: Addison-Wesley, 1994).

Peck, Abe. *Uncovering the Sixties: The Life and Times of the Underground Press* (New York: Pantheon, 1985).

Peters, Nancy J., ed. *War After War* (San Francisco: City Lights Books, 1992).

Petras, James et al., eds. *We Accuse* (Berkeley: Diablo Press, 1965).

Pfiffner, James P. *The President, the Budget and Congress: Impoundment and the 1974 Budget Act* (Boulder, CO: Westview, 1979).

Piehl, Mel. *Breaking Bread: The Catholic Worker and the Origins of Catholic Radicalism in America* (Philadelphia: Temple University Press, 1982).

*Plato's Epistles*, trans. G. R. Morrow (Indianapolis: Bobbs-Merrill, 1962).

Podhoretz, Norman. *Why We Were in Vietnam* (New York: Simon & Schuster, 1983).

Porter, Gareth. *A Peace Denied: The United States, Vietnam, and the Paris Agreement* (Bloomington: Indiana University Press, 1975).

Powers, Thomas. *The War at Home: Vietnam and the American People, 1964-1968* (New York: Grossman, 1973).

*Quotations from Chairman LBJ.* (New York: Simon & Schuster, 1968).

Raskin, Marcus. *The Common Good: Its Politics, Policies and Philosophy* (New York: Routledge and Kegan Paul, 1986).

Reiff, Philip. *The Triumph of the Therapeutic: The Uses of Faith After Freud* (New York: Harper & Row, 1966).

Riesman, David. *The Lonely Crowd: A Study of the Changing American Character* (New Haven, CT: Yale University Press, 1961).

Robbins, Tom. *Still Life with Woodpecker* (New York: Bantam, 1980).

Rorabaugh, William. *Berkeley at War: The 1960s* (New York: Oxford University Press, 1989).

Rosenberg, Milton, Verba, Sidney, and Converse, Philip E. *Vietnam and the Silent Majority: The Dove's Guide* (New York: Harper & Row, 1970).

Roszak, Theodore. *The Making of a Counter Culture: Reflections on the Technocratic Society and Its Youthful Opposition* (Garden City, NY: Doubleday-Anchor, 1969).

Roszak, Theodore, ed. *The Dissenting Academy* (New York: Pantheon, 1968).

Rothman, Stanley, and Lichter, S. Robert. *Roots of Radicalism: Jews, Christians and the New Left* (New York: Oxford University Press, 1982).

Rowe, John Carlos, and Berg, Rick, eds. *The Vietnam War and American Culture* (New York: Columbia University Press, 1991).

Rubin, Jerry. *Do It! Scenarios of the Revolution* (New York: Simon & Schuster, 1970).

——. *Growing Up (at 37)* (New York: M. Evans and Company, 1976).

Rusk, Dean. *As I Saw It* (New York: W. W. Norton, 1990).

Ryan, William. *Dr. Excitement's Elixir of Longevity* (New York: Dell, 1987).

Safire, William. *Before the Fall* (Garden City, NY: Doubleday, 1975).

Sale, Kirkpatrick. *SDS* (New York: Vintage, 1973).

——. *Human Scale* (New York: Coward, McCann and Geogheagan, 1980).

——. *The Green Revolution: The American Environmental Movement 1962-1992* (New York: Hill & Wang, 1993).

Salisbury, Harrison, ed. *Vietnam Reconsidered: Lessons From a War* (New York: Harper & Row, 1984).

Sayres, Sohnya, et al., eds. *The Sixties Without Apology* (Minneapolis: University of Minnesota Press, 1984).

Schandler, Herbert. *Lyndon Johnson and Vietnam: The Unmaking of a President* (Princeton, NJ: Princeton University Press, 1977).

Schlesinger, Arthur M., Jr. *The Disuniting of America* (New York: W. W. Norton, 1992).

Schoultz, Lars. *Human Rights and United States Policy Towards Latin America* (Princeton, NJ: Princeton University Press, 1981).

Schumacher, E. F. *Small Is Beautiful: Economics as if People Mattered* (New York: Harper & Row, 1973).

Scruggs, James. *To Heal a Nation* (New York: Harper & Row, 1985).

Sevy, Grace, ed. *The American Experience in Vietnam: A Reader* (Norman: University of Oklahoma Press, 1989).

Shawcross, William. *Sideshow* (New York: Simon and Schuster, 1979).

Sheehan, Neil et al. *The Pentagon Papers* (New York: Bantam, 1970).

——. *A Bright Shining Lie* (New York: Random House, 1988).

——. *After the War was Over: Hanoi and Saigon* (New York: Random House, 1992).

Skolnick, Jerome H. *The Politics of Protest* (New York: Ballantine, 1969).

Small, Melvin. *Johnson, Nixon and the Doves* (New Brunswick, NJ: Rutgers University Press, 1988).

Small, Melvin, and Hoover, William D., eds. *Give Peace a Chance* (Syracuse, NY: Syracuse University Press, 1992).

Smith, R. B. *An International History of the Vietnam War* (New York: St. Martin's, 1985).

Snepp, Frank, *Decent Interval: An Insider's Account of Saigon's Indecent End* (New York: Random House, 1977).

Solo, Pam. *From Protest to Policy: Beyond the Freeze to Common Security* (Cambridge, MA: Ballinger, 1988).

Sontag, Susan. *Styles of Radical Will* (New York: Dell Publishing, 1969).

Spitz, Robert Steven. *Barefoot in Babylon: The Creation of the Woodstock Music Festival, 1969* (New York: Viking, 1979).

Spretnak, Charlene. *The Spiritual Dimension of Green Politics* (Santa Fe, NM: Bear & Co., 1986).

Stansill, Peter, and Mairowitz, David Zane, eds. *BAMN (By Any Means Necessary): Outlaw Manifestos and Ephemera* (Hammondsworth, UK: Penguin, 1971).

Starr, Jerald M. *The Lessons of the Vietnam War: A Modular Textbook* (Pittsburgh: Center for Social Studies Education, 1988).

Stavis, Ben. *We Were the Campaign: New Hampshire to Chicago for McCarthy* (Boston: Beacon, 1970).

Stein, David Lewis. *Living the Revolution: The Yippies in Chicago* (Indianapolis: Bobbs-Merrill, 1969).

Stevens, Jay. *Storming Heaven* (New York: Harper & Row, 1988).

Stillman, William, and Pfaff, Edward. *The Politics of Hysteria* (New York: Harper & Row, 1964).

————. *Power and Impotence: The Failure of American Foreign Policy* (New York: Random House, 1966).

Stolz, Matthew, ed. *Politics of the New Left* (Beverly Hills, CA: Glencoe Press, 1971).

Stone, Gregory, and Lowenstein, Douglas, eds. *Lowenstein: Acts of Courage and Belief* (New York: Harcourt Brace Jovanovich, 1983).

Sullivan, Michael P. *The Vietnam War: A Study in the Making of American Policy* (Lexington, KY: University of Kentucky Press, 1986).

Summers, Harry G., Jr. *On Strategy: A Critical Analysis of the Vietnam War* (Novato, CA: Presidio, 1982).

Swerdlow, Amy. *Women Strike for Peace* (Chicago: University of Chicago Press, 1993).

Talmon, Jacob. *The Origins of Totalitarian Democracy* (London: Secker & Warburg, 1952).

Tatum, Arlo, and Tuchinsky, Joseph S. *Guide to the Draft* (Boston: Beacon Press, 1968).

Teodori, Massimo, ed. *The New Left: A Documentary History* (Indianapolis: Bobbs-Merrill, 1969).

Thayer, Thomas C. *War Without Fronts: The American Experience in Vietnam* (Boulder, CO: Westview Press, 1985).

Thompson, Hunter S. *Fear and Loathing on the Campaign Trail, 1972* (New York: Fawcett, 1973).

Thompson, W. Scott, and Frizzell, Donaldson D., eds. *The Lessons of Vietnam* (London: Macdonald and Jane's, 1977).

Thoreau, Henry David. *Essays on The Duty of Civil Disobedience and Walden* (New York: Lancer, 1968).

Thornton, Richard C. *The Carter Years: Toward a New Global Order* (Washington: Paragon, 1991).

Thrall, Charles A., and Starr, Jerold M., eds. *Technology, Power, and Social Change* (Carbondale: Southern Illinois University Press, 1972).

Toai, Doan Van, and Chanoff, David. *Vietnamese Gulag* (New York: Harcourt, Brace, 1985).

Tocqueville, Alexis de. *Democracy in America* (New York: Harper & Row, 1966)

Tompkins, Berkeley. *Anti-Imperialism in the United States: The Great Debate, 1898-1920* (Philadelphia: University of Pennsylvania Press, 1970).

Trilling, Lionel. *Beyond Culture* (New York: Viking, 1965).

————. *Sincerity and Authenticity* (Cambridge, MA: Harvard University Press, 1972).

Tucker, Robert W., and Hendrickson, David C., *The Imperial Temptation: The New World Order and America's Purpose* (New York: Council on Foreign Relations, 1992).

Turley, William S. *The Second Indochina War* (New York: New American Library, 1986).

Unger, Irwin. *The Movement: A History of the American New Left, 1959-1972* (New York: Dodd, Mead, 1974).

————, and Unger, Debi. *Turning Point, 1968* (New York: Scribner's, 1989).

Useem, Michael. *Conscription, Protest and Social Conflict: The Life and Death of a Draft Resistance Movement* (New York: John Wiley & Sons, 1973).

Van Deburg, William L. *New Day in Babylon* (Chicago: University of Chicago Press, 1992).

Veysey, Laurence. *The Communal Experience: Anarchist and Mystical Counter-Cultures in America* (New York: Harper & Row, 1973).

Vickers, George R. *The Formation of the New Left: The Early Years* (Lexington, MA: D.C. Heath, 1975).

*The Vietnam Hearings* (New York: Random House, 1966).

Viorst, Milton. *Fire in the Streets: America in the 1960s* (New York: Simon & Schuster, 1979).

Vogelgesang, Sandy. *The Long Dark Night of the Soul: The American Intellectual Left and the Vietnam War* (New York: Harper & Row, 1974).

Walton, Richard. *The Remnants of Power* (New York: Coward McCann, 1968).

Walzer, Michael. *The Revolution of the Saints* (Cambridge, MA: Harvard University Press, 1965).
Waskow, Arthur. *From Race Riot to Sit-in* (New York: Doubleday, 1966).
Wattenberg, Ben. *The Good News Is the Bad News Is Wrong* (New York: Simon & Schuster, 1985).
Weigel, George. *Tranquillitas Ordinis* (New York: Oxford University Press, 1986).
Weinstein, James. *Ambiguous Legacy: The Left in American Politics* (New York: New Viewpoints, 1975).
Wells, Tom. *The War Within: America's Battle Over Vietnam* (Berkeley, CA: University of California Press, 1994).
Westbrook, Robert B. *John Dewey and American Democracy* (Ithaca, NY: Cornell University Press, 1992).
Westmoreland, William. *A Soldier Reports* (Garden City, NY: Doubleday, 1976).
Wiener, Jon. *Come Together: John Lennon in His Times* (New York: Random House, 1984).
Willenson, Kim. *The Bad War: An Oral History of the War in Vietnam* (New York: New American Library, 1988).
Williams, Reese, ed. *Unwinding the Vietnam War: From War into Peace* (Seattle, WA: Real Comet Press, 1987).
Wills, Gary. *The Kennedy Imprisonment: A Meditation on Power* (New York: Pocket Books, 1982).
Wittner, Lawrence S. *Rebels Against War: The American Peace Movement, 1933-1983* (Philadelphia: Temple University Press, 1984).
Wolfe, Tom. *The Electric Kool-Aid Acid Test* (New York: Farrar, Straus & Giroux, 1968).
———. *Radical Chic and Mau Mau-ing the Flak Catchers* (New York: Farrar, Straus & Giroux, 1970).
———. *The New Journalism* (New York: Harper & Row, 1973).
Yack, Bernard. *The Logic of Total Revolution* (Princeton, NJ: Princeton University Press, 1986),
Young, Marilyn B. *The Vietnam Wars, 1945-1990* (New York: HarperCollins, 1991).
Young, Nigel. *An Infantile Disorder? The Crisis and Decline of the New Left* (Boulder, CO: Westview, 1977).
Yousaf, Mohammed, and Adkin, Mark. *The Bear Trap: Afghanistan's Untold Story* (London: Leo Cooper, 1992).
Zaroulis, Nancy, and Sullivan, Gerald. *Who Spoke Up? American Protest Against the War in Vietnam* (New York: Doubleday, 1984).

## Journal Essays, Magazine Articles, and Book Chapters

Adams, Nina S. "The Women Who Left Them Behind." In Melvin Small and William D. Hoover, eds., *Give Peace a Chance* (Syracuse, NY: Syracuse University Press, 1992).
Adelson, Joseph. "What Generation Gap?" *New York Times Magazine,* January 18, 1970.
Adler, Renata. "Letter From Palmer House." *The New Yorker,* September 23, 1967.
Altbach, Philip G. "From Revolution to Apathy: American Student Activism in the 1970s." In Philip G. Altbach, *Student Politics* (Metuchen, NJ: Scarecrow Press, 1981).
Anderson, Terry H. "Pop Music and the Vietnam War." *Peace and Change* 11,2 (Spring 1986).
Andrews, Bruce. "Public Constraint and American Policy in Vietnam." *International Studies Series,* Sage Publications, Series 02-042, Vol. 4, May 1976.
"An Elegy for the New Left." *Time,* August 15, 1977.
"An Interview with Henry Kissinger." *Penthouse* (December 1986).
"Annals of Political Correctness." *Second Thoughts* 1,3 (Spring 1991).
Asch, Solomon. "Effects of Group Pressures in the Modification and Position of Judgments." In H. Guetzkow, ed., *Groups, Leadership and Man* (Pittsburgh: The Carnegie Press, 1951).
"Back to the Fifties." *The New Republic,* December 10, 1990.
Barton, Allen H. "The Columbia Crisis: Campus, Vietnam, and the Ghetto." *Public Opinion Quarterly* 32,3 (Fall 1968).
Bell, Daniel. "A Return to the Sacred." In *The Winding Passage* (Cambridge: Abt Books, 1980).
Bell, Tom. "We Won't Go—A Case Study." *New Left Notes,* March 27, 1967.
Berger, Peter. "Indochina & the American Conscience," *Commentary* (February 1980).
———. "Religion in Post-Protestant America." *Commentary* (May 1986).
Berger, Suzanne. "Politics and Antipolitics in Western Europe," *Daedelus* 108,1 (Winter 1979).
Berkowitz, William R. "The Impact of Anti-Vietnam War Demonstrations Upon National Public Opinion and Military Indicators." *Social Science Research* 2,1 (March 1973).
Berlin, Isaiah. "The Bent Twig." *Foreign Affairs* 51,1 (October 1972).
Berman, Paul. "Don't Follow Leaders." *The New Republic,* August 10 & 17, 1987.

———. "The Fog of Political Correctness." *Tikkun* 7,1 (January/February 1992).

Bernstein, Michael Andre. "Murder and the Utopian Moment." *The American Scholar* (Spring 1992).

Billingsley, K. L. "A Vietnam Memorial: The NCC and Indochina." *This World* (Fall 1988).

———. "Blood for Ink." *Second Thoughts* 1,3 (Spring 1991).

Blumenthal, Sidney. "The Wonks." *The New Republic,* August 3, 1992.

Bookchin, Murray. "Listen Marxist." In *Post-Scarcity Anarchism* (San Francisco: Ramparts Press, 1971).

de Borchgrave, Arnaud. "The Role of the Media in the Vietnam War." In John Norton Moore, ed., *The Vietnam Debate* (Lanham, MD: University Press of America, 1990).

Boyer, Paul. "From Activism to Apathy: The American People and Nuclear Weapons, 1963-1980." *Journal of American History* 70,4 (March 1984).

———. "Where Have All the Sit-Ins Gone," *Tikkun* 7,1 (January/February 1992).

"Briefingspeak." *The Nation,* March 11, 1991.

Brinkley, Alan. "Dreams of the Sixties." *New York Review of Books,* October 22, 1987.

Brown, Sam. "The Politics of Peace." *Washington Monthly* 2,6 (August 1970).

———. "The Defeat of the Antiwar Movement." In Anthony Lake, ed., *The Vietnam Legacy* (New York: New York University Press, 1976).

———. "The Legacy of Choices." In Grace Sevy, ed., *The American Experience in Vietnam: A Reader* (Norman: University of Oklahoma Press, 1989).

Brumburg, Abraham. "Changes in Russia and the American Right." *Dissent* (Winter 1992).

Bundy, William P. "The Path to Viet Nam: Ten Decisions." *Orbis* (Fall 1967).

Burstein, Paul, and Freudenberg, William. "Changing Public Policy: The Impact of Public Opinion, Antiwar Demonstrations, and War Costs on Senate Voting on Vietnam War Motions." *American Journal of Sociology* 84,3 (July 1978).

Buzzanco, Bob. "The American Military's Rationale Against the Vietnam War." *Political Science Quarterly* 101,4 (Winter 1986).

Calvert, Gregory. "In White America: Radical Consciousness and Social Change." In M. Teodori, ed., *The New Left: A Documentary Record* (Indianapolis: Bobbs-Merrill, 1969).

Carter, Jimmy. "New Approach to Foreign Policy." In *The Presidential Campaign 1976, Volume One, Part One, Jimmy Carter* (Washington: U.S. Government Printing Office, 1978).

Casciato, Art. "Upton Sinclair." In Bernard K. Johnpoll and Harvey Klehr, eds., *Biographical Dictionary of the American Left* (Westport, CT: Greenwood, 1986).

Chafets, Ze'ev. "An Invitation to Tikkunstock." *Jerusalem Report,* June 20, 1991.

Chase, Alston. "The Great, Green Deep-Ecology Revolution." *Rolling Stone,* April 23, 1987.

Chomsky, Noam. "The Responsibility of the Intellectuals." *New York Review of Books,* February 23, 1967.

———. "Mayday: The Case for Civil Disobedience." *New York Review of Books,* June 17, 1971.

Cleaver, Eldridge. "Introduction." In Jerry Rubin, *Do It! Scenarios of the Revolution* (New York: Simon & Schuster, 1970).

Clifford, Clark. "A Viet Nam Reappraisal: The Personal History of One Man's View and How It Evolved." *Foreign Affairs* 47,4 (July 1969).

Collier, Peter. "The Other War They Lost." *Second Thoughts* 1,3 (Spring 1991).

Collier, Peter, and Horowitz, David. "Panthers, Contras and Other Wars," *The New Republic,* June 26, 1989.

Converse, Philip, and Schuman, H. "'Silent Majorities' and the Vietnam War." *Scientific American* (June 1970).

Cooper, David. "Beyond Words." In *To Free a Generation* (New York: Collier, 1968).

Cortright, David. "Responsibilities of the US Peace Movement." *Middle East Report* (November/December 1990).

Davidson, Osha. "Recruiters for Peace: Giving the Lie to Rambo." *The Nation,* February 14, 1987.

Davis, Rennie. "Facing Up to Repression." *Liberation* (June 1969).

Dellinger, David. "April 15: Telling off the Taxman." *WIN* 6 (May 15, 1970).

DelVecchio, John M. "Memorial Days." *The World & I* (May 1992).

Doctorow, E. L. "Open Letter to the President." *The Nation,* January 7/14, 1991.

Dornan, Robert K. "Hanoi Hilton: Too True to Make It at the Box Office?" *The World & I* (August 1987).

"Down the Memory Hole." *The Nation,* May 11, 1992.

Draper, Theodore. "The Ghosts of Vietnam." *Dissent* (Winter 1979).

————. "Podhoretz's Vietnam War." *The New Republic,* March 10, 1982.

————. "The Class Struggle." *The New Republic,* January 26, 1987.

Echols, Alice. "'Women Power' and Women's Liberation: Exploring the Relationship between the Antiwar Movement and the Women's Liberation Movement." In Melvin Small and William D. Hoover, eds., *Give Peace a Chance* (Syracuse, NY: Syracuse University Press, 1992).

Eisenstadt, S. N. "Generational Conflict and Intellectual Antinomianism." *Annals of the American Academy of Political and Social Science* 395 (May 1971).

Englehardt, Tom. "Pentagon-Media Presents: The Gulf War as Total Television." *The Nation,* May 11, 1992.

Fairclough, Adam. "Martin Luther King, Jr., and the War in Vietnam." *Phylon* (March 1984).

Fairlie, Henry. "War Against Reason." *The New Republic,* November 6, 1989.

Falcoff, Mark. "Let's Be Honest About Vietnam." *The American Spectator,* December 1987.

————. "Uncomfortable Allies: U.S. Relations with Pinochet's Chile." In Daniel Pipes and Adam Garfinkle, eds., *Friendly Tyrants: An American Dilemma* (New York: St. Martin's, 1991).

Falk, Richard. "What War?" *The Nation,* February 3, 1992.

Fallows, James. "What Did You Do in the Class War, Daddy," *The Atlantic Monthly* (October 1975).

Farber, David. "The Counterculture and the Antiwar Movement," in Melvin Small and William D. Hoover, eds., *Give Peace a Chance* (Syracuse, NY: Syracuse University Press, 1992).

Field, Anne. "Harassment on Campus: Sex in a Tenured Position." *Ms.* (September 1981).

"Final Examination: Gulf War 101." *Friends Journal* (October 1991).

Flacks, Richard. "What Happened to the New Left." *Socialist Review* (January/March 1989).

Forman, David J. "Rules of the Protest Game." *Jerusalem Post,* May 5, 1993.

Fricke, David. "Roger McGuinn." *Rolling Stone,* August 23, 1990.

Fromkin, David, and Chace, James. "What Are the Lessons of Vietnam?" *Foreign Affairs* 63,4 (Spring 1985).

Gallup, George. "Public Opinion and the Vietnam War." *Gallup Opinion Index,* Report 52 (October 1969).

Garfinkle, Adam. "Friendly Tyrants: Historical Reckoning." In Daniel Pipes and Adam Garfinkle, eds., *Friendly Tyrants: An American Dilemma* (New York: St. Martin's, 1991).

————. "Psychobabble and Its Discontents." *Heterodoxy* 1,3 (June 1992).

Gellner, Ernest. "Homeland of the Unrevolution." *Daedelus* 122,3 (Summer 1993).

Genovese, Eugene D. "The Question." *Dissent* (Summer 1994.

Gershman, Carl, "The Rise and Fall of the New Foreign Policy Establishment." *Commentary* (July 1980).

Gitlin, Todd. "The Radical Potential of the Poor." *Internationalist Socialist Journal* 5,24 (1966).

————. "What Are We Doing to Dismantle the System and What to Decorate It." *Liberation News Service,* 1968.

————. "Jump-Start for the Peace Forces." *The Nation,* January 7/14, 1991.

————. "From Universality to Difference: Notes on the Fragmentation of the Idea of the Left," *Contentions* (Winter 1993).

————. "The Rise of 'Identity Politics.'" *Dissent* (Spring 1993).

————. "Reflections on 1968." *Dissent* (Fall 1993).

Glass, Andrew J. "Defense Report/Draftees Shoulder Burden of Fighting and Dying in Vietnam." *National Journal* 2,33 (August 15, 1970).

Goldstein, Jonathan. "Vietnam Research on Campus: The Summit/Spicerack Controversy at the University of Pennsylvania 1965-67." *Peace & Change* 11,2 (Spring 1986).

Goodman, Walter. "Liberals vs. Radicals—War in the Peace Camp." *New York Times Magazine,* December 3, 1967.

Gottlieb, Sanford. "State Within a State: What Is the Military-Industrial Complex?" In Michael Harrington and Irving Howe, eds., *The Seventies: Problems and Proposals* (New York: Harper & Row, 1972).

Greenfeld, Liah. "Transcending the Nation's Worth." *Daedelus* 122,3 (Summer 1993).

Greider, William. "Hell, No, We Won't Go." *Rolling Stone* (April 1988).

————. "Learning Wrong Lessons From the Gulf Crisis." *Rolling Stone,* October 4, 1990.

Grenier, Richard. "Hollywood's Foreign Policy: Utopianism Tempered by Greed." *The National Interest* (Summer 1991).

Gress, David. "Neutralism and World Order." In William R. Kintner, ed., *Arms Control: The American Dilemma* (Washington: Washington Institute Press, 1987).

Gusfield, Joseph R. "The (F)utilty of Knowledge? The Relation of Social Science to Public Policy toward Drugs." *Annals of the American Academy of Political and Social Science,* no. 417 (January 1975).

Gutmann, David. "The New Mythologies and Premature Aging in the Youth Culture." *Social Research* 40,2 (Summer 1973).

———. "The Subjective Politics of Power: The Dilemma of Postsuperego Man." *Social Research* 40,4 (Winter 1973).

Hackney, Sheldon. "On the War in the Persian Gulf." *Almanac* (University of Pennsylvania), January 22, 1991.

Hahn, Harlan. "Dove Sentiments Among Blue-collar Workers." *Dissent* (May/June 1970).

Halberstam, David. "McCarthy and the Divided Left." *Harper's* (March 1968).

Hallin, Daniel C. "The Media, the War in Vietnam and Political Support: A Critique of the Thesis of an Oppositional Media." *The Journal of Politics* 46,1 (February 1984).

———. "Correlates of Public Sentiment about War: Local Referenda on the Vietnam Issue." *American Political Science Review* 64,4 (December 1970).

Hardwick, Elizabeth. "Selma, Alabama: The Charms of Goodness." *New York Review of Books,* April 22, 1965.

Hayes, James R. "The Dialectics of Resistance: An Analysis of the GI Movement." *Journal of Social Issues* 31,1 (Fall 1975).

Heilbrunn, Jacob. "The Revision Thing." *The New Republic,* August 15, 1994.

Heineman, Kenneth. "The Silent Majority Speaks: Antiwar Protest and Backlash, 1965-1972." *Peace & Change* 17,4 (October 1992).

Herf, Jeffrey. "The New Left and Its Fading Aura." *Partisan Review* 53,2 (Spring 1986).

———. "Reliving the Sixties." *Partisan Review* 57,2 (Spring 1990).

Heritage Foundation. "Making the World Safe for America: A U.S. Foreign Policy Blueprint." April 1992.

Herring, George C. "America and Vietnam: The Debate Continues." *The American Historical Review* 92,2 (April 1987).

Hilsman, Roger. "Vietnam: The Decision to Intervene." In Jonathan R. Adelman, ed., *Superpowers and Revolution* (New York: Praeger, 1986).

Hollander, Paul. "The Survival of the Adversary Culture." *Partisan Review* 53,3 (Summer 1986).

Holsti, Ole K., and Rosenau, James. "Does Where You Stand Depend on When You Were Born? The Impact of Generation of Post-Vietnam Foreign Policy Beliefs." *Public Opinion Quarterly* 44,1 (Spring 1980).

Hoopes, Townsend. "The Fight for the President's Mind—and the Men Who Won It." *The Atlantic Monthly* (October 1969).

Hopkins, George W. "'May Day' 1971: Civil Disobedience and the Vietnam Antiwar Movement." In Melvin Small and William D. Hoover, eds., *Give Peace a Chance* (Syracuse, NY: Syracuse University Press, 1992).

Horowitz, David J. "Revolutionary Kharma versus Revolutionary Politics." *Ramparts* 9,8 (March 1971).

———. "Nicaragua: A Speech to My Former Colleagues on the Left." *Commentary* (June 1986).

———. "My Vietnam Lessons." *The World & I* (April 1987).

———. "A Letter to a Political Friend." In John Bunzel, *Political Passages: Journeys of Change Through Two Decades, 1968-1988* (New York: Free Press, 1988).

———. "The Anti-war Movement: Vietnam Lessons." In John Norton Moore, ed., *The Vietnam Debate: A Fresh Look at the Arguments* (Lanham, MD: University Press of America, 1990).

Horowitz, David, and Collier, Peter. "Another 'Low Dishonest Decade' on the Left." *Commentary* (January 1987).

Horowitz, Helen Lefkowitz. "The 1960s and the Transformation of Campus Cultures." *History of Education Quarterly* 26,2 (Spring 1986).

Hosenball, Mark. "Captive Minds." *The New Republic,* January 18, 1993.

Howard, Michael. "Cold War, Chill Peace." *World Policy Journal* 10,4 (Winter 1994).

Hunt, R. N. Carew. "Willi Muezenberg." In David Footman, ed., *International Communism,* St. Anthony's Paper, no. 9 (Carbondale: Southern Illinois University, 1960).

"Interview with Tom Hayden." *Rolling Stone,* October 26, 1972.

Isserman, Maurice. "You Don't Need a Weathervane but a Postman Can Be Helpful." In Melvin Small and William D. Hoover, eds., *Give Peace a Chance* (Syracuse, NY: Syracuse University Press, 1992).

Jahanbegloo, Ramin. "Philosophy and Life: An Interview [with Sir Isaiah Berlin]." *New York Review of Books,* May 28, 1992.

Jennings, M. Kent. "Residues of a Movement: The Aging of the American Protest Generation." *American Political Science Review* 81,2 (June 1987).

Johnson, Paul. "The Litany of Anti-Americanism." *The National Interest,* no. 27 (Spring 1982).

Judis, John B. "The Strange Case of Ramsey Clark." *The New Republic,* April 22, 1991.

Kakutani, Michiko. "Our Woman of Letters." *New York Times Magazine,* March 29, 1987.

Karnow, Stanley. "Giap Remembers." *New York Times Magazine,* June 24, 1990.

Kaus, Mickey. "Washington Diarist." *The New Republic,* September 10 & 17, 1990.

Kelley, Michael. "Before the Storm." *The New Republic,* February 4, 1991.

Ketwig, John. ". . . and a hard rain fell." In Reese Williams, ed. *Unwinding The Vietnam War: From War into Peace* (Seattle, WA: Real Comet Press, 1987).

Khong, Yuen Foong. "Vietnam, the Gulf and U.S. Choices: a Comparison." *Security Studies* 2,1 (Autumn 1992).

Kimball, Warren. "The Cold War Warmed Over." *American Historical Review* 79,3 (October 1974).

Kimmel, Michael S. "The Sixties without Metaphor." *Society* 26,3 (March/April 1989).

Kirkpatrick, Jeane. "Dictatorships and Double Standards." *Commentary* (November 1979).

Klima, Ivan. "No Blood for Oil." *Index on Censorship* 4 & 5 (1991).

Klare, Michael T. "The Peace Movement's Next Steps." *The Nation,* March 25, 1991.

————. "High-Death Weapons of the Gulf War." *The Nation,* June 3, 1991.

Kohn, Richard H. "Out of Control." *The National Interest,* no. 35 (Spring 1994).

Kondracke, Morton. "The Aspin Papers." *The New Republic,* April 27, 1992

Kopkind, Andrew. "Anti-Vietnam Politics: Peace Candidates in Oregon, California." *The New Republic,* June 4, 1966.

Kramer, Hilton. "Notes & Comments: April 1993." *The New Criterion* 2,8 (April 1983).

————. "The Life and Death of Lillian Hellman." *The New Criterion* 3,2 (October 1984).

Krassner, Paul. "Abbie." *The Nation,* May 8, 1989.

————. "Disorder in Judge Hoffman's Court." *The Nation,* October 11, 1993.

Krauthammer, Charles. "Stretch Marx." *The New Republic,* August 16-23, 1982.

————. "Morality and the Reagan Doctrine." *The New Republic,* September 8, 1986.

Laird, Melvin S. "The Secretary's Summary." *Defense Department Report, FY-1973: The Foundation of a Strategy for Peace* (Washington: GPO, February 15, 1972).

Lasky, Melvin. "The Ideas of '68." *Encounter* (November 1988).

Laufer, Robert S. "Sources of Generational Consciousness and Conflict." *Annals of the American Academy of Political and Social Science Annals* (May 1971).

Leary, Timothy, Alpert, Richard, and Metzner, Ralph. "Rationale of the Mexican Psychedelic Training Center." In Richard Blum and Associates, *Utopiates: The Use and Users of LSD* (New York: Atherton Press, 1965).

Lemann, Nicholas. "The Post Vietnam Generation." In A. D. Horne, *The Wounded Generation* (Englewood Cliffs, NJ: Prentice-Hall, 1981).

"Letters." *Playboy* (June 1981).

Levy, Peter B. "The New Left, Labor, and the Vietnam War." *Peace & Change* 15,1 (January 1990).

Lewy, Guenter. "Does America Need a *Verfassungsschutzbericht?" Orbis* (Fall 1987).

Lipset, Seymour Martin. "The President, the Polls and Vietnam." *Transaction* (September/October 1966).

Lunch, William L., and Sperlich, Peter W. "American Public Opinion and the War in Vietnam." *Western Political Quarterly* 32,1 (March 1979).

Mailer, Norman. "Statement on Vietnam." *Partisan Review* 32,4 (Fall 1965),

Mandelbaum, Michael. "Not So Slick." *The New Republic,* June 1, 1992.

"Mark Twain on American Imperialism." *The Atlantic Monthly* (April 1992).

McGovern, George. "Foreword." In Melvin Small and William D. Hoover, eds., *Give Peace a Chance* (Syracuse, NY: Syracuse University Press, 1992).

McReynolds, David. "U.S.-Iraq: More Than a Few Wild Cards." *Nonviolent Activist* (October/November 1990).

——. "Pacifists and the Movement." In Melvin Small and William D. Hoover, eds., *Give Peace a Chance* (Syracuse, NY: Syracuse University Press, 1992).

Menard, Louis. "Life in the Stone Age." *The New Republic,* January 7 & 14, 1991.

——. "What Are Universities For?" *Harper's* (December 1991).

Miller, Arthur H. "Political Issues and Trust in the Government." *American Political Science Review* 68,3 (September 1974).

Miller, Frederick D. "The End of SDS and the Emergence of the Weathermen." In Jo Freeman, ed., *Social Movements of the Sixties and Seventies* (New York: Longman, 1983).

Mirsky, Jonathan. "Reconsidering Vietnam." *New York Review of Books,* October 10, 1991.

Modigliani, Andre. "Hawks and Doves, Isolationism and Political Distrust: An Analysis of Public Opinion on Military Policy," *American Political Science Review* 66,3 (September 1972).

Mueller, John E. "Reflections on the Vietnam Antiwar Movement and on the Curious Calm at the War's End." In Peter Braestrup, ed., *Vietnam as History: Ten Years After the Paris Peace Accords* (Washington: Wilson Center and University Press of America, 1984).

Murallo, Sam, Chute, Alexandra, and Colwell, Mary Anna. "Pacific and Nonpacifist Groups in the U.S. Peace Movement of the 1980s." *Peace & Change* 16,3 (July 1991).

Muravchik, Joshua. "Mississippi Burning: Airbrushing History." *World & I* (March 1989).

——. "The End of the Vietnam Paradigm?" *Commentary* (May 1991).

Neuhaus, Richard John. "The War, the Churches, and Civil Religion." *Annals of the American Academy of Political and Social Science,* vol. 387 (January 1970).

Niebuhr, Reinhold. "Two Forms of Utopianism." *Christianity and Society* 12,4 (Autumn 1947).

Nisbet, Robert. "Who Killed the Student Revolution?" *Encounter* (February 1970).

"Notebook." *The New Republic,* March 18, 1991.

O'Donnell, K. "LBJ and the Kennedys." *Life,* August 7, 1970.

Oglesby, Carl. "An Open Letter to McCarthy Supporters." In Matthew Stolz, ed., *Politics of the New Left* (Beverly Hills, CA: Glencoe Press, 1971).

Olsen, Edward A. "South Korea under Military Rule: Friendly Tyrant?" In Daniel Pipes and Adam Garfinkle, eds., *Friendly Tyrants: An American Dilemma* (New York: St. Martin's, 1991).

Olsson, Peter A. "Media Power: The Vietnam and Gulf Wars," *Mind & Human Interaction* 3,3 (May 1992).

O'Rourke, P. J. "What Went Wrong?" *Wilson Quarterly* (Autumn 1988).

Peck, Sidney. "Notes on the Strategy and Tactics of the Movement Against the War." *New Politics* (August 1968).

Pike, Douglas. "South Vietnam: Autopsy of a Compound Crisis." In Daniel Pipes and Adam Garfinkle, eds., *Friendly Tyrants: An American Dilemma* (New York: St. Martin's, 1991).

Pike, Douglas, and Ward, Benjamin. "Korea and Vietnam: U.S. Success Stories." *Washington Quarterly* (Summer 1987).

Podhoretz, Norman. "The Reagan Road to Détente." *Foreign Affairs* 63,3 (America and the World, 1984).

Political Ecology Group. "War in the Gulf: An Environmental Perspective." Action Paper #1 (January 1991).

"Prayers and Protest." *Newsweek,* January 28, 1991.

Radosh, Ronald. "The Know-Nothing Left." *Second Thoughts* 1,1 (Summer 1989).

——. "Jon Wiener's Pop Marxism." *The New Criterion* 10,7 (March 1992).

Ransford, H. Edward. "Blue Collar Anger: Reaction to Student and Black Protest." *American Sociological Review* 27,3 (June 1972).

Robinson, John P. "Public Reaction to Political Protest: Chicago 1968." *Public Opinion Quarterly* 34,1 (Spring 1970).

——. "Balance Theory and Vietnam-Related Attitudes." *Social Science Quarterly* 53,1 (December 1970).

Rorty, Richard. "Demonizing the Academy," *Harper's* (January 1995).

Roszak, Theodore. "The Disease Called Politics." In Paul Goodman, ed., *Seeds of Liberation* (New York: Braziller, 1965).

Rudd, Mark. "University in Revolt." In Jerry Avorn, *Up Against the Ivy Wall* (New York: Atheneum, 1968).

Rustin, Bayard. "From Protest to Politics." *Commentary* (February 1965).

Savio, Mario. "An End to History." In Matthew Stolz, ed., *Politics of the New Left* (Beverly Hills, CA: Glencoe Press, 1971).

Schell, Jonathan. "Speak Loudly, Carry a Small Stick." *Harper's* (March 1989).

Schreiber, E. M. "Anti-War Demonstrations and American Public Opinion on the War in Vietnam." *British Journal of Sociology* 27,2 (June 1976).

Shapiro, Bruce. "Dr. Fulani's Snake-Oil Show." *The Nation,* May 4, 1992.

Shapiro, Herbert. "The Vietnam War and the American Civil Rights Movement." *Journal of Ethnic Studies* 16 (Winter 1989).

Shils, Edward. "Dreams of Plentitude, Nightmares of Scarcity." In Seymour M. Lipset and Philip G. Altbach, eds., *Students in Revolt* (Boston: Houghton Mifflin, 1969).

————. "Totalitarians and Antinomians." In John Bunzel, ed., *Political Passages: Journeys of Change Through Two Decades, 1968-1988* (New York: Free Press, 1988).

Small, Melvin. "The Impact of the Antiwar Movement on Lyndon Johnson, 1965-68: A Preliminary Report." *Peace & Change* (Spring 1984).

Solarz, Stephen J. "The Stakes in the Gulf." *The New Republic,* January 7/14, 1991.

Solomon, Kim. "The Peace Movement: An Anti-Establishment Movement." *Journal of Peace Research* 23,2 (June 1986).

Starr, Paul. "No Vietnam." *The New Republic,* February 18, 1991.

Steel, Ronald. "The End and the Beginning." In Michael J. Hogan, ed., *The End of the Cold War: Its Meaning and Implications* (New York: Cambridge University Press, 1992).

Stone, I. F. "A Reply to the White Paper." *I. F. Stone's Weekly,* March 8, 1965.

Stone, Victoria. "From Words to Actions: Haverford Responds to War in the Persian Gulf." *Haverford* (Spring 1991).

"Student Protest." *Annals of the American Academy of Political and Social Science* (May 1971).

"The Student's March on Washington." In Matthew Stolz, ed., *Politics of the New Left* (Beverly Hills, CA: Glencoe Press, 1971).

Szamuely, George. "Casualties of War: A Review." *Second Thoughts* 1,2 (Fall 1989).

Talbott, Strobe. "Why Bosnia Is Not Vietnam." *Time,* August 24, 1992.

Tannenbaum, Rob. "The Disciples of Pot." *Rolling Stone,* May 28, 1992.

Thompson, E. P. "Notes on Exterminism, the Last Stage of Civilization." In *Exterminism and Cold War* (London: Verso, 1982).

Toai, Doan Van, and Chanoff, David. "El Salvador: Lessons from the Vietnam Experience." *Washington Quarterly* (Fall 1984).

Todorov, Tzvetan. "Stalled Thinkers." *The New Republic,* April 13, 1987.

Tolson, Jay. "By Theory Possessed." *Wilson Quarterly* 18,3 (Summer 1994).

"Trotskyism." *Encyclopedia of the Left* (New York: Garland, 1990).

Turkle, S. R. "Symbol and Festival in the French Student Uprising." In Sally Falk Moore and Barbara Meyerhoff, eds., *Symbol and Politics in Communal Ideology: Cases in Question* (Ithaca, NY: Cornell University Press, 1975).

Tuttleton, James W. "American Literary Radicalism in the Twenties." *The New Criterion* 3,7 (March 1985).

Unger, Craig. "Tom Hayden's Original Sin: Looking for Absolution in All the Wrong Places." *Esquire* (June 1989).

Updike, John. "On Not Being a Dove." *Commentary* (March 1989).

Urgo, Joseph R. "Comedic Impulses and Society Propriety: The Yippie Carnival." *Studies in Popular Culture* 10,1 (Winter 1987).

Verba, Sidney, and Brody, Richard. "Participation, Policy Preferences, and the War in Vietnam." *Public Opinion Quarterly* 34,3 (Fall 1970).

Verba, Sidney, Brody, Richard, Nie, Norman H., Polsby, Nelson W., Erdman, Paul, and Black, Gordon. "Public Opinion and the War in Vietnam." *American Political Science Review* 61,2 (June 1967).

Volkan, Kurt. "The Vietnam War Memorial." *Mind & Human Interaction* 2,2 (May 1992).

Walzer, Michael. "On the Role of Symbolism in Political Thought." *Political Science Quarterly* 82,2 (June 1967).

Waskow, Arthur. "The Meaning of Creative Disorder." In *From Race Riot to Sit-in* (New York: Doubleday, 1966).

————. "Jews and the Gulf War: The View From 'In Between.'" *The Nation,* May 27, 1991.

Wasserman, Steve, "Cuba and the Panacea of Revolution." *Tikkun* 2,2 (March/April 1987).

Weisberg, Jacob. "Means of Dissent." *The New Republic,* February 25, 1991.

Wenner, Jann S. "Jerry Brown for President." *Rolling Stone,* April 30, 1992.

Wheeler, John. "Coming to Grips with Vietnam." *Foreign Affairs* 63,4 (Spring 1985).

Wildavsky, Aaron. "The Empty-head Blues: Black Rebellion and White Reaction." *The Public Interest* (Spring 1968).

Wolin, Merle Linda. "Tales of the Hollyleft." *Second Thoughts* 1,3 (Spring 1991).

Woodward, C. Vann. "The Dreams of Martin Luther King." *New York Review of Books,* January 15, 1987.

Woodward, Kenneth L. "Soulful Matters." *Newsweek,* October 31, 1994.

Yankelovich, Daniel et al., "Trend Reference Book." (New York: Yankelovich Monitor, 1985).

Young, Charles M. "Noam Chomsky." *Rolling Stone,* May 28, 1992.

Zeidler, Jeanne. "Speaking Out, Selling Out, Working Out: The Changing Politics of Jane Fonda." In Edward Crapol, ed., *Women and American Foreign Policy: Lobbyists, Critics, and Insiders* (Westport, CT: Greenwood Press, 1987).

Zinn, Howard. "Marxism and the New Left." In Matthew Stolz, ed., *Politics of the New Left* (Beverly Hills, CA: Glencoe Press, 1971).

## Newspaper Articles

Allen, Henry. "C'mon Lighten Up America!" *Philadelphia Inquirer,* May 14, 1992.

Alterman, Eric. "Is the Vietnam Syndrome Dead? No, Hussein Was One of a Kind," *New York Times,* March 4, 1991.

Apple, R. W., Jr. "Views on the Gulf: Lawmakers Versed in Vietnam." *New York Times,* September 16, 1990.

————. "Defining the Issue: The White House Works to Evoke World War II Memory, Not Vietnam." *New York Times,* January 17, 1991.

————. "Devil of a War: It May Not Be Vietnam, but Parallels are Inescapable." *New York Times,* January 27, 1991.

Applebome, Peter. "Backers of Policy Seize Initiative in the Streets." *New York Times,* February 6, 1991.

————. "Sense of Pride Outweighs Fear of War," *New York Times,* February 24, 1991.

Ayers, B. Drummond, Jr. "For Foes of Gulf War, Nation's Victory Is Bitter," *New York Times,* March 12, 1991.

Berman, Paul. "Protestors Are Fighting the Last War." *New York Times,* January 31, 1991.

Bishara, Ghassan. "Anti-war Activists in Washington: Bring All the Troops Back Home." *Al-Fajr,* February 4, 1991.

Bishop, Katherine. "The 60's Legacy: From the Inside Out." *New York Times Education Section,* January 8, 1989.

Blonston, Gary, and Rankin, Robert. "Stars Turn out Along with the Faithful." *Miami Herald,* January 21, 1993.

Braestrup, Peter. "Ho Chi Minh's Tricks Won't Work for Saddam." *Wall Street Journal,* February 5, 1991.

Buchwald, Art. "'We Have the Enemy on the Run' Says Gen. Custer at Big Horn." *Washington Post,* February 6, 1968.

Butterworth, Fox. "'I Am Ready,' McGovern Says, Again." *New York Times,* January 25, 1991.

Califano, Joseph A., Jr. "Don't Blame L.B.J." *New York Times,* May 14, 1992.

Canellos, Peter. "Students to Probe War Censorship." *Boston Globe,* April 25, 1991.

Carter, Stephen L. "Conservatives' Faith, Liberals' Disdain." *New York Times,* August 15, 1993.

Cassel, Andrew. "Anti-war Forces Relive '68 Democratic Meeting." *Philadelphia Inquirer,* August 29, 1988.

Cooper, Kenneth J. "Campus-Based Activists Organize Against War," *Washington Post,* January 28, 1991.

DePalma, Anthony. "On Campuses, Coordinated Antiwar Protests." *New York Times,* February 22, 1991.

Dillin, John. "Jane Fonda Regrets 'Hurt' Caused by Vietnam Deeds." *Christian Science Monitor,* June 17, 1988.

————. "Public Backs Gulf War Only If Quick." *Christian Science Monitor,* January 11, 1991.

Doloff, Steven. "Woodstock's Message Is Still True." *Philadelphia Inquirer,* August 8, 1991.

Dowd, Maureen. "Quayle Aims at Protests, a la Agnew." *New York Times,* January 24, 1991.

Eizenstat, Stuart E. "Will the Democrats Go British Labor's Route?" *New York Times*, June 18, 1987.

Erlanger, Steven. "Church Convocation Calls for Cease-Fire In Persian Gulf War." *New York Times*, February 11, 1991.

Feaver, Peter D. "Vietnam's Wrong Lesson in the Gulf." *Christian Science Monitor*, November 23, 1990.

Fialka, John J. "The Climactic Battle: Iraqis Are Stunned By Ferocious Assault." *Wall Street Journal*, March 1, 1991.

Fisher, Marc. "Demonstrations Embody the Fear and Pride of Two Nations." *Washington Post*, January 21, 1991.

Forman, David J. "Rules of the Protest Game." *Jerusalem Post*, May 5, 1993.

Fox, Richard Wightman. "The Reality Box." *New York Times Book Review*, May 4, 1992.

Friedman, Thomas L. "Any War in Bosnia Would Carry a Domestic Price." *New York Times*, May 2, 1993.

Freund, Charles Paul. "The View from Over 30." *New York Times Book Review*, August 14, 1988.

Gelb, Leslie. "Policy Monotheism." *New York Times*, March 17, 1991.

——. "Kissinger vs. Kerry," *New York Times*, September 27, 1992.

——. "'Chris' and Aspin and Lake." *New York Times*, January 24, 1993.

Gold, Erna. "Look at Vietnam Generation Now." *New York Times*, July 16, 1994.

Goldman, Ari L. "Praying for Gulf Peace." *New York Times*, December 29, 1990.

Goldman, Daniel. "In Memory, People Re-Create Their Lives to Suit Their Images of the Present." *New York Times*, June 23, 1987.

Gonzales, David. "Some in Military Now Resist Combat." *New York Times*, November 26, 1990.

——. "Talk of Ground War Intensifies Mood at Antiwar Demonstrations." *New York Times*, February 18, 1991.

Goodman, Ellen. "Which 'Vietnam' Won't This War Be?" *Des Moines Register*, January 8, 1991.

Gordon, Michael R. "Hitting Hussein With a Stick, With a Sledgehammer in Reserve." *New York Times*, January 14, 1993.

Greene, Jonathan. "Will the Sixties Ever End?" *London Evening Standard*, August 1, 1988.

Greenhouse, Steven. "Senate Urges End to U.S. Embargo Against Vietnam." *New York Times*, January 28, 1994.

Gross, Jane. "The Vietnam Generation Surrenders Its Certainty." *New York Times*, January 13, 1991.

Halloran, Richard. "Officers Shaped by Vietnam Taking Control of the Army." *New York Times*, June 28, 1987.

Harmon, Chris A. "Never Saw a Protest I Didn't Like, but Not This Time." *New York Times*, February 3, 1991.

Hentoff, Nat. "Review of the Press." *The Village Voice*, June 24, 1965.

Hinckle, Warren. "Ross Perot: Hero of the Counterculture." *New York Times*, July 10, 1992.

Hinds, Michael deCourcy. "Drawing on Vietnam Legacy, Antiwar Effort Buds Quickly." *New York Times*, January 11, 1991.

Honan, William H. "Schlesinger Sees Free Speech in Peril." *New York Times*, May 27, 1994.

Hooper, Trish. "Today's Generation at Kent State." *Wall Street Journal*, February 6, 1991.

Horwitz, Tony. "Iraq Is a Hard Place, American Pacifists Ruefully Discover." *Wall Street Journal*, November 5, 1990.

Johnson, Haynes. "Oh, Those 'Splendid Little Wars.'" *Washington Post*, July 26, 1991.

Kagay, Michael R. "Public Shows Support for Land War." *New York Times*, February 26, 1991.

Kaufman, Marc. "Many Jews Shun Anti-war Movement," *Philadelphia Inquirer*, February 11, 1991.

Kleinfield, N. R. "Abbie, Eldridge and RFK: Heavy Flashback, Man." *New York Times*, January 3, 1993.

Kondracke, Morton. "Leaning on the Left." *New York Times*, March 15, 1992.

Kopkind, Andrew. "Anti-Vietnam Politics: Peace Candidates in Oregon, California." *The New Republic*, June 4, 1966.

Kolbert, Elizabeth. "When 'the War' Means Vietnam, Politics Gets Muddy." *New York Times*, February 9, 1992.

Lehman, David. "Time for a New Generation to Shout." *Chicago Tribune*, August 30, 1993.

Lewis, Anthony. "Guilt for Vietnam." *New York Times*, May 30, 1994.

Lewis, Neil A. "Lawmakers Lose a Suit on War Powers." *New York Times*, December 14, 1990.

Lindorff, David. "War in Peace." *The Village Voice*, April 20, 1982.

Lippmann, Thomas W. "Conservationists Oppose 'Oil War.'" *Washington Post*, November 2, 1990.

Loeb, Vernon. "Battle Cry." *Philadelphia Inquirer,* May 27, 1990.

Marable, Bill. "Gregory Discusses Problems." *The Earlham Post* (Earlham College, Richmond, IN), October 8, 1968.

McCarthy, Colman. "The Cowards' Air War." *Washington Post,* February 17, 1991.

McDougall, Walter A. "What We Do for Our Country." *New York Times,* February 17, 1992.

McFadden, Robert D. "General Who Planned Air Assault, With Lessons of Vietnam: Charles Albert Horner." *New York Times,* January 19, 1991.

———. "Amid Prayers for Peace, Preachers Split on War." *New York Times,* January 21, 1991.

McKinley, Jesse. "A Song Slipped in Enriches a Killer." *New York Times,* December 11, 1993.

Meyer, Josh. "Ron Kovic Calls for Pullout from Gulf." *Los Angeles Times,* August 23, 1990.

Miller, Jim. "The Anti-War Movement, This Time." *New York Times,* January 18, 1991.

Moore, Alexis. "As L.A. Raged, '60s Activists Saw Similarities and Contrasts." *Philadelphia Inquirer,* May 24, 1992.

Mueller, John E. "A Quick Victory? It Better Be." *New York Times,* January 19, 1991.

Nisbet, Robert. "War, Crisis and Intellectuals." *Wall Street Journal,* January 25, 1971.

Opon, Kathleen Ryan. "Dissent is Patriotic." *New York Times,* February 3, 1991.

Pace, Eric. "Jerry Rubin, 56, Flashy 60's Radical, Dies; 'Yippies' Founder and Chicago 7 Defendant." *New York Times,* November 30, 1994.

Quindlen, Anna. "Rumor Has It." *New York Times,* October 11, 1992.

Rafsky, Robert. "A Better Life for Having Acted Up." *New York Times,* April 19, 1992.

Raines, Howell. "Reagan Calls Arms Race Essential to Avoid a 'Surrender' or 'Defeat'." *New York Times,* August 19, 1980.

Reinhold, Robert. "The 60's Legacy: The Past Examined." *New York Times Education Section,* January 8, 1989.

Rense, Rip. "Country Joe Is Back, Without Anti-war Songs." *Philadelphia Inquirer,* February 17, 1991.

Reston, James. "Washington: The Stupidity of Intelligence." *New York Times,* October 17, 1965.

Rich, Frank. "Peace and Love, '94 Style." *New York Times,* July 10, 1994.

Richardson, Valerie. "Tinseltown Insiders Create Forum to Shed the Right Light." *Washington Times,* November 23, 1991.

Richburg, Keith B. "Historians From U.S., Vietnam Confer on War." *Washington Post,* December 11, 1988.

Rigdon, Joan E. "Students Prepare to Dodge a Draft That Doesn't Exist." *Wall Street Journal,* February 8, 1991.

Rorty, Richard. "The Unpatriotic Academy." *New York Times,* February 13, 1994.

Rosenthal, Andrew. "Bush Writes to College Papers In Appeal for Support on Gulf." *New York Times,* January 11, 1991.

———. "Bush's Tight Control." *New York Times,* January 23, 1991.

Roth, Kenneth. "Civilians Are Off-Limits—Right?" *Los Angeles Times,* February 4, 1991.

Royko, Mike. "Threat of a Draft Wouldn't Be Worth the Effort." *Philadelphia Daily News,* October 11, 1990.

Ryan, Desmond. "Martin Sheen: Man with a Mission." *Philadelphia Inquirer,* February 17, 1991.

Schmookler, Andrew. "New Role for Progressives." *Christian Science Monitor,* April 1, 1994.

Shatzkin, Kate, and Birkland, Dave. "Minor Storm over Visit of Schwarzkopf." *Seattle Times,* April 10, 1991.

Shor, Francis. "We Learned the Wrong Lessons in Vietnam." *New York Times,* January 20, 1991.

Shribman, David. "Victory in Gulf War Exorcises the Demons of the Vietnam Years." *Wall Street Journal,* March 1, 1991.

Socol, Ira. "Trained to Do Our Dirty Work for Us." *New York Times,* May 2, 1992.

Sozby, Steve. "From Vietnam to Iraq: The Players are Different, All Else is the Same." *Al-Fajr,* February 4, 1991.

Stanley, Alessandra. "As War Looms: Marches and Vigils, Talk and Fear." *New York Times,* January 15, 1991.

Steinfels, Peter. "Debate on Persian Gulf Enlivens Bishops' Meeting." *New York Times,* November 13, 1990.

———. "Cardinal Says Iraqi's Acts Prove Bush Right." *New York Times,* January 26, 1991.

Stepp, Laura Sessions, and Dione, E. J. "Churches' Anti-War Effort Marks Departure." *Washington Post,* January 26, 1991.

Summers, Harry. "Another Atrocity about Vietnam." *Washington Times,* August 31, 1989.

———. "Waging War as the Media Watches," *Washington Times,* September 7, 1989.

Tolchin, Martin. "54 in House Sue to Bar Bush From Acting Without Congress." *New York Times,* November 21, 1990.

Toner, Robin. "Liberals in Search of Values Run into Discord over War." *New York Times,* January 27, 1991.

Tovish, Aaron. "The Only Winner in Peruvian President's Coup Is the Military." *New York Times,* April 26, 1992.

Turner, Wallace. "Tip Leads to Arrest of Radical Sought in 1970 Case." *New York Times,* January 22, 1987.

Walsh, Elsa. "Local Activist Finds Fame in Baghdad." *Washington Post,* January 31, 1991.

———. "Antiwar Movement Is Fighting a Losing Battle." *Washington Post,* March 5, 1991.

Weinraub, Bernard. "Hollywood Takes Politics Seriously, But Wants a Little Respect." *New York Times,* June 28, 1992.

Wicker, Tom. "Broadening the Choice." *New York Times,* January 2, 1991.

———. "Ghosts of Vietnam." *New York Times,* January 26, 1991.

———. "Winners and Losers." *New York Times,* March 16, 1991.

———. "An Unwinnable War." *New York Times,* June 12, 1991.

Williams, Juan. "Double Talk From War Protesters." *Washington Post,* February 7, 1991.

Wines, Michael. "Parade for Gulf Victory Draws 200,000 in Capital." *New York Times,* June 9, 1990.

Zakheim, Dov S. "Is the Vietnam Syndrome Dead? Happily, It's Buried in the Gulf." *New York Times,* March 4, 1991.

## Discography

Country Joe McDonald and the Fish. *The I Feel Like I'm Fixing to Die Rag.* Vanguard 79266, 1967.

Crosby, Stills, Nash, and Young. *Four Way Street.* Atlantic SD 2-902, 1971.

Louvin Brothers. *The Louvin Brothers.* Rounder Records Specialty Series No. 07, 1980.

Laura Nyro. *Christmas and the Beads of Sweat.* Columbia KC30259, 1970.

Peter Rowan. *Peter Rowan.* Flying Fish 071, 1978.

Earl Scruggs. *Family and Friends.* Columbia C30584, 1970.

Simon and Garfunkel. *Parsley, Sage, Rosemary and Thyme.* Columbia CS 9363, 1966.

# Subject Index*

Abolitionists 25, 35, 237, 296
Abraham Lincoln Brigade 106, 184
academia 6, 23, 209, 219-22, 288
The Action Network 242
adversary culture 6, 23-4, 34, 37, 39-45, 66,
    71, 83, 106, 149, 209, 220, 223, 237-38,
    253, 288-294
Afghanistan War 217-18
Age of Aquarius 146
AIDS Coalition to Unleash Power (ACT-UP)
    232-33, 242
Aldermaston marches 51
*Alice's Restaurant* 230
alienation 8, 70, 124, 136-142
American Association for International
    Conciliation 36
American Federation of Labor 38, 202
American Friends Service Committee (AFSC)
    36, 43-4, 99, 193, 243, 292
American Institute for Marxist Studies 82
American Peace Society 36
American Security Council 257
Americans for Democratic Action 67, 88, 172
anarchism 5, 8, 34, 38, 41, 94, 169, 245, 294,
    295-96
Angola 201, 217, 220-21, 241
Anti-Imperialist League 36
*Apocalypse Now* 224, 230
*Armies of the Night* 10, 11
Arms Control and Disarmament Agency
    (ACDA) 44, 156
asceticism 95, 122, 127-29
ASEAN 269
Assembly of Unrepresented Peoples 77-78
Association for the Reform and Codification of
    the Law of Nations 36

baby boom 8, 57
"Back in the U.S.S.R." 190
balkanization of radicalism 58, 193-94
"Ballad of the Green Berets" 65, 82
ban the bomb 42, 50, 68, 237
*Bananas* 231
Bay of Pigs 57
The Beatles 147, 190, 227
beatniks 47, 94, 106
behaviorism 132, 138
*The Beverly Hillbillies* 178
Bien Hoa attack 58

*The Big Chill* 230
Birmingham bus boycott 49
black nationalism 5, 98, 111-15
Black Panthers 18, 49, 112, 167-68, 171, 173,
    183-84, 232
*Bonnie and Clyde* 168, 178
boredom 122, 153
*Born on the Fourth of July* 230
Bosnia 221, 260-61, 264, 288
Boston Five 107, 292
Brandywine Peace Community 243
*A Bright Shining Lie* 228, 230
*Brown v. the Board of Education* 49
Budget Reform Act of 1974 283
Bush administration 24, 251-53
The Byrds 81, 93, 226

"A Call to Mobilize the Conscience of America" 79
"A Call to Resist Illegitimate Authority" 150
Cambodia 154, 187, 191, 199, 201-03, 209,
    217, 225, 230, 241, 261, 267-69
Campaign for Peace in the Middle East 241, 243
capitalism 23, 39, 63, 179, 191, 276, 292, 294
Carnegie Endowment for International Peace 37
Carter administration 210-14, 218, 221
*Casualties of War* 230
Catonsville 9 184
The Catholic Worker 41, 53-4, 72
Central American sanctuary movement 127
Chicago Peace Council 97, 176
Chicago riots, 1968 11, 70, 95, 161-62, 165,
    169, 185
Chicago Seven 144, 167, 171, 176, 185, 191,
    231
China 120, 164, 203-04, 215, 221, 269
Christianity 39-40, 164
Christmas 147
Christmas bombing 197, 204, 209
"Christmas in My Soul" 147
Church of the Brethren 42
*Cinderella* 47
civil disobedience 54, 152, 161, 188, 193, 245
Civil Rights Act 52, 62
civil rights movement 4, 9, 22, 34, 44-50, 55, 65-
    66, 72, 75, 82, 91, 93, 131, 181, 233, 271
Civil War 24, 35, 197
Clark Amendment 200-01
Clergy and Laity Concerned (About the War in
    Vietnam) 25, 67, 79, 99, 176, 254

---

\* Some subjects that are mentioned only once and in passing and do not directly concern the subject
at hand are not indexed. Material in endnotes is not indexed.

Clinton administration 260-61
A Clockwork Orange 231
Coalition Against Intervention, see National Coalition Against Intervention in the Middle East)
Coalition for America at Risk 256
Coalition for a New Foreign and Military Policy 211
Cold War 30, 43, 49, 62, 68, 105, 108, 132, 142, 182, 204, 218-20, 267, 278, 282
comedy 94, 281
Commentary 107
Committee for Non-Violent Action (CNVA) 54, 68, 72
Committee for Peace and Security in the Gulf 257
Committee in Solidarity with the People of El Salvador (CISPES) 243, 245, 289, 294
Committees of Liaison 76
Committees of Correspondence 295
communism 5, 8, 17, 23, 26, 38, 41, 46, 59, 73, 105, 109, 118, 121, 175, 203, 218, 269
Communist League of America 40
Communist Party USA 39, 42, 73, 97-99, 176, 242, 245
The Conspiracy 170, 176, 180, 183, 188
conspiracy theories 145, 294
Containment 48, 71, 203, 205-06
Cooper-Church amendment 202
Council on Foreign Relations 60
Council for a Liveable World 172
counterculture 21, 25, 64, 81, 94-95, 109-10, 124-25, 133-34, 145-46, 152, 161, 169, 184-85, 197, 272, 277, 286-88, 294-96
Counterinaugural 171, 179, 194
Country Joe and the Fish 81, 170
Crazies 167, 171, 180
creative disorder 129, 254
credibility gap 1, 59, 274
Crosby, Stills, Nash, and Young 170, 187, 226
Cuba 50, 52, 54, 57, 112, 120, 164, 169, 184, 201, 213
Cuban Missile Crisis 51, 57

Days of Rage 177, 179, 184
The Deer Hunter 230
Democratic Leadership Conference 282
Democratic Party 4, 6, 10, 14, 17-18, 35, 41, 53, 71, 87, 89-90, 159-61, 164, 166, 182, 193, 199-200, 205, 217, 256, 266, 280-82, 291
Democratic Socialists of America 243
détente 203-07, 211, 216-18, 220,
Diggers 91, 143, 245
Dissent 107
Dominican Republic 75
The Doors 93

Dow Chemical Corporation 274
draft (selective service) 52, 65, 70, 77-78, 81, 94, 127, 150, 170, 190, 195, 233-34, 239, 245, 250, 271-72, 278
draft card burning 77-78, 245
student deferment (II-S) 65, 122
"Draft Dodger Rag" 82
drugs 43, 91, 94, 139, 141, 170, 235, 273, 277
Du Bois Clubs 94
Dump Johnson movement 88, 172

Earth Day 249
Easter Peace Walk 51
Easy Rider 230
eco-anarchism 25, 294-96
Economic Research and Action Project (ERAP) 63
"Eight Miles High" 93
Eisenhower administration 105
El Salvador 220, 223-34, 240-41, 289
escalation 1, 14-16, 60-61, 77, 83, 85, 88, 102, 111, 154, 185, 189, 203
"Eve of Destruction" 82

Federal Bureau of Investigation (FBI) 22, 44, 87, 131, 178
Federation of Atomic Scientists 44
Fellowship of Reconciliation (FOR) 36, 40, 43, 53-4, 68, 72, 243, 249
feminism 123, 129-30, 194-95
Fifth Avenue Parade 79-80, 87-8, 171, 176, 242, 290
"Find the Cost of Freedom" 187-88
The Fire Next Time 105, 112
"Foggy Mountain Breakdown" 178
Fourth International (Trotskyite) 40
Fourth Internationalist Tendency 241, 243
free love 92, 269
Free Speech Movement 47, 65-66, 76, 83, 121
Freedom Summer 112
friendly tyrants problem 30, 273-74, 279
Friends Committee on National Legislation 199
The Fugs 81
Full Metal Jacket 230

Gallup polls, see public opinion
game theory 7, 132
generational conflict 25, 42, 119-20, 130-31, 136, 138-43, 276, 285, 297
The Gift of the Magi 9
"Give Peace a Chance" 180
God 46, 140, 147
Good Morning Vietnam 230
graduated response 132, 248
Grateful Dead 81, 93
"The Great Atomic Power" 43
Great Depression 38-41, 122, 140
Great Society 60, 232

Greenpeace 243, 248, 294
guerilla theater 79, 151, 247

*Hair* 230, 276
Hands Off Cuba Coalition 243
*Hanoi Hilton* 221
"Hell, No! I Ain't Gonna Go!" 112
hippies 7, 18, 91, 94-5, 165, 184, 191, 261
Hollywood 230, 251
Honolulu Conference 89
human rights movement 213-14, 227, 240

"identity politics" 5, 288
"I Feel Like I'm Fixin' To Die Rag" 81
Industrial Workers of the World (IWW) 41
Institute for Policy Studies 44, 72, 213, 242,
    259, 292
Intercollegiate Socialist Society 37, 61
Intermediate-range Nuclear Forces Treaty 218,
    223
International Communist League 241
International Days of Protest 78-79, 87-88, 102
Inter-University Committee for a Public
    Hearing on Vietnam 75
*Invisible Man* 112
Iraq 237, 247-48, 254-55, 259-60, 284, 288
isolationism 39, 41, 211, 278-79
Israel 24, 224, 254-55

Jackson State University 187
Jefferson Airplane 81, 93
*Jesus Christ Superstar* 147
Jews 38, 49, 109, 138, 142, 183, 254-55
Johnson administration 1-2, 4, 8, 19, 30, 58-
    61, 72, 85-87, 96, 101, 149, 251, 265-66,
    268, 284
    March 31, 1968 policy shift 2, 19, 29, 160,
        170, 173-74, 266
*Joseph and the Technicolor Dreamcoat* 147, 276
journalism, *see* media

Kennedy administration 1, 9, 44-45, 51, 54-56,
    59, 111, 131,
Kent State University 187-88, 250
*Killing Fields* 230
Kirkpatrick Doctrine 214
Korean War 2, 14, 45, 59, 71, 267
Ku Klux Klan 18, 112
Kuwait Crisis (1990-91) 6, 24, 221, 237-64,
    293

labor movement 18, 25, 37, 39, 41, 83, 98,
    119-20, 122, 202, 237, 281, 296
Laos 58, 199
Lawyers Committee on Nuclear Policy 243
League for Industrial Democracy (LID) 61-2
League to Enforce Peace 37
Lebanon 215-6, 221, 241

Left-Liberalism 44, 54, 60, 64, 67, 102, 160,
    164, 173, 179, 183, 193, 203, 246, 256, 292
Lesbian/Gay Labor Alliance 243
liberalism (and liberals) 5, 37-9, 50-2, 56, 102-
    07, 111, 124, 131-32, 134, 142, 145-47,
    159-61, 166, 171-73, 175, 182-83, 186,
    189, 196, 200-03, 205-06, 213-14, 218-
    19, 224, 243-46, 251, 253, 266, 272, 279-
    81, 288-93,
*Liberation* 81, 96, 176
Liberation News Service 194
*Life* 77, 153
"Light My Fire" 93
"Like a Rolling Stone" 82
*Listen Yankee* 50
literary Left 104-11, 251
"Little Old Lady from Pasadena" 82
*The Lonely Crowd* 104
Los Angeles riots 231-32
LSD 91-93, 95, 123, 144, 277
"Lucy in the Sky with Diamonds" 93

Mad Dogs 167, 180
magic 143-45, 148, 287
*Manifeste des 121* 52
Mansfield sense of the Senate resolution 202
*The Many Loves of Dobie Gillis* 46
"March Against Death" 179-80, 247
"March on the Pentagon to Confront the
    Warmakers" 19, 93, 96, 144, 149-53
March on Washington 52, 111-12
marijuana 92-3, 153, 169, 197, 234, 261, 277-78
Marxism (also Marxism-Leninism) 8, 23, 33,
    35, 39, 42, 44, 63, 69, 94-5, 99, 118, 138,
    146, 168, 180, 191, 275, 294
*M\*A\*S\*H* 230
MassPax 172, 179
May Day Tribes 183, 193, 195, 247, 254, 262
May 2nd Movement (M2M) 52-3, 73, 94
Mayaguez incident 207
McGovern-Hatfield "end-the-war" amendment
    199, 201
media 4, 6, 20, 53, 160, 238, 252, 284-85, 290
Mennonite Church 42
mescaline 93
Mighty Mouse 46, 58, 131
millenarianism 34
Military Families Support Network 245
military-industrial complex 39, 62-3, 81, 211,
    269, 275-76, 292
Minnesota Peace Drum 246
Mississippi Summer 112
"Mister Tamborine Man" 93
Mobe, *see* Spring Mobilization to End the War
    and New Mobilzation to End the War
*The Mobilizer* 150
Moratorium, *see* Vietnam Moratorium
    Committee

Movement for a New Congress 202
*Mr. Natural* 122
multiculturalism 5, 126, 286-88
music 42, 46, 81-82, 91-94, 146-47, 170, 180, 187-88, 225-27, 277
My Lai massacre 197, 199, 203, 239

*The Nation* 107, 247, 292
National Action Group (NAG) 161, 175
National African-American Network Against U.S. Intervention in the Gulf 244
National Alliance Against Political and Racist Oppression 243
National Arbitration League 36
National Coalition to Stop U.S. Intervention in the Middle East 241-43
National Coalition Against War, Racism, and Repression (NCAWRR) 193
National Conference for a New Politics (NCNP) 114-15
National Coordination Committee to End the War in Vietnam (NCCEWV) 67, 78-80, 87-88, 97-88, 114, 150-52
National Council of Churches 253
National Mobilization to End the War in Vietnam 103
National Organization for Women (NOW) 245
National Peace Action Coalition (NPAC) 193
Nazi-Soviet Non-Aggression Pact (also Molotov–von Ribbentrop Pact) 41, 73, 98, 120
negative follower effect 10-12, 14, 17-8
"Negotiations Now" 103
New Christy Minstrals 82
New Deal 42, 55, 165
New Frontier 55, 60
New Left 4, 5, 9, 20, 23, 25, 34, 63-4, 68-9, 91-2, 96, 98, 109, 117-127, 145, 149-50, 160-64, 177, 191, 193-94, 197, 287, 291, 294
*New Left Review* 81
New Mobilization Committee to End the War in Vietnam 169, 171-73, 175-80, 187-89, 193, 202
new pacifism 41, 60, 64-5, 68-71, 73, 77, 87, 96, 102, 120, 124, 150, 161, 171, 177, 193, 294
definition of violence 39-40, 65, 129, 294
New Politics 4, 218, 281
*The New Republic* 107, 179, 234, 269
*The New Yorker* 105, 112
*The New York Review of Books* 105, 107-08, 150
*The New York Times* 9, 12, 19, 175, 225, 239-40, 249, 252, 254-55, 260, 264
Nicaragua 211-15, 217, 221, 283
Nicaragua National Network 243
Nixon administration 2, 16, 30, 167, 172, 174, 178, 183-86, 189-90, 196, 198-99, 207, 216-17, 284, 290
Nixon Doctrine 204-05

nuclear freeze movement 127, 240, 254, 293-94
nuclear weapons 44-45, 185-86, 223-24
Nye Commission Report 39

obscenity 8, 13, 118-19, 123, 128
"Ohio" 187-88
old Left 4-5, 44, 60, 63, 69, 94, 109, 117-24, 177, 287, 291
Operation Pursestrings 193, 201-02
*On the Road* 47
*Ozzie and Harriet* 46

*Pacem in Terris* 51
Pacifica News Service 262, 276
pacifism 4, 23, 34, 38-42, 49, 53, 69, 246
Palestine Human Rights Committee 243
Palestine Solidarity Committee 243, 245
Palmer House 114-15, 244
"Panama Red" 93
Paris Accords 10, 29, 248, 267
Partial Test Ban Treaty 50, 57
participatory democracy 98, 124, 126, 167-68, 296
*Partisan Review* 107
Pax Christi 243, 254
*The Pentagon Papers* 16, 30, 87, 197, 203
Peoples Coalition for Peace and Justice (PCPJ) 193, 195
personalism 14, 121
Peter, Paul and Mary 74, 82
Physicians for Social Responsibility 243
*Platoon* 230
Pledge of Resistance 242
political correctness 286-88
political pilgrimage 19, 76, 82-3, 151, 249
polls, *see* public opinion
pollsterism 6, 283-85
Popular Front for the Liberation of Palestine 245
Port Huron Statement 62-63, 120, 168
positive intolerance 239
presidential election
    1896 36
    1900 36
    1948 42, 200
    1964 53, 58-605
    1968 18, 156, 159, 165-66, 181, 185, 265, 280-81
    1972 200, 202-03, 217, 265, 267
    1976 206, 212, 214, 217, 230, 281
    1980 281
    1984 281
    1988 281
    1992 233-35, 295
Procol Harem 93
Progressive Era 34, 36
Progressive Labor Party 52, 73, 95, 113, 163, 167-68, 241, 290

Progressive Student Alliance 242
Progressive Student Network 243
Project Camelot 45
Provisional Committee to Stop Nuclear Tests 44
public opinion 3, 7, 11, 13-20, 158-60, 174, 180, 189-90, 199, 251-52, 265, 278-79, 284

Quadrapartite Agreement on Berlin 206
Quakers 35, 42, 123, 250, 262

Rainbow Coalition 200, 276
*Ramparts* 81, 99, 235
Reagan administration 210, 214-18, 220
Reagan Doctrine 216
red diaper babies 62-3, 95, 110, 123
religion 3, 34-5, 40, 43, 46, 101, 117, 125-27, 133, 140, 142-48, 184, 235, 253-55, 292, 296-97
Republican Party 14, 17-8, 54, 175, 181-82, 202, 215, 266, 291
Republic of South Vietnam, *see* South Vietnam
Revolutionary Communist Brigades 245
Revolutionary Communist Party, U.S.A. 245
Revolutionary Workers League 243, 245
Revolutionary Youth Movement (RYM) 168
Riverside Church Disarmament group 179, 245
"rocket rattle" 43, 220
*Rolling Stone* 225-26
The Rolling Stones 240
"Rolling Thunder" 54
ROTC 191
Russian Revolution (1917) 37, 40

Saigon, fall of 10, 206, 209, 217, 267, 274
San Antonio Formula 156
SANE (Committee for a SANE Nuclear Policy) 25, 44, 50-51, 53, 60, 67-8, 71, 73, 75, 78, 80, 83, 86, 88-89, 98, 102-03, 172, 193, 199, 201, 239, 243, 292
"Satisfaction" 82
*Saturday Review* 107
search-and-destroy tactics 27, 30
Seattle 8 262
sectarianism 4, 5, 38, 87
selective service, *see* draft
Sergeant Bilko 46
sex 43, 46, 122-23, 127-30, 144-45
"silent majority" 179
"Silent Night" 93
"A Simple Desultory Philippic (Or How I was Robert McNamara'ed Into Submission)" 92
*Slaughterhouse Five* 230
social gospel movement 34-6, 38, 292
socialism 23, 37, 41-42, 44, 61, 83, 96, 123, 151, 211, 241, 275
Socialist Party 37, 41, 44

Socialist Workers Party 5, 51, 68, 99, 152, 161, 168, 175-76, 188-89, 193, 243, 290
*Soul on Ice* 112
"The Sounds of Silence," 92
South Vietnam 7, 28, 30-1, 64, 89, 174, 201, 206, 209, 265-66, 268
    antiwar movement image of 151
    as "friendly tyranny" 279-80
    U.S. commitment to 71, 223, 268
Southern Christian Leadership Conference 91, 99-100
Soviet Union 23, 42, 97, 201, 203-04, 206, 214-15, 218
Spanish-American War 34, 36, 211
Spanish Civil War 14, 106, 184
Sparticist League 241
Spring Mobilization Committee to End the War in Vietnam (SMCEWV) 99-100, 102-03, 115
Stalinism 8, 63, 105, 163
"Stop the Draft Week" 150, 153
streaking 191-92
Student League for Industrial Democracy (SLID) 61
Student Mobilization Committee to End the War in Vietnam 176, 202
Student Non-Violent Coordinating Committee (SNCC) 66, 74, 77, 88, 91, 100, 112, 114, 232
Student Peace Union 51-5, 72
Students for a Democratic Society (SDS) 5, 9, 11, 18, 34, 52, 54, 61-65, 72-73, 79, 86, 91-92, 94-96, 98, 104-05, 114-15, 124, 126, 128, 131, 137, 149, 152, 161, 163, 165-69, 177, 180, 191-92, 202, 235, 241, 290
    death of 166-69, 191
*Studies on the Left* 81, 97-98
"Strawberry Fields" 93
sunken costs 14, 17
Symbionese Liberation Army 227

teach-in movement 72, 75-6, 85, 108, 239
Teamsters Union 122
technocratic mentality 8, 47, 133-36, 146, 295-96
    and applied social science 43-45
    and "technowar" 45
television 20, 48, 58, 100-01, 157-58, 209, 252, 261-62, 291
Tet offensive 5, 9, 16, 19, 28-9, 101, 149, 154-56, 158, 160, 169, 252, 266-67, 284-85
Third World 203, 249, 270
tiger cages 31
Tonkin Gulf Resolution 53, 89, 90, 253
Trotskyites 8, 41, 97, 120, 161, 171, 175, 241
truth squads 85-6, 251

Turn Toward Peace 44
The Twist 46

United Automobile Workers 61-2, 122, 202
United States, impact of antiwar movement on 270-97
United World Federalists 44
Universal Peace Union 37
university 22, 48, 96, 120, 135-36, 143, 162, 190-91, 198, 250, 285
"Up Against the Wall, Motherfuckers" 160, 163-64, 167, 245
U.S. Congress 2, 16, 65, 75, 77, 89, 100, 166, 178, 193, 199-204, 207, 228, 253, 256, 266-68, 282
U.S. Peace Council 243, 245
utopianism 22, 70, 135

vanguardism 5, 23, 99, 112-13, 122, 128, 152, 154, 167-68, 171, 177-78, 184-85, 193-94, 232, 290, 292
Venceremos Brigade 184
Vietcong (National Liberation Front/NLF) 9, 27, 29, 65, 70, 76, 80, 102, 112, 151, 154-55, 170, 173, 180, 252, 289
Vietnam antiwar movement
  backlash from 91, 101-02, 111, 165
  compared to Kuwait antiwar movement 6, 258-64
  factionalism 67-76, 87-88, 94-5, 289-90
  literature about 221-22
  phases of 1-2, 83, 96-99, 102-04, 115, 151-53, 169, 186-87
  violence 70, 78, 87, 105, 115, 161, 177, 183-84, 195-96
Vietnam antiwar movement rallies
  December 1964 54
  April 1965 72-75, 79, 241
  June 1965 73-75, 241
  November 1965 79-81
  April 1967 94-100, 103
  October 1967 17, 19, 93, 96, 131, 144, 149-53, 169-72
  October 1969 177-80
  November 1969 183-85
  May 1970 1988-90, 201, 285
  April 1971 195-97
Vietnam Day (Berkeley) 76
Vietnam generation 21, 23, 43, 45-9, 66, 117, 137-38, 147-48, 198, 235, 240, 270-78, 286-87
  socialization of 45-49, 117, 137-43
Vietnam Memorial 261
Vietnam Moratorium Committee (Moratorium) 5, 169, 172-75, 178-80, 187, 191, 201, 266
Vietnam Summer 103-04
Vietnam syndrome 212, 257, 261, 278

Vietnam Veterans Against the War (VVAW) 196-97, 242, 252
Vietnam War
  compared to Kuwait War 6, 237-64
  images of 3, 7-9, 11, 26-27, 219-20, 223, 230-31, 280
  "lessons" of 210-11, 257
  literature on 209, 221-22
  as metaphor 209-35
  moral judgments about 268-70
  phases of 20
  U.S. military strategy in 27-31
  winnability of 26-31, 267-69
The Village Voice 74
"Voter's Pledge Peace Campaign" 88, 202

War Powers Resolution 200, 216, 253, 283
War Resisters League (WRL) 40, 43, 51, 53-54, 68, 70, 72-3, 81, 88, 176, 223, 243, 246-47
Watergate scandal 20, 183, 197, 199, 206, 214, 274, 284
Watts riots 77-78
Weathermen (Weather Underground) 166, 168, 177, 180, 183-85, 193, 227
White House Festival of the Arts 108
The White Negro 105
White Paper on El Salvador (1981) 215
White Paper on Vietnam (1965) 72, 215
"White Rabbit" 93
"Whiter Shade of Pale" 93
"whiz kids" 45, 89
Wise Men 5, 9, 19-20, 90, 157-60, 266-67, 290
"With a Little Help from My Friends" 227
Women's Christian Temperance Union 36
Women's International League for Peace and Freedom 25, 37, 50, 52, 68, 72, 243, 292
Women's Strike for Peace (WSP) 50, 53, 72, 75, 81, 176
women's suffrage 25, 237
Woodstock 170, 186, 227-28, 271
World Peace Foundation 37
World War I 34, 36-40, 133-35, 263
World War II 34, 41-2, 48, 55, 147, 211, 238, 252, 263, 273

Yippies 5, 94, 129, 169, 180, 266
Young Communist League 243, 245
Young Socialist Alliance 52, 68, 80, 92, 94-95, 171, 175, 243, 290
youth 43, 47-48, 50, 57, 64, 81-82, 91, 104-06, 109, 117, 125, 130-31, 135, 137-39, 142, 147-48, 160, 163, 168, 172, 183, 185, 219, 222, 225, 228, 234, 261, 265-66, 290, 293, 297
Youth Against War and Fascism 98
yuppies 49, 228

# Name Index**

Abzug, Bella 196, 239
Acheson, Dean 90, 156-57, 198
Agnew, Spiro 165, 229, 251
Allen, Donna 83
Alsop, Joseph 264
Anderson, Henry 96
Aptheker, Herbert 82
Arnett, Peter 249, 252, 285
Aspin, Les 260

Baez, Joan 52, 66, 74, 127, 223, 251
Baldwin, James 112
Ball, George 56, 90, 157, 205
Becker, Norma 88, 176
Belafonte, Harry 82
Bell, Daniel 132
Bellow, Saul 80
Berlin, Isaiah 134, 297
Berrigan, Daniel 52
Berrigan, Philip 52, 238, 246
Blaine, James Gillespie 36
Boudin, Kathy 176
Boulding, Kenneth 108
Bourne, Randolph 133
Boyle, Kay 74
Bradley, Omar 90, 159
Bridges, Harry 123
Brown, Chester L. 252
Brown, H. Rapp 112, 114, 244
Brown, Harold 212
Brown, Jerry 225
Brown, Norman O. 133
Brown, Sam 11, 70, 85, 131, 154, 172, 180, 190, 228, 257
Bruce, Lenny 93-4
Bryan, William Jennings 36
Brzezinski, Zbigniew 75, 212
Buchanan, Patrick 206
Bundy, McGeorge 12, 19, 60-61, 64, 75, 80, 90, 159
Bundy, William P. 156-57
Burgess, Anthony 231

Burlage, Robb 111
Burnham, James 132
Burroughs, William S. 47
Bush, George 220, 233, 246, 249, 251-53, 257-58, 260, 283
Butterfield, Jeanne 245

Califano, Joseph A., Jr. 48, 232
Calley, William 197, 199
Calvert, Greg 69, 104
Camus, Albert 133, 168
Carmichael, Stokely 91, 100, 103, 113
Carter, Jimmy 157, 212, 214-15, 218, 230, 281
Carver, George 156-57
Castaneda, Carlos 144
Castro, Fidel 50, 103, 213
Charles, Ray 227
Cheever, John 106
Cheney, Dick 246, 248, 262
Chomsky, Noam 105, 196, 225
Christopher, Warren 261
Church, Frank 64, 202
Clark, Ramsey 83, 241, 246
Cleaver, Eldridge 112
Clifford, Clark 12, 155-57, 285
Clinton, Bill 228, 233-35, 261, 278, 282
Clinton, Hillary Rodham 235
Cocker, Joe 227
Coffin, William Sloane 179, 245
Collier, Peter 23, 263-64
Collins, Judy 74
Cooper, David 118
Cortright, David 239, 292
Cotton, Elizabeth 82
Cousins, Norman 44, 64, 292
Cronkite, Walter 20, 101, 153, 157-58

Daley, Richard J. 144, 281
Darrow, Clarence 61
Davidson, Carl 343
Davis, Rennie 161-62, 171, 176-77, 183, 193, 195, 247, 254
Day, Dorothy 34, 41, 121
Dean, Arthur 90, 157
Dean, James 46, 147
Debray, Regis 121
Dellinger, David 51-3, 64, 70, 73, 76-7, 80, 96, 100, 107, 151-53, 161, 167, 171, 173, 175-77, 180, 183, 185, 187-88, 193, 195, 198, 223
Dellums, Ronald 196
De Palma, Brian 230
Deutscher, Isaac 76
Dewey, John 132, 134-35
Dillon, Douglas 90, 157
Doctorow, E. L. 251
Dodd, Thomas 44
Dohrn, Bernardine 167-68, 177, 184
Dowd, Douglas 83, 108, 176
Draper, Theodore 110
Dukakis, Michael 281
Dulles, John Foster 105, 181
DuPuy, William E. 157
Duvall, Robert 228
Dylan, Bob 74, 82, 93, 167

Eagleburger, Lawrence 261
Eisenhower, Dwight David 42, 57, 182, 205, 213
Eizenstat, Stuart 282
Ellison, Ralph 112
Ellsberg, Daniel 197
Epton, Bill 113

Fall, Bernard 75
Fanon, Franz 113, 121
Farber, David 11, 161
Feiffer, Jules 43, 80

---

** Some names that are mentioned only once and in passing and do not directly concern the subject at hand are not indexed. Persons not contemporaneous with narrated events are also not indexed. Material in endnotes is not indexed.

Feinberg, Rabbi Abraham 52
Ferber, Michael 292
Feuer, Louis 138-39, 141
Fitzgerald, Frances 270
Flacks, Richard 123, 276
Fonda, Jane 83, 229-30
Forbes, James 245
Ford, Gerald 206, 281
Forman, James 114
Fortas, Abe 90, 157
Freidenberg, Edgar Z. 133
Fromm, Erich 108, 122, 133
Fulbright, William 53, 77,
    89-91

Gandhi, Mahatmas 70
Gans, Curtis 88
Garson, Marvin 83
Gavin, James M. 27
Genovese, Eugene 123, 127
Gilmore, Bob 44
Gingrich, Newt 228
Ginsberg, Allen 47, 94, 96
Gitlin, Todd 11, 21-23, 46,
    92, 129, 165,
    168, 240, 287-88
Goldberg, Arthur 80, 90,
    157, 175
Goldman, Emma 34, 94, 122
Goldwater, Barry 53, 58-60,
    181
Gompers, Samuel 38
Goodell, Charles 178, 180
Goodman, Mitchell 107
Goodman, Paul 74, 105,
    108, 111, 133,
    162, 296
Gore, Albert, Jr. 199, 235
Gottlieb, Sanford 80
Gramsci, Antonio 109
Gregory, Dick 76, 94, 281
Grossman, Jerome 172
Gruening, Ernst 51, 56, 74,
    76, 166
Guevara, Che 104, 122, 152
Gumbleton, Thomas 254
Guthrie, Woodie 82
Gutmann, David 139-43

Haber, Al 61-3, 129
Haber, Barbara 129
Habib, Philip 157
Haggard, Merle 82
Haig, Alexander, Jr. 215, 261
Halberstam, David 285
Halstead, Fred 51, 64, 161,
    175-76, 188, 198
Hampton, Fred 177

Harkin, Tom 214
Harriman, W. Averell 157,
    175
Harrington, Michael 6203,
    106, 110
Hart, Philip 180
Hartman, Chester 104
Hayden, Tom 9, 13, 47,
    62-3, 82-3, 92, 113,
    122, 131, 160-62,
    165, 167, 177
Hawk, David 172, 175-76
Hearst, Patricia 227
Helms, Richard 157
Hendrix, Jimi 169, 224
Hentoff, Nat 74
Herf, Jeffrey 126, 198
Herr, Michael 285
Hersh, Seymour 203, 285
Hesse, Herman 33, 133
Ho Chi Minh 19, 79, 168,
    248-49
Hoffer, Eric 123
Hoffman, Abbie 21, 47,
    129, 142, 144, 161,
    171, 180, 188, 191,
    228, 270
Hoffmann, Julius 231
Holbrooke, Richard 212
Hoopes, Townsend 56
Horowitz, David 10, 13, 23
Horowitz, Irving Louis 145
Howe, Irving 105, 107
Hughes, H. Stuart 73
Humphrey, Hubert H. 65,
    77, 161, 165-66, 182,
    280-81
Hurt, Mississippi John 82
Hussein, Saddam 242, 256,
    259, 284, 288
Huxley, Aldous 93

Ives, Burl 82

Jackson, Jesse 200, 245, 248
Jacobs, John 184
James, William 132, 134
Javits, Jacob 71, 77
Jennings, Peter 225
John XXIII, Pope 51
Johnson, Lady Bird 90-91
Johnson, Lyndon Baines 2,
    15-17, 19-20, 29, 52-
    53, 58-60, 71, 85-86,
    88-91, 100, 108, 110,
    155-60, 164, 170, 174,
    181-82, 189, 213, 216,
    232, 256, 266, 284

Kafka, Franz 124, 133
Kahin, George McT. 108
Katzenbach, Nicholas 157
Kelly, Thomas 248
Kennan, George 71, 89
Kennedy, John F. 45, 54-57,
    131, 134, 181, 213
Kennedy, Robert F. 5, 71,
    88, 131, 160, 164, 169,
    178
Kerouac, Jack 47, 94
Kerrey, Bob 235
Kerry, John F. 196, 227, 252
Kesey, Ken 47, 91, 94, 96
Keynes, John Maynard 134,
    182, 205
Keys, Donald 292
Khrushchev, Nikita 42, 99
King, Coretta Scott 75, 80
King, Martin Luther, Jr. 52,
    75, 91, 100, 103, 111,
    169
Kirk, Grayson 163
Kirkpatrick, Jeanne 214
Kissinger, Henry 28, 111,
    172, 203-04, 206, 248,
    261
Klare, Michael T. 259
Klonsky, Michael 168
Kolko, Gabriel 108
Kopkind, Andrew 105
Kovic, Ron 239
Krassner, Paul 144-45, 162
Kristopherson, Kris 251
Kunstler, William 242-43

Laing, R. D. 118
Laird, Melvin S. 205
Lake, Anthony 212, 260-61
Lasch, Christopher 106, 123
Law, Bernard Cardinal 254
Lawrence, Anthony 249
Leary, Timothy 91, 96
Lemann, Nicholas 274-75,
    297
Lennon, John 147, 170, 180,
    190
Lens, Sidney 97, 107, 169,
    175, 180, 185
Lerner, Michael 262-63
Lewis, John 112
Lifton, Robert Jay 108
Lippman, Walter 61
Lodge, Henry Cabot 80, 90,
    157
London, Jack 61
Lowell, Robert 108
Lowenstein, Allard 88, 172

Luce, Phillip 52
Lynd, Staughton 73-77, 82-83, 88, 107, 109
Lyttle, Bradford 178, 188, 193

Macdonald, Dwight 74, 105-06
Mailer, Norman 76, 93, 105, 109-11, 182, 281
Malcolm X 112
Manson, Charles 167, 228-29
Marcuse, Herbert 105, 108, 120, 136, 296
Maurin, Peter 41, 121
McCarthy, Eugene 5, 64, 88, 156, 158, 160, 162, 164-66, 180, 290
McCarthy, Joseph 42, 181
McCarthy, Mary 105-06, 109-11, 153
McCloy, John J. 90, 157
McDonald, Country Joe 81, 240
McGovern, George 10-1, 64, 77, 180, 199-204, 228, 240, 280-81
McGuinn, Jim 226, 282-83
McGuire, Barry 82
McLuhan, Marshall 296
McNamara, Robert S. 45, 64, 80, 85-86, 90, 92, 100-01, 135, 152, 155, 299-302
McReynolds, David 54, 73-74, 107, 239-40
Meacham, Steward 44, 175-76, 179, 183, 185, 247
Meany, George 202
Melman, Seymour 44, 75, 108, 292
Meyer, William H. 74
Millay, Edna St. Vincent 61
Miller, Arthur 80
Mills, C. Wright 50, 62, 97-98, 108, 133, 168, 275
Mitchell, Parren 196
Morgenthau, Hans 71, 74, 203
Morse, Wayne 51, 56, 75, 166
Moses, Robert 74, 76-77, 80
Mumford, Lewis 133
Mungo, Raymond 118
Muravchik, Joshua 9, 259
Murphy, Robert 90, 157

Muskie, Edmund 175
Muste, Abraham Johannes 34, 40, 55, 51, 73, 87, 97, 107, 151, 240

Nash, Graham 170
Nelson, Gaylord 64, 77
Newport, Gus 243
Newton, Huey 228
Niebuhr, Reinhold 70
Ngo Dinh Diem 28, 52, 58, 60, 134
Ngo Dinh Nhu 52
Nguyen Loc Loan 155
Nguyen Thi Binh 76
Nisbet, Robert 126, 134
Nitze, Paul 157
Nixon, Richard 2-3, 12, 17-19, 111, 165-66, 169-75, 180-83, 185, 187, 189-90, 197, 203-04, 206, 215-16, 251, 266-67, 280-81, 284
Nunn, Sam 282
Nyro, Laura 147

Ochs, Phil 82
O'Dell, Jack 243
Odetta 82
Oglesby, Carl 72, 78, 80, 96, 131, 154, 168, 235
Orwell, George 123, 200

Pauling, Linus 44, 80
Peck, Sidney 64, 97-98, 102, 107, 129-30, 149, 152-53, 169, 171, 173, 176-77, 183, 185, 188, 193, 198, 290
Peirce, Charles Sanders 132
Peretz, Martin 179
Perot, Ross 227, 235
Picasso, Pablo 109
Pickett, Clarence 44
Pickus, Robert 73, 76
Pol Pot 227, 268
Potter, Paul 74, 76
Presley, Elvis 42, 58

Quayle, Dan 234, 251, 291

Rand, Ayn 93
Randall, Tony 80
Randolph, A. Philip 54, 112
Rangel, Charles 196, 245
Rapoport, Anatol 108
Raskin, Marcus 44, 105, 150, 292

Reagan, Ronald 43, 206, 215-16, 218, 220, 224, 291
Reed, John 61
Reston, James 19
Ridgeway, Mathew 90, 157
Riesman, David 104, 124, 133
Robb, Charles 282
Robbins, Tim 245, 251
Rogers, Will 94
Rogers, William 201
Roosevelt, Franklin 55, 182, 280
Rose, Axl 229
Ross, Diana 230
Rostow, Walt 12, 75, 157
Roszak, Theodore 105, 111, 296
Roth, Philip 106
Rowen, Peter 277
Rubin, Jerry 9, 13, 88, 94-95, 110, 119, 129, 144, 150, 169, 171, 180, 188, 191, 228
Ruby, Ron 242
Rudd, Mark 115, 163, 176-77
Rush, Bobby 232
Rusk, Dean 12, 16, 19, 57, 157
Russell, Bertrand 51, 246
Rustin, Bayard 53, 73, 75, 106, 112

Sabin, Albert 80
Sadler, Barry 65, 82, 93
Sanburo, Angela 245
Sanders, Ed 81
Sarandon, Susan 245, 251
Savio, Mario 65-66, 129
Scheer, Robert 88
Schell, Jonathan 215-6, 285
Schlesinger, Arthur, Jr. 215-16, 285
Schlesinger, James 45
Scott, Lawrence 44
Scruggs, Earl 177-78
Seale, Bobby 112, 167, 232
Sebastian, John 228
Seeger, Pete 82
Sheehan, Neil 228, 285
Sheen, Martin 223-24, 251
Simon, Paul 93, 225
Simpson, Alan 252
Sinclair, John 95
Sinclair, Upton 95
Skinner, B. F. 132, 134, 136, 138

Smith, Danu 244
Smith, Robert C. 228
Snepp, Frank 209
Solarz, Stephen 199, 214, 257
Sontag, Susan 107, 109, 119, 127
Spock, Benjamin 44, 68, 74, 76, 80, 99-100, 103, 140, 179
Stanton, Frederick Perry 36
Steel, Ronald 105, 205, 264
Stevenson, Adlai 74
Stills, Stephen 188
Stone, I. F. 63, 73, 108, 133
Stone, Oliver 251, 275
Swados, Harvey 74

Talbott, Strobe 260-61
Tarnoff, Peter 260
Tate, Doris 167
Tate, Sharon 167
Taylor, Frederick 134
Taylor, Maxwell 90, 93, 157
Teague, Walter 80
Terkel, Studs 243

Thomas, Norman 44, 54, 61, 73, 76, 105, 154, 240, 263
Thompson, Hunter S. 200
Trudeau, Garry 246
Truman, Harry S. 55, 205
Twain, Mark 36

Udall, Stewart 175

Vance, Cyrus 90, 157, 212
Vann, John 228
Vo Nguyen Giap 19, 29
Vonnegut, Kurt 230, 251

Wallace, George 18, 165-66, 182, 204
Wallace, Henry 42, 44, 200
Walzer, Michael 106, 110, 137, 146
Ware, Bobby 232
Warnke, Paul 156-57
Waskow, Arthur 72, 105, 150, 254-55
Watts, Alan 94
Weber, Max 133
Weinberg, Jack 65

Weinberger, Caspar 220, 278
Weinglass, Leonard 242
Weiss, Cora 76, 176, 187
Wenner, Jann S. 225
Westmoreland, William 12, 27, 29, 155
Wheeler, Earl 157
Whyte, William H., Jr. 133
Wilkerson, Cathy 194-95
Wilkins, Roy 112
Williams, Robert 113
Wilson, Charles 218
Wilson, Sloan 133
Wilson, Will R. 171
Wilson, Woodrow 38, 134, 282
Wisner, Frank 260
Wolfe, Robert 81
Wolfe, Tom 124
Wolin, Sheldon 108

Yard, Molly 245
Young, Andrew 100
Young, Neil 226
Young, Stephen 64

Zinn, Howard 108, 242-43